CENSORSHIP

Anna Wiśniewska-Grabarczyk

CENSORSHIP

OF LITERATURE IN POST-WAR POLAND:

IN LIGHT OF THE CONFIDENTIAL BULLETINS FOR CENSORS FROM 1945 TO 1956

Lodz–Cracow 2022

Anna Wiśniewska-Grabarczyk (ORCID: 0000-0002-3005-200X) – University of Łódź
Faculty of Philology, Department of the 20th and 21st Century Polish Literature
90-236 Łódź, 171/173 Pomorska St., Poland

Published by Łódź University Press & Jagiellonian University Press
First edition, Łódź–Kraków 2022
W.10454.21.0.M

ISBN 978-83-8220-938-9 – paperback Łódź University Press
e-ISBN 978-83-8220-939-6 – electronic version Łódź University Press
ISBN 978-83-233-5191-7 – paperback Jagiellonian University Press
e-ISBN 978-83-233-7388-9 – electronic version Jagiellonian University Press

https://doi.org/10.18778/8220-938-9

Łódź University Press
90-237 Łódź, 34a Matejki St., Poland
www.wydawnictwo.uni.lodz.pl
e-mail: ksiegarnia@uni.lodz.pl
phone +48 42 665 55 77

Distribution outside Poland
Jagiellonian University Press
31-126 Kraków, 9/2 Michałowskiego St., Poland
Phone: +48 12 631 01 97, +48 12 663 23 81, fax +48 12 663 23 83
Cell Phone: + 48 506 006 674, e-mail: sprzedaz@wuj.pl
Bank: PEKAO SA, IBAN PL 80 1240 4722 1111 0000 4856 3325
www.wuj.pl

I dedicate this book to my mother

TABLE OF CONTENTS

INTRODUCTION

Censorship is like a long-time mistress.
You're often fed up with her, sometimes she's tiresome
and frustrating,
and you know her inside out.
And yet, it's difficult to leave her.[1]

Some Remarks about Censorship in Poland
in the Years 1944–1990

My book is about censorship in Poland in the years 1945–1956.[2] It does not, of course, describe all aspects of the activity of the institution responsible for limiting speech in that period, as such a work would require several thousand pages of elaboration. In the book, I mainly focus on the ways of censoring literature described in the confidential Bulletins for censors.[3]

The efforts to establish a censorship institution in Poland began even before the end of World War II. The first censorship unit was created as early as 1944. In 1945, Centralne Biuro Kontroli Prasy (CBKP, the Central Press Control Bureau) was formed. In that same year, it was renamed Główny Urząd Kontroli Prasy, Publikacji i Widowisk (GUKPPiW, the Main Office for the Control of the Press, Publications and Public Performances), and in 1981 – Główny Urząd Kontroli Publikacji i Widowisk (GUKPiW, the Main Office for the Control of Publications

---

[1] "Wypowiedzi pracowników UKPPiW," *Biuletyn Informacyjno-Instrukcyjny* no. 1 (37), January 1955, p. 63 (APG, WUKPPiW, file ref. no. 110). A statement by one of the censors quoted in a survey conducted by the editors of the Bulletin on the tenth anniversary of the existence of the censorship office.

[2] This book is based on a monograph originally published in Polish in 2021 (*Książki z Mysiej. Literatura w świetle poufnych Biuletynów urzędu cenzury z lat 1945–1956*, Warszawa: IBL PAN). In this revised edition, the author added an introduction and explanatory notes, while also expanding some parts and shortening others, but the most significant modification has been adapting the book to non-Polish-language readers.

[3] Throughout the book, the word is capitalized when it refers to the discussed Bulletins for censors.

and Public Performances). Apart from the GUKPPiW, censors worked in the field, and in voivodeship or district censorship offices scattered all over Poland. They comprised a network that enveloped the country and constituted the basic censorship institutions controlling the written word, media, as well as intellectual and artistic life in post-war Poland.

The Russians had a deep influence on shaping the censorship system in Poland. The employees of Glavlit (Central Board for Literature and Press Affairs), Piotr Gładin and Kazimierz Jarmuż, came to Lublin in 1944 to take part in the initial work on the establishment of censorship, including the creation of documents defining the scope of the institution's activity on Polish territory. The censorship office was to be subordinate to the Central Committee of the Polish Workers' Party (KC PPR) and, from 1948, to the Central Committee of the Polish United Workers' Party (KC PZPR, which emerged when the Polish Workers' Party and the Polish Socialist Party were combined). Institutional censorship in Poland was reliant on the USSR, although the degree of that dependency varied throughout its operation.

Censorship in the form developed in the 1940s and early 1950s functioned practically until the end of the Polish People's Republic,[4] although not always in equal intensity. After the socio-political upheavals of 1956, 1968 and 1970, it usually eased for some time, resulting in periods of so-called "Thaw" (*odwilż*). Attempts were also made to fight it through open protests and the creation of an alternative publishing circuit, so-called "second circulation" (*drugi obieg*): a system of underground publishing houses, which printed outside the scrutiny of censorship. During the entire period of the Office's existence, there was preventive censorship – assessing materials before publication, and secondary censorship – evaluating materials already published.

Institutional censorship was abolished in Poland by the decree of April 11, 1990, which came into force on June 6 of the same year.[5]

It is worth remembering that post-war censorship functioned in Poland against the officially binding constitution of March 1921, recognized by the government. According to its article 105: "Freedom of the press is guaranteed. Cen-

---

[4] The Polish People's Republic (Polska Rzeczpospolita Ludowa, henceforth PRL) was the official name of Poland from 1952 until 1989. From 1918 to 1952, the official name was the Republic of Poland (Rzeczpospolita Polska, henceforth RP). People's Poland (Polska Ludowa) was a semi-official, propagandistic name of the state from 1944 to 1989.

[5] "Ustawa z dnia 11 kwietnia 1990 r. o uchyleniu ustawy o kontroli publikacji i widowisk, zniesieniu organów tej kontroli oraz o zmianie ustawy – Prawo prasowe" (Dz.U. 1990, nr 27, poz. 173, s. 378–389, http://isap.sejm.gov.pl/isap.nsf/DocDetails. xsp?id=WDU19900290173 (accessed July 27, 2021)).

sorship, or the system of licensing printed matter, may not be introduced."[6] Similarly, when the constitution of the Polish People's Republic was enacted on July 22, 1952, the existence of censorship was contrary to its article 71, which read: "The Polish People's Republic shall guarantee its citizens freedom of speech, of the press, of meetings and assemblies, of processions and demonstrations."[7]

Research Assumptions

> *The censor has no right to abuse the scissors,*
> *he is not allowed to trim a work according to his*
> *literary or political taste.*[8]

During the period of institutional control of speech, which was imposed in the Polish People's Republic in the years 1944–1990, every cultural text related to literature, journalism, painting, music, theater or film, was subjected to assessment by functionaries of the censorship office.[9] The supervisory system was total, at least according to the assumptions of its creators: there were attempts to extend the state "care" to all products of human creative activity, as a result of which "censorship numbers were found on bread stickers."[10] However, the invigilation apparatus designed in this way was not perfect; for example, underground publications and samizdat issued without state supervision found their way to the publishing market. This phenomenon appeared on a larger scale in the 1970s, but examples of such activities can already be found in the earlier

---

[6] "Ustawa z dnia 17 marca 1921 r. – Konstytucja Rzeczypospolitej Polskiej," http://libr.sejm.gov.pl/tek01/txt/kpol/e1921.html (accessed September 1, 2021).

[7] "Konstytucja Polskiej Rzeczypospolitej Ludowej uchwalona przez Sejm Ustawodawczy w dniu 22 lipca 1952 r.," http://libr.sejm.gov.pl/tek01/txt/kpol/e1952a.html (accessed September 1, 2021).

[8] "Ocena pracy cenzury prewencyjnej. Uwagi ogólne," *Biuletyn Instrukcyjny* no. 1, May 1945, p. 1v (*"Biuletyny Instrukcyjno-Szkoleniowe 1945–1951"* (APP, WUKPPiW, file ref. no. 4)).

[9] On the difficulties of defining the word cluster "cultural text" see, e.g.: *Słownik pojęć i tekstów kultury. Terytoria słowa*, Third Revised Edition, ed. E. Szczęsna, Warszawa: WSiP, [2004], p. 307 et seq.; S. Żółkiewski, *Teksty kultury. Studia*, Warszawa: PWN, 1988; M. Rygielska, "O 'tekście kultury,'" *Zeszyty Etnologii Wrocławskiej* 2015, no. 1, pp. 27–43; cf. also S.J. Żurek, "Koncepcja podstawy programowej z języka polskiego," [in:] *Podstawa programowa z komentarzami* vol. 2: *Język polski w szkole podstawowej, gimnazjum i liceum*, Warszawa: Ministerstwo Edukacji Narodowej, 2009, pp. 55–59.

[10] "Druki ulotne," *Biuletyn Informacyjno-Instrukcyjny* no. 8, August 1952, p. 28 (APG, WUKPPiW, file ref. no. 81).

period.[11] Books published by Instytut Literacki and other émigré publishing houses also reached Poland, smuggled across the borders (which involved considerable difficulty and risk).[12]

Aware of the existence of those "islands of freedom," I have chosen to focus on the art which was, to varying degrees, enslaved and mutilated; the art which was born in direct confrontation with the censorship office. This choice was a consequence of my multi-year research into constraints put on freedom of speech. In my earlier works, I also described post-war Polish culture in the context of the activities of the censorship office,[13] but in this case, I decided to investigate poorly explored sources, namely, the confidential Bulletins for censors. I was primarily interested in the articles published there devoted to fiction, although my research also covered materials on non-fiction and other texts of culture.

Once again, my several years of studying the Bulletins confirmed that it is impossible to discuss the history of the literature of People's Poland without outlining the political context. This is evident from reading the articles published there, which did not conceal the fact that the reviews of literary, film or dramatic works were meant to bolster ideology. Censors discussed specific texts, referring to current political events and adjusting their assessment to the guidelines formulated by the leadership of the Polish Workers' Party, and from 1948, the Polish United Workers' Party.

Taking into account both of these contexts – cultural and political – had a fundamental influence on the shape of this book. An additional role was also played by the way in which I decided to present materials published in censorship periodicals. Bulletins, like any serial publications, can be read and analyzed chronologically – according to the order of their appearance – or problematically – devoting attention to selected topics and questions; both types of reading perform slightly different functions. The former allows us to look at the periodicals in their historical development; the latter, to isolate and discuss only the topics

---

[11] W. Kajtoch [W. K.], "Drugi obieg," [in:] *Encyklopedia książki* vol. 1: *Eseje. A–J*, eds. A. Żbikowska-Migoń, M. Skalska-Zlat, Wrocław: Wydawnictwo UWr, 2017, pp. 539–540.

[12] Instytut Literacki (The Literary Institute) – one of the most important Polish émigré publishing houses, established in Rome in 1946 (in 1947, it was moved to Maisons-Laffitte near Paris). It was founded by Jerzy Giedroyc, Zofia Hertz, Zygmunt Hertz, Józef Czapski and Gustaw Herling-Grudziński, and published many Polish and foreign writers whose works were banned in communist Poland (e.g., Czesław Miłosz, Witold Gombrowicz, George Orwell) as well as very important magazines: *Kultura* and *Zeszyty Historyczne*.

[13] See, e.g.: A. Wiśniewska-Grabarczyk, "The censorship review in the Polish People's Republic as cryptotext," *The Polish Review* 2019, vol. 64, no. 1, pp. 31–49; eadem, *"Czytelnik" ocenzurowany. Literatura w kryptotekstach – recenzjach cenzorskich okresu stalinizmu (na materiale GUKPPiW z 1950 roku)*, Warszawa: Wydawnictwo IPN, 2018.

of interest. However, even if we forgo a linear reading and focus on selected problems, considering the chronology is still possible during the presentation of the material, and in the case of texts so politically entangled, it even seems necessary.

Bearing this in mind, I have adopted a problem-based system, devoting subsequent chapters to separate topics, the selection of which organizes the main structure of the book. Although the chronological order has been applied to the presentation of the censorship documents only in a few cases, this system is strongly present in all parts of the work. My goal was to analyze the material in relation to the time in which it was created and in the context of the cultural and political situation. In this way, I have avoided "reading out of context,"[14] whether it was historical, political, social, or cultural factors. I hope that I have reconciled the two systems, because I do not believe that a "pure alternative: either by chronology or by problems"[15] could have been employed.

This book could not possibly cover all the topics that had surfaced over the eleven years of my research.[16] However, I have tried to point out the problems that garnered particular attention, recurred in the censors' "reflections" or shed new light on previous knowledge about "Mysia Street and its environs" (throughout its existence, the Main Office for the Control was located at 5 Mysia Street in Warsaw).[17]

---

[14] A. Nasiłowska, "Problemowo czy chronologicznie? Kilka argumentów," *Zeszyty Szkolne. Edukacja humanistyczna* 2007, no. 2, p. 47 (The author discusses two systems in the teaching of literature in secondary schools, but certain insights and findings seem to be universal and applicable to the teaching and research of various humanities disciplines, not only at the level of school education).

[15] Ibidem, p. 48.

[16] The selection I had to make will be complemented by the "Appendix" (forthcoming) in which I record all the authors and their works appearing in the Bulletins.

[17] I use this expression in reference to censorship understood as an institutionalized phenomenon occurring in Poland in the years 1944–1990. It is worth noting that the building at Mysia Street, which housed the censorship office, had not been completed until 1950. When the Central Press Control Bureau moved from Lublin to Warsaw, it first took the building at Szeroka Street, then 31 Koszykowa Street (see: K. Kamińska-Chełminiak, "Przeniesienie Centralnego Biura Kontroli Prasy z Lublina do Warszawy," [in:] eadem, *Cenzura w Polsce 1944–1960. Organizacja. Kadry. Metody pracy*, Warszawa: Wydział Dziennikarstwa, Informacji i Bibliologii UW i Oficyna Wydawnicza ASPRA-JR, 2019, pp. 73–75). The Bureau's new office in Warsaw was mentioned in the Bulletin from June 1945; this may have been the premises at 31 Koszykowa Street, to which it moved in August 1945 (see: "Przemówienie dyrektora ob. Zabłudowskiego," *Biuletyn Instrukcyjny* no. 2, June 1945, p. 18 (APG, WUKPPiW, file ref. no. 210)). While the censorship office was located at 5 Mysia Street, in some publications we can find the address 6/8 Bracka Street – both refer to the same block; I thank PhD, Eng. of Architecture Tomasz Majda for the consultation on this matter (see, e.g.: M. Leśniakowska, *Architektura w Warszawie*, Third Revised Edition, Warszawa: Arkada. Pracownia Historii

Considering the above, I have divided the book into three main parts, preceded by the "Introduction" and concluded with the "Summary."

In the first part, entitled "In Search of a Definition: What Were the Confidential Bulletins for Censors? Characteristics of the Source Material," I have presented basic information about the Bulletins: the purposes they served, their structure and the nature of the material presented in them. The reflections end with a definition of confidential Bulletins for censors.

The main objective of the second part, "Literature and Current Literary Phenomena," was to reconstruct the picture of literary life as it was presented in the Bulletins in the years 1945–1956. I was interested in how texts that were produced in the post-war geopolitical conditions were discussed, as well as in the attitude towards the past – broadly understood as the domestic and foreign heritage, from the early literary activity to the texts describing the war and occupation. Do the periodicals contain familiar strategies with which "Mysia Street" attempted to train or eliminate authors? Did subsequent issues of the magazine reflect the changes that the post-war literary era was undergoing? To what extent did contemporary writing constitute an important segment of the Bulletins' reflections?

In order to answer these and other questions, it was necessary to include not only materials discussing literary phenomena, but also those which explored other issues, especially cultural ones. In the last part entitled "'Camera Censorica.' What Else Was Discussed in the Bulletins?" I briefly outlined the matters that were not the subject of previous discussion, including those concerning film, radio and plays, as well as the institutional base of control. The last section of the main considerations is devoted to censors who were also artists. In the chapter "Before the Proper Summary, or… the Censor as an Artist: The Literary Work of the Functionaries of 'Mysia Street and Its Environs,'" I provide "evidence" for the literary bent of the political functionaries, as the censors were called in the 1950s. Employees of the Main Office and those in field branches scattered around Poland not only practiced the difficult skill of controlling others; some of them aspired to create their own literary works. The main reflections are concluded with one such poem.

In the "Summary," I synthesized the results of my observations on how literature and other arts were presented in the confidential Bulletins for censors produced from 1945 to 1956.

The book ends with "Bibliography," including the List of Authors and Works Documented in the Bulletins for Censors from 1945–1956 (Selection) and the List of the Bulletins for Censors and *Biblioteczki Biuletynu Informacyjno-Instrukcyjnego GUKPPiW* – I treat these elements as inherent parts of the story of communist censorship that require no comment.

Sztuki, 2005, p. 104; J. Rutkowska, R. Zdziarska, H. Szwankowska, *Warszawa. Przewodnik*, Warszawa: Wydawnictwo Sport i Turystyka, 1966, p. 296).

State of the Art

Compiled information is fruit for thought,
therefore, it is harmful.[18]

The bibliography on literary issues discussed in the confidential Bulletins for censors from 1945–1956 is relatively modest.

The journal is part of a large collection of training and instructional materials produced by "Mysia Street" and most often appears in this context in the statements of researchers describing the specificity and division of labor in the institution. The training and instructional materials created in the Main Office were investigated by the representatives of different fields – historians, historians of the press and the publishing market, political analysts, bibliologists and library scholars, including Zbigniew Romek, Bogusław Gogol, Dariusz Jarosz, Kamila Kamińska-Chełminiak, Daria Nałęcz, Piotr Nowak, Andrzej Paczkowski, Stanisław Adam Kondek, Aleksander Pawlicki and Robert Looby.[19] In some of the studies, issues related to the publishing market appeared, however, the censors' "reflections" on specific literary works or analyses of the country's cultural life presented in the Bulletins were only on the margins of the main deliberations (if they were discussed at all).

The first literary studies fully devoted to the Bulletins were published by Kamila Budrowska. In 2011, she published the article "Tajne pismo cenzury. *Biuletyn*

---

[18] "Uzasadnienie ingerencji," *Biuletyn Informacyjno-Szkoleniowy* no. 1, October 30, 1948, fol. 80r (APP, WUKPPiW, file ref. no. 4).

[19] See, e.g.: Z. Romek, *Cenzura a nauka historyczna w Polsce 1944–1970*, Warszawa: Wydawnictwo Neriton, 2010; B. Gogol, *"Fabryka fałszywych tekstów." Z działalności Wojewódzkiego Urzędu Kontroli Prasy, Publikacji i Widowisk w Gdańsku w latach 1945–1958*, Warszawa: Wydawnictwo Neriton, 2012; D. Jarosz, "Zapisy cenzury z lat 1948–1955," *Regiony* 1996, no. 3, pp. 2–37; K. Kamińska-Chełminiak, *Cenzura w Polsce 1944–1960…*; *Główny Urząd Kontroli Prasy 1945–1949*, compiled by D. Nałęcz, Warszawa: ISP PAN, 1994, series *Dokumenty do Dziejów PRL* issue 6; P. Nowak, *Cenzura wobec rynku książki. Wojewódzki Urząd Kontroli Prasy, Publikacji i Widowisk w Poznaniu w latach 1946–1955*, Poznań: Wydawnictwo Naukowe UAM, 2012; A. Paczkowski, "Cenzura 1946–1949. Statystyka działalności," *Zeszyty Historyczne* 1996, issue 116, pp. 22–57; S.A. Kondek, *Władza i wydawcy. Polityczne uwarunkowania produkcji książek w Polsce w latach 1944–1949*, Warszawa: Biblioteka Narodowa, 1993; idem, *Papierowa rewolucja. Oficjalny obieg książek w Polsce w latach 1948–1955*, Warszawa: Biblioteka Narodowa, 1999; A. Pawlicki, *Kompletna szarość. Cenzura w latach 1965–1972. Instytucja i ludzie*, Warszawa: Wydawnictwo Trio, 2001; R. Looby, *Censorship, Translation and English Language Fiction in People's Poland*, Leiden (Netherlands)–Boston (Massachusetts): Brill Rodopi, 2015.

Informacyjno-Instrukcyjny w latach 1952–1955"[20] [The secret journal of censorship. *Informational and Instructional Bulletin* between 1952–1955]. In the subsequent essay, "Wewnętrzne pismo cenzury. *Biuletyn Informacyjno-Instrukcyjny* w latach 1952–1955" [The internal journal of censorship. *Informational and Instructional Bulletin* between 1952–1955], the researcher offered an overview of the content of the indicated resource,[21] while in the article "Od orderu do 'zapisu.' Jak GUKPPiW oceniał pisarzy w latach 1952–1955?" [From honors to "the Index." How did the GUKPPiW rate writers in the years 1952–1955?], she focused on a specific issue, namely, the "relationship: writer – state," which was precarious and ambiguous in People's Poland.[22] She used the Bulletin records as the basis for her considerations.

Three years later Budrowska published "archival material from the fonds of the Main Office for the Control of the Press, Publications, and Public Performances from mid-1955" on Kazimiera Iłłakowiczówna's work – the text indicated came from a Bulletin issued in July of that year.[23] Work on the confidential Bulletins from 1955 continued in the Białystok fonds. Its effect was a selection of documents from the journal from that year, published under Budrowska's editorship.[24] It should be added that already in 2009, the researcher had made several references to the advisories in question, and in 2013, she pointed to the latest findings on what period these confidential advisories were written.[25]

In the works mentioned so far, the main focus was on the Bulletins from 1952–1955. In the resources of the State Archive in Gdańsk, I found subsequent

---

[20] K. Budrowska, "Tajne pismo cenzury. *Biuletyn Informacyjno-Instrukcyjny* w latach 1952–1955," [in:] *Komunikowanie się Polaków w latach 1944–1989*, eds. K. Stępnik, M. Rajewski, Lublin: Wydawnictwo UMCS, 2011, pp. 51–61.

[21] Eadem, "Wewnętrzne pismo cenzury. *Biuletyn Informacyjno-Instrukcyjny* w latach 1952–1955," [in:] eadem, *Studia i szkice o cenzurze w Polsce Ludowej w latach 40. i 50. XX wieku*, Białystok: Wydawnictwo Alter Studio, 2014, pp. 95–106. See also: eadem, "Przeszłość ocenzurowana. GUKPPiW a obraz historii Polski w literaturze lat 1945–1958," [in:] eadem, *Studia i szkice o cenzurze w Polsce Ludowej…*, pp. 28–29.

[22] Eadem, "Od orderu do 'zapisu.' Jak GUKPPiW oceniał pisarzy w latach 1952–1955?," [in:] *Kariera pisarza w PRL-u*, eds. M. Budnik, K. Budrowska, E. Dąbrowicz, K. Kościewicz, Warszawa: IBL PAN, 2014, series *Badania Filologiczne nad Cenzurą PRL* vol. 4, p. 79.

[23] Eadem, "O twórczości Kazimiery Iłłakowiczówny. Materiał archiwalny z zespołu Głównego Urzędu Kontroli Prasy, Publikacji i Widowisk z połowy 1955 r.," *Napis. Pismo poświęcone literaturze okolicznościowej i użytkowej* 2017, series 23, pp. 364–386.

[24] "*Biuletyn Informacyjno-Instrukcyjny.*" *Wybór dokumentów z 1955 r.*, eds. K. Budrowska, M. Budnik, W. Gardocki, Białystok: Wydawnictwo Alter Studio, 2018, series *Cenzura w PRL. Archiwalia* vol. 3.

[25] K. Budrowska, *Writers, Literature and Censorship in Poland. 1948–1956*, Berlin: Peter Lang, 2020, p. 27 et seq.; K. Budrowska, *Zatrzymane przez cenzurę. Inedita z połowy wieku XX*, Warszawa: IBL PAN, 2013, series *Badania Filologiczne nad Cenzurą PRL* vol. 2, p. 33.

issues of the journal (from 1945, 1949, 1950 and 1956), which at that time had been poorly studied or lacked any analyses. This was an important addition to the considerations, which helped complement the previous findings. The results of my research were published in 2017 and 2019 in the articles "'O wyższy poziom pracy nad książką' – biuletyny urzędu cenzury z lat 1945–1956 w perspektywie literaturoznawczej. Rekonesans" ["For a higher level of work on the book" – bulletins for censors from 1945 to 1956 from a literary studies perspective. A reconnaissance study] and "Bulletins of the Polish censorship office from 1945 to 1956. A reconnaissance study."[26] The resources of the State Archive in Poznań also turned out to be helpful; they contained other issues, which were little known and absent from literary studies. I presented the results of my work on the voluminous folder containing 291 folia of Bulletins from the years 1945–1951 in the article "Archiwalia 'pionierskiego' okresu powojennej cenzury. Literatura w poufnych biuletynach urzędu cenzury (1945–1951)"[27] [Archival records of the "pioneer" period of post-war censorship. Literature in the confidential bulletins for censors (1945–1951)].

In 2020, I published two more texts about the Bulletins. This time I examined the "Competition for a censorship review of Wanda Wasilewska's novel *Rzeki Płoną*," which was announced in one of the Bulletins published in 1952.[28] In a popular science article entitled "'Cenzura jest jak stara kochanka…,' czyli o czym pisano w poufnych poradnikach dla cenzorów" ["Censorship is like a long-time mistress…," or the content of confidential advisories for censors],

---

[26] A. Wiśniewska-Grabarczyk, "'O wyższy poziom pracy nad książką' – biuletyny urzędu cenzury z lat 1945–1956 w perspektywie literaturoznawczej. Rekonesans," [in:] *Cenzura w PRL. Analiza zjawiska*, eds. Z. Romek, K. Kamińska-Chełminiak, Warszawa: Oficyna Wydawnicza ASPRA-JR, 2017, p. 61–74; eadem, "Bulletins of the Polish censorship office from 1945 to 1956. A reconnaissance study," *Acta Universitatis Lodziensis. Folia Litteraria Polonica* 2019, no. 4, pp. 311–331 (this is a slightly revised and expanded version of the 2017 article cited above).

[27] Eadem, "Archiwalia 'pionierskiego' okresu powojennej cenzury. Literatura w poufnych biuletynach urzędu cenzury (1945–1951)," *Sztuka Edycji. Studia Tekstologiczne i Edytorskie* 2021, issue 2 (20), pp. 51–62; see also: "*Biuletyny Instrukcyjno-Szkoleniowe 1945–1951*" (APP, WUKPPiW, file ref. no. 4). At this point, I would like to correct the incomplete information I gave in my article "'O wyższy poziom pracy nad książką…'": I wrote there that Daria Nałęcz did not provide the file reference numbers of the Bulletins from 1945 and did not characterize their contents; indeed there was no characteristic of the collections, however, the reference numbers were given on p. 45, which I overlooked (see: *Główny Urząd Kontroli Prasy…*, p. 45).

[28] A. Wiśniewska-Grabarczyk, "Konkurs na recenzję cenzorską powieści Wandy Wasilewskiej pt. *Rzeki płoną*. Materiał archiwalny z poufnego biuletynu dla cenzorów z roku 1952," *Bibliotekarz Podlaski* 2020, issue 1, pp. 215–233, https://bibliotekarzpodlaski.pl/index.php/bp/article/view/427/489 (accessed January 21, 2021).

I synthesized the results of previous research, while also examining the censors' own creative work presented in the advisories.[29]

In recent years there have been several literary studies articles based on instructional materials from "Mysia Street." One of them is Barbara Tyszkiewicz's text from 2016, entitled "Sztuka czytania między wierszami. Z problematyki cenzorskich instruktaży drugiej połowy lat 70."[30] [The art of reading between the lines: on censorship instructions from the second half of the 1970s]. The researcher studied *Informacje Instruktażowe* from this very period and analyzed cultural problems presented there. *Sygnały* – another type of instructional document, which featured typescripts of contested texts – was the subject of Budrowska's article from 2014. She described the material deposited in the GUKPPiW as "a confidential, internal bulletin of the office."[31] Training materials were also used by such authors as Wiktor Gardocki and Joanna Hobot.[32] However, despite the frequent convergence of nomenclature, not all instructional archives analyzed in the above-mentioned articles could be defined as "Bulletins for censors."[33]

Source Material

Not a single word (generally speaking) shall be printed
or distributed without our scrutiny or knowledge.[34]

The basic source material used in the book were Bulletins for censors issued in the years 1945–1956. These documents are deposited in several state archives in Poland, e.g., in Gdańsk, Poznań and the Central Archives of Mod-

---

[29] Eadem, "'Cenzura jest jak stara kochanka…,' czyli o czym pisano w poufnych poradnikach dla cenzorów," *Informator Polski* 2020, no. 3–4, pp. 13–16, https://www.fede-racja-polonia.dk/pliki/pdf/IP-110.pdf (accessed January 21, 2021).

[30] B. Tyszkiewicz, "Sztuka czytania między wierszami. Z problematyki cenzorskich instruktaży drugiej połowy lat 70.," [in:] *"Sztuka czytania między wierszami." Cenzura w komunikacji literackiej w Polsce w latach 1965–1989*, eds. K. Budrowska, M. Kotowska-Kachel, Warszawa: IBL PAN, 2016, series *Badania Filologiczne nad Cenzurą PRL* vol. 6, pp. 127–158.

[31] K. Budrowska, "O niestosownych zastosowaniach literatury przez cenzurę PRL," [in:] eadem, *Studia i szkice o cenzurze w Polsce Ludowej…*, p. 107.

[32] W. Gardocki, *Cenzura wobec literatury polskiej w latach osiemdziesiątych XX w.*, Warszawa: IBL PAN, 2019, series *Badania Filologiczne nad Cenzurą PRL* vol. 8; J. Hobot, *Gra z cenzurą w poezji Nowej Fali (1968–1976)*, Kraków: Wydawnictwo Literackie, 2000.

[33] Below I present my own definition of Bulletins for censors, which, I hope, will serve as a stimulus for further genre and classification study on instructional materials produced by the censorship office.

[34] "Z krajowej odprawy w GUKP," *Biuletyn Informacyjno-Instrukcyjny* no. 7, July 1952, p. 15 (APG, WUKPPiW, file ref. no. 84).

ern Records in Warsaw.[35] I have compared the individual issues of the periodicals stored in the above-mentioned centers and can confirm that there are no major differences between them; most of the deviations that I have noticed, e.g., missing pages in some of the issues, were hardly intentional action on the part of the editors of the magazine, but had to do with archival work done later or some unforeseen circumstances or mistakes.[36] Some of the copies bear handwritten annotations, which, of course, cannot be treated as a difference in the actual content of the periodical.[37] The hypothesis of variance in the vocabulary used in different copies of the same issue of the Bulletin requires further research.[38]

The oldest Bulletin I have located is dated May 1945, while the last one comes from February 1956. In total, I have analyzed all the Bulletins from the years 1945–1956 that I was able to find in the archives, i.e., four complete years from 1952 to 1955, twelve issues a year (some appeared as double issues); eleven other issues (or possibly thirteen, which is discussed below) – one each

---

[35] In this book, I have primarily made references to the resources of the Gdańsk archives, because I studied them first and they formed the basis of my initial research of the subject, see: Archiwum Państwowe Gdańsk (State Archives in Gdańsk), fonds: Wojewódzki Urząd Kontroli Prasy, Publikacji i Widowisk (The Voivodeship Office for the Control of the Press, Publications and Public Performances; hereafter cited as APG, WUKPPiW). See also: Archiwum Państwowe w Poznaniu (State Archives in Poznań), fonds: Wojewódzki Urząd Kontroli Prasy, Publikacji i Widowisk (The Voivodeship Office for the Control of the Press, Publications and Public Performances; hereafter cited as APP, WUKPPiW); Archiwum Akt Nowych (Central Archives of Modern Records), fonds: Główny Urząd Kontroli Prasy, Publikacji i Widowisk (The Main Office for the Control of the Press, Publications and Public Performances; hereafter cited as AAN, GUKPPiW).

[36] Some of the issues have missing pages, e.g., page 23 is missing from the April 1953 issue of the AAN Bulletin, while the August issue of the same year has no page XIII; in the Gdańsk resources, in the June/July 1953 issue of the Bulletin there is no errata, which can be found in the same issue housed in the AAN (the page is clipped between pages 30 and 31); two copies of the Bulletin from March 1950 included in the Poznań resources in the folder *"Biuletyny Instrukcyjno-Szkoleniowe 1945–1951"* contain no "Addendum," which preceded that same issue found in the AAN – this is a significant omission, as the "Addendum" reported a delay in publishing the issue, which eventually came out not, as the title page indicates, in March, but in May (see: *Biuletyn Szkoleniowy* no. 1, March (May) 1950, p. 1 (APG, WUKPPiW, file ref. no. 328)).

[37] Cf., e.g., annotations made on the last page of *Biuletyn Instrukcyjny* no. 2 from June 1945, held in the APP (APP, WUKPPiW, file ref. no. 4, fol. 13r) and lack of these in the copy stored in APG (APG, WUKPPiW, file ref. no. 210, p. 19).

[38] See, e.g.: an excerpt about "things of interference" and "things of interpretation" in the chapter "On the Works of Kazimiera Iłłakowiczówna."

from 1950 and 1951, and two each from 1945, 1948, 1949, and 1956; and one undated Bulletin, referenced only with the number 4 (prepared certainly after November 1946 and before October 30, 1948). Due to the lack of the title page, it is difficult to determine whether two additional documents, i.e., ["Materiały z odprawy"; Briefing materials] and "Na marginesie narodowej dyskusji" [On the margin of the national discussion], filed in the folder *"Biuletyny Instrukcyjno-Szkoleniowe* 1945–1951", can be regarded as two subsequent issues of the periodical in question.[39] It is possible considering that both texts were placed in the folder with other Bulletins; furthermore, this collection, as well as others, contain the so-called special issues presenting transcripts of conferences, briefings and meetings. It seems, however, that it is too early to settle the status of these "problematic" materials, which could have found their way into this collection accidentally.[40]

The discussed periodicals had a supplement entitled *Biblioteczki Biuletynu Informacyjno-Instrukcyjnego GUKPPiW*, also published by the censorship office. So far, I have managed to find seven issues of the supplement, all dated 1955.[41]

Narrowing the material down only to the issues that could unquestionably be classified as confidential Bulletins for censors, I have analyzed 59 issues of the periodical and seven *Biblioteczki*, that is, about 2,670 typewritten pages in total.

While working on the book, I also used other archival materials, mainly documents created in the Main Office or the Voivodeship Offices for the Control of the Press, Publications and Public Performances. When it was justified, I quoted some of them, confronting the information contained therein with the position presented in the Bulletins, e.g., in the case of censorship reviews featured in the magazine.

---

[39] ["Materiały z odprawy"]; "Na marginesie ogólnonarodowej dyskusji," fol. 14r–48r, fol. 247r–252r ("*Biuletyny Instrukcyjno-Szkoleniowe* 1945–1951" (APP, WUKPPiW, file ref. no. 4)). The title ["Materiały z odprawy"] is my proposal – in the resource analyzed, the collection was not provided with a title; the fact that it is a separate entity is evidenced by the subject matter, the continuous numbering within the document, and its "appearance" (the material is damaged and often illegible).

[40] I write more about this subject in the article "Archiwalia 'pionierskiego' okresu powojennej cenzury…"

[41] *Biblioteczka Biuletynu Informacyjno-Instrukcyjnego GUKPPiW* no. 18, 1955 (APG, WUKPPiW, file ref. no. 215); no. 19, 1955 (APG, WUKPPiW, file ref. no. 213); no. 20, 1955 (APG, WUKPPiW, file ref. no. 214); no. 21, 1955 (APG, WUKPPiW, file ref. no. 212); no. 22, 1955 (APG, WUKPPiW, file ref. no. 195); no. 23, 1955 (APG, WUKP-PiW, file ref. no. 194); no. 24, 1955 (APG, WUKPPiW, file ref. no. 193).

Rules for Presenting the Material

*The censor's pencil should resemble a surgical lancet
rather than a Stone Age club.*[42]

The archival sources sometimes contained errors. In most cases, it was not possible to render them in English, but the most glaring mistakes have been indicated by the phrase [*sic*]. My additions to quotations are put in square brackets [...]. The abbreviations appearing in the statements of censors and other functionaries of the censorship office are not expounded; in exceptional cases (e.g., when the abbreviation makes it impossible to understand the text) I provide full names, for example, Non-per[iodical] Public[ations] Department. A list of all abbreviations used is provided at the end of the book.

In a few places, the Bulletins transformed into a kind of "palimpsest," thanks to deletions, corrections and extra information added to the original version. I include this variability in the citations because it reveals the process of working on the text, changes in the censor's thinking or differences in the assessments made by the Office's staff.

In a censor's sheet, also known as a "review form,"[43] there are usually two or three dates: 1) the date the work was submitted to the reviewer (meaning, the date a particular censor was assigned to the task; not to be confused with the date the publication reached the Office); 2) the date below the reviewer's motion (i.e., the date the evaluation was completed); 3) finally, the date when the supervisor evaluating the motion issued a decision. In this book, the default date is the one when the first assessment was made. In exceptional cases, if it is essential for the argument, I include all three dates.

In light of the subject of the work, I have taken particular care in quoting the full titles of the texts reviewed, as well as the names and surnames of the authors, which the editors of the Bulletin repeatedly failed to do. The Bulletin versions that were inaccurate and incomplete, and sometimes erroneous, are signaled in the footnote the first time a given author or title appears.

---

[42] "Podsumowanie dyskusji nad wierszem Roztworowskiego pt. 'Oskarżam,'" *Biuletyn Informacyjno-Instrukcyjny* no. 11/12 (23/24), November/December 1953, p. 16 (APG, WUKPPiW, file ref. no. 9). This metaphor also appeared in other censorship documents, cf. *"Lancetem, a nie maczugą." Cenzura wobec literatury i jej twórców w latach 1945–1965*, eds. K. Budrowska, M. Woźniak-Łabieniec, Warszawa: IBL PAN, 2012, series *Badania Filologiczne nad Cenzurą PRL* vol. 1.

[43] "Recenzja z pozycji literackiej, cz. I" (in the series *O wyższy poziom pracy nad książką*), *Biuletyn Informacyjno-Instrukcyjny* no. 8, August 1952, p. 21, 23 (APG, WUKPPiW, file ref. no. 81). "A censor's sheet" is *arkusz recenzyjny* and "a review form" is *blankiet recenzyjny*.

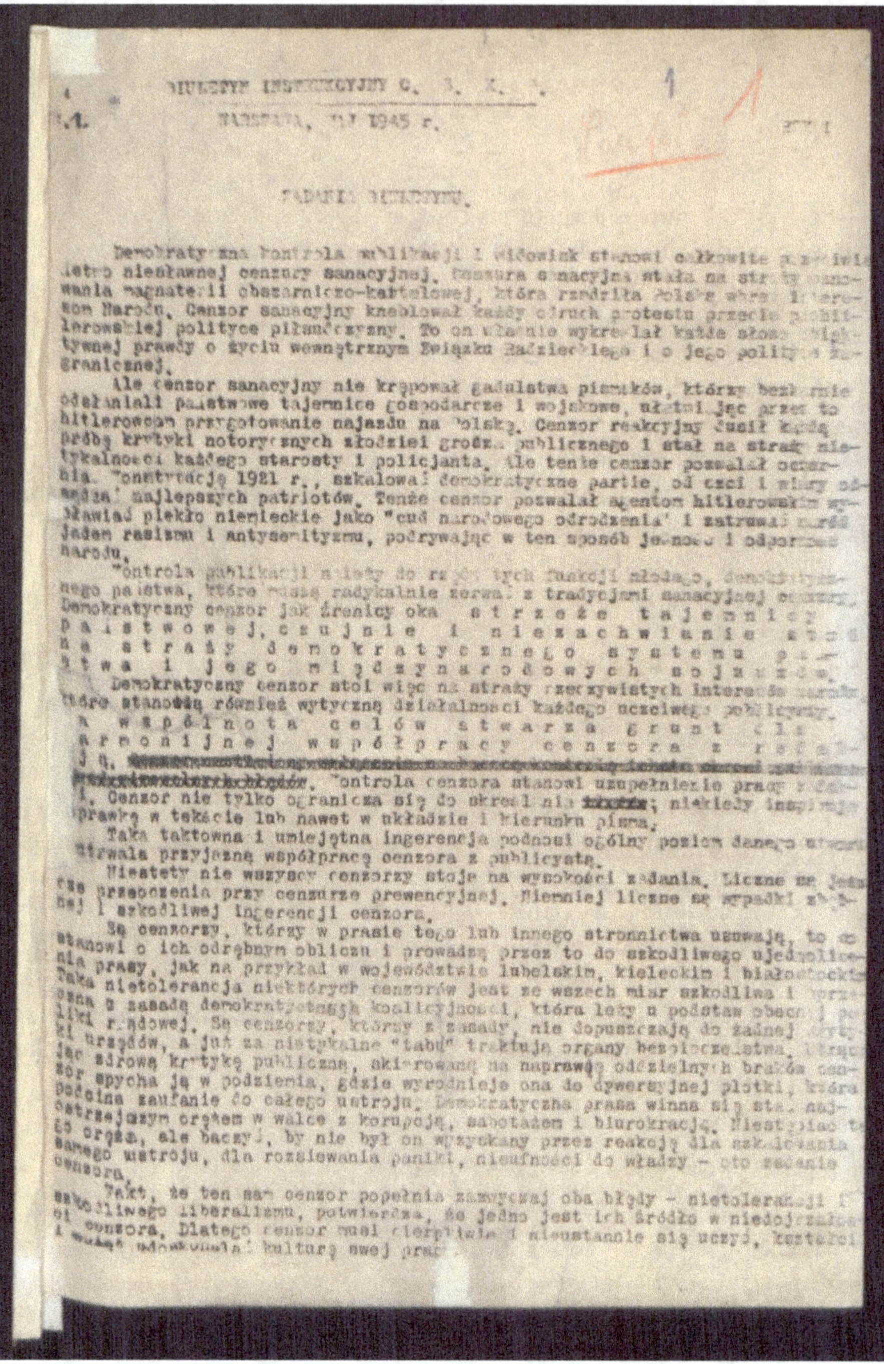

Fig. 1. The first page of the oldest Bulletin yet found, *Biuletyn Instrukcyjny* no. 1, dated May 1945 (APP, WUKPPiW, file ref. no. 4, fol. 1r).

Part One

**IN SEARCH OF A DEFINITION:
WHAT WERE THE CONFIDENTIAL
BULLETINS FOR CENSORS?
CHARACTERISTICS OF THE SOURCE
MATERIAL**

1. THE PURPOSE OF CREATING
A CONFIDENTIAL PERIODICAL FOR CENSORS

What do you think about all this, dear GUKP?[1]

The decision to start publishing the Bulletin for censors was made "as a result of the agreement between the party apparatus and the chief censorship institutions."[2] It was largely a response to the grassroots voices of functionaries, who complained that they had no instructional manual. The fact that censorship practice required theoretical foundations was repeatedly stressed in the Bulletins from the very beginning.[3] In 1945, the June Bulletin quoted relevant statements from the First National Conference of Managers and Delegates of Voivodeship Offices for the Control of the Press, Publications and Public Performances, which took place in Warsaw from May 23 to 25, 1945.[4] The then deputy head of the Propaganda Department of the Central Committee of the Polish Workers' Party, Ferdynand Chaber, argued that it was necessary to create something like a "book of

---

[1] B. Sołtan (WUKPPiW Gdańsk), "Na marginesie pewnej ingerencji" (correspondence in "Dział Listów"), *Biuletyn Informacyjno-Instrukcyjny* no. 12 (48), December 1955, p. 58 (APG, WUKPPiW, file ref. no. 117).

[2] *Główny Urząd Kontroli Prasy 1945–1949*, compiled by D. Nałęcz, Warszawa: ISP PAN, 1994, series *Dokumenty do Dziejów PRL* issue 6, p. 10. I have also discussed the circumstances surrounding the creation of the Bulletins in the articles "Bulletins of the Polish censorship office from 1945 to 1956. A reconnaissance study," *Acta Universitatis Lodziensis. Folia Litteraria Polonica* 2019, no. 4, pp. 315–318; and "'O wyższy poziom pracy nad książką' – biuletyny urzędu cenzury z lat 1945–1956 w perspektywie literaturoznawczej. Rekonesans," [in:] *Cenzura w PRL. Analiza zjawiska*, eds. Z. Romek, K. Kamińska-Chełminiak, Warszawa: Oficyna Wydawnicza ASPRA-JR, 2017, pp. 65–67.

[3] See, e.g.: "Dyskusja nad nr 1 *Biuletynu Informacyjno-Szkoleniowego*," *Biuletyn Informacyjno-Szkoleniowy* no. 1/3, January 1949, p. 47 (APG, WUKPPiW, file ref. no. 196); "Od Redakcji," *Biuletyn Informacyjno-Szkoleniowy* no. 3, March 1952, p. 1 (APG, WUKPPiW, file ref. no. 96); "Artykuł wstępny," *Biuletyn Informacyjno-Szkoleniowy* no. 1 (13), January 1953, pp. 2–8 (APG, WUKPPiW, file ref. no. 19).

[4] *Biuletyn Instrukcyjny* no. 2, June 1945 (APG, WUKPPiW, file ref. no. 210); *Główny Urząd Kontroli Prasy 1945–1949...*, pp. 29–78.

censorship wisdom."[5] According to him, the functionaries of the Office worked "in a segment" that had "no established tradition nor literature."[6] It may have been the first attempt to create a user-friendly and comprehensible instructional manual for censors, which would go beyond the rigid framework of regulations that often deterred the functionaries.

The first preserved issue formulated the Bulletin's tasks: "to showcase the work of a good censor and disseminate positive achievements, to reveal mistakes and warn against them, to improve the activities of our offices and raise their standards."[7] Subsequent issues repeatedly set up essentially the same objectives, sometimes supplementing them with additional guidelines or elaborating on certain elements, an example of which is the "Introduction" to the 1950 *Biuletyn Szkoleniowy*:

> We present Issue No. 1 of the Training Bulletin. Leaning on our censorship practice, this bulletin will examine the challenges we encounter in the segment of the press, publications and performances. The problems will be arranged thematically, and they primarily include omissions and interferences as well as overlooked ideological distortions (when, instead of interference, a signal to GUKP would have sufficed).[8]

The content of this issue of the Bulletin confirms these assumptions: the material was sorted by problems and the "training" contained in the title of the magazine was based on "learning from mistakes"; drawing not from regulations, but the censorship practice. The articles focused on omissions and unnecessary intrusions, which usually came with a commentary. In most of the periodicals analyzed, this was a typical approach to presenting the material.

It was also the case in the January 1952 issue, which reiterated the reasons for creating the internal censorship magazine:

> The decision to publish the Informational and Instructional Bulletin systematically was prompted by the need to provide collective assistance to the GUKP employees both in Warsaw and in the field to aid them in their difficult and responsible work.[9]

---

[5] "Seminarium prasy (wyjątki z protokółu)," *Biuletyn Instrukcyjny* no. 2, June 1945, p. 2 (APG, WUKPPiW, file ref. no. 210).

[6] Ibidem, p. 1.

[7] "Zadania biuletynu," *Biuletyn Instrukcyjny* no. 1, May 1945, fol. 1v (APP, WUKPPiW, file ref. no. 4).

[8] "Wstęp," *Biuletyn Szkoleniowy* no. 1, March (May) 1950, p. 3 (APG, WUKPPiW, file ref. no. 328). See also: "Zabezpieczyć stałe i systematyczne szkolenie zespołów cenzorskich," *Biuletyn Informacyjno-Szkoleniowy* no. 10, October 1952, p. 1 (APG, WUKPPiW, file ref. no. 75); "Artykuł wstępny," *Biuletyn Informacyjno-Instrukcyjny* no. 1 (13), January 1953, pp. 2–8 (APG, WUKPPiW, file ref. no. 19).

[9] "Podwyższyć poziom naszej pracy," *Biuletyn Informacyjno-Instrukcyjny* no. 1, January 1952, p. 1 (APG, WUKPPiW, file ref. no. 100).

It seems that the magazine was not immediately embraced by the rank-and-file functionaries, because as late as July 1952 attempts were made to persuade them to make use of the periodical more regularly and to take an active part in its creation:

> There is another major aid to training and instruction – not yet sufficiently appreciated and applied – and that is our Bulletin. There is no doubt that its regular publication is an extraordinary achievement in our work. The material it contains serves to help every censor. In the course of our work on the Bulletin, we have made a fair share of mistakes, and we have had to overcome a number of difficulties. Above all, it has been a question of establishing the right character and profile of the Bulletin.
> The further development of the Bulletin largely depends on the co-operation of our comrades from voivodeship offices.
> Is it normal that the majority of comrades from the head offices have not written a single article for the Bulletin in six months? Is there really nothing to write about? In our opinion, there is. We must admit to ourselves that at times, the attitude towards the Bulletin testifies to a political underestimation of its importance for our work. Therefore, the key task in this segment is to radically change this attitude and have every political worker treat the Bulletin as their auxiliary instrument in their work for the Office.[10]

Also in December 1952 and in January of the following year, there were complaints about the insufficient use of the Bulletin in censorship practice, about the lack of materials sent from voivodeship offices and the little interest in co-operating with the magazine's editorial board. There were reminders that some "collectives have not yet sent a single word to the Bulletin."[11] Other materials, on the other hand, emphasized the benefits of reading the Bulletin: according to the censors' testimonies, the number of omissions and unjustified interferences supposedly decreased and there was a noticeable improvement in the level of professional competence of the functionaries.[12]

To recapitulate, confidential Bulletins for censors were designed to go beyond the dry regulations and guidelines formulated by the state apparatus. Indeed, the

---

[10] "Z krajowej odprawy w GUKP," *Biuletyn Informacyjno-Instrukcyjny* no. 7, July 1952, p. 14 (APG, WUKPPiW, file ref. no. 84).

[11] "Artykuł wstępny," *Biuletyn Informacyjno-Instrukcyjny* no. 1 (13), January 1953, p. 7 (APG, WUKPPiW, file ref. no. 19); see also: B. Gutkowski, "O wyższy poziom pracy Urzędu," *Biuletyn Informacyjno-Instrukcyjny* no. 12, December 1952, p. 7 (APG, WUKPPiW, file ref. no. 70).

[12] "Artykuł wstępny; O realizację wyników odprawy grudniowej GUKPPiW," *Biuletyn Informacyjno-Instrukcyjny* no. 1 (13), January 1953, pp. 2–8, 12 (APG, WUKPPiW, file ref. no. 19).

journal placed great emphasis on their explication, citing and discussing a number of specific interferences. Thanks to this, the periodical often provided answers to questions and doubts, constituting a concrete "aid in the work of censors"[13] and an excellent conduit for the exchange of professional experience. However, even though it also published texts written by rank-and-file functionaries, the Bulletin retained the classic structure of an instructional text.

---

[13] "Zabezpieczyć stałe i systematyczne szkolenie zespołów cenzorskich," *Biuletyn Informacyjno-Instrukcyjny* no. 10, October 1952, p. 1 (APG, WUKPPiW, file ref. no. 75).

2. THE CENSOR AS THE CO-AUTHOR OF BULLETINS FOR CENSORS

The Bulletins of "The Ministry of Truth" (as the censorship office might be called after Orwell's *1984*, which was banned in communist Poland[15]) were dominated by instructional and training texts, whose task was to advise and educate the model censor. The vast majority of such articles were written by the "Bulletin's Editorial Board,"[16] which as a rule, remained unknown to the average reader of the magazine. None of the analyzed issues mentioned its members, and only once was the editorial material signed with a specific name; this was in February 1956, when the introduction of the "Bulletin's editor," S. Wilner, was published.[17] While most of the editorials were anonymous, sometimes it was signaled that a text was sent by an administrative unit of the Office, such as Departament Nadzoru i Instruktażu [Department of Supervision and Instruction].[18]

---

[14] "Z krajowej odprawy w GUKP," *Biuletyn Informacyjno-Instrukcyjny* no. 7, July 1952, p. 15 (APG, WUKPPiW, sygn. 84). I have also discussed the co-authorship of the Bulletins in the articles "Bulletins of the Polish censorship office from 1945 to 1956…," pp. 322–327; "'O wyższy poziom pracy nad książką'…," pp. 71–73.

[15] Orwell's dystopia from 1949 was first published in Polish by Instytut Literacki in 1953, then (officially) not until 1988; G. Orwell, *1984*, London: Secker & Warburg, 1949.

[16] The journal usually used capital letters ("Bulletin's Editorial Board"), although there were also times when a lowercase letter was used with the second part ("Bulletin's editorial board"), see, e.g.: Departament Nadzoru i Instruktażu, "Uwagi o instruktażu," *Biuletyn Informacyjno-Instrukcyjny* no. 2 (50), February 1956, p. 33 (APG, WUKPPiW, file ref. no. 6).

[17] S. Wilner, "I co dalej?… (refleksje redaktora Biuletynu)," *Biuletyn Informacyjno--Instrukcyjny* no. 2 (50), February 1956, pp. 2–8 (APG, WUKPPiW, file ref. no. 6).

[18] See, e.g.: Departament Nadzoru i Instruktażu, "Uwagi o instruktażu," *Biuletyn Informacyjno-Instrukcyjny* no. 2 (50), February 1956, pp. 24–36 (APG, WUKPPiW, file ref. no. 6). In the book I specify the authors of the articles, also if the author of the text is an administrative unit of the Office or simply "the Editorial Board"; I also include other information given by the author, e.g., the branch and the city; see, e.g.: Bieliński (WUKP Łódź), "Z terenowych prac wtórnych. Uwagi krytyczne na temat popularyzacji spółdzielczości produkcyjnej na łamach prasy terenowej," *Biuletyn Informacyjno-Instrukcyjny* no. 2 (14),

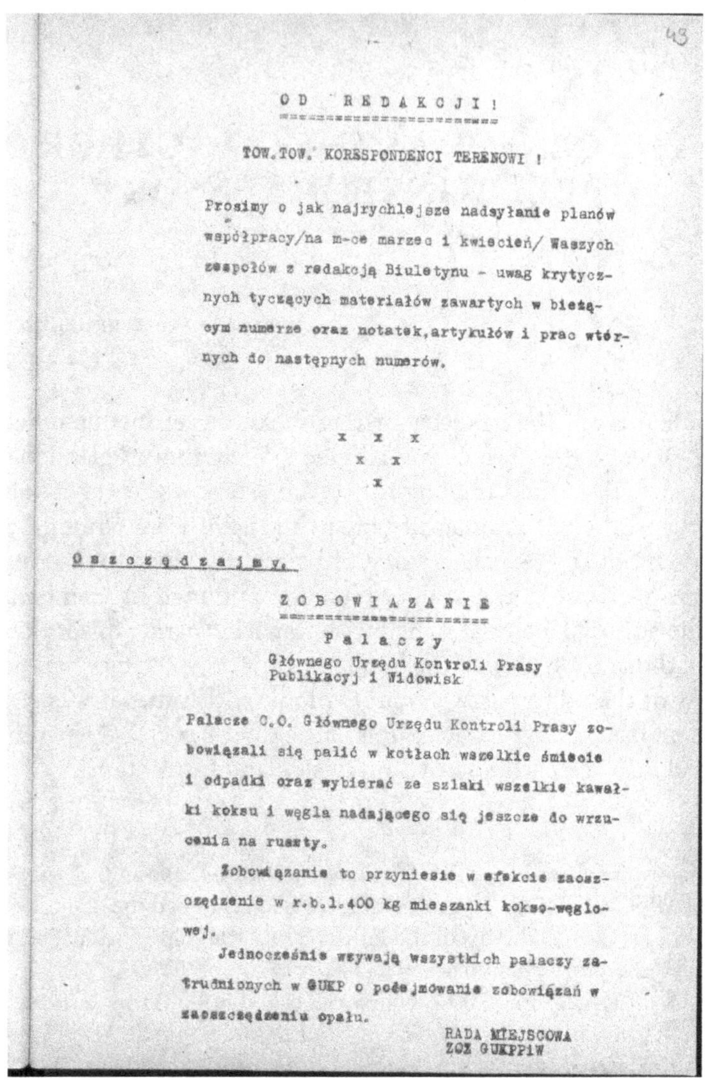

Fig. 2. The appeal by the Bulletin's editorial board encouraging censors to cooperate with the magazine, published in the February 1953 issue (APG, WUKPPiW, file ref. no. 18, p. 43): "Please send us the plans for your teams' cooperation with the Bulletin's editors for the months of March and April as soon as possible. Feel free to send critical remarks on the material contained in the recent issue as well as notes, articles, and secondary works for future issues."

February 1953, pp. 38–42 (APG, WUKPPiW, file ref. no. 18); Editorial board, "50 numerów *Biuletynu*," *Biuletyn Informacyjno-Instrukcyjny* no. 12 (48), December 1955, pp. 2–3 (APG, WUKPPiW, file ref. no. 117).

In addition to this type of training and instructional material, we can find reports, balance sheets, and summaries, which came from field centers. The purpose of these reports was, among other things, to boast about the team's achievements and possibly to help colleagues from other branches. However, in most publications of this type, the monologue prevailed over the dialogue, and an official clerical style was maintained.[19]

Nonetheless, an effort was made to offset this somewhat authoritarian tone and the subjunctive nature of the statements with materials in which both heads of field branches and rank-and-file political workers wrote more freely. The magazine encouraged correspondent-censors to provide such testimonies and to contribute to the work of the editorial board by submitting plans for cooperation, notes, articles, and critical comments.[20]

Obviously, the editorial board could not be open to a real dialogue: the only critical materials that were published were those that could be used to attack or lecture selected censorship teams, individual functionaries, or even the entire censorship community, but never the system as a whole. However, the encouragement of free expression, different from tedious reports and balance sheets, was certainly intended to loosen the rigid editorial form of the periodical and make it more "friendly" and accessible than other materials created in the Office.

Some materials about the Bulletins, including letters to the editors (also those printed in the magazine), have been preserved in censorship documents in archives scattered around Poland. The following materials from Poznań may serve as an example: "Dyskusja nad Biuletynem" [A discussion about the Bulletin] and "Terenowy głos w dyskusji" [The field's voice in the discussion].

---

[19] WUKP Bydgoszcz, "Radio Polskie – Bydgoszcz. Uwagi krytyczne za okres 1–25.09.1952," *Biuletyn Informacyjno-Instrukcyjny* no. 10, October 1952, pp. 16–21 (APG, WUKPPiW, file ref. no. 75).

[20] See, e.g.: "Zadania biuletynu," *Biuletyn Instrukcyjny* no. 1, May 1945, fol. 1v (APP, WUKPPiW, file ref. no. 4); "Seminarium prasy (wyjątki z protokółu). O stylu pracy w terenie," *Biuletyn Instrukcyjny* no. 1, June 1945, p. 10 (APG, WUKPPiW, file ref. no. 210); "Instrukcje-wytyczne," *Biuletyn Informacyjno-Szkoleniowy* no. 1, 1951, fol. 271r (APP, WUKPPiW, file ref. no. 4); "Od Redakcji," *Biuletyn Informacyjno-Instrukcyjny* no. 1, January 1952, p. 48 (APG, WUKPPiW, file ref. no. 100); "Od Redakcji," *Biuletyn Informacyjno-Instrukcyjny* no. 2 (14), February 1953, p. 43 (APG, WUKPPiW, file ref. no. 18). See also: Fig. 2, and Fig. 3.

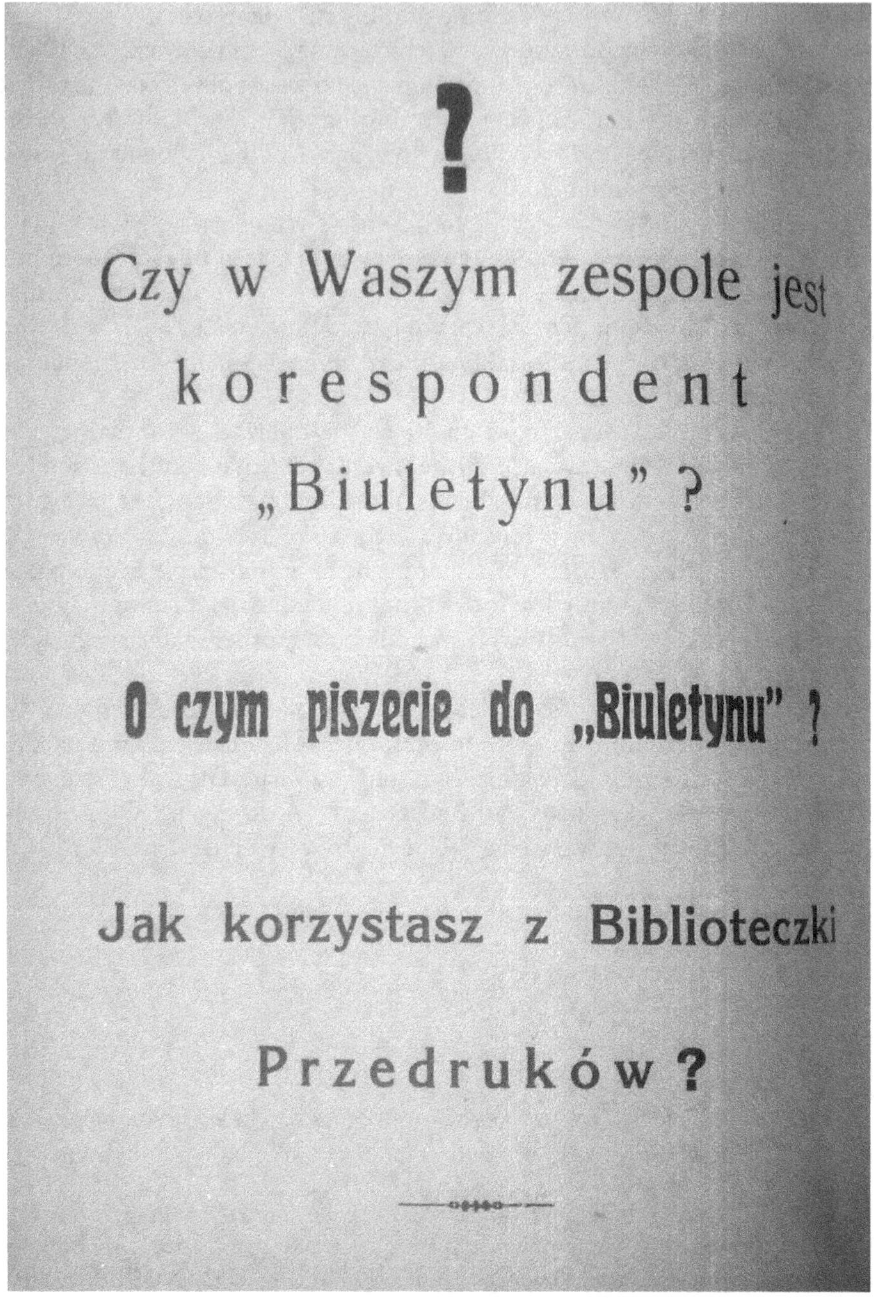

Fig. 3. The appeal of the Bulletin's editorial board encouraging censors to cooperate with the magazine, included in the September 1953 issue (AAN, GUKPPiW, file ref. no. 22, p. 552): "What's your contribution to the *Bulletin*? How do you use the Reprint Library?".

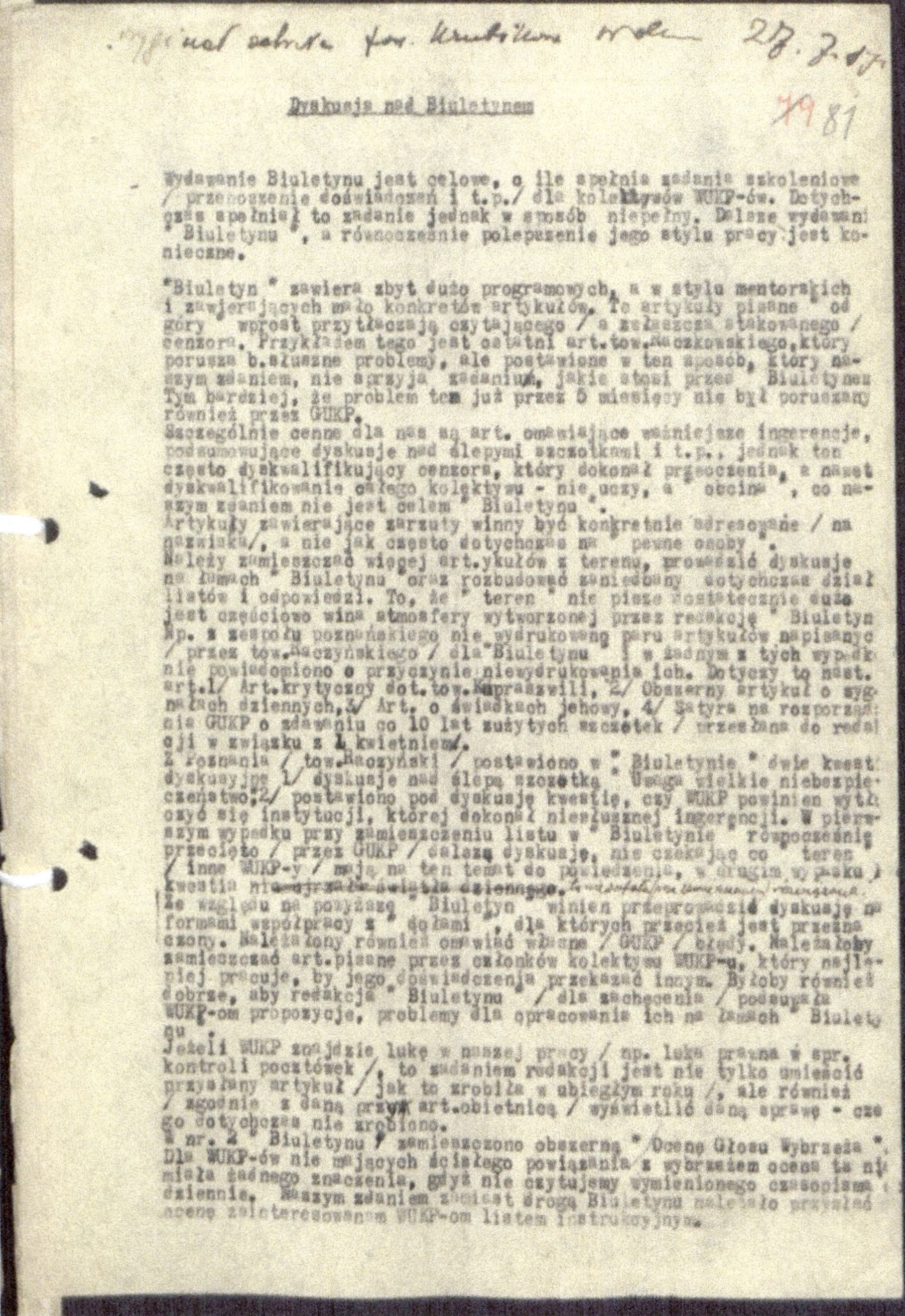

Dyskusja nad Biuletynem

Wydawanie Biuletynu jest celowe, o ile spełnia zadania szkoleniowe /przekazywanie doświadczeń i t.p./ dla kolektywów WUKP-ów. Dotychczas spełniał to zadanie jednak w sposób niepełny. Dalsze wydawani[e] "Biuletynu", a równocześnie polepszenie jego stylu pracy jest konieczne.

"Biuletyn" zawiera zbyt dużo programowych, a w stylu mentorskich i zawierających mało konkretów artykułów. Te artykuły pisane "od góry" wprost przytłaczają czytającego /a zwłaszcza stłoczonego/ cenzora. Przykładem tego jest ostatni art.tow.Raczkowskiego, który porusza b.słuszne problemy, ale postawione w ten sposób, który naszym zdaniem, nie sprzyja zadaniu, jakie stawi przed "Biuletynem". Tym bardziej, że problem ten już przez 5 miesięcy nie był poruszany również przez GUKP.
Szczególnie cenne dla nas są art. omawiające ważniejsze ingerencje, podsumowujące dyskusje nad ślepymi szczotkami i t.p.., jednak ten często dyskwalifikujący cenzora, który dokonał przeoczenia, a nawet dyskwalifikowanie całego kolektywu - nie uczy, a "obcina", co naszym zdaniem nie jest celem "Biuletynu".
Artykuły zawierające zarzuty winny być konkretnie adresowane /na nazwiska/, a nie jak często dotychczas na "pewne osoby".
Należy zamieszczać więcej art.ykułów z terenu, prowadzić dyskusje na łamach "Biuletynu" oraz rozbudować zaniedbany dotychczas dział listów i odpowiedzi. To, że "teren" nie pisze dostatecznie dużo, jest częściowo winą atmosfery wytworzonej przez redakcję "Biuletyn". Np. z zespołu poznańskiego nie wydrukowano paru artykułów napisanyc[h] /przez tow.Raczyńskiego/ dla "Biuletynu" i w żadnym z tych wypadk[ów] nie powiadomiono o przyczynie niewydrukowania ich. Dotyczy to nast. art.1/ Art.krytyczny dot.tow.Kupraszwili, 2/ Obszerny artykuł o sygnałach dziennych, 3/ Art. o świadkach jehowy, 4/ Satyra na rozporządzenie GUKP o zdawaniu co 10 lat zużytych szczotek /przesłana do redakcji w związku z 1 kwietniem/.
Z Poznania /tow.Raczyński / postawiono w "Biuletynie" dwie kwestie dyskusyjne 1/ dyskusje nad ślepą szczotką: Uwaga wielkie niebezpieczeństwo;2/ postawiono pod dyskusję kwestię, czy WUKP powinien wytłoczyć się instytucji, której dokonał niesłusznej ingerencji. W pierwszym wypadku przy zamieszczeniu listu w "Biuletynie" równocześnie przecięto /przez GUKP/ dalszą dyskusję, nie czekając co "teren" /inne WUKP-y/ mają na ten temat do powiedzenia, w drugim wypadku kwestia nierozstrzygnięta świadka dziennego.
Ze względu na powyższą "Biuletyn" winien przeprowadzić dyskusję [nad] formami współpracy z "dołami", dla których przecież jest przeznaczony. Należałoby również omawiać własne /GUKP/ błędy. Należałoby zamieszczać art.pisane przez członków kolektywu WUKP-u, który najlepiej pracuje, by jego doświadczenia przekazać innym. Byłoby również dobrze, aby redakcja "Biuletynu" /dla zachęcenia/ podsuwała WUKP-om propozycje, problemy dla opracowania ich na łamach "Biuletynu".
Jeżeli WUKP znajdzie lukę w naszej pracy /np. luka prawna w spr. kontroli pocztówek /, to zadaniem redakcji jest nie tylko umieścić przysłany artykuł /jak to zrobiła w ubiegłym roku /, ale również /zgodnie z daną przez art.obietnicą / wyświetlić daną sprawę - czego dotychczas nie zrobiono.
W nr. 2 "Biuletynu" zamieszczono obszerną "Ocenę Głosu Wybrzeża". Dla WUKP-ów nie mających ścisłego powiązania z wybrzeżem ocena ta nie miała żadnego znaczenia, gdyż nie czytujemy wymienionego czasopisma dziennie. Naszym zdaniem zamiast drogą Biuletynu należało przysłać ocenę zainteresowanym WUKP-om listem instrukcyjnym.

Fig. 4a. The first page of "Dyskusja nad Biuletynem" – material from 1955 from the branch in Poznań (APP, WUKPPiW, file ref. no. 18, fol. 81r).

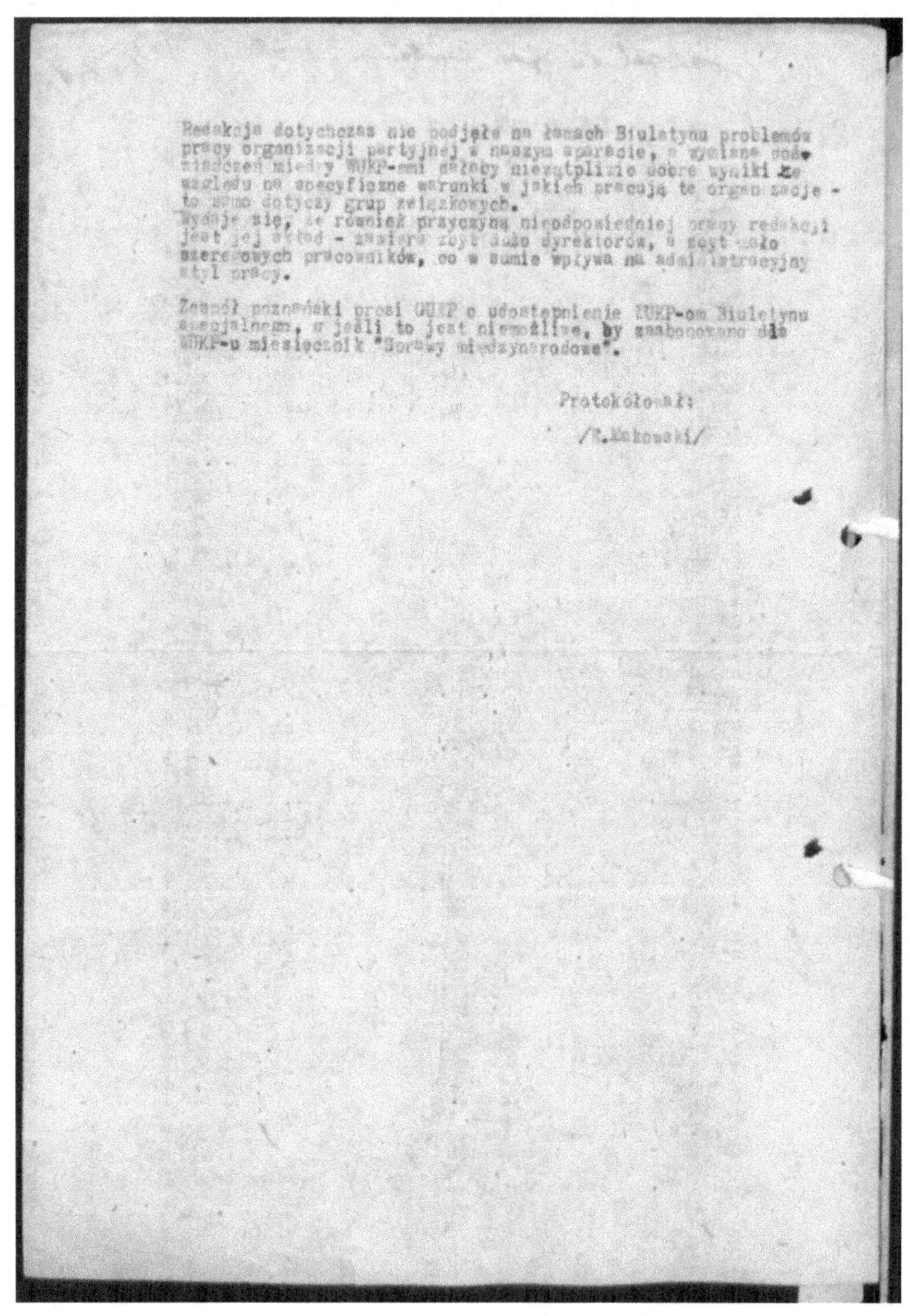

Fig. 4b. The second page of "Dyskusja nad Biuletynem" – material from 1955 from the branch in Poznań (APP, WUKPPiW, file ref. no. 18, fol. 81v).

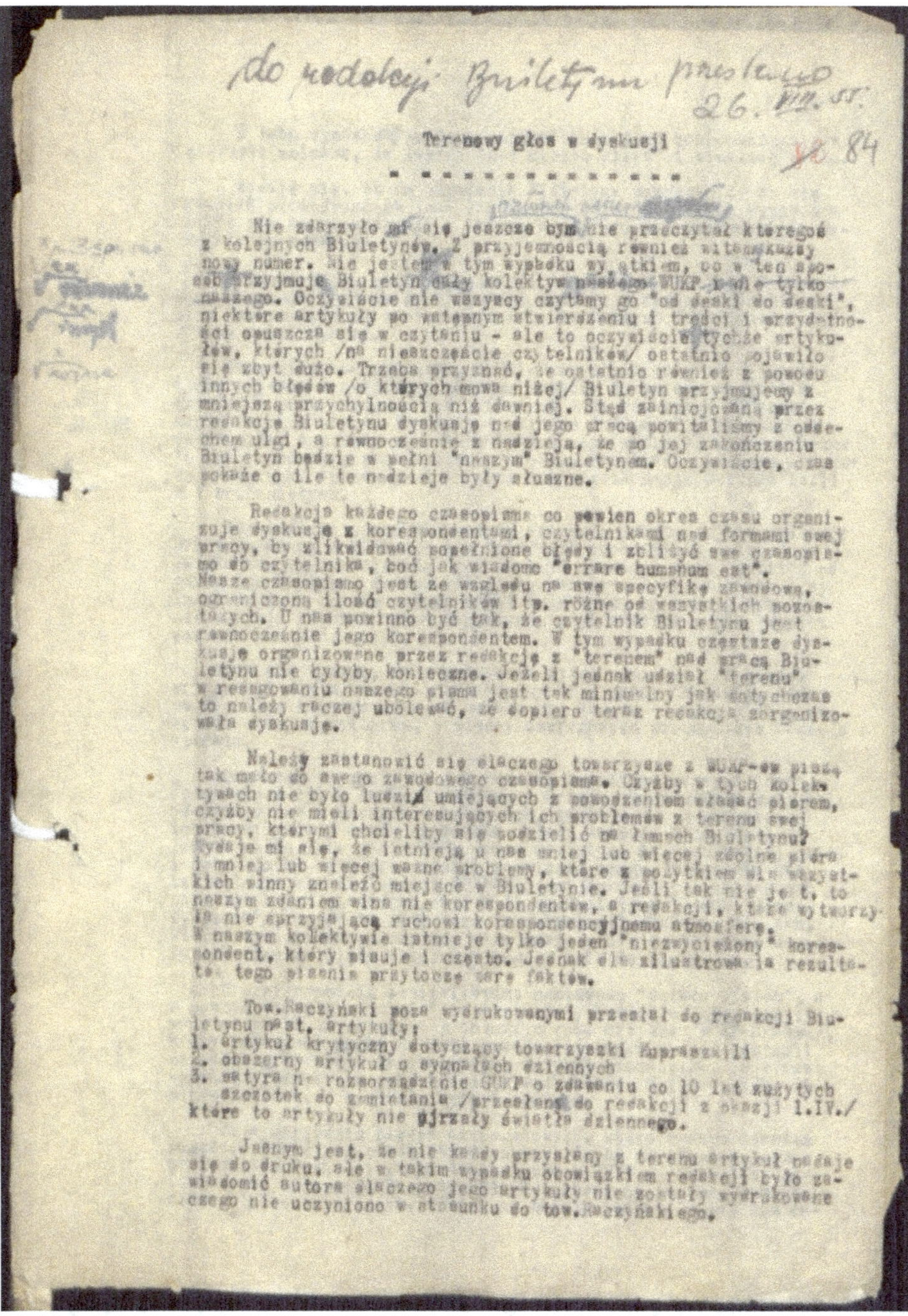

Terenowy głos w dyskusji

Nie zdarzyło mi się jeszcze bym nie przeczytał któregoś z kolejnych Biuletynów. Z przyjemnością również witam każdy nowy numer. Nie jestem w tym wypadku wyjątkiem, co w ten sposób przyjmuje Biuletyn cały kolektyw naszego WUKP, a nie tylko naszego. Oczywiście nie wszyscy czytamy go "od deski do deski", niektóre artykuły po wstępnym stwierdzeniu i treści i przydatności opuszcza się w czytaniu – ale to oczywiście tychże artykułów, których /na nieszczęście czytelników/ ostatnio pojawiło się zbyt dużo. Trzeba przyznać, że ostatnio również z powodu innych błędów /o których mowa niżej/ Biuletyn przyjmujemy z mniejszą przychylnością niż dawniej. Stąd zainicjowaną przez redakcję Biuletynu dyskusję nad jego pracą powitaliśmy z ogólnem ulgą, a równocześnie z nadzieją, że po jej zakończeniu Biuletyn będzie w pełni "naszym" Biuletynem. Oczywiście, czas pokaże o ile te nadzieje były słuszne.

Redakcja każdego czasopisma co pewien okres czasu organizuje dyskusję z korespondentami, czytelnikami nad formami swej pracy, by zlikwidować popełnione błędy i zbliżyć swe czasopismo do czytelnika, bo jak wiadomo "errare humanum est". Nasze czasopismo jest ze względu na swą specyfikę zawodową, ograniczoną ilość czytelników itp. różne od wszystkich pozostałych. U nas powinno być tak, że czytelnik Biuletynu jest równocześnie jego korespondentem. W tym wypadku częstsze dyskusje organizowane przez redakcję z "terenem" nad pracą Biuletynu nie byłyby konieczne. Jeżeli jednak udział "terenu" w redagowaniu naszego pisma jest tak minimalny jak dotychczas to należy raczej ubolewać, że dopiero teraz redakcja zorganizowała dyskusję.

Należy zastanowić się dlaczego towarzysze z WUKP-ów piszą tak mało do swego zawodowego czasopisma. Czyżby w tych kolektywach nie było ludzi umiejących z powodzeniem władać piórem, czyżby nie mieli interesujących ich problemów z terenu swej pracy, którymi chcieliby się podzielić na łamach Biuletynu? Wydaje mi się, że istnieją u nas mniej lub więcej zdolne pióra i mniej lub więcej ważne problemy, które z pożytkiem dla wszystkich winny znaleźć miejsce w Biuletynie. Jeśli tak nie jest, to naszym zdaniem wina nie korespondentów, a redakcji, która wytworzyła nie sprzyjającą ruchowi korespondencyjnemu atmosferę. W naszym kolektywie istnieje tylko jeden "niezwyciężony" korespondent, który pisuje i często. Jednak dla zilustrowania rezultatów tego pisania przytoczę parę faktów.

Tow. Raczyński poza wydrukowanymi przesłał do redakcji Biuletynu m-st. artykuły:
1. artykuł krytyczny dotyczący towarzyszki Kuprzszyli
2. obszerny artykuł o sygnałach dziennych
3. satyra na rozporządzenie GUKP o zdawaniu co 10 lat zużytych szczotek do zamietania /przesłane do redakcji z sesji 1.IV./
które to artykuły nie ujrzały światła dziennego.

Jasnym jest, że nie każdy przysłany z terenu artykuł nadaje się do druku, ale w takim wypadku obowiązkiem redakcji było zawiadomić autora dlaczego jego artykuły nie zostały wydrukowane czego nie uczyniono w stosunku do tow. Raczyńskiego.

Fig. 5a. The first page of "Terenowy głos w dyskusji" – material from 1955 from the branch in Poznań (APP, WUKPPiW, file ref. no. 18, fol. 84r).

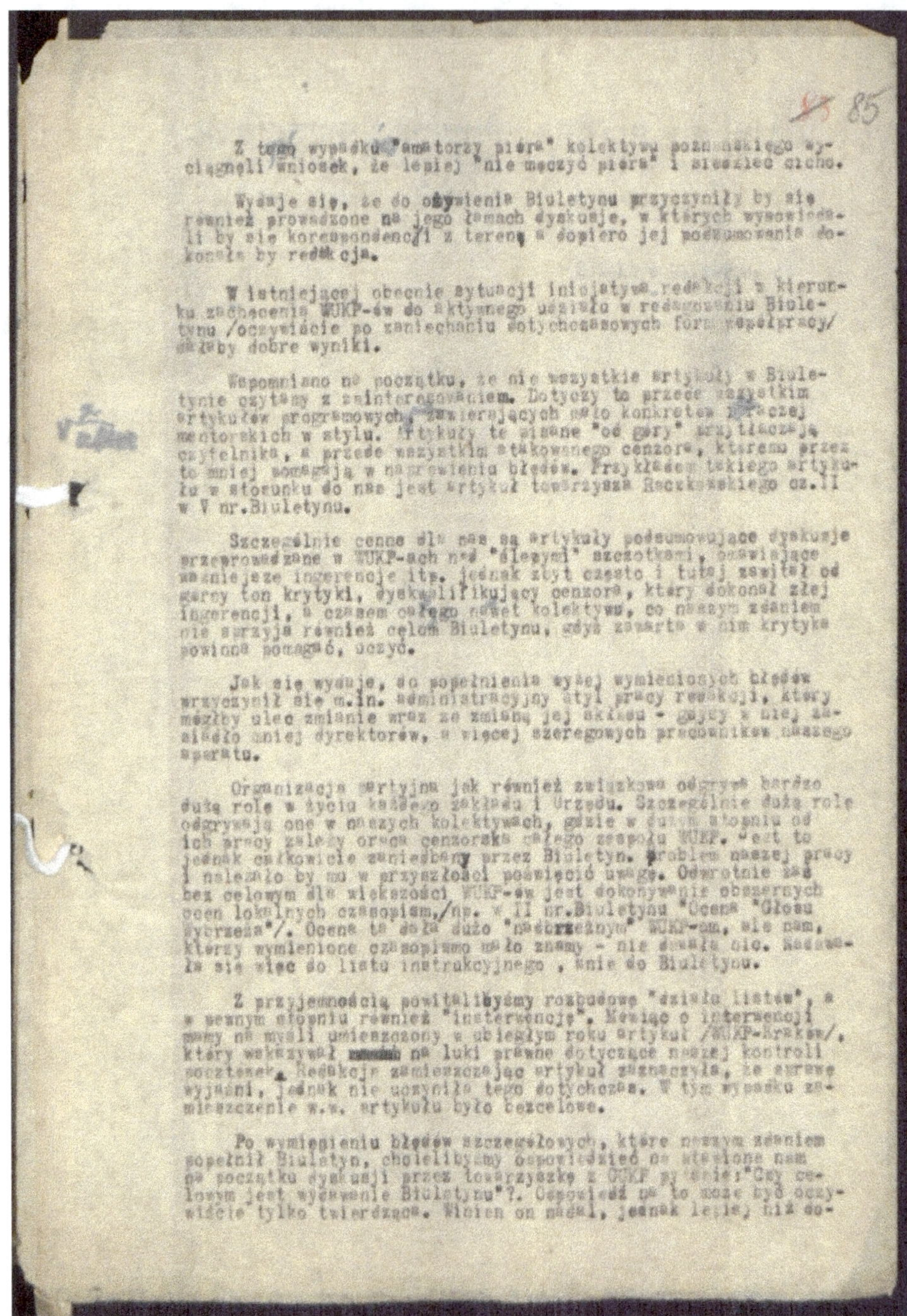

Fig. 5b. The second page of "Terenowy głos w dyskusji" – material from 1955 from the branch in Poznań (APP, WUKPPiW, file ref. no. 18, fol. 85r).

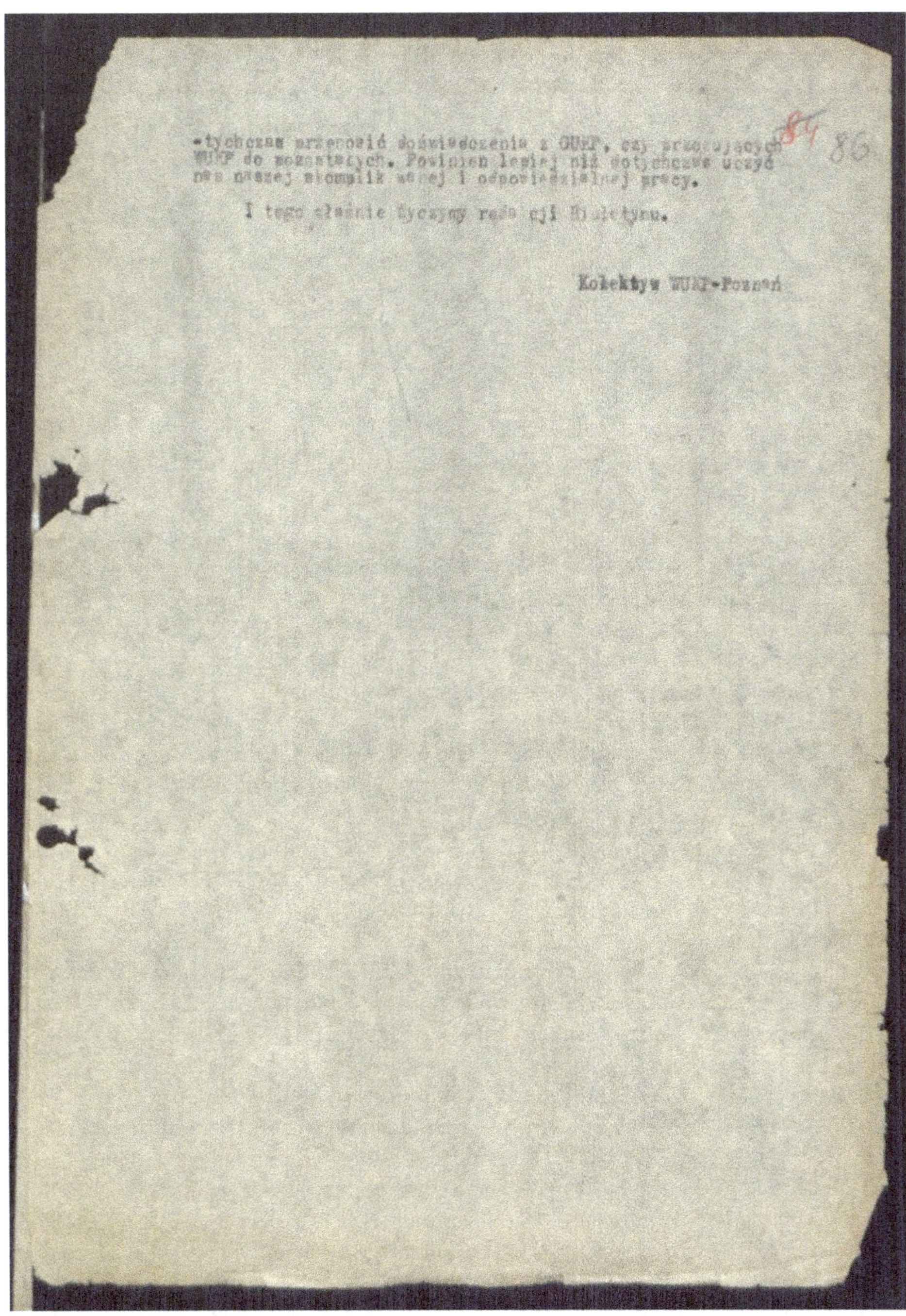

Fig. 5c. The third page of "Terenowy głos w dyskusji" – material from 1955 from the branch in Poznań (APP, WUKPPiW, file ref. no. 18, fol. 86r).

The magazine published reports and letters sent from various centers both by lower-level functionaries and by "decision-makers," that is, their superiors, usually heads of voivodeship offices or heads of departments or divisions.[21] Some of this correspondence, e.g., from Łódź, Kraków, Olsztyn, Poznań, and Katowice (the Bulletins consistently used the name Stalinogród that was enforced by communists after Stalin's death[22]), was also presented in a separate "Dział Listów" [Letters section].[23] The most frequently discussed topics were related to organization and working conditions in the office, as well as the assessment of cultural texts; the authors analyzed the difficulties in everyday censorship practice or shared innovative solutions to help overcome them.[24] Furthermore, in numerous materials, the Bulletin itself was evaluated by individual functionaries or entire censor collectives.[25]

While the majority of the correspondence – especially reports – maintained the official clerical style, there were some examples of more casual messages,

---

[21]   See, e.g.: Bieliński (WUKP Łódź), "Z terenowych prac wtórnych. Uwagi krytyczne na temat popularyzacji spółdzielczości produkcyjnej na łamach prasy terenowej," *Biuletyn Informacyjno-Instrukcyjny* no. 2 (14), February 1953, pp. 38–42 (APG, WUKPPiW, file ref. no. 18); W. Wierciak (Kraków), "Dobra organizacja ważnym ogniwem w podnoszeniu jakości pracy," *Biuletyn Informacyjno-Instrukcyjny* no. 1 (25), January 1954, pp. 23–25 (APG, WUKPPiW, file ref. no. 39).

[22]   The enforced name Stalinogród (*Stalin* + *gród* (archaic: city)) functioned from March 7, 1953 to October 21, 1956 and was used in correspondence between censorship offices, see, e.g.: K. Dworecki (Stalinogród), "O wyższy poziom organizacji pracy," *Biuletyn Informacyjno-Instrukcyjny* no. 1 (25), January 1954, pp. 7–14 (APG, WUKPPiW, file ref. no. 39); "O wynikach dyskusji nad opowiadaniem Kubalskiego, 'Wyrok,'" *Biuletyn Informacyjno-Instrukcyjny* no. 2 (26), February 1954, pp. 25–26 (APG, WUKPPiW, file ref. no. 42).

[23]   Usually "Dział Listów" was one of the modules of the Bulletin and was included at the end. See, e.g.: "Dział Listów" in the Bulletins from September 1952, pp. 48–49; January 1953, pp. 69–72; March 1953, pp. 60–75; January 1954, pp. 39–44; January 1956, pp. 51–59.

[24]   See, e.g.: "Korespondencja," *Biuletyn Informacyjno-Instrukcyjny* no. 3, March 1952, pp. 31–33 (APG, WUKPPiW, file ref. no. 96; Tadeusz Warchoł's letter from the Gdańsk branch); A. Żmijewska, "Kilka uwag 'młodego cenzora,'" *Biuletyn Informacyjno-Instrukcyjny* no. 7, July 1952, pp. 39–42 (APG, WUKPPiW, file ref. no. 84); "Dział Listów" *Biuletyn Informacyjno-Instrukcyjny* no. 11, November 1952, pp. 67–68 (APG, WUKPPiW, file ref. no. 72); "Dział Listów," *Biuletyn Informacyjno-Instrukcyjny* no. 12, December 1952, pp. 41–44 (APG, WUKPPiW, file ref. no. 70).

[25]   "Korespondencja," *Biuletyn Informacyjno-Instrukcyjny* no. 3, March 1952, pp. 29–31 (APG, WUKPPiW, file ref. no. 96; the letter from Olsztyn presents the discussion on the January issue of the Bulletin); "Artykuł wstępny," *Biuletyn Informacyjno-Instrukcyjny* no. 1 (13), January 1953, pp. 2–8 (APG, WUKPPiW, file ref. no. 19).

which resembled a feature article or even a rather personal confession. Such was the tone in the letter from the censor in Olsztyn entitled "Spójrzmy sobie w oczy towarzysze…" [Let us look each other in the eyes, comrades…], which began with the following self-reflection:

> Sitting alone at night with People's Poland and awaiting the columns, I began to draw up a balance sheet of my annual censorship work. I remember vividly the period when I took my first steps, or rather when I started to learn the "craft" of censorship under the guidance of comrades Rotnicka, Majzner, Wachowiak and others.[26]

Thanks to such testimonies, the magazine became not only a venue to exchange expertise, but also a kind of censor's confessional, where personal experiences were shared. One could often hear voices of self-criticism and resolutions to improve (more or less honest); unsurprisingly, in the first post-war decade, the "self-criticism ceremonial"[27] also reached "Mysia Street," becoming another element of the game between the authorities and rank-and-file reviewers, comrades, political workers or advisors (in the Bulletins, these terms were used synonymously with the word "censor").[28]

Employees of the censorship office were also encouraged to compete in the field of "censorship criticism," which I understand as the assessment of cultural works supervised by the state and subordinated to its political interests. This was the case, for example, in August 1952, when a competition for the "best collective book review" was announced.[29] Unfortunately, only a fraction of the field branches responded to the challenge presented by the head of the Łódź center, Maria

---

[26] S. Paź (WUKPPiW Olsztyn), "Spójrzmy sobie w oczy, towarzysze…" (correspondence in "Dział Listów"), *Biuletyn Informacyjno-Instrukcyjny* no. 1 (49), January 1956, p. 51 (APG, WUKPPiW, file ref. no. 4). See also: "Sam na sam z Polską Ludową," interview with an anonymous censor conducted by Joanna Pruszyńska, *Rzeczpospolita* April 15–16, 2000, no. 90, pp. D4–D5.

[27] J. Putrament, "Pół wieku," vol. 4: *Literaci*, Warszawa: "Czytelnik," 1970, p. 62.

[28] See, e.g.: "Na marginesie dyskusji nad *Pokoleniem* Czeszki"; S. Borowik (Gdańsk), "O pracy WUKP Gdańsk z referentami społeczno-administracyjnymi," *Biuletyn Informacyjno-Instrukcyjny* no. 4, April 1952, p. 16, 33 (APG, WUKPPiW, file ref. no. 93); "Niektóre zagadnienia międzynarodowe w świetle naszych doświadczeń," *Biuletyn Informacyjno-Instrukcyjny* no. 11, November 1952, pp. 12–14 (APG, WUKPPiW, file ref. no. 72); "Śladem naszych recenzji," *Biuletyn Informacyjno-Instrukcyjny* no. 1 (13), January 1953, p. 46 (APG, WUKPPiW, file ref. no 19). The censor as "advisor" to the press appears in ["Materiały z odprawy"], fol. 43r et seq. (*"Biuletyny Instrukcyjno-Szkoleniowe 1945–1951"* (APP, WUKPPiW, file ref. no. 4)).

[29] "Konkurs na recenzję," *Biuletyn Informacyjno-Instrukcyjny* no. 8, August 1952, p. 41 (APG, WUKPPiW, file ref. no. 81).

Lorber. From the four submissions that were sent to "Mysia Street," the winners were selected and published in the November issue of that year's Bulletin.[30] In addition, the censors' contributions to *Mały Słownik Historyczny* [Little dictionary of history] were awarded – the best entries were published in the periodical.[31]

Finally, the magazine also featured the censors' own literary works, which is somewhat surprising. Later in the book, I will analyze a few such examples, including theatrical works produced on the stage of "Mysia Street."

------

[30] "Trzy recenzje," *Biuletyn Informacyjno-Instrukcyjny* no. 11, November 1952, pp. 47–66 (APG, WUKPPiW, file ref. no. 72). I write about the competition in the chapter "Competition for a Censorship Review of Wanda Wasilewska's Novel *Rzeki płoną.*"

[31] See: "Z problematyki naszych prac specjalnych," *Biuletyn Informacyjno-Instrukcyjny* no. 11/12 (23/24), November/December 1953, pp. 45–49 (APG, WUKPPiW, file ref. no. 9); "Z problematyki naszych prac specjalnych" (correspondence in "Dział Listów"), *Biuletyn Informacyjno-Instrukcyjny* no. 1 (25), January 1954, pp. 49–54 (APG, WUKPPiW, file ref. no. 39); "Z problematyki naszych prac specjalnych," *Biuletyn Informacyjno-Instrukcyjny* no. 2 (26), February 1954, pp. 34–39 (APG, WUKPPiW, file ref. no. 42).

3. CHARACTERISTICS OF THE SOURCE MATERIAL AND THE ISSUE OF THE BULLETINS' IDENTITY[32]

In the tradition of censorship, there were times when
we blamed… beavers for being a Mexican species.[33]

Over a period of eleven years, between 1945 and 1956, the confidential periodical for censors changed its titles five times. In May and June 1945, *Biuletyn Instrukcyjny* [Instructional bulletin] was published; the next preserved issue was titled *Biuletyn Głównego Urzędu Kontroli Prasy* [Bulletin of the Main Office for the Control of the Press]; in October and November 1948, January and May 1949, and in 1951 – *Biuletyn Informacyjno-Szkoleniowy* [Informational and training bulletin]; in March 1950 – *Biuletyn Szkoleniowy* [Training bulletin]; and from 1952 to 1956 – *Biuletyn Informacyjno-Instrukcyjny* [Informational and instructional bulletin].

The issues published between 1952 and 1956 are unquestionably one continuous publication, which is evidenced, e.g., by its numeration covering more than one calendar year.[34] Considering that for over four years, the Bulletin was published as a monthly, I also use this term to refer to it. The continuity of the Bulletin is further confirmed by materials from the editors, who wrote, for example, in the December 1955 issue that it was entering its fifth year.[35] Despite that remark, the earlier issues of the magazine should also be treated as a part of the

---

[32] I discuss the issue of the Bulletin's identity in the articles "Bulletins of the Polish censorship office from 1945 to 1956…," pp. 312–315; "'O wyższy poziom pracy nad książką'…," pp. 63–64.

[33] L. Majzner, "Na marginesie niektórych zbędnych ingerencji," *Biuletyn Informacyjno-Instrukcyjny* no. 7 (43), July 1955, p. 4 (APG, WUKPPiW, file ref. no. 103).

[34] The issues from 1953–1956 have double numeration, covering the calendar year and the period from January 1952, e.g., *Biuletyn Informacyjno-Instrukcyjny* no. 1 (13) 1953 or the last of the analyzed issues *Biuletyn Informacyjno-Instrukcyjny* no. 2 (50) 1956, et seq.

[35] Editorial board, "50 numerów *Biuletynu*," *Biuletyn Informacyjno-Instrukcyjny* no. 12 (48), December 1955, p. 2 (APG, WUKPPiW, file ref. no. 117). See also: "Artykuł wstępny," *Biuletyn Informacyjno-Instrukcyjny* no. 1 (13), January 1953, p. 2 (APG, WUK-PPiW, file ref. no. 19).

same periodical and a continuum of one title. This claim is supported by the type and the layout of the presented content (in the Bulletins from 1952–1956 and in some earlier issues), the purpose the Bulletins served, the address of the recipient and issuer (in spite of some modifications), the title pages (including the cover, when it has been preserved) and, of course, the method of distribution.[36]

Before the above-mentioned characteristics of the magazine are discussed, it is worth considering why the journal became a monthly in 1952. The reasons for this should be sought in the dramatic political and systemic changes brought about by the year 1952, in which the Constitution was adopted, the new name of the Polish People's Republic was introduced, but also a series of political trials with death sentences took place (including the officers of the General Staff of the Polish Army, Air Force and Navy). These transformations also affected the "factory of false texts,"[37] as Stefan Kisielewski referred to the censorship office. At that time, more stable forms of internal communication were developed, as evidenced, for example, by the regularly published Bulletin. Thus, we can say that the censorship of the PRL, in the strict sense of the word, existed since 1952; all the earlier activities can be viewed as the "pioneer" period, when both the Office itself and its Bulletin were experimenting with their formula. For this reason, the issues published between 1945 and 1951 appear to be an inhomogeneous collection (perhaps, if subsequent issues from this period are discovered, more similarities in the layout and organization of the Bulletin's contributions over the years will emerge).[38]

Returning to the characteristics of the source material, it can be assumed that the modifications to the Office's name were meant to reflect the successive stages of its reorganization, or were a response to some internal regulations that shifted the balance of power and influence at "Mysia Street." One of the most import-

---

[36] According to the Press Law Act of January 26, 1984, the press "shall be considered periodical publications that do not constitute a limitative and homogenous entirety, are published at least once a year and bear a permanent title or a name, a number and a date, including, but not limited to: daily newspapers and magazines, newswires, telex messages, bulletins, radio and television broadcasts, film chronicles […]" ("Obwieszczenie Marszałka Sejmu Rzeczypospolitej Polskiej z dnia 14 września 2018 r. w sprawie ogłoszenia jednolitego tekstu ustawy – Prawo prasowe" (Dz.U. 2018, poz. 1914, s. 1–17), http://isap.sejm.gov.pl/isap.nsf/DocDetails.xsp?id=WDU20180001914 (accessed July 27, 2021)).

[37] S. Kisielewski, "Przeciw cenzurze – legalnie (garść wspomnień)," *Zapis* 1977, no. 4, p. 59. Stefan Kisielewski (1911–1991; pseud. *Kisiel*) – a Polish writer and columnist, repeatedly banned from print during the communist era; in 1990, *Nagroda Kisiela* (Kisiel Prize) was established and it is presented in three categories: publicist, politician (public figure) and entrepreneur.

[38] I elaborate on this topic in the article "Archiwalia 'pionierskiego' okresu powojennej cenzury. Literatura w poufnych biuletynach urzędu cenzury (1945–1951)," *Sztuka Edycji. Studia Tekstologiczne i Edytorskie* 2021, issue 2 (20), pp. 51–62.

ant changes that took place in the discussed period is dated November 15, 1945, when – by a resolution of the Council of Ministers – the Central Press Control Bureau established on January 19, 1945 was transformed into the Main Office for the Control of the Press, Publications and Public Performances.[39] Next, on July 5, 1946, a decree on the creation of the GUKPPiW provided the legal framework for the institution.[40] Most likely, the fourth issue (undated) of the *Bulletin of the Main Office for the Control of the Press* owes its title to the latter change. In the rest of the Bulletins found so far, the name of the Office was not a component of the title, although the issues from May and June placed its name under the monthly's title – *Informational Bulletin* of the Central Press Control Bureau. It was pointed out at briefings that certain changes affecting the Office, e.g., "the transition from the Ministry of Public Security to the Presidium of the Council of Ministers,"[41] impacted the way it operated (in this case, the censors were less expansive). It seems, however, that despite the above-mentioned transformations, which could explain the modifications to the name of the periodical, there are no fundamental formal or content-related reasons why the magazine should not be treated as one continuous publication.

The other data identifying the publishing house on the title page were very similar. In the case of the 1952–1956 issues, the title page served also as the cover of the magazine; it was printed on slightly thicker gray-blue or gray paper, and had a similar layout.[42]

---

[39] The initial stage "in the history of our censorship" was also discussed in the Bulletins, see, e.g.: "Przemówienie dyrektora ob. Zabłudowskiego," *Biuletyn Instrukcyjny* no. 2, June 1945 r., pp. 17–19 (APG, WUKPPiW, file ref. no. 210).

[40] The decree entered into force less than a month later, on August 2, 1946. See, e.g.: "Główny Urząd Kontroli Prasy 1945–1949…," pp. 15–17, 27–28; W. Janowski, "Główny Urząd Kontroli Prasy, Publikacji i Widowisk w latach 1945–1947. Problemy wewnątrzorganizacyjne," [in:] *Literatura w granicach prawa (XIX–XX w.)*, eds. K. Budrowska, E. Dąbrowicz, M. Lul, Warszawa: IBL PAN, 2013, series *Badania Filologiczne nad Cenzurą PRL* vol. 3, pp. 152–156; K. Kamińska-Chełminiak, "Utworzenie Centralnego Biura Kontroli Prasy; Utworzenie Głównego Urzędu Kontroli Prasy, Publikacji i Widowisk," [in:] eadem, *Cenzura w Polsce 1944–1960. Organizacja. Kadry. Metody pracy*, Warszawa: Wydział Dziennikarstwa, Informacji i Bibliologii UW i Oficyna Wydawnicza ASPRA-JR, 2019, pp. 50–57, 75–85. See also: "Dekret z dnia 5 lipca 1946 r. o utworzeniu Głównego Urzędu Kontroli Prasy, Publikacji i Widowisk" (*Journal of Laws* 1946 no. 34, item 210, p. 379, http://isap.sejm.gov.pl/isap.nsf/DocDetails.xsp?id=wdu19460340210 (accessed July 27, 2021)).

[41] ["Materiały z odprawy"], fol. 46r (*"Biuletyny Instrukcyjno-Szkoleniowe 1945–1951"* (APP, WUKPPiW, file ref. no. 4)).

[42] All the covers from those years, which were also the title pages, were almost identical; they differed in minor details, e.g., font size or color. However, it is difficult to view these changes as anything other than "revamping" the magazine or as changes dictated by the specificity of the photocopying equipment used during those five years.

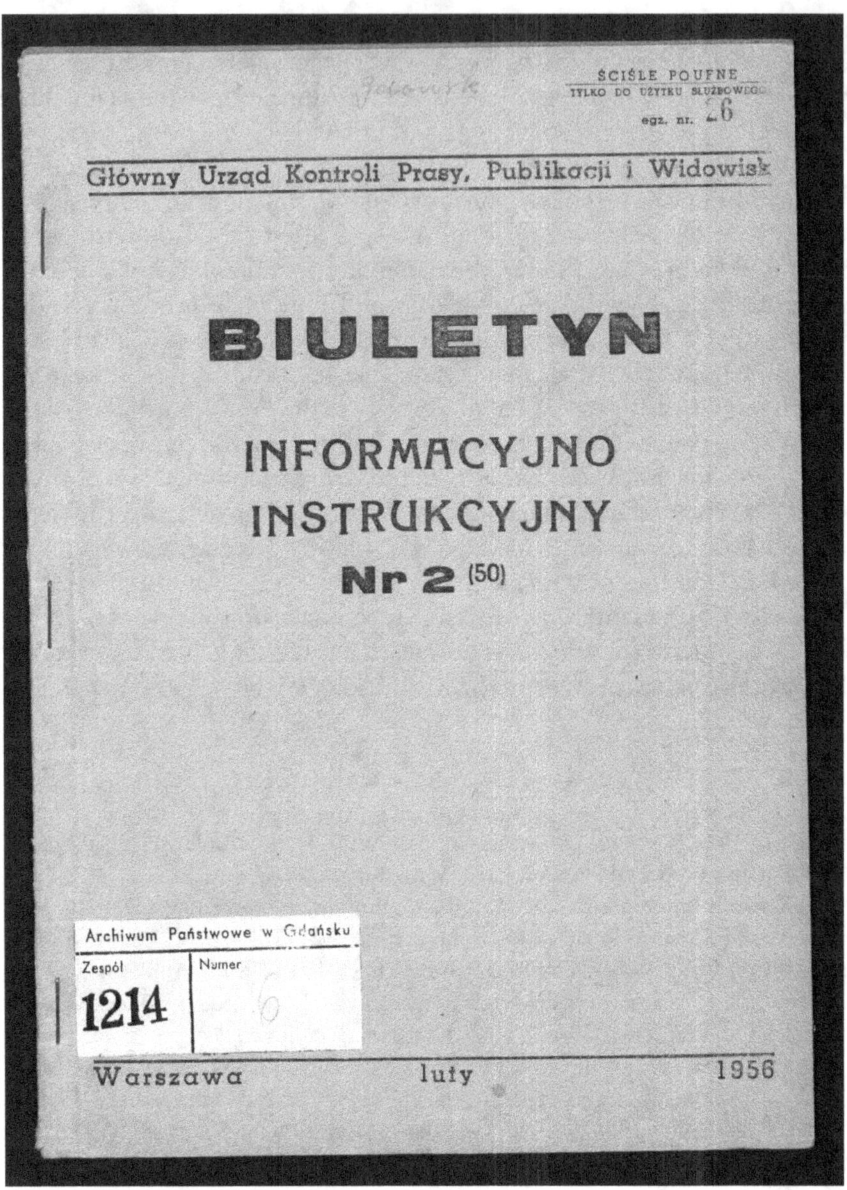

Fig. 6. The cover of the last of the analyzed Bulletins, *Biuletyn Informacyjno-Instrukcyjny* dated February 1956 (APG, WUKPPiW, file ref. no. 6).

A separate title page can also be found in the undated Bulletin marked as issue no. 4 and in the Bulletins from 1950 and 1951. In other periodicals, it was part of the first page, on which the proper content of the issue or the table of contents was published (perhaps some of these "coverless" issues were accompanied by title pages, although this seems unlikely).[43] In almost all of the issues, we find basic information identifying the periodical, which consisted of 1) the core of the title "Bulletin," whose scope of meaning was narrowed down by the modifiers "instructional," "training," "informational and instructional" or "informational and training" and, in one issue, the noun modifier – (Bulletin) of "The Main Office for the Control of the Press";[44] 2) title and number of the issue; 3) date and place of the publication (year, month, city – Warsaw);[45] 4) the name "The Main Office for the Control of the Press, Publications and Public Performances" placed at the top of the page[46] and the statement "Strictly confidential. For official use only" (in Bulletins from 1952–1956, it was printed in the upper right corner of the cover). The confidentiality of the periodical was also indicated in earlier issues.[47]

The address of the recipient and the issuer also suggest that the Bulletins are one continuous publication. The periodicals were published by the Main Office for the Control of the Press, Publications and Public Performances (the issues from May and June 1945 indicate that the periodical was printed by the Publishing House of the Central Press Control Bureau in Warsaw[48]) and their recipients were mainly censors, although they also reached other employees of the Office.

---

[43] The "Table of Contents" was placed at the end or at the beginning of the journal; it did not appear in a few issues, e.g., from May and June 1945 (I reconstructed it based on the contents of the issue), while in the March (May) 1950 issue, it was placed after the "Introduction" on page 4. Sometimes the titles of the chapters in the "Table of Contents" differed slightly from those within the issue and were their abbreviated versions – in this work, I usually quote the titles in accordance with the actual "Table of Contents." In exceptional situations, I quote the title found within the issue.

[44] If we recognize ["Materiały z odprawy"] and "Na marginesie narodowej dyskusji" as separate Bulletins, it should be noted that they feature neither the title of the journal nor other identifying data of the periodical.

[45] The issue marked as no. 4 provides no date and place of the publication (however, it can be assumed that the information about the place of the publication was included in the title of the magazine – *Bulletin of the Main Office for the Control of the Press*), while in the issues from January 1949 and 1951, there is no information about the place of the publication.

[46] For obvious reasons, the name "CBKP" appears in the first two preserved Bulletins. However, the Office's name was not given in the issues from January 1949 and 1951.

[47] The Bulletin from May 1945 included the note "Confidential," handwritten in red pencil; the June issue from the same year was marked with "Confidential. For official use only"; issue no. 4 – "For official use only"; the issue from October 1948 – "Confidential"; the November issue from the same year – "Highly classified"; the 1949 and 1950 issues, instead of the note, bore a purple stamp "Classified"; and the issue no. 1 from 1951 read "Classified."

[48] *Biuletyn Instrukcyjny* no. 1, May 1945, fol. 3r (APP, WUKPPiW, file ref. no. 4); *Biuletyn Instrukcyjny* no. 2, June 1945, p. 19 (APG, WUKPPiW, file ref. no. 210).

The way the Bulletins were distributed was also important: they were circulated only within the Office, as indicated by the above-mentioned confidentiality clause of the document.

Another piece of strong evidence supporting the hypothesis of the title's continuity are the goals formulated for the magazine, and the type and layout of the materials presented in it. Since the former have been discussed in the previous subchapters, I will focus now on the contents of the periodical.[49]

The magazine published articles discussing various aspects of the functioning of "Mysia Street and its environs," from the organization of work in the Office to matters concerning the censorship of specific texts. Each Bulletin featured several articles dealing with various topics, though always related to censorship. A departure from this arrangement of the presented contents was visible in special issues, which focused on particular matters, e.g., conferences or national councils of the Office's employees, or jubilees celebrating the tenth anniversary of the founding of the institution.[50]

Proof of the continuity of the title is also provided by the series of articles published in subsequent issues of the magazine, e.g., "O wyższy poziom pracy nad książką"[51] [For a higher level of work on the book], "O wyższy poziom naszej pracy"[52] [For a higher level of our work], successive reports on the implementa-

---

[49] The content is "in the bibliological sense, a set of all the meaningful components of a work, including the way in which they are formed, arranged, and communicated. From an editorial and bibliographic standpoint, the content of a book consists of an introduction, the main text, a critical apparatus, a commentary, indexes, bibliographies, as well as figures, tables, lists, maps, etc. These elements are sometimes listed in the table of contents." ("Zawartość," [in:] *Encyklopedia wiedzy o książce*, eds. A. Birkenmajer, B. Kocowski, J. Trzynadlowski, Wrocław: Ossolineum, 1971, p. 2584).

[50] It applies to the June 1945 issue, undated issue no. 4, and the issues from July/August 1953 and February 1956. If we recognize ["Materiały z odprawy"] and "Na marginesie narodowej dyskusji" as Bulletins, they should be treated as special issues.

[51] Articles published in the series *O wyższy poziom pracy nad książką*: "Uwagi ogólne o recenzji," *Biuletyn Informacyjno-Instrukcyjny* no. 7, July 1952, pp. 26–29 (APG, WUKPPiW, file ref. no. 84); "Recenzja z pozycji literackiej, cz. I," *Biuletyn Informacyjno-Instrukcyjny* no. 8, August 1952, pp. 18–24 (APG, WUKPPiW, file ref. no. 81); "Recenzja z pozycji literackiej (cd.)," *Biuletyn Informacyjno-Instrukcyjny* no. 9, September 1952, pp. 24–33 (APG, WUKPPiW, file ref. no. 78); "O wyższy poziom pracy nad książką (cd.)," *Biuletyn Informacyjno-Instrukcyjny* no. 11, November 1952, pp. 37–42 (APG, WUKPPiW, file ref. no. 72). See also the chapter "Books Discussed as Part of the Series *For a Higher Level of Work on the Book*: (Not Only) Nałkowska, Czeszko, Lācis, Meisner, and Jackiewicz."

[52] Selected articles published in the series *O wyższy poziom naszej pracy*: "O właściwe wykorzystywanie prasy periodycznej w naszej pracy codziennej," *Biuletyn Informacyjno-Instrukcyjny* no. 2, February 1952, pp. 29–34 (APG, WUKPPiW, file ref. no. 99); "Przez sprawniejszą organizację – do lepszej pracy," *Biuletyn Informacyjno-Instrukcyjny* no. 3, March 1952, pp. 21–25 (APG, WUKPPiW, file ref. no. 96).

tion of a project aimed at discussing selected titles[53] and correspondence from censors, who referred to the contents presented in the Bulletins.[54] Apart from this, the readers-censors and the Bulletin's editorial board often commented on the materials included in earlier issues.[55] For example, the January 1949 issue featured a discussion of issue no. 1 of *Biuletyn Informacyjno-Szkoleniowy*; unfortunately, the information identifying the year of its publication was not provided. Only a detailed comparative analysis of the Bulletins revealed that the reference was made to Bulletin no. 1 from 1948[56] (interestingly, Zbigniew Romek wrote that "two confidential bulletins designed for training purposes" were published at that time[57]).

All the above-mentioned arguments demonstrate that the analyzed Bulletins for censors were parts of the same continuous publication.

---

[53] See the chapter: "Books Selected for Discussion in Censorship Offices between 1952 and 1956."

[54] See, e.g.: "Korespondencja," *Biuletyn Informacyjno-Instrukcyjny* no. 3, March 1952, pp. 29–31 (APG, WUKPPiW, file ref. no. 96); A. Żmijewska, "Na temat szkolenia," *Biuletyn Informacyjno-Instrukcyjny* no. 11, November 1952, pp. 67–68 (APG, WUKPPiW, file ref. no. 72); "Nasze zdanie o 'Wynikach dyskusji nad opowiadaniem Kubalskiego, "Wyrok,"'" *Biuletyn Informacyjno-Instrukcyjny* no. 5 (29), May 1954, pp. 50–53 (APG, WUKPPiW, file ref. no. 49).

[55] See, e.g.: "Oszczędność – systemem w naszej pracy," *Biuletyn Informacyjno-Instrukcyjny* no. 3, March 1952, p. 18 (APG, WUKPPiW, file ref. no. 96).

[56] "Sprawozdania z procesów o charakterze politycznym"; "Aprowizacja"; "Zagadnienie krytyki"; "Dyskusja nad nr 1 *Biuletynu Informacyjno-Szkoleniowego*," *Biuletyn Informacyjno-Szkoleniowy* no. 1/3, January 1949, pp. 4–5, 45–47 (APG, WUKPPiW, file ref. no. 196).

[57] Z. Romek, *Cenzura a nauka historyczna w Polsce 1944–1970*, Warszawa: Wydawnictwo Neriton, 2010, p. 63.

4. THE BULLETIN FOR CENSORS AS
A CRYPTOTEXT. A DEFINITION OF THE GENRE

*The censors at the Press Office considered themselves "supermen"
whose job was of the greatest importance.*[58]

Słownik terminologii medialnej [Dictionary of the media and communications terminology] states that bulletins are "publications of various institutions for their internal use."[59] *Encyklopedia wiedzy o prasie* [Encyclopedia of press knowledge], on the other hand, specifies that the internal character of a bulletin may also stem from "reasons of professional secrecy."[60] However, this component in the definition of the periodicals from "Mysia Street" seems insufficient, because in this case, more than professional secrecy was at stake.

Using the available definitions, one could characterize the Bulletins for censors as "an internal publication of The Main Office for the Control of the Press, Publications and Public Performances." The definition constructed in this way is only partially correct, because it does not highlight the key features of this genre, namely, the fact that it was a confidential publication, covered by the secrecy clause, and anchored in the state apparatus. Even if we consider that the suggestion of confidentiality is contained in the phrase "internal publication," this is information that should be highlighted in the definition itself, just as the fact that the Bulletin was a periodical created on the order of the state, since both pieces of information are fundamental in the context of the existence of institutional control of the speech. At this point, my earlier findings on restricted-distribution texts and cryptotexts, which I presented in my article "The censorship review in the Polish People's Republic as cryptotext" as well as other publications, will prove essential.[61]

---

[58] K. Dworecki, "O wyższy poziom organizacji pracy," *Biuletyn Informacyjno-Instrukcyjny* no. 1 (25), January 1954, p. 7 (APG, WUKPPiW, file ref. no. 39).

[59] S. Dziki [SD], "Biuletyn," [in:] *Słownik terminologii medialnej*, ed. W. Pisarek, Kraków: Universitas, 2006, p. 18.

[60] S. Dziki [S. Dz.], "Biuletyn," [in:] *Encyklopedia wiedzy o prasie*, ed. J. Maślanka, Wrocław: Ossolineum, 1976, p. 33. Of the many works on press and journalistic genres, the following was particularly useful: M. Wojtak, *Analiza gatunków prasowych*, Lublin: Wydawnictwo UMCS, 2010.

[61] A. Wiśniewska-Grabarczyk, "The censorship review in the Polish People's Republic as cryptotext," *The Polish Review* 2019, vol. 64, no. 1, pp. 31–49; eadem, "Recenzja

Bulletins for censors as secret documents, intended only for a selected circle of readers (mainly for the employees of the censorship office), meet the definition criteria of cryptotexts, which are confidential texts with deliberately limited distribution (that is why in this work, I use this name synonymously).[62] Cryptotexts can be categorized into texts produced by the state apparatus or without its participation. Bulletins, as internal journals of the CBKP and later GUKPPiW, were obviously examples of the first type of texts. On the other hand, underground publications, which escaped censorship and were distributed unofficially among the citizens, were examples of texts unfounded in the state apparatus, created with an intentional evasion of the authorities.

The importance of other cryptotexts employed in censorship work should also be stressed. One of them was *Sygnały* [Signals], which featured instructional letters, reviews of interferences and various other guidelines and instructions.[63] All the above-mentioned cryptotexts varied slightly in their tasks, contents and presentation of the material. However, they were all anchored in the state apparatus, shared the secrecy clause, and their distribution was deliberately limited. The censorship review was similar in this respect, however, unlike the aforementioned texts, it was not instructional but evaluative in nature. Therefore, it was the result of a practical application of the guidelines included in the analyzed instructional cryptotexts.[64]

---

cenzorska jako kryptotekst," [in:] eadem, *"Czytelnik" ocenzurowany. Literatura w kryptotekstach – recenzjach cenzorskich okresu stalinizmu (na materiale GUKPPiW z 1950 roku)*, Warszawa: Wydawnictwo IPN, 2018, pp. 97–114. Here I will only mention those fragments of the concept which are crucial to a definition of the Bulletin for censors.

[62] Among the limited-distribution texts, we also distinguish printings with unintentionally limited distribution. Examples are publications of local folklore, ephemera, or simply self-published materials – in these cases, limited distribution is usually the result of insufficient funds for publication. It should be emphasized that such texts are not confidential. To put it another way, every confidential document is a document with limited distribution, but not every document with limited distribution is a confidential document.

[63] See, e.g.: classified instructions, documents and other materials published by the former censor, Tomasz Strzyżewski, featured in "Książka Zapisów i Zaleceń GUKPPiW": T. Strzyżewski, *Czarna Księga Cenzury PRL* vol. 1: London: Wydawnictwo Aneks, 1977, vol. 2: ibidem 1978; idem, *Czarna Księga Cenzury PRL*, Warszawa: Niezależna Oficyna Wydawnicza "Nowa," 1981; idem, *Wielka Księga Cenzury PRL w dokumentach*, Warszawa: Wydawnictwo Prohibita, 2015; see also: *The Black Book of Polish Censorship*, trans. and ed. by J. Leftwich Curry, New York: Vintage Books, 1984.

[64] A. Wiśniewska-Grabarczyk, "Recenzja cenzorska Polski Ludowej," *Zagadnienia Rodzajów Literackich* 2016, vol. 59, no. 1 (117), pp. 97–103. Here I would like to thank Prof. Iwona Loewe for consulting me on meta- and paratexts and for confirming my intuition that the censorship review represents the latter genre (the author's email correspondence with Prof. I. Loewe, April 10, 2018).

Considering the above-listed arguments, I propose the following definition:

Anchored in the state apparatus, **the Bulletin for censors** was a confidential, internal journal of the Central Press Control Bureau, then of the Main Office for the Control of the Press, Publications and Public Performances, predominantly addressed to censors; the Bulletin presented materials primarily on censorship and the activities of the Office for the Control; it published editorial articles and materials from the field (censorship reviews, reports, balance sheets and letters sent by censor teams or specific employees of the censorship office, press articles, regulations, etc.); in terms of its purpose, the Bulletin fulfilled a training, instructional, and informational function; in terms of its distribution method, it was a cryptotext, that is, a confidential text with deliberately limited distribution.

PART TWO

LITERATURE AND CURRENT
LITERARY PHENOMENA

I. Fiction

1. THE CENSOR'S STRUGGLE WITH THE TEXT
SOME PRELIMINARY REMARKS

1.1. Literary and Cultural Issues on the Pages of the Bulletins

Censors should always keep their "ear to the ground"
when it comes to current cultural issues.[1]

There was a widespread belief in the Office for the Control that "the Non-Periodical Publications Department mainly reviews literary publications"[2] and that it was fiction that was most often discussed at work briefings. It is difficult to argue with this view, although the selection of material presented in the Bulletins suggests that texts on domestic, international, and social policy, or history and economics were equally popular. While literature and culture were only one of the many thematic threads discussed in the periodical, they were indeed presented in the Bulletins quite regularly. This should not come as a surprise considering that over a period of eleven years, almost sixty issues of the journal were published.

These topics appeared in various forms – from extensive analyses to shorter materials, the latter of which were definitely more numerous. Some matters were discussed cyclically, others recurred sporadically, and yet others appeared only once in the magazine. It is noteworthy that the first preserved Bulletin contains no examples of textual control in the field of broadly understood art. This slim issue (only five pages long) is limited to perfunctory remarks about the need to protect the press, books, radio, and theater life from the machinations of vicious "reaction."[3] The censorial succinctness may have stemmed from the volume of the issue, but the functionaries also showed restraint in later years; from the very beginning, the Bulletins proved that the organization of post-war cultural life was, in most periods, secondary to the organization of political, social, and economic life (although, of course, it is difficult to draw a clear demarcation line between literature and life in an era of socialized culture).

---

[1] "Recenzja z pozycji literackiej, cz. I" (in the series *O wyższy poziom pracy nad książką*), *Biuletyn Informacyjno-Instrukcyjny* no. 8, August 1952, pp. 23–24 (APG, WUK-PPiW, file ref. no. 81).

[2] Ibidem, p. 18.

[3] "Zadania biuletynu," *Biuletyn Instrukcyjny* no. 1, May 1945, fol. 1v (APP, WUKP-PiW, file ref. no. 4).

Exclusive chapters on one author or one work were rare. The writers who received such special coverage include Bogdan Brzeziński, Bohdan Czeszko, Zofia Dróżdż-Satanowska, Konstanty Ildefons Gałczyński, Kazimiera Iłłakowiczówna, Stanisław Kowalewski, Zdzisław Kubalski, Józef Kuśmierek, Marian Promiński, Jan Rostworowski, Jerzy Stadnicki, Wanda Wasilewska and Stefan Żeromski (some of whom will be discussed later).

Occasionally, articles were fully devoted to a few selected works, which were analyzed with great censorial "care."[4] More often, however, several works appeared in one text treating them as exemplifications of the problem at hand and, thus, not devoting much attention to other aspects of the work. In certain cases, the author was mentioned only briefly, without any details that might have made it easier to interpret the example. Other times, the author was not mentioned at all, or his or her name and the title of the discussed work were distorted.[5] Given the nature of the Bulletins as tools for training, such a practice was unexpected, especially in the case of editorial materials.

A good example of this was a letter from the Kraków branch, whose author complained about "Mysia Street's" cooperation with field offices. At one point, he mentioned problems with the assessment of Mrożek,[6] but the writer's name

---

[4] "Spółdzielczość produkcyjna w naszej literaturze," *Biuletyn Informacyjno-Instrukcyjny* no. 3 (27), March 1954, pp. 28–46 (APG, WUKPPiW, file ref. no. 45); T. Zaręba, "O wynikach dyskusji," *Biuletyn Informacyjno-Instrukcyjny* no. 8 (44), August 1955, p. 33 (APG, WUKPPiW, file ref. no. 124); L. Rutkowski (Depart. of Cultural Publications), "Nareszcie żywa dyskusja… (podsumowanie głosów z dyskusji nad utworami Andrzejewskiego, Rudnickiego i Flaszena)," *Biuletyn Informacyjno-Instrukcyjny* no. 1 (49), January 1956, pp. 13–23 (APG, WUKPPiW, file ref. no. 4); "Głosy w dyskusji," *Biuletyn Informacyjno-Instrukcyjny* no. 1 (49), January 1956, pp. 13–23 (APG, WUKPPiW, file ref. no. 4).

[5] Authors whose works were discussed without providing the authors' names: Gabriela Zapolska (Józef Maskoff), author of the play *Tamten* (the June 1945 Bulletin, p. 13); Adam Bilski and Zygmunt Jaski, authors of the series *Psoty Kleksa* (the January 1949 Bulletin, p. 8); Robert Rydz, author of the play *Ułan i Młynarka* (the May 1949 Bulletin, fol. 142r–142v); Zofia Jaremko-Żytyńska, author of the book *Odbudowa i rozwój życia kulturalnego w Polsce 1944–1948* (the May 1949 Bulletin, fol. 157v-157r); authors whose last names were spelled incorrectly: Zofia Meisner misspelled as Zofia Meissner (the September 1952 Bulletin, p. 24), Janusz Trzcieniecki as Trzcieniewski (the May 1949 Bulletin, fol. 154v); author whose first name was provided inaccurately: Stanisław Kowalewski as Mirosław Kowalewski (the February 1955 Bulletin, pp. 1–2).

[6] Sławomir Mrożek (1930–2013) – one of the most popular Polish playwrights; a prose writer, satirist, and cartoonist. He used the poetics of absurdity, satire, and surrealism to ridicule the absurdity of life in communist Poland. His works have been translated into many languages, including English, e.g., *Police* and *Tango*. In 1954, the year when the letter was issued, the writer was still employed at the editorial office of *Dziennik Polski*.

only appeared as an illustration of the disrespectful attitude of the Main Office's employees towards their colleagues from field branches:

> In whatever form we send our objections to Warsaw (we are talking about signals), they do not merit a response. This is not about the "grand gesture" of answering questions. The matter is much more serious. For example, we had reservations about Mrożek's article in *Dziennik Polski*. The secondary assessment did not agree with the preventive one. At the briefing, the votes were divided. So we sent a signal with all our remarks to the GUKP waiting for a response. After a few days, the editors posted an article on a similar issue, framing it similarly. While evaluating another article of this kind we were again not sure if we were not making an oversight. Although there were no serious consequences, there is a simple conclusion for the future: the National Press Department should respond to the objections raised in the signals. Not to all of them – because clearly this would be neither necessary nor possible with the current staffing of the Press Department – but to the important ones.[7]

In this particular case, Mrożek only served as an illustration of a specific problem. The readers-censors were not interested in the nature of the interpretative challenge faced by their colleagues; what was more important was the need to improve the situation between "us" (the field offices) and "them" (the Main Office).

Many remarks on literature and culture appeared in the form of short notes (like the one quoted above), comments or glosses on the margins of other considerations, e.g., in chapters devoted to the crucial issues of the era. Naturally, the tables of contents, included in almost every Bulletin, did not list such marginalia; it was only after reading through the journal that one could discover them. Sometimes, however, more substantial materials on art were also absent from the contents lists. A prime example was the 1950 *Biuletyn Szkoleniowy*, in which several books, poems, films, as well as journalistic and feature texts were discussed, sometimes quite extensively. These included *Lata walki* [Years of struggle] by Stanisława Sowińska, *Morgi* [The morgen] by Zofia Przęczek, *Przebudzenie* [Awakening] by Maria Witkowska, the third volume of *Urbanistyka* [Urban planning] by Tadeusz Tołwiński, the poems "Warszawskoje szosse" [Warsaw high road] by Leon

---

[7] J. Nowak (WUKP Kraków), "Uwagi krytyczne na temat współpracy GUKP z terenem na odcinku prasowym" (correspondence in "Dział Listów"), *Biuletyn Informacyjno-Instrukcyjny* no. 1 (25), January 1954, p. 41 (APG, WUKPPiW, file ref. no. 39). Kajetan Mojsak focused on the censorship of Mrożek's "early works," i.e., those from the late 1950s and early 1960s. Therefore, he does not provide any information about red-penciling the writer's work from the period of his employment at *Dziennik Polski*, see: K. Mojsak, "Wczesna twórczość Stanisława Mrożka w dokumentach cenzury," [in:] idem, *Cenzura wobec prozy nowoczesnej. 1956–1965*, Warszawa: IBL PAN, 2016, series *Badania Filologiczne nad Cenzurą PRL* vol. 7, pp. 123–154.

Pasternak and "Posiedzeniarze" [Loafers] by Vladimir Mayakovsky, as well as the films *Zakazane piosenki* [Forbidden songs] and *Dom na pustkowiu* [House in the wilderness]. The issue's table of contents was not helpful in this case, but reflected the tumultuous changes that were taking place on the political scene at the time, as evidenced by the titles of the pieces: "Polish-Soviet Friendship," "The Titov Diversion," "The National Front," "The Road to Socialism," "The Question of the Class Struggle," "The Role of the Party and the Working Class," "The Traditions of the Labor Movement," "The German Question," and "The Struggle for Peace."[8]

Literature usually appeared in the Bulletins as a subject of censorship assessment. Sometimes, however, certain works were also used to support the evaluation of another title. Most often, to illustrate their thesis, the functionaries used quotations (more or less aptly) by famous artists. Of course, their selection was biased, one example of which was using a quote from Mark Twain in an article on the Great Depression and Roosevelt's reforms: "It is by the goodness of God that in our country we have those three unspeakably precious things: freedom of speech, freedom of conscience, and the prudence never to practice either of them."[9]

1.2. The Censorship of Fiction

By raising our level,
we raise the level of our work on the book.[10]

The censorship office on Mysia Street and its local branches received titles representing various fields of writing, which also translated into the selection of contents presented in the Bulletins. They assessed works of fiction and ephemera, school textbooks, scientific and popular science books, as well as other non-fiction and borderline genres, e.g., reportages.[11] Considerable attention was paid to

---

[8] *Biuletyn Szkoleniowy* no. 1, March (May) 1950 (APG, WUKPPiW, file ref. no. 328).

[9] "Czy Reformy Roosevelta były postępowe," *Biuletyn Informacyjno-Instrukcyjny* no. 1 (13), January 1953, p. 36 (APG, WUKPPiW, file ref. no. 19). The quote comes from the novel by M. Twain, *Following the Equator. A Journey Around the World*, Hartford–New York: The American Publishing Co., Doubleday&McClure Co., 1897, p. 195.

[10] "Recenzja z pozycji literackiej (cd.)" (in the series *O wyższy poziom pracy nad książką*), *Biuletyn Informacyjno-Instrukcyjny* no. 9, September 1952, p. 33 (APG, WUKPPiW, file ref. no. 78).

[11] I define non-fiction as "informative, didactic, scholarly or journalistic writing which (in contrast to fiction) typically strives for precision and clarity in conveying its message" (*Podręczny słownik bibliotekarza*, compiled by G. Czapnik, Z. Gruszka in co-operation with H. Tadeusiewicz, Warszawa: Wydawnictwo Stowarzyszenia Bibliotekarzy Polskich, 2011, p. 182). I understand the term "borderline genre" as "genres which

the analysis of the publishing industry, however, censors were more interested in the socio-political rather than cultural issues discussed there, thus, only in exceptional cases were literary works and their reviews published in the press.

The editors of the Bulletins admitted that "most of our shortcomings and deficiencies in the work on literature extend to other types of assessments,"[12] which meant that some of the guidelines concerning censorship were universal and applied to any type of creative activity. This was the case, for example, when making sure that reviews considered the proper ideological realization of a work and that state secrets were not disclosed. Similarly, the instructions to fight against "the 'allism' of postulates in censorship evaluations, that is, against unrealistic demands made on a particular work"[13] found application in a wide range of censorial work. In their assessments, censors were obliged to take into account the author, the publisher and the nature of the publication, as well as its goals and the target reader.[14] However, functionaries often committed the sin of overzealousness, placing unreasonable expectations on specific works, which could not possibly demonstrate the defining characteristics of randomly selected genres. The Bulletin's readers were repeatedly reminded that "the censor's pencil should resemble a surgical lancet rather than a Stone Age club,"[15] or that "it is evidence of poor censorship to disqualify an entire work while pointing to a number of erroneous and harmful moments, and completely disregarding its strong points."[16] In ignoring the above-mentioned recommendations of superiors, one can see that

---

display both features regarded as characteristic of fine literature in a given period of time, as well as features of those forms of expression, which are generally not guided by aesthetic aims, primarily scholarly, philosophical and journalistic texts" (*Słownik terminów literackich*, ed J. Sławiński, Revised and Expanded Third Edition, Wrocław: Ossolineum, 1988, p. 163).

[12] "Recenzja z pozycji literackiej, cz. I" (in the series *O wyższy poziom pracy nad książką*), *Biuletyn Informacyjno-Instrukcyjny* no. 8, August 1952, p. 19 (APG, WUKPPiW, file ref. no. 81).

[13] "O wyższy poziom pracy nad książką (cd.)" (in the series *O wyższy poziom pracy nad książką*), *Biuletyn Informacyjno-Instrukcyjny* no. 11, November 1952, p. 39 (APG, WUKPPiW, file ref. no. 72).

[14] See, e.g.: "Uwagi ogólne o recenzji (in the series *O wyższy poziom pracy nad książką*)," *Biuletyn Informacyjno-Instrukcyjny* no. 7, July 1952, pp. 26–29 (APG, WUKPPiW, file ref. no. 84); "Podsumowanie dyskusji nad wierszem Roztworowskiego pt. 'Oskarżam,'" *Biuletyn Informacyjno-Instrukcyjny* no. 11/12 (23/24), November/December 1953, p. 16 (APG, WUKPPiW, file ref. no. 9).

[15] "Podsumowanie dyskusji nad wierszem Roztworowskiego pt. 'Oskarżam,'" *Biuletyn Informacyjno-Instrukcyjny* no. 11/12 (23/24), November/December 1953, p. 16 (APG, WUKPPiW, file ref. no. 9).

[16] Ibidem.

a certain hedging approach was exercised when a rank-and-file functionary of the "Ministry of Truth" was unable to give any concrete arguments against a work, but felt the need (justified or unjustified by the text itself) to point out the author's trespasses. However, the abuse of censorial pen was also to be avoided, because employees were held accountable not only for their oversights, but also for overzealousness: the 1945 Bulletin reported the dismissal of two censors for "corseting" the religious press.[17]

To reduce both types of errors, more detailed guidelines were formulated for censoring specific literary types and genres. The need for such instructions was signaled by those concerned, who in their daily practice encountered a great variety of works, assessing "both novels, and plays, narrative poems, collections of poems, literary reportages, essays, classics and contemporary authors."[18] Not all political workers were aware of the diversified assessment criteria, which may not come as a surprise given the small percentage of functionaries with higher education at the time.[19] Blatant errors in the interpretation and evaluation of works were rampant, so guidance on how to avoid them was valuable to a rank-and-file employee:

> After all, we will not measure Stryjkowski and Prus with the same yardstick. However, there were cases when one of our assessments alleged that "Prus is far from Marxism" and Thackeray's book was denied any social and artistic value. These are, of course, glaring examples and the result of exceptional ignorance, but the danger of applying one frame to every work, regardless of who wrote it and when, is still acute.[20]

---

[17] "Seminarium prasy (wyjątki z protokółu). Jedność narodowa," *Biuletyn Instrukcyjny* no. 2, June 1945, p. 4 (APG, WUKPPiW, file ref. no. 210).

[18] "Recenzja z pozycji literackiej, cz. I" (in the series *O wyższy poziom pracy nad książką*), *Biuletyn Informacyjno-Instrukcyjny* no. 8, August 1952, p. 19 (APG, WUKPPiW, file ref. no. 81).

[19] See, e.g.: K. Budrowska, "Social background and education," [in:] eadem, *Writers, Literature and Censorship in Poland. 1948–1956*, Berlin: Peter Lang, 2020, pp. 131–133; K. Kamińska-Chełminiak, "Wykształcenie," [in:] eadem, *Cenzura w Polsce 1944–1960. Organizacja. Kadry. Metody pracy*, Warszawa: Wydział Dziennikarstwa, Informacji i Bibliologii UW i Oficyna Wydawnicza ASPRA-JR, 2019, pp. 64–65; P. Nowak, "Wojewódzki Urząd Kontroli Prasy, Publikacji i Widowisk w okresie nacjonalizacji rynku książki w Poznaniu (1946–1955)," *Biblioteka* 2011, no. 15, p. 164; see also: A. Pawlicki, *Kompletna szarość. Cenzura w latach 1965–1972. Instytucja i ludzie*, Warszawa: Wydawnictwo Trio, 2001, p. 81.

[20] "Recenzja z pozycji literackiej, cz. I" (in the series *O wyższy poziom pracy nad książką*), *Biuletyn Informacyjno-Instrukcyjny* no. 8, August 1952, p. 19 (APG, WUKPPiW, file ref. no. 81).

Julian Stryjkowski (1905–1996) – a Polish prose writer, playwright and journalist of Jewish origin, author of, e.g., the novel *Austeria*; Bolesław Prus (1847–1912) – one of the most popular Polish writers of the Positivist period, author of such novels as *The Doll* and *Pharaoh*.

The aforementioned guidelines, however, were of a rather general nature, as it was believed that the censor's "clear reason and democratic conscience"[21] would dictate the right decisions in assessing specific cases. Obviously, this remark should be put in quotation marks, since the censor was supposed to follow the guidelines and instructions (and not display his or her creative invention), but the fact remains that the Bulletins lacked exhaustive, programmatic statements on what criteria to apply to a given genre of literature, although the need for such input was signaled, for example, in the case of children's literature,[22] reportage,[23] satire[24] or socialist realist novels[25] (different criteria were also recommended for different press titles[26]). Usually, minor remarks accompanying the evaluation of a particular work were formulated. I have extracted them from these individual contexts and presented them in the following parts of the book as collective guidelines concerning censorship of a particular literary genre.

At this point, however, I would like to elaborate on the guidelines for censoring fiction *au bloc*. Not only do the Bulletins draw attention to the differences in evaluating various literary genres, but they also make a more general distinction, highlighting the differences in the evaluation of fiction and other types of

---

[21] "Seminarium prasy (wyjątki z protokółu). Granice dopuszczalnej krytyki," *Biuletyn Informacyjno-Instrukcyjny* no. 2, June 1945, p. 8 (APG, WUKPPiW, file ref. no. 210; see also: p. 18).

[22] See, e.g.: A. Purowska, "O pracy nad książką dziecięcą," *Biuletyn Informacyjno-Instrukcyjny* 1955, no. 5 (41), pp. 19–24 (APG, WUKPPiW, file ref. no. 131).

[23] See, e.g.: "O dyskusji nad książką J. Kuśmierka *Uwaga człowiek*," *Biuletyn Informacyjno-Instrukcyjny* no. 2, February 1952, p. 37 (APG, WUKPPiW, file ref. no. 99); "Zagadnienia przemysłu w prasie poznańskiej (luty–marzec 1953 r.)," *Biuletyn Informacyjno-Instrukcyjny* no. 5 (17), May 1953, p. 51 (APG, WUKPPiW, file ref. no. 15).

[24] See, e.g.: J. Kleyny, "Uwagi na temat satyry," *Biuletyn Informacyjno-Instrukcyjny* no. 10, October 1952, p. 35 (APG, WUKPPiW, file ref. no. 75); idem, "Z problemów satyry," *Biuletyn Informacyjno-Instrukcyjny* no. 7/8 (31/32), July/August 1954, pp. 21–36 (APG, WUKPPiW, file ref. no. 65); idem, "I jeszcze raz o satyrze," *Biuletyn Informacyjno-Instrukcyjny* no. 4 (40), April 1955, pp. 9–25 (APG, WUKPPiW, file ref. no. 65); K. Bażańska, "Satyra w terenie. Uwagi o dyskusji nad tekstami Brzezińskiego," *Biuletyn Informacyjno-Instrukcyjny* no. 11/12 (35/36), November/December 1954, pp. 27–36 (APG, WUKPPiW, file ref. no. 59).

[25] See, e.g.: "O dyskusji nad książką J. Kuśmierka, *Uwaga człowiek*," *Biuletyn Informacyjno-Instrukcyjny* no. 2, February 1952, p. 37 (APG, WUKPPiW, file ref. no. 99).

[26] See, e.g.: "Seminarium prasy (Wyjątki z protokółu). Jedność narodowa," *Biuletyn Instrukcyjny* no. 2, June 1945, p. 3 (APG, WUKPPiW, file ref. no. 210); "O właściwe wykorzystywanie prasy periodycznej w naszej pracy codziennej" (in the series *O wyższy poziom naszej pracy*), *Biuletyn Informacyjno-Instrukcyjny* no. 2, February 1952, pp. 29–34 (APG, WUKPPiW, file ref. no. 99). See also: the chapter "Literary and Cultural Issues in the Press."

writing. This issue was discussed quite extensively in one of the articles in the series *O wyższy poziom pracy nad książką*:

> A literary work is a complex thing. In addition to the often rich socio-political subject matter, it contains a number of other elements that often become decisive factors in the assessment. Above all, there is the artistic value and everything connected with its extraction and analysis: the question of form, language, style, etc.[27]

According to the above, the evaluation criteria applied to fiction should also consider "the writer's creative idea" and "his artistic independence,"[28] which could soften the blow of the censor's evaluation (though it was not a given): *licencia poetica* did not free the author from writing under the dictates of the rules. The margin of freedom enjoyed by artistic expression was not afforded to journalism, popular science works, socio-political positions and school textbooks, which had to be subjected to more stringent evaluation criteria than fiction (different criteria were also applied to different publishing houses).[29]

It often came down to finding only mistakes, shortcomings and defects in reviewed works, including literary ones. The censors saw this as their basic task, although in cases of unjustified criticism they could, as I have mentioned, be held responsible – several Bulletins wrote about "responsibility and culpability in censorial work."[30] While the censor's inquisitiveness was often rewarded, many Bulletins also stressed the need to "see the strong points and qualities"[31] of a work. It was pointed out that "the censor's failure to see the positive values of a book, especially in fiction, threatens to turn censorship into an instrument retarding the development of our young literature"[32] (this particular remark was made in January 1953, hence, it is not difficult to guess in what direction this "young literature" was supposed to develop).

----

[27] "Recenzja z pozycji literackiej, cz. I" (in the series *O wyższy poziom pracy nad książką*), *Biuletyn Informacyjno-Instrukcyjny* no. 8, August 1952, p. 20 (APG, WUKPPiW, file ref. no. 81). See also: "O wynikach dyskusji nad opowiadaniem Kubalskiego, 'Wyrok,'" *Biuletyn Informacyjno-Instrukcyjny* no. 2 (26), February 1954, pp. 32–33 (APG, WUKPPiW, file ref. no. 42).

[28] "Uwagi ogólne o recenzji" (in the series *O wyższy poziom pracy nad książką*), *Biuletyn Informacyjno-Instrukcyjny* no. 7, July 1952, p. 29 (APG, WUKPPiW, file ref no. 84).

[29] Ibidem; "O wyższy poziom pracy nad książką (cd.)" (in the series *O wyższy poziom pracy nad książką*), *Biuletyn Informacyjno-Instrukcyjny* no. 11, November 1952, p. 37 (APG, WUKPPiW, file ref. no. 72).

[30] See, e.g.: K. Dworecki, "Odpowiedzialność i wina w pracy cenzorskiej," *Biuletyn Informacyjno-Instrukcyjny* no. 7 (43), July 1955, pp. 37–47 (APG, WUKPPiW, file ref. no. 103).

[31] "Śladem naszych recenzji," *Biuletyn Informacyjno-Instrukcyjny* no. 1 (13), January 1953, p. 45 (APG, WUKPPiW, file ref. no. 19).

[32] Ibidem.

This compulsive focus on errors and shortcomings of a text is one of the hedging strategies signaled earlier. I have mentioned that in the 1940s and 1950s, the training and competences of censors left much to be desired. In the Bulletins, even the heads were "reproached" for gross spelling errors.[33] Most of the functionaries had no training in literary criticism. Moreover, at this stage of the Office's existence, they had not yet mastered the minutia of "censorship criticism" due to poor professional training, but also the lack of specialization in the area of evaluated literature; one week, a functionary assessed, for example, Różewicz's poetry; another – Tołwiński's *Urbanistyka*, and the next – operetta art (such examples appeared in the Bulletins).[34] Most employees deplored this practice, but some heads boasted that they made sure that their subordinates received "diverse texts for inspection."[35]

Nonetheless, the superiors were aware of their subordinates' limited education, so a recurring issue in the Bulletins was the question of training the functionaries and raising their professional qualifications. This was to be achieved via cycles of dedicated articles on the subject[36] and lists of titles recommended either for individual reading or for joint discussion during briefings and meetings. These were mainly texts on politics and history, but those interested were also encouraged to peruse titles penned by the literary critics known at the time: *Spór o realizm* [The dispute over realism] by Melania Kierczyńska, *Literatura na przełomie* [Literature at the turn] and *Literatura międzywojenna* [Inter-war literature] by Ryszard Matuszewski, as well as books written by famous writers: *Prawo*

---

[33] "Na marginesie sprawozdań kwartalnych WUKPPiW," *Biuletyn Informacyjno-Instrukcyjny* no. 7/8 (31/32), July/August 1954, p. 11 (APG, WUKPPiW, file ref. no. 65).

[34] "Recenzje," *Biuletyn Informacyjno-Szkoleniowy* no. 1/3, January 1949, p. 9 (APG, WUKPPiW, file ref. no. 196); "O wyższy poziom pracy na odcinku widowisk," *Biuletyn Informacyjno-Szkoleniowy* no. 3 (15), March 1953, p. 39 (APG, WUKPPiW, file ref. no. 17). Cf. "Kilka uwag o programach 'Artosu,'" *Biuletyn Informacyjno-Szkoleniowy* no. 1, January 1952, p. 45 (APG, WUKPPiW, file ref. no. 100); "Przez sprawniejszą organizację – do lepszej pracy" (in the series *O wyższy poziom naszej pracy*), *Biuletyn Informacyjno-Szkoleniowy* no. 3, March 1952, pp. 23–24 (APG, WUKPPiW, file ref. no. 96).

[35] K. Dworecki (Stalinogród), "O wyższy poziom organizacji pracy," *Biuletyn Informacyjno-Szkoleniowy* no. 1 (25), January 1954, pp. 10–11 (APG, WUKPPiW, file ref. no. 39). See also: "Ze sprawozdań Kierowników Wojewódzkich Biur," *Biuletyn Instrukcyjny* no. 2, June 1945 r., p. 14 (APG, WUKPPiW, file ref. no. 210); ["Materiały z odprawy"], fol. 22r ("*Biuletyny Instrukcyjno-Szkoleniowe* 1945–1951" (APP, WUKPPiW, file ref. no. 4)); S. Paź (WUKPPiW Olsztyn), "Spójrzmy sobie w oczy towarzysze…" (correspondence in "Dział Listów"), *Biuletyn Informacyjno-Szkoleniowy* no. 1 (49), January 1956, pp. 51–52 (APG, WUKPPiW, file ref. no. 4).

[36] See, e.g.: the aforementioned series of articles *O wyższy poziom pracy nad książką* and *O wyższy poziom naszej pracy*.

do kultury [The right to culture] by Leon Kruczkowski, *Obywatele* [Citizens] by Kazimierz Brandys and *Władza* [Authorities] by Tadeusz Konwicki.[37]

Another plague of "censorship criticism" was its tolerance of the low artistic value of a work. In consequence, mediocre texts of no literary value were allowed for print, simply because they were politically correct.[38] This issue was raised, among others, in 1952, following the publication of the article "Nowy Zoil, czyli o schematyzmie"[39] [The new Zoilus: on schematism] written by Ludwik Flaszen.[40] It cannot be denied, however, that the Bulletins made various attempts to assess the artistic value of works and track down "linguistic sloppiness," or even, as one of the issues put it, "the abuse of the Polish language."[41]

There was also a discussion on the need to move away from the evaluation focused only on the analysis of the parts of the book without considering it as a whole (this guideline appeared most often in the assessment of fiction). The result of such an attitude towards a work could be either a ban on publication – if the censor extrapolated individual errors to the whole – or on the contrary, acceptance of a work which as a whole was not effective, but passed through the sieve of the censor's detail-oriented evaluation. In some cases, these lapses may have stemmed from the system of "fragmentary 'reading' of the same book by several censors,"[42] which was criticized in the June 1954 issue.

The above-mentioned censorship strategies were used mainly with regard to contemporary literature, as it was this kind that most often reached

---

[37] "Noty," *Biuletyn Informacyjno-Szkoleniowy* no. 1, January 1952, pp. 48–49 (APG, WUKPPiW, file ref. no. 100); "Noty," *Biuletyn Informacyjno-Szkoleniowy* no. 2, February 1952, p. 50 (APG, WUKPPiW, file ref. no. 99); J. Kupraszwili (the Head of the National Division of the Department of Non-Periodical Publications), "Nowości wydawnicze," *Biuletyn Informacyjno-Szkoleniowy* no. 6, June 1955, pp. 42–43 (APG, WUKPPiW, file ref. no. 52).

[38] See, e.g.: "Recenzja z pozycji literackiej, cz. I" (in the series *O wyższy poziom pracy nad książką*), *Biuletyn Informacyjno-Szkoleniowy* no. 8, August 1952, p. 20 (APG, WUKPPiW, file ref. no. 81).

[39] See, e.g.: L. Flaszen, "Nowy Zoil, czyli o schematyzmie," *Życie Literackie* January 6, 1952, no. 1, pp. 3–4.

Zoilus: a caustic, excessively harsh, and unjust literary critic; the term comes from the Ancient philosopher and rhetorician, Zoilus of Amphipolis (4th century B.C.), who famously criticized Homer's works, thus earning himself the nickname Homeromastix (The scourge of Homer).

[40] Ludwik Flaszen – a publicist and critic, later a co-founder of the Laboratory Theatre (along with Jerzy Grotowski (1930–2020)).

[41] "Kilka uwag o programach 'Artosu,'" *Biuletyn Pnformacyjno-Instrukcyjny* no. 1, January 1952, p. 45 (APG, WUKPPiW, file ref. no. 100).

[42] "Wnioski z narady krajowej tyczące kontroli prewencyjnej książek," *Biuletyn Informacyjno-Instrukcyjny* no. 6 (30), June 1954, p. 13 (APG, WUKPPiW, file ref. no. 52).

the desks of the functionaries. It should come as no surprise then that pre-war literature was presented in the Bulletins with moderate restraint. A reading of the periodicals suggests that the editors were more interested in the present and the future rather than the past, which is why works created before 1945 were featured relatively rarely. Despite the fact that the authorities moved quite quickly to form a new literary canon,[43] in the preserved periodicals, the adaptation of the cultural past to the requirements of the present appeared to be less important than the training of censors proficient in the art of assessing the latest literature and art.

There may have been several reasons for this. First, it was easier to create precise guidelines for what was already a closed literary past. Secondly, the publishing market was dominated by contemporary literature, which – along with the redefined classics – was to shape the new citizenry.

The Bulletins, therefore, played a primarily normative role, indicating what criteria should be used to evaluate current events and cultural phenomena. The instructions for the inspection of pre-war literature did not differ from those applied to contemporary works, although, over the years, the guidelines for the assessment of this particular segment of writing also emerged. In the material analyzed, they are illustrated by minor mentions (e.g., about the works of Mickiewicz, Norwid or Sienkiewicz – authors who wrote at a time when Poland lost its independence and disappeared from the map of the world for one hundred and twenty-three years).[44] The first and probably the most substantial statement on the censorship of classics appeared in the July 1952 issue:

---

[43] See, e.g.: M. Zawodniak, "Klasycy literatury i klasycy marksizmu. Dwa w jednym," [in:] *Komunistyczni bohaterowie* vol. 1: *Tradycja, kult, rytuał*, eds. M. Bogusławska, Z. Grębecka, E. Wróblewska-Trochimiuk, Warszawa–Kraków: Wydział Polonistyki UW and Wydawnictwo Libron, 2011, series *Wschód–Zachód–Konfrontacje*, pp. 13–20; idem, "Zaraz po wojnie, a nawet przed… O przygotowaniach do socrealizmu," *Teksty Drugie* 2000, no. 1–2, pp. 141–151; P. Dakowicz, "Walka ideologiczna z Norwidem i o Norwida (1944–1948)," *Pamiętnik Literacki* 2009, issue 2, pp. 5–30.

[44] See, e.g.: "Recenzje"; "Zagadnienie suwerenności państwowej"; "Konfiskata 'słówek' przy niewidzeniu całości"; "'Szantaż' Mickiewiczem," *Biuletyn Informacyjno-Szkoleniowy* no. 1/3, January 1949, p. 8, 17, 37–38, 40–41 (APG, WUKPPiW, file ref. no. 196); "Sugerowanie prześladowań religijnych," *Biuletyn Informacyjno-Szkoleniowy* no. 4, May 1949, fol. 145v ("*Biuletyny Instrukcyjno-Szkoleniowe 1945–1951*" (APP, WUKPPiW, file ref. no. 4)); "Kilka uwag o pracy nad wstępem, przypisami i posłowiem," *Biuletyn Informacyjno-Szkoleniowy* no. 9 (21), September 1953, pp. 542–549 (AAN, GUKPPiW, file ref. no. 22).

Adam Mickiewicz (1798–1855) – one of the most prominent and best known Polish writers of the Romantic era; author of such works as *Forefathers' Eve* and *Pan Tadeusz*; Cyprian Kamil Norwid (1821–1883) – a notable poet of Romanticism; a selection of

> When it comes to a classic of domestic or foreign literature, we should lean to-
> wards either permission to publish or a suggestion not to publish. As a rule, inter-
> ference with classics is not advisable, unless it concerns works by authors who are
> not very well known, and only minor deletions are recommended.
> An introduction or afterword and footnotes should provide an appropriate expo-
> sition and context.[45]

It should be remembered that we have only nine issues from the years 1945–1951, and it was at this time that the work on transforming the literary tradition and adapting it to the requirements of the new reality began. Therefore, the subject of the cultural past may have been dealt with in the issues that have not yet been found.

1.3. The Specifics of Book Inspection

> *The titles we received for inspection were not always*
> *turned over to the publisher on schedule.*
> *It was believed that titles should "ripen"*
> *for at least 2 weeks.[46]*

It was the responsibility of political functionaries to assess all texts submitted to the Office for the Control. However, work did not always proceed smoothly, and one of the maladies were delays in evaluating materials, which obstructed the entire publishing process.

Long delays were also observed in the Non-Periodical Publications Offices, were books were assessed.[47] Dozens of "unread books 'waiting' their turn"[48] were

---

his poems was published in English (see: *Poems*). Henryk Sienkiewicz (1846–1916) – a key Polish writer of Positivism, a Nobel laureate in Literature (1905); author of such novels as *Quo Vadis, With Fire and Sword, The Deluge, Fire in the Steppe*. The Partitions of Poland, which lasted between 1772 and 1918, is a period when Poland – divided between Austria, Prussia, and Russia – disappeared from the map.

[45] "Uwagi ogólne o recenzji" (in the series *O wyższy poziom pracy nad książką*), *Biuletyn Informacyjno-Instrukcyjny* no. 7, July 1952, p. 27 (APG, WUKPPiW, file ref. no. 84).

[46] K. Dworecki (Stalinogród), "O wyższy poziom organizacji pracy," *Biuletyn Informacyjno-Instrukcyjny* no. 1 (25), January 1954, p. 9 (APG, WUKPPiW, file ref. no. 39).

[47] See, e.g.: "Dwie recenzje," *Biuletyn Informacyjno-Szkoleniowy* no. 4, maj 1949, fol. 157r (APP, WUKPPiW, file ref. no. 4); "Oszczędność – systemem w naszej pracy," *Biuletyn Informacyjno-Szkoleniowy* no. 3, March 1952, pp. 16–17 (APG, WUKPPiW, file ref. no. 96).

[48] Rak (WUKPPiW Poznań), "WUKP Poznań. Brygada Młodzieżowa im. J. Bruna wita Zlot," *Biuletyn Informacyjno-Instrukcyjny* no. 7, July 1952, p. 35 (APG, WUKPPiW, file ref. no. 84).

piling up in huge warehouses; political functionaries could not keep up with the reading, which was certainly due to staff shortages, although there were also other reasons. At one of the briefings, as early as in the 1940s, it was written that "the Press Office must be the director's pet project."[49] The following quotation shows that, even in 1954, serial publications occupied a major, if not the most important, place:

> It was convenient for the staff of the Non-Periodical Publications Office or the Performances Office that their matters were not "on the tapis" of the work briefings. They were happy to leave this "honor" to the "pressmen." For them, the briefings, during which press matters were discussed, became an hour of downtime on softly cushioned armchairs and sofas. When the discussion revolved around press interference, which for them was some kind of higher math, the employees of the "deprived" offices either snoozed or daydreamed.
> [...]
> Strolls and chats – which for some employees were an integral part of their workday – were a "taboo" that could not be violated; otherwise, work at the Office would "lose its charm."[50]

The privileging of some offices at the expense of others had a negative impact on the "ethics" and work results of the "deprived" teams. Attempts were made to remedy this situation by reorganizing the Non-Periodical Publications Department, e.g., by creating divisions according to the criterion of publications,[51] or by streamlining the review process, and delegating new responsibilities to staff.[52] Some solutions had surprising results:

> When comrades from the Press Office received books for inspection, you could see fear in their eyes. Initially, quite a few could not cope with writing a review. These comrades realized that the inspection of non-periodical titles was not as trivial as they had previously assumed.[53]

---

[49] See: ["Materiały z odprawy"], fol. 33r ("*Biuletyny Instrukcyjno-Szkoleniowe 1945–1951*" (APP, WUKPPiW, file ref. no. 4)).

[50] K. Dworecki (Stalinogród), "O wyższy poziom organizacji pracy," *Biuletyn Informacyjno-Instrukcyjny* no. 1 (25), January 1954, pp. 7–8 (APG, WUKPPiW, file ref. no. 39).

[51] "Przez sprawniejszą organizację – do lepszej pracy" (in the series *O wyższy poziom naszej pracy*), *Biuletyn Informacyjno-Instrukcyjny* no. 3, March 1952, pp. 21–25 (APG, WUKPPiW, file ref. no. 96).

[52] K. Dworecki (Stalinogród), "O wyższy poziom organizacji pracy," *Biuletyn Informacyjno-Instrukcyjny* no. 1 (25), January 1954, pp. 7–14 (APG, WUKPPiW, file ref. no. 39).

[53] Ibidem, p. 12.

Another way to solve the problem of delayed book reviews was through additional staff commitments made on holidays, anniversaries, and important political events. Functionaries of the so-called Periodicals (that is, Periodical Publications Department) and Non-Periodicals (Non-Periodical Publications Department) declared, for example, that they would read an additional number of pages meant for inspection. Censors from the capital and voivodeship offices, e.g., in Kraków and Wrocław, made such an offer. The latter informed about the effort of "reading 15 books sent by the GUKP as part of a secondary inspection, during off-duty hours."[54] However, not all of them fulfilled these supererogatory duties in an exemplary manner, as one functionary of the Poznań branch reported:

> And when we jointly decided at a work briefing that we would cut the number of people on duty from two to one in order to secure the entire afternoon and night edition, a problem arose as to who would read the modified pages arriving at the Office at 3 p.m., i.e., at a time when the entire team was finishing work and the censor on duty hadn't started his shift yet. It was decided that it would get sorted, we would rotate and stay after hours and read these additional four pages. But when it came to actually doing the reading, not a soul could be found in the censor's room![55]

The issue of work efficiency in terms of the number of inspected pages recurred in several Bulletins. The situation in the capital office appeared to be the best. According to one of the articles, an average employee of the Warsaw office read more than his or her colleague in any voivodeship department, that is, from 4,500 to 5,500 pages a month.[56] Taking the average figure of 5,000 pages per month and assuming that a censor worked five days a week, seven hours a day,[57] he or she had to read 220 pages every day, which is not a small number.

---

[54] "Z akcji współzawodnictwa zobowiązaniowego," *Biuletyn Informacyjno-Instrukcyjny* no. 10, October 1952, p. 49 (APG, WUKPPiW, file ref. no. 75). See also: "Odpowiadamy na apel pracowników 'Pafawagu,'" *Biuletyn Informacyjno-Instrukcyjny* no. 3, March 1952, p. 36 (APG, WUKPPiW, file ref. no. 96); B. Gutkowski, "O wyższy poziom pracy Urzędu," *Biuletyn Informacyjno-Instrukcyjny* no. 12, December 1952, p. 6 (APG, WUKPPiW, file ref. no. 70; see also: Fig. 2 with the GUKPPiW stokers' commitment (visible at the bottom of the page) to save fuel.

[55] Rak (WUKPPiW), "WUKP Poznań. Brygada Młodzieżowa im. J. Bruna wita Zlot," *Biuletyn Informacyjno-Instrukcyjny* no. 7, July 1952, pp. 34–35 (APG, WUKPPiW, file ref. no. 84).

[56] "Z krajowej odprawy w GUKP," *Biuletyn Informacyjno-Instrukcyjny* no. 7, July 1952, p. 3 (APG, WUKPPiW, file ref. no. 84).

[57] "Wypowiedzi w dyskusji. Wierciak" (WUKPPiW Kraków), *Biuletyn Informacyjno-Instrukcyjny* no. 6/7 (18/19), June/July 1953, p. 67 (APG, WUKPPiW, file ref. no. 14). Cf. "Wnioski usprawniające sprawozdawczość" (in the series *Z naszych doświadczeń*), *Biuletyn Informacyjno-Instrukcyjny* no. 3, March 1952, p. 27 (APG, WUKPPiW, file ref. no. 96).

What exactly was the situation in the field branches? According to the Bulletins, it varied considerably, depending on the period and the staffing levels in individual offices; however, the prevailing view was that productivity in these centers was lacking. A censor in the Non-Periodical section of the Bydgoszcz office read an average of 108 to 135 pages a day, while a functionary at the voivodeship censorship office in Kraków read between 60 and 200.[58] The Katowice office fared poorly, with three or sometimes four censors (depending on the current employment levels) reading a total of only 8,000 pages a month.[59]

One of the urgent issues, raised especially in the context of Non-Periodicals' inspection, was low censor competence that could be remedied by "outsourcing experts." Such a solution would bring the domestic inspection system closer to the one used in the USSR, where experts "worked in tandem with publishers in the course of producing a book."[60] Certainly, attempts at such cooperation were made at "Mysia Street" and in the field branches, but to an unsatisfactory degree, as was noted, for example, in March 1952.

---

[58] J. Garlicki, "Kilka uwag na temat organizacji pracy w WUKPPiW" (correspondence in "Dział listów"), *Biuletyn Informacyjno-Instrukcyjny* no. 12, December 1952, p. 44 (APG, WUKPPiW, file ref. no. 70); "Dobra organizacja ważnym ogniwem w podnoszeniu jakości pracy," *Biuletyn Informacyjno-Instrukcyjny* no. 1 (25), January 1954, p. 23 (APG, WUKPPiW, file ref. no. 39).

[59] K. Dworecki (Stalinogród), "O wyższy poziom organizacji pracy," *Biuletyn Informacyjno-Instrukcyjny* no. 1 (25), January 1954, p. 9 (APG, WUKPPiW, file ref. no. 39).

[60] "Przez sprawniejszą organizację – do lepszej pracy" (in the series *O wyższy poziom naszej pracy*), *Biuletyn Informacyjno-Instrukcyjny* no. 3, March 1952, p. 24 (APG, WUKPPiW, file ref. no. 96).

2. COMPETITION FOR A CENSORSHIP REVIEW OF WANDA WASILEWSKA'S NOVEL *RZEKI PŁONĄ*

*The enthusiasm with which the author talks about
the Soviet man, about his cordial and brotherly
attitude to the Poles, makes the book a lasting
contribution to Polish-Soviet friendship.*[61]

One of the most frequent accusations made (not only) in the Bulletins against censors was their lack of expertise and, consequently, their inability to properly assess materials submitted to the Office for the Control. Therefore, as part of the training, the journal's editorial staff discussed a number of erroneous censorship interferences, reviews and decisions. The mistakes were analyzed in order to "emphasize and even exaggerate those bad tendencies, which must be eliminated,"[62] and to present the only correct interpretation of a work.

The situation was different in November 1952, when the Bulletin printed three almost exemplary works awarded in a competition for censors for the best collective book review, that is, written by the employees of a given Office.[63] Maria Lorber, a censor and initiator of the action, hoped that it would be a good test of the ability to combine theory with practice. In a letter sent to the Bulletin's editors, she proposed that Wanda Wasilewska's novel *Rzeki płoną* [Burning rivers]

---

[61] "Trzy recenzje," *Biuletyn Informacyjno-Instrukcyjny* no. 11, November 1952, p. 62 (APG, WUKPPiW, file ref. no. 72). I wrote about the censorship rivalry in the article "Konkurs na recenzję cenzorską powieści Wandy Wasilewskiej pt. *Rzeki płoną*. Materiał archiwalny z poufnego biuletynu dla cenzorów z roku 1952," *Bibliotekarz Podlaski* 2020, vol. 46, no. 1, pp. 215–233; therefore, at this point, I will only present the main theses of the article.

[62] "Seminarium prasy (wyjątki z protokółu). Jedność narodowa," *Biuletyn Instrukcyjny* no. 2, June 1945, p. 5 (APG, WUKPPiW, file ref. no. 210).

[63] "O wynikach konkursu na recenzje powieści W. Wasilewskiej *Rzeki płoną*," *Biuletyn Informacyjno-Instrukcyjny* no. 11, November 1952, pp. 43–47 (APG, WUKPPiW, file ref. no. 72); "Trzy recenzje," *Biuletyn Informacyjno-Instrukcyjny* no. 11, November 1952, pp. 47–66 (APG, WUKPPiW, file ref. no. 72). See also: K. Budrowska, "Od orderu do 'zapisu.' Jak GUKPPiW oceniał pisarzy w latach 1952–1955?," [in:] *Kariera pisarza w PRL-u*, eds. M. Budnik, K. Budrowska, E. Dąbrowicz, K. Kościewicz, Warszawa : IBL PAN, 2014, series *Badania Filologiczne nad Cenzurą PRL* vol. 4, pp. 83–84.

be the subject of the censors' reflection.[64] The competition was announced in the August issue. The Non-Periodical Publications Department of the GUKPPiW as well as the Bulletin's editors encouraged the contestants to take part.[65]

However, the idea did not meet with much enthusiasm on the part of the staff, as only four out of sixteen then existing field centers submitted collective reviews: the offices of Łódź, Poznań, Katowice and Kraków.[66] The September issue printed a reminder about the contest, and the Bulletin from October communicated that individual reviews could also compete, that sets of valuable books awaited the winners, and the entries would be judged by a committee consisting of Niereńska, Kupraszwili, Landsberg, Tajer and Michlewicz.[67]

Collective reviews were received by the Bulletin's editors by September 25, 1952. In November, the three winning works by the teams from Poznań, Kraków and Łódź were published *in extenso*, and it was concluded that the former collective deserved the main prize.[68] The article preceding the winning texts justified the verdict of the committee and summarized the highlights of the reviewed texts.[69]

The Bulletin did not specify why it supported the proposal of the "censor from Ryki"[70] – Lorber came from the city of Ryki – to make Wasilewska's novel

---

[64] "Konkurs na recenzję," *Biuletyn Informacyjno-Instrukcyjny* no. 8, August 1952, pp. 41–42 (APG, WUKPPiW, file ref. no. 81). See also: W. Wasilewska, *Pieśń nad wodami*, part 3: *Rzeki płoną*, Warszawa: Wydawnictwo MON, 1952.

[65] "Konkurs na recenzję," *Biuletyn Informacyjno-Instrukcyjny* no. 8, August 1952, p. 42 (APG, WUKPPiW, file ref. no. 81).

[66] "List z Krakowa" (correspondence in "Dział listów"), *Biuletyn Informacyjno-Instrukcyjny* no. 9, October 1952, p. 48 (APG, WUKPPiW, file ref. no. 78); "Artykuł wstępny," *Biuletyn Informacyjno-Instrukcyjny* no. 1 (13), January 1953, p. 7 (APG, WUKPPiW, file ref. no. 19).

[67] Editorial board, [A reminder about the censorship competition], *Biuletyn Informacyjno-Instrukcyjny* no. 9, September 1952, p. 49 (APG, WUKPPiW, file ref. no. 78); "Komunikat o konkursie," *Biuletyn Informacyjno-Instrukcyjny* no. 10, October 1952, p. 48 (APG, WUKPPiW, file ref. no. 75).

[68] "O wynikach konkursu na recenzje powieści W. Wasilewskiej *Rzeki płoną*," *Biuletyn Informacyjno-Instrukcyjny* no. 11, November 1952, pp. 43–47 (APG, WUKPPiW, file ref. no. 72); "Trzy recenzje," *Biuletyn Informacyjno-Instrukcyjny* no. 11, November 1952, pp. 47–66 (APG, WUKPPiW, file ref. no. 72). See also: Fig. 7a–7b.

[69] "O wynikach konkursu na recenzje powieści W. Wasilewskiej *Rzeki płoną*," *Biuletyn Informacyjno-Instrukcyjny* no. 11, November 1952, pp. 43–47 (APG, WUKPPiW, file ref. no. 72).

[70] A.B. Cieśla, *Mania – cenzorka z Ryk*, http://www.ryki-dawniej.com/yewish-ryki/zide-z-ryk-ve-svete/mania---cenzorka-z-ryk?tmpl=%2Fsystem%2Fapp%2Ftemplates%2Fprint%2F&showPrintDialog=1 (accessed January 31, 2021). See also: S. Redlich, *Na rozdrożu. Żydzi w powojennej Łodzi 1945–1950*, Łódź: Wydawnictwo IPN, 2012, p. 54.

the focus of the competition. What gave Lorber credentials was her role as an active censor who contributed to and was praised in the Bulletins. Furthermore, in the year when the competition was announced, she had become the head of the voivodeship censorship office in Łódź.[71] Perhaps the idea was simply appealing; the subject matter of the book and the fact that its author, Wanda Wasilewska, was a well-known figure and a person of merit to the new order (which was mentioned in the awarded reviews) were certainly significant. Wasilewska, a writer and long-time communist activist, had an established position on the political and literary scene. Despite the fact that after the war she stayed in Kiev, thriving in the state structures of the USSR and in diplomacy, she did not lose her influence at home and maintained contact with Poland.[72]

The choice of the work may also have been influenced by the fact that in 1952, *Rzeki płoną* was awarded the Stalin Prize.[73] Moreover, the entire novel cycle, *Pieśń nad wodami* [Song by the waters], enjoyed the acclaim of both readers and critics, as evidenced by numerous reprints and translations, as well as literary reviews appearing in the press of the day (the book was analyzed by Henryk Bereza, Ryszard Matuszewski, and Jerzy Putrament, among others, who at that time were well-known literary critics).[74] Thus, the censors were given one of the more popular works to evaluate.

Wasilewska's work, like many others of its kind, was a biased account of the fate of Poles staying in the territory of the USSR during World War II (this issue appeared marginally in Zofia Przęczek's *Morgi*, also discussed in the Bulletin[75]). One of the important aims of this type of literature was to convince the reader

---

[71] See, e.g.: "Z krajowej odprawy w GUKP," *Biuletyn Informacyjno-Instrukcyjny* no. 7, July 1952, p. 5, 11 (APG, WUKPPiW, file ref. no. 84); "Nasz Bilans," *Biuletyn Informacyjno-Instrukcyjny* no. 1 (37), January 1955, p. 68 (APG, WUKPPiW, file ref. no. 110).

[72] I list the works devoted to Wasilewska in the aforementioned article devoted to her: see A. Wiśniewska-Grabarczyk, "Konkurs na recenzję cenzorską powieści Wandy Wasilewskiej pt. *Rzeki płoną…*"

[73] J. Kuczawa, "Bumerang stalinowskiej laureatki," *Orzeł Biały* [London] 1952, no. 31/32, pp. 6–7; no. 34, pp. 4–5.

[74] Reviews of the novel and the entire series, as well as subsequent editions of the work, are presented in the aforementioned article on the writer. A fragment of the competition novel entitled *Warszawa 1945* also appeared [in:] W. Wasilewska, *Wieczór literacki*, compiled by A. Naborowska, Warszawa: "Czytelnik," 1954, pp. 96–99.

[75] Przęczek's play deals with repatriation, among other issues; Katarzyna Walocha, the daughter of the protagonist, returns with her children from behind the Bug River, while the fate of her husband remains unknown for a long time; his family fears that he might have fallen victim to the UPA (The Ukrainian Insurgent Army) (see Z. Przęczek, *Morgi. Współczesna sztuka obyczajowa w 3 aktach*, Warszawa: "Książka i Wiedza," 1949).

that the post-Yalta geopolitical order and its aftermath – the Recovered Territories, the western border on the Oder, the eastern border along the Bug River, and the loss of the Borderlands to the USSR (which, of course, was not referred to as such) – was, in fact, a return to the original boundaries. The western border was even presented as reinstating the "ancient Piast lands,"[76] while the slogan "the eastern border as a line of friendship"[77] appeared already in 1945 as one of the key issues tackled by the Kraków branch. The Bulletins show that the censors learned the difficult art of describing the history of "Western Ukraine" or "Western Belarus"; both terms replaced the phrase Borderlands (*Kresy*), which was being eliminated from the dictionary.[78]

In the exemplary censorship reviews of the exemplary novel, the ideological realization of the work received the most attention. The presentation of the events leading up to the new geopolitical situation, which was in accordance with the interpretation of the time, found recognition. The reviewers praised the selection of material that served as the canvas for the story; it was highlighted that the author tried not to omit any of the important events, which was not easy in the context of the turbulent history of that period. Obviously, the selection and presentation of the contents and the tendentiously constructed characters were ideologically driven; the book was meant to dispel the doubts of those who still wavered and reaffirm the political faith of the already convinced.

---

[76] K. Gieba, "Próba epopei. O narracjach założycielskich tzw. Ziem Odzyskanych," *Teksty Drugie* 2015, no. 5, p. 325.

[77] "Ze sprawozdań Kierowników Wojewódzkich Biur," *Biuletyn Instrukcyjny* no. 2, June 1945, p. 16 (APG, WUKPPiW, file ref. no. 210).

On the Eastern Borderlands and the censorship of that topic, see, e.g.: K. Budrowska, "Cenzurowanie tematyki pogranicza w Polsce Ludowej w latach 1945–1956. Przegląd problematyki badań," *Studia Wschodniosłowiańskie* 2015, vol. 15, pp. 533–542.

For an extensive bibliography on the Borderlands, Borderlands literature, and the definitional problems associated with the term, see, e.g.: *Pogranicza, Kresy, Wschód a idee Europy*, series 2: *Wiktor Choriew in memoriam*, concept and introduction by J. Ławski, scholarly edition A. Janicka, G. Kowalski, Ł. Zabielski, Białystok: Książnica Podlaska im. Łukasza Górnickiego, 2013; J. Kolbuszewski, *Kresy*, Wrocław: Wydawnictwo Dolnośląskie, 2006; *Kresy – pojęcie i rzeczywistość. Zbiór studiów*, ed. K. Handke, Warszawa: Slawistyczny Ośrodek Wydawniczy, 1997; B. Hadaczek, *Kresy w literaturze polskiej XX wieku. Szkice*, Szczecin: Wydawnictwo Ottonianum, 1993; A. Gall, "Kresy w polskiej literaturze," [in:] *Interakcje. Leksykon komunikowania polsko-niemieckiego*, http://www.polska-niemcy-interakcje.pl/articles/show/3 (accessed January 31, 2021).

[78] "The so-called Eastern Borderlands" appear in one of the analyzed reviews, see: "Trzy recenzje," *Biuletyn Informacyjno-Instrukcyjny* no. 11, November 1952, pp. 50, 64 (APG, WUKPPiW, file ref. no. 72).

Wasilewska's lyrical and personal description of the events, in which she took an active part, was also rated positively. An extensive section of the winning review was devoted to presenting the profile of the writer and revolutionary, a person of such great merit for the propagation of communist ideals. Her political and literary activity was appreciated and the pioneering role she played in the implementation of socialist realism in Poland was emphasized.

Referring to the writer's biography was one of the censorship strategies, as was leaning on the authorities in the field. The latter maneuver was used in the material preceding the discussion of the awarded reviews. Ryszard Matuszewski – deputy editor-in-chief of *Nowa Kultura*, a respected literary historian and critic at the time – was quoted several times by the Bulletin's editors (for example, his line about "blasting the epic framework of the novel"[79]). While the competition reviews contained no such direct quotations from Matuszewski, the teams were certainly familiar with both this and other articles written about the novel, as indicated by a number of similar formulations and evaluations.[80]

The three winning reviews mostly praised the novel. There were also critical comments, but they did not affect the final positive evaluation of the book. One of the criticisms of the novel concerned the narrative method and minor inconsistencies in the psychological portrayal of the characters, especially in depicting their ideological transformations. According to the Łódź and Kraków teams, the shift from realistic descriptions to inner monologues conflicted with the assumptions of social realism and could have been a prelude to psychologism. At that time, psychologism and unrealistic poetics (along with formalism and "the detachment of literature from life") were blacklisted, and were one of the charges that could lead to the blocking of a book or the need for corrections.[81] In spite of this, the jurors did not agree with the reservations expressed by the two teams; they leaned more towards the evaluation of the comrades from Poznań,

---

[79] R. Matuszewski, "Trylogia Wasilewskiej," *Nowa Kultura* May 18, 1952, no. 20, p. 11; see also: R. Matuszewski, *Literatura na przełomie*, Warszawa: "Czytelnik," 1951. Matuszewski was deputy editor-in-chief of *Nowa Kultura* from April 1950 to December 1955 (see, e.g.: J. Zawadzka [J. Z.], "Matuszewski Ryszard," [in:] *Współcześni polscy pisarze i badacze literatury. Słownik biobibliograficzny* vol. 5: *L–M*, eds. J. Czachowska, A. Szałagan, Warszawa: WSiP, 1997, pp. 327–331).

[80] Cf., e.g. : 1) Wasilewska's novel is "a lasting contribution to Polish-Soviet friendship" (quoted in the November 1952 Bulletin, p. 62) and 2) Wasilewska's novel is "a valuable and lasting contribution to the Polish-Soviet friendship" (R. Matuszewski, "Trylogia Wasilewskiej…," p. 2).

[81] See, e.g.: K. Budrowska, *Writers, Literature and Censorship…*, p. 234. I present "Mysia Street's" attitude towards formalism and literature "detached from life" in the chapter "An Evaluation of the Poetic Publications Printed by the 'Czytelnik' Publishing Cooperative in 1951."

78   Literature and Current Literary Phenomena

who "noticed the consequences of the incomplete narration better."[82] Namely, they pointed out that the descriptions of the best representatives of the working class were too fragmentary and that the role of Polish communists in the plot of the novel was underrepresented.

It was also to the credit of the winning review that its authors appreciated yet another compositional trick of Wasilewska's, that is, the "splendid battle scenes"[83] of great dramatic intensity (they were also praised by Matuszewski, quoted once again by the Bulletin's editors[84]). In their descriptions of military operations and the realities of World War II, the censorship teams used "the dichotomous division of reality, characteristic of newspeak,"[85] with a sharp distinction between "ingroups" and "outgroups." This means of expression dominated the assessment of books on the subject at the time.

The jurors evaluating the competition entries, however, did not agree with the interpretation presented by the Łódź team, who complained that by giving voice to too many characters, Wasilewska did not create a single, coherent, realistic picture of the Battle of Lenino[86]. In response to this accusation, which the committee believed to be unfounded, they quoted a relevant passage from the *Report* of the 19th Congress of the Communist Party of the Soviet Union (KPZR). In the report, Georgy Malenkov – one of Stalin's closest collaborators – spoke about the category of typicality in art, redefining and adapting the concept to fit the creative method of socialist realism.[87] Citing high government officials, not

---

[82] "O wynikach konkursu na recenzje powieści W. Wasilewskiej *Rzeki płoną,*" *Biuletyn Informacyjno-Instrukcyjny* no. 11, November 1952, p. 45 (APG, WUKPPiW, file ref. no. 72).

[83] Ibidem, p. 46.

[84] Ibidem; cf. also R. Matuszewski, "Trylogia Wasilewskiej…", p. 11.

[85] A. Wiśniewska-Grabarczyk, *"Czytelnik" ocenzurowany. Literatura w kryptotekstach – recenzjach cenzorskich okresu stalinizmu (na materiale GUKPPiW z 1950 roku),* Warszawa: Wydawnictwo IPN, 2018, p. 38. See, e.g.: "Trzy recenzje," *Biuletyn Informacyjno-Instrukcyjny* no. 11, November 1952, pp. 48, 53–54, 58, 60–64 (APG, WU-KPPiW, file ref. no. 72). See also: A. Kloc, *Cenzura wobec tematu II wojny światowej i podziemia powojennego w literaturze polskiej 1956–1958,* Warszawa: Wydawnictwo IPN, 2018.

[86] Battle of Lenino – an armed clash that took place on October 12 and 13, 1943 near the town of Lenino in Belarus, in which the Wehrmacht was defeated by the Red Army; in the battle, alongside the Red Army, Polish troops fought, including the 1st Tadeusz Kościuszko Infantry Division; in socialist Poland, the battle became a symbol and was used for propaganda purposes, and October 12 was celebrated as the Polish Army Day.

[87] "O wynikach konkursu na recenzje powieści W. Wasilewskiej *Rzeki płoną,*" *Biuletyn Informacyjno-Instrukcyjny* no. 11, November 1952, p. 46 (APG, WUKPPiW, file ref. no. 72); cf. G.M. Malenkow, *Referat sprawozdawczy na XIX Zjeździe Partii o działalności KC WKP(b),* Warszawa: "Książka i Wiedza," 1952.

necessarily specialists in a given field, obviously had propagandistic value and, in a sense, cut off further discussion. In this case, the reference also had a training bent: the paper had been presented less than a month before the Bulletin was published.[88] By drawing on the latest materials, the censors suggested that they kept up with the ongoing changes (especially considering that the speech was widely discussed in the press and in the same year, was published by "Książka i Wiedza"[89]).

At that time (in November 1952), the category of "typicality" mentioned in Malenkov's paper was a relevant problem. As noted earlier, Ludwik Flaszen's article published in January 1952 sparked up discussion in the press about schematism in literature. According to the critic, it was the misunderstood "typicality" that was the source of schematism, from which there was an increasing effort to depart. This topic appeared several times in the Bulletins, for example, in the material on the censorship of prose selections (which I discuss below).

The winning analyses of Wasilewska's novel took into account all elements that should be present in any censorship evaluation: the ideological realization and issues raised in the work, its educational and artistic value, the author's achievements and stance, as well as the circumstances in which the work was created. The reviews also tried to balance the positive assessment with critical remarks. According to the jury, the Poznań team made the most accurate observations and the fewest mistakes, while its "attractive language and meticulous presentation"[90] made it stand out from its competitors.

On the categories of typicality in literature, see, e.g.: W. Tomasik, "Realizm socjalistyczny. Zasada typowości," [in:] idem, *Słowo o socrealizmie. Szkice*, Bydgoszcz: Wydawnictwo Wyższej Szkoły Pedagogicznej w Bydgoszczy, 1993, pp. 7–8; H. Markiewicz, "O typowości w literaturze. Z historii problemu," *Pamiętnik Literacki* 1957, issue 1, pp. 46–82; A. Wasilewski, "O kilku problemach typowości," *Nowa Kultura* August 23, 1953, no. 34, pp. 1–2.

[88] The 19th Congress of the KPZR, which was established to replace the All-Union Communist Party (Bolsheviks), took place between October 5 and 14, 1952.

[89] See, e.g.: G.M. Malenkow, *Referat sprawozdawczy na XIX Zjeździe Partii…*; J. Putrament, "Idea staje się życiem," *Nowa Kultura* October 5, 1952, no. 40, pp. 1–2; "XIX Zjazd KPZR. O sprawach kultury i sztuki," *Życie Literackie* October 26, 1952, no. 22, pp. 2, 15.

[90] "O wynikach konkursu na recenzje powieści W. Wasilewskiej *Rzeki płoną*," *Biuletyn Informacyjno-Instrukcyjny* no. 11, November 1952, p. 47 (APG, WUKPPiW, file ref. no. 72).

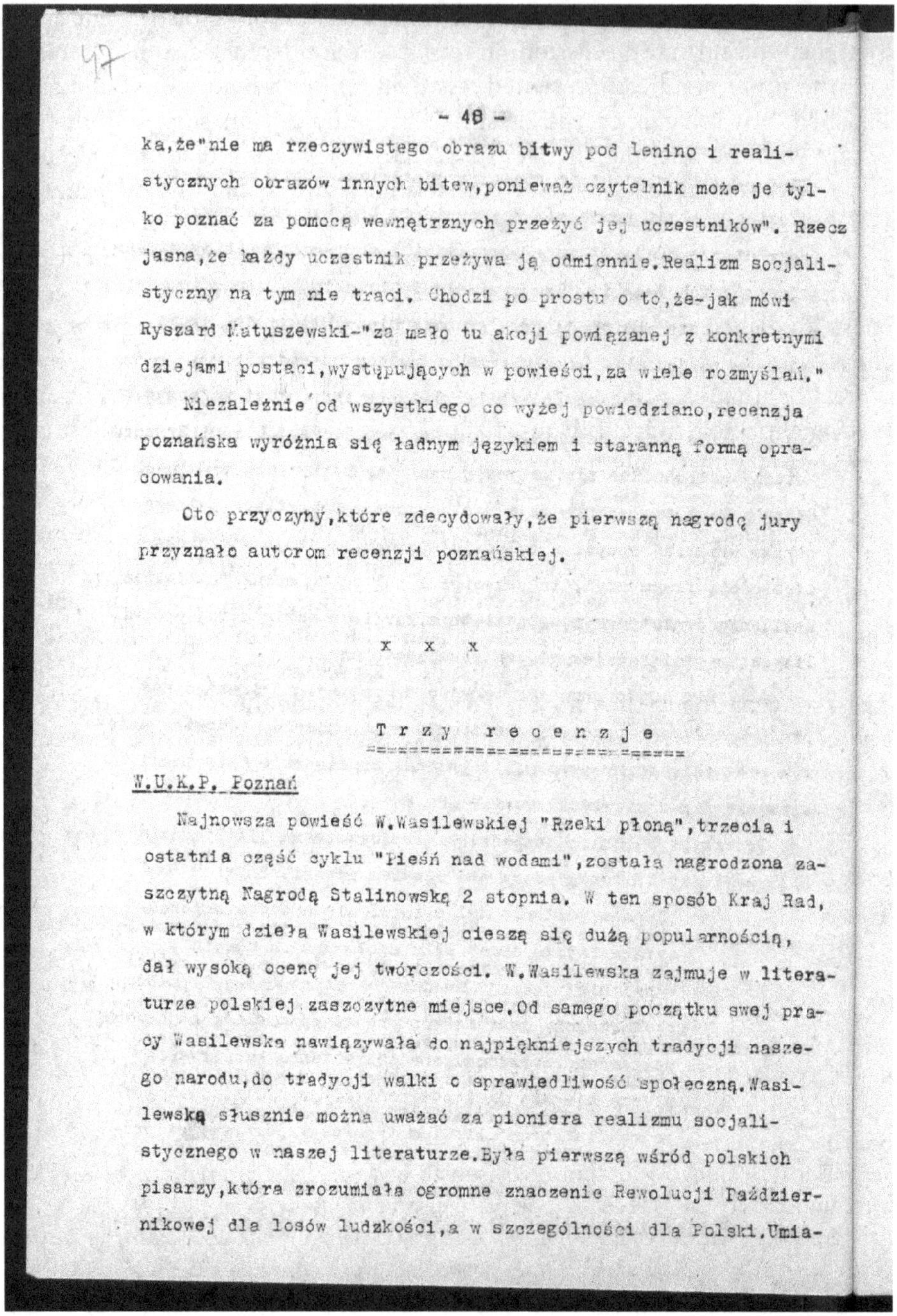

- 48 -

ka,że"nie ma rzeczywistego obrazu bitwy pod lenino i reali-
stycznych obrazów innych bitew,ponieważ czytelnik może je tylko poznać za pomocą wewnętrznych przeżyć jej uczestników". Rzecz
jasna,że każdy uczestnik przeżywa ją odmiennie.Realizm socjalistyczny na tym nie traci. Chodzi po prostu o to,że-jak mówi
Ryszard Matuszewski-"za mało tu akcji powiązanej z konkretnymi
dziejami postaci,występujących w powieści,za wiele rozmyślań."

Niezależnie od wszystkiego co wyżej powiedziano,recenzja
poznańska wyróżnia się ładnym językiem i staranną formą opracowania.

Oto przyczyny,które zdecydowały,że pierwszą nagrodę jury
przyznało autorom recenzji poznańskiej.

x   x   x

Trzy   recenzje
===

W.U.K.P. Poznań

Najnowsza powieść W.Wasilewskiej "Rzeki płoną",trzecia i
ostatnia część cyklu "Pieśń nad wodami",została nagrodzona za-
szczytną Nagrodą Stalinowską 2 stopnia. W ten sposób Kraj Rad,
w którym dzieła Wasilewskiej cieszą się dużą popularnością,
dał wysoką ocenę jej twórczości. W.Wasilewska zajmuje w literaturze polskiej zaszczytne miejsce.Od samego początku swej pracy Wasilewska nawiązywała do najpiękniejszych tradycji naszego narodu,do tradycji walki o sprawiedliwość społeczną.Wasi-
lewską słusznie można uważać za pioniera realizmu socjalistycznego w naszej literaturze.Była pierwszą wśród polskich
pisarzy,która zrozumiała ogromne znaczenie Rewolucji Paździer-
nikowej dla losów ludzkości,a w szczególności dla Polski.Umia-

Fig. 7a. The first page of the winning censorship review of Wanda Wasilewska's *Rzeki płoną* ("Trzy recenzje," *Biuletyn Informacyjno-Instrukcyjny* no. 11, November 1952, p. 47 (APG, WUKPPiW, file ref. no. 72)).

- 49 -

ła od pierwszej chwili dostrzec jedyną drogę wiodącą nasz naród do zwycięstwa w walce o wyzwolenie narodowe i społeczne-
drogę rewolucyjnej walki klasy robotniczej.Płomienny patriotyzm łączył się u Wasilewskiej z głębokim internacjonalizmem,
uczuciem miłości i zaufania do pierwszego w dziejach państwa
robotników i chłopów.W państwie tym widziała Wasilewska rę-
kojmię zwycięstwa nad ustrojem wyzysku i ucisku na całym świecie,a przede wszystkim w swej ojczyźnie. Dlatego właśnie jej
twórczość mogła w latach Polski sanacyjnej zagrzewać ludzi do
walki z faszyzmem,z wszelkim wstecznictwem i niesprawiedliwoś-
cią,mogła ich natchnąć wiarą w zwycięstwo słusznej sprawy od-
grywając tym samym rolę rzeczywiście rewolucyjną.

Dzieła Wasilewskiej doczekały się w Polsce Ludowej wielo-
tysięcznych nakładów i należą do najpopularniejszych,najlepiej
znanych każdemu człowiekowi pracy.Wasilewska pozostaje wielką
pisarką rewolucjonistką do naszych dni.W swej najnowszej powieści"Rzeki płoną" jako pierwsza w naszej literaturze sięga
po kluczowy temat przyjaźni Polsko-Radzieckiej i początków
Polski Ludowej. "Rzeki płoną" to epopea historyczna o dziejach
Polaków w ZSRR w latach 1941-1945,o powstaniu I Armii i działalności Związku Patriotów Polskich.Daleka od schematyzmu i
wszelkich uproszczeń,autorka nie sięga do jednego środowiska
Polaków w ZSRR,ale stara się przedstawić przekrojowo niejako
całe społeczeństwo polskie,od klasy robotniczej i jej działaczy poprzez drobnomieszczaństwo do przedstawicieli klas posia-
dających i wodzirejów sanacyjno-faszystowskich.Utwór jej ce-
chuje przede wszystkim wielka wiara w człowieka,w jego nie-
przebrane siły,w jego miłość i braterstwo ze wszystkimi uczci-
wymi ludźmi na całym świecie.

Wasilewska,pisarz rewolucjonista,zdaje sobie doskonale

Fig. 7b. The second page of the winning censorship review of Wanda Wasilewska's *Rzeki płoną* ("Trzy recenzje," *Biuletyn Informacyjno-Instrukcyjny* no. 11, November 1952, p. 48 (APG, WUKPPiW, file ref. no. 72)).

3. POETRY

*Wydawnictwo Literackie has only existed for a year
and has displayed a tendency towards objectivist
coverage, avoiding taking a stand.*[91]

Issues concerning poetry appeared sporadically in the Bulletins. Usually, they were general remarks on the censorship of poetry; in a few cases, references were made to specific authors and works. Some attention was also paid to poetry in the report on the catalog of the "Czytelnik" Publishing House, while special "care" was given to the works of Mikołaj Rostworowski and Kazimiera Iłłakowiczówna, as well as the poems of Bogdan Brzeziński, a "satirist in the field"[92] (all three artists were discussed in separate articles). Additionally, one of the *Biblioteczki Biuletynu* devoted considerable material to Konstanty Ildefons Gałczyński, analyzing consecutive stages of the artist's work from his debut to 1951.[93]

3.1. How to Review Poetry Selections? Ginczanka, Hollender Słonimski, Ważyk, and an Unknown Red Army Man

It is the censor's job to indicate whether a book requires a framing introduction, a possible addition, or, on the contrary, the omission of certain works.[94]

---

[91] J. Kupraszwili, "Odpowiedź na list Kolegi prasowca," *Biuletyn Informacyjno-Instrukcyjny* no. 9 (33), September 1954, p. 40 (APG, WUKPPiW, file ref. no. 56).

[92] B. Brzeziński, *Satyryk w terenie*, Warszawa: Wydawnictwo Literackie, 1954.
Bogdan Brzeziński (1911–1980) – a Polish satirist, columnist, contributor to the Polish Radio, for which he wrote skits, radio plays for children, satirical and cabaret programs.

[93] J. Trębicki (Department of Cultural Publications), "Konfrontacja Gałczyńskiego," *Biblioteczka Biuletynu Informacyjno-Instrukcyjnego GUKPPiW* no. 24, 1955, p. 40 (APG, WUKPPiW, file ref. no. 193).
Konstanty Ildefons Gałczyński (1905–1953) – a Polish poet, prose writer, playwright and translator; author of satirical and grotesque works, as well as song lyrics; he wrote the collection of poems *Zaczarowana dorożka* [Enchanted carriage], among other works.

[94] "O recenzjach zbiorków literackich," *Biuletyn Informacyjno-Instrukcyjny* no. 4 (16), April 1953, p. 27 (APG, WUKPPiW, file ref. no. 16).

In the August 1952 issue of the monthly, a few general remarks on the subject of evaluating poetry were made. It was deplored that "good, analytical reviews of books of poetry"[95] were rare, that censors were unable to formulate decent assessment of a work because they did not understand the specificity of the literary material. It was further reminded that:

> in books of poetry containing selections from longer periods of the work of a given poet, the important thing is the creative and ideological evolution of the author, which such a collection should exhibit. In the case of books of recent poems, written by an author of late, it is important to remember about his previous output and evaluate the book after comparing it with his earlier works.[96]

The above quotation perfectly captures the essence of the censor's "reflections" not only on poetry; the same remarks applied to prose, selections of short stories, and collected works. Functionaries were repeatedly reminded that, when assessing a work, one must take into account whether it was a debut or yet another publication. In both cases, the artist's creative and ideological stance was important, but in the context of a writer who had been on the publishing market for some time, his or her previous worldview was also a factor.

This issue in relation to poetry was raised eight months later, when another important element of assessing a text was pointed out:

> As far as the poetry selections are concerned, they mostly characterize the ideological and artistic development of the author; it must be remembered that in their youth, some of our greatest poets went through a period when they formally and ideologically succumbed to the influence of a decadent, bourgeois culture. A selection of these authors' poetry from a longer period reflects a process of ideological change; a process of sometimes grappling with oneself, with the influence of the environment and culture in which one grew up. Such a book ought to shed a light on their path to our party, expose their hesitations. The reader, taking such a book into their hands, should understand what led the author to our ranks, or how they were pulled in another direction.[97]

The last sentence quoted shows how important it was to correctly prepare a text for print. This was to be achieved by means of tailored paratexts, i.e., prefaces,

---

[95] "Recenzja z pozycji literackiej, cz. I" (in the series *O wyższy poziom pracy nad książką*), *Biuletyn Informacyjno-Instrukcyjny* no. 8, August 1952, p. 21 (APG, WUKPPiW, file ref. no. 81).

[96] Ibidem, p. 22.

[97] "O recenzjach zbiorków literackich," *Biuletyn Informacyjno-Instrukcyjny* no. 4 (16), April 1953, p. 27 (APG, WUKPPiW, file ref. no. 16).

afterwords, introductions, notes from the publisher, footnotes, etc.[98] (the fact that one of the Bulletins published a separate article on drafting the introduction, footnotes and afterword speaks to the importance of this strategy[99]). In the case of collected works, censors were quick to avail themselves of the opportunity to omit certain inconvenient texts to ensure such "collections, selections, and montages"[100] would conform to the core idea. As previously mentioned, paratexts also played an extremely important role in the publication of "classics." For instance, in a Bulletin from 1949, several inferences in the National Edition of Adam Mickiewicz's Works were criticized. The censors pointed out that such unnecessary interventions only "ridiculed the Office." They also admonished their colleagues for overlooking comments that, in their opinion, were fundamentally false: "neither in the introduction nor in the various glosses was it emphasized that the poet was also a fierce fighter for progress and democracy."[101]

All of the above-mentioned publishing and censorship strategies played a special role in periods of increased terror and control of creativity, as evidenced by the many books mutilated by censorial "inventiveness" during (not only) the Stalinist period.[102] If it was decided that a work required additional preparation, it was usually handled by the publishing house. This solution was adopted, among others, in the case of dead writers, and those whose developmental line was

---

[98] G. Genette, *Palimpsesty. Literatura drugiego stopnia*, trans. T. Stróżyński, A. Milecki, Gdańsk: Wydawnictwo słowo/obraz terytoria, 2014; idem, "Palimpsesty. Literatura drugiego stopnia," trans. A. Milecki, [in:] *Współczesna teoria badań literackich za granicą. Antologia* vol. 4, part 2: *Literatura jako produkcja i ideologia. Poststrukturalizm. Badanie intertekstualne. Problemy syntezy historycznoliterackiej*, compiled by H. Markiewicz, Kraków: Wydawnictwo Literackie, 1992, pp. 319–321.

[99] "Kilka uwag o pracy nad wstępem, przypisami i posłowiem," *Biuletyn Informacyjno--Instrukcyjny* no. 9 (21), September 1953, pp. 542–549 (AAN, GUKPPiW, file ref. no. 22).

[100] "O recenzjach zbiorków literackich," *Biuletyn Informacyjno-Instrukcyjny* no. 4 (16), April 1953, p. 27 (APG, WUKPPiW, file ref. no. 16).

[101] "Konfiskata 'słówek' przy niewidzeniu całości," *Biuletyn Informacyjno-Instrukcyjny* no. 1/3, January 1949, p. 38 (APG, WUKPPiW, file ref. no. 196). See also: L. Płoszewski, "O Wydaniu Narodowym *Dzieł* Mickiewicza," *Pamiętnik Literacki* 1956, issue 2, pp. 317–340. Cf. "Uwagi ogólne o recenzji" (in the series *O wyższy poziom pracy nad książką*), *Biuletyn Informacyjno-Instrukcyjny* no. 7, July 1952, p. 27 (APG, WUKPPiW, file ref. no. 84).

[102] See, e.g.: M. Budnik, "Skróty w utworach"; "Wstępy i posłowia"; "Przypisy"; "Opracowanie typograficzne," [in:] eadem, *"Książka Nowego Czytelnika." Literatura dla byłych analfabetów przeszkolonych w Polsce w latach 1948–1951*, Białystok: Wydawnictwo UwB, 2014, pp. 175–202; J. Dygul, "Parateksty polskich przekładów z literatury włoskiej w czasach stalinowskich," *Italica Wratislaviensia* 2010, no. 1, pp. 80–92.

deemed incomplete.[103] Zuzanna Ginczanka and Tadeusz Hollender were mentioned as examples. Their names appear (probably inadvertently) in the fragment devoted to prose (Hollender also wrote children's stories, satires and reportages; nonetheless, poetry was his basic means of expression).[104] Unfortunately, only the last names of the poets were listed, and no titles. The analysis below fills in these gaps.

In 1953, "Czytelnik" published Ginczanka's *Wybór wierszy*[105] [Selected poems], the poet's first post-war edition and the second book in her bibliography. *O centaurach* [On centaurs] from 1936 was her only book published in her lifetime.[106] The introduction to the 1953 edition was written by Jan Śpiewak, Ginczanka's colleague from Rivne in Volhynia, a poet, translator and author of many reviews and critical texts. Several of the works that Śpiewak evaluated in literary magazines became the subject of quite different "critical and literary" censorship reflection in the Bulletins.[107]

---

[103] "O recenzjach zbiorków literackich," *Biuletyn Informacyjno-Instrukcyjny* no. 4 (16), April 1953, p. 28 (APG, WUKPPiW, file ref. no. 16).

[104] See the chapter "How to Review Select Prose? Nałkowska, Borowski, and Bartelski."

On Zuzanna Ginczanka, see, e.g.: J. Mikołajewski, *Cień w cień. Za cieniem Zuzanny Ginczanki*, Warszawa: Wydawnictwo Dowody na Istnienie, 2019; *Ginczanka. Na stulecie poetki*, eds. K. Kuczyńska-Kochany, K. Szymańska, Kraków: Wydawnictwo Pasaże, 2018; A. Araszkiewicz, *Wypowiadam wam moje życie. Melancholia Zuzanny Ginczanki*, Warszawa: Fundacja Ośka, 2001; I. Kiec, *Ginczanka. Życie i twórczość*, Poznań: Wydawnictwo Obserwator, 1991; Z. Ginczanka, *Udźwignąć własne szczęście. Poezje*, introduction and compilation by I. Kiec, Poznań: "Brama" – Książnica Włóczęgów i Uczonych, 1991.

On Tadeusz Hollender see, e.g.: J. Chwastyk-Kowalczyk, "Tadeusz Hollender – enfant terrible de Léopo," *Respectus Philologicus* 2007, no. 12, pp. 64–76; *Tadeusz Hollender – poeta rozstrzelany*, compiled by T. Żółciński, Polskie Radio May 30, 1973, https://www.polskieradio.pl/39/156/Artykul/1452163,Tadeusz-Hollender-satyra-w-czasach-Apokalipsy (accessed January 31, 2021); *Szkic do portretu Tadeusza Hollendra*, Polskie Radio August 19, 1978, https://www.polskieradio.pl/39/156/Artykul/1452163,Tadeusz-Hollender-satyra-w-czasach-Apokalipsy (accessed January 31, 2021).

[105] Z. Ginczanka, *Wiersze wybrane*, selection and introduction by J. Śpiewak, Warszawa: "Czytelnik," 1953.

[106] Eadem, *O centaurach*, Warszawa: Wydawnictwo J. Przeworskiego, 1936.

[107] J. Śpiewak on Ginczanka, see, e.g.: "Zuzanna, gawęda tragiczna," [in:] idem, *Przyjaźnie i animozje*, Warszawa: PIW, 1965, pp. 167–217; J. Łobodowski, *Pamięci Sulamity*, Toronto: Polish-Canadian Publishing Fund, 1987. Other books that Jan Śpiewak reviewed include Mandalian and Gaworski's, also discussed in the Bulletins (see the chapter "An Evaluation of the Poetic Publications Printed by the 'Czytelnik' Publishing Cooperative in 1951").

In 1949, *Wiersze. Satyry. Fraszki* [Poems. Satires. Epigrams] by Tadeusz Hollender was published.[108] The volume was compiled by two poets and an outstanding editor; the material was selected and prefaced by Aleksander Maliszewski, a critic, playwright, columnist, and member of the pre-war literary group *Kwadryga*; recollections about the author were written by Jerzy Zagórski, whose poems were also reviewed in the Bulletins; the bibliography and footnotes were compiled by Juliusz Wiktor Gomulicki, an expert on Warsaw and the author of a number of books on literature.

It is difficult to say in which direction the literary career of Ginczanka and Hollender would have developed. The Bulletin categorized them as artists who never got to spread their wings (despite the fact that they both had several publications to their credit[109]). Was it right to assume, though, that they would have shared the ideas of the architects of post-war art? Ginczanka came from the circle of *Skamander* and *Wiadomości Literackie*.[110] In her "Lviv period,"[111] she was a member of the Union of Soviet Writers of Ukraine. How would she have found herself in the new reality? Would a Jewish boy arrested by the Gestapo for underground activity, a satirist, mocker, and poet, have embraced socialism? We do not know: Hollender was shot in 1943; Ginczanka the following year.[112]

---

[108] T. Hollender, *Wiersze. Satyry. Fraszki*, selection and introduction by A. Maliszewski, recollections about the author by J. Zagórski, critical supplement by J.W. Gomulicki, Warszawa: "Książka i Wiedza," 1949.

[109] Ginczanka had one book of poetry, but her work also appeared in the press; Hollender's list of publications, on the other hand, included several books; see B. Tyszkiewicz [B. T.], "Ginczanka Zuzanna," [in:] *Współcześni polscy pisarze i badacze literatury. Słownik biobibliograficzny* vol. 3: *G–J*, eds. J. Czachowska, A. Szałagan, Warszawa: WSiP, 1994, pp. 46–47; J. Czachowska [J. Cz.], "Hollender Tadeusz," [in:] *Współcześni polscy pisarze i badacze literatury. Słownik biobibliograficzny* vol. 3: *G–J...*, pp. 264–265.

[110] *Skamander* and *Wiadomości Literackie* were two very popular and opinion-forming cultural and literary magazines of the interwar period in Poland.

[111] On the "Lviv period" of writers coming to Poland from the USSR, see, e.g.: M. Zawodniak, *Zaraz po wojnie, a nawet przed...*, p. 144. See also: M. Inglot, *Polska kultura literacka Lwowa lat 1939–1941*, Wrocław: Towarzystwo Przyjaciół Polonistyki Wrocławskiej, 1995.

[112] In her poem from 1942, Ginczanka mentions "a zealous informant" – the superintendent of a Lviv tenement house who denounced her to the Gestapo (she managed to escape that time, but unfortunately, another denunciation – in Kraków – proved tragic for the poet), see Z. Ginczanka, "[Non omnis moriar...]," [in:] eadem, *Wiersze wybrane...*, p. 77.
On the circumstances surrounding Ginaczanka's death, see: R. Kotarba, "Śmierć poetki. Historia okupacyjna," *Ale Historia. Tygodnik Historyczny* December 14, 2015, no. 50, pp. 12–13 (in the article, the historian writes that Ginczanka may not have been executed in the fall in Montelupich Prison in Kraków, as it was previously assumed, but

When publishing the works of living authors, sometimes the explanatory para-text was replaced by a metatext, i.e., "a word from the author." It could take various forms but played the same role as the paratext.[113] This was the case, for example, with the collection of poems by Antoni Słonimski, who was asked to provide an "introduction explaining" his development. What did the poet do? "He wrote a poem that served as a poetic introduction perfectly illustrating the book's main theme."[114]

The Bulletin states neither the title of the poem nor the book from which it came. However, the quoted fragment suggests that it was the poem "Do Czytelnika" [To the Reader] from the collection *Poezje*, published in 1951.[115] The material on Słonimski appeared in April 1953, so the editors of the monthly referred to the situation from two years earlier. The poet's self-criticism recurred in another selection from 1954, and even 1955, that is, in slightly different circumstances, when the impending Thaw was palpable:[116]

[fragment of Antoni Słonimski's poem "Do Czytelnika," quoted in the Bulletin]

Pójdź za tą pieśnią, która błądziła
Przez mgły polskiego ćwierćwiecza.
Łamiąc się z sobą, nim zwyciężyła
Sprawa człowiecza.

Bo pieśń, choć nieba sięgnie wyniosła
Gdy samej sobie zaczyna kłamać,
Trzeba, jak rękę, co się źle zrosła,
Na nowo łamać.[117]

---

in the spring of 1944 in the concentration camp in Płaszów; the same place of execution, along with the fall date, is also given in the 1994 dictionary *Współcześni polscy pisarze i badacze literatury. Słownik biobibliograficzny* vol. 3: *G–J…*, p. 46).

[113] The authorship criterion marks the difference between a paratext, i.e., a third-party text, and a metatext, i.e., a text by the author on their own work (to this day, the distinction between paratextuality and metatextuality is being debated, see, e.g.: I. Loewe, *Gatunki paratekstowe w komunikacji medialnej*, Kraków: Wydawnictwo UŚ, 2007, pp. 66–78).

[114] "O recenzjach zbiorków literackich," *Biuletyn Informacyjno-Instrukcyjny* no. 4 (16), April 1953, p. 27 (APG, WUKPPiW, file ref. no. 16).

[115] A. Słonimski, "Do Czytelnika," [in:] idem, *Poezje*, Warszawa: "Czytelnik," 1951, p. 5.

[116] Idem, "Do Czytelnika," [in:] idem, *Poezje*, Second Edition, Warszawa: "Czytelnik," 1954, p. 5; Third Edition, ibidem 1955, p. 5. The poem "Do Czytelnika" was also featured in *Poezje zebrane* in 1964 (A. Słonimski, *Poezje zebrane*, Warszawa: PIW, 1964, p. 499), but it was not included in the slim collection *Poezje zebrane* from 1972 (A. Słonimski, *Poezje wybrane*, Warszawa: Ludowa Spółdzielnia Wydawnicza, 1972).

[117] "O recenzjach zbiorków literackich," *Biuletyn Informacyjno-Instrukcyjny* no. 4 (16), April 1953, p. 27 (APG, WUKPPiW, file ref. no. 16).

[Follow the song that erred
Through the mists of a quarter-century of Poland.
The human cause,
At war with itself, before it won.

For the song, though it may be sublime
When it begins to lie to itself,
Ought to be broken again
Much like a badly healed arm.]

The Bulletin quotes the above two stanzas, but the entire work consists of five stanzas; the last three are as follows:

Jeślim, co marzył, syn marnotrawny,
Goryczy pełen samotnik,
Dziś tym marzeniom kształt daje jawny
Chłop i robotnik.

Chociaż mnie nieraz złudnym urokiem
Nęciły świata cienie i blaski,
Pozwól dziś krok mój zrównać z twym krokiem,
Ludu warszawski.

Kto nie żył dumą, wiarą i troską
Dni naszych, tych dni ogromnych,
Ten nie odżyje, nawet i zgłoską
W sercu potomnych.[118]

[Whatever I dreamed, the prodigal son,
A lonely embittered man,
Today those dreams are made concrete
By a peasant and a laborer.

Though I have been seduced
By the world's shadows and glamours
Today, let me fall into step with you,
People of Warsaw.

Who did not live with pride, faith and verity
Of our days, those tremendous days,
He will not return as much as an echo
In the hearts of posterity.]

---

[118] A. Słonimski, "Do Czytelnika," [in:] idem, *Poezje*, Warszawa: "Czytelnik," 1951, p. 5.

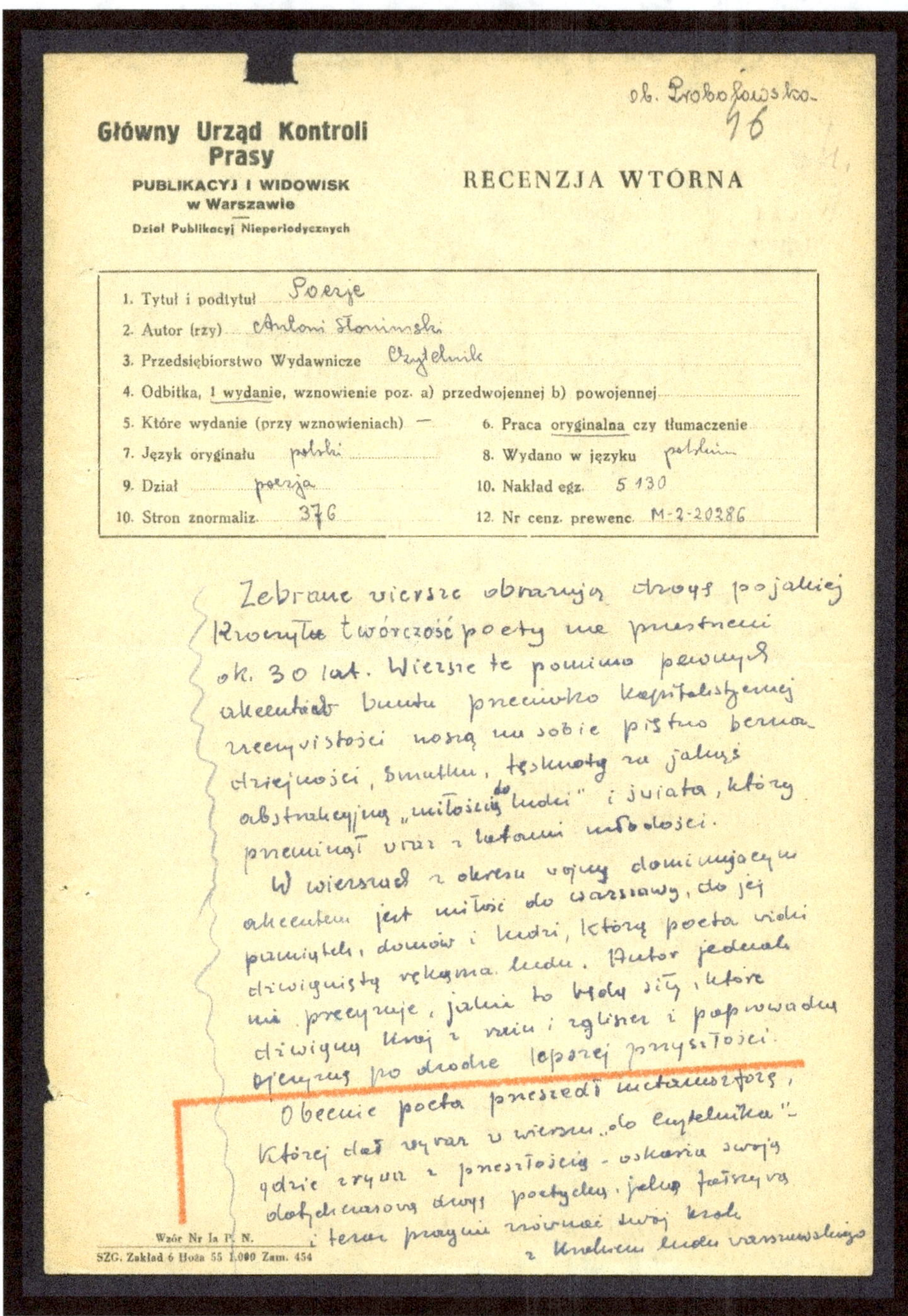

Główny Urząd Kontroli Prasy

PUBLIKACYJ I WIDOWISK
w Warszawie

Dział Publikacyj Nieperiodycznych

RECENZJA WTÓRNA

1. Tytuł i podtytuł   *Poezje*
2. Autor (rzy)   *Antoni Słonimski*
3. Przedsiębiorstwo Wydawnicze   *Czytelnik*
4. Odbitka, 1 wydanie, wznowienie poz. a) przedwojennej b) powojennej
5. Które wydanie (przy wznowieniach) —   6. Praca oryginalna czy tłumaczenie
7. Język oryginału   *polski*   8. Wydano w języku   *polskim*
9. Dział   *poezja*   10. Nakład egz.   *5 130*
10. Stron znormaliz.   *376*   12. Nr cenz. prewenc.   *M-2-20286*

Fig. 8a. The first page of the secondary censorship review of *Poezje* by Antoni Słonimski from January 11, 1952 (AAN, GUKPPiW, file ref. no. 2919, fol. 46r). The translated passage is framed in red.

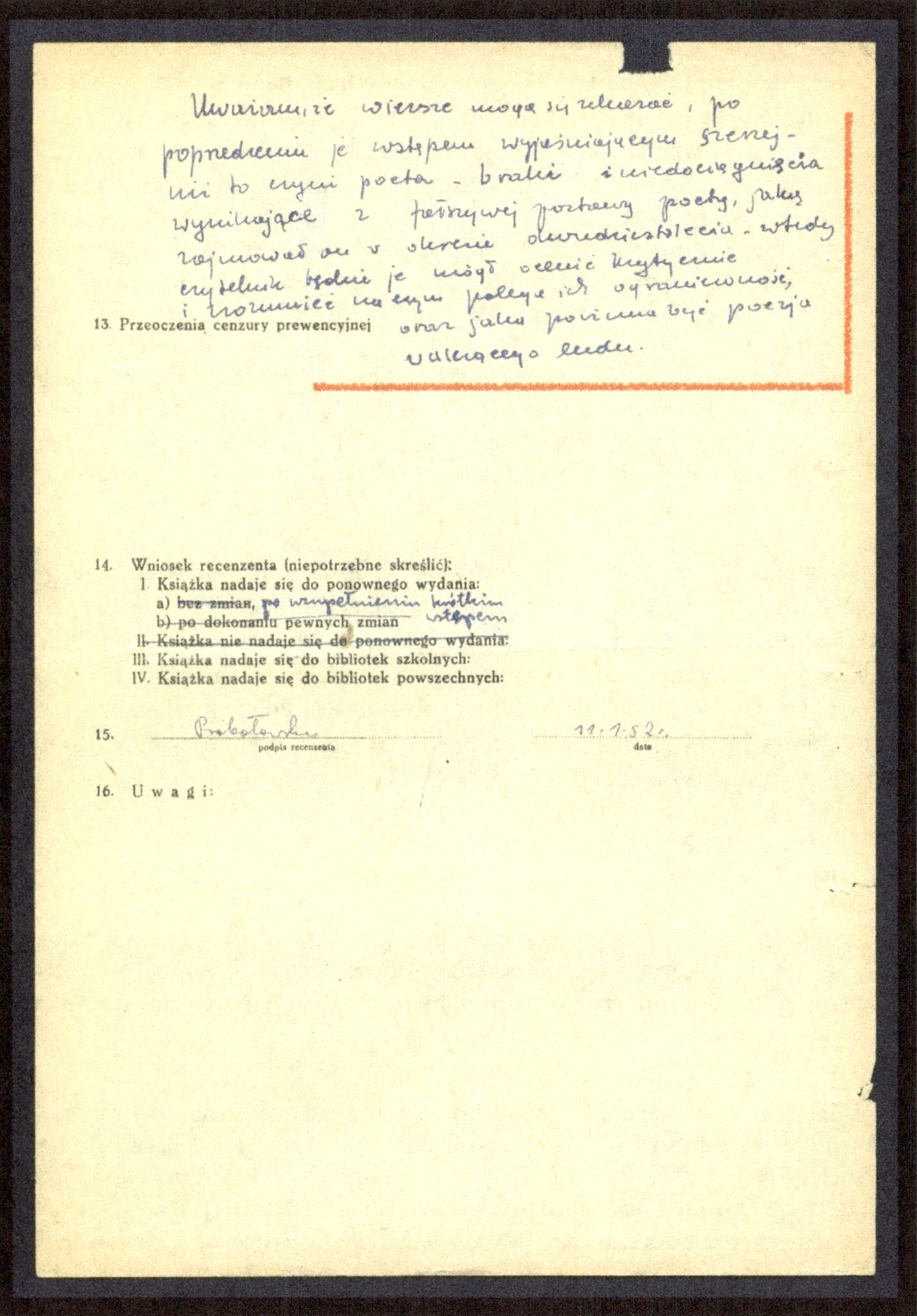

Fig. 8b. The second page of the secondary censorship review of *Poezje* by Antoni Słonimski from January 11, 1952 (AAN, GUKPPiW, file ref. no. 2919, fol. 46v). The translated passage is framed in red.

Interestingly, Słonimski's case had been discussed in the press and presented as "an example of exceptionally beautiful self-criticism" already in 1951.[119] Despite this, the "Ministry of Truth" required an additional "explanatory introduction" to the subsequent editions of *Poezje*. Such a suggestion can be found in the secondary review written on January 11, 1952 by comrade Probołowska.[120] In a document stored in the GUKPPiW fonds at the AAN, the censor writes:

> The poet has undergone a metamorphosis, which he expressed in the poem "Do czytelnika" – where he cuts himself off from the past – accusing his previous poetic path as false and now wants to level his step with the step of the people of Warsaw.
> I believe that the poems can be published if preceded by an introduction explaining – more broadly than the poet does – the shortcomings and deficiencies resulting from the false stance the poet had taken in the interwar period. Then the reader will be able to evaluate them critically and understand what their limitations are and what the poetry of a people that fights should be like.[121]

After 1956, Słonimski took a decidedly different position, became engaged in many anti-government initiatives, and criticized the state authorities. Below are two important, yet very different documents directly related to the writer. The first is his two-sentence *List 34* [Letter 34] submitted on March 14, 1964 to the Office of the Council of Ministers. It was a protest of Polish intellectuals against censorship (which was also signed by other "Bulletin" writers:[122] Andrzejewski, Jastrun, Ważyk, and Zagórski):

> To the Prime Minister
> Józef Cyrankiewicz
>
> Restrictions on paper allocation for printing books and magazines, and imposing stricter press censorship are becoming a threat to the development of national culture. We, the undersigned, driven by civic concern, recognizing the existence

---

[119] See, e.g.: P. Hoffman, "O niektórych problemach realizmu socjalistycznego," *Nowa Kultura* November 18, 1951, no. 46, p. 2; idem, "O niektórych problemach realizmu socjalistycznego," *Materiały do Studiów i Dyskusji z Zakresu Teorii i Historii Sztuki, Krytyki Artystycznej oraz Badań nad Sztuką* November 1952, no. 1, p. 89.

[120] "Ingerencje cenzorskie GUKPPiW, WUKPPiW w Bydgoszczy, Krakowie, Wrocławiu w okresie VII 1951, I 1952–II 1953 w publikacjach nieperiodycznych. Recenzje prewencyjne i wtórne" (AAN, GUKPPiW, file ref. no. 2919, fol. 46r–46v; A. Słonimski, *Poezje*; censorship review from January 11, 1952).

[121] Ibidem. See also: D. Jarosz, "Zapisy cenzury z lat 1948–1955," *Regiony* 1996, no. 3, p. 34.

[122] I use this term to refer to authors whose work was discussed in the Bulletins.

of public opinion, the right to criticism, free discussion and reliable information as a necessary element of progress, demand a change in Polish cultural policy in the spirit of the rights guaranteed by the Constitution of the Polish state and in agreement with the good of the nation.[123]

In 1976, Słonimski was one of the thirty-seven authors whose names appeared in the secret instructions of the censorship office (the list also included such "Bulletin" authors as Andrzejewski, Bocheński, Mandalian, Matuszewski, and Szczepański), which read:

> All original publications of the following authors, reported by the press and book publishers, and any mentions of their names should be signaled to the management of the Office, which will decide whether such materials will be allowed for print. This provision does not apply to radio and television, the management of which shall ensure compliance with these rules. The contents of this provision is intended exclusively for the information of the censors.[124]

The poet's earlier choices and attitudes – his forced emigration, return to Poland, and the scars of Stalinism – left their mark not only on the poet's work, as evidenced by the above quoted self-criticism, but also on the extremely polarized evaluation of the poet himself, as Joanna Kuciel-Frydryszak, the poet's biographer, writes:

> Tadeusz Konwicki, to whom Antoni Słonimski bequeathed a Sony television set, was not surprised when the coffin containing his friend's body did not fit into the grave and the pit had to be widened.

---

[123] The reaction of the PRL authorities to *List 34* was the so-called Counter-Letter, signed by around six hundred writers (many of whom later claimed that they had signed a different version of the published text). *List 34* crossed the borders of the country, provoking reactions in the international press, see, e.g.: "Lost liberty," *The Observer*; "Polish intellectuals protest against censorship," *The New York Times*; cf. "Protest pisarzy przeciw antypolskiej kampanii. Polityka kulturalna jest wspólną sprawą inteligencji twórczej i kierownictwa politycznego," *Dziennik Polski* May 12, 1964, no. 111, p. 2. See also, e.g.: J. Kuciel-Frydryszak, "Antoni Słonimski i *List 34*," Biuletyn IPN "Pamięć.pl," 2012, no. 1, pp. 38–41; J. Eisler, *List 34*, Warszawa: PWN, 1993; *List 34* (in the series *Dźwiękowy Przewodnik Po Historii Najnowszej – Polska*), compiled by K. Kobylecka, Polskie Radio February 4, 1997, https://www.polskieradio.pl/39/156/Artykul/565503,Trzydziestu-czterech-w-obronie-kultury-polskiej (accessed January 31, 2021); *List 34 – reakcja zachodnich mediów na list wystosowany do premiera Cyrankiewicza*, RWE 1964, https://www.polskieradio.pl/39/156/Artykul/565503,Trzydziestu-czterech-w-obronie-kultury-polskiej (accessed January 31, 2021).

[124] T. Strzyżewski, *Wielka Księga Cenzury PRL w dokumentach*, Warszawa: Wydawnictwo Prohibita, 2015, p. 95.

"He was bigger than the norm. But it wasn't news to me," he wrote.
Not only did Słonimski not fit in the grave, but he always eluded any attempts to classify and label him, and there were many such attempts.[125]

In the piece written "on demand," Słonimski's way of settling accounts with the past was quite radical. He was clearly distancing himself from his previous actions and poems, which – as the censorship officials described them – were "ideologically and formally foreign."[126] However, this type of testimony was not a universal requirement. If it was deemed that a selection of poems presented an ideological breakthrough in a "dramatic and transparent"[127] manner, no editorial or authorial commentary was necessary. Adam Ważyk's *Nowy wybór wierszy*[128] [A new selection of poems], published by "Czytelnik" in 1950, was one example. As in the case of Słonimski, the censors were making a reference to a book that had been published several years earlier (this was a frequent practice in the magazine[129]). The Bulletin juxtaposed fragments of two works included in the aforementioned collection: "Dobranoc" [Goodnight], the closing poem in the volume *Oczy i usta* [Eyes and lips], published in 1927; and the poem "Odpowiedź" [Answer] "written after the tragic September,"[130] which opened the volume *Serce granatu* [The heart of the grenade]. According to the authors of the article, a comparison of these two works clearly showed the ideological breakthrough and the great shock that the poet experienced as a result of the September defeat:

---

[125] J. Kuciel-Frydryszak, *Słonimski. Heretyk na ambonie*, Warszawa: W.A.B., 2012, p. 9. See also: M. Shore, "Powrót Antoniego Słonimskiego"; "Skamander traci poetę," [in:] eadem, *Kawior i popiół. Życie i śmierć pokolenia oczarowanych i rozczarowanych marksizmem*, trans. M. Szuster, Warszawa: Świat Książki, 2008, pp. 323–326, 353–356 et seq. (cf. M. Shore, *The Taste of Ashes: The Afterlife of Totalitarianism in Eastern Europe*, London: Windmill Books, 2014); J. Kumaniecka, *Saga rodu Słonimskich*, Warszawa: Iskry, 2003.

[126] "O recenzjach zbiorków literackich," *Biuletyn Informacyjno-Instrukcyjny* no. 4 (16), April 1953, p. 28 (APG, WUKPPiW, file ref. no. 16).

[127] Ibidem.

[128] A. Ważyk, *Nowy wybór wierszy*, Warszawa: "Czytelnik," 1950.

[129] The Bulletins referred to various materials prepared or published much earlier, including books and literary or censorship reviews (see, for example, the April 1953 Bulletin (p. 26), which referred to a censorship review of Zofia Nałkowska's *Medallions* written on September 19, 1951; I discuss it in the chapter "How to Review Select Prose? Nałkowska, Borowski, and Bartelski."

[130] "O recenzjach zbiorków literackich," *Biuletyn Informacyjno-Instrukcyjny* no. 4 (16), April 1953, p. 28 (APG, WUKPPiW, file ref. no. 16).

[the last stanza of the poem "Dobranoc," quoted in the Bulletin]

To gorzkie gwiazdy gasną nad głową
To gaśnie moja lampa słodka
to sygnałem nagłym przemija słowo
którego już nigdy nie spotka[m].[131]

[The bitter stars are growing dim
Burning out is my sweet lamp
The word fades with a sudden sound
Never shall I have it back.]

[the first two stanzas of the poem "Odpowiedź" quoted in the Bulletin]

Głosem poległych wołają
Krwawiące mury Warszawy:
Jaki wasz będzie rachunek?
Nasza odpowiedź:
          Krwawy.

Czym odpłacicie za najazd,
za obłąkaną kobietę,
za kulę w piersi dziecięcej?
Nasza odpowiedź:
          Bagnetem![132]

[The bleeding walls of Warsaw
Call out with the voice of the fallen:
What will be your score?
Our answer:
          Bloody.

What's your payback for the invasion,
for a crazed woman,
for a bullet in a child's chest?
Our answer:
          A bayonet!]

---

[131] Ibidem. Cf. Also A. Ważyk, "Dobranoc," [in:] idem, *Oczy i usta*, Warszawa: Zwrotnica, 1926, p. 49; A. Ważyk, "Dobranoc," [in:] idem, *Nowy wybór wierszy…*, p. 59.
[132] "O recenzjach zbiorków literackich," *Biuletyn Informacyjno-Instrukcyjny* no. 4 (16), April 1953, p. 28 (APG, WUKPPiW, file ref. no. 16). See also: A. Ważyk, "Odpowiedź," [in:] idem, *Serce granatu*, Moscow: Związek Patriotów Polskich w ZSRR, 1943; Second Edition expanded with poems written in 1944: Lublin: Związek Zawodowy Literatów Polskich, 1944, p. 5; A. Ważyk, "Odpowiedź," [in:] idem, *Nowy wybór wierszy…*, p. 60.

The selection of these two works was certainly not accidental. They come from two completely different periods in the poet's work. They vary in their subject matter and literary imagery (although both books share certain features), but, above all, in the circumstances in which the books were created, their poetic program and the goals ascribed to art. *Oczy i usta* was written during the Kraków Avant-garde period, while *Serce granatu* is not only proof of the poet's shift, which afforded him the goodwill of his comrades from "Mysia Street." It also testifies to his concern about his wife, expressed in the most moving poems of the volume, with the motif of a fighting woman.[133] In 1943, Ważyk found himself in deep Russia, dreaming, above all, of being reunited with his wife; at the time, he did not realize "she had been fooled by the scheme with the so-called Polish Hotel":[134] lured by the promise of a passport, she checked in voluntarily, and after covering the costs of her "freedom," was gassed in the camp along with many others.[135] At the same time, Ważyk also dreamed of returning to Poland and, like numerous others, placed his only hope in the alliance between Poland and the USSR, which was to overthrow Nazi Germany. The question is whether *Serce granatu*, published in Moscow in 1943 by the Union of Polish Patriots in the USSR, was written by Adam Ważyk the poet or was it already the work of Ważyk the political officer of the Tadeusz Kościuszko First Infantry Division? It is difficult to give an unequivocal answer, even if we bear in mind that "Serce granatu" opened the collection *Wiersze i Pieśni Pierwszej Armii Polskiej w ZSRR* [The poems and songs of the First Polish Army of the USSR], printed two years later.[136]

It is much easier to establish that, in 1953, when this short material about Ważyk appeared in the Bulletin, the poet was still on the "right" side, as evidenced by the State Literary Award of the 2nd degree, which he received at that time. It was not until the following year that the artist started exhibiting an "ideological breakthrough"; in 1954, Ważyk stopped being the head of *Twórczość*, and in 1955, his most famous text, *Poemat dla dorosłych* [Poem for adults] – also discussed in the Bulletins – was published. However, the primary focus here is on Ważyk the "socialist realist" and what attempts were made to control the publication of collective volumes in general.

To recapitulate: Słonimski was "asked" to write an introduction to the collection, while in Ważyk's case, no additional explanatory text was needed. I have already mentioned another strategy used in publishing collected volumes and se-

---

[133] See, e.g.: A. Sandauer, *Byłem…*, Warszawa: PIW, 1991, pp. 97–98.

[134] Ibidem, p. 97.

[135] Gizela Giza née Szejman, Ważyk's first wife, was gassed in Oświęcim in 1943 (see, e.g.: A. Sandauer, *Byłem…*, pp. 97–98).

[136] A. Ważyk, "Serce granatu," [in:] *Wiersze i Pieśni Pierwszej Armii Polskiej w ZSRR*, Łódź: Wydawnictwo Oddziału Propagandy Głównego Zarządu Polityczno-Wychowawczego Wojska Polskiego, 1945, series *Biblioteczka Utworów Literackich* no. 22, p. 5.

lected works, which was data selection. This solution was used in preparing the publication of the volume *Na dziesięciolecie ZWM* [For the 10th anniversary of the Union of Youth Struggle].[137] The jubilee collection included "bellicose materials testifying to the struggle and fortitude of the members of the ZWM during the occupation and in the first period of building People's Poland."[138] According to the Bulletin, a poem by an unnamed Soviet prisoner of war who had escaped from a Nazi camp was removed from the collection.[139] This decision was explained by formal considerations: the poem did not fit in with the concept of the volume, which contained, above all, works encouraging people to fight. Against this background, the literary testimony filled with sadness, resignation, and depression, was demotivating, which was all the more dangerous, because it was penned by a Soviet soldier. Below is the entire poem cited in the Bulletin:

"A poem by a Red Army man who escaped from captivity"

Kiedyś bajki bajały babuszki
O wojnach minionych lat.
Dziś nie bajkę – zranionej jęk duszy
ślę tą pieśnią w krwawiący świat.

Jakże ciężka jest wojny dola –
Wiek za wiekiem powtarza te słowa.
Śmierć na polu, kalectwo, niewola –
Jakże mało mówi ludzka mowa.

I dziś znowu strumieniem wypływa
jasna młodość w zakrwawione pola,
I dziś znowu jako krew zastyga
młodość rwąca przed słowa – niewola.

Nie ja jeden przeżyłem tę mękę,
nas tysiące ginęły od plag,
Zmarłym światom podałem tam rękę,
własnej śmierci witałem już znak.

I już nie wiem, jak przyszła święta owa noc
I spowiła nas w mrok
Jakem umknął – już nie pamiętam.
Wiem, że w lesie znalazłem ślad.

---

[137] The ZWM, created in 1943, was as an extension of the Polish Workers' Party.

[138] "O recenzjach zbiorków literackich," *Biuletyn Informacyjno-Instrukcyjny* no. 4 (16), April 1953, pp. 31–32 (APG, WUKPPiW, file ref. no. 16).

[139] Ibidem, p. 32.

Wokół cicho drzewa szumiały
i witałem wolności cud.
Byłem sam, zgubiony i mały,
A przede mną nieznany trud.

Ludzie człeka zwierzętom nie dali,
Ludzie – bracia, przeciwko nim siła.
Jaki los mnie znów woła z oddali?
Może trawą porośnie mogiła?[140]

[Babushkas used to spin tales
About the bygone wars.
Today not a tale but – a wounded soul's moan
I send out to the bleeding world.

How heavy's the burden of war –
This line is repeated age after age,
Death in a battle, mayhem, gore –
Words are merely rearranged.

And today again bright youth
Is flowing in the bloodstained field,
And today again youth curdles
like blood rushing before it surrenders.

Not only I suffered the torment,
Thousands of us have died from the plague,
Prepared to go where the dead went,
I had one foot in the grave.

And I know not how that holy night came
And shrouded us in darkness
How I escaped – I cannot recall.
I know I found a trace in the forest.

The trees were humming quietly
And I welcomed the miracle of freedom.
I was alone, lost and small,
And before me unknown dole.

People did not sell me to the beasts,
People – my brothers, with might against them.
What fate beckons at me from afar?
Will the grass overgrow my grave?]

---

[140] Ibidem.

A short note was included under the poem, which read: "Written by a Red Army man who escaped from German captivity, hid in Warsaw and later fought in the Polish partisan – translated by Zofia Jaroszewicz."[141] The origin of the work outlined in the Bulletin is highly probable: the unnamed soldier-poet and the translator of the work may have met. Zofia Jaroszewicz was an activist of the Union of Youth Struggle, poet, publicist, and member of the Marxist discussion circle. She organized support for the defenders of Warsaw as early as September 1939 thanks to her involvement in the Workers' Welfare Committee, where she supervised medical posts, as well as stations distributing food and clothing. Hiding under the pseudonym "Kasia," she also engaged in underground activity, distributing the PPR press and co-operating in the publication of *Biuletyn Radiowy*.[142] By the time the collection *Na dziesięciolecie ZWM* was published, Jaroszewicz had already been dead. She died on September 17, 1944 as a result of complications from a gunshot wound.[143]

It was recommended that the poem by the Red Army man be removed from the collection *Na dziesięciolecie ZWM*. Indeed, in 1953, an ephemeron with this title was published, and the poem was not included.[144] Aware of the nonchalance of the Bulletin's editors in quoting book titles, I also checked another collection published that year, which could be identified as the one mentioned in the Bulletin. It was an extensive, almost three hundred-page anthology compiled by Tadeusz Drewnowski under the title *Zrodził nas czyn. Zbiór wierszy i pieśni na dziesięciolecie ZWM* [Borne out of action. A collection of poems and songs for the 10th anniversary of the ZWM]. It was prefaced by Bohdan Czeszko, the author of *Pokolenie* [Generation] (discussed in the Bulletins), and, more importantly in this context, a member of the ZWM.[145] However, I did not find the quoted poem in this publication either. It was also not included in the only book of poetry by the poet-translator published so far, that is, *Pola zakwitną makami* [The field will blossom with poppies]; probably because it was not a collection of translations, but her original works, compiled by Witold Kozłowski, who met "Kasia" in March 1940.[146] I also

---

[141] Ibidem.

[142] A bulletin published from 1941 by an underground socialist organization called the Radio Bulletin Group, which co-operated with other socialist and communist organizations in the occupied Warsaw.

[143] W. Kozłowski, "Jaroszewicz Zofia," [in:] *Słownik biograficzny działaczy polskiego ruchu robotniczego*, ed. F. Tych, vol. 2: *E–J*, Warszawa: "Książka i Wiedza," 1987, p. 661.

[144] *Na dziesięciolecie ZWM*, Warszawa: Iskry, 1953, series *Materiał do Szkolenia Zetempowskiego*.

[145] *Zrodził nas czyn. Zbiór wierszy i pieśni na dziesięciolecie ZWM*, compiled by T. Drewnowski, introduction B. Czeszko, Warszawa: Iskry, 1953.

[146] W. Kozłowski, "Wstęp," [in:] idem, *Pola zakwitną makami*, Warszawa: Wydawnictwo Harcerskie "Horyzonty," 1970, p. 7; Second Edition: Warszawa: Młodzieżowa Agencja Wydawnicza, 1978; Third Edition: ibidem 1983.

checked other publications on the Union of Youth Struggle, in which the removed poem could have been placed, but, ultimately, I was unable to locate it.[147] Perhaps further library and archival searches will reveal the place of the poem's original publication, or maybe it was never printed, adding to the large collection of works withheld by the PRL's censorship and unpublished to this date.

3.2. An Evaluation of the Poetic Publications Printed by the "Czytelnik" Publishing Cooperative in 1951

> *Różewicz's poetry is difficult to absorb.*
> *I bought two books of his poetry*
> *and burned them both.*[148]
>
> Jan Bolesław Ożóg

Some of the above-described problems also appeared in the evaluation of the "Czytelnik" Publishing House, where a large part of its catalog, including poetry, was inspected.[149] The most attention was devoted to the newest poetry, although the report also mentioned two selections of Russian and Polish classics: *Dwa wieki poezji rosyjskiej* [Two centuries of Russian poetry] selected by Mieczysław Jastrun and Seweryn Pollak, and *Wiersze, które lubimy* [Poems we like], edited by Jan Kott and Adam Ważyk (the two volumes will be discussed below).

The authors of the report assessed "Czytelnik's" policy on the publication of contemporary poetry favorably. The only major complaint, which resurfaced with regard to poetry as well as other types of literature, was the insufficient number of translations. The report bemoaned that neither the contemporary poetry of the Soviet Union and the countries of people's democracy nor the poems of progressive poets from capitalist countries were included in the company's catalog.[150]

---

[147] *Zrodził nas czyn. Szlakiem bojowym ZWM*, compiled by A. Drożdżyński, Warszawa: Wydawnictwo RSW "Prasa," 1953; *Zrodził nas czyn. W XX rocznicę powstania Związku Walki Młodych i ZMP "Grunwald,"* Warszawa: Związek Młodzieży Socjalistycznej, 1963; *Zrodził nas czyn. W 30-lecie powstania Związku Walki Młodych*, Warszawa: Wydawca Miesięcznik "Kultura i Ty," 1973.

[148] "Dyskusja o poezji Różewicza," *Życie Literackie* August 8, 1954, no. 31, p. 10 (speakers in the discussion were well-known literary critics and writers: Jan Błoński, Adam Włodek, Henryk Vogler, Julian Przyboś, Jan Bolesław Ożóg, Ludwik Flaszen, and Jerzy Zagórski).

[149] "Czytelnik," founded in 1944 by Jerzy Borejsza and still in existence today, was one of the most important publishing houses in socialist Poland.

[150] "Działalność wydawnictwa 'Czytelnik' w 1951 r.," *Biuletyn Informacyjno-Instrukcyjny* no. 5, May 1952, p. 21 (APG, WUKPPiW, file ref. no. 90).

Having perused the collections of contemporary Polish poets published in 1951 by "Czytelnik," the censors concluded that, at least "in this segment," Borejsza's publishing house successfully engaged in "fighting the remnants of formalism, detachment from life, individualism, etc."[151] As stated earlier, these categories were some of the most common charges against not only poetic works; they appeared in the Bulletins and in numerous censorship reviews of the time as central arguments against the publication of a given work.[152] The censors were, therefore, pleased that there were books which took other approaches.

In publishing practice, new content in poetic works was achieved, for instance, through the selection of appropriate poems "from different periods of creativity, illustrating the poet's development."[153] Furthermore, the catalog included "selections of poetry by both well-known authors (e.g., Jastrun) and emerging authors (Gisges, Fenikowski, Miller)."[154] Once more, the Bulletin offered scant information; in most cases, however, it was easy to determine which books were referenced.

Jastrun, whose *Wiersze dawne i nowe* [Old and new poems] was published by Borejsza in 1951,[155] appeared in the material as a well-known author. On the other hand, the books of Jerzy Zagórski, who debuted around the same time as Jastrun, and Tadeusz Różewicz – the youngest of the three – were placed in a separate category.[156] According to the censors, they were "shining examples of transformations in authors who moved away from decidedly foreign positions."[157] Before the legitimacy of this statement is considered, it should be stressed that Różewicz came from a different generation than Zagórski. The latter was assessed by comparing his pre- and post-war work; Różewicz – if one can really speak here of evolution – was evaluated only on the basis of the volumes published after 1945. The war-time *Echa leśne* [Forest echoes] was a volume unknown to the censors, so they rated the poet only on the basis of the transformations he had undergone from *Niepokój* [Disquiet] to *Czas, który idzie* [The time that is coming].

---

[151] Ibidem.

[152] See, e.g.: K. Budrowska, *Writers, Literature and Censorship...*, pp. 230–234; A. Wiśniewska-Grabarczyk, *"Czytelnik" ocenzurowany. Literatura w kryptotekstach...*, pp. 89–93.

[153] "Działalność wydawnictwa 'Czytelnik' w 1951 r.," *Biuletyn Informacyjno-Instrukcyjny* no. 5, May 1952, p. 21 (APG, WUKPPiW, file ref. no. 90).

[154] Ibidem.

[155] M. Jastrun. *Wiersze dawne i nowe*, Warszawa: "Czytelnik," 1951.

[156] Mieczysław Jastrun debuted in 1929 with his book of poems *Spotkanie w czasie*; Jerzy Zagórski in 1933 with *Ostrze mostu*; Tadeusz Różewicz in 1944 with *Echa leśne*.

[157] "Działalność wydawnictwa 'Czytelnik' w 1951 r.," *Biuletyn Informacyjno-Instrukcyjny* no. 5, May 1952, p. 21 (APG, WUKPPiW, file ref. no. 90).

In 1951, Różewicz returned to Poland after a year-long cultural exchange in Hungary. He described his impressions in a series of reportages entitled *Kartki z Węgier*[158] [Postcards from Hungary], published two years later. The expressionistic and catastrophic books *Niepokój* and *Czerwona rękawiczka* [The red glove], published before his departure in 1947 and 1948, provoked extreme feelings from the critics, ranging from Przyboś's admiration to accusations of nihilism.[159] Today, they serve as rather indisputable proof of the "universal revolution"[160] that the young poet had initiated at the time. On the other hand, the two collections of poems published in "Czytelnik" after his return to Poland – *Pięć poematów* [Five poems] from 1950 and *Czas, który idzie* from 1951 – were received with moderate approval, and certainly did not evoke such extreme emotions as the first two post-war collections. This is what Włodzimierz Maciąg – a literary critic, a fresh graduate of Kraków's Polish Studies Department and the future professor of the humanities – wrote about *Pięć poematów*:[161]

> It is not surprising that a poet who struggles to see a positive hero also struggles to write about building socialism. There is no trace of this subject in Różewicz's collection. However, it should be pointed out that the outline of a serious ideological breakthrough can be seen in the poems printed throughout 1950 in *Nowa Kultura*. This is most clearly visible in the poems with Hungarian themes. However, there are not enough of them to make a proper assessment of this breakthrough.[162]

---

[158] T. Różewicz, *Kartki z Węgier*, Warszawa: "Czytelnik," 1953.

[159] B. Ostromęcki, "Niepokój," *Nowiny Literackie* October 5, 1947, no. 29, p. 6; J. Zawieyski, "Poezja niepokoju," *Odrodzenie* October 19, 1947, no. 42, p. 5; "Dyskusja o poezji Różewicza…," p. 10.

[160] T. Drewnowski, *Próba scalenia. Obiegi-Wzorce-Style*, Warszawa: PWN, 1997, p. 84. On the two above-mentioned books, see also: P. Pietrych, "*Niepokój* – niemal zapomniany tom poetycki Tadeusza Różewicza z 1947 roku," *Pamiętnik Literacki* 2017, issue 2, pp. 143–166; idem, "Tadeusz Różewicz pisze wiersze w roku 1946, czyli poeta modernistyczny wobec wojny," *Poznańskie Studia Polonistyczne. Seria Literacka* 2014, no. 24, pp. 256–267; A. Skrendo, "Przyboś i Różewicz. Paralela," [in:] idem, *Poezja modernizmu. Interpretacje*, Kraków: Universitas, 2005, pp. 140–174; T. Kłak, "Konteksty *Niepokoju*," [in:] idem, *Spojrzenia. Szkice o poezji Tadeusza Różewicza*, Katowice: Wydawnictwo Biblioteka Śląska, 1999, pp. 81–115; T. Drewnowski, *Walka o oddech. O pisarstwie Tadeusza Różewicza*, Warszawa: Wydawnictwa Artystyczne i Filmowe, 1990, pp. 73–86 et seq.

[161] See the chapter "On a Discussion of Marian Promiński's Novella 'Toreador i Mściciel.'"

[162] W. Maciąg, [Review: T. Różewicz, *Pięć poematów*, Warszawa: "Czytelnik," 1950], *Życie Literackie* April 1, 1951, no. 5, p. 3 (review in the article "Poezja polska 1950"). See also: T. Różewicz, *Pięć poematów*, Warszawa: "Czytelnik," 1950; idem, *Czas, który idzie*, Warszawa: "Czytelnik," 1951. See also: J. Błoński, "Pogłosy i zapowiedzi," *Wieś* 1950, no. 25, p. 5.

Even today, both *Pięć poematów* and *Czas, który idzie* pose interpretative difficulties and, according to some researchers, are proof that Różewicz "joined the ranks of those artists who, perhaps without excessive humility or zeal, became champions of the new reality."[163] This view was at least partly shared by the Main Office if it categorized the poet as "moving from decidedly foreign positions." Różewicz's potential for an ideological breakthrough was also noticed in his poems published in the press at the time.

The elements of the writing evolution of Jerzy Zagórski (a former member of the literary group "Żagary" and a "Righteous Among the Nations") that likely gained the censors' approval were his turn towards new, classicist forms of writing and abandoning catastrophism (the "remnants" of which were still noticeable in Różewicz's poetry[164]). In this case, the Bulletin also did not specify the title of the collection. However, they were certainly referring to *Wiersze wybrane* [Selected poems] published in 1951 by "Czytelnik," which was comprised of "old poems" and "new poems."[165]

Różewicz, Jastrun and Zagórski appeared in the Bulletin as artists who had cemented their place in Polish literature. Simultaneously, Borejsza's publishing house carried out the postulate to promote new poetry. As observed in the report, it presented "emerging authors,"[166] which included three poets who debuted in the first five years after the war, namely Jan Maria Gisges, Franciszek

---

Nowa Kultura – one of the most important national social and literary weeklies, published in Warsaw between 1950–1963; initially, the magazine propagated socialist realism; during the Thaw, it took part in the liberalization of cultural life in the country; many of the titles discussed in this book were reviewed in *Nowa Kultura*.

[163] E. Mazur, "'Składam słowa/dźwigam swój czas.' Kilka uwag do dyskursu o ocaleniu w poezji Tadeusza Różewicza (na lekcjach języka polskiego w szkołach ponadgimnazjalnych)," *Zeszyty Naukowe Uniwersytetu Rzeszowskiego* 2014, issue 86, p. 44. On the two above-mentioned collections and Różewicz's attitude to socialist realism, see, e.g.: A. Ściepuro, "Wobec stalinizmu. Wiersze Tadeusza Różewicza z lat 1949–1956," *Pamiętnik Literacki* 1997, issue 2, pp. 33–49; A. Skrendo, "Tadeusza Różewicza 'dochodzenie do socrealizmu,' czyli o *Uśmiechach*," [in:] idem, *Poezja modernizmu. Interpretacje...*, pp. 186–203; T. Drewnowski, *Walka o oddech...*, pp. 95–111 et seq.

[164] J. Błoński, *Pogłosy i zapowiedzi...*, p. 5.

[165] J. Zagórski, *Wiersze wybrane*, Warszawa: "Czytelnik," 1951. For reviews of *Wiersze wybrane*, see, e.g.: L. Herdegen, "'Pierścienie strof' Jerzego Zagórskiego," *Życie Literackie* September 30, 1951, no. 18, p. 12; J. Preger, [Review: J. Zagórski, *Wiersze wybrane*, Warszawa: "Czytelnik," 1951] (in the series *Wśród Książek*), *Twórczość* 1951, no. 11, pp. 165–167; S. Błaut, "Poezja Jerzego Zagórskiego," *Tygodnik Powszechny* February 10, 1952, no. 6, pp. 4–5.

[166] "Działalność wydawnictwa 'Czytelnik' w 1951 r.," *Biuletyn Informacyjno-Instrukcyjny* no. 5, May 1952, p. 21 (APG, WUKPPiW, file ref. no. 90).

Fenikowski and Jerzy Miller.[167] In 1951, "Czytelnik" published their collections, respectively: *Pierwsza miłość* [First love], *Lewy brzeg* [Left bank], and *Słowa na pozycji* [Words in position].[168] In the case of Gisges and Miller, these were their second collections of poetry. *Lewy brzeg* was Fenikowski's first book of poetry; his earlier poems had been included in a book that broached the difficult subject of the Regained Territories, *Odra szumi po polsku*[169] [The Oder hums in Polish].

All three volumes mentioned in the Bulletin were reviewed in *Życie Literackie* by Jan Błoński, one of the most famous representatives of the Kraków school of literary criticism.[170] Błoński, along with Flaszen, Kijowski and Puzyna were the leading students of Kazimierz Wyka's seminar, which in the 1950s produced the

---

[167] Jan Maria Gisges was born in 1914, Franciszek Fenikowski in 1922, and Jerzy Miller a year later (see: E. Głębicka [E. G.], "Gisges Jan Maria," [in:] *Współcześni polscy pisarze i badacze literatury. Słownik biobibliograficzny* vol. 5: *L–M…*, pp. 50–52; A. Szałagan [A. Sz.], "Fenikowski Franciszek," [in:] *Współcześni polscy pisarze i badacze literatury. Słownik biobibliograficzny* vol. 2: *C–F*, eds. J. Czachowska, A. Szałagan, Warszawa: WSiP, 1994, pp. 285–288; J. Zawadzka [J. Z.], "Miller Jerzy," [in:] *Współcześni polscy pisarze i badacze literatury. Słownik biobibliograficzny* vol. 5: *L–M…*, pp. 396–398).

[168] J.M. Gisges, *Pierwsza miłość*, Warszawa: "Czytelnik," 1951; F. Fenikowski, *Lewy brzeg*, Warszawa: "Czytelnik," 1951; J. Miller, *Słowa na pozycji*, Warszawa: "Czytelnik," 1951.

[169] L. Goliński, F. Fenikowski, *Odra szumi po polsku*, Poznań: Wydawnictwo Zachodnie, 1946.

[170] See the review of *Pierwsza miłość* and *Słowa na pozycji*: J. Błoński, "U poetów (I)," *Życie Literackie* September 16, 1951, no. 17, p. 4, 11 (in the article, Błoński also reviewed the volume of Stanisław Ostrowski *Tłumaczę słowo pokój* and Henryk Gaworski *Przed nami życie*; the passage devoted to Miller was entitled "Na nowych pozycjach"); see the review of *Lewy brzeg*: J. Błoński, "U poetów (III)," *Życie Literackie* December 9, 1951, no. 23, p. 10 (in the article, Błoński reviewed three books, including *Pierwsza linia pokoju* by Wiktor Woroszylski and *Nowa ziemia* by Jan Koprowski; the passage devoted to Fenikowski was entitled "Pomyślna ewolucja"). Also see the reviews: A Kamieńska, [Review: J.M. Gisges, *Pierwsza miłość*, Warszawa: "Czytelnik," 1951] (in the series *Wśród Książek*), *Twórczość* 1951, no. 2, pp. 144–147; J.J. Lipski, [Review: F. Fenikowski, Warszawa: *Lewy brzeg*, "Czytelnik," 1951] (in the series *Wśród Książek*), *Twórczość* 1952, no. 6, pp. 166–168.
Życie Literackie (Literary Life) – one of the most important Polish literary and social magazines, published in Kraków in 1951–1990. In the first half of the 1950s, it implemented the postulates of socialist realism (similarly to *Nowa Kultura* and almost all other magazines published at the time); from 1955/1956, *Życie Literackie* took an active part in the reconstruction of Polish culture, thanks to the publication of the previously unwelcome Western literature, the works of emigrant writers and the rehabilitation of the works from the interwar period; many of the titles discussed in this book were reviewed in *Życie Literackie*.

most influential literary criticism. As critics, they tried to make a measured use of the only correct theory at the time – the Marxist theory of literature. Rosiek writes that essentially, it was Wyka and his students who comprised "the Polish critique" in the thirty years after the war.[171] Members of the group were very active, which is why many a book discussed in the Bulletins was sooner or later evaluated in the press by them.

The three poets reviewed by Błoński – Gisges, Fenikowski and Miller – were entering the Polish literary scene with difficult wartime baggage. In their later artistic work, they pursued various fields, from writing song lyrics (Miller) to creating radio plays (Fenikowski). The case of Gisges, successfully persuaded to cooperate with the Secret Service, illustrates the ambiguous and challenging times, in which they were forced to create.[172]

In 1951, in addition to the already established and "emerging" poets, "Czytelnik" started publishing debuts. The Bulletins noted two authors (only by their last names): Andrzej Mandalian and Henryk Gaworski. Mandalian, born in Shanghai in 1926, the son of Polish-Armenian communist activists, was repatriated from the USSR in 1947 and became permanently linked to Poland. Four years after his arrival, he published his debut poem "Dzisiaj" [Today], with which he fitted perfectly into the cultural program of the time, although not without running into some pitfalls along the way.[173] Leszek Herdegen – the author of an extremely enthusiastic review of Wisława Szymborska's debut volume[174] – also praised Mandalian's poem for its struggle "for a new socio-political face of the Polish countryside" and its literary imagery, unusually mature for a poet of his age.[175]

---

[171] S. Rosiek, "Mówienie a milczenie. O biografii duchowej krytyka literackiego w Polsce," [in:] S. Chwin, S. Rosiek, *Bez autorytetu*, Gdańsk: Wydawnictwo Gdańskie, 1981, p. 71. See also: M. Szumna, "Uczeń Kazimierza Wyki," *Nowa Dekada Krakowska* 2018, no. 1, pp. 16–26 (cf. the issue devoted mainly to Kazimierz Wyka); J. Błoński, "Krakowska szkoła krytyki," the interview with Jan Błoński conducted by Maciej Szybist, *Gazeta Krakowska* January 1, 1981, no. 11, pp. 3, 5.

[172] J. Siedlecka, *Kryptonim "Liryka." Bezpieka wobec literatów*, Warszawa: Prószyński Media, 2009, p. 280.

[173] L. Herdegen, "Poemat Andrzeja Mandaliana," *Życie Literackie* June 22, 1952, no. 13, p. 6. See also: A. Mandalian, *Dzisiaj*, Warszawa: "Czytelnik," 1951.

[174] See the review of the Nobel laureate's book *Dlatego żyjemy*: L. Herdegen, "Dwa tomiki poezji" (in the series *Świat Książek*), *Świat. Tygodnik Ilustrowany* 1953, no. 27, p. 14.

[175] L. Herdegen, "Poemat Andrzeja Mandaliana…," p. 6. See other reviews of the poem: G. Lasota, "Patos walki," *Nowa Kultura* May 11, 1952, no. 19, pp. 9–10; J. Śpiewak, [Review: A. Mandalian, *Dzisiaj*, Warszawa: "Czytelnik," 1951] (in the series *Wśród Książek*), *Twórczość* 1952, no. 3, pp. 150–152.

LESZEK HERDEGEN

POEMAT ANDRZEJA MANDALIANA

Andrzej Mandalian
Rys. Sławomir Mrożek

ZBIGNIEW SZYMAŃSKI

DO POETY

Mieczysławowi Jastrunowi

Za wiersz sprawdzalny jak algebra,
Za słowa prawdy, strofy piękne,
Brzmiące jak ton czystego srebra
I jak pieśń gminna nieulękłe,
Za walkę o szczęśliwszy wiek
O jasne jutro, wolność, prawo,
Za rym jak nurt głębokich rzek,
Dyszący męską, gniewną sławą.

Za wiersze, w których dłutem mistrza
Zaklęty został kształt epoki,
Jak w krystalicznych gamach Liszta
Szum drzewa, szept i cień obłoków.
Za trud, za ciężkie, duszne noce
Pełne wyrzeczeń i radości, —
Nad Twoją księgą jasne oczy
Będą uśmiechać się z ufnością.

I z niej to będą przyszli czerpać
Historię naszych dni i wieku,
W których zastygły jest ślad cierpień
I echa walk i trosk człowieka.
Bo nie umiera wiersz spiżowy,
Pochmurny wiersz, gdy w nim się mieści
I dziecka płacz i czas surowy
Pełen głębokiej, ludzkiej treści.

LESZEK HERDEGEN

Fig. 9. L. Herdegen, "Poemat Andrzeja Mandaliana," *Życie Literackie* June 22, 1952, no. 13, p. 6 (with a portrait of Mandalian, drawn by Sławomir Mrożek). Source: Małopolska Biblioteka Cyfrowa.

Mandalian's position as one of the leading poets of socialist realism and a representative of the "pimple generation" (*pryszczaci*) was strengthened two years later by his collection entitled *Słowa na co dzień* [Words for every day], which included "Towarzyszom z Bezpieczeństwa" [To Comrades from the Security]: a poem glorifying the work of the Ministry of Public Security functionaries.[176] This is by no means an exceptional work; support for the activities of the people's government took many different forms in that period. Although poems portraying the employees of the Ministry of Public Security and the Security Service in a positive light did not dominate the editorial offer at the time, they did appear in the works written by various writers.[177] Mandalian, like several other artists mentioned in the Bulletins, made a difficult journey from the "pet of the authorities" to the author banned from printing.[178] This was the repressive measure taken against the writer after he signed *Memoriał 101* in 1976, in which Polish intellectuals expressed their opposition to the planned changes to the Constitution of the PRL.[179]

The other debutant, Henryk Gaworski had published poems and translations in magazines before his first collection of poetry, *Przed nami* życie [Life ahead of us], came out in 1951 with "Czytelnik." The volume was reviewed in *Twórczość* and *Życie Literackie* by the aforementioned Jan Śpiewak and Jan Błoński.[180] The

---

[176] A. Mandalian, "Towarzyszom z Bezpieczeństwa," [in:] idem, *Słowa na co dzień*, Warszawa: "Czytelnik," 1953, pp. 9–15.

Pryszczaci – a group of young Polish writers at the turn of the 1950s, radical enthusiasts of subordinating literary works to the requirements of the ideology of the communist party, according to the assumptions of the so-called socialist realism; the most important representatives of this milieu were Tadeusz Borowski, Wiktor Woroszylski, Andrzej Braun, Wisława Szymborska, Tadeusz Konwicki, Witold Wirpsza, Andrzej Mandalian and Witold Zalewski; the term refers to the young age of the people associated with the group.

[177] See, e.g.: *Wieczny płomień. Wybór wierszy poetów radzieckich i polskich o Feliksie Dzierżyńskim*, compiled by W. Woroszylski, Warszawa: PIW, 1951; *Wiersze i pieśni poświęcone pracownikom bezpieczeństwa*, Warszawa 1954.

[178] T. Mielczarek, "Pisarze w PRL: 'pieszczochy władzy' czy ofiary systemu," [in:] *Niewygodne dla władzy. Ograniczanie wolności słowa na ziemiach polskich w XIX i XX wieku*, eds. D. Degen, J. Gzella, Toruń: Wydawnictwo Naukowe UMK, 2010, pp. 213–231.

[179] *Memoriał 101* was filed on January 31, 1976; the opposed changes would have introduced the PZPR's leading role in the state and a permanent and inviolable alliance with the USSR.

[180] H. Gaworski, *Przed nami życie*, Warszawa: "Czytelnik," 1951. See the reviews of the book: J. Śpiewak, [Review: H. Gaworski, *Przed nami życie*, Warszawa: "Czytelnik," 1951] (in the series *Wśród Książek*), *Twórczość* 1952, no. 5, pp. 207–211; J. Błoński, "U poetów (I)...," pp. 4, 11 (the passage devoted to Gaworski was entitled "Uważajmy").

Twórczość – the oldest Polish monthly publishing prose, poetry, literary criticism and essays. It was established in August 1945 and exists to this day.

latter praised Gaworski for his desire to "write socialistically also about nature, love and many different matters, hitherto avoided by some poets."[181] Despite this praise, Błoński's reception of the volume by the "debutant from Warsaw" was not uncritical. The excessive idyllic nature of some of the works was seen as flawed: "these poems by Gaworski smack of an after-dinner siesta."[182]

In later years, Gaworski's books were assessed differently. Here is what Stanisław Barańczak, a Polish poet, translator, and a lecturer at Harvard University, wrote in his subjective selection *Książki najgrosze* [The worst books] about the novel *Jelenie jedzą klejnoty* [Deer eat jewels], published in 1978: "the reader has to wade through two hundred pages of Henryk Gaworski's prose, as tasty as artificial honey and as nutritious as 'I Can't Believe It's Not Butter!'"[183]

Similarly to Gisges, Gaworski – a former Home Army soldier and Warsaw insurgent – succumbed to the persuasions of the Security Service.[184] This information is crucial in the context of literary considerations, because "Mysia Street and its environs" functioned in a complicated network of mutual connections, and an agreement to collaborate may have been a factor in the assessment of a given artist's work. As Barbara Tyszkiewicz writes:

> The rank-and-file employees of the GUKPPiW were not informed about the operational activities carried out by the security department. After all, state censorship was one of the most important instruments of exerting pressure on writers. It was applied by means of threads which, as a rule, do not leave a trace on paper.[185]

---

[181] J. Błoński, "U poetów (I)…," p. 4.

[182] Ibidem.

[183] S. Barańczak, "Fredek, jesteś cudowny, czyli major w kamaszach," [in:] idem, *Książki najgorsze i parę innych ekscesów krytycznoliterackich*, Second Revised Edition, Poznań: Wydawnictwo a5, 1990, pp. 100–101; see also: H. Gaworski, *Jelenie jedzą klejnoty*, Warszawa: Iskry, 1978.

Stanisław Barańczak (1946–2014) – a Polish poet, literary critic, translator, scholar and editor; he was a prominent representative of the Polish poetic formation "New Wave" (*Nowa Fala*) and is generally regarded as one of the greatest translators of English poetry into Polish and Polish poetry into English; in 1976, both Barańczak's and Słonimski's names appeared in one of the secret instructions of the GUKPPiW.

[184] Joanna Siedlecka writes that Gaworski was an operational contact of the Secret Service (see J. Siedlecka, *Kryptonim "Liryka"*…, p. 422). While some of Siedlecka's findings are legitimate, I agree with most of the criticism leveled against both her research methods and her "cheap rhetorical tricks," see, e.g. the following reviews: *Kryptonim "Liryka"*…: S. Buryła, "Artyści i ich opiekunowie," *Znak* 2009, no. 7/8, pp. 138–143; B. Kaliski, "Jedynie donos jest ciekawy?," *Nowe Książki* 2009, no. 4, pp. 49–50.

[185] B. Tyszkiewicz, "'Pod prąd.' Jerzy Zawieyski wobec zmian w polityce kulturalnej państwa w latach 1945–1955," [in:] *"Lancetem, a nie maczugą." Cenzura wobec literatury*

All the above-presented poets were praised in the Bulletin for "their strong connection with current social and political issues."[186] Indeed, the afore-quoted titles tried to meet the expectations placed on literature at the time. In a similar vein, the poetic proposals of three other authors included in the report, namely Witold Wirpsza, Jan Brzechwa and Jan Koprowski, acquainted the reader "with building socialism in Poland and the struggle for peace."[187] As usual, no titles were provided but it can be assumed that Wirpsza was praised for his *Polemiki i pieśni* [Polemics and songs], Brzechwa for his collection *Pokój zwycięży. Wiersze i satyry* [Peace will prevail. Poems and satires] and *Strofy o Planie sześcioletnim* [Verses on the six-year plan], while Koprowski for *Pejzaże polskie* [Polish landscapes], all of which were published by "Czytelnik" in 1951.

This small section devoted to the poetry published by "Czytelnik" in 1951, there is no major polarization of attitudes among artists, simply because it was not an option. It was still a time when publication was determined not by the artistic value of a work, but by the political declarations of the author – expressed in the poetry itself, in programmatic texts or press articles, etc. The time for seeking one's own formal solutions and poetic language, as well as new, challenging ideological declarations, would come later. However, not everyone decided to go through the "difficult art of vomiting," the way Ważyk, Mandalian or Wirpsza did. Also, not everyone arrived there by following the "three rules": "you should vomit what you've consumed," "if you vomit, vomit all the way," and "you should not vomit monumentally, but like a sweaty mouse."[188] These rules come from the 1955 article by Ludwik Flaszen *O trudnym kunszcie womitowania* [On the difficult art of vomiting], who was critical of the anti-socialist speeches of Ważyk and Brandys (to be discussed later). Flaszen's charges were that "such a tone could have been taken by someone who stood outside the errors, someone with a conscience not split by the complicity in errors, who never naively idealized or acted against oneself."[189] It seems, however, that Flaszen lost this battle, as both testimonies were considered relevant. The Bulletins from 1956 elaborate on the difficulties of assessing Flaszen's article (analyzed below).

---

i jej twórców w latach 1945–1965, eds. K. Budrowska, M. Woźniak-Łabieniec, Warszawa: IBL PAN, 2012, series *Badania Filologiczne nad Cenzurą PRL* vol. 1, p. 40.

[186] "Działalność wydawnictwa 'Czytelnik' w 1951 r.," *Biuletyn Informacyjno-Instrukcyjny* no. 5, May 1952, p. 21 (APG, WUKPPiW, file ref. no. 90).

[187] Ibidem.

[188] L. Flaszen, "O trudnym kunszcie womitowania" (in the series *Z notatnika szalonego recenzenta*), *Życie Literackie* October 30, 1955, no. 44, p. 5.

[189] Ibidem.

3.3. On the Works of Kazimiera Iłłakowiczówna

And yet, in 1954, Iłłakowiczówna's jubilee
was not celebrated.[190]

In July 1955, the Bulletin published a long piece "O twórczości Kazimiery Iłłakowiczówny" [On the works of Kazimiera Iłłakowiczówna]. When the writer returned to the country in 1947, she probably had no illusions regarding her career back home.[191] The second half of the 1940s and the beginning of the 1950s were a difficult time for artists, especially those with an ambiguous past, incompatible with the requirements of the new authorities. In the case of Iłłakowiczówna, tangible proof of this was that she was delegated to translation work and did not obtain the desired position at the Ministry of Foreign Affairs. Essentially, she could have expected this: as Joanna Kuciel-Frydryszak – the poet's biographer – concludes, "employing Piłsudski's former secretary in the ministry was simply out of the question."[192]

Kazimierz Królik, a censor and author of the Bulletin article in question, did, however, recognize the writer's accomplishments, listing three of the numerous awards she received for her artistic activity: the City of Vilnius Award (1930), the state award (1935) and the Polish PEN Club Award for translation work

---

[190] B. Mamoń, "O wierszach Kazimiery Iłłakowiczówny," *Tygodnik Powszechny* Easter 1955, no. 15, p. 12.

[191] Since this material was published with commentary by Kamila Budrowska: "O twórczości Kazimiery Iłłakowiczówny. Materiał archiwalny z zespołu Głównego Urzędu Kontroli Prasy, Publikacji i Widowisk z połowy 1955 r.," *Napis. Pismo poświęcone literaturze okolicznościowej i użytkowej* 2017, series 23, I only provide the main theses of the Bulletin article, elaborating on its selected aspects.

[192] *"Iłła" – opowieść o Kazimierze Iłłakowiczównie* [Joanna Kuciel-Frydryszak interviewed by Agata Szwedowicz (PAP)], Dzieje.pl, October 7, 2017, https://dzieje.pl/ksiazki/illa-opowiesc-o-kazimierze-illakowiczownie (accessed January 22, 2021). See also: Z. Chojnowski, *Postacie kobiecości. O poezji Kazimiery Iłłakowiczówny*, Kraków–Bielsko-Biała: Instytut Literacki–Wydawnictwo Naukowe UKSW, 2019; J. Kuciel-Frydryszak, *Iłła. Opowieść o Kazimierze Iłłakowiczównie*, Warszawa: Marginesy, 2017; I. Kienzler, "Kazimiera Iłłakowiczówna – zakochana poetka," [in:] eadem, *Kobiety w życiu Marszałka Piłsudskiego*, Warszawa: Bellona, 2014, pp. 241–274.
Józef Piłsudski (1867–1935) – a Polish statesman who served as the Chief of State (1918–1922) and First Marshal of Poland (from 1920); considered the *de facto* leader (1926–35) of the Second Republic as the Minister of Military Affairs; after World War I, he exercised increasing influence on Polish politics and actively participated in international diplomacy; considered the father of the Second Republic of Poland.

(1954).[193] Iłła (Iłłakowiczówna) had embarked on translating fiction already before the war. She translated from English, German, French, Romanian, and Hungarian. The aforementioned report on "Czytelnik's" activities mentioned Sándor Petőfi's *Wybór poezji* [Poetry selection], which, included a poem translated by Iłłakowiczówna. Furthermore, the volume of *Poezje* published exactly twenty years later already contained four such poems.[194]

The question arises as to why a long article devoted to the poet's work was published in July 1955. Although she had appeared in the Bulletins earlier, these were only minor mentions, dwarfed by Królik's material.[195] The opening of the text may provide a clue, although naturally, one should read carefully between the lines, as it was always the case with the documents created by the censorship office:

> Since the relatively abundant poetic output of Iłłakowiczówna is little known in our country, and recently some Catholic publishing houses have made strenuous attempts to publish some of her poems (PAX 1954, Pallotinum 1955), the poet's output and the nature of her work ought to be examined. This orientation is required in concrete censorship work.[196]

Indeed, these were the first editions of Iłła's poems since 1949 (Kamila Budrowska mentions the unsuccessful attempt to publish a collection of her *Wiersze wybrane* in 1948).[197] In 1954, PAX published *Poezje 1940–1954* [Poems 1940–1954], while in 1955, *Wiersze religijne. 1912–1954* [Religious poems. 1912–1954] came out, however, not with Pallotinum, as it was claimed in the Bulletin,

---

[193] K. Królik, "O twórczości Kazimiery Iłłakowiczówny," *Biuletyn Informacyjno-Instrukcyjny* no. 7 (43), July 1955, pp. 18–19 (APG, WUKPPiW, file ref. no. 103). The article contains a few minor factual errors and several inaccuracies, such as the information that Iłła began her poetic career in 1904 (when, in fact, her debut took place a year later). This and other inaccuracies were pointed out by Kamila Budrowska in her publication "O twórczości Kazimiery Iłłakowiczówny…," passim.

[194] K. Iłłakowiczówna, "Do Stefanka," [in:] S. Petőfi, *Wybór poezji*, Warszawa: "Czytelnik," 1951, pp. 46–47; K. Iłłakowiczówna, "Stoję na rozdrożu…"; "Do Stefanka"; "Gdyby Pan Bóg…"; "Przy końcu września," [in:] S. Petőfi, *Poezje*, Warszawa: PIW, 1971, pp. 26–28, 38–39, 96. See also: "Działalność wydawnictwa 'Czytelnik' w 1951 r.," *Biuletyn Informacyjno-Instrukcyjny* no. 5, May 1952, p. 19 (APG, WUKPPiW, file ref. no. 90).

[195] Iłłakowiczówna was mentioned, e.g., in the Bulletin from October 1953 (see: p. 5).

[196] K. Królik, "O twórczości Kazimiery Iłłakowiczówny," *Biuletyn Informacyjno-Instrukcyjny* no. 7 (43), July 1955, p. 18 (APG, WUKPPiW, file ref. no. 103).

[197] See: K. Iłłakowiczówna, *Wiersze wybrane. 1912–1947*, Łódź–Poznań: Wydawnictwo W. Bąka, 1949, and K. Budrowska, "O twórczości Kazimiery Iłłakowiczówny…," pp. 365–366.

but with another religious publishing house, Albertinum from Poznań.[198] The discussed article by Królik appeared in the July issue of the Bulletin, thus, at least four months before the publication of *Wiersze religijne*, the printing of which was completed in November of the same year.[199]

The heightened interest in the poet's works was indeed one of the reasons for the appearance of the material, which was simply meant to serve a training function. It was necessary to create the most comfortable conditions for censors to evaluate her future works, as the period in which the poet remained silent (publishing her poems only in the press and working on translations) was coming to an end. The changes that were occurring on the political and cultural scene translated to a "turbulent time of impending thaw"[200] at the GUKPPiW, as well. Materials for censors started featuring instructions about "how to assess the works of previously unpublished writers,"[201] such as Iłłakowiczówna. It was also significant that religious publishing houses became interested in her work and that the author's biography abounded in moments that could be weaponized in the publishing "negotiations." Therefore, the rest of the Bulletin material recapitulates the poet's literary résumé and biography, beginning with "encyclopedic data"[202] about her works.

Naturally, her activity as a translator was mentioned, including her translation of *Anna Karenina* by Leo Tolstoy and *Egmont* by Goethe (which, interestingly, would be published the following year, i.e., in 1956). There is also a note on her translation of *How to Win Friends and Influence People* by Dale Carnegie, who gained popularity thanks to his self-help guides.[203] That book translated by Iłła was published in 1948 by the aforementioned Albertinum Publishing House. Perhaps

---

[198] K. Iłłakowiczówna, *Poezje 1940–1954*, Warszawa: Instytut Wydawniczy "Pax," 1954; eadem, *Wiersze religijne. 1912–1954*, Poznań: Albertinum, 1955. The erroneous information that the title was published by Pallotinum was also repeated on page 25 of the Bulletin. About the Albertinum Publishing House see, e.g.: P. Nowak, "Skuteczna czy nieskuteczna. Socjalistyczna cenzura w czasach terroru stalinowskiego. Studium przypadku poznańskiego wydawnictwa Albertinum," *Toruńskie Studia Bibliologiczne* 2013, no. 2, pp. 31–47.

[199] K. Budrowska, "O twórczości Kazimiery Iłłakowiczówny…," p. 365.

[200] Ibidem, p. 364.

[201] Ibidem.

[202] K. Królik, "O twórczości Kazimiery Iłłakowiczówny," *Biuletyn Informacyjno-Instrukcyjny* no. 7 (43), July 1955, p. 19 (APG, WUKPPiW, file ref. no. 103).

[203] L. Tolstoy, *Anna Karenina. Powieść* vol. 1–4, trans. K. Iłłakowiczówna, Warszawa: PIW, 1952–1953; J.W. Goethe, *Egmont. Tragedia*, compiled by Z. Ciechanowska, trans. K. Iłłakowiczówna, Wrocław: Ossolineum, 1956; D. Carnegie, *Jak uszczęśliwiać innych i samemu być szczęśliwym?*, summarized by K. Iłłakowiczówna, Poznań: Albertinum, 1948 (cf. also the abridged title *Jak uszczęśliwiać innych i być szczęśliwym* [in:] K. Budrowska, "O twórczości Kazimiery Iłłakowiczówny…," p. 371).

it is a coincidence, but for the second time, the article omits Albertinum, suggesting that the two above-mentioned works were published by "Książka i Wiedza":

> The period of her [Iłłakowiczówna's – AWG] stay in People's Poland involves primarily translation work. In 1948, "Książka i Wiedza" publishes her translation of Aron Tomasi's *Alek na puszczy* [Ábel a rengetegben] and Dale Carnegie's *Jak uszczęśliwiać i być szczęśliwym*.[204]

A minor error also appeared in reference to Tomasi's book, which was printed by "Wiedza," and not "Książka i Wiedza." In 1948, "Książka i Wiedza" Publishing and Trading Cooperative was established by merging the "Wiedza" Publishing House, affiliated with the PPS, and the "Książka" Publishing Cooperative, affiliated with the PPR.

Once again, the titles of the reviewed works were not given precisely; in the first case, the name of the protagonist was changed from Abel to Alek; in the second, the title was shortened. These flaws, however, are less important than the fact that already the following year, the Office for the Control blocked the publication of Carnegie's work, which was not reprinted in Iłła's translation until 1991.[205] The preserved, negative censorship review of the self-help book states that it promotes an "American way of life,"[206] perceiving happiness in terms of income, popularity, success, and fame:

> it makes an explicit connection between moral motives and material gains, and as such, is completely unsuited to the psyche of the Polish reader. Numerous praises of American people and their way of thinking make this book completely expendable.[207]

The Bulletin, however, did not mention these unsuccessful attempts to publish the book; neither in the first part, which only offered an overview of the author's literary biography, nor later – where it would have been possible, because in

---

[204] K. Królik, "O twórczości Kazimiery Iłłakowiczówny," *Biuletyn Informacyjno-Instrukcyjny* no. 7 (43), July 1955, p. 19 (APG, WUKPPiW, file ref. no. 103). See A. Tamási, *Abel w puszczy*, trans. K. Iłłakowiczówna, Warszawa: "Wiedza," 1948.

[205] D. Carnegie, *Jak zjednywać przyjaciół i osiągnąć sukces w życiu*, edition revised, amended, trans. into Polish and summarized by K. Iłłakowiczówna, Warszawa: Oficyna Literatów "Rój," 1991.

[206] "Recenzje książkowe 1949" (APP, WUKPPiW, file ref. no. 234, fol. 6; D. Carnegie, *Jak uszczęśliwiać innych i samemu być szczęśliwym*, censorship review written on October 14, 1949); see also: P. Nowak, "Wojewódzki Urząd Kontroli Prasy, Publikacji i Widowisk w okresie nacjonalizacji rynku książki…," p. 178.

[207] "Recenzje książkowe 1949" (APP, WUKPPiW, file ref. no. 234, fol. 6; D. Carnegie, *Jak uszczęśliwiać innych…*).

that section reconstructing the poet's "factual life path," her work was discussed in more detail,[208] Apart from literature, the editors were interested in two more issues – Iłła's cooperation and relationship with Piłsudski, and her attitude towards the USSR.

The report reads that Iłłakowiczówna met the Marshal "via her sister who was Piłsudski's personal secretary in the period before World War I."[209] The poet maintained very close contact with him, which over time "turned into boundless and almost blind adoration for the future Marshal."[210] Piłsudski's attitude to his associate was quite different, and, according to the testimony in the Bulletin, the Commander did not have the best opinion of her.[211] Regardless of the actual relationship between the two, the material clearly ridicules Iłłakowiczówna, painting her as an exalted and "capricious"[212] person obsessed with the Marshal. To finally discredit Iłła using her own weapon, Królik cites the poet's memoir, noting that after such testimony "there is no need for further commentary":[213] "In an incomprehensible and irrational way, these four years proved my faith in Józef Piłsudski to be complete, ardent and boundless."[214]

Using excerpts from the writer's works, the material repeatedly described the poet's hostile, even hateful attitude towards the USSR and her bottomless faith in Piłsudski and the entire Sanation Camp.[215] Most of the quotations provided the title of the poem or the book from which they came. The works that supposedly illustrated the poet's "blind and boundless"[216] faith in Piłsudski included *Wiersze belwederskie* [Belvedere poems] and *Wiersze o Marszałku Piłsudskim* [Poems

---

[208] K. Królik, "O twórczości Kazimiery Iłłakowiczówny," *Biuletyn Informacyjno-Instrukcyjny* no. 7 (43), July 1955, p. 19 (APG, WUKPPiW, file ref. no. 103).

[209] Ibidem, p. 20. On Barbara, Kazimiera's elder sister, see, e.g.: A. Poppa, "Siostra znanej siostry czy poetka nieusłyszana? Twórczość Barbary Czerwijowskiej," [in:] *Twórczość niepozorna. Szkice o literaturze*, eds. J. Grądziel-Wójcik, A. Kwiatkowska, L. Marzec, Kraków: Wydawnictwo Pasaże, 2015, pp. 52–62; J. Ratajczak, "*Wspomnienia* Barbary Czerwijowskiej," *W Drodze* 1991, no. 2, pp. 60–64.

[210] K. Królik, "O twórczości Kazimiery Iłłakowiczówny," *Biuletyn Informacyjno-Instrukcyjny* no. 7 (43), July 1955, p. 20 (APG, WUKPPiW, file ref. no. 103).

[211] Ibidem, pp. 19–20. Commander is one of the nicknames of Piłsudski, who was also referred to as Grandfather, Marshal and Ziuk.

[212] Ibidem, p. 20.

[213] Ibidem, p. 23.

[214] Ibidem.

[215] Ibidem, p. 20. Cf. K. Iłłakowiczówna, *Ścieżka obok drogi*, Warszawa: Rój, 1939, *passim*.

Sanacja (Sanation Camp) – a colloquial name for the camp that ruled in Poland from 1926 to 1939, established and functioning initially under the leadership of Józef Piłsudski.

[216] K. Królik, "O twórczości Kazimiery Iłłakowiczówny," *Biuletyn Informacyjno-Instrukcyjny* no. 7 (43), July 1955, p. 22 (APG, WUKPPiW, file ref. no. 103).

about Marshal Piłsudski].[217] Such overtone reportedly resonated in two poems for children quoted by the censor – "Strzelcy" [Riflemen] and "Pomnik" [The monument] – which came from the series *Wiersze belwederskie* (but this time were included in the volume *Ballady bohaterskie* [Heroic ballads] from 1934).[218]

However, the most important book revealing Iłła's attitude to Piłsudski was believed to be *Ścieżka obok drogi* [A path beside the road]. This is the poet's memoir describing her work at the Ministry of Military Affairs, when she was secretary to the Marshal. Królik criticized the author's total adoration of her superior, which dominated the narrative, although it was not *Ścieżka obok drogi* that he thought was "the most foolish memoir in the history of Poland."[219] That title was earned by *Strzępy meldunków* [Scraps of reports] by Felicjan Sławoj Składkowski, which Iłłakowiczówna drew on and which she evaluated extremely highly.[220] Królik's assessment should not come as a surprise considering that Składkowski, a supporter of Sanation and Minister of the Interior in Józef Piłsudski's cabinet, was supposedly fanatically attached to his superior, as evidenced by the above-mentioned book describing his cooperation with the Marshal.[221]

Iłłakowiczówna's narrative poem entitled "Opowieść o moskiewskim męczeństwie" [A story of the Moscow martyrdom] and her poem "Dusza księdza Butkiewicza"[222] [The soul of Father Butkiewicz] were given as examples of works

---

[217] K. Iłłakowiczówna, *Wiersze belwederskie*, [in:] eadem, *Słowik litewski. Poezje*, Warszawa: Gebethner and Wolff, 1936, pp. 49–70; eadem, *Wiersze o Marszałku Piłsudskim. 1912–1935*, Warszawa: Główna Księgarnia Wojskowa, 1936.

[218] K. Królik, "O twórczości Kazimiery Iłłakowiczówny," *Biuletyn Informacyjno-Instrukcyjny* no. 7 (43), July 1955, pp. 22–23 (APG, WUKPPiW, file ref. no. 103). Cf. K. Iłłakowiczówna, "Strzelcy"; "Pomnik," [in:] eadem, *Ballady bohaterskie*, Lviv: Ossolineum, 1934, pp. 71, 79.

[219] K. Królik, "O twórczości Kazimiery Iłłakowiczówny," *Biuletyn Informacyjno-Instrukcyjny* no. 7 (43), July 1955, p. 23 (APG, WUKPPiW, file ref. no. 103).

[220] F.S. Składkowski, *Strzępy meldunków*, Warszawa: Instytut Badania Najnowszej Historii Polski, 1936.

[221] "Zmiana Rządu. Gen. dr. Sławoj-Składkowski premjerem i ministrem spraw wewn.," *Gazeta Lwowska* May 17, 1936, no. 113, p. 1. See also: *Kto był kim w Drugiej Rzeczypospolitej*, ed. J.M. Majchrowski in co-operation with G. Mazur and K. Stepan, Warszawa: "BGW," 1994, p. 27 et seq.; M. Czarniawski, *Sławoj Składkowski w legendzie*, Białystok: Wydawca Marek Czarniawski, 2007; M. Sioma, "Obcy wśród swoich: losy gen. dyw. Sławoja Felicjana Składkowskiego w latach 1939–1941," *Annales Universitatis Mariae Curie-Skłodowska* 2005, vol. 60, pp. 193–207; Z. Landau, "Sławoj Felicjan Składkowski," [in:] *Polski Słownik Biograficzny*, ed. H. Markiewicz, co-operation with M. Adrianek et al., vol. 38: *Skarbek Aleksander–Słomka Jan*, Warszawa–Kraków: PAN, 1997–1998, pp. 193–197.

[222] K. Iłłakowiczówna, *Opowieść o moskiewskim męczeństwie. Złoty wianek*, Warszawa: Księgarnia F. Hoesick, 1927; K. Iłłakowiczówna, "Dusza księdza Butkiewicza," [in:]

characterized by "boundless stupidity and fabrications, modeled after the official propaganda and slanders of the ruling circles of Sanation Poland."[223] Both were dedicated to a Polish priest and social activist, who before World War I, had made great contributions to the development of Polish education in St. Petersburg, where he served as a priest. After 1919, he decided to remain in the USSR in order to support his Polish congregation, but his activities – for example, as vicar general of Archbishop Jan Feliks Cieplak – obviously did not meet with the approval of the authorities. Budkiewicz (along with several other priests, including Cieplak) was arrested and tried in Moscow on charges of spreading anti-Soviet propaganda and opposing the separation of church and state.[224] He was executed on March 31, 1923, in Moscow's Lubyanka Prison. Both the trial and murder were reported in the press of the time.[225]

The Bulletin presented Budkiewicz as a counterrevolutionary and mocked Iłłakowiczówna for trying to portray him as a "national hero, who like the original Christians, died a 'martyr's death' in defense of the 'faith' of Christ."[226] The poem "Opowieść o moskiewskim męczeństwie" was also accused of being "a disgraceful and unseemly libel against Lenin and the Soviet power"[227] as exemplified by the fragment of the poem quoted in the Bulletin.[228] According to Królik, the choice of works translated by Iłłakowiczówna further reflected her hostile attitude towards the USSR. As an example, he gave the translation of what he considered the "arch-reactionary"[229] book, *The Bolshevik Persecution of Christianity* by Francis McCullagh, who was a witness at Budkiewicz's trial. His account, which was decidedly unfavorable to the accusers, was published in London in 1924; Iłła's translation appeared in Kraków in the same year.[230]

---

eadem, *Słowik litewski…*, p. 164. The Bulletin and the article by Józef Kłos use the spelling "Butkiewicz"; in other materials, I have encountered the form "Budkiewicz."

[223] K. Królik, "O twórczości Kazimiery Iłłakowiczówny," *Biuletyn Informacyjno-Instrukcyjny* no. 7 (43), July 1955, p. 21 (APG, WUKPPiW, file ref. no. 103).

[224] On K.R. Budkiewicz see, e.g.: "Budkiewicz Konstanty Romuald," [in:] M. Korzeniowski, K. Latawiec, M. Gabryś-Sławińska, D. Tarasiuk, *Leksykon uchodźstwa polskiego w Rosji w latach I wojny światowej*, Lublin: Wydawnictwo UMCS, 2018, pp. 135–137.

[225] See, e.g.: J. Kłos, "Grymas szatana," *Wiadomości dla Duchowieństwa* 1923, no. 4, pp. 60–63; "Zamordowanie księdza prałata Budkiewicza," *Kurier Warszawski* April 4, 1923, no. 92, p. 1.

[226] K. Królik, "O twórczości Kazimiery Iłłakowiczówny," *Biuletyn Informacyjno-Instrukcyjny* no. 7 (43), July 1955, p. 22 (APG, WUKPPiW, file ref. no. 103).

[227] Ibidem, p. 21.

[228] Ibidem. Cf. K. Iłłakowiczówna, "Opowieść o moskiewskim męczeństwie…"

[229] K. Królik, "O twórczości Kazimiery Iłłakowiczówny," *Biuletyn Informacyjno-Instrukcyjny* no. 7 (43), July 1955, p. 22 (APG, WUKPPiW, file ref. no. 103).

[230] F. McCullagh, *The Bolshevik Persecution of Christianity*, London 1924; F. McCullagh, *Prześladowanie chrześcijaństwa przez bolszewizm rosyjski*, trans. K. Iłłakowiczówna, Kraków: Wydawnictwo Księży Jezuitów, 1924.

The issues discussed so far comprised the first part of Królik's article, while in the second part, the author moved on to a "political assessment"[231] of the two volumes mentioned at the beginning, *Poezje 1940–1954* and *Wiersze religijne. 1912–1954*. According to his testimony, the censor's office was completely indifferent to the religious poems included in the first of them. Absolutely unacceptable, on the other hand, and – from the censor's point of view – constituting intrusive elements[232] were the poems which reeked of "a conspicuous Home-Army theory about two enemies, which has been extended to our times."[233] As an example, he quoted two poems: "Zmroził mróz" [Chilled by frost] and "Wiersz na styczeń 1944" [A poem for January 1944]. As Budrowska noted, the latter poem was blocked by "Mysia Street" and had not been published until 1954.[234]

Another accusation, common in the "censorship criticism" of the first half of the 1950s, was leveled against *Poezje 1940–1954* for its lack of works affirming the post-war reality. However, it was somewhat balanced by "the poet's great sensitivity to the poetic nature of facts and things, to the lyricism of everyday matters of peasants, Gypsies, children, and the rural poor, which is particularly visible in the poems written during her stay in Romania."[235] In the assessment of the volume *Wiersze religijne. 1912–1954*, Iłła's insights about social problems, class inequality, and the plight of the working masses were also highlighted, especially in the poems written in the 1930s, such as "Kolęda Marianny" [Marianna's carol] and "Ballada o śpiewającym nożowcu" [The ballad of the singing knifer]; as an exemplification of these

---

[231] K. Królik, "O twórczości Kazimiery Iłłakowiczówny," *Biuletyn Informacyjno-Instrukcyjny* no. 7 (43), July 1955, p. 24 (APG, WUKPPiW, file ref. no. 103).

[232] Ibidem. The material quoted by Kamila Budrowska contains the form "interpretative elements," to which the researcher attached the qualifier *[sic!]*, which helped her signal "factual errors and fragments reflecting the peculiar worldview of the author." (K. Budrowska, "O twórczości Kazimiery Iłłakowiczówny…," p. 369). Thus, it may be another example of minor differences between the same issues of the Bulletins. Budrowska used the Bulletin which was in the fonds of documents with the reference number AAN, GUKPPiW, 420, folder 165/4 (this is the old reference number, i.e., before the changes were made to the GUKPPiW fonds at the beginning of 2019), while I used the resources after the aforementioned change and, therefore, received a folder with the reference number AAN, GUKPPiW, file ref. no 24. The Bulletin found there contains the phrase "intrusive elements" (p. 357/p. 23), which is the same as in the material from Gdańsk. Did the researcher use some other Bulletin, now unavailable?

[233] K. Królik, "O twórczości Kazimiery Iłłakowiczówny," *Biuletyn Informacyjno-Instrukcyjny* no. 7 (43), July 1955, p. 24 (APG, WUKPPiW, file ref. no. 103).

[234] Ibidem, pp. 24–25. Cf. K. Iłłakowiczówna, "Zmroził mróz," [in:] eadem, *Poezje 1940–1954…*, p. 145; eadem, "Wiersz na styczeń 1944," [in:] eadem, *Lekkomyślne serce*, Warszawa: "Czytelnik," 1959, p. 20.

[235] K. Królik, "O twórczości Kazimiery Iłłakowiczówny," *Biuletyn Informacyjno-Instrukcyjny* no. 7 (43), July 1955, p. 25 (APG, WUKPPiW, file ref. no. 103).

issues, the Bulletin quoted extensive excerpts from the poem "Do chrześcijan"[236] [To the Christians]. Królik also drew attention to those poems in which the religious vocabulary was, in his opinion, "merely a cover for the proclamation of outright secular aims."[237] As an example, he used two poems, "Wybraniec" [The chosen one] and "Walka" [The fight].[238] Two other poems, "Dzwony zadumane" [Bells of reflection] and "Słyszycie, jak się Polska modli" [Hear ye how Poland prays], were also classified as only ostensibly religious. The latter was seen as a longing for the Poland of the nobility, which did not fit into the new socialist order.[239]

The analysis of the material devoted to Iłłakowiczówna suggests that her two post-war poetry selections – or at least their ideological realizations – were received poorly by the Main Office, The assessment of the poet's skills was more favorable, though still ambiguous. According to Królik, some poems struck with simplicity and gave the "impression of naivety, carelessness, or even ineptitude."[240] It seems, however, that the censor did not treat this as an accusation, because this is what he wrote about the poem "Były lilie" [There were lilies] and the whole series *Z wycieczki jesiennej* [From the autumn trip], which included the above-mentioned poem: "It should be emphasized that Iłłakowiczówna's recent poems, written in 1955, are far removed in content from her pre-war work and represent a high artistic level."[241] As an illustration, he quoted three poems from the cycle – "Były lilie," "Pasł się obłok" [A cloud was grazing] and "Liście" [Leaves].[242] What the censor disliked was trivial

---

[236] Ibidem, p. 26. Cf. K. Iłłakowiczówna, "Do chrześcijan," [in:] eadem, *Słowik litewski...*, pp. 83–87; eadem, "Do chrześcijan," [in:] eadem, *Wiersze religijne. 1912–1954...*, pp. 101–103.

[237] K. Królik, "O twórczości Kazimiery Iłłakowiczówny," *Biuletyn Informacyjno-Instrukcyjny* no. 7 (43), July 1955, p. 25 (APG, WUKPPiW, file ref. no. 103).

[238] Ibidem, pp. 25–26. K. Iłłakowiczówna, "Walka"; "Wybraniec," [in:] eadem, *Z głębi serca*, Warszawa: Gebethner and Wolff, 1928, pp. 32–33; eadem, "Wybraniec"; "Walka," [in:] eadem, *Wiersze o Marszałku Piłsudskim...*, pp. 17, 19. Cf. eadem, "Walka," [in:] eadem, *Wiersze religijne. 1912–1954...*, p. 68.

[239] K. Królik, "O twórczości Kazimiery Iłłakowiczówny," *Biuletyn Informacyjno-Instrukcyjny* no. 7 (43), July 1955, p. 26 (APG, WUKPPiW, file ref. no. 103). Cf. K. Iłłakowiczówna, "Słyszycie, jak się Polska modli," [in:] eadem, *Trzy struny*, Petrograd: Skł. gł. Księg. Polska, 1917; eadem, "Słyszycie, jak się Polska modli," [in:] eadem, *Trzy struny*, Warszawa–Kraków: Towarzystwo Wydawnicze, 1919, pp. 5–7; eadem, "Słyszycie, jak się Polska modli," [in:] eadem, *Wiersze religijne. 1912–1954...*, pp. 12–13.

[240] K. Królik, "O twórczości Kazimiery Iłłakowiczówny," *Biuletyn Informacyjno-Instrukcyjny* no. 7 (43), July 1955, p. 28 (APG, WUKPPiW, file ref. no. 103).

[241] Ibidem. See: K. Iłłakowiczówna, "Z wycieczki jesiennej," *Twórczość* 1952, no. 2, pp. 3–4.

[242] K. Królik, "O twórczości Kazimiery Iłłakowiczówny," *Biuletyn Informacyjno-Instrukcyjny* no. 7 (43), July 1955, pp. 28–29 (APG, WUKPPiW, file ref. no. 103). Cf. K. Iłłakowiczówna, "Liście," "Były lilie," "Pasł się obłok," *Twórczość* 1952, no. 2, pp. 3–4.

subject matter, the detachment of works from real problems, and reducing literature to "strictly private"[243] issues. The above-listed criticism was in line with that voiced by "Mysia Street" against a number of works published in the first post-war decade (although with varying intensity, depending on the tightness of the censorship corset).

Before issuing a final opinion on Iłłakowiczówna's output, another subject was raised, namely, the evaluation of her poetry by Catholic literary critics. A remark was made that it was during the interwar period that the poet was criticized primarily for her religious works. One of the harsher texts that appeared at the time was *Pliszka w jaskini lwa. Rozważania nad książką panny Iłłakowiczówny Ścieżka obok drogi*[244] [A wagtail in the lion's cave: reflections on Miss Iłłakowiczówna's book *Ścieżka obok drogi*]. The example was not accidental, as in that case, the criticism came from the poet's own camp: Maria Jehanne Wielopolska, another supporter of Piłsudski, anticlerical atheist, writer, critic and publicist famous for her sharp tongue.[245]

However, as Królik writes, for the post-war literary critics, Iłłakowiczówna became one of the most outstanding poets, who skillfully combined patriotism and religion with folk and social themes. Her work was valued for its "transparency, realism, all-human aspect, originality, etc."[246] It was also appreciated for building a poetic statement on the models of folk songs and storytelling, giving primacy to imagination, ambience and emotion, concentrating on moral and religious issues, and finally, for projecting "'the poetic self' as a bard, a sorceress of her country and her people."[247] In the conclusion, Królik subscribes to this assessment of Iłłakowiczówna's work. He points out, however, that a serious part of her writing

---

[243] K. Królik, "O twórczości Kazimiery Iłłakowiczówny," *Biuletyn Informacyjno-Instrukcyjny* no. 7 (43), July 1955, p. 28 (APG, WUKPPiW, file ref. no. 103).

[244] M.J. Wielopolska, *Pliszka w jaskini lwa. Rozważania nad książką panny Iłłakowiczówny* Ścieżka obok drogi, Warszawa: Drukarnia J. Zielony, 1939.

[245] On M.J. Wielopolska see, e.g.: H. Faryna-Paszkiewicz, *Polemira. Niesłusznie zapomniana*, Warszawa: Wydawnictwo Nisza i Narodowe Centrum Kultury, 2016; M. Jaworska, "Prababka polskiej rewolucji kobiecej – Maria Jehanne Wielopolska," *Akant* 2007, no. 12, pp. 22–23; L. Marzec, *Maria-Jehanne Wielopolska, Wielkopolski Słownik Pisarek*, https://pisarki.fandom.com/wiki/Maria-Jehanne_Wielopolska (accessed January 31, 2021).

[246] K. Królik, "O twórczości Kazimiery Iłłakowiczówny," *Biuletyn Informacyjno-Instrukcyjny* no. 7 (43), July 1955, p. 29 (APG, WUKPPiW, file ref. no. 103).

[247] Ibidem. See, e.g. the reviews of her post-war works published before 1955: W. Bąk, "Kazimiera Iłłakowiczówna," *Świat* October 24, 1948, no. 43, p. 2; M. Głowiński, "O sztuce miniatury" (in the series *Wśród Książek*), *Twórczość* 1955, no. 7, pp. 162–165; B. Mamoń, "O wierszach Kazimiery Iłłakowiczówny…," pp. 12, 15.

devoted to glorifying Sanation and its leaders, and full of hatred towards the Soviet Union, has an objectively harmful political overtone. Therefore, the positive sides of Iłłakowiczówna's work cannot obscure what cannot be condoned.

This means that when assessing Iłłakowiczówna's poetry, one should see both sides of her work.[248]

3.4. On a Discussion of the Poem "Oskarżam" by Mikołaj Rostworowski

> *The attitude of the voivodeship censors towards Roztworowski's poem is a clear example of using a club, instead of a lancet.*[249]

Between 1952–1956, censorship offices held discussions on selected titles. In the majority of cases, these were prose works which I analyze in the next section of the book. Poetry was examined only twice. One poem was Bogdan Brzeziński's "Egzamin" [Examination] presented at the end of 1954; the other poem was "Oskarżam" [I accuse] by Mikołaj Rostworowski,[250] reviewed at the end of 1953. It comes from the collection *Przeciw nocy* [Against the night] published in the same year by "Pax."[251] As Zbigniew Banderczak noted in his review of the volume in *Tygodnik Powszechny*, almost all the poems from that collection (as well as its review) had been printed in the weekly *Dziś i Jutro*.[252]

The censorship teams that undertook the effort to interpret the work were not kind to the poet: they unanimously called for the removal of the poem in

---

[248] K. Królik, "O twórczości Kazimiery Iłłakowiczówny," *Biuletyn Informacyjno-Instrukcyjny* no. 7 (43), July 1955, p. 30 (APG, WUKPPiW, file ref. no. 103).

[249] "Podsumowanie dyskusji nad wierszem Roztworowskiego pt. 'Oskarżam,'" *Biuletyn Informacyjno-Instrukcyjny* no. 11/12 (23/24), November/December 1953, p. 16 (APG, WUKPPiW, file ref. no. 9).

[250] In the Bulletin spelled Roztworowski. Both forms of the surname occur in the literature, but the "Rostworowski" spelling is more common.

[251] M. Rostworowski, "Oskarżam," [in:] idem, *Przeciw nocy*, Warszawa: Instytut Wydawniczy "Pax," 1953, p. 25; K. Bażańska, "Satyra w terenie. Uwagi o dyskusji nad tekstami Brzezińskiego," *Biuletyn Informacyjno-Instrukcyjny* no. 11/12 (35/36), November/December 1954, pp. 27–36 (APG, WUKPPiW, file ref. no. 59). See also: K. Budrowska, "Od orderu do 'zapisu'…," pp. 86–87.

[252] See the reviews of the collection: J. Górski, "Moje trzy grosze," *Dziś i Jutro* April 11, 1954, no. 15, p. 4; Z. Jastrzębski, "Sprawy trudne i bliskie"; Z. Banderczak, "Przeciw nocy," *Tygodnik Powszechny* February 7, 1954, no. 6, pp. 5–6.

its entirety, deeming it erroneous, diversionary and harmful.[253] The results of the discussion were quite conclusive, as the text had been inspected in a number of offices, including in Bydgoszcz, Gdańsk, Kraków, Lublin, Łódź and Wrocław. In spite of this, the superiors defended the work, pointing out numerous mistakes and shortcomings in the subordinates' interpretations.

One could say, paraphrasing the Bulletin's newspeak, that the secular but nonetheless Catholic Rostworowski came "from foreign positions."[254] What the editorial board thought the rank-and-file functionaries failed to recognize was the processes that had been occurring within the Catholic intelligentsia community. As early as 1947, the "Pax" Association was established by the group centered around the weekly *Dziś i Jutro* (of which the poet soon became the editor-in-chief) and directed by Bolesław Piasecki. It allowed the communists to at least partially surveil the Polish Church, not only in its "soc-Pax" version.[255] In 1953, several difficult years began for the whole "Pax" environment. After the arrest of the Primate of the Millennium, and the election of Bishop Michał Klepacz (subordinate to the communists) as the chairman of the Polish Episcopate, "Pax" ceased to play the role of an intermediary between the communists and the Episcopate, and thus its significance – in the political sense – diminished in the eyes of the authorities.[256]

All this, however, did not seem to have much influence on the assessment of the poem presented in the Bulletin, because the censors did not refer to the aforementioned events nor "did [they] pay attention to the fact that the author was a Catholic who wrote for a particular reader – and that the publisher was 'Pax.'"[257]

---

[253] "Podsumowanie dyskusji nad wierszem Roztworowskiego pt. 'Oskarżam,'" *Biuletyn Informacyjno-Instrukcyjny* no. 11/12 (23/24), November/December 1953, p. 16 (APG, WUKPPiW, file ref. no. 9).

[254] "Działalność wydawnictwa 'Czytelnik' w 1951 r.," *Biuletyn Informacyjno-Instrukcyjny* no. 5, May 1952, p. 21 (APG, WUKPPiW, file ref. no. 90).

[255] M. Głowiński, "Powieść na miarę naszych czasów (*Obywatele* Kazimierza Brandysa)," [in:] idem, *Rytuał i demagogia. Trzynaście szkiców o sztuce zdegradowanej*, Warszawa: Wydawnictwo "Open," 1992, p. 57. See, e.g.: Z. Przetakiewicz, *Od ONR-u do Pax-u*, Warszawa: Wydawnictwo Prasy Lokalnej, 2010; A. Kołodziejczyk, "Bolesław Piasecki i jego idea," [in:] *Komu służył PAX. Materiały z sympozjum "Od Pax-u do Civitas Christiana" zorganizowanego przez Katolickie Stowarzyszenie Civitas Christiana, 30–31 stycznia 2008 roku*, ed. S. Bober, Warszawa: Instytut Wydawniczy "Pax," 2008, pp. 27–50. See also: "Słowa a fakty. Przyczynek do oceny postawy episkopatu polskiego," *Biuletyn Informacyjno-Instrukcyjny* no. 3 (15), March 1953, pp. 29–35 (APG, WUKPPiW, file ref. no. 17).

[256] M. Tunak, *1953–1955 – trudne lata dla środowiska Pax*, Historia.org.pl, February 26, 2018, https://historia.org.pl/2018/02/26/1953-1956-trudne-lata-dla-srodowiska-pax/ (accessed January 31, 2021).

[257] "Podsumowanie dyskusji nad wierszem Roztworowskiego pt. 'Oskarżam,'" *Biuletyn Informacyjno-Instrukcyjny* no. 11/12 (23/24), November/December 1953, p. 17 (APG, WUKPPiW, file ref. no. 9).

Without taking into account the poet's ideological background, the functionaries could not appreciate the fact that he explored current topics, which most of his colleagues had avoided. Rostworowski's poem tells the tragic fate of Major Jerzy Sosnowski, an outstanding intelligence officer of the Second Republic of Poland. Wrongly accused of treason by the Sanation authorities, he died during World War II in circumstances that remain unexplained to this day.[258]

The Bulletin pointed out another consequence of the censors' ignorance: the fact that they applied the same assessment rules to a Catholic writer as to a Marxist author, which was a grave mistake. In the case of writers whose ideology was not exactly orthodox, one should always appreciate those aspects that were taken for granted with ideologically correct writers; in "Oskarżam," it was the stigmatization of the hostile activities of American imperialists. As mentioned earlier, the criteria of censorship were supposed to vary not only depending on the medium (books, film, radio), the method of distribution (titles intended only for libraries, etc.), the types of writing (fiction, scientific and professional literature, etc.), but also on the attitude and biography of the author and the publisher. The example of Rostworowski's evaluation shows once again that "employees of voivodeship branches are afraid to show leniency lest they fall out of favor and expose themselves to reprimand," and they forget that "a Catholic writer must be won over to the cause by meeting his or her attempts to fit into the new reality."[259]

Hence, if the rank-and-file functionaries were unable to see the positives, what errors did they notice in the work? Their attention was focused on details: they made "reservations about almost every stanza and every line."[260] According to them, the poem contained numerous attacks on People's Poland, as well as attempts to justify Sosnowski's actions as a spy and evoke pity in the reader for his tragic fate. They also made a range of other minor interpretative errors and criticized the artistic dimension of the poem. In her negative assessment, Lorber (the conceiver of the idea for the competition involving Wasilewska's novel), compared Rostworowski's work to Maria Konopnicka's poetry. However, according to the editors, "the very comparison of the poem's author to Konopnicka – contrary to the intention of comrade Lorber – suggested a high artistic level of the poem."[261]

---

[258] P. Kołakowski, A. Krzak, *Sprawa majora Jerzego Sosnowskiego w świetle dokumentów analitycznych Oddziału II SGWP i zeznań Franza Heinricha Pfeifera*, Warszawa: Wydawnictwo Demart, 2015.

[259] K. Budrowska, "Od orderu do 'zapisu'…," p. 86.

[260] "Podsumowanie dyskusji nad wierszem Roztworowskiego pt. 'Oskarżam,'" *Biuletyn Informacyjno-Instrukcyjny* no. 11/12 (23/24), November/December 1953, p. 18 (APG, WUKPPiW, file ref. no. 9).

[261] Ibidem, p. 20.

With so many negative evaluations, what was the solution? The Bulletin writes about the following compromise:

> The critical moments were discussed with the editors, who agreed with our arguments. As a result of the editor's discussions with the author, the poem was reworked and included in the collection. The author not only corrected the indicated lines, but inserted two more stanzas to give the whole a clearer emphasis.[262]

Considering that the report on the discussion of the poem was included in the last, double issue of the Bulletin in 1953, and the volume *Przeciw nocy* was published at the end of that year, it is highly probable that some of the suggestions presented during the debates and later in the Bulletin were incorporated into the new version of the poem. This is confirmed by the material in which the fragments criticized by the censors look different in the printed version, but also by the comparison of the "final draft" of the poem quoted in the Bulletin with the version published in the volume *Przeciw nocy*: apart from the change in the second line, no other modifications were made. The first illustration below shows the "final" draft of the poem as printed in the Bulletin; the second illustration is the actual final version from the "Pax" edition. The passages that were discussed in the Bulletin are shown in the table.

Tab. 1. Mikołaj Rostworowski, "Oskarżam" – changes introduced to the final version of the poem, signaled in the Bulletin.

Excerpts from the original version that were discussed in the Bulletin	The version published by "Pax"
[stanza did not appear in the original version]	…Z paniczami po społu polerował Dionizy kontuszowy konterfekt małorolnej Oj-czyzny. […Along with the lords, Dionizy po-lished the kontusz image of smallholder Home-land.]

Maria Konopnicka (1842–1910) – a Polish poet, novelist, literary critic, and translator of the Positivist period; an activist for women's equality and Poland regaining independence; one of the most prominent Polish writers.

[262] Ibidem.

Tab. 1 (continued)

Excerpts from the original version that were discussed in the Bulletin	The version published by "Pax"
Na sędziowskim, na stole z pruskim kwasem ampułki. **Jaką Polskę żeś kochał od frasunku pożółkły?** [On the judge's table Prussian acid ampoules. **What Poland did you love, yellowed with vexation?**]	Na sędziowskim, na stole z pruskim kwasem ampułki. Jakiej Polski żeś szukał, od frasunku pożółkły? [On the judge's table Prussian acid ampoules. What Poland did you seek out, yellowed with vexation?]
Pańska miłość to była. Innej ziemi krajobraz w twoją duszę wpisało wilcze prawo niedobre. [**It was a lord's love**. The wicked jungle law instilled in your soul another country's landscape.]	Pańska droga to była. Innej ziemi krajobraz w twoją duszę wpisało wilcze prawo niedobre. [It was a lord's way. The wicked jungle law instilled in your soul another country's landscape.]
[stanza did not appear in the original version] […] **Z zajadłością biedniacką dźwigasz dolę szyderczą** – cudzoziemski najmita, najsmutniejszy dywersant. [**With pauper's viciousness you bear the mordant plight** – a foreign mercenary, most woeful saboteur.]	Łacno nawet zza morza takim synem frymarczyć, szczuć na ojców gdy z braćmi radlą ugór folwarczny. [Even from overseas it is easy to peddle such a son, to bait the fathers who with their brothers are tilling the fallow land. […] Z zajadłością oślepłą dźwigasz dolę szyderczą – cudzoziemski najmita, najsmutniejszy dywersant. [With blind viciousness you bear the mordant plight – a foreign mercenary, most woeful saboteur.]

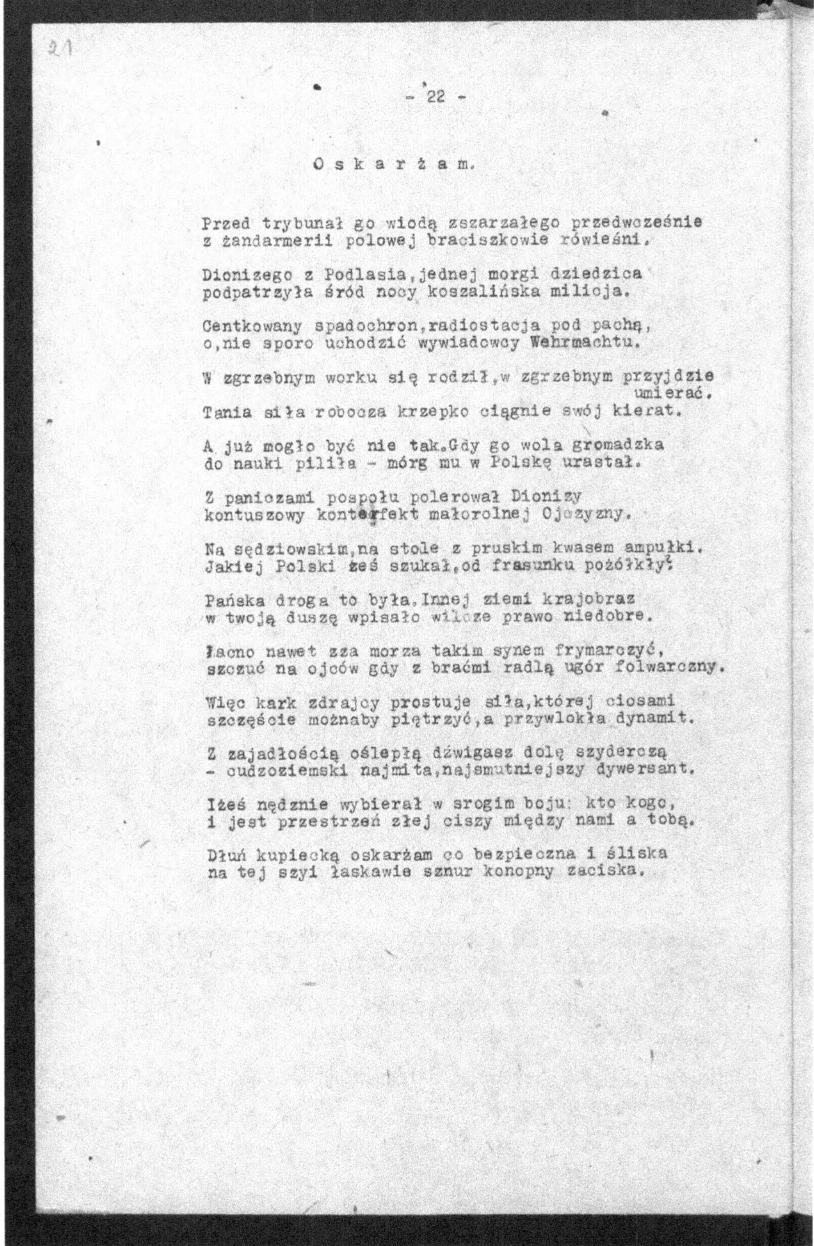

```
                          - 22 -


                    O s k a r ż a m.


Przed trybunał go wiodą zszarzałego przedwcześnie
z żandarmerii polowej braciszkowie rówieśni.

Dionizego z Podlasia,jednej morgi dziedzica
podpatrzyła śród nocy koszalińska milicja.

Centkowany spadochron,radiostacja pod pachą,
o,nie sporo uchodzić wywiadowcy Wehrmachtu.

W zgrzebnym worku się rodził,w zgrzebnym przyjdzie
                                            umierać.
Tania siła robocza krzepko ciągnie swój kierat.

A już mogło być nie tak.Gdy go wola gromadzka
do nauki piliła - mórg mu w Polskę urastał.

Z paniczami pospołu polerował Dionizy
kontuszowy kontrefekt małorolnej Ojczyzny.

Na sędziowskim,na stole z pruskim kwasem ampułki.
Jakiej Polski żeś szukał,od frasunku pożółkły?

Pańska droga to była.Innej ziemi krajobraz
w twoją duszę wpisało wilcze prawo niedobre.

Łacno nawet zza morza takim synem frymarczyć,
szczuć na ojców gdy z braćmi radlą ugór folwarczny.

Więc kark zdrajcy prostuje siła,której ciosami
szczęście możnaby piętrzyć,a przywlokła dynamit.

Z zajadłością oślepłą dźwigasz dolę szyderczą
- cudzoziemski najmita,najsmutniejszy dywersant.

Iżeś nędznie wybierał w srogim boju: kto kogo,
i jest przestrzeń złej ciszy między nami a tobą.

Dłuń kupiecką oskarżam co bezpieczna i śliska
na tej szyi łaskawie sznur konopny zaciska.
```

Fig. 10a. The version of Mikołaj Rostworowski's poem published in the Bulletin: a compromise between the censorship office, the editors of "Pax" and the author ("Podsumowanie dyskusji nad wierszem Roztworowskiego pt. 'Oskarżam,'" *Biuletyn Informacyjno-Instrukcyjny* no. 11/12 (23/24), November/December 1953, p. 20 (APG, WUKPPiW, file ref. no. 9)).

O   S   K   A   R   Ż   A   M

Przed trybunał go wiodą, zszarzałego przedwcześnie,
w mundurowej eskorcie braciszkowie rówieśni.

Dionizego z Podlasia, jednej morgi dziedzica,
podpatrzyła śród nocy koszalińska milicja.

Centkowany spadochron, radiostacja pod pachą,
o, niesporo uchodzić wywiadowcy Wehrmachtu.

W zgrzebnym worku się rodził, w zgrzebnym przyjdzie umierać.
Tania siła robocza krzepko ciągnie swój kierat.

A już mogło być nie tak. Gdy go wola gromadzka
do nauki piliła — mórg mu w Polskę urastał.

. . . Z paniczami po społu polerował Dionizy
kontuszowy konterfekt małorolnej Ojczyzny.

Na sędziowskim, na stole z pruskim kwasem ampułki.
Jakiej Polski żeś szukał, od frasunku pożółkły?

Pańska droga to była. Innej ziemi krajobraz
w twoją duszę wpisało wilcze prawo niedobre.

Łacno nawet zza morza takim synem frymarczyć,
szczuć na ojców, gdy z braćmi radlą ugór folwarczny.

Więc kark zdrajcy prostuje siła, której ciosami
szczęście można by piętrzyć, a przywlokła dynamit.

Z zajadłością oślepłą dźwigasz dolę szyderczą
— cudzoziemski najmita, najsmutniejszy dywersant.

Iżeś nędznie wybierał w srogim boju: kto kogo
i jest przestrzeń złej ciszy między nami a tobą,

dłoń kupiecką oskarżam, co bezpieczna i śliska
na tej szyi łaskawie sznur konopny zaciska.

— 25 —

Fig. 10b. The final version of Mikołaj Rostworowski's poem "Oskarżam," published in the volume *Przeciw nocy*: a compromise between the censorship office, the editors of "Pax" and the author (M. Rostworowski, "Oskarżam," [in:] idem, *Przeciw nocy*, Warszawa: Instytut Wydawniczy "Pax," 1953, p. 25).

3.5. Other Poetic Works Discussed in the Bulletins: (Not Only) Norwid, Pasternak, Lenin, Mayakovsky, and Jasieński

> *How to recognize the enemy, how to distinguish*
> *healthy criticism from poisoned, what should not be*
> *questioned, and what must not be published*
> *– no magic wand can show censors these things.*[263]

Apart from the examples discussed so far, poetic works appeared relatively rarely in the Bulletins. In January 1949, it was noted that one of the recurring "tricks" of the Catholic press was to include poems from the period of the partitions, which supposedly suggested that "Poland is not a sovereign country." The provided example was Norwid's poem "Do lilii polnej" [To the lily of the field], which was blocked from printing in *Posłaniec Matki Boskiej Saletyńskiej*.[264] Indeed, the issue of that journal did not contain the litany "Do Najświętszej Panny Maryi" [To the Blessed Virgin Mary] (because that is the actual title of the work), although it did appear in the same year in the anthology *Polska poezja Maryjna* [Polish Marian poetry].[265]

In March 1950, a fragment of Pasternak's poem "Warszawskoje szosse," published several times after 1943, was analyzed:

> Idą chłopy i pany, idą razem zbratani,
> idą z lagrów, z posiółków, z zesłania,
> idą śląskie pieruny, osiwiałe leguny,
> wspólnej drogi już nic nie przesłania.
> U nas wszyscy koledzy. Idzie więzień z Berezy,
> były glina i hrabia Chorąży, idzie cieśla spod Omska,
> idzie ślusarz z Radomska, hełm bojowy jednako im ciąży.[266]

---

[263] "Seminarium prasy (wyjątki z protokółu). Granice dopuszczalnej krytyki," *Biuletyn Instrukcyjny* no. 2, June 1945, p. 8 (APG, WUKPPiW, file ref. no. 210).

[264] "Zagadnienie suwerenności państwowej," *Biuletyn Informacyjno-Szkoleniowy* no. 1/3, January 1949, p. 17 (APG, WUKPPiW, file ref. no. 196).

[265] Cf. *Posłaniec Matki Boskiej Saletyńskiej* R: 28, 12.1948 and C.K. Norwid, "Do Najświętszej Panny Maryi Litania," [in:] *Polska poezja Maryjna*, anthology laid out by T. Jodełka, preface by J. Zawieyski, cover and vignettes by T. Gronowski, Niepokalanów: Centrala "Milicji Niepokalanej," 1949, pp. 187–196.

[266] "Front Narodowy," *Biuletyn Szkoleniowy* no. 1, March (May) 1950, p. 27 (APG, WUKPPiW, file ref. no. 328). Cf. L. Pasternak, "Warszawskoje szosse," [in:] idem, *Słowa z daleka*, Moscow: Związek Patriotów Polskich w ZSRR, 1944, pp. 18–19; idem, "Warszawskoje szossé," [in:] *Wiersze i pieśni Pierwszej Armii Polskiej w ZSRR...*, p. 21; idem, "Warszawskoje szosse," *Co Dzień Niesie. Nowiny dla Żołnierzy* 1946, no. 6, p. 4.

[The peasants and the lords are coming, fraternized
Returning from forced labor, *poseloks*[267] and exiles,
Silesian Hanyses, gray-haired legionaries
There's nothing to stop them walking side by side.
We are all friends. Here comes a prisoner from Bereza,
An ex-copper and count Ensign, a carpenter from Omsk,
A locksmith from Radomsko, a combat helmet weighs all the same.]

The material did not provide the poet's surname, but it obviously referred to Leon Pasternak, a satirist and writer, communist activist, and, what is important in this context, an officer of the 1st Division of the Polish Army. He was the author of the extremely popular song of the 1st Division entitled *Oka* [The Oka] and, according to some, the author of the lyrics to the song-hymn *My, Pierwsza Dywizja* [We, the 1st Division].[268]

The poet was accused of portraying the formation of the division in an unfair way, i.e., in a manner inconsistent with the prevailing interpretation of the time. Pasternak allegedly ignored the fact that both the 1st Division established in the USSR, as well as People's Guard and People's Army formed in Poland, were "<u>based on a broad national front, at the head of which stood the working class,</u> [...] revolutionaries, activists and fighters of the KPP [Communist Party of Poland – AWG]"[269] (original emphasis):

On Pasternak's poem see, e.g.: A. Morawiec, "Brr, Bereza. Polish Literature towards the Confinement Centre in Bereza Kartuska. 1934–1939," *Acta Universitatis Lodziensis. Folia Litteraria Polonica* 2019, no. 4, pp. 250–251; J. Przymanowski, *Ze 101 frontowych nocy*, Warszawa: "Książka i Wiedza," 1961, pp. 35–38; *Wybór poezji o żołnierzach PSZ na Zachodzie, związanych z żołnierzami Polski Podziemnej i Powstania Warszawskiego wspólną ideą wywalczenia Polski wolnej i niepodległej* (in the series *Dodatek Literacki* no. 774), compiled by E. Romiszewski, Polskie Radio May 10, 1975, https://www.polskieradio.pl/13/3707/Audio/291108,Dodatek-literacki-nr-774 (accessed January 31, 2021).

[267] Settlements, mostly farms in the USSR, were exiled families were sent.

[268] It was sung to the tune of *My, Pierwsza Brygada* [We, the First Brigade].
See, e.g.: A. Romanowski, "'My, Pierwsza Brygada': powstanie pieśni – przemiany – recepcja społeczna," *Pamiętnik Literacki* 1988, issue 2, pp. 267–296.

[269] "Front Narodowy," *Biuletyn Szkoleniowy* no. 1, March (May) 1950, p. 27 (APG, WUKPPiW, file ref. no. 328).
Gwardia Ludowa (GL, People's Guard) – a communist underground armed organization created in 1942 by the communist Polish Workers' Party in German-occupied Poland with sponsorship from the USSR; in 1944, it was incorporated in Armia Ludowa (AL, People's Army): a communist Soviet-backed partisan force whose aims were to fight against Nazi Germany in occupied Poland, support the Soviet Red Army against the German forces and aid in the creation of a pro-Soviet communist government in Poland.

the fact that the ranks of this army included a "count" and a "copper" resulted from the specific conditions, from the fact that they happened to be in the territory of the USSR. In Poland, the "count" and "copper" stood on the opposite side of the barricade. That is why it is harmful to register uncritically the wrongly generalized fact that the count fought side by side with a worker, and a National Democrat next to a communist.[270]

Since the poem by the former Bereza prisoner had been written "when the Army was being formed,"[271] the recommendation was not to remove it from the collections published then, but reprints in the press were forbidden. This was of course a severe punishment for the poet, but not as severe as the one inflicted on him a few years earlier, when he had to pay a much higher price "for his creative freedom"[272]; as Arkadiusz Morawiec writes, it was for his literary work that Pasternak had been sent to Bereza.

In April 1954, the Bulletin printed a small note, showing what criteria were taken into consideration when evaluating translations of (not only) poetic texts:

> In the work *O W.I. Leninie. Zbiór recytacji i pieśni w 30-tą rocznicę śmierci W.I. Lenina* [On V.I. Lenin. A collection of recitations and songs on the 30th anniversary of V.I. Lenin's death], published by the KW PZPR[273] in Poznań – Mayakovsky's poem "Nie wierzymy" [We cannot believe] translated by Bruno Jasieński was included. The Poznań office overlooked the name of the translator. Bruno Jasieński had been exposed in the USSR as a spy and saboteur.[274]

---

[270] Ibidem.

[271] Ibidem.
Miejsce Odosobnienia w Berezie Kartuskiej (Bereza Kartuska Prison) – a prison operated by Poland's Sanation government from 1934 to 1939 in the town Bereza Kartuska in Poland (today Belarus); it was established to isolate and demoralize political opponents of the Sanation government such as National Democrats, communists, members of the Polish People's Party, as well as Ukrainian and Belarusian nationalists.

[272] A. Morawiec, "Brr, Bereza. Polish Literature towards the Confinement Centre in Bereza Kartuska. 1934–1939…," pp. 250–251 (see the respective chapter "Pasternak's Case").

[273] Komitet Wojewódzki (KW) PZPR – the Regional Committee of the Polish United Workers' Party.

[274] "Przegląd ingerencji nr 3/54 Departamentu Publikacyj Nieperiodycznych GUKPPiW poświęcony omówieniu kilku różnorodnych zagadnień," *Biuletyn Informacyjno-Instrukcyjny* no. 4 (28), April 1954, p. 32 (APG, WUKPPiW, file ref. no. 48); cf. W. Majakowski, "Nie wierzymy," trans. B. Jasieński, [in:] *O W.I. Leninie. Zbiór recytacji i pieśni w 30-tą rocznicę śmierci W.I. Lenina*, trans. A. Ważyk et al., Poznań: KW PZPR, 1954, pp. 12–13.

In this case, it was not the translation itself that was criticized, but the choice of the translator. Bruno Jasieński, one of the most famous Polish futurists, could not count on the goodwill of "Mysia Street" (unlike other translators featured in the collection, such as Adam Ważyk and Antoni Słonimski). In 1929, Jasieński had moved to the USSR and fit easily into the Soviet reality. However, in 1937, during the great purge, he was arrested by the NKVD and shot a year later.

***

Aside from the poetic works discussed so far, the Bulletins contained some additional comments or slightly longer materials on poetry. Most often, post-war works or those created during the inferno were presented.[275] Apart from the aforementioned Norwid, only a few references were made to the poetic tradition of the 19th century,[276] even though the country was constantly working to adapt its literary tradition to the requirements of the new reality, while the fathers of the "refurbished" canon explained "the essence of assimilating cultural heritage."[277]

---

[275] "Ze sprawozdań Kierowników Wojewódzkich Biur," *Biuletyn Instrukcyjny* no. 2, June 1945, p. 14 (APG, WUKPPiW, file ref. no. 210).

[276] See: "Przegląd ingerencji nr 3/54 Departamentu Publikacyj Nieperiodycznych GUKPPiW poświęcony omówieniu kilku różnorodnych zagadnień," *Biuletyn Informacyjno-Instrukcyjny* no. 4 (28), April 1954, pp. 35–36 (APG, WUKPPiW, file ref. no. 48).

[277] M. Zawodniak, *Klasycy literatury i klasycy marksizmu…*, p. 14.

4. PROSE WORKS

In their youth, our functionaries absorbed a view
that profiteers or cooperative directors deserve better
treatment than writers or artists.[278]

Prose works were the most frequently discussed literary subject in the Bulletins. The monthly presented works of fiction (novels, short stories), borderline genres (reportages) as well as scholarly and popular science books. Some of them were the topic of separate articles, others were discussed in collective studies. The review of the Bulletin's prose works will begin with one of the synthesized studies, which reflected on how to properly assess literary selections.

4.1. How to Review Select Prose? Nałkowska, Borowski and Bartelski

A censor must not fall from one extreme into another
and interfere "mindlessly."[279]

Censors, both those assessing prose and those evaluating poetry, reported major problems with inspecting so-called non-homogenous titles, that is "collections or selections, which are compiled works often on the most varied topics, written in different periods."[280] According to their superiors, the most common mistake made by the "foot soldiers" was to treat such publications as a collection of independent parts and "discuss each work separately, without a generalizing synthesis."[281] Such a strategy usually made it difficult to arrive at a clearly formulated decision, which was, ultimately, the essence of censorial evaluation.

---

[278] "Konfiskata 'słówek' przy niewidzeniu całości," *Biuletyn Informacyjno-Szkoleniowy* no. 1/3, January 1949, p. 36 (APG, WUKPPiW, file ref. no. 196).

[279] "Przykłady dobrych i złych ingerencji gospodarczych," *Biuletyn Informacyjno-Instrukcyjny* no. 10, October 1952, p. 24 (APG, WUKPPiW, file ref. no. 75).

[280] "O recenzjach zbiorków literackich," *Biuletyn Informacyjno-Instrukcyjny* no. 4 (16), April 1953, p. 26 (APG, WUKPPiW, file ref. no. 16).

[281] Ibidem.

For instance, the censorship review of Zofia Nałkowska's *Medallions*, fragments of which are quoted in the article on the assessment of collections of literary works, was presented as an outcome of such practices.[282] Indeed, it appears that the censor evaluated each of the eight short stories individually, without trying to formulate an opinion about the whole publication. In the following "manner the entire volume was parceled out,"[283] and the final request to discontinue the publication took into account neither its ideological rating, "nor the significance and value of the entire book, nor the person of the author"[284]:

[excerpts from the censorship review of Zofia Nałkowska's *Medallions* quoted in the Bulletin].

The novella "The Hole" – The author describes the suffering of a woman who survived the Pawiak prison, the transport to the camp, and the camp. The novella is completely apolitical, naturalistic.
The novella "The Cemetery Lady." The action takes place in a cemetery during the occupation; reflections. The novella is apolitical, strong accents of pessimism.
The novella "By the Railway Track." The content of the novella – escape from a railroad transport during the Nazi occupation, naturalistic.[285]

Medallions was first published in 1946. By 1953, the year when the discussed Bulletin was printed, there had been four editions of the book.[286] The above-quoted fragment probably comes from a censorship review drafted in September 1951.[287]

---

[282] Zofia Nałkowska (1884–1954) – a Polish writer, journalist and playwright; after World War II, she was a member of the Main Commission for the Investigation of German Crimes in Poland committed between 1939 and 1945 in Poland or abroad against Polish citizens or persons of Polish nationality and against foreigners who were in Poland at the time.

[283] "O recenzjach zbiorków literackich," *Biuletyn Informacyjno-Instrukcyjny* no. 4 (16), April 1953, p. 26 (APG, WUKPPiW, file ref. no. 16).

[284] Ibidem.

[285] Ibidem.

[286] Z. Nałkowska, *Medaliony*, Warszawa: "Czytelnik," 1946; Second Edition: ibidem 1949; Third Edition: ibidem 1952; Fourth Edition: ibidem 1953. English version: Z. Nałkowska, *Medallions*, trans. D. Kuprel, Evanston: Northwestern University Press, 2000.

[287] "Ingerencje cenzorskie GUKPPiW, WUKPPiW w Bydgoszczy, Gdańsku, Katowicach, Krakowie, Łodzi w okresie VI 1950–XI 1950, IV 1951–XII 1951 w publikacjach nieperiodycznych Spółdzielni Wydawniczej 'Czytelnik'. Recenzje prewencyjne i wtórne" (AAN, GUKPPiW, file ref. no. 2854, pp. 716–717; Z. Nałkowska, *Medaliony*, censorship review from September 19, 1951). See also: Fig. 11a–c.

GŁÓWNY URZĄD KONTROLI PRASY,
PUBLIKACJI i WIDOWISK

Dział Publikacji Nieperiodycznych

1. Tytuł i podtytuł *Medaliony*

2. Autor (rzy) *Z. Nałkowska*

3. Przedsiębiorstwo wydawnicze *Czytelnik*

4. Wysokość nakładu *7130*   5. Książka nowa, czy wznowienie

6. Praca oryginalna, czy tłumaczenie   7. Język oryginału

8. Data przekazania pracy recenzentowi *19.9.51 r.*

U W A G I: Recenzja powinna między innymi dawać odpowiedź na następujące kwestie:
a) Tematyka i problematyka książki.
b) Ideologiczne i społeczno-wychowawcze znaczenie książki.

RECENZJA

Z bioru nowel.

Nowela I " Profesor Spanner"

Autorka opisuje badanie pracownika instytutu anatomicznego zeznajacego jak uczeni niemieccy fabrykowali mydło z tłuszczu zamordowanych ludzi Nowela naturalistyczna, problematyka wydaje się obecnie niewskazana, co innego w roku 45,6 a nawet jeszcze w 1947.

Nowela II "Dno"

Autorka opisuje cierpienia kobiety która przeszła przez "Pawiak", transport do obozu i obóz. Nowela chociaż wiele apolityczna, naturalistyczna.

Nowela III "Kobieta cmentarna"

akcja noweli rozgrywa się na cmentarzu, w czasie okupacji, refleksje. Nowela apolityczna, duże akcenty pesymizmu, (str 36 słowa wypowiedziane przez antysemitkę winny być skreślone)

Nowela IV "Przy torze kolejowym"

Treść noweli - ucieczka z transportu kolejowego w okresie okupacji hitlerowskiej, naturalistyczna.

Nowela V "Dwojra Zielona"

Treść noweli- żydówka opowiada swe okupacyjne przeżycia. (str 56 żargon niewłaściwe) nowela naturalistyczna, politycznie bardzo słaba.

Nowela VI " wiza "

I zdania noweli politycznie szkodliwe, (str 64 linia 20, szkodliwe) Treść noweli wspomnienia z obozu.

G. U. K. P. wzór № 1 (P.N.)

SZG. Zakł. 6 Zam: 455

Fig. 11a. The first page of the censorship review of Zofia Nałkowska's *Medallions* from September 19, 1951 (AAN, GUKPPiW, file ref. no. 2854, p. 716).

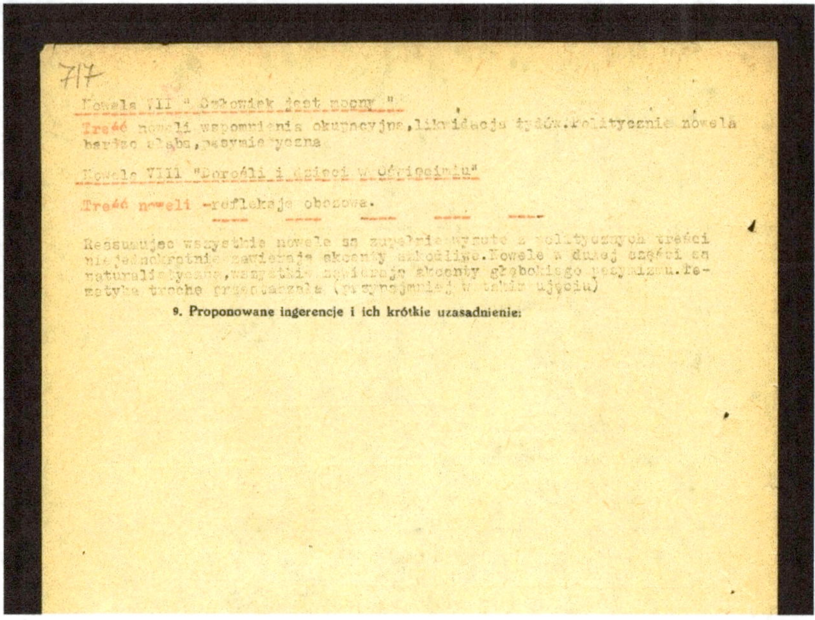

Fig. 11b. The upper part of the second page of the censorship review of Zofia Nałkowska's *Medallions* from September 19, 1951 (AAN, GUKPPiW, file ref. no. 2854, p. 717).

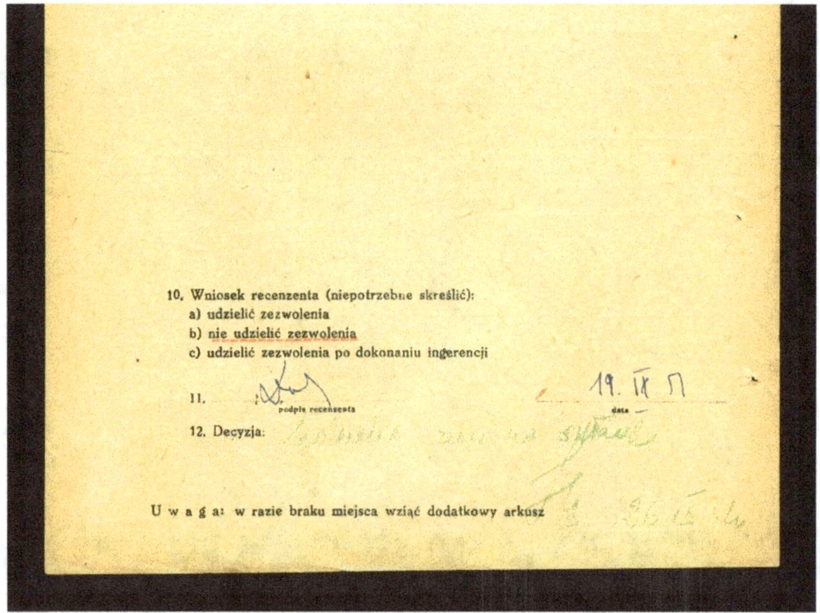

Fig. 11c. The lower part of the second page of the censorship review of Zofia Nałkowska's *Medallions* from September 19, 1951 (AAN, GUKPPiW, file ref. no. 2854, p. 717).

The Bulletin faithfully reproduced the text of the review, modifying only the layout and removing an interjection that had been placed next to the paragraph about the novella "The Cemetery Lady": "(p. 38, the words uttered by the antisemitic woman should be deleted)."[288] The whole quoted review was, in fact, divided into eight separate fragments corresponding to the eight novellas – this arrangement was additionally emphasized by the numbering: novella 1. "Professor Spanner," novella 2. "The Hole"… etc.

Thus, there should be no doubt that the parts quoted in the Bulletin were transcribed from this very review. However, the Bulletin indicated the lack of a summary, whereas at the end of the review, a succinct assessment of the whole collection was given:

> To recapitulate, all the novellas are completely devoid of political elements; they often contain harmful accents. The novellas are mostly naturalistic, all of them have accents of deep pessimism. The subject matter is somewhat outdated (at least in this formulation).[289]

Indeed, this brief summary can hardly be considered exhaustive, but it was, nevertheless, an attempt at a synthesis. One can, of course, assume that the Bulletin's article was based on yet another review, devoid of this final fragment, but remarkably similar to the one from September 1951, or simply one that copied the theses of that very review, omitting the criticized summary. After all, we know that censors copied their colleagues' reviews (one Bulletin wrote about two identical reviews of Boris Zhitkov's booklet[290]), so this possibility should be taken into account. Perhaps the censors referred to the cited review, but did not find its summary satisfactory. The fact that at least some of the functionaries read the above-mentioned "synthesis" is evidenced by its fragment quoted in the Bulletin from August 1952.[291] The editors considered it a gross display of ignorance and

---

[288] Ibidem, p. 716. See: Fig. 11a and cf. "O recenzjach zbiorków literackich," *Biuletyn Informacyjno-Instrukcyjny* no. 4 (16), April 1953, p. 26 (APG, WUKPPiW, file ref. no. 16).

[289] "Ingerencje cenzorskie GUKPPiW, WUKPPiW w Bydgoszczy, Gdańsku, Katowicach, Krakowie, Łodzi w okresie VI 1950–XI 1950, IV 1951–XII 1951 w publikacjach nieperiodycznych Spółdzielni Wydawniczej 'Czytelnik.' Recenzje prewencyjne i wtórne" (AAN, GUKPPiW, file ref. no. 2854, p. 717 (Z. Nałkowska, *Medaliony*; censorship review from September 19, 1951)). See: Fig. 11b.

[290] I present the case of copying the review of Zhitkov's booklet *O słoniu* in the chapter "On the Work on Children's Books."

[291] "Recenzja z pozycji literackiej, cz. I" (in the series *O wyższy poziom pracy nad książką*), *Biuletyn Informacyjno-Instrukcyjny* no. 8, August 1952, p. 19 (APG, WUKPPiW, file ref. no. 81).

agreed that the request of the reviewer to withhold permission should be denied. Thanks to the September 1951 review preserved in the archives, we can confirm that the request was declined by a supervisor's decision a week later, allowing for the book's typesetting.[292]

Finally, the censorship review from September 19, 1951 is quoted by Dariusz Jarosz – it is identical to the one preserved in the GUKPPiW fonds in the AAN.[293] According to Kamila Budrowska, fragments of this review are quoted in the August 1952 issue of the Bulletin, which affirms one of the presented hypotheses. On the other hand, the researcher writes that it is in this review that we find a "grossly stupid" postulate to incorporate a story portraying a positive Polish character into the *Medallions*; neither in Jarosz's piece, nor in the review preserved in the AAN (which he quotes), nor in the August issue of the Bulletin did I find such a thoughtless postulate. Was there a different review?[294]

The second problem faced by the censors of non-homogenous titles was to present the evolution of a given author's writing "reliably" (i.e., in accordance with the political line at the time). The solution, similarly to poetry selections, was to provide the publication with appropriate explanatory paratexts:

> When it comes to today's writers, the fighters for socialist realism in literature (e.g., Putrament) whose line of development is not direct, or when it comes to a selection of dead writers for whom this line was not completed (Hollender, Ginczanka) – the inclusion of an introduction defining the writer's stance and ideological development is almost always necessary and we should demand such an introduction from the publisher.[295]

In Jerzy Putrament's case, explanatory introductions played a completely different role than in the case of Ginczanka and Hollender, both of whom were discussed in the part devoted to poetry. Putrament, a former "Żagary" member, easily found his way around the structures of the new government, so there was no need to elaborate on his choices from that period. On the other hand, the "flaw" of his biography, which required an explanation, was his sympathizing with the pre-war organizations that adhered to Catholic-nationalist ideals. Furthermore,

---

[292] See: Fig. 11c.

[293] Cf. D. Jarosz, *Zapisy cenzury z lat 1948–1955…*, p. 31 and "Ingerencje cenzorskie GUKPPiW, WUKPPiW w Bydgoszczy, Gdańsku, Katowicach, Krakowie, Łodzi w okresie VI 1950–XI 1950, IV 1951–XII 1951 w publikacjach nieperiodycznych Spółdzielni Wydawniczej 'Czytelnik'. Recenzje prewencyjne i wtórne" (AAN, GUKPPiW, file ref. no. 2854), pp. 716–717; Z. Nałkowska, *Medaliony*; censorship review from September 19, 1951.

[294] K. Budrowska, *Writers, Literature and Censorship…*, p. 42.

[295] "O recenzjach zbiorków literackich," *Biuletyn Informacyjno-Instrukcyjny* no. 4 (16), April 1953, p. 28 (APG, WUKPPiW, file ref. no. 16).

he had been the vice-president of the Academic Association of All-Polish Youth, which was, after all, an offshoot of the National Party. The post-war communist authorities dealt brutally with the latter, and with National Democrats in general.[296] Putrament, however, did not share the fate of many All-Polish Youth activists who were sentenced to death in show trials, because even before the war, he had become a loyal follower of the only correct ideology, the beginning of which had been a break "with the All-Polish Youth and a veering to leftist positions."[297] His "devotion" to the new Poland afforded him the honorable title of a mediocre writer, but an excellent communist.[298]

What could be striking in the context of this very "episode" with the All-Polish Youth is that, according to the editors of the Bulletin, Putrament realized a literary scenario that could have also been extended to Ginczanka. The bench ghetto and the total elimination or limiting the number of students of Jewish origin (the so-called *numerus nullus* and *numerus clausus*) promoted by the All-Polish Youth had a direct impact on the poet, who precisely for that reason resigned from attending the lectures at the University of Warsaw.[299] Nonetheless, in the "Lviv period," like many others, both of them became part of the same order, joining the Union of Soviet Writers of Ukraine and publishing in *Nowe Widnokręgi*, the organ of the Union of Writers of the USSR.

Returning to the subject of the censorship of so-called non-homogenous works, however, even if a given selection of prose or poetry satisfactorily showed the developmental path of an artist, it was sometimes necessary to remove works that were politically harmful or presented the artist in an inappropriate light.[300] In the Bulletin from April 1953, we read that such a need was signaled in the case

---

[296] On the national camp, see, e.g.: A. Friszke, *Grzechy endecji* (in the series *Spory historyków*), Biuletyn IPN "Pamięć.pl" 2012, no. 9, pp. 25–29, http://www.polska1918-89.pl/pdf/grzechy-endecji,2094.pdf (accessed January 31, 2021); J. Żaryn, *Endecja – cenne dziedzictwo* (in the series *Spory historyków*) Biuletyn IPN "Pamięć.pl" 2012, no. 9, pp. 30–34, http://www.polska1918-89.pl/pdf/endecja---cenne-dziedzictwo,2095.pdf (accessed January 31, 2021); L. Kulińska, M. Ostrowski, R. Sierchuła, *Narodowcy. Myśl polityczna i społeczna Obozu Narodowego w Polsce w latach 1944–47*, Warszawa: PWN, 2001. See also: K. Szwagrzyk, *Zbrodnie w majestacie prawa 1944–1955*, Warszawa: Wydawnictwo ABC Future, 2000; T. Swat, *Niewinnie straceni w Warszawie 1944–1956*, Warszawa: Fundacja Ochrony Zabytków, 1994.

[297] M. Zaleski, *Przygoda drugiej awangardy*, Second Revised and Supplemented Edition, Wrocław: Ossolineum, 2000, pp. 74–75.

[298] M. Hemar, *Moja przekora. Satyry polityczne z lat 1943–1971*, selected and compiled by A.K. Kunert, Kraków: Wydawnictwo Literackie, 2001, p. 41.

[299] A. Araszkiewicz, *Wypowiadam wam moje życie…*, p. 36.

[300] "O recenzjach zbiorków literackich," *Biuletyn Informacyjno-Instrukcyjny* no. 4 (16), April 1953, p. 28 (APG, WUKPPiW, file ref. no. 16).

of Tadeusz Borowski's[301] *Wybór pism* [Selected texts] submitted by Państwowy Instytut Wydawniczy (PIW). It is possible that the collection reached "Mysia Street" under this working title, but in the end, it was published in 1954 as the five-volume *Utwory zebrane* [Collected works], hence, after the material had appeared in the journal.[302] This should not come as a surprise, since the censorship evaluation, which had already been carried out at that time, was only one of the stages of the publishing process, which apparently had not yet been completed.

The quality of the PIW publication is evidenced by the opinion of one of its editors, Tadeusz Drewnowski, who half a century later prepared a new – this time four-volume edition – of Borowski's texts.[303] The renowned expert of the author of "Here in Our Auschwitz" complained that "apart from *Utwory zebrane* from 1954, which is hasty and dilettante, and does not do justice to its title"[304] the writer still had no reliably edited collected works (interestingly, in the meantime, Drewnowski had prepared several editions of Borowski's works for none other than PIW).[305] The materials of the censorship office from 1953, however, reveal the inner workings of this incomplete and mutilated first edition of the collected works.

---

[301] From the extensive bibliography on Borowski, see, e.g.: S. Buryła, *Prawda mitu i literatury. O pisarstwie Tadeusza Borowskiego i Leopolda Buczkowskiego*, Kraków: Universitas, 2003; T. Drewnowski, *Ucieczka z kamiennego świata (o Tadeuszu Borowskim)*, Warszawa: PIW, 1961; J. Szczęsna, *Tadeusz Borowski – poeta*, Poznań: Poznańskie Studia Polonistyczne, 2000. See also: [Tadeusz Drewnowski reminisces about Tadeusz Borowski], Polskie Radio October 16, 1973, https://www.polskieradio.pl/39/156/ Artykul/1469874,Tadeusz-Borowski-zdac-relacje-w-obronie-umarlych (accessed January 31, 2021).

[302] See: T. Borowski, *Utwory zebrane*, eds. T. Drewnowski, J. Piórkowski, foreword by W. Woroszylski, vol. 1: *Wiersze*, Warszawa: PIW, 1954; vol. 2: *Proza 1945–1947*: ibidem; vol. 3: *Krytyka literacka i artystyczna*: ibidem; vol. 4: *Publicystyka*: ibidem; vol. 5: *Proza 1948–1951*: ibidem.

[303] T. Borowski, *Pisma w czterech tomach*, vol. 1: *Poezja*, compiled by T. Drewnowski, J. Szczęsna, Kraków: Wydawnictwo Literackie, 2003; vol. 2: *Proza (1)*, compiled by S. Buryła, ibidem 2004; vol. 3: *Proza (2)*, compiled by S. Buryła, ibidem 2004; vol. 4: *Krytyka*, compiled by T. Drewnowski, ibidem 2005.

[304] T. Drewnowski, *Wstęp*, [in:] T. Borowski, *Niedyskrecje pocztowe. Korespondencja Tadeusza Borowskiego*, compiled by T. Drewnowski, Warszawa: Prószyński i S-ka, 2001, p. 7.

[305] See, e.g.: T. Borowski, *Wspomnienia, wiersze, opowiadania*, afterword, selection and illustrations by T. Drewnowski, footnotes by W. Jesionowska, Warszawa: PIW, 1974; T. Borowski, *Poezje*, selection and preface by T. Drewnowski, Warszawa: PIW, 1972; T. Borowski, *Opowiadania wybrane*, selection and layout by T. Drewnowski, Warszawa: PIW, 1971. See also: T. Borowski, *Rozmowa z przyjacielem. Wiersze*, submitted for print and prefaced by T. Drewnowski, Wrocław: Wydawnictwo Dolnośląskie, 1999.

Why were there plans to make cuts to the selection proposed by PIW? According to the evaluators, the publishing house failed to ensure the coherence of the collection, which was supposed to present Borowski "as a militant writer of the young generation, ruthlessly combating all manifestations of backwardness and obscurantism; as a writer fighting for socialist realism in literature."[306] According to Wiktor Woroszylski's "Preface," written between August and September 1953, this was supposed to be the guiding idea for the whole collection.[307] However, the evaluators felt that the actual contents did not comport with this pronouncement.

The censors objected to "decadent stories written in the early period of [the author's] career,"[308] which did not toe the ideological line of the publishing house and, according to the functionaries, would have been particularly harmful if published in a volume with a mass circulation. This is what the censor quoted in the Bulletin wrote about these texts, which ultimately, were not removed:

> It seems improbable but they are nationalistic, religiose (e.g., "Tropione zwierzęta" [Hunted animals]), they apotheosize the Warsaw Uprising and the pre-war scouting, and contain anti-Soviet accents. Two short stories entitled "This way for the gas, ladies and gentlemen" and "Bitwa pod Grunwaldem" [The Battle of Grunwald] describe life in the Nazi and American camps. They are repugnant for their cynicism, naturalism, bringing to the surface the animal essence of man, and their lack of ideology. The Katyń case is framed ambiguously at best.[309]

According to the decision of rank-and-file employees of the Office for the Control, the three stories mentioned in the quotation were supposed to be cut from the volume, but their superiors found these accusations groundless and, eventually, all the texts were published.[310] It is noteworthy that the stories had

---

[306] "O recenzjach zbiorków literackich," *Biuletyn Informacyjno-Instrukcyjny* no. 4 (16), April 1953, p. 29 (APG, WUKPPiW, file ref. no. 16).

[307] W. Woroszylski, *O Tadeuszu Borowskim, jego życiu i twórczości*, [in:] T. Borowski, *Utwory zebrane*, eds. T. Drewnowski, J. Piórkowski, preface by W. Woroszylski, vol.1: *Wiersze…*, pp. 5–116.

[308] "O recenzjach zbiorków literackich," *Biuletyn Informacyjno-Instrukcyjny* no. 4 (16), April 1953, p. 29 (APG, WUKPPiW, file ref. no. 16).

[309] Ibidem.
Zbrodnia Katyńska, Katyń, Las Katyński (the Katyń Massacre) – mass executions of nearly 22,000 Polish military officers and intelligentsia carried out by the USSR in April and May 1940; The USSR claimed the Nazis had killed the victims, and it continued to deny responsibility for the massacres until 1990.

[310] T. Borowski, "Proszę państwa do gazu"; "Bitwa pod Grunwaldem"; "Tropione zwierzęta," [in:] idem, *Utwory zebrane*, eds. T. Drewnowski, J. Piórkowski, preface by W. Woroszylski, vol. 2: *Proza 1945–1947…*, pp. 80–100, 171–216, 226–232.

already been published, including in book editions: in 1946 (and 1948) – "This Way for the Gas, Ladies and Gentlemen"[311]; in 1947 – "Tropione zwierzęta," and in 1948 – "Bitwa pod Grunwaldem."[312] This was before the shift in publishing policy and the tightening of evaluation criteria, which – more or less from 1949 onwards – were aimed at increasing control over published content. The censors felt that the selection of works proposed by PIW – intended to show the ideological evolution Borowski had undergone – was inadequate, and they recommended against commemorating that period of his creativity "in favor of presenting its most mature, peak phase."[313] Which is what? – one might ask. The simplest answer would be the one that came after 1948, and testified to what one could call a desperate turn towards socialist realism.[314] How did the artist see this turn? "My writer's path has been very banal,"[315] he told a Polish Radio editor in 1951:

> First, I wrote a few poems, which were read by a handful of my friends. It was during the war. Back then, I liked those poems and proclaimed myself a poet. Then I stopped liking them. Something was happening to me during that time, as it was with many of us. I had been in the camp, I saw with my own eyes the so-called liberation of Germany by American imperialists. At that time, my friends and I wrote a memoir volume on Oświęcim, *We Were in Auschwitz*. Some of the reportages from this volume were printed in the national press, and two stories were included in the collection *A Farewell to Maria*. […] Shortly afterwards, I published another [volume – AWG], *The World of Stone* – twenty very unsuccessful stories, short sketches, which combined were supposed to form a pamphlet on certain literary fads in Poland. The polemic was so disguised it was invisible. Well… it was a flop.
> And that was that.[316]

---

[311] In the Bulletin, "Panowie, proszę do gazu" – Gentlemen, this way for the gas.

[312] See, e.g.: 1) "Proszę państwa do gazu": 6643 J. Nel Siedlecki, 75817 K. Olszewski, 119198 T. Borowski, *Byliśmy w Oświęcimiu*, Munich: Oficyna Warszawska na Obczyźnie, 1946, pp. 93–111; T. Borowski, *Pożegnanie z Marią. Opowiadania*, Warszawa: "Wiedza," 1948, pp. 80–106; 2) "Tropione zwierzęta": T. Borowski, *Pewien żołnierz. Opowieści szkolne*, Warszawa: Spółdzielnia Wydawnicza "Płomienie," 1947, pp. 16–22; 3) "Bitwa pod Grunwaldem": T. Borowski, *Pożegnanie z Marią. Opowiadania*, Warszawa: "Wiedza," 1948, pp. 127–179.

[313] "O recenzjach zbiorków literackich," *Biuletyn Informacyjno-Instrukcyjny* no. 4 (16), April 1953, p. 29 (APG, WUKPPiW, file ref. no. 16).

[314] J. Błoński, "Piekła Borowskiego," *Teksty* 1972, no. 6, p. 160.

[315] [Interview with Tadeusz Borowski after the publication of *Opowiadania z książek i gazet*], Polskie Radio 1951, https://www.polskieradio.pl/39/156/Artykul/1469874,Tadeusz-Borowski-zdac-relacje-w-obronie-umarlych (accessed January 31, 2021). The transcript is quoted from a radio broadcast.

[316] Ibidem.

However, this ideological transformation – understandably, described by Czesław Miłosz in an entirely different manner from the one presented above and in the Bulletin[317] (that is, extremely critically) – was a process during which non-obvious books were written; books "which were, in a way, a meaningful continuation of his earlier works,"[318] such as *Pewien żołnierz…* [One soldier] or *Opowiadania z książek i gazet* [Stories from books and newspapers]. Like the writer's previous works, they too were a testimony to his personal, creative and moral dramas.

"Mysia Street" was certainly interested in showing the new, changed Borowski, who three years earlier, in 1950, had admitted on the pages of *Odrodzenie* to his profound socialist realist faith.[319] In the article, Borowski took a critical look at his earlier lack of involvement in the creation of new, socialist literature. Ultimately, he praised the political duties of this literature and aligned himself with the writers who, immersed in the slogans of class struggle, put their talent in the service of the state and built a new socialist order. "Mysia Street's" goal to show the "changed" Borowski was accomplished; for example, *Utwory zebrane* [The collected works] contained almost all the stories from the meaningful *Czerwony maj* [Red May]. The latter was prefaced in 1953 by another representative of the

---

[317] Cz. Miłosz, "Beta, czyli nieszczęśliwy kochanek," [in:] idem, *Zniewolony umysł*, Kraków: Wydawnictwo Literackie, 1999, pp. 137–161. Cf. the poem "Na śmierć Tadeusza Borowskiego" with an entirely different tone, written by Miłosz after the writer's death (Cz. Miłosz, "Na śmierć Tadeusza Borowskiego," [in:] idem, *Światło dzienne*, Paris: Instytut Literacki, 1953, p. 146). See also: A. Bikont, J. Szczęsna, *Lawina i kamienie. Pisarze wobec komunizmu*, Warszawa: Prószyński i S-ka, 2006, pp. 68–79; M. Głowiński, "Od katastrofizmu do poezji politycznej" (in the series *Wśród książek*), *Twórczość* 1956, no. 1, pp. 140–144.
Czesław Miłosz (1911–2004) – one of the most famous Polish poets, prose writers, and translators; he was awarded the Nobel Prize for Literature in 1980; in 1951, he left Poland and became one of the most important Polish émigré authors and intellectuals; due to his decision to emigrate, his work was banned in Poland during the communist era; he was a lecturer at the University of California, Berkeley and at Harvard University; he wrote, among others: *The Captive Mind, Private Obligations, The Issa Valley* (see also several volumes of English translations of his poetry, e.g.: *The Collected Poems 1931–1987, Provinces*).
[318] S. Buryła, "Wstęp," [in:] T. Borowski, *Pisma w czterech tomach* vol. 3: *Proza (2)…*, p. 19.
[319] T. Borowski, "Rozmowy. Dla towarzyszy: Jerzego Andrzejewskiego i Wiktora Woroszylskiego," *Odrodzenie* February 19, 1950, no. 8, pp. 5–6.
Odrodzenie (Revival) (1944–1950) – Poland's first post-war socio-cultural weekly; the magazine supported the cultural policy of the authorities, but avoided formulating an unambiguous ideological and artistic program in order to consolidate various artistic circles in post-war Poland; in 1950, it merged with the weekly *Kuźnica* (which had a decidedly less liberal profile and openly supported Marxism), resulting in the creation of the previously mentioned weekly *Nowa Kultura*.

Columbus generation who was ideologically committed to the authorities, Kazimierz Koźniewski.[320] However, if the "decision-makers" had not rejected the proposal of the rank-and-file censors to remove an important testimony of this ideological transformation from *Utwory Zebrane*, PIW's publication would have contained texts with a decidedly uniform tone, written by a member of P(Z)PR, a declared communist.

The question of Borowski's change of worldview resurfaced when discussing *Miejsce urodzenia* [The birthplace], a collection of short stories by Lesław Bartelski, in whose work the Columbuses occupy an important, if not the most important place.[321] PIW submitted the book to the Office for the Control "in a period of heated discussion about the so-called schematism in literature."[322] Undoubtedly, the debates in 1953 were extensive, but a decent "Thaw" campaign was yet to come.[323] The distortions of socialist realism had been signaled as early as 1949 by Adam Ważyk, but the nationwide discussion was started by the above mentioned Flaszen's article, "Nowy Zoil, czyli o schematyzmie," from January 1952[324] (delivered a year earlier at a meeting of the prose section of the Union of Polish Writers – the ZLP). Flaszen argued that literature at the time was warping the postulate for "typicality," which resulted in schematism (as previously noted, the problem also resurfaced in the Bulletins while discussing Wanda Wasilewska's book *Rzeki Płoną*). This was evidenced by "political formulas" and "the allism" (overloading works with commentary and "efforts to represent everything in a book"), as well as "happy-ends" and creating black and white characters, among other issues.[325]

"Nowy Zoil…," which provoked an avalanche of objections, was discussed in the press and at the sessions of the General Board of the ZLP from January 17–18 and June 20–21, 1952.[326] Speakers at this nationwide discussion included

---

[320] Koźniewski's *Piątka z ulicy Barskiej* [Five from Barska Street] was also discussed in the Bulletins, more on which later.

[321] L. Bartelski, *Miejsce urodzenia. Opowiadania*, Warszawa: PIW, 1953. See also: idem, *Termopile literackie. Polska 1939–1945*, Warszawa: Instytut Wydawniczy "Pax," 2002; idem, *Genealogia ocalonych. Szkice o latach 1939–1944*, Warszawa: Wydawnictwo Literackie, 1963.

[322] "O recenzjach zbiorków literackich," *Biuletyn Informacyjno-Instrukcyjny* no. 4 (16), April 1953, p. 30 (APG, WUKPPiW, file ref. no. 16).

[323] J. Smulski, *Pękanie lodów. (Krótkie formy narracyjne w literaturze polskiej 1954–1955)*, Toruń: Wydawnictwo UMK, 1995, p. 4.

[324] A. Ważyk, *W stronę humanizmu*, Warszawa: "Książka," 1949; L. Flaszen, "Nowy Zoil, czyli o schematyzmie…"

[325] L. Flaszen, "Nowy Zoil, czyli o schematyzmie…," p. 4.

[326] See, e.g.: "Kronika życia literackiego w PRL. 1952," compiled by H. Filipkowska, [in:] *Kronika życia literackiego Polski Ludowej 1944–1969. Materiały*, collaborative work edited by E. Korzeniewska (until 1963) and J. Stradecki (1964–1969), written between 1963–1970, pp. 3–6, 50–52.

key literary critics and authors at the time: Henryk Markiewicz, Maria Janion, Tadeusz Konwicki, Adama Tadeusz Ważyk, Drewnowski, Jerzy Putrament, and Melania Kierczyńska, who refuted the charges, writing that Flaszen "presented a distorted and partial picture of contemporary literature because he based his analysis on the weakest novels."[327]

The discussion continued the following year, and some of the points raised in it translated into an evaluation of Bartelski's short stories, whose artistic level was rated favorably, but a "certain unhealthy tendency"[328] throughout the volume was noticed (more on this below). This was already the sixth book in the output of the writer, who two years earlier had received the State Award of the Third Degree and the Award of the Minister of Culture and Art for his "very schematic"[329] novel *Ludzie zza rzeki* [People from behind the river] (also evaluated in the Bulletin).[330] The censors assessing *Miejsce urodzenia* were certainly aware of these distinctions, which did not exempt them from a reliable evaluation of his subsequent works. On the contrary, such recognition might have invited greater vigilance, in accordance with the principle – often repeated in Bulletins and other censorship documents – that "loyal" texts should be thoroughly scrutinized.[331]

In the end, the collection published by PIW consisted of twelve stories, but probably it should be assumed that the volume received by the Main Office was longer.[332] The Bulletin mentioned three novellas, which were removed from the

---

[327] M. Kierczyńska, "O schematyzmie," *Nowa Kultura* January 20, 1952, no. 3, p. 2. See also other statements from 1952: H. Markiewicz, "Krytyka literacka w latach 1945–1951. Referat wygłoszony na plenum ZLP poświęconym zagadnieniom krytyki literackiej"; Z. Bieńkowski, "Po plenum krytyki," *Twórczość* 1952, no. 3, pp. 117–144; L. Flaszen, "Odpowiedź Zoila, czyli o akcentach," *Życie Literackie* June 8, 1952, no. 12, pp. 7, 13; M. Janion, "'Dopływy' krytyki literackiej," *Wieś* January 10, 1952, no. 6, p. 4; T. Konwicki, "Z zapisków schematysty," *Nowa Kultura* November 23, 1952, no. 47, p. 6; H. Zaworska, "Wokół 'schematyzmu,'" *Wieś* January 13, 1952, no. 2, p. 4; A. Sandauer, "O typowości i schematyzmie," *Nowa Kultura* May 18, 1952, no. 20, pp. 5–6. See also: E. Możejko, *Realizm socjalistyczny. Teoria. Rozwój. Upadek*, Kraków: Universitas, 2001; M. Pietrzak, "Socrealistyczna krytyka literacka w ujęciu diachronicznym," *Acta Universitatis Lodziensis. Folia Litteraria Polonica* 2008, no. 10, pp. 237–251.

[328] "O recenzjach zbiorków literackich," *Biuletyn Informacyjno-Instrukcyjny* no. 4 (16), April 1953, p. 30 (APG, WUKPPiW, file ref. no. 16).

[329] Ibidem.

[330] L. Bartelski, *Ludzie zza rzeki*, Warszawa: PIW, 1951.

[331] See, e.g.: *Biuletyn Głównego Urzędu Kontroli Prasy* no. 4, fol. 52r–54r (APP WU-KPPiW, file ref. no. 4); "Recenzja z pozycji literackiej (cd.)" (in the series *O wyższy poziom pracy nad książką*), *Biuletyn Informacyjno-Instrukcyjny* no. 9, September 1952, p. 27 (APG, WUKPPiW, file ref. no. 78).

[332] The fact that the "golden dictionary" – a bio-bibliographical dictionary edited by Czachowska and Szałagan – suggests that there should be thirteen stories in the PIW

collection, thus depriving it of "the conceptual blade in the alleged fight against schematism."[333] Which stories were they? Unfortunately, no titles were given. However, a comparison of the fragments about them with the PIW edition suggests that indeed, the three "problematic" texts were probably not published in the volume. It seems that two short stories that "characterized the relationships in the army and the militia in the first period after the Liberation in a malicious and defamatory manner"[334] did not make their way into the collection (although this problem resurfaces in several places, which works against the presented hypothesis): "These stories – in which the author is a character somewhat caught up in the vortex of events and struck by the bluntness and malice of the new authorities in the first period – were intended to justify his hesitation and distrust in what the people's government represented."[335]

It seems that the third of the indicated works will not be found either, but let us stop for a moment to reflect on how Bartelski described the process of writers' growing into the new reality.[336] The functionaries were not thrilled with the examples selected by the author, because "he was attracted to those writers who, in spite of their intense struggle with themselves, did not manage to have a breakthrough – for example, Adolf Rudnicki or the already late, ideologically foreign, and plagued with doubts, Tadeusz Gaycy"[337] (original spelling). The editors did not specify to which stories they were referring, but in this case, the collection itself was helpful. It was relatively easy to interpret the words about Gajcy, a catastrophist, the editor of *Sztuka i Naród* (centered around the Confederation of the Nation, to which the poet belonged) who polemicized with Borowski, Baczyński and the group "Płomienie" [Flames] (from the PPS). For the censors, these credentials sufficiently proved the ideological foreignness of the protagonist of the story "Ciężar domu"[338] [The burden of home].

It was much more difficult to interpret the fragment concerning Adolf Rudnicki. The quotation clearly suggests that Rudnicki failed to live up to expectations, was unable to "have a breakthrough," to adapt to... Well, to what exactly? It

---

edition may be treated as an editorial oversight (probably, the story "Żona, kamień węgielny" was inadvertently made into two separate stories; see: A. Szałagan [A. Sz.], "Bartelski Lesław Marian," [in:] *Współcześni polscy pisarze i badacze literatury. Słownik biobibliograficzny* vol. 1: *A–B*, eds. J. Czachowska, A. Szałagan, Warszawa: WSiP, 1994, p. 110).

[333] "O recenzjach zbiorków literackich," *Biuletyn Informacyjno-Instrukcyjny* no. 4 (16), April 1953, p. 31 (APG, WUKPPiW, file ref. no. 16).

[334] Ibidem, p. 30.

[335] Ibidem.

[336] Ibidem.

[337] Ibidem.

[338] L. Bartelski, "Ciężar domu," [in:] idem, *Miejsce urodzenia...*, pp. 31–43. See also S. Bereś, *Gajcy. W pierścieniu śmierci*, Wołowiec: Wydawnictwo Czarne, 2016.

seems that already during the war, in the "Lviv period," the author of *Epoka pieców* [The epoch of the ovens] fit well into the new reality.[339] The choices he made (or perhaps surrendered to unknowingly) benefited him later. These included co-operation with the Union of Soviet Writers of Ukraine and communist journals published in the Polish territories occupied by the USSR after the USSR's attack on Poland on September 17, 1941: *Nowe Widnokręgi* and *Czerwony Sztandar*.[340]

However, in spite of several state awards and his considerable popularity with the readers, the writer was not always pampered by the critics; the most famous criticism, by Artur Sandauer, was yet to come.[341] He was repeatedly accused of being an "outsider," and this is most likely what the censor had in mind when he or she wrote about his inability to "have a breakthrough." Rudnicki was "a Jew among Poles and the Other among Jews,"[342] and this "separateness" did not result only from his conscious decision, as the critics of the time wanted to believe, but was a question of identity for a man who – after the tragedy of the Shoah – had to work out the "beautiful art of writing" anew.[343]

The third story that was cut from *Miejsce urodzenia*, this time a story about Borowski, once again raises the issue of the writer's ideological breakthrough. Bartelski was accused of portraying the author of *A Farewell to Maria* "at a point when his worldview had not yet crystallized."[344] Indeed, the two quotations from the story used in the Bulletin describe incidents that took place during his school period. According to the censors, Bartelski made a mistake suggesting that this educationally inappropriate episode from the protagonist's youth made "his

---

[339] A. Rudnicki, *Szekspir*, Warszawa: "Książka," 1948, p. 244.

[340] *Nowe Widnokręgi* – a socio-literary magazine published between 1941–1946, an organ of the communist Writers' Union of the USSR; *Czerwony Sztandar* – a daily journal published between 1939–1941 in Polish, mainly in Lviv.

J. Wróbel, *Miara cierpienia. O pisarstwie Adolfa Rudnickiego*, Kraków: Universitas, 2004; A. Wal, *Twórczość w cieniu menory. O prozie Adolfa Rudnickiego*, Rzeszów: Wydawnictwo URz, 2001; A. Molisak, "Adolfa Rudnickiego odmiany żydowskości," [in:] *Pisarze polsko-żydowscy. Przybliżenia*, eds. M. Dąbrowski, A. Molisak, Warszawa: Dom Wydawniczy Elipsa, 2006, pp. 67–79; E. Prokop-Janiec, "Żyd – Polak – artysta. O budowaniu tożsamości po Zagładzie," *Teksty Drugie* 2001, no. 1, pp. 120–134. See also: A. Rudnicki, "Z zapisków 1947," transcribed from manuscript and compiled by M. Rudnicki-Schlumberger, M. Tukaj, *Twórczość* 2015, no. 2, pp. 54–97.

[341] A. Sandauer, *Bez taryfy ulgowej*, Warszawa: "Czytelnik," 1959, pp. 7–30.

[342] S. Buryła, [Review: J. Wróbel, *Miara cierpienia. O pisarstwie Adolfa Rudnickiego*, Kraków: Universitas, 2004], *Pamiętnik Literacki* 2006, issue 2, p. 234.

[343] A. Rudnicki, "Piękna sztuka pisania," [in:] idem, *Szekspir...*, pp. 209–218. See also: H. Zaworska-Trznadlowa, "O powojennej twórczości Adolfa Rudnickiego," *Pamiętnik Literacki* 1953, issue 3–4, pp. 151–189.

[344] "O recenzjach zbiorków literackich," *Biuletyn Informacyjno-Instrukcyjny* no. 4 (16), April 1953, p. 30 (APG, WUKPPiW, file ref. no. 16).

path to the party of progress very difficult."[345] In *Miejsce urodzenia*, we find neither the fragments quoted in the Bulletin (provided below), nor the story about the author of *The World of Stone*; nor can we find them in the sketch devoted to Borowski, *Dzień jego* śmierci [The day of his death], which was included in a collection of Bartelski's short stories published in 1967. What fragments were quoted in the cryptotext, then?

[the statements of Borowski, the protagonist of the short story, quoted in the Bulletin].

– People can be trained, they need to be trained. Ethics is not a matter of the individual, but of the society. Like society, like person. The year was 1932, and the event I'm going to describe took place in a public school in the Soviet Ukraine, in the autonomous region of Marchlevsk. Of course, the school had Polish as the language of instruction. So, at this public school, the editor of the bulletin board purchased decals in a corner store and, taking advantage of the incredible demand for them, traded them to his schoolmates at a profit. One day, a clumsy drawing appeared in the bulletin depicting a gallows with a man hanging from it. Across the body of the hanged read a large caption: "Our editor-in-chief," and underneath, another "Away with speculation."
– Did it help?
– He treated my question as an impulsive reflex…
[…]
… – I was trained too! – he laughed with slight irony. – My Schoolmates, dear Schoolmates, once drew a gallows, putting my name underneath it. – You asked if it helped? My friend, by changing social conditions you can change a person…[346]
(original emphasis)

4.2. Books Selected for Discussion in Censorship Offices Between 1952 and 1956

The Bulletin used to have articles that talked about the censor's work on a book, about writing reviews, etc. It has been a long time now that our Bulletin has featured any material that would help the censor directly in inspecting non-periodical titles or in writing reviews.[347]

---

[345] Ibidem.

[346] Ibidem. See also: L. Bartelski, "Dzień jego śmierci," [in:] idem, *W kręgu bliskich. Szkice do portretów*, Kraków: Wydawnictwo Literackie, 1967, pp. 31–41.

[347] W. Wierciak (WUKP Kraków), "O czym chcemy czytać w Biuletynie" (correspondence in "Dział Listów"), *Biuletyn Informacyjno-Instrukcyjny* no. 9 (45), September 1955, p. 66 (APG, WUKPPiW, file ref. no. 120).

As noted earlier, detailed and extensive book reviews appeared quite rarely in the Bulletins. Most titles were discussed in a few or a dozen sentences in collective articles. Sometimes, however, selected titles were analyzed with more care in devoted articles. Over the course of eleven years, several dozen such materials were included. Some of them were examined as part of a "nationwide discussion of selected books of fiction,"[348] probably initiated in 1952 (or at the end of 1951); "nationwide," that is, involving censorship offices all over Poland. Titles were sent to field branches to be analyzed at work briefings, and the conclusions (often along with the minutes) of the discussion were presented in the Bulletins. During these four years, mainly prose texts were reviewed, and poetic works were considered only twice.

It is worth noting that the subjects of these large-scale debates were also press articles, mainly on political and social issues, but also artistic or historical ones.[349] Perhaps a suggestion put forward by the readers of the Bulletin was taken into account and the formula of the discussion was broadened to include genres other than fiction in the censorship "reflection."[350] Maybe the coverage of the debates on non-fiction presented in the Bulletins comprised a separate program of the Office; what is most significant is that all the above-mentioned texts were discussed in offices across the country.

The presented considerations focused on new releases: when the material on a particular title was published, the book had already been on the market; thus, the reports in the magazine were a training tool for readers-censors. However, at least some of the discussions – at the moment when they were being held in the offices – might have had a preventive character: censors could debate the texts before they were published. Sometimes a discussion of a work which had been blocked by the censors was presented. The reports featured in the Bulletins certainly did not exhaust the debates on selected titles that were taking place in branches all over the country. In the censorship materials, information can be found about these types of undertakings, an example of which are documents from the Head Office and voivodeship offices, where titles intended for discussion are provided.[351]

---

[348] "O dyskusji nad książką J. Kuśmierka, *Uwaga człowiek*," *Biuletyn Informacyjno-Instrukcyjny* no. 2, February 1952, p. 35 (APG, WUKPPiW, file ref. no. 99). See also: K. Budrowska, "Od orderu do 'zapisu'…," pp. 78–95.

[349] See, e.g.: "O właściwe stosowanie w naszej pracy cenzorskiej wytycznych VII Plenum (cd.)," *Biuletyn Informacyjno-Instrukcyjny* no. 9, September 1952, pp. 14–17 (APG, WUKPPiW, file ref. no. 78).

[350] "Artykuł wstępny," *Biuletyn Informacyjno-Instrukcyjny* no. 1 (13), January 1953, p. 4 (APG, WUKPPiW, file ref. no. 19).

[351] "Materiały dyskusyjno-szkoleniowe 1954–1955" (APP, WUKPPiW, file ref. no. 18, fol. 99r, 100r); cf. Fig. 12.

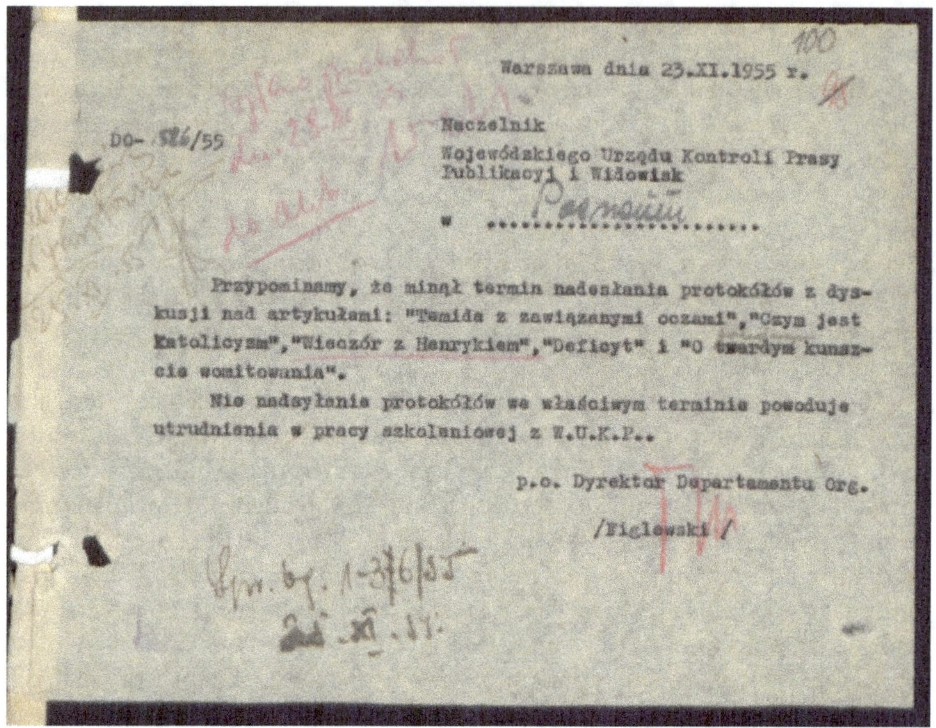

Fig. 12. A letter dated November 23, 1955 from the GUKPPiW to the WUKPPiW in Poznań informing about the failure to send the minutes of discussions on controversial press articles within the specified time limit (APP, WUKPPiW, file ref. no. 18, fol. 100r).

It is rather transparent "what the meaning and purpose of organizing"[352] such nationwide discussions about books was, but consider how the idea was justified by those who conceived of it:

> We realized that it is artificial, unjustified, and harmful for censors of individual departments, divisions, or offices to be isolated.
> We realized the necessity of discussing our mistakes and work achievements collectively, in full teams, and collectively passing on our experiences to each other. Our daily practice demanded that the already decayed dams inhibiting the quality and efficiency of our work be overcome. It demanded the creation of such forms of training and organization which would allow press censors to familiarize themselves with the work of non-periodical publications and vice versa. Organiz-

---

[352] "O dyskusji nad książką J. Kuśmierka, *Uwaga człowiek*," *Biuletyn Informacyjno-Instrukcyjny* no. 2, February 1952, p. 35 (APG, WUKPPiW, file ref. no. 99).

ing book discussions was conceived as one of the forms that could serve this very purpose[353] (original emphasis).

The quoted passage may suggest that the improvement of cooperation between the departments of the Office was the real aim of these discussions, and the book itself was only a pretext and a means to achieve it. There is certainly some truth to this, as the Bulletins regularly commented on the lack of cooperation between the Office's departments, and even signaled expectations of censors from the voivodeship centers to receive reports on the work of "the apparatus at the level of the headquarters."[354] However, it was assumed that the discussion would not only have a positive impact on the cooperation between the departments and on so-called interpersonal dynamics, but also that it would improve strictly professional competence, that is, related to the assessment of cultural texts.

4.2.1. Titles Selected for Discussion in Censorship Offices in 1952: (Not Only) Kuśmierek and Czeszko

> *And do you, comrade, even know what censorship is*
> *and what role it has in our system?*[355]

In 1952, a report was published on the discussion of the article entitled "Od Statutu Wiślickiego do Konstytucji Polskiej Rzeczpospolitej Ludowej"[356] [From the Wiślicki's Statute to the Constitution of the Polish People's Republic]. Furthermore, two extensive reports on the deliberations had taken place in the censorship offices concerning the collection of reportages *Uwaga! Człowiek* [Attention! Human] by Józef Kuśmierek[357] and the novel *Pokolenie* by Bohdan Czeszko. The material on Kuśmierek was published in February, while the one on Czeszko in April. Thus, in both cases it was after the publication of Flaszen's article, which set the tone for the entire year's worth of press coverage.

---

[353] Ibidem.

[354] "Korespondencja," *Biuletyn Informacyjno-Instrukcyjny* no. 3, March 1952, p. 30 (APG, WUKPPiW, file ref. no. 96).

[355] "Wypowiedź pracowników UKPPiW," *Biuletyn Informacyjno-Instrukcyjny* no. 1 (37), January 1955, p. 15 (APG, WUKPPiW, file ref. no. 110). A statement by one of the censors quoted in a survey conducted by the editors of the Bulletin on the occasion of the tenth anniversary of the Office for the Control.

[356] "Podsumowanie dyskusji," *Biuletyn Informacyjno-Instrukcyjny* no. 11, November 1952, pp. 24–36 (APG, WUKPPiW, file ref. no. 72). I write about the article in the chapter "Literary and Cultural Issues in the Press."

[357] In the Bulletin – *Uwaga człowiek.*

Unfortunately, it is unclear when the books were discussed, but both articles show the problems that the critic framed so explicitly. This should not come as a surprise, since the shortcomings of socialist realism had been pointed out even before "Nowy Zoil…" and some of the rationalizing ideas – for example, on how to deal with schematism – came from the very co-creators of the system. In a way, they were inscribed in this dialogue, which was not yet dangerous because it was still unfolding in the spirit of the doctrine. This was evidenced by Jakub Berman's paper in which he demanded "a full ideological engagement of artists and closer contact with life in order to overcome schematism."[358] The presentation took place in October 1951 at a meeting devoted to artistic creation, attended by more than two hundred representatives from various fields of art.[359] In the article on Kuśmierek, there are echoes of the paper, although a direct reference was made to another of Berman's slogans, the "struggle for the quality of literature." This slogan was coined "at the September meeting of writers and artists"[360] in 1951; it seems, however, that the Bulletin's editors may have been referring to the October meeting.

A significant part of the problems formulated when discussing Kuśmierek's reportages also appeared in the course of deliberations on *Pokolenie* (and in subsequent years): the necessity of maintaining correct proportions when assessing the ideological and artistic realization of the work; the necessity of evaluating the work as a whole, rather than as a collection of fragments and details that contribute insignificantly to a proper assessment; the necessity of a deeper analysis of the work and its evaluation in a broader context than before. Of course, all of the above-mentioned guidelines had to be implemented in accordance with the prevailing creative method and value system, but they were also a signal of the transformations that the literature of the time was undergoing. This section will consider how these changes resonated in the case of the evaluations of these two books.

✳✳✳

---

[358] M. Fik, *Kultura polska po Jałcie. Kronika lat 1944–1981*, London: Polonia Book Fund, 1989, p. 160. See also: J. Berman, "Pokażcie wielkość naszych czasów," *Materiały do Studiów i Dyskusji z Zakresu Teorii i Historii Sztuki, Krytyki Artystycznej oraz Badań nad Sztuką* 1952, no. 1, pp. 33–37.

[359] "Kronika życia literackiego w PRL. 1951," compiled by M. Wosiek, [in:] *Kronika życia literackiego Polski Ludowej 1944–1969. Materiały*, collaborative work edited by E. Korzeniewska (until 1963) and J. Stradecki (1964–1969), written between 1963–1970, pp. 59–61.

[360] "O dyskusji nad książką J. Kuśmierka, *Uwaga człowiek*," *Biuletyn Informacyjno-Instrukcyjny* no. 2, February 1952, p. 36 (APG, WUKPPiW, file ref. no. 99).

On a Discussion of J. Kuśmierek's Book *Uwaga! Człowiek*

*The apparatus people were afraid of him, that's why he got
away with "Bieda Adachowej."*[361]
Stefan Bratkowski

*They were afraid of him because he could put his foot down
– he had no problem calling the minister a schmuck.*[362]
Adam Michnik

The report on the discussion of Kuśmierek's book was the first to be presented as part of the project; therefore, apart from purely literary issues – that
is, the evaluation of the reportages – the material contained several introductory
remarks about the program. From the statements quoted in the Bulletins, it can
be concluded that the debates on the volume were organized in the Main Office,
as well as in Kielce, Łódź, Olsztyn, Poznań, Rzeszów and Wrocław. The collection
itself became a pretext for deliberations on raising the qualifications of professional censors, but also for discussions on the proper assessment of literature.

As for the author of the book, Józef Kuśmierek (1927–1992) was a Warsaw
insurgent, a one-year member of the Polish United Workers' Party, and a long-
time freelance publicist and writer. He practiced various genres of journalism, but
was most attracted to reportage (the Bulletins discussed several of them, which is
presented below).[363] The volume *Uwaga! Człowiek* was published by "Czytelnik"
in 1951 and was comprised of three reportages: "Bieda Adachowej" [Adachowa's
poverty], "Sprawa jednego konia" [The case of one horse] and "Pożar" [Fire]).[364]
It was the second book in the output of the author who had previously won

---

[361] M. Grochowska, "Uwaga! Kuśmierek. Opowieść o szlachetnym warchole," *Gazeta Wyborcza* March 31–April 1, 2012, no. 77, p. 36.

[362] Ibidem.

[363] "Z doświadczeń prewencyjnej kontroli niektórych pism literackich," *Biuletyn Informacyjno-Instrukcyjny* no. 4 (16), April 1953, p. 21 (APG, WUKPPiW, file ref. no. 16);
L. Rutkowski, "J. Kuśmierek – 'Uwaga, wielkie niebezpieczeństwo,'" *Biuletyn Informacyjno-Instrukcyjny* no. 9 (33), September 1954, pp. 9–16 (APG, WUKPPiW, file ref.
no. 56). On the censorship of other reportages by Kuśmierek, see: M. Budnik, *"Książka
Nowego Czytelnika"…*, pp. 156–157. Sample collections of the author's reportages include: *Opowiadania reportera*, Warszawa: "Czytelnik," 1954; *Obecny (reportaże 1945–
1990)*, London: Wydawnictwo Aneks, 1991.

[364] J. Kuśmierek, *Uwaga! Człowiek*, Warszawa: "Czytelnik," 1951; Second Edition:
ibidem 1955; reprinted in *Uwaga! Człowiek i inne opowiadania*, Warszawa: "Książka
i Wiedza," 1955. See, e.g.: B. Dorosz [B. D.], "Kuśmierek Józef," [in:] *Współcześni polscy pisarze i badacze literatury. Słownik biobibliograficzny* vol. 4: *K*, eds. J. Czachowska,
A. Szałagan, Warszawa: WSiP, 1994, pp. 498–501.

a prize in a competition for a film treatment and had already been publishing in the press. The book was noticed and appreciated by critics; reviews appeared in such journals as *Nowa Kultura, Twórczość,* and *Życie Literackie*.[365] In February 1952, the book was discussed at a meeting of the Warsaw branch of the ZLP (during the meetings, other titles which had been written about in Bulletins, such as *Pokolenie* and *Piątka z ulicy Barskiej*, were also discussed).[366]

The work posed the censors considerable difficulties with interpretation and was mentioned in the Bulletins several times, e.g., in May 1952, when it was considered to be politically immature (similarly to another reportage by the writer that was assessed in the Bulletins[367]). The accusations formulated in February against the reviews that were produced after the discussion of the book boiled down to two things: taking into account only or primarily the ideological realization of the work, and focusing on its flaws and shortcomings. The mistake "of overlooking the essential values of the book"[368] and thus creating one-sided assessments was displayed on the example of a review sent by the Poznań team, in which the dominant tone was indeed doleful and not a single word was said about the artistic layer of the work:

> In his collection of reportages, the author paints a very fragmentary picture of the Polish countryside, partly from the pre-war times but mainly from the period after the war. J. Kuśmierek sees our countryside in the darkest colors. Bribery and villainy are the order of the day. He fails to see the creative elements of our reality: no one helps the peasants in the class struggle against the kulaks.[369] The activities of the party are neither seen nor heard. Such a picture of the countryside is contrary to reality. Even when the author describes the life of a production cooperative (*Pożar*), he does not steer clear of these misapprehensions.
> Overall, it must be concluded that a reader will not benefit from reading the book *Uwaga człowiek*.[370]

---

[365] T. Drewnowski, "Uwaga! Nowy człowiek," *Nowa Kultura* October 14, 1951, no. 41, p. 5; A. Kijowski, "Opowiadania niecierpliwe," *Życie Literackie* February 17, 1952, no. 4, p. 6; A. Mauersberger, [Review: J. Kuśmierek, *Uwaga! Człowiek*, Warszawa: "Czytelnik," 1951], *Twórczość* 1952, no. 2, pp. 150–153.

[366] "Kronika życia literackiego w PRL. 1952…," p. 7.

[367] "Działalność wydawnictwa 'Czytelnik' w 1951 r.," *Biuletyn Informacyjno-Instrukcyjny* no. 5, May 1952, p. 22 (APG, WUKPPiW, file ref. no. 90); L. Rutkowski, "J. Kuśmierek – 'Uwaga, wielkie niebezpieczeństwo,'" *Biuletyn Informacyjno-Instrukcyjny* no. 9 (33), September 1954, pp. 9–16 (APG, WUKPPiW, file ref. no. 56).

[368] "O dyskusji nad książką J. Kuśmierka, *Uwaga człowiek*," *Biuletyn Informacyjno-Instrukcyjny* no. 2, February 1952, p. 38 (APG, WUKPPiW, file ref. no. 99).

[369] A pejorative term used to refer to a rich peasant who was considered an extortionist and a class enemy.

[370] "O dyskusji nad książką J. Kuśmierka, *Uwaga człowiek*," *Biuletyn Informacyjno-Instrukcyjny* no. 2, February 1952, p. 36 (APG, WUKPPiW, file ref. no. 99).

Even if in other reviews the functionaries tried to evaluate something more than the ideological layer of the work, such as the reality of life in the countryside, their interpretation did not meet with the approval of their superiors, providing further evidence of the censors' lack of skill:

> Some comrades (e.g., comrade Zagórowska) accused the book of unfamiliarity with relationships in the countryside and falsely framing the "two souls" of the middle-sized farmer. This accusation is groundless and wrong because one of the positive sides of the book is the insightful, pertinent and correct presentation of the "two souls" of the middle-sized farmer (the character of Wrzosek).[371]

According to the superiors, the reviews sent by the field branches, which were the result of discussions on Kuśmierek, left no illusions as to the competence of professional censors and the value of these particular evaluations (despite some quite decently written reviews):

> While for the most part rightly pointing out the errors and defects of Kuśmierek's book, the com[rades] hardly paid any attention to its serious artistic achievements, to the fact that the reportages strongly appeal to the reader, that they are evocative and convincing. While they rightly put the main emphasis on the political meaning of the reportages, on their atypicality, and even on a certain distortion of reality, they failed to notice the serious, positive, anti-kulak character of the reportages, which, written with such zest, are an unquestionable positive. In fact, it is still a common sin for many of our censors not to notice the strong and positive things in the works they evaluate.[372]

What did the censor assessing the work of his colleagues have in mind when he wrote about artistic achievements? It would be difficult to point to any criteria, other than intuitive ones, which enabled uneducated censors to judge the artistic value of a book. From the context, it seems that the idea was to break with naïve schematism, with a black-and-white and simplified presentation of the world. Was this not what Berman meant when he demanded that artists "come into closer contact with life in order to overcome schematism"?[373]

In the first period of the socialist realist offensive, the artistic value of a work indeed was pushed into the background, giving way to the ideological correctness of the text and to the "true" reflection of social reality. And that reality was described using comprehensible artistic means, always from the position of the

---

[371] Ibidem, p. 37.
[372] Ibidem, p. 36.
[373] M. Fik, *Kultura polska po Jałcie…*, p. 160.

socialist worldview and the historical interests of the working class.[374] This was understandable in the context of propagandistic and paideutic art, whose aim was to push forward the only correct vision of the world and to prepare the citizen to function in the proclaimed reality as seamlessly as possible. However, with the development of the trend, the postulates underwent modifications; debates and discussions took place, and as a result, "production literature" – that is, literature created in accordance with the poetics of socialist realism – also transformed.

These changes translated into guidelines formulated for censors. "Appropriate censorship instructions," written during the over forty-five year period of the Office's existence, "were intended to provide a suitable basis"[375] for its work during the rise of socialist realism, including all of its more and less orthodox phases. In the documents, guidelines can be found concerning the artistic and ideological realization of works. For example, in 1949 it was established that "permission must be granted to a novel, even if it is artistically weaker, but there is a guarantee that the author will become a progressive, militant and productive writer in the future."[376] Such declarations appeared in the materials from the 1950s (e.g., in reports from interferences) and were usually an additional argument in favor of the publication of a work. However, in the analyzed Bulletins (including those from before 1950), I have not found similar postulates; on the contrary, a completely different tone resounded in all of them:

> on the territory of the Kraków Voivodeship, we take into account the artistic level, and for this reason, advisors were involved so as not to let a low-level publication slip by.[377]

> It should be strongly emphasized that an artistically worthless, garish, graphomaniac publication, even if it is politically correct, is in fact harmful.[378]

> A similar tone can be found in the analyzed report from the discussion of Kuśmierek:

---

[374] B. Owczarek, "Realizm socjalistyczny," [in:] *Słownik literatury polskiej XX wieku,* eds. A. Brodzka, M. Puchalska, M. Semczuk, A. Sobolewska, E. Szary-Matywiecka, Wrocław: Ossolineum, 1995, p. 922.

[375] *Główny Urząd Kontroli Prasy 1945–1949,* compiled by D. Nałęcz, Warszawa: ISP PAN, 1994, series *Dokumenty do Dziejów PRL* issue 6, p. 24 (see also p. 19).

[376] "Narady i odprawy naczelników WUKP i kierowników referatów widowisk w dniach: 7–9 II 1949, 26–28 VI 1949, 5 VIII 1949, 11 XII 1949. Protokoły, stenogramy" (AAN, GUKPPiW, file ref. no. 4, p. 125); cf. *Główny Urząd Kontroli Prasy 1945–1949…,* p. 24.

[377] "Ze sprawozdań Kierowników Wojewódzkich Biur," *Biuletyn Instrukcyjny* no. 2, June 1945, p. 16 (APG, WUKPPiW, file ref. no. 210).

[378] "Recenzja z pozycji literackiej, cz. I" (in the series *O wyższy poziom pracy nad książką*), *Biuletyn Informacyjno-Instrukcyjny* no. 8, August 1952, p. 20 (APG, WUKPPiW, file ref. no. 81).

It is unquestionable that the issue of the quality of the works we review, especially fiction, is still at the bottom of the list. We have not yet been able to fully grasp the obvious truth that even if a novel sets up and solves certain problems very well, but its artistic level is extremely low, then the novel is undoubtedly harmful and should not be published.[379]

For the sake of comparison, consider a passage from Flaszen's article published only a month earlier, in which the same accusations appear, this time formulated not against "censorship criticism" but against literary criticism:

A dangerous precedent of praise for the material itself was created. The artistic layer was treated as something of secondary importance, set aside for later. It was said: the book is good because the direction for development is correct, instead of saying: the book is poor but the direction for development is correct.[380]

Thus, one can see that the censorship office tried to keep up with the changes occurring in literature (assuming that at times, it was not the motor behind them) and that, with obvious and unquestionable differences, "censorship criticism" was to some extent guided by the same principles as literary, open criticism. However, it was one thing to construct guidelines and indicate the proper direction of work in various instructional materials (e.g., in the Bulletins), and another to assimilate and apply the new guidelines by rank-and-file functionaries. The heads of the GUKPPiW and their superiors realized the need for the continuous training of censors, and one of the most interesting forms of professional development were lectures by invited guests.

This opportunity emerged in November 1951, when a meeting was organized with Paweł Hoffman (the same person who sang the praises of Słonimski's self-criticism). At that time, Hoffman was the head of the Cultural Department of the Central Committee of the PZPR and editor-in-chief of *Nowa Kultura*. Not long before that, he had also been the head of *Kuźnica* and earlier, of *Rzeczpospolita* (one of the most important dailies published since 1944).[381] A fragment of Hoffman's paper was quoted in the article devoted to Kuśmierek for a reason:

If we would like to recapitulate what we expect from our literature and artists, we should say that we expect our ideological truth to be alive in art. We have been accused, and deservingly, that our creators write the appropriate things that will, however, not get through to people, because this truth is purely cognitive… We remember what we said two years ago, that the works that were created… were

---

[379] "O dyskusji nad książką J. Kuśmierka, *Uwaga człowiek*," *Biuletyn Informacyjno-Instrukcyjny* no. 2, February 1952, p. 35 (APG, WUKPPiW, file ref. no. 99).

[380] L. Flaszen, "Nowy Zoil, czyli o schematyzmie…," p. 3.

[381] C. Budzyńska, "Hoffman Paweł Maksymilian," [in:] *Słownik biograficzny działaczy polskiego ruchu robotniczego*, ed. F. Tych, vol. 2: *E–J…*, pp. 635–636.

potboilers. But this was a developmental stage. The first task was new subject matter. Today we are taking another step – we say to the authors: it is wonderful that you have started writing about it, but write about the fact that human things are happening there, give us the truth about living people...[382]

The Bulletin authors certainly did not choose this particular quote by accident. Hoffman's comment about the transformations of the newest Polish literature hit the nail on the head when it stressed that what was acceptable at an earlier stage of development was not acceptable today (in 1952). In fact, together with Berman, Andrzejewski, Kruczkowski and many others, the publicist had discussed the changes affecting literature a month earlier (that is, in October 1951), at the above-mentioned meeting devoted to artistic creativity. The conclusions of that meeting were presented in one of the November issues of *Nowa Kultura*; apart from Hoffman's "keynote" article, the speakers were Włodzimierz Sokorski, Jan Kott and Kazimierz Dejmek.[383]

Based on the fragment quoted in the Bulletin, it can be assumed that the editor's tone during the meeting with censors was the same as during the October sessions; he encouraged writing about "living people," which was derived from Berman's proposal to "close the gap between creativity and life."[384] In addition, he drew attention to an extremely important problem at the time, namely the failure to take into account the artistic value of texts ("the works that were created... were potboilers"). These guidelines, emphasizing the need to break with schematism and pay attention to the artistic value of works, certainly made sense in the context of the mediocre or extremely low-grade books, simplified in form and content, which flooded the publishing market after the proclamation of socialist realism. It should not be assumed, however, that they relieved censors of the most important task, that is, the assessment of ideological correctness, which – importantly – was the primary criterion of a review during the entire period of the operation of the office at Mysia Street. Furthermore, it also applied to the evaluation of borderline genres, to which Kuśmierek's reportages belonged. The next chapter will explore whether the genre classification had any bearing on the assessment of his work.

***

---

[382] "O dyskusji nad książką J. Kuśmierka, *Uwaga człowiek*," *Biuletyn Informacyjno-Instrukcyjny* no. 2, February 1952, p. 35 (APG, WUKPPiW, file ref. no. 99).

[383] P. Hoffman, "O niektórych problemach realizmu socjalistycznego," *Nowa Kultura* November 18, 1951, no. 46, pp. 1–2; see also the featured statements by W. Sokorski, "Wnioski z narady" (pp. 3–4), J. Kott, "Wiedza i głębokie przeżycie tematu – warunkiem rozwoju naszej plastyki" (p. 3), K. Dejmek, "Nie ma nowego teatru bez nowej dramaturgii" (p. 2).

[384] "Kronika życia literackiego w PRL. 1951...," p. 60.

Attention! Reportage[385]

*Reading the reportage, one has
the impression that the BBC is speaking.
The author uses the same propaganda
as the BBC.*[386]

In 1951, two reportages by Kuśmierek were published: the discussed collection *Uwaga! Człowiek* and *Sprawa jednego konia*. The books were published at a time when reportage created in Poland was on the defensive (the most outstanding works of the genre by Wańkowicz, Pruszyński and Fiedler were written during the war and/or in exile).[387] The popularity of this type of work started to decline around 1948, after one of the main representatives of the genre, Franciszek Gil[388] – whose reportages were also assessed in the Bulletins – had gone silent. The reactivation and renewal of the genre's formula were possible thanks to Kuśmierek, who stood out among other reporters of the time with his "critical attitude and avoidance of simplification."[389] This is what Anna Nasalska says about Kuśmierek, the winner of the Kisiel Prize, in the context of his collection *Uwaga! Człowiek*:

> His analysis of the complex reality and a detective's search for the truth revealing the hidden mechanisms of human injustice are also presented from the perspective of the triumphant justice guaranteed by the party at various levels of its territorial reach.[390]

In the program of socialist realism, reportage took "a high position, according to the importance attached to it in Soviet literature."[391] Apart from Kuśmierek,

---

[385] The title of this chapter is a reference to Kuśmierek's works: "Uwaga! Człowiek"; "Uwaga, wielkie niebezpieczeństwo"; "Uwaga! Polska" and "Uwaga! Kuśmierek" (a series of articles in *Gazeta Wyborcza*).

[386] L. Rutkowski, "J. Kuśmierek – 'Uwaga, wielkie niebezpieczeństwo,'" *Biuletyn Informacyjno-Instrukcyjny* no. 9 (33), September 1954, p. 15 (APG, WUKPPiW, file ref. no. 56).

[387] See, e.g.: K. Pruszyński, *Droga wiodła przez Narvik*, London: M.I. Kolin, 1941; A. Fiedler, *Dywizjon 303*, London: M.I. Kolin, 1942; M. Wańkowicz, *Ziele na kraterze*, New York: Roy, 1951.

[388] See: K. Kąkolewski, "Reportaż," [in:] *Słownik literatury polskiej XX wieku...*, p. 931.

[389] A. Nasalska, "Reportaż," [in:] *Słownik realizmu socjalistycznego*, eds. Z. Łapiński, W. Tomasik, Kraków: Universitas, 2004, p. 291.

[390] Ibidem.

[391] Ibidem, p. 286.

one should mention, for instance, the works of Maria Jarochowska, documenting the life of the Polish peasant and worker; numerous publications in *Odrodzenie* and *Nowa Kultura*, or the "front page" debut of Mrożek in *Przekrój* in July 1950.[392] Reportage also appeared in the catalog of such publishing houses as "Czytelnik," "Książki i Wiedza" and "Nasza Księgarnia," covering a variety of topics, from local to international affairs.[393] The fact that it appeared several times in the Bulletins further points to the importance of the genre.[394]

Returning to 1952 and the part of the reportage that classified the genre of the collection, as it turns out, an inappropriate genological classification was supposedly the reason why several censors evaluated the book incorrectly. Treating Kuśmierek's work as a typical novel resulted in it being subjected to the same requirements "as a novel of socialist realism"[395] (it is partly justified by the fact that up to that point, the title had been treated either as a collection of reportages or reportage-style short stories[396]). In that case, what were the expectations of the Office's rank-and-file functionaries regarding Kuśmierek? They wanted the author to give a comprehensive view of reality, and according to their superiors,

> it is obvious that reportage cannot offer a complete picture of reality, and it is not its task in the first place. A reportage is only supposed to offer a picture of a fragment of reality; of course, it should have a discernible value, be communicative, and typical for the given period and environment.[397]

---

[392] See, e.g.: M. Jarochowska, "Pierwsze kombajny" (in the series *Wycieczka chłopów do ZSRR*); S. Mrożek, "Młode Miasto," *Przekrój* July 22, 1950, no. 276, pp. 4, 8–9; M. Jarochowska, *Niebieskie okulary. Reportaże z huty Częstochowa*, Warszawa: "Czytelnik," 1952; See also: A.Z. Makowiecki, "'Odrodzenie' (1944–1950)," [in:] *Słownik literatury polskiej XX wieku…*, p. 756.

[393] See, e.g.: A. Fiedler, *Rio de Oro. Na ścieżkach Indian brazylijskich*, Warszawa: "Nasza Księgarnia," 1950; A. Ścibor-Rylski, *Górnicze gołębie pokoju. O Wiktorze Markiefce*, Warszawa: "Książka i Wiedza," 1950.

[394] See, e.g.: "Z doświadczeń prewencyjnej kontroli niektórych pism literackich," *Biuletyn Informacyjno-Instrukcyjny* no. 4 (16), April 1953, pp. 18–25 (APG, WUKPPiW, file ref. no. 16); "Trzy listy," *Biuletyn Informacyjno-Instrukcyjny* no. 5 (17), May 1953, pp. 53–54 (APG, WUKPPiW, file ref. no. 15).

[395] "O dyskusji nad książką J. Kuśmierka, *Uwaga człowiek*," *Biuletyn Informacyjno-Instrukcyjny* no. 2, February 1952, p. 37 (APG, WUKPPiW, file ref. no. 99).

[396] Cf., e.g.: K. Kąkolewski, "Reportaż," [in:] *Słownik literatury polskiej XX wieku…*, p. 931; B. Dorosz [B. D.], "Kuśmierek Józef," [in:] *Współcześni polscy pisarze i badacze literatury. Słownik biobibliograficzny* vol. 4: *K…*, p. 499.

[397] "O dyskusji nad książką J. Kuśmierka, *Uwaga człowiek*," *Biuletyn Informacyjno-Instrukcyjny* no. 2, February 1952, p. 37 (APG, WUKPPiW, file ref. no. 99).

Did Kuśmierek's reportages meet at least the other demands? Not exactly, replied the supervisors:

> Clearly, none of the three works collected in this book offers a typical picture of our reality. And clearly, the lack of resistance and fight against exploitation, as well as showing the party on the defensive is not typical in our country. For example, the character of Kociek – the prosecutor, or the activity of the administrative authorities, etc. are unusual. These are undoubtedly important and serious factual errors, however, one must also see the positives which prevail and qualify the book for publication.[398]

This was the response of the "decision makers" who, despite noticing serious flaws in the work, did not block it. Thus, what for some was a weak but acceptable point, for others was a reason to give the book a negative evaluation. Perhaps this was because Kuśmierek was not an obvious author – he "corrected" and adapted the reality he presented to the requirements of the dominant ideology because he had no other option. He tried to reconcile the contradictory expectations that were (indirectly) placed on reportage – namely, the presentation of a true picture of reality – while at the same time adjusting this picture to the requirements of the prevailing ideology.

The quoted fragment shows that, at least in this case, the "decision-makers" expected something more from censors than just tracking down dangerous theses or formulations in a book. The functionaries should be able to evaluate and appreciate the work not only as a collection of parts, but as a whole; they should be able to see potential and solutions worthy of praise in a faltering or novel idea (to the extent the system allowed it).

Firstly, this corresponded to warnings already formulated in the second half of the 1940s against "confiscating 'words' while ignoring the whole"[399] (the creative ingenuity of the management also warned against putting on "horse blinkers which allowed one to only see words but not the whole"[400] and against a propensity for "chasing after harsh words"[401]). While in the above-mentioned cases, the

---

[398] Ibidem.

[399] "Konfiskata 'słówek' przy niewidzeniu całości," *Biuletyn Informacyjno-Szkoleniowy* no. 1/3, January 1949, pp. 34–38 (APG, WUKPPiW, file ref. no. 196). See also ["Materiały z odprawy"], fol. 35r (*"Biuletyny Instrukcyjno-Szkoleniowe 1945–1951"* (APP, WUKPPiW, file ref. no. 4)).

[400] ["Materiały z odprawy"], fol. 34r (*"Biuletyny Instrukcyjno-Szkoleniowe 1945–1951"* (APP, WUKPPiW, file ref. no. 4)). This metaphor also appeared in other censorship documents, cf. "Z krajowej odprawy w GUKP," *Biuletyn Informacyjno-Instrukcyjny* no. 7, July 1952, p. 19 (APG, WUKPPiW, file ref. no. 84).

[401] *Biuletyn Głównego Urzędu Kontroli Prasy* no. 4, fol. 55r (APP WUKPPiW, file ref. no. 4).

censors' offense was removing minor errors at the expense of more serious omissions, in the case of *Uwaga! Człowiek*, the point was not to condemn the work to oblivion by extrapolating individual errors to the whole.

Secondly, it fit in with the fight against schematism, which was being carried on at the time, and valuing a work only for the material and substance from which it was created, while treating the artistic "tooling" as secondary. The necessity of fighting schematism and "not obfuscating" the image of reality presented in reportage was also argued for later, for example, in April 1953, when several examples of bad reportage were discussed.[402]

Evidently, genological classification was not fundamental to the discussion of Kuśmierek's work, but it did affect its assessment. Based on these few succinct excerpts, it is clear that in 1952, the Office for the Control expected its staff to use evaluative criteria appropriate for the type of writing. The report from the discussion noted the need for different standards of reviewing so-called fictional literature (citing the novel of socialist realism as an example) and non-fictional literature (that is, reportage). Whether reportage-specific issues were really discussed in this case is a different matter. A number of the problems raised in these excerpts also concerned the evaluation of works of fiction.

***

On a Discussion of Bohdan Czeszko's Book *Pokolenie*

It is "our" book, a party book,
written with a deep passion.[403]

Another title discussed at the "Ministry of Truth" in 1952 was Bohdan Czeszko's *Pokolenie*, a novel dealing with the political and moral choices of young people coming of age during the war.[404] The Bulletin does not give a definite answer as to how many branches held debates; it was generally reported that the book

---

[402] "Z doświadczeń prewencyjnej kontroli niektórych pism literackich," *Biuletyn Informacyjno-Instrukcyjny* no. 4 (16), April 1953, pp. 18–25 (APG, WUKPPiW, file ref. no. 16).

[403] "Na marginesie dyskusji nad *Pokoleniem* Czeszki," *Biuletyn Informacyjno-Instrukcyjny* no. 4, April 1952, p. 18 (APG, WUKPPiW, file ref. no. 93). The quote refers to Bohdan Czeszko's *Pokolenie*.

[404] See also: K. Budrowska, "Wewnętrzne pismo cenzury. *Biuletyn Informacyjno-Instrukcyjny* w latach 1952–1955," [in:] eadem, *Studia i szkice o cenzurze w Polsce Ludowej w latach 40. i 50. XX wieku*, Białystok: Wydawnictwo Alter Studio, 2014, pp. 99–101.

was discussed in the Non-Periodical Publications Department.[405] On the other hand, in August 1952, one of the instructional texts referred to reviews of *Pokolenie* specifically because they were "generally familiar to the entire censorship apparatus."[406] It must, therefore, be assumed that at least several teams approached the discussion. The novel itself was still written about in the May 1952 Bulletin.[407]

The book was published in November 1951 by "Czytelnik"; however, it had already been presented in installments in *Twórczość* since May.[408] Critics received the book favorably, although some shortcomings were pointed out to the author. Reviews appeared in, e.g., *Życie Literackie*, *Dziś i Jutro* and *Wieś*, while *Nowa Kultura* organized a discussion about the book due to the enormous interest among readers. *Pokolenie* garnered critical attention from Drawicz, Flaszen, Kott, Żukrowski and others.[409] The work was also discussed at a meeting of the Warsaw branch of the Polish Literary Society in February 1952. In the same year, the author received the State Award of the Second Degree for the novel. Already in 1953, a film script had been written based on the book, and a movie adaptation, directed by Andrzej Wajda (which probably surpassed the literary original) was released in 1954.[410]

The discussion reports on Kuśmierek and Czeszko were only two months apart, which is perhaps why both pointed out many similar flaws in the evaluation of the books. The censors were accused, broadly speaking, of schematism in assessment, zeroing in on errors and criticism that was disproportionate to what the titles represented. Two quotations of note:

---

[405] "Na marginesie dyskusji nad *Pokoleniem* Czeszki," *Biuletyn Informacyjno-Instrukcyjny* no. 4, April 1952, p. 16 (APG, WUKPPiW, file ref. no. 93).

[406] "Recenzja z pozycji literackiej, cz. I" (in the series *O wyższy poziom pracy nad książką*), *Biuletyn Informacyjno-Instrukcyjny* no. 8, August 1952, p. 22 (APG, WUKPPiW, file ref. no. 81).

[407] "Działalność wydawnictwa 'Czytelnik' w 1951 r.," *Biuletyn Informacyjno-Instrukcyjny* no. 5, May 1952, p. 22 (APG, WUKPPiW, file ref. no. 90).

[408] B. Czeszko, *Pokolenie*, *Twórczość* 1951, no. 5, pp. 51–91; no. 6, pp. 82–108; no. 7, pp. 30–66; no. 8, pp. 17–52; B. Czeszko, *Pokolenie*, Warszawa: "Czytelnik," 1951.

[409] J. Kott, "Świadomość i pasja (O *Pokoleniu* Bohdana Czeszki)"; W. Żukrowski, "Walczące pokolenie," *Nowa Kultura* January 27, 1952, no. 4, pp. 6–7; L. Flaszen, "Rozmowa o *Pokoleniu*," *Życie Literackie* February 17, 1952, no. 4, p. 5; A. Drawicz, "Jeszcze o *Pokoleniu*," *Wieś* May 11, 1952, no. 19, p. 6; Z. Lichniak, "Z dziejów zwycięskiej generacji," *Dziś i Jutro* March 9, 1952, no. 10, pp. 5–6; Z. Macużanka, "Powieść o bohaterskiej młodzieży," *Polonistyka* 1952, no. 5, pp. 55–57.

[410] *Pokolenie* (*A Generation*), directed by A. Wajda, script by B. Czeszko, starring T. Łomnicki, U. Modrzyńska, Z. Cybulski, R. Polański, prod. Wytwórnia Filmów Fabularnych, 1954.

> while generally pointing out legitimate errors and shortcomings of Kuśmierek's book, for the most part [the censors – AWG] hardly paid any attention to its major artistic achievements.[411]

and a fragment about *Pokolenie*:

> This book, which is still hotly debated today, was initially not evaluated in sufficient depth. It fell victim to a certain schematism in the evaluation, a dogged search for errors in formulations without seeing the book as a whole.[412]

In the material on Czeszko, this set of observations present in both reports was expanded by several new remarks, some of which were directly related to the content of *Pokolenie*. The layout of the report was also updated: for obvious reasons, the re-explication of the project's aims was abandoned. As a result, essentially all of the material was devoted exclusively to Czeszko. Secondly, the article was divided into three distinct parts: a presentation of the accusations pointed out by the censors; a recounting of the discussion of the book[413]; and a rebuttal of the accusations by the Bulletin's editors, which was very important from the point of view of the monthly's training and instructional goals.

Undoubtedly, the board evaluating the report was most struck by the statements of the "botchers" Tyrman and Probołowska.[414] According to their superiors, these censors deserved this epithet for their simplified and erroneous interpretations of the events presented in the novel. For instance, comrade Tyrman accused Czeszko of naturalism in the descriptions of the protagonists' experiences, characterizations and images from the ghetto.[415] Probołowska, on the other hand, felt the book lacked a strongly outlined positive hero, which was refuted according to the postulate of "literature closer to life": "A positive hero does not have to be a knight without blemish; he must be true and human and may be prone to mistakes and hesitations. The fact that Stacho got drunk over a certain period by no means disqualifies him as one of the heroes."[416]

---

[411] "O dyskusji nad książką J. Kuśmierka, *Uwaga człowiek*," *Biuletyn Informacyjno-Instrukcyjny* no. 2, February 1952, p. 36 (APG, WUKPPiW, file ref. no. 99).

[412] "Na marginesie dyskusji nad *Pokoleniem* Czeszki," *Biuletyn Informacyjno-Instrukcyjny* no. 4, April 1952, p. 16 (APG, WUKPPiW, file ref. no. 93).

[413] Comrade Bażańska, Dobrzyński, Mortimor, Światycka, Pomykało, Tyrman and Wilner had taken part in the discussion.

[414] "Na marginesie dyskusji nad *Pokoleniem* Czeszki," *Biuletyn Informacyjno-Instrukcyjny* no. 4, April 1952, p. 16 (APG, WUKPPiW, file ref. no. 93).

[415] Ibidem.

[416] Ibidem.

Probołowska also failed to distinguish between an evaluation of a work and its summary, which was a frequent error committed by the staff. According to the editors, she did not present a censorship review but a schematic note from the publisher. This problem was raised in numerous Bulletins, including in August 1952, when the subject of *Pokolenie* was rehashed:

> There are times when a very broad review is limited to a more or less detailed summary of the novel's plot. At best, it is a list of basic problems, but without any attempt to analyze them, to show <u>how</u> these problems were posed. And yet, this is the <u>how</u> that interests us the most. A review should certainly provide a kind of summary, but its fundamental part must be an analysis of the value of the book, an assessment.[417] (original emphasis)

Technically, this objection applied only to Probołowska's review, because the other assessments of *Pokolenie* were written with more care.

In the next part, the April report goes on to present the comments of subsequent censors, emphasizing (not without disappointment) that they focused primarily on the failings of the novel. Many comments were critical of the portrayal of the People's Army and the National Front, and of the insufficient "unmasking of the essence of the Warsaw Uprising."[418] The latter issue was revisited four months later, and the accusation was supplemented by a lack of emphasis on the treacherous role of the Home Army and the National Armed Forces.[419] In the April issue, however, the proper politicization of the book was still on the agenda; it was, of course, necessary, although there were warnings against mechanically saturating the novel with remarks of a political nature, as this could have produced a discrepancy between form and content. The functionaries paid attention to the psychological outlining of the characters, the composition of the novel, and the direction of the plot.

The statement of the censor Światycka took into account the above elements in her evaluation, but also the author's education. Bear in mind that Czeszko graduated from a high school of fine arts, and then studied at the Academy of Fine Arts in Warsaw and occasionally worked as an interior designer:

> Comrade Światycka maintains the charge of a discrepancy between the form and content of *Pokolenie*. The content of the novel is the struggle of the communists,

---

[417] "Recenzja z pozycji literackiej, cz. I" (in the series *O wyższy poziom pracy nad książką*), *Biuletyn Informacyjno-Instrukcyjny* no. 8, August 1952, p. 22 (APG, WUKPPiW, file ref. no. 81).

[418] "Na marginesie dyskusji nad *Pokoleniem* Czeszki," *Biuletyn Informacyjno-Instrukcyjny* no. 4, April 1952, p. 18 (APG, WUKPPiW, file ref. no. 93).

[419] "Recenzja z pozycji literackiej, cz. I" (in the series *O wyższy poziom pracy nad książką*), *Biuletyn Informacyjno-Instrukcyjny* no. 8, August 1952, p. 22 (APG, WUKPPiW, file ref. no. 81).

and the memoirs of a National Armed Forces member, Władek, fare the best. Major drawbacks of the book include narrowing down the issues, its fragmentary nature, a series of chaotic, disjointed scenes, a lack of dynamism, and unresolved problems. Comrade Światycka attributes the fragmentary nature, a lack of a generalizing view, and the shallowing of psychological experiences to the fact that the author is also a painter, which contributed to the static nature of the portrayal. The Jewish society is shown as sheep going to the slaughter, no resistance is visible.[420]

The reference to the author's biography was justified, although Czeszko's education was certainly less important for the censor's evaluation than his attitude and choices during the war. Czeszko, a soldier of the People's Guard, People's Army and People's Army of Poland, member of the Union of Youth Struggle, participant of the Warsaw Uprising, described *Pokolenie* from the perspective of his own experiences, which was noticed and appreciated in some reviews: "Such a true picture could only be given by a man who knew the life of the youth of that time, their ups and downs; someone who had an emotional, affectionate attitude to this 'coming of age' of the young generation."[421] The fact that after the war, as an ideological communist, the author joined the only righteous side – legitimizing the new order with his works – was certainly significant for this assessment.

Throughout the debate, there was much criticism of the work, but there were also voices appreciating the novel. Some censors, regardless of the accusations against Czeszko, admitted that the book gave a fair picture of the events, showed real, flesh-and-blood people, and was even interesting and devoid of cheap tricks.[422] However, the most favorable review was given to *Pokolenie* by functionary Pomykało. Although the ideological charge was present in his evaluation, a certain critical reflection cannot be denied. For the censor, Czeszko's novel was an expression of "a breakthrough in our literature."[423] None of his colleagues formulated such a strong thesis, or at least it was not quoted in the Bulletins. Pomykało also commended the realistic portrayal of the protagonists and criticized the assessments, which focused on the book's flaws while ignoring its merits. This aspect of the censorship evaluation was also pointed out in August 1952, when it was bemoaned that the one-sidedness of the perspective did not allow the reviewers for "a deep, analytical rating of the value of the book, which has received

---

[420] "Na marginesie dyskusji nad *Pokoleniem* Czeszki," *Biuletyn Informacyjno-Instrukcyjny* no. 4, April 1952, p. 17 (APG, WUKPPiW, file ref. no. 93). Czeszko passed his *matura* (final secondary education) exam in 1947 at the State High School of Fine Arts in Warsaw, and from 1947 to 1951, he studied at the Academy of Fine Arts in Warsaw.

[421] Ibidem, p. 18.

[422] Ibidem, p. 17.

[423] Ibidem.

this year's State Award."[424] Such a balanced evaluation, which did not disregard the flaws of the work but made sure to note its qualities, was discussed in the press and at numerous meetings and conventions.

Recapitulating the discussion of *Pokolenie*, the authors of the Bulletin stated that "this interesting title did not find its full and proper evaluation by the team."[425] Although they also pointed out the work's shortcomings (the defects in portraying the characters, "a failure to show the full hideousness of the Home Army's role in organizing the uprising,"[426] and to sufficiently highlight the role of the People's Guard and People's Army in the national struggle for liberation), they considered *Pokolenie* to be an ideologically valuable title, representing a major achievement in the literature of the time:

> It is "our" book, a party book, written with deep passion. It presents characters that are living and real; ones that hesitate, grapple, possess all human traits and weaknesses, while following the line of development. The characters of the book are very simple, they grow by gaining awareness, struggle in hardship, fulfill their duties. They display no easy heroism, declamation, cheap pathos. They are compelling.
> The protagonist of the book actually is the "Generation"; those young people who during the occupation – under the influence of the party and their older, more informed comrades – learned to fight and developed their awareness and morality. It is worth mentioning here how beautifully the author portrayed the characters of the old communists, how mature and full of moderation they are in their statements and actions. At the same time, there is so much care for the young characters, so much effort not to warp them.[427]

The final question is why the superiors recognized the Polish Hemingway's[428] book as "absolutely engrossing,"[429] sparing no praise for it, while the other censors could not fully appreciate the work that was tailored according to the obligatory

---

[424] "Recenzja z pozycji literackiej, cz. I" (in the series *O wyższy poziom pracy nad książką*), *Biuletyn Informacyjno-Instrukcyjny* no. 8, August 1952, p. 23 (APG, WUKPPiW, file ref. no. 81).

[425] "Na marginesie dyskusji nad *Pokoleniem* Czeszki," *Biuletyn Informacyjno-Instrukcyjny* no. 4, April 1952, p. 18 (APG, WUKPPiW, file ref. no. 93).

[426] Ibidem, p. 20.

[427] Ibidem, pp. 18–19.

[428] A. Lisiecka, "Drogi do wolności Bohdana Czeszki," [in:] eadem, *Pokolenie "pryszczatych,"* Warszawa: PIW, 1964, p. 101. See also: *Bohdan Czeszko* (in the series *Literackie Portrety*), prepared by W. Holewiński, guests: A. Robiński, J. Termer, Polskie Radio program 2 June 14, 2018, https://polskieradio24.pl/8/3869/Artykul/2149212,Literackie-portrety-Bohdan-Czeszko (accessed January 31, 2021).

[429] "Na marginesie dyskusji nad *Pokoleniem* Czeszki," *Biuletyn Informacyjno-Instrukcyjny* no. 4, April 1952, p. 18 (APG, WUKPPiW, file ref. no. 93).

model? There could have been several reasons. Before these are elaborated on, it is worth asking whether the selection of reviews of *Pokolenie* presented in the Bulletins was not biased by the training character of the monthly. After all, the editors made no secret of the fact that they primarily discussed incorrect and damaging reviews in order to point out what mistakes rank-and-file employees should avoid. In this case, I was able to verify the hypothesis by studying the reviews of *Pokolenie* preserved in other censorship documents. This allowed me to confirm my initial observation that the functionaries indeed had quite a few reservations about the book.

According to the superiors, one of the reasons for such an erroneous assessment of *Pokolenie* could have been the low competence of censors (in the 1950s, this was not surprising) and the fact that Czeszko's book – as a socialist realist production – was subjected to meticulous scrutiny according to the aforementioned rule "of sharp interference and constant chiseling of 'loyal' texts."[430] The report on the discussion showed unambiguously that the employees of field branches evaluated the novel according to previous standards, that is, zeroing in on errors in ideological realization and neglecting artistic solutions, while their superiors expected something more. Of course, this "more" was still within the universe of the socialist-realist recipe for books, because in 1952, a real "breakthrough in literature" was still out of the question.

These two reasons seem unquestionable, but one could – with some caution – look for another in the novel itself. It is indisputable that *Pokolenie* is a book created "according to the official model,"[431] the work of an ardent communist, repeating lies about Katyń, the Home Army and the Warsaw Uprising. However, it could not be denied that the book contained some relatively new solutions, which made it less of a typical, "flat"[432] production piece, to which the censors were accustomed. An ordinary functionary might not have appreciated either the work's original, own language (considering the Stalinist conditions) or the nuances in the portrayal of the characters realized with considerable authenticity. If these were noticed at all, they were treated as an unauthorized departure from the novelistic orthodoxy. And how was diverging even a little from the existing rules of writing handled? Typically, censors adopted a hedging attitude, because the fear of being held responsible for an oversight made the staff look for errors even where there were none.

Perhaps this was also the reason for such an evaluation of *Pokolenie*: only a censor meticulously following literary criticism and the instructions of the Office would have been able to produce a nuanced evaluation, forgo tracking down errors and appreciate the artistic value of the book, well-received by superiors

---

[430] K. Budrowska, "Wewnętrzne pismo cenzury…," p. 101.

[431] Ibidem.

[432] J. Abramow-Newerly, *Lwy STS-u*, Warszawa: Wydawnictwo Rosner&Wspólnicy, 2005, p. 41.

and the press. It is possible to accept such a hypothesis, although it should be made clear once again that the book was still within the universe of the socialist-realist formula for a novel, and as such, could defend itself as good – albeit imperfect – production literature (if not for the censors' "obsession" with pointing out errors). Everything depended on how the censors would evaluate the novel: as a model product of the socialist-realist method or as a "semi-finished product" trying to realize new – but still socialist-realist – standards of writing.

4.2.2. Books Selected for Discussion in Censorship Offices in 1953

> *The importance of excellent library management is*
> *illustrated by the fact that*
> *while writing his work The Development of*
> *Capitalism in Russia, Lenin used 583 books.*[433]

In 1953, a report was presented on the discussion of the aforementioned poem "Oskarżam" by Mikołaj Rostworowski. In fact, this was the only literary text reviewed in the 1953 Bulletins as part of the nationwide discussions. This does not mean, however, that other materials were not examined. This time, it was press publications that became the focus of censorial reflection, all of which dealt with topics quite different from literary ones. The titles of the articles speak for themselves: "The Struggle for Peace – the Pivotal Matter,"[434] "Are Socialism and Communism Different Systems?"[435], "Why Did the Countryside Not Receive Compensation?"[436], "The Wall-Street–Nowogrodzka Axis,"[437] "Traditions

---

[433] "Z terenowych prac ocenowych," *Biuletyn Informacyjno-Instrukcyjny* no. 9, September 1952, p. 46 (APG, WUKPPiW, file ref. no. 78; a fragment of the radio broadcast entitled *Przystępujemy do skompletowania gminnych bibliotek*, July 1952).

[434] "Śladem dyskusji nad artykułem 'Walka o pokój sprawą najważniejszą,'" *Biuletyn Informacyjno-Instrukcyjny* no. 2 (14), February 1953, pp. 3–9 (APG, WUKPPiW, file ref. no. 18).

[435] "Jakie ingerencje były konieczne w artykule pt. 'Czy socjalizm i komunizm to inne ustroje' (Kurier Szczeciński no. 297)," *Biuletyn Informacyjno-Instrukcyjny* no. 2 (14), February 1953, pp. 16–22 (APG, WUKPPiW, file ref. no. 18).

[436] "O błędach artykułu pod tytułem 'Dlaczego wieś nie otrzymała ekwiwalentu' w świetle niektórych zagadnień Uchwały Rządu z dn. 3.I.53 r.," *Biuletyn Informacyjno-Instrukcyjny* no. 2 (14), February 1953, pp. 23–32 (APG, WUKPPiW, file ref. no. 18).

[437] "W sprawie dyskusji nad art. 'Oś Wall-Street–Nowogrodzka,'" *Biuletyn Informacyjno-Instrukcyjny* no. 4 (16), April 1953, pp. 2–10 (APG, WUKPPiW, file ref. no. 16). In this case, after the report, the discussed article was featured in the Bulletin, see "Załącznik," *Biuletyn Informacyjno-Instrukcyjny* no. 4 (16), April 1953, pp. 11–17 (APG, WUKPPiW, file ref. no. 16).

of Friendship: *The Great Proletariat* and *Narodnaya Volya*,"[438] "The Battle for Sucha Wola,"[439] "Poland Has Returned to the Oder and Neisse Rivers and Is There to Stay."[440]

4.2.3. Books Selected for Discussion in Censorship Offices in 1954: (Not Only) Brzeziński, Kuśmierek, Kubalski, and Promiński

In 1954, further discussion reports were presented; this time, the focus was on the poetic output of Bogdan Brzeziński,[441] a "satirist in the field," and author of the monologues for *Podwieczorek przy mikrofonie* [Afternoon tea at the microphone], as well as two works of fiction, which are presented below. As in the previous year, press articles were also assessed (although there were far fewer of them[442]). In addition, another reportage by Józef Kuśmierek discussed in the series was reviewed, this time examining Polish schools. "Uwaga, wielkie niebez-

---

[438] "Uwagi o przebiegu dyskusji na temat artykułu 'Tradycje przyjaźni. *Wielki Proletariat i Narodnaja Wola*,'" *Biuletyn Informacyjno-Instrukcyjny* no. 5 (17), May 1953, pp. 2–9 (APG, WUKPPiW, file ref. no. 15). Also in this case, the report was followed by the discussed text, see: "Tradycje przyjaźni. *Wielki Proletariat i Narodnaja Wola*," *Biuletyn Informacyjno-Instrukcyjny* no. 5 (17), May 1953, pp. 10–12 (APG, WUKPPiW, file ref. no. 15).

[439] "Podsumowanie dyskusji nad artykułem 'Bitwa o Suchą Wolę,'" *Biuletyn Informacyjno-Instrukcyjny* no. 8 (20), August 1953, pp. 31–41 (APG, WUKPPiW, file ref. no. 13). Also in this case, the report was followed by the discussed text, see "Załącznik art. 'Bitwa o Suchą Wolę,'" *Biuletyn Informacyjno-Instrukcyjny* no. 8 (20), August 1953, pp. 42–50 (APG, WUKPPiW, file ref. no. 15).

[440] "Na marginesie dyskusji nad artykułem Jakuba Barycza pt. 'Polska wróciła nad Odrę i Nysę i nad nimi pozostanie,'" *Biuletyn Informacyjno-Instrukcyjny* no. 11/12 (23/24), November/December 1953, pp. 22–31 (APG, WUKPPiW, file ref. no. 9).

[441] K. Bażańska, "Satyra w terenie. Uwagi o dyskusji nad tekstami Brzezińskiego," *Biuletyn Informacyjno-Instrukcyjny* no. 11/12 (35/36), November/December 1954, pp. 27–36 (APG, WUKPPiW, file ref. no. 59).

[442] "O wynikach dyskusji," *Biuletyn Informacyjno-Instrukcyjny* no. 3 (27), March 1954, pp. 10–19 (APG, WUKPPiW, file ref. no. 45; the discussion was about the article "Pionierzy rewolucji" by Henryk Dobrowolski); L. Majzner, "Podsumowanie dyskusji," *Biuletyn Informacyjno-Instrukcyjny* no. 7/8 (31/32), July/August 1954, pp. 12–20 (APG, WUKPPiW, file ref. no. 65; the discussion was about "O polityce ograniczania kułactwa"); L. Kimlowski, "Kilka uwag o tygodniku *Dookoła świata* (January–June 1954)," *Biuletyn Informacyjno-Instrukcyjny* no. 9 (33), September 1954, pp. 25–32 (APG, WUKPPiW, file ref. no. 56); J. Raczkowski, "W związku z dyskusją na temat problematyki II Zjazdu PZPR," *Biuletyn Informacyjno-Instrukcyjny* no. 11/12 (35/36), November/December 1954, pp. 14–26 (APG, WUKPPiW, file ref. no. 59; the discussion was about "Zadania górnictwa węglowego w świetle wytycznych II Zjazdu PZPR").

pieczeństwo" [Attention, grave danger] was not viewed favorably by the "deci-sion-makers," who recommended that the text be blocked. Some of the censors agreed with this verdict, however, they polemicized with certain opinions presented in the report. In the Bulletins, a peculiar discussion ensued between censors Rutkowski and Raczyński, who, in subsequent statements, presented their arguments about the justification for withholding the work. The titles of the articles and letters sent to the Bulletin's editors testify to the emotional involvement in Kuśmierek's case: "J. Kuśmierek – 'Uwaga, wielkie niebezpieczeństwo,'" "Czy Kuśmierek jest wrogiem?" [Is Kuśmierek the enemy?] and "Trzeba by chyba coś zmienić… (Rehabilitujemy Kuśmierka)" [We ought to do something… (Rehabilitating Kuśmierek)].[443]

***

On a Discussion of Zdzisław Kubalski's Short Story "Wyrok"

Burewicz is no Stefek Burczymucha[444]

"Wyrok," [The sentence] discussed that year, also triggered a letter from the censorship collective, dissatisfied with the criticism it had received for its evaluation of the selected title.[445] It is one of the short stories that comprise Zdzisław[446] Kubalski's book *W Redłowie i gdzie indziej* [In Redłowo and elsewhere]. The book was published in 1954 but some of the stories were printed earlier in

---

[443] L. Rutkowski, "J. Kuśmierek – 'Uwaga, wielkie niebezpieczeństwo,'" *Biuletyn Informacyjno-Instrukcyjny* no. 9 (33), September 1954, pp. 9–16 (APG, WUKPPiW, file ref. no. 56); J. Raczyński (WUKPPiW Poznań), "Czy Kuśmierek jest wrogiem?," *Biuletyn Informacyjno-Instrukcyjny* no. 10 (34), October 1954, pp. 35–37 (APG, WUKPPiW, file ref. no. 58); idem, "Trzeba by chyba coś zmienić… (Rehabilitujemy Kuśmierka)" (correspondence in "Dział Listów"), *Biuletyn Informacyjno-Instrukcyjny* nr 3 (39), marzec 1955, pp. 38–40 (APG, WUKPPiW, sygn. 107).

[444] "Nasze zdanie o 'Wynikach dyskusji nad opowiadaniem Kubalskiego, "Wyrok,"'" (correspondence in "Dział Listów"), *Biuletyn Informacyjno-Instrukcyjny* no. 5 (29), May 1954, p. 52. Burewicz, a member of the Communist Party of Poland, is the protagonist in Kubalski's story. Stefek Burczymucha is the titular hero of Maria Konopnicka's poem, see: M. Konopnicka, *Stefek Burczymucha*, ill. by A. Zieleńcowa, Warszawa: "Nasza Księgarnia," 1955 (the first edition was published in 1895).

[445] See: "Nasze zdanie o 'Wynikach dyskusji nad opowiadaniem Kubalskiego, "Wyrok,"'" (correspondence in "Dział Listów"), *Biuletyn Informacyjno-Instrukcyjny* no. 5 (29), May 1954, pp. 50–53 (APG, WUKPPiW, file ref. no. 49).

[446] In the Bulletin – Zbigniew.

Zielony Sztandar.[447] The volume was received by critics with mild enthusiasm, as evidenced by the title of Jan Józef Lipski's review of the collection, "O czytankach"[448] [On little tales].

The editors praised the interesting polemics and the "lively reaction" evoked by the material, which – according to the quoted statements – was discussed in the branches in Gdańsk, Katowice (referred consistently in the Bulletins as Stalinogród), Kraków, Lublin, Łódź, Poznań and Wrocław. The reports sent to "Mysia Street" showed that all the voivodeship collectives were in favor of removing the text, which only a few comrades assessed positively, adding it to the pool of materials evaluated extremely differently by the rank-and-file employees and "decision-makers" of the censorship office.

For those readers of the Bulletin who were unfamiliar with the story, the editors included a concise summary, which was, obviously, of considerable educational value. Supplementing the details provided by the anonymous editorial board, it can be noted that Kubalski specialized in rural issues, which was the basic theme of this collection as well. This time, the protagonist of Kubalski's short story is a certain Burewicz, a member of the Communist Party of Poland (KPP) "who during the Soviet Union's war against the Nazi invaders is employed in Soviet work battalions behind the front line."[449] Unfortunately, while logging, the protagonist twice falls asleep: "The first time Burewicz was caught sleeping in the woods during working hours (and it was a week ago), it was not reported outside the company."[450]

Burewicz was awakened from his second, several-hour nap by the "good, but impulsive"[451] company commander, Manilov. This, of course, has disastrous (though not tragic) consequences for Burewicz's fate shown in the story, but it also does not escape the attention of the censors, who were convinced that "a member of the KPP, a Sanation prisoner, could not have acted the way Burewicz did: falling asleep on the job."[452] Almost all the censors feared that Kubalski ridiculed the Polish communists; only some saw the character as a departure from "a cliché and stereotype."[453] The latter opinion was shared by the superiors

---

[447] Z. Kubalski, "Wyrok," [in:] *W Redłowie i gdzie indziej. Opowiadania*, Warszawa: Ludowa Spółdzielnia Wydawnicza, 1954, pp. 68–79. Cf. e.g.: idem, "O głośnym wydarzeniu w cichej wsi Skorupki," *Zielony Sztandar* December 27, 1953, no. 52, p. 16 (part one); January 1–3, 1954, no. 1, p. 11 (part two) and idem, *W Redłowie i gdzie indziej...*, pp. 45–54.

[448] J.J. Lipski, "O czytankach," *Nowa Kultura* July 11, 1954, no. 28, p. 7.

[449] "O wynikach dyskusji nad opowiadaniem Kubalskiego, 'Wyrok,'" *Biuletyn Informacyjno-Instrukcyjny* no. 2 (26), February 1954, p. 25 (APG, WUKPPiW, file ref. no. 42).

[450] Z. Kubalski, "Wyrok...," p. 71.

[451] Ibidem.

[452] "O wynikach dyskusji nad opowiadaniem Kubalskiego, 'Wyrok,'" *Biuletyn Informacyjno-Instrukcyjny* no. 2 (26), February 1954, p. 26 (APG, WUKPPiW, file ref. no. 42).

[453] Ibidem.

who warned against creating flawless heroes, even communists, because it would "make them flat and schematic, detached from the actual phenomena of everyday life."[454] Clearly, the fight against schematism was not over yet.

The protagonist of the novella was brought before the field court of the Soviet Army for his actions. According to most censors, this provisional legal system, which operated during the war, reflected unfairly and unfavorably on the USSR. In their view, the story suggested that the penalties applied by the local judiciary were disproportionate to the offenses; that there were similarities between the Sanation judiciary and the Soviet Army's field court; and that the protagonist's actions were sabotage. However, the superiors felt that these opinions were an exaggeration and that, ultimately, Burewicz did not fall asleep "on purpose, with premeditation" but "out of ordinary fatigue, while reminiscing about the old days."[455] Refuting the charges of their subordinates, the editors referred to specific fragments in the text – including a quotation from the novella – that contradicted the censors' theses and demonstrated numerous errors and shortcomings, or even caricatural consequences of their interpretation. They noted again the need to apply different standards of evaluation to press and scholarly texts, and to fiction. According to the editors, "many comrades overlooked the fact that the short story should have been considered a literary creation,"[456] and the discussion itself "clearly indicated a lack of flexibility in assessing the novella and its value in terms of both content and form."[457]

The discussion of "Wyrok" was presented in February 1954. The analysis of the material evidently showed that many problems boomeranged, which is aptly recapitulated by the following excerpt from the report that could probably summarize the discussion on Kuśmierek, Czeszko, and others:

> In their work as censors, the voivodeship collectives are mainly focused on catching the harmful moments, completely ignoring whether it is a newspaper article or literary fiction. Meanwhile, this is of fundamental importance for the evaluation of the whole. In addition, they pay little or no attention to the positive aspects; in this case, the high educational and artistic value of the novella.
> When assessing any work of literature, one should beware of schematism and mechanistic application of pigeonholing, as well as scholastic and unrealistic criteria.[458]

***

---

[454] Ibidem, p. 27.

[455] Ibidem. Cf. Z. Kubalski, "Wyrok…," pp. 71–72.

[456] "O wynikach dyskusji nad opowiadaniem Kubalskiego, 'Wyrok,'" *Biuletyn Informacyjno-Instrukcyjny* no. 2 (26), February 1954, p. 33 (APG, WUKPPiW, file ref. no. 42).

[457] Ibidem.

[458] Ibidem.

The February 1954 material on "Wyrok" was not the last devoted to the short story. In May of that year, the editors printed a letter from the Łódź team, who "decided to 'chime in' on the novella and the summary of the discussion."[459] The functionaries felt clearly hurt by how the Bulletin's editors assessed their opinions. However, the Łódź collective was not rebuked any more than the others; what is more, one of the employees of this branch was praised for giving the novella a positive evaluation.[460]

Nevertheless, Łódź made an accusation about taking statements out of context and a biased selection of quotations, which made the whole discussion shallow. The functionaries attempted to refute their superiors' arguments with the same weapon that was used on them, that is, they accused the editors of taking a schematic approach to evaluation, failing to see the work as a whole, and focusing on details. According to the censors, the editors made the same mistake both in evaluating the story and in assessing the evaluations submitted to them; they approached the task too formally, that is, they made an unauthorized dissection of the story into partial, disconnected sentences, losing sight of the text as a whole and the entire discussion.

In the letter, the censors addressed most of the accusations, including the one about the unfounded notion of "red terror"[461] in the work and the atmosphere of fear that supposedly prevailed in the Soviet unit. Admittedly, the censors from Łódź defended their position in an unusual manner, making a reference to Stefek Burczymucha:

> After all, Burewicz is no Stefek Burczymucha, who "was afraid of nothing, even if it was a bear, he'd fight it," but made a fuss about "a mouse."
> Burewicz is a seasoned KPP member, who ought to evaluate his misdemeanor self-critically. He probably knows what "punishment" he might get, so the gradation of moods from anxiety to fear is an expression of disbelief in the Soviet justice, an expression of Burewicz's breakdown.[462]

It is unclear what the reaction of the Bulletin's editors was because there was no response either in this or the following issues. The letter probably did not

---

[459] "Nasze zdanie o 'Wynikach dyskusji nad opowiadaniem Kubalskiego, "Wyrok,"'" (correspondence in "Dział Listów"), *Biuletyn Informacyjno-Instrukcyjny* no. 5 (29), May 1954, p. 50 (APG, WUKPPiW, file ref. no. 49).

[460] "O wynikach dyskusji nad opowiadaniem Kubalskiego, 'Wyrok,'" *Biuletyn Informacyjno-Instrukcyjny* no. 2 (26), February 1954, p. 25 (APG, WUKPPiW, file ref. no. 42).

[461] Ibidem, p. 31.

[462] "Nasze zdanie o 'Wynikach dyskusji nad opowiadaniem Kubalskiego, "Wyrok,"'" (correspondence in "Dział Listów"), *Biuletyn Informacyjno-Instrukcyjny* no. 5 (29), May 1954, p. 52 (APG, WUKPPiW, file ref. no. 49).

change much; rather, it was meant to show that, despite the disagreement with the assessment presented by the Main Office, the discussion of the novella was very beneficial, and the storm that erupted in the Łódź branch after reading the summary was proof that "the team was deeply 'touched' by the novella."[463]

***

On a Discussion of Marian Promiński's Novella "Toreador i Mściciel"

> *"The Belgians carried their liberators – the Allied soldiers*
> *– on their shoulders, singing their national anthems."*
> *Deleted because of the one-sided exposure of joy only*
> *in relation to the Allied soldiers: what about the Soviet*
> *soldiers?*[464]

Another report on a discussion was featured in the same May issue in which the letter on "Wyrok" was published. The idea of discussing books in groups was again met with great interest, as Marian Promiński's novella "Toreador i Mściciel" [The Toreador and the Avenger] was analyzed in most branches. Promiński, a graduate of Polish Studies in Lviv, who since 1945 had been connected with Kraków and for many years with "Czytelnik," had already had several publications. Similarly to other "Bulletin" authors (e.g., Flaszen, Husarski, Mrożek, Zagórski), a year earlier he had signed a resolution of the Kraków branch of the ZLP which supported Stalinist death sentences in a show trial of priests from the Kraków Curia.[465]

In contrast to previous reports, which presented mostly erroneous judgments about the selected titles, this time the supervisors felt that "the participants in the discussion gave a generally correct evaluation of the novella."[466] "Correct" did not equal positive; already at the beginning, the functionaries were praised for

---

[463] Ibidem, p. 53.

[464] An interference (rated as unnecessary) in an article from *Dziennik Polski* from May 11, 1945 (see *Biuletyn Instrukcyjny* no. 2, June 1945, p. 4 (APG, WUKPPiW, file ref. no. 210)).

[465] See, e.g.: W. Czuchnowski, *Blizna. Proces kurii krakowskiej 1953*, Kraków: Społeczny Instytut Wydawniczy "Znak," 2003. The ZLP's resolution on the Kraków trial was also signed by other cultural representatives appearing in this work, such as the literary critics who evaluated the texts discussed in the Bulletins: Jan Błoński, Leszek Herdegen, Andrzej Kijowski, and Włodzimierz Maciąg, among others.

[466] "Podsumowanie dyskusji," *Biuletyn Informacyjno-Instrukcyjny* no. 5 (29), May 1954, p. 21 (APG, WUKPPiW, file ref. no. 49).

accurately pointing out the shortcomings of the work and for formulating a motion not to grant permission to print. However, not all the flaws were caught by the censors and it is on these overlooked errors that the report focuses.

As in the case of the short story "Wyrok," the plot of the novella was summarized. Once again, it was a war story, this time shown from the perspective of air combat. The protagonists were a German Air Force ace, a "toreador" at the height of his fame, Rudolf (Rudi) Schätzke, and the Soviet pilot Wania Siemionowicz Podlaszenko. According to the functionaries from the field branches, Promiński made the German into a "complex, interesting character with a rich spiritual life,"[467] while rendering Podlaszenko as a primitive with impoverished inner life, driven primarily by personal revenge for the murder of his family (hence, the titular Mściciel – Avenger), and not – as befits a Soviet soldier – by patriotic motives.

Unsurprisingly, this portrayal of two soldiers fighting against each other provoked opposition from the censors. Suffice it to say that we get to know Rudi, "sentimental like all Austrians,"[468] through letters written to his beloved Liesel, while Podlaszenko, "of athletic build, with a misshapen head and a funny potato for a nose,"[469] is seen in the canteen in the company of Natasha, Zoya and Matushka, three young female soldiers. Furthermore, in the scene where two airmen clashed, Schätzke – loyal to the principles of noble sportsmanship – did not leverage his advantageous position and did not shoot at Podlaszenko, which cost him his own defeat.[470] This indignation was shared by the censors' superiors. They felt, however, that their subordinates failed to clearly highlight that Promiński was trying to rehabilitate not just any Nazi, but a German Air Force officer with nearly two hundred downed machines to his credit, and a representative of the possessing class at that. If Promiński's aim was to showcase the difference "between the command of the Nazi army and the simple soldiers who were the instruments carrying out the criminal objectives of Nazi aggression,"[471] it was a failed attempt.

"Toreador i Mściciel" arrived at "Mysia Street" almost five years after the division of Germany; West Germany was created on September 7, 1949, and East Germany exactly one month later. This had a considerable impact on the evaluation of books with a German motif; the censor's pencil was wielded differently depending on whether the book dealt with the East or West German states.[472]

---

[467] Ibidem, p. 26.

[468] M. Promiński, "Toreador i Mściciel," [in:] idem, *Salamandra*, Kraków: Wydawnictwo Literackie, 1956, p. 58.

[469] Ibidem, p. 63.

[470] Ibidem, p. 22.

[471] Ibidem, p. 36.

[472] See, e.g.: J.M. Bates, "Cenzura wobec problemu niemieckiego w literaturze polskiej (1948–1955)," [in:] *Presja i ekspresja. Zjazd szczeciński i socrealizm*, eds. D. Dąbrowska, P. Michałowski, Szczecin: Wydawnictwo Naukowe US, 2002, pp. 79–92.

The report on Promiński did not raise this issue explicitly, but this is probably what the Kraków censor meant when he or she wrote that "not every German was a fascist and not everyone who fought on the side of the Nazis was convinced of the righteousness of their cause."[473]

The majority of the debaters put forward a motion not to grant permission to print; interestingly, the superiors approved of this decision. However, the possibility of corrections was allowed and the story was eventually published in the collection *Salamandra*, but not until 1956. The text was certainly submitted for another review by the Office for the Control, but further research is needed to trace Mysia Street's influence on the final shape of the novella.[474]

4.2.4. Books Selected for Discussion in Censorship Offices in 1955: (Not Only) Kowalewski, Dróżdż-Satanowska, Stadnicki, and Bednorz

In 1955, several more reports of discussions on socio-political press publications were featured.[475] There were also debates on prose works, and in all of these discussions, the assessments of rank-and-file employees differed significantly from those of their superiors. According to the latter, a whole range of lower-level functionaries were still stuck "in the thinking schematism"[476] and issued opinions that failed to take into account the changes that were sweeping through the literary world.

This type of assessment of subordinates' skills had been given on other occasions: right before and during the challenging and not obvious "Thaw" discussions. However, what made these reports different was the fact that they were

---

[473] "Podsumowanie dyskusji," *Biuletyn Informacyjno-Instrukcyjny* no. 5 (29), May 1954, p. 24 (APG, WUKPPiW, file ref. no. 49).

[474] M. Promiński, "Toreador i Mściciel...," pp. 57–74. See also the reviews of the collection: L. Grzeniewski, "Nowelistyka Promińskiego," *Życie Literackie* December 16, 1956, no. 51, p. 4; Z. Pędziński, "Piórkiem Promińskiego," *Nowe Sygnały* November 25, 1956, no. 8, p. 5.

[475] L. Kimlowski (Dept. of Socio-Political Publications), "W związku z dyskusją nad artykułem Z. Lichniaka 'Droga przez historię'"; M. Owczarczyk (Dep. Publik. Społ.-Polit.), "W kręgu Temidy (w sprawie dyskusji nad artykułem 'Temida z zawiązanymi oczami')," *Biuletyn Informacyjno-Instrukcyjny* no. 12 (48), December 1955, pp. 28–46 (APG, WUKPPiW, file ref. no. 117).

[476] H. Landsberg, "O dyskusji nad opowiadaniem Mirosława Kowalewskiego 'Dwa pokoje,'" *Biuletyn Informacyjno-Instrukcyjny* no. 2 (38), February 1955, p. 4 (APG, WUKPPiW, file ref. no. 108). "*Biuletyn Informacyjno-Instrukcyjny.*" *Wybór dokumentów z 1955 r.*, eds. K. Budrowska, M. Budnik, W. Gardocki, Białystok: Wydawnictwo Alter Studio, 2018, series *Cenzura w PRL. Archiwalia* vol. 3, reprinted the articles discussed below on Kowalewski, Stadnicki, and the stories about the Recovered Territories.

drawn up not by anonymous editors, but by censors indicated by name, including those holding managerial positions. Almost all of the previous reports – that is, those on Kuśmierek, Czeszko, Rostworowski, Kubalski and Promiński – were not signed by a concrete superior or even a lower-ranking employee (the exception being Brzeziński's evaluation signed by the censor Bażańska). Meanwhile, every report from 1955 (and from 1956) bears the author's signature, sometimes with a censor's "affiliation."[477] Perhaps this is proof of the growing "tension" between the management and the rest of the staff, who were not able to keep up with the rapidly changing guidelines of that period. Admittedly, it was not easy to simultaneously "loosen" the censorship corset, and continue to "keep one's ear to the ground."[478]

***

On a Discussion of Stanisław Kowalewski's Short Story "Dwa Pokoje"

> *Even a seasoned communist should be allowed*
> *to make mistakes, as long as he believes that his*
> *behavior is fully justified.*[479]

The material on the discussion of "Dwa pokoje" [Two rooms] is evidence that censorship documents should be read and researched with reserve. The Bulletins are filled with various, rather minor mistakes and inaccuracies, which could easily be explained or corrected; a similar negligence occurred in the case of this material. The title of the article – "On a discussion of Mirosław Kowalewski's short story 'Dwa pokoje'" – misled the reader-censor because, in fact, the author of the work was not Mirosław, as some contemporary studies also claim, but Stanisław Kowalewski.[480] The mistake may be explained by the fact that in

---

477 See: L. Rutkowski (Depart. of Cultural Publications), "Nareszcie żywa dyskusja… (podsumowanie głosów z dyskusji nad utworami Andrzejewskiego, Rudnickiego i Flaszena)," *Biuletyn Informacyjno-Instrukcyjny* no. 1 (49), January 1956, p. 12 (APG, WUKPPiW, file ref. no. 4).

478 See: J. Kleyny, "O sztuce dla dorosłych," *Biuletyn Informacyjno-Instrukcyjny* no. 10 (45), October 1955, p. 11 (APG, WUKPPiW, file ref. no. 119); see also: "Recenzja z pozycji literackiej, cz. I" (in the series *O wyższy poziom pracy nad książką*), *Biuletyn Informacyjno-Instrukcyjn* no. 8, August 1952, pp. 23–24 (APG, WUKPPiW, file ref. no. 81).

479 J. Kasper (WUKP Bydgoszcz), "Na marginesie dyskusji. 'Bronię żywego człowieka,'" *Biuletyn Informacyjno-Instrukcyjny* no. 2 (38), February 1955, p. 12 (APG, WUKP-PiW, file ref. no. 108).

480 See: K. Budrowska, "Od orderu do 'zapisu'…," pp. 87–88; *"Biuletyn Informacyjno--Instrukcyjny." Wybór dokumentów z 1955 r…*, p. 67 et seq. See also: J. Zawadzka [J. Z.],

the discussed period, there were at least three Kowalewskis (to name the most popular ones): Janusz, Stanisław and Mirosław. The latter was a prose writer and popularizer of science, whose writing skills were described by Michał Głowiński in the following way: "[…] I did not want to make my task easier by paying attention to the productions of authors such as Jan Wilczek or Mirosław Kowalewski. On the contrary, I adopted the principle that whenever possible, I would examine the texts of authors who have played some role in Polish literature […]."[481]

The discussion of Stanislaw Kowalewski's short story had both a training and preventative function. The staff received the text for review after it had been published in *Nowa Kultura*, but before it was reprinted in the author's forthcoming collection of short stories.[482] However, for most of the functionaries, this turned out to be their first contact with the work, as only two censorship teams had done their homework from the press briefing and knew about the publication. Helena Landsberg, the head of Non-Periodicals and, simultaneously, the author of the report, did not conceal her indignation at such incompetence on the part of the censors.[483]

Kowalewski's short story centered on the conflict between the engineer Witold Piaskowski, part of the old intelligentsia class, and the "chairman," a representative of the new authorities, who was in charge of housing allocation. The latter issue was the axis of the conflict between the characters. The work was a testimony to difficult class problems, which some functionaries felt were presented in an incompetent, even dangerous way. The author was criticized for his mocking of both the intelligentsia and the working class. The reviews of the work varied from a handful of positive opinions to mostly unfavorable ones. For instance, the Łódź team considered the publication of the short story to be an oversight; other teams, also reluctant to stir up class antagonisms, mostly suggested either preventing the text from going to print or introducing corrections.

"Kowalewski Mirosław," [in:] *Współcześni polscy pisarze i badacze literatury. Słownik biobibliograficzny* vol. 4: *K…*, pp. 318–319; E. Głębicka [E. G.], "Kowalewski Stanisław," [in:] *Współcześni polscy pisarze i badacze literatury. Słownik biobibliograficzny* vol. 4: *K…*, pp. 319–322; J. Czachowska [J. Cz.], "Kowalewski Janusz," [in:] *Współcześni polscy pisarze i badacze literatury. Słownik biobibliograficzny* vol. 4: *K…*, pp. 317–318.

[481] M. Głowiński, *Rytuał i demagogia…*, p. 7.

[482] S. Kowalewski, "Dwa pokoje," *Nowa Kultura* November 14, 1954, no. 46, p. 5; idem, "Dwa pokoje," [in:] idem, *Kiedy mija noc. Opowiadania*, Warszawa: "Czytelnik," 1955, pp. 206–219; idem, "Dwa pokoje," [in:] idem, *Opowiadania niemodne*, Warszawa: "Czytelnik," 1956, pp. 310–326.

[483] H. Landsberg, "O dyskusji nad opowiadaniem Mirosława Kowalewskiego 'Dwa pokoje,'" *Biuletyn Informacyjno-Instrukcyjny* no. 2 (38), February 1955, p. 2 (APG, WUK-PPiW, file ref. no. 108).

STANISŁAW KOWALEWSKI

DWA POKOJE

Fig. 13. The first page of Stanisław Kowalewski's short story "Dwa pokoje"
(*Nowa Kultura* November 14, 1954, no. 46, p. 5).

Helena Landsberg, who had been mentioned earlier, disagreed with the diagnosis of her colleagues. She stated that, despite several errors in the construction and motivation of the characters, Kowalewski's story was "human, direct and fresh"[484] and certainly deserved to be published. The head of Non-Periodicals castigated the censors for too hasty a dismissal of the author and overusing an accusatory tone.[485] She also tried to prove that the censors misunderstood the text and presented her interpretation of the work. She believed that the basic error of her colleagues from the Office for the Control was rooted in their misjudgment of the protagonists, for example, the engineer, who was not – as the functionaries claimed – a representative of the bourgeoisie, but of that part of the old intelligentsia that joined the efforts of building socialism: "In our conditions, he is a working man and that is how we should see him. We define him according to the position he has taken towards our reality. And this position is positive."[486]

According to Landsberg, her censor colleagues were also wrong in their assessment of the ending of the work, as it was not the representative of the old intelligentsia who came out of the conflict on the winning side, but the former Bereza prisoner (so-called Bereziak), the representative of the authorities. Landsberg's report on the discussion did not exhaust the topic of "Dwa pokoje," because it was immediately followed by a letter from Juliusz Kasper, who at that time was still a rank-and-file functionary in the Kraków branch.[487] His opinion was similar to Landsberg's. He appreciated Kowalewski mostly for departing from schematism and clichés, and for daring to create vivid and realistic, and, above all, fallible and erring characters. The censor's statement clearly echoed what was expected of literature at the time: "We do not want crystal characters! We do not want bronze statues of classical shapes. We want a living human being"[488] – albeit one tailored to the expectations of the time.

***

---

[484] Ibidem, p. 10.

[485] Ibidem, p. 3.

[486] Ibidem, p. 6.

[487] J. Kasper (WUKP Bydgoszcz), "Na marginesie dyskusji. 'Bronię żywego człowieka,'" *Biuletyn Informacyjno-Instrukcyjny* no. 2 (38), February 1955, pp. 11–13 (APG, WUKPPiW, file ref. no. 108). In later years, Kasper became the head of the Non-Periodical Publications Office.

[488] Ibidem, p. 13.

On a Discussion of Zofia Dróżdż-Satanowska's Book *Pod wiatr*

The report on a discussion of Zofia Dróżdż-Satanowska's *Pod wiatr* [Against the wind] was released after a long delay, for which its author – again Helena Landsberg – blamed her comrades from the voivodeship offices: "despite repeated requests and admonitions, only ten WUKPs [voivodeship offices] submitted discussion materials; three of them not in the form of a discussion and summary, but as a general opinion of the collective on the title, without detailing the positions of individual debaters."[489] Published in two volumes, the novel appeared with almost no corrections, which, according to the head of Non-Periodicals, was a serious oversight.[490] Despite the fact that most comrades considered the book to be weak,[491] they ultimately showed excessive leniency toward the author, who could boast of a legitimate left-wing biography and easily settled in the post-war realities. During the occupation, the writer cooperated with *Nowe Widnokręgi*, and for her post-war social, journalistic, and writing activities, she received numerous state awards, including the Knight's Cross of the Order of Polonia Restituta.[492] Perhaps this is what influenced the censors' opinion.

Landsberg, however, was intransigent in her assessment. She believed that the first volume of the diptych, which told the story of the struggle between the farmhands and the manor's owners, could be defended, while the second volume was a testimony to the author's complete misunderstanding of the interwar reality and lack of knowledge about the history of the workers' movement, the activities of the Polish Socialist Party, the Communist Party of Poland, etc. In her statement, Landsberg pointed out a number of examples confirming her opinion, recreating selected scenes in meticulous detail and citing quotations from the novel.

Although some comrades noticed the errors mentioned by the supervisor, the vast majority of the censors were unable to formulate a comprehensive and correct evaluation that met the supervisor's expectations. Landsberg bemoaned the low competence of her subordinates, criticizing both those who let the book

---

489 H. Landsberg, "O wynikach dyskusji nad książką Drożdż-Satanowskiej pt. *Pod wiatr*," *Biuletyn Informacyjno-Instrukcyjny* no. 3 (39), March 1955, p. 19 (APG, WUKP-PiW, file ref. no. 107).

490 Ibidem, p. 25. See also: Z. Dróżdż-Satanowska, *Pod wiatr*, Warszawa: Ludowa Spółdzielnia Wydawnicza, vol. 1: 1953, vol. 2: ibidem 1954. See also: K. Budrowska, "Od orderu do 'zapisu'…," p. 89.

491 H. Landsberg, "O wynikach dyskusji nad książką Drożdż-Satanowskiej pt. *Pod wiatr*," *Biuletyn Informacyjno-Instrukcyjny* no. 3 (39), March 1955, p. 20 (APG, WUKP-PiW, file ref. no. 107).

492 Z. Terech, "Zofia Dróżdż-Satanowska," [in:] *Pisarze regionu świętokrzyskiego*, series 1, vol. 3, ed. J. Pacławski, Kielce: Kieleckie Towarzystwo Naukowe i Wyższa Szkoła Pedagogiczna im. J. Kochanowskiego w Kielcach, 1990, pp. 32–47.

pass uncorrected and those who condemned it across the board: "if we had caught the errors in time," Landsberg wrote, "the author could have consulted the Department of Party History about her book and corrected it, especially since you cannot deny it some authenticity."[493]

***

On a Discussion of Jerzy Stadnicki's Short Stories "Prawo Do Skargi" and "Badania Dodatkowe"

In August 1955, material was presented on two short stories by Jerzy Stadnicki, "Prawo do skargi" [The right to complain] and "Badania dodatkowe" [Additional studies].[494] They were part of a collection published in 1955 under the title *Kurz na miłości. Opowiadania* [Dust on love: Stories].[495] The discussed works focused on the broadly defined issue of old age and the situation of post-war health care. Reviews praised the pioneering attitude of the author, who was "one of the first to explore a previously ignored topic."[496]

The censors admitted that these were not easy texts to review, and the author of the report, Wanda Jesionowska, noted that the most difficult task for the staff was to assess the writer's attitude and to properly understand the characters he portrayed.[497] One of the reasons for this was undoubtedly the writer's predilection for using internal monologue, which allowed him "to evaluate facts through the eyes of the character he created."[498] Some censors accused Stadnicki of wanting to discard the elderly from society and presenting an excessively critical assessment of Polish social health care; however, this interpretation was wrong according to Jesionowska. In her opinion, by pointing out the shortcomings of the medical service, Stadnicki hoped to shock the public opinion and improve the

---

[493] H. Landsberg, "O wynikach dyskusji nad książką Drożdż-Satanowskiej pt. *Pod wiatr,*" *Biuletyn Informacyjno-Instrukcyjny* no. 3 (39), March 1955, p. 27 (APG, WUKPPiW, file ref. no. 107).

[494] W. Jesionowska, "O opowiadaniach Stadnickiego," *Biuletyn Informacyjno-Instrukcyjny* no. 8 (44), August 1955, pp. 23–32 (APG, WUKPPiW, file ref. no. 124).

[495] J. Stadnicki, "Badania dodatkowe"; "Prawo do skargi," [in:] idem, *Kurz na miłości. Opowiadania,* preface S. Lichański, Warszawa: Instytut Wydawniczy "Pax," 1955, pp. 57–104. See the reviews of the collection: S. Grochowiak, "Opowiadania okrutne," *Wrocławski Tygodnik Katolicki* June 19, 1955, no. 25, p. 11.

[496] W. Jesionowska, "O opowiadaniach Stadnickiego," *Biuletyn Informacyjno-Instrukcyjny* no. 8 (44), August 1955, p. 28 (APG, WUKPPiW, file ref. no. 124).

[497] Ibidem, p. 23.

[498] Ibidem.

lot of the weakest, which – according to the censor – was the role of the writer: "After all, we are striving for a militant, realistic literature that truthfully portrays life with its positives and shortcomings. Meanwhile, the comrades would prefer that the writer simply practiced the art of varnishing."[499]

Jesionowska's opinion on Stadnicki basically confirmed what Landsberg and Kasper had previously written about Kowalewski's short stories: in the second half of 1955, there was appreciation for the voices in literature that were critical of reality; not all of them, of course, but selected ones. On the other hand, among the many skeptical opinions about Stadnicki, there was also much praise, particularly for the artistic execution of his works. The censors appreciated the author's literary artistry and his commitment to what and how he wrote. The best recommendation was given in the conclusion by Jesionowska, who classified the discussed texts as "solid literature."[500]

***

On a Discussion of the Works "Bąk Brzmi… w Trzcinie," "Decyzja, Czyli Rzecz o Człowieku Odzyskanym" and "Lotny Finisz"

> *By generalizing isolated facts of inhospitality, the author revives and reignites outdated regional antagonisms and frightens repatriates from the East with the supposedly diabolic soul of the West.*[501]

In August 1955, yet another account of a discussion was published. This time a collective article presented three works, all of which concerned "nationality problems in the Recovered Territories."[502] These matters (also in relation to literature) appeared quite rarely in the Bulletins.[503] In a similar way, the works presented for

---

[499] Ibidem, p. 28.

[500] Ibidem, p. 32.

[501] "Seminarium prasy (wyjątki z protokółu). Granice dopuszczalnej krytyki," *Biuletyn Instrukcyjny* no. 2, June 1945, p. 7 (APG, WUKPPiW, file ref. no. 210).

[502] T. Zaręba, "O wynikach dyskusji," *Biuletyn Informacyjno-Instrukcyjny* no. 8 (44), August 1955, p. 33 (APG, WUKPPiW, file ref. no. 124). I would like to thank Professor Grzegorz Strauchold for consultation on the literature of the Recovered Territories (e-mail correspondence, March 20–29, 2020).

[503] See, e.g.: "Seminarium prasy (wyjątki z protokółu). Granice dopuszczalnej krytyki"; "Ze sprawozdań Kierowników Wojewódzkich Biur," *Biuletyn Instrukcyjny* no. 2, June 1945, pp. 7, 13 (APG, WUKPPiW, file ref. no. 210); "'Wścibstwo' cenzorskie," *Biuletyn Informacyjno-Szkoleniowy* no. 1, October 30, 1948, fol. 79r (APP, WUKPPiW, file ref. no. 4); "Na przykładzie problemów Warmii i Mazur," *Biuletyn Informacyjno-Instrukcyjny* no. 6 (30), June 1954, pp. 3–10 (APG, WUKPPiW, file ref. no. 52); J. Raczyński (WUKPPiW Poznań),

discussion, "Bąk brzmi… w trzcinie"[504] [Blunder rings… in the reeds], "Decyzja, czyli rzecz o człowieku odzyskanym" [A decision, or a thing about a recovered man], and "Lotny finisz" [A flying finish], expounded on the myth of the Recovered Territories that had formed since the end of World War II.[505] The rulers of the new Poland successfully created myth-making slogans about the return of the primordial Polish lands to the Motherland, expecting similar declarations in literature. As early as 1946, a volume by the duo Goliński-Fenikowski entitled *Odra szumi po polsku* was published. And this is just one of many examples of literature that described – in a manner consistent with the expectations of the authorities – the lives of displaced persons, re-emigrants and natives, who comprised the post-migration melting pot.

According to the author of the report, Tadeusz Zaręba, the three short stories selected for discussion did not rise to the challenge. All of them were excessively focused on the harm done to the natives, which, according to the reviewer, could have been "fuel for the flame of revisionism"[506] and could have led to an escalation of the conflict in these areas. The censor also stressed the fact that the novellas emphasized the barbarity of the Polish settlers and made various unfair generalizations, for instance, depicting them "as looters, thieves, and slobs."[507] Much of this type of presentation was ignored or unnoticed by the other functionaries, the vast majority of whom were in favor of publishing the stories. Zaręba postulated that all three texts should be blocked – this proposal was at least partly carried out, since "Decyzja, czyli rzecz o człowieku odzyskanym" was not published until 1978, and the other two stories have not been located so far (the fact that the Bulletin provides no names of the authors of the works does not help the search).[508]

"Zagadnienie niemieckie na łamach *Przeglądu Zachodniego*"; W. Stankiewicz (WUKPPiW Opole), "Problem autochtonów na łamach *Trybuny Opolskiej*," *Biuletyn Informacyjno-Instrukcyjny* no. 10 (34), October 1954, pp. 8–18, 19–26 (APG, WUKPPiW, file ref. no. 58).

[504] The title is a reference to Jan Brzechwa's children's poem "Chrząszcz."

[505] On the Western borders (Recovered Territories) and the censorship of the Borderlands, see, e.g.: M. Wakar, "Mit Ziem Odzyskanych – geneza i tropy w literaturze," [in:] *"Ziemie Odzyskane." W poszukiwaniu nowych narracji*, eds. E. Kledzik, M. Michalski, M. Praczyk, Poznań: Instytut Historii UAM, 2018, pp. 127–143; K. Gieba, "Próba epopei…"; J. Szydłowska, *Narracje pojałtańskiego Okcydentu. Literatura polska wobec pogranicza na przykładzie Warmii i Mazur (1945–1989)*, Olsztyn: Wydawnictwo UWM, 2013; G. Strauchold, "Ludność rodzima pod 'opieką' cenzury (1945–1948). Przyczynek do polityki informacyjnej lat 40," *Wrocławskie Studia z Historii Najnowszej* 2001, vol. 8, pp. 277–286; "Rocznik Ziem Odzyskanych," https://www.rocznikziemzachodnich.pl/rzz (accessed January 31, 2021).

[506] T. Zaręba, "O wynikach dyskusji," *Biuletyn Informacyjno-Instrukcyjny* no. 8 (44), August 1955, p. 34 (APG, WUKPPiW, file ref. no. 124).

[507] Ibidem, p. 36.

[508] Z. Bednorz, "Decyzja, czyli rzecz o człowieku odzyskanym," [in:] idem, *Na zapiecku trzy okna*, Warszawa: Instytut Wydawniczy "Pax," 1978, pp. 86–107. See also: *"Biuletyn Informacyjno-Instrukcyjny." Wybór dokumentów z 1955 r…*, p. 192.

Perhaps "Lotny finisz" and "Bąk brzmi w… trzcinie" joined the collection of unpublished texts blocked by the PRL's censorship.

It is worth considering another hypothesis according to which all three texts had been published earlier and were going to be reprinted, which is why they were submitted to "Mysia Street" for assessment. This was the case with Zbyszek Bednorz's short story: I found the first printing in *Tygodnik Powszechny* from November 1948, hence, the story had been published almost seven years before the failed attempt at reprinting it. From the editor's note, we learn that the text was awarded in a short story competition at the beginning of 1948 and was being printed "only now because the author wanted to make some changes in the novella."[509] It may be a code for modifications forced by the censorship office already in 1948, all the more so that the two versions – the one from 1948 and from 1978 – differ.

4.2.5. Titles Selected for Discussion in Censorship Offices in 1956: (Not Only) Andrzejewski, Rudnicki, and Flaszen

In January 1956, three "Thaw" articles were discussed: by Andrzejewski, Rudnicki, and Flaszen. In the February issue, the project was not continued: there is no information whether the selected books were also discussed in the following months, as only the first two issues of the Bulletins from that year have been found so far.

***

On a Discussion of the Works "Wieczór z Henrykiem" by Jerzy Andrzejewski, "Deficyt" by Adolf Rudnicki and "O Trudnym Kunszcie Womitowania" by Ludwik Flaszen

> *Our discussion has partly revealed that our censorship community does not live in isolation and that the fluctuations of the creative community also seep into it.*[510]

The discussion protocols of the three works sent to "Mysia Street" were presented in one report by censor Rutkowski from the Department of Cultural Publications; the same person who had earlier analyzed Kuśmierek. The material was a continu-

---

[509] Z. Bednorz, "Decyzja, czyli rzecz o człowieku odzyskanym," *Tygodnik Powszechny* November 14, 1948, no. 46, p. 6.

[510] L. Rutkowski (Depart. of Cultural Publications), "Nareszcie żywa dyskusja… (podsumowanie głosów z dyskusji nad utworami Andrzejewskiego, Rudnickiego i Flaszena)," *Biuletyn Informacyjno-Instrukcyjny* no. 1 (49), January 1956, p. 3 (APG, WUK-PPiW, file ref. no. 4).

ation of the "Thaw" discussion initiated the previous year, in the course of which the indicated texts were also examined.[511] In fact, the 1956 report did not specify the title of Flaszen's article, however, thanks to the "vomiting" metaphor and citations from the analyzed text, it was easy to establish that it was the (aforementioned) editorial "O trudnym kunszcie womitowania." Also in Rudnicki's case, the material lacked precision and only provided the series in which the redacted text appeared, namely, the famous *Niebieskie kartki* [The blue pages]. Nevertheless, here too, an analysis of the text suggested that the discussed article referred to "Deficyt." As for Andrzejewski, the report mentioned "Rozmowy z Henrykiem" [Conversations with Henryk], but the actual title was "Wieczór z Henrykiem" [An evening with Henryk].[512]

When the Bulletin was published, the texts had already been functioning successfully in the public space. Rudnicki's article was printed on October 23, and the other two a week later, that is, on October 30, 1955. It can be assumed that the discussions in the voivodeship offices were held after the publication of the editorials, because according to the aforementioned censorship documents from November 9 and 23, 1955, the three texts in question were listed as material for discussion in all the WUKP. (The first document mentioned "Rozmowy z Henrykiem" and *Niebieskie kartki*, which might have been the source of the inaccuracies repeated in the Bulletin).[513] However, some of the statements presented in the Bulletin material may suggest that the articles had been discussed even before publication, an example of which is the sentence about Flaszen's text: "The article should be published if only because it will not cause political harm, and the author will be duly reprimanded in the press."[514] Did the article not cause political harm? The answer varies depending on who is asked. What is undeniable, however, is that the editorial "O trudnym kunszcie womitowania" caused a great deal of ferment on the literary scene at the time (similarly to the other aforementioned text by the critic from Kraków, "Nowy Zoil…").

---

[511] J. Kleyny, "O sztuce dla dorosłych," *Biuletyn Informacyjno-Instrukcyjny* no. 10 (45), October 1955, pp. 10–22 (APG, WUKPPiW, file ref. no. 119). See also: M. Woźniak-Łabieniec, "Cenzura w okresie odwilży jako temat tabu," *Acta Universitatis Lodziensis. Folia Litteraria Polonica* 2013, no. 1, pp. 89–97.

[512] A. Rudnicki, "Deficyt (1)" (in the series *Niebieskie kartki*), *Świat* October 23, 1955, no. 42, p. 9; J. Andrzejewski, "Wieczór z Henrykiem" (in the series *Kartki z dziennika*), *Nowa Kultura* October 30, 1955, no. 44, p. 2; cf. Fig. 14 and 15.

[513] "Materiały dyskusyjno-szkoleniowe 1954–1955" (APP, WUKPPiW, file ref. no. 18, p. 99, 100). Cf. Fig. 12 and a scan of the document from November 9, 1955: M. Woźniak-Łabieniec, *Obecny nieobecny. Krajowa recepcja Czesława Miłosza w krytyce literackiej lat pięćdziesiątych w świetle dokumentów cenzury*, Łódź: Wydawnictwo UŁ, 2012, p. 182.

[514] L. Rutkowski (Depart. of Cultural Publications), "Nareszcie żywa dyskusja… (podsumowanie głosów z dyskusji nad utworami Andrzejewskiego, Rudnickiego i Flaszena)," *Biuletyn Informacyjno-Instrukcyjny* no. 1 (49), January 1956, p. 5 (APG, WUKPPiW, file ref. no. 4).

Nowa Kultura Nr 44 (293)

Kartki z dziennika

Wieczór z Henrykiem

JERZY ANDRZEJEWSKI

Fig. 14. J. Andrzejewski, "Wieczór z Henrykiem," *Nowa Kultura* October 30, 1955, no. 44, p. 2 (in the series *Kartki z dziennika*).

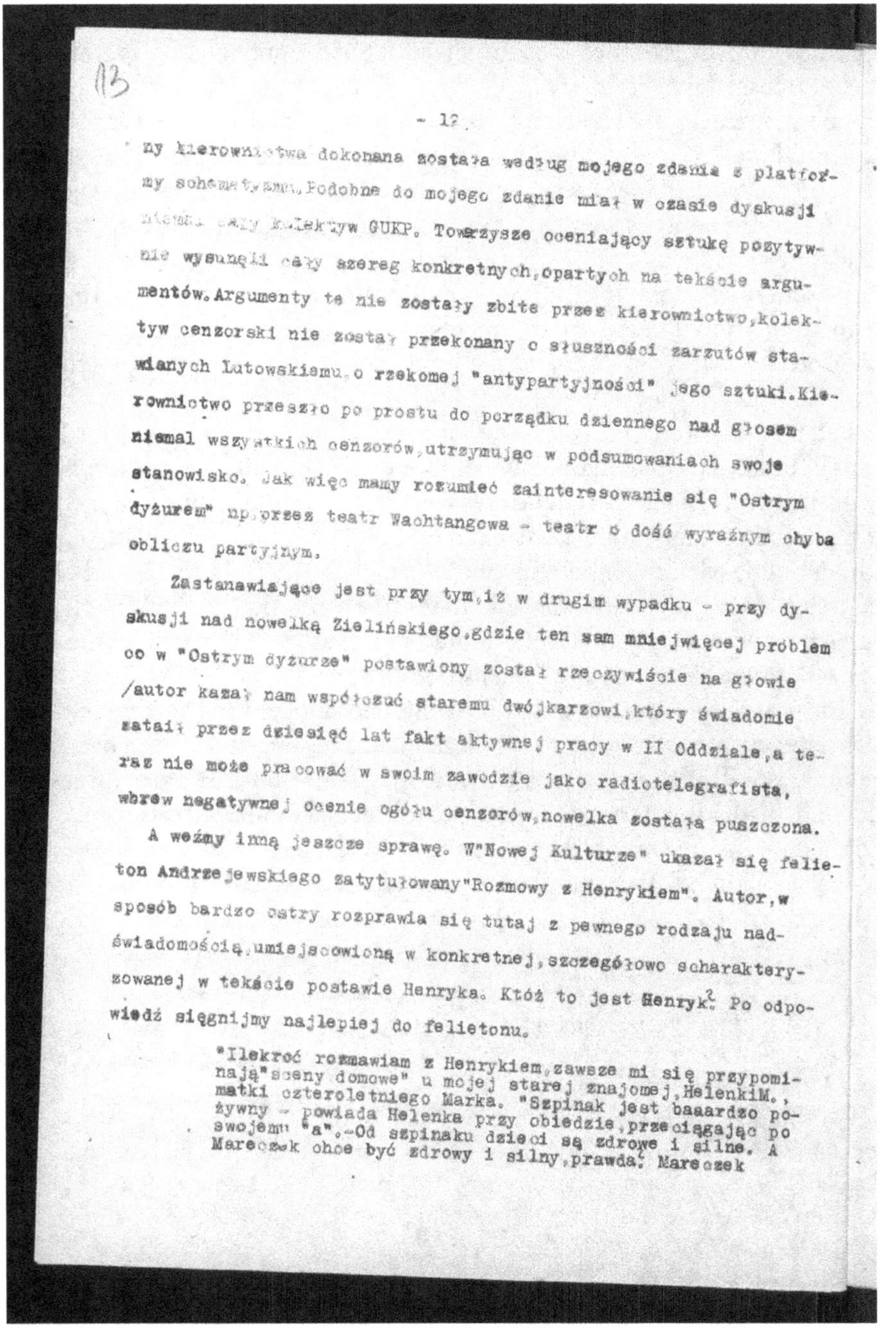

- 13 -

ny kierownictwa dokonana została według mojego zdania z platfor-
my schematyzmu. Podobne do mojego zdanie miał w czasie dyskusji
niemal cały kolektyw GUKP. Towarzysze oceniający sztukę pozytyw-
nie wysunęli cały szereg konkretnych, opartych na tekście argumentów. Argumenty te nie zostały zbite przez kierownictwo, kolektyw cenzorski nie został przekonany o słuszności zarzutów sta-
wianych Lutowskiemu, o rzekomej "antypartyjności" jego sztuki. Kierownictwo przeszło po prostu do porządku dziennego nad głosem
niemal wszystkich cenzorów, utrzymując w podsumowaniach swoje
stanowisko. Jak więc mamy rozumieć zainteresowanie się "Ostrym
dyżurem" np. przez teatr Wachtangowa – teatr o dość wyraźnym chyba
obliczu partyjnym.

Zastanawiające jest przy tym, iż w drugim wypadku – przy dyskusji nad nowelką Zielińskiego, gdzie ten sam mniej więcej problem
co w "Ostrym dyżurze" postawiony został rzeczywiście na głowie
/autor kazał nam współczuć staremu dwójkarzowi, który świadomie
zatail przez dziesięć lat fakt aktywnej pracy w II Oddziale, a teraz nie może pracować w swoim zawodzie jako radiotelegrafista,
wbrew negatywnej ocenie ogółu cenzorów, nowelka została puszczona.

A weźmy inną jeszcze sprawę. W "Nowej Kulturze" ukazał się felie-
ton Andrzejewskiego zatytułowany "Rozmowy z Henrykiem". Autor, w
sposób bardzo ostry rozprawia się tutaj z pewnego rodzaju nad-
świadomością, umiejscowioną w konkretnej, szczegółowo scharaktery-
zowanej w tekście postawie Henryka. Któż to jest Henryk? Po odpowiedź sięgnijmy najlepiej do felietonu.

> "Ilekroć rozmawiam z Henrykiem, zawsze mi się przypomi-
> nają "sceny domowe" u mojej starej znajomej, Helenki M.,
> matki czteroletniego Marka. "Szpinak jest baaardzo po-
> żywny – powiada Helenka przy obiedzie, przeciągając po
> swojemu "a". – Od szpinaku dzieci są zdrowe i silne. A
> Mareczek chce być zdrowy i silny, prawda? Mareczek

Fig. 15. An excerpt from Jerzy Kleyny's article with a fragment on "Wieczór [Rozmowy] z Henrykiem" (J. Kleyny, "O sztuce dla dorosłych," *Biuletyn Informacyjno-Instrukcyjny* no. 12 (48), December 1955, p. 13 (APG, WUKPPiW, file ref. no. 117)).

The articles by Rudnicki, Flaszen and Andrzejewski, sent for evaluation in 1955, offered an overview of the cultural output of the previous decade, raising the widely-discussed issue of party-steered creativity. Some of the artists had repeatedly commented on this topic, also in programmatic texts; the Bulletins from February and June 1952 recommended for self-study *Partia i twórczość pisarza* [The party and the work of the writer] by one of our discussants, Jerzy Andrzejewski.[515]

Clearly, the censors were not indifferent to the topic either, since Rutkowski praised the collectives for their mass participation in the action, which attracted around ninety debaters "from all voivodeship and even city offices."[516] Apparently, the functionaries differed greatly in their assessments of the texts submitted, which proves that for a rank-and-file employee of the "Ministry of Truth," the minutia – which (especially during this period) determined the fate of often similar statements – were difficult to understand. Despite this (or perhaps because of this), Rutkowski appreciated the non-schematic and diverse contributions, especially those in which the employees went beyond discussions of the editorials and shared their views on the current situation in culture, particularly literature, without hiding what they thought "about the whole, v[ery] difficult and complicated issue of the party's ideological influence on artistic creativity."[517] The most interesting and apt opinions were quoted in full as a supplement to the discussion, which also had a training dimension.[518]

The overall positive impression of the debates held in the offices did not, however, prevent Rutkowski from pointing out a few erroneous and overly harsh opinions, as well as those that were too liberal, to his mind. The employees of the field branches had a lot to say about the reviewed materials, but ultimately, almost all of them were in favor of letting the analyzed texts pass "on the wave of the ongoing discussion."[519] According to Rutkowski, such a decision could be accepted in the case of Andrzejewski and Rudnicki, but not Flaszen. The latter's article

---

[515] "Noty," *Biuletyn Informacyjno-Instrukcyjny* no. 2, February 1952, p. 50 (APG, WUKPPiW, file ref. no. 99); "Noty," *Biuletyn Informacyjno-Instrukcyjny* no. 6, June 1952, p. 46 (APG, WUKPPiW, file ref. no. 87).

[516] L. Rutkowski (Depart. of Cultural Publications), "Nareszcie żywa dyskusja… (podsumowanie głosów z dyskusji nad utworami Andrzejewskiego, Rudnickiego i Flaszena)," *Biuletyn Informacyjno-Instrukcyjny* no. 1 (49), January 1956, p. 2 (APG, WUKPPiW, file ref. no. 4).

[517] Ibidem, p. 1.

[518] "Głosy w dyskusji," *Biuletyn Informacyjno-Instrukcyjny* no. 1 (49), January 1956, pp. 13–23 (APG, WUKPPiW, file ref. no. 4).

[519] L. Rutkowski (Depart. of Cultural Publications), "Nareszcie żywa dyskusja… (podsumowanie głosów z dyskusji nad utworami Andrzejewskiego, Rudnickiego i Flaszena)," *Biuletyn Informacyjno-Instrukcyjny* no. 1 (49), January 1956, pp. 3, 7 (APG, WUKPPiW, file ref. no. 4).

was a reaction to Ważyk's "Poemat dla dorosłych," published in *Nowa Kultura* on August 21, and to a short story entitled "Nim będzie zapomniany" [Before he is forgotten] by Kazimierz Brandys, published there on September 18.[520] Brandys's statement was intended as a "pamphlet on the traitor,"[521] that is Czesław Miłosz, whom the future signatory of *Memoriał 101* would not forgive for escaping to the West. Quoting Marzena Woźniak-Łabieniec, it can be added that Flaszen's article was the first voice in defense of the Nobel laureate.[522] We should also note by way of digression the "reckoning" statement of one of the other "Bulletin" authors, Aleksander Ścibor-Rylski. The following declaration, dated October 1955, was the writer's reaction to the publication of Jan Józef Szczepański's *Polska jesień* [Polish autumn], which had waited on the censor's shelf for "a full six years":[523]

> That is why I look with such anger at the censors, editors, publishers and secretaries of all sorts, in a word, at the people who were the literary gatekeepers at that time. I am ready to generously split the blame with them, without inquiring whose share was greater, but I have no intention of taking it upon myself alone! Meanwhile, will you look at that, hardly any of those people now feel that they have sinned; they are all pure, undefiled, impeccable; any reproach surprises them and, what is worse, offends them. After all, they had no say, the blind media of directives, the poor sleepwalkers following the "chain of command"![524]

Returning to Flaszen, according to Rutkowski, Flaszen's nihilistic evaluation of the entire literary decade, as well as the negation of the positive role played by the party in steering art, should not have been accepted by the functionaries. Why then, Rutkowski asks, did the article – discussed with such passion – receive Kraków's imprimatur?[525] It was the result of insufficient substantive preparation

---

[520] A. Ważyk, "Poemat dla dorosłych," *Nowa Kultura* August 21, 1955, no. 34, pp. 1–2; K. Brandys, "Nim będzie zapomniany," *Nowa Kultura* September 18, 1955, no. 38, pp. 1, 4–5, 7. See also, e.g.: S. Burkot, "Poezja w latach 1955–1968," [in:] idem, *Literatura polska 1939–2009*, Third Revised Edition, Warszawa: PWN, 2014, pp. 126–177; J. Smulski, "Odwilżowe w formie, stalinowskie w treści (o opowiadaniu Kazimierza Brandysa 'Nim będzie zapomniany')," *Acta Universitatis Nicolai Copernici. Nauki Humanistyczno-Społeczne. Filologia Polska* 1996, no. 47, pp. 47–60.
[521] L. Flaszen, "O trudnym kunszcie womitowania…," p. 5.
[522] M. Woźniak-Łabieniec, *Obecny nieobecny…*, p. 184.
[523] A. Ścibor-Rylski, "W poszukiwaniu epickiego klucza," *Nowa Kultura* October 30, 1955, no. 44, p. 3 (this is a review article on the 1955 edition of *Czas nieutracony* by Stanisław Lem). See also: J.J. Szczepański, *Polska jesień*, Kraków: Wydawnictwo Literackie, 1955.
[524] A. Ścibor-Rylski, "W poszukiwaniu epickiego klucza…," p. 3.
[525] L. Rutkowski (Depart. of Cultural Publications), "Nareszcie żywa dyskusja… (podsumowanie głosów z dyskusji nad utworami Andrzejewskiego, Rudnickiego

of the team from Kraków. According to the superior, only some censors noticed the dangerous content of Flaszen's article and in a very categorical tone demanded that it be removed. Rutkowski supported this opinion, just as he supported removing fragments from Adolf Rudnicki's editorial that the censors felt were inappropriate.[526]

The fragment was accused of being anti-party and promoting an anti-social vision of art, according to which the artist was supposed to create in isolation from society. However, in the opinion of most censors, these errors could be corrected with suggested modifications. The censors turned out to be relatively understanding towards the transgressions of the writer, whose attitude was explained by the trauma of the occupation, something that could not be said about their sentiments towards Flaszen:

> If Rudnicki's stance results from the writer's personal traumas brought on by his experiences during the occupation, and from the fact that he was not always allowed to express them fully, Flaszen depreciates the writing of Ważyk, Brandys and Putrament in a v[ery] malicious way, accusing them of insincerity, hypocrisy and duplicity.[527]

It is also worth noting the rather lenient tone of the Office's employee towards the failings of the author of "Poemat dla dorosłych": "Ważyk's mistakes cannot devalue him as a writer and it should be assumed that he will understand his mistake and try to document this with his further work."[528]

Rutkowski responded positively to the decision to publish "Wieczór z Henrykiem," nevertheless, he did not fail to reproach the censors for their excessive restraint in evaluating Andrzejewski's editorial. The supervisor appreciated that the reviews noted the uncurbed criticism of the author of *Partia i twórczość* towards his native art, but he complained that most of the functionaries did not take the trouble

---

i Flaszena)," *Biuletyn Informacyjno-Instrukcyjny* no. 1 (49), January 1956, p. 11 (APG, WUKPPiW, file ref. no. 4).

[526] Ibidem, p. 6.

The text was part of the series, which was published since 1952: first in the *Świat* weekly, then in *Przekrój*, to finally appear in a (widely reviewed) book form; *Niebieskie kartki* was examined by one of the protagonists of the discussion, Jerzy Andrzejewski.

See, e.g.: A. Rudnicki, "Deficyt," [in:] idem *Niebieskie kartki. Ślepe lustro tych lat*, Kraków: Wydawnictwo Literackie, 1956, pp. 226–234. See also: J. Andrzejewski, "O *Niebieskich kartkach* Adolfa Rudnickiego" (in the series *Kartki z dziennika lektury*), *Nowa Kultura* April 24, 1955, no. 17, p. 2.

[527] L. Rutkowski (Depart. of Cultural Publications), "Nareszcie żywa dyskusja… (podsumowanie głosów z dyskusji nad utworami Andrzejewskiego, Rudnickiego i Flaszena)," *Biuletyn Informacyjno-Instrukcyjny* no. 1 (49), January 1956, p. 6 (APG, WUKPPiW, file ref. no. 4).

[528] Ibidem, p. 7.

to analyze and reflect on his more recent statements, from the famous "Lament papierowej głowy" [Lament of a paper head] to the editorial "Mój chłopięcy ideał" [My boyhood ideal].[529] It is difficult to disagree with the censor's opinion, according to which both texts constituted a closed system of views on the issue of party-steered literature and could have made the work on the assigned article easier. This was evidenced by the complicated publishing history of the former of the titles. It was first printed in the *Świat* weekly in 1956, and earlier and later attempts to publish the work were effectively blocked by the censors, until 1967, when the story appeared again in the volume *Niby gaj* [A quasi grove]. Some studies note that "Wielki lament…" had been printed only once before 1967. However, apart from its publication in *Świat*, in that same year (1956) the story appeared again in the second expanded edition of the collection *Złoty lis* [Golden Fox].[530]

Returning to "Wieczór z Henrykiem," according to Rutkowski, the ignorance of Andrzejewski's previous statements meant that only a handful of functionaries correctly diagnosed the dangerous allusiveness of "Wieczór z Henrykiem," which concealed an attack on the party leadership. Aware of all these shortcomings, Rutkowski explained his decision to publish the text as follows:

> We let this editorial go to print because it was not explicit; it contained a lot of correct remarks, and moreover, it could have been interpreted as an attack on manipulators and dogmatists. The comrades who saw through the veiled content of the editorial essentially judged it right, but the conclusion not to let it go to print was too far-reaching. Only where there is an overt attack on our basic principles will we apply the censorship pencil, although sometimes this too will depend on a number of circumstances (see: the Chałasiński-Schaff discussion).[531]

---

[529] Ibidem, p. 8.

[530] J. Andrzejewski, "Wielki lament papierowej głowy," *Świat* September 2, 1956, no. 36, pp. 20–21; idem, "Wielki lament papierowej głowy," [in:] idem, *Złoty Lis*, Expanded Second Edition, Warszawa: PIW, 1956, pp. 93–106; idem, "Mój chłopięcy ideał," [in:] idem, *Niby gaj. Opowiadania 1933–1958*, Warszawa: PIW, 1959, pp. 607–613. Cf. K. Budrowska, *Writers, Literature and Censorship…*, pp. 141–143.

[531] L. Rutkowski (Depart. of Cultural Publications), "Nareszcie żywa dyskusja… (podsumowanie głosów z dyskusji nad utworami Andrzejewskiego, Rudnickiego i Flaszena)," *Biuletyn Informacyjno-Instrukcyjny* no. 1 (49), January 1956, p. 9 (APG, WUKPPiW, file ref. no. 4). The issue was the debate within Polish sociological thought between Józef Chałasiński and Adam Schaff, but also the "sphere of influence" in the editorial committees of various sociological and philosophical publishing series; see, e.g.: P. Grabarczyk, *Directival Theory of Meaning. From Syntax and Pragmatics to Narrow Linguistic Content*, Cham: Springer, 2019, pp. 1–20; W. Winclawski, "*Studia Socjologiczne – okoliczności powstania i status czasopisma w socjologii polskiej*," *Studia Socjologiczne* 2011, no. 1, pp. 11–38; K. Ajdukiewicz, "W sprawie artykułu prof. A. Schaffa o moich poglądach filozoficznych," *Myśl Filozoficzna* 1953, no. 2, pp. 292–334.

Thus, in Rutkowski's view, the publication of "Wieczór z Henrykiem" was a calculated step, which could not be said about the publication of Flaszen's article. "The censors began to study [the columnist from Kraków] more closely, removing all attempts to defend both the critic and his article about vomiting."[532] This was just one example of efforts to suppress the "Thaw" tendencies.

4.3. Books Discussed as Part of the Series *For a Higher Level of Work on the Book*: (Not Only) Nałkowska, Czeszko, Lācis Meisner, and Jackiewicz

> *No one claims that every novel must contain everything, but censors reviewing a given title must see everything and should remember that they are responsible for their every word, their every judgment.*[533]

From July to November 1952, a series of articles entitled *O wyższy poziom pracy nad książką* [For a higher level of work on the book] was published in the Bulletins.[534] A total of four texts were designed to aid censors in evaluating non-periodical publications. The materials included many general instructions for the censorship of fiction, scientific publications and political pamphlets; there were also more formal guidelines useful for constructing a censorship review.

The foreword to the series states that the editors will analyze topics and problems based on selected examples of good and bad reviews.[535] However, in the first two articles, the argument "was maintained in a rather general tone and referred more to the construction of the reviews themselves and the approach to

---

[532] M. Woźniak-Łabieniec, *Obecny nieobecny...*, p. 186.

[533] "Recenzja z pozycji literackiej (cd.)" (in the series *O wyższy poziom pracy nad książką*), *Biuletyn Informacyjno-Instrukcyjny* no. 9, September 1952, p. 28 (APG, WUKPPiW, file ref. no. 78).

[534] Articles published in the series *O wyższy poziom pracy nad książką*: "Uwagi ogólne o recenzji," *Biuletyn Informacyjno-Instrukcyjny* no. 7, July 1952, pp. 26–29 (APG, WUKPPiW, file ref. no. 84); "Recenzja z pozycji literackiej, cz. I," *Biuletyn Informacyjno-Instrukcyjny* no. 8, August 1952, pp. 18–24 (APG, WUKPPiW, file ref. no. 81); "Recenzja z pozycji literackiej (cd.)," *Biuletyn Informacyjno-Instrukcyjny* no. 9, September 1952, pp. 24–33 (APG, WUKPPiW, file ref. no. 78); "O wyższy poziom pracy nad książką (cd.)," *Biuletyn Informacyjno-Instrukcyjny* no. 11, November 1952, pp. 37–42 (APG, WUKPPiW, file ref. no. 72).

[535] "Uwagi ogólne o recenzji" (in the series *O wyższy poziom pracy nad książką*), *Biuletyn Informacyjno-Instrukcyjny* no. 7, July 1952, p. 26 (APG, WUKPPiW, file ref. no. 84).

the reviewed work rather than to the contents of specific reviews."[536] Only in the
third article were there more specific references to the literary texts and the evaluations devoted to them, while the closing material discussed non-fiction writing.
Below are the books examined throughout the series.

***

As mentioned earlier, general issues and guidelines for censoring fiction dominated the second part of the series. On the margins of these considerations, a mention
was made about the schematic review of Zofia Nałkowska's *Medallions* (more material on the book appeared the following April),[537] the censorship reviews of Czeszko's
Pokolenie discussed in offices across Poland (a separate article on the novel appeared
four months earlier, in April 1952),[538] and the publication of the mediocre play for
community centers *Głos Narodu* [Voice of the Nation].[539] The decision to allow such
a weak work to be published was largely the fault of censorship reviews, which

> were primarily focused on detailed interference and less on deeper analysis. As
> a result, by drawing attention to the harmfulness of fragments, they lost sight of
> the whole, which remained harmful even after the interference.
> The factor that should have determined the final decision in this case was the lack
> of any artistic value, as the political element was more or less straightened out by
> the detailed interference.[540]

The quotation shows two very important failings of "censorship criticism" at that
time, which were signaled in the Bulletins on multiple occasions: focusing on

---

[536] "Recenzja z pozycji literackiej (cd.)" (in the series *O wyższy poziom pracy nad
książką*), *Biuletyn Informacyjno-Instrukcyjny* no. 9, September 1952, p. 24 (APG, WUK-
PPiW, file ref. no. 78).

[537] "Recenzja z pozycji literackiej, cz. I" (in the series *O wyższy poziom pracy nad
książką*), *Biuletyn Informacyjno-Instrukcyjny* no. 8, August 1952, p. 19 (APG, WUKP-
PiW, file ref. no. 81). See also the chapter "How to Review Select Prose? Nałkowska,
Borowski, and Bartelski."

[538] "Recenzja z pozycji literackiej, cz. I" (in the series *O wyższy poziom pracy nad
książką*), *Biuletyn Informacyjno-Instrukcyjny* no. 8, August 1952, p. 22 (APG, WUKPPiW,
file ref. no. 81).

[539] The Polish Literary Bibliography does not record the title in either 1950, 1951 or
1952. From the information in the Bulletin, it can be concluded that *Głos Narodu* was
published by the CRZZ Publishing House.

[540] "Recenzja z pozycji literackiej, cz. I" (in the series *O wyższy poziom pracy nad
książką*), *Biuletyn Informacyjno-Instrukcyjny* no. 8, August 1952, p. 20 (APG, WUKPPiW,
file ref. no. 81).

details, which resulted in an incorrect evaluation of the work as a whole; and not taking into account the literary value of the assessed work.

The monthly also addressed the excessive succinctness of many reviews. As an example, the review of *The Fisherman's Son* by Vilis Lācis, a Latvian-Soviet politician and writer, twice awarded the Stalin Prize, was quoted.[541] The entire review reads as follows: "A novel about the life of Latvian fishermen in the interwar years. Translation is beyond reproach."[542] Clearly, the censor took the principle of *brevitas* to heart.

***

The third article in the series discussed censorship reviews of two books, *Wiedeńska wiosna* [Viennese spring] by Aleksander Jackiewicz and *Wrak 103* [Wreck 103] by Zofia Meisner. In both cases, "extensive, thorough, often even analytical"[543] assessments were made, which – as the supervisors admitted – at first glance, could not be criticized in any way. However, they soon found out that the initial diagnosis was deeply wrong, as they formulated a number of very similar accusations against the reviews. Interestingly, in spite of similar evaluations, the fate of the two texts proved quite different: Jackiewicz's book was published in 1952, while Meisner's has not been published to this day, adding to the collection of unpublished texts blocked by the PRL's censorship.

Zofia Meisner,[544] born in 1900, was a teacher, activist of the Polish Scouting Association, and author of novels of manners that were popular before the war. After the war, she was quite effectively sentenced to oblivion by communist censors: to this day, her works are known only to a small circle of specialists and the

---

[541] V. Lācis, *Syn rybaka. Powieść z życia łotewskiego*, trans. W. Olda, Warszawa: "Książka i Wiedza," 1950; Second Edition: ibidem 1953, trans. W. Giełżyński; Third Edition: ibidem 1954; see English edition: V. Lācis, *The Fisherman's Son*, trans. I. and T. Litvinov, Moscow: Foreign Languages Publishing House, 1954. On the "controversy" sparked by another novel by Lācis, *Towards New Shores*, see: "Życie przeciwko schematowi. List do redakcji dziennika *Prawda* w sprawie krytyki powieści W. Łacisa," *Nowa Kultura* March 23, 1952, no. 12, p. 3 (see: Fig. 24 with a review of Fedor Panfierov's novel *Bruski*, discussed later in the book).

[542] Recenzja z pozycji literackiej, cz. I" (in the series *O wyższy poziom pracy nad książką*), *Biuletyn Informacyjno-Instrukcyjny* no. 8, August 1952, p. 21 (APG, WUKPPiW, file ref. no. 81).

[543] "Recenzja z pozycji literackiej (cd.)" (in the series *O wyższy poziom pracy nad książką*), *Biuletyn Informacyjno-Instrukcyjny* no. 9, September 1952, p. 24 (APG, WUKPPiW, file ref. no. 78).

[544] In the Bulletin – misspelled Meissner.

author herself is sometimes confused with "Zofia Meissner, a translator of English and American literature."[545]

Indeed, Zofia Meisner's literary career was virtually nonexistent after 1945, except for a few works printed in the press and her *Obrońcy Westerplatte*[546] [Defenders of Westerplatte] published posthumously. Magdalena Budnik observes that from 1948 on, the author tried to publish the aforementioned book with four different publishing houses, but the unstable situation on the publishing market (such as closing down private publishing houses) and the subject matter of the novel caused the book to lie on the shelf for nine years. It was not published until the wave of the "Thaw" in 1957, two years after the writer's death.[547] We also know that after 1945, she failed to publish at least four more books: *Bursztyny* [Ambers], *Po prostu skandal* [Simply outrageous], *Cztery Elżbiety* [Four Elizabeths], and *Wrak 103*, which was mentioned in the September 1952 Bulletin.[548] Thanks to the preserved material, we can establish that the title definitely made it to "Mysia Street" and was meticulously evaluated by the functionaries from Warsaw and Gdańsk. The Bulletin's editors made a reference to a folder of materials on this particular novel, which contained a total of six reviews. This information is important because, according to various testimonies, Meisner was also the author of a novel entitled *Wraki* [Wrecks]. However, she supposedly destroyed the manuscript after Janusz Meissner, a pilot and journalist, author of several dozen books on aviation, and military and maritime studies, published a work in 1953 with not only the same title but also the same subject matter.[549]

---

[545] M. Budnik, "Przedwojenna pisarka w realiach wczesnego PRL-u. Przypadek Zofii Meisner," [in:] *Kariera pisarza w PRL-u…*, p. 214.

In point of fact, Meissner translated Howard Fast's play *Thirty Pieces of Silver*, mentioned in the Bulletins. See the chapter "Dramatic Works."

[546] Z. Meisner, *Obrońcy Westerplatte*, Warszawa: Wydawnictwo MON, 1957. See, e.g.: *Gdańsk w literaturze. Bibliografia od roku 997 do dzisiaj* vol. 5: *1945–1979*, ed. L. Rybicki, Gdańsk: Wydawnictwo słowo/obraz terytoria, 2007, pp. 139–140. Z. Meisner published, e.g., in: *Płomyczek, Tygodnik Powszechny, Rejsy,* and *Pomorze*.

[547] See: M. Budnik, "Przedwojenna pisarka w realiach wczesnego PRL-u…," pp. 212–231; "Zmarła Zofia Meisner," *Głos Wybrzeża* October 8–9, 1955, no. 240, p. 2; "Zofia Meisner-Denis nie żyje," *Dziennik Bałtycki* October 9–10, 1955, no. 241, p. 4.

[548] A. Flisikowska, *Gdańsk literacki: od kontrolowanego do wolnego słowa (1945–2005)*, Gdańsk: Wydawnictwo "Mestwin" i Wojewódzka i Miejska Biblioteka Publiczna im. Josepha Conrada-Korzeniowskiego w Gdańsku, 2011, pp. 16, 18–19, 37; S. Poręba, "Zofia Meisner – między szkołą i literaturą," *Nowości. Gazeta Pomorza i Kujaw* July 9, 1997, no. 158, p. 9; E. Kochanowska, "Zofia Meisner. Meisnerówna przez jedno 's,'" [in:] eadem, *Odeszli w cień*, Gdańsk: Wydawnictwo Morskie, 1981, pp. 75–88; M. Budnik, "Przedwojenna pisarka w realiach wczesnego PRL-u…," pp. 214, 229–230.

[549] E. Kochanowska, "Zofia Meisner. Meisnerówna przez jedno 's'…," pp. 79–80; S. Poręba, "Zofia Meisner – między szkołą i literaturą…," p. 9. See also: J. Meissner, *Wraki*, Warszawa: Iskry, 1953.

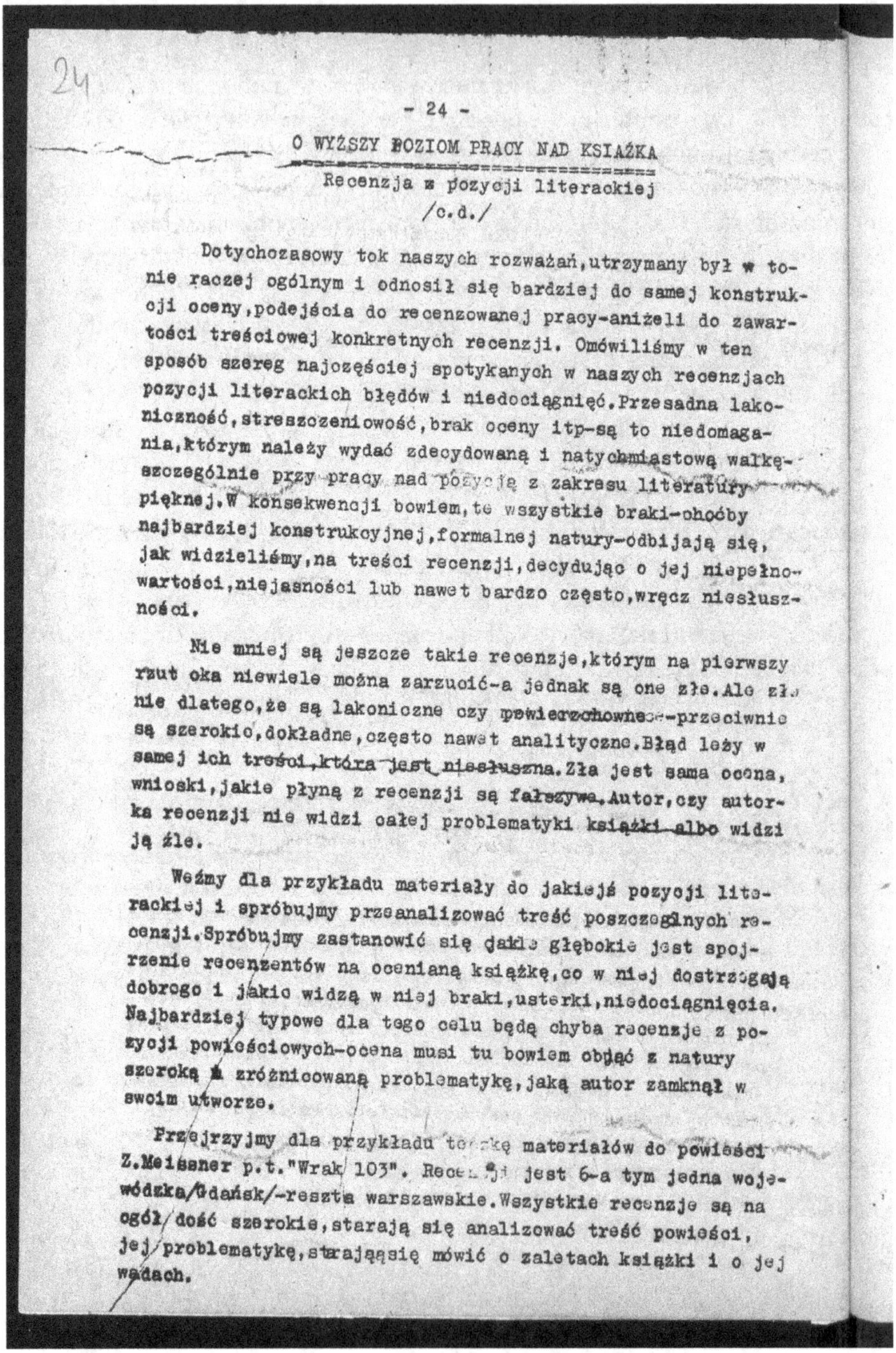

24

- 24 -

O WYŻSZY POZIOM PRACY NAD KSIĄŻKĄ
Recenzja z pozycji literackiej
/c.d./

    Dotychczasowy tok naszych rozważań,utrzymany był w tonie raczej ogólnym i odnosił się bardziej do samej konstrukcji oceny,podejścia do recenzowanej pracy-aniżeli do zawartości treściowej konkretnych recenzji. Omówiliśmy w ten sposób szereg najczęściej spotykanych w naszych recenzjach pozycji literackich błędów i niedociągnięć.Przesadna lakoniczność,streszczeniowość,brak oceny itp-są to niedomagania,którym należy wydać zdecydowaną i natychmiastową walkę-szczególnie przy pracy nad pozycję z zakresu literatury pięknej.W konsekwencji bowiem,te wszystkie braki-choćby najbardziej konstrukcyjnej,formalnej natury-odbijają się, jak widzieliśmy,na treści recenzji,decydując o jej niepełnowartości,niejasności lub nawet bardzo często,wręcz niesłuszności.

    Nie mniej są jeszcze takie recenzje,którym na pierwszy rzut oka niewiele można zarzucić-a jednak są one złe.Ale złe nie dlatego,że są lakoniczne czy ~~powierzchowne~~-przeciwnie są szerokie,dokładne,często nawet analityczne.Błąd leży w samej ich treści,która ~~jest niesłuszna~~.Zła jest sama ocena, wnioski,jakie płyną z recenzji są ~~fałszywe~~.Autor,czy autorka recenzji nie widzi całej problematyki ~~książki albo~~ widzi ją źle.

    Weźmy dla przykładu materiały do jakiejś pozycji literackiej i spróbujmy przeanalizować treść poszczególnych recenzji.Spróbujmy zastanowić się jakie głębokie jest spojrzenie recenzentów na ocenianą książkę,co w niej dostrzegają dobrego i jakie widzą w niej braki,usterki,niedociągnięcia. Najbardziej typowe dla tego celu będą chyba recenzje z pozycji powieściowych-ocena musi tu bowiem objąć z natury szeroką i zróżnicowaną problematykę,jaką autor zamknął w swoim utworze.

    Przejrzyjmy dla przykładu te ~~pkę~~ materiałów do powieści Z.Meisner p.t."Wrak 103". Recenzji jest 6-a tym jedna wojewódzka/Gdańsk/-reszta warszawskie.Wszystkie recenzje są na ogół dość szerokie,starają się analizować treść powieści, jej problematykę,starają się mówić o zaletach książki i o jej wadach.

Fig. 16a. A fragment of the material on *Wrak 103* by Zofia Meisner featured in the Bulletin from September 1952 (APG, WUKPPiW, file ref. no. 78, p. 24).

- 25 -

Książka należy do gatunku t.zw."lekkiej" literatury,ma
dużo elementów sensacyjności.

Czasokres trwania akcji obejmuje pierwsze lata po wyzwo-
leniu.Terenem akcji jest Gdańsk.Autorka pokazuje w zasadzie
dwa środowiska: robotnicze i szabrowników,szpiegów itp.Na
takim tle rozwija się główny wątek powieści,który stanowią
dzieje Jana Bończy-szabrownika i spekulanta-przechodzącego
                        pod
poważną ewolucję i awansującego koniec powieści na cał-
kiem pozytywnego bohatera.W fabułę wplątany jest ponadto
cały szereg innych wątków,np.sprawa tajemniczego wynalaz-
ku i związana z tym działalność grupy szpiegowskiej,praca
kolektywu robotniczego przy usuwaniu wraków itp.

Wyliczając i omawiając pozytywne strony powieści,pod-
kreślając wydobycie ciekawej i mało dotychczas znanej
tematyki,wszystkie recenzje są na ogół zgodne.

Tak naprzykład mówi o pozytywach powieści recenzja tow.
Sowadskiego/Warszawa/:"Powieść ...obrazuje bohaterską walkę
robotnika polskiego o uruchamianie portów,pracę wykonywaną w
trudnych warunkach,nieraz z narażeniem życia,podkreśla czo-
łową mobilizującą rolę partii,demaskuje agresywną,dywersyj-
ną działalność wywiadów imperialistycznych i sprzymierzonego
z nimi wroga klasowego,pokazuje patriotyzm i świadomość kla-
sową robotników Kaszubów".

Inne recenzje zawierają mniej więcej to samo.Ale w powieści jest właśnie dosyć dużo al . I recenzje nasze widzą to,
recenzenci piszą o tym.Jednak nie wszyscy i nie wszyscy tak
samo.Np.recenzja tow.Krutikowej jest w zasadzie wyłącznie
pozytywną, a jej wniosek to :"...do wydania jej nie mam za-
strzeżeń". Oprócz dwóch szczegółowych ingerencji i dość nie-
jasnych sformułowań o tym,że:"...w powieści przebijają
pewne idealistyczne naleciałości u autorki" lub:"pewna nie-
zręczność stylu"- autorka recenzji nie ma pod adresem książki
żadnych poważniejszych zastrzeżeń-przeciwnie,stwierdza,iż:
"...autorka trafnie ujmuje zagadnienia,słusznie podkreśla
przodującą rolę partii i prawdziwie proletariackiej inteligencji". Abstrahując od tego,iż taki sposób oceny właściwie
nic nie mówi-gdyż czytający dalej nie wie jak są ujęte zagadnienia i jakie to są zagadnienia,-trzebaby bliżej się
przyjrzeć merytorycznej słuszności tej oceny-czy rzeczywiś-

Fig. 16b. A fragment of the material on *Wrak 103* by Zofia Meisner featured in the Bulletin from September 1952 (APG, WUKPPiW, file ref. no. 78, p. 25).

Is it possible the censorship reviews of *Wrak 103* that have been found are actually reviews of the author's allegedly destroyed *Wraki*? It is too early to give a definitive answer; especially that until now, these titles have been treated as two separate works.[550] However, there are many indications that they may indeed have been the same book, or two novels on a very similar subject. *Wraki*, destroyed by the writer due to the remarkable similarity to Meissner's book, supposedly told the story of extracting ships sunken during the war from the bottom of the sea (Meissner wrote about a German ship called Adlernest; in the film adaptation, for which he and Czeszko wrote dialogues, ultimately, it was the famous Dzierżyński[551]). If Meisner indeed destroyed the manuscript, we will never learn whether her book was about wreck extraction, unless it really was the same book; then we can try to reconstruct the plot of the novel by relying on the censors' accounts. After all, the writer might have given up on publishing the book after it had already been submitted to the Main Office.

From the excerpts of the reviews quoted in the Bulletin, we learn that the novel, set in Gdańsk, "deals with efforts to extract shipwrecks on our coast after the last war,"[552] and its plot, besides the main motif – the fate of Jan Bończa – is built on a number of twists and turns of a sensational and spy nature. Thus, the hypothesis about a single book, circulated in the corridors of "Mysia Street" and existing in the author's manuscript under two different titles, does not seem unfounded. It must be clearly emphasized, however, that the Bulletin did not address any of the aforementioned issues. Reviews of *Wrak 103* were treated as training material. Obviously, the fact that no mention was made of the similarity of the title to Meissner's *Wraki* may or may not be evidence that the books told different stories. This was 1952, so at least one of Meisner's books had already been put "on halt," while Meissner continued to publish successfully, although he soon faced reprisals when his books about the Polish Air Force in England started to be removed from the shelves.[553]

---

[550] See, e.g.: M. Budnik, "Przedwojenna pisarka w realiach wczesnego PRL-u…," pp. 214, 229, 230; A. Flisikowska, *Gdańsk literacki: od kontrolowanego do wolnego słowa…*, p. 19; S. Poręba, "Zofia Meisner – między szkołą i literaturą…," p. 9.

[551] *Wraki*, directed by E. Petelska, Cz. Petelski, script by E. Petelska, Cz. Petelski, J. Meissner, dialogues J. Meissner, B. Czeszko, starring Z. Józefowicz, Z. Cybulski, U. Modrzyńska, produced by Wytwórnia Filmów Fabularnych w Łodzi, Polska 1957.

[552] "Recenzja z pozycji literackiej (cd.)" (in the series *O wyższy poziom pracy nad książką*), *Biuletyn Informacyjno-Instrukcyjny* no. 9, September 1952, p. 28 (APG, WUK-PPiW, file ref. no. 78).

[553] See, e.g.: K. Budrowska, *Writers, Literature and Censorship…*, p. 92. The MS Dzierżyński was a ship built for the British fleet, then incorporated into the German fleet and sunk in 1944; the vessel was recovered in 1954 and later became part of the Polish fleet.

To recapitulate the censors' standpoint on *Wrak 103* we may return to the Bulletins. Most of the reviews appreciated the positive aspects of the novel, including its innovative theme and the depiction of the heroic struggle of the workers to open ports. Almost all the censors also recognized the shortcomings of the work, which in some reviews clearly dominated over the praise; only comrade Krutikowa offered virtually no criticism. Voices of dissatisfaction included limiting the book's subject matter to "one backyard"[554] and the inadequate portrayal of the party, the technical intelligentsia, and the workers. On this occasion, the author was reproached for being rather biased when characterizing the latter group: "it is unclear why but according to all our writers, the workers must 'slurp' when eating,"[555] one censor wrote. More "foibles" of this kind were noticed in the novel, for example, in the case of the entire spy plot and the activities of intelligence, counterintelligence and the State Security.

According to superiors, some of the reviewers were unable to diagnose the errors and therefore concluded that the book should be accepted for print without any interference. What is worse, even if they noticed and pointed out the defects, they were in favor of publishing the work, for example, because of the "novelty of the topic."[556] The supervisors did not support such decisions, viewing them as the consequences of an erroneous assessment of both specific plots and the novel as a whole, rather than a collection of isolated components.

Similar accusations were leveled against the second book reviewed in this article, *Wiedeńska wiosna* by Aleksander Jackiewicz. The author, who in 1944 had escaped from forced labor in Germany to Vienna, returned to Poland in 1947 and continued his literary work, but his main area of interest became film criticism and history. The material analyzed excerpts from four censorship reviews of *Wiedeńska wiosna*, which, similarly to the reviews of *Wrak 103*, were characterized by considerable attention to detail, suggesting that they were written correctly and in accordance with the prevailing ideology. However, even in this case, a closer analysis revealed that some of the evaluations had several shortcomings. The editors wanted to sensitize the censors to such cases and to make them realize that, even with seemingly easy books, their vigilance should not be lulled.

The novel was published in 1952 by "Książka i Wiedza," and therefore the material in the Bulletin was most likely published afterwards.[557] The subject of Jackiewicz's novel was the post-war fate of the Busch family: the sons Egon and

---

[554] "Recenzja z pozycji literackiej (cd.)" (in the series *O wyższy poziom pracy nad książką*), *Biuletyn Informacyjno-Instrukcyjny* no. 9, September 1952, p. 26 (APG, WUK-PPiW, file ref. no. 78).

[555] Ibidem, p. 25.

[556] Ibidem, p. 28.

[557] A. Jackiewicz, *Wiedeńska wiosna*, Warszawa: "Książka i Wiedza," 1952.

Rudolf, as well as their father, Hans Busch, an Austrian writer who, "having withdrawn during the years of Nazi rule from any participation in the social and political life of the country, returns to Vienna liberated by the Soviet army."[558] The activities of Egon, a fascist, and the testimony of Rudolf, a concentration camp prisoner, trigger a transformation in their father from a "bourgeois liberal-humanist"[559] to a supporter of proletarian ideology. Some censors saw a certain resemblance to Leon Kruczkowski's *Niemcy* [The Germans], for instance, in the emphasis on the psychological portrayal of Busch, the father, "who appears to be the Austrian equivalent of Professor Sonnenbruch."[560]

All the reviews gave a similar, rather balanced assessment of the positive aspects of the book: the quality artistic execution and the skillful presentation of the difficult subject of the Austrians' struggle for the post-war shape of their country. Only comrade Leszczyński's assessment was surprisingly one-sided: he made no critical comments about the book. The differences in opinion only became apparent in the evaluation of the book's shortcomings and errors, which were zealously traced by comrade Rajska, the author of an extremely one-sided and "caustic"[561] evaluation (the "overzealous" reviewers of *Wrak 103*, Krutikowa and Pomykało, were also noticed by the editors[562]).

Some censors drew attention to the failure to show the links between resurgent fascism and the imperialist forces; for others the bland, two-dimensional characters of the communists were unacceptable; yet others felt that the contrast between the Soviet and Western occupation zones was insufficiently emphasized, while the rest saw this as the novel's strength. Perhaps these differences in the evaluation of the shortcomings were the biggest surprise for the superiors, who inquired about the reasons for such diverse positions.

In reply, the editors pointed to the need for more reliable substantive preparation of the censors, continuous improvement of their qualifications, supporting their evaluation with source materials, historical studies, etc., and especially, strong knowledge of the subject matter of the assessed work; this applied both to the evaluation of *Wiedeńska wiosna* and *Wrak 103*. According to the "deci-

---

[558] "Recenzja z pozycji literackiej (cd.)" (in the series *O wyższy poziom pracy nad książką*), *Biuletyn Informacyjno-Instrukcyjny* no. 9, September 1952, p. 28 (APG, WUK-PPiW, file ref. no. 78).

[559] Ibidem, p. 27.

[560] Ibidem, p. 32.

Niemcy [The Germans] – a drama by Leon Kruczkowski published in 1949; the work shows different attitudes of the Germans towards Nazism – from the internal detachment of the father of the family, Professor Walter Sonnenbruch (who neither actively opposed nor supported Nazism), to the acceptance and opposition to Nazism of his two sons.

[561] Ibidem, p. 30.

[562] Ibidem, pp. 25–28.

sion-makers," only this could have prevented the censors from writing reviews that did not give a full and analytical picture of the novel; such a view could be drawn only after reading all the evaluations, which – as an approach – was not satisfying for the superiors.

✱✱✱

In the last article of the series, problems related to the assessment of non-fiction works were raised. Several examples of censorship interventions in scholarly texts that were absurd or simply wrong (according to the superiors) were pointed out, but in most cases, without giving the titles of the analyzed works.[563] There were also evaluations of various pamphlets, from agitational and electoral ones to a brochure/manufacture sheet on textile spinning, from which the assessment of *Korespondencja Jana Śniadeckiego* [Jan Śniadecki's correspondence] seems to be slightly more interesting for a literature specialist.

The Bulletin quoted an excerpt from "a Kraków review of the work of the PAU."[564] To clarify, the first volume of correspondence was indeed published by the PAU (Polish Academy of Arts and Sciences), but this was in 1932. It is unlikely that the functionaries were evaluating a pre-war book; it is more probable that a second volume of correspondence was maturing on the censor's desk and did not get published until two years later, in 1954. It is possible that the collection was submitted to the Office for the Control by the PAU but ultimately, it was the PAN (Polish Academy of Sciences) and Ossolineum that became the book's publisher.[565]

Like any scholarly work, the book was accompanied by a number of footnotes. As mentioned earlier, in the times of the "Ministry of Truth," all kinds of paratexts – thanks to which works could be properly "framed" – were appreciated. The situation was no different in the case of footnotes in scholarly publications, where the critical apparatus often became a place of political manipulation and "ideological expression" of editors and censors, and was subject to the same verification of the Office as the main body of the text. That is why the Kraków censors evaluating

---

[563] "O wyższy poziom pracy nad książką (cd)" (in the series *O wyższy poziom pracy nad książką*), *Biuletyn Informacyjno-Instrukcyjny* no. 11, November 1952, pp. 37–42 (APG, WUKPPiW, file ref. no. 72).

[564] Ibidem, p. 38.

[565] *Korespondencja Jana Śniadeckiego* vol. 1: *Listy z Krakowa 1780–1787*, compiled by L. Kamykowski, Kraków: PAU, 1932; vol. 2: *Listy z Krakowa 1787–1807*, compiled by M. Chamcówna, S. Tync, Wrocław: Ossolineum i Komitet Historii Nauki PAN, 1954. See also, e.g.: Ł. Wróbel, "Korespondencja Jana Śniadeckiego jako źródło w edukacji historycznej," *Wiadomości Historyczne. Czasopismo dla nauczycieli* 2013, no. 3, pp. 17–21.

Korespondencja… also paid attention to this part of the publication. The accusation of the lack of ideological evaluation of the presented content in the critical apparatus was curious, but not surprising in the Stalinist era. The superiors appreciated this inquisitiveness of the team from Kraków, however, they complained that their report was missing concrete examples confirming the lack of this "ideological" framing of the comments (indeed, the report provided only one example).

4.4. Other Prose Works Discussed in the Bulletins: (Not Only) Sowińska, Koźniewski, Strumph-Wojtkiewicz, Gil, Zalewski Bocheński, Bartelski, Dębnicki, Dobraczyński, and Żeromski

> *There are some unnecessary interferences. They stem from the fact that sometimes the censor makes an interference "just in case," not being 100% convinced of its validity and assuming that it is better to have an unnecessary interference than an oversight.* [566]

Apart from the above-listed books, the monthly reviewed (in a more or less concise form) dozens of other prose titles. The evaluations usually pointed out the same problems, including schematism in the analysis and interpretation of the work, disregard for who the author and the target audience were, and the lack of a comprehensive evaluation that should take into account the ideological and artistic realization as well as the advantages and disadvantages of the work. The dominant and most general accusation that was frequently leveled at the censors' was their lack of competence. What follows is a modest selection of the titles that appeared in the Bulletins over the eleven years after the war.

***

Nine Bulletins from the years 1945–1951 have been found so far, and only some of them include a discussion about the control of specific cultural works. In the March 1950 Bulletin, several works were analyzed, including *Lata walki,* a memoir by Stanisława Sowińska – Władysław Gomułka's supporter and Marian Spychalski's close collaborator – which had a considerable impact on the assessment of her book. The memoirs appeared in print in *Głos Ludu* as early as 1946 and in 1948 the book was published. The title was reviewed by such critics as

---

[566] W. Wierciak (WUKPPiW Kraków), "Na przykładzie jednego przypisu," *Biuletyn Informacyjno-Instrukcyjny* no. 7/8 (31/32), July/August 1954, p. 37 (APG, WUKPPiW, file ref. no. 65).

Stefan Żółkiewski, a Stalinizer of Polish culture, who began his article by stating: "A surprisingly excellent book. And unfairly undervalued."[567] The publishing market of the 1950s had no place for the "independent communist's"[568] memoirs; the internal party fights between Bolesław Bierut and the supporters of adopting the Moscow model of ruling in Poland, and the Gomułka faction – which proposed a separate, Polish road to socialism – were becoming increasingly fierce.[569]

The material in the Bulletin appeared about six months after the arrest of Sowińska, who was imprisoned in Stalinist prisons from October 19, 1949 to December 8, 1954. The writer sat on the defendant's bench along with Gomułka and Spychalski; the former was released on December 13, 1954; Spychalski was imprisoned in Stalinist prisons from May 13, 1950 to March 1956. Morever, Gomułka, who was on leave, was arrested by Józef Światło, the same person who escaped to the West in December 1953 and who later revealed the crimes of Stalinism in Poland, in his program *Za kulisami bezpieki i Partii* (*Behind the Scene of the Party and Bezpieka: Josef Swiatlo Reveals the Secrets of the Regime and Security Apparatus*) on Radio Free Europe; it is worth mentioning that Światło, already a lieutenant-colonel, also took part in the investigation of Stanisława Sowińska.[570]

---

[567] S. Żółkiewski, "Pamiętnik 'Barbary' Sowińskiej," *Kuźnica* June 6, 1948, no. 23, p. 10. See also: S. Sowińska, *Lata walki*, Warszawa: "Książka," 1948; cf. other review of *Lata walki*: T. Borowski, "Małe i wielkie legendy," *Odrodzenie* February 29, 1948, no. 9, pp. 1, 3. Stefan Żółkiewski (1911–1991) – a Polish theorist, historian of literature and literary critic; one of the most loyal and highly positioned communist politicians, a co-founder of Polish Workers' Party, the Minister of Higher Education.

[568] M. Przeperski, "Suwerenność komunistki," *Nowe Książki* 2017, no. 9, pp. 28–29 (a review of S. Sowińska's book, *Gorzkie lata. Z wyżyn władzy do stalinowskiego więzienia*, edited and compiled by Ł. Bertram, Warszawa: Wydawnictwo Ośrodek Karta, 2017). See also other review of *Gorzkie lata…*: A. Mrozik, "Czy komunistka może być ofiarą?," *Bez dogmatu* 2017, no. 112, pp. 29–31.

[569] K. Trembicka, "Dwie wizje komunistycznej Polski czy spór o sposób sprawowania władzy? Refleksje o myśli politycznej Władysława Gomułki i Bolesława Bieruta," *Annales Universitatis Paedagogicae Cracoviensis. Studia Politologica* 2013, no. 9, pp. 32–45; J. Jagiełło, *O polską drogę do socjalizmu. Dyskusje w PPR i PPS w latach 1944–1948*, Second Edition, Warszawa–Kraków: PWN, 1983. See also: *Towarzysz Wiesław*, script and direction by P. Boruszkowski, produced by Telewizja Polska, 2013, https://www.cda.pl/video/1306845d5 (accessed March 31, 2021); P. Boruszkowski, J. Eisler, *Towarzysz Wiesław* (in the series *Cafe Historia*), interview conducted by A. Górniakowska, ed. U. Dubowska, prod. APTiF for TVP Historia, TVP SA 2014, https://vod.tvp.pl/video/cafe-historia,towarzysz-wieslaw,17022431 (accessed January 10, 2021).

[570] Światło's accounts were published numerous times, also in book form, see, e.g.: J. Światło, *Za kulisami bezpieki i partii. Józef Światło ujawnia tajniki partii, reżymu i aparatu bezpieczeństwa*, Warszawa: Niezależna Oficyna Wydawnicza NOWA, 1981; see English edition: J. Swiatlo, *Behind the Scene of the Party and Bezpieka: Josef Swiatlo Reveals the*

By the time the Bulletin was published, Sowińska had already been interrogated by Stalinist prison functionaries, as she recounted in her memoir *Gorzkie lata. Z wyżyn władzy do stalinowskiego więzienia* [Bitter years: from the heights of power to a Stalinist prison]:

> I saw a prisoner walking under escort, like me. His appearance made me shudder. He was so swollen he resembled a rubber sack bloated to its limit. Pierce the epidermis, and water will leak out in streams, leaving a man-shaped tatter with dangling rags for arms. His face was leaden in color – it barely resembled a human face. There was nothing in the gaze, not a trace of thought, as if his brain had undergone a thorough washing…[571]

In this context, the decision, probably made at the turn of 1950, to withdraw *Lata walki* from circulation seems to be an insignificant episode. The fact that only political accusations were leveled against the novel justifies the hypothesis that its removal from the publishing market was determined primarily by changes on the political scene: the purges within the PPR, the ousting of Gomułka and his comrades, and the consolidation of new elites around the only correct vision of history. If Sowińska had not been associated with Spychalski and Gomułka, at most the book would have been redacted and the author would not have been imprisoned.

Stanisława Sowińska – an agent of the intelligence service of the GL, firmly embedded in the occupational and post-war structures of the Polish state, and a close collaborator of her colleagues who were sentenced in successive trials – did not escape a similar fate. She was, above all, a communist activist; in *Lata walki*, she constructed a legend about those who at that time were being removed from power.[572] This interpretation is confirmed by the author; in the introduction to the second, 1957 edition of her work, she reminisced that:

> I was accused of not really writing *Lata walki* myself. It was Gomułka and Spychalski who jointly wrote it – each their part; I only "lent" them my name to espouse the false and hypocritical legends manufactured by the two above-mentioned fig-

---

Secrets of the Regime and Security Apparatus, New York: Free Europe Committee, 1955. See also: S. Sowińska, *Gorzkie lata…*, pp. 47, 63.

[571] S. Sowińska, *Gorzkie lata…*, p. 50. Sowińska's first interrogations began shortly after her arrest; the author writes about these and subsequent ones on pages: 62–66 (on November 2, 1949, the first interrogation of Sowińska took place after she was transported from the Mokotów prison to the "Spacer" facility – a secret prison at the disposal of the "Special Group/Bureau (from the end of 1951 – Department X of the Ministry of Public Security) tasked with combating the 'internal enemy' in the bosom of the PZPR" (S. Sowińska, *Gorzkie lata…*, p. 63). The writer's account quoted above describes the appearance of the inmates after their interrogations with the experts at the "school" of the investigation.

[572] Ł. Bertram, "Od Redaktora," [in:] *Gorzkie lata…*, p. 7.

ures around my own person, and around ninety-eight out of one hundred people mentioned in the book, who turned out to be spies, provocateurs, traitors, ordinary thugs and, of course, just like me, "deservedly" repented in prison.
After many furious battles, when I "convinced" my tormentors that it was I, myself, of my own free will, who wrote it, I was accused of deliberately and consciously propagating those false legends and glorifying those persons – first and foremost, naturally, Spychalski and Gomułka.[573]

While it seems that *Lata walki* should have been blacklisted, it does not appear in two directories and indices drawn up in 1950,[574] nor in the largest (at the time) *List of Books Subject to Immediate Withdrawal*,[575] dated October 1, 1951. Perhaps the title was not on any of these lists; the activities of the censorship office were liable to a "human" element, understood as a simple oversight or negligence.[576] It is worth adding, however, that on the cited list from 1951, under no. 1376 of *List no. 1*, there was a record of the removal of all titles by Marian Spychalski, whose wife unsuccessfully interceded with Maria Dąbrowska.[577] The author of *Noce i dnie* [Nights and days] was not an accidental addressee of the request: in spite of her opposition to the actions of the new authorities and her growing awareness that even Borejsza – whom she valued (not without reciprocation) – was made of the same clay as the State Security tormentor Różański,[578] she still received awards, made efforts to have her works published, and attended writers' conventions. As a pre-war socialist, she was "a choice morsel for the post-war communist rulers of our country."[579]

***

---

[573] S. Sowińska, *Wstęp do drugiego wydania*, [in:] eadem, *Lata walki*, Warszawa: "Książka i Wiedza," 1957, p. 10. *Lata walki* was also published in 1962 and 1966, both by "Książka i Wiedza."

[574] *Cenzura PRL. Wykaz książek podlegających niezwłocznemu wycofaniu 1 X 1951 r.*, afterward by Z. Żmigrodzki, Wrocław: Wydawnictwo "Nortom," 2002.

[575] "Wykaz książek wycofanych z bibliotek 1945–1956" (APP, WUKPPiW, file ref. no. 13, pp. 35–36).

[576] See, e.g.: K. Dworecki, "O wyższy poziom organizacji pracy," *Biuletyn Informacyjno-Instrukcyjny* no. 1 (25), January 1954, pp. 9–10 (APG, WUKPPiW, file ref. no. 39).

[577] J. Giedroyc, J. Stempowski, *Listy 1946–1969. Część 1*, Warszawa: "Czytelnik," 1998, p. 342.

[578] Jerzy Borejsza (born Beniamin Goldberg) and Józef Różański (born Jozef Goldberg) were brothers.

[579] I. Kienzler, *Prowokatorka. Fascynujące życie Marii Dąbrowskiej*, Warszawa: Bellona, 2017, p. 324. On Dąbrowska's tough choices and decisions, and the price she paid for them, see, e.g.: M. Dąbrowska, *Dzienniki powojenne* vol. 1: *1945–1949*; vol. 2: *1950–1954*, selection, introduction and footnotes by T. Drewnowski, Warszawa: "Czytelnik," 1996.

The first issue from 1953 reviewed Kazimierz Koźniewski's novel *Piątka z ulicy Barskiej*.[580] The supervisors once again criticized the censors for their overzealousness in tracing the work's flaws and errors while overlooking its advantages and strong points.[581] A certain novelty in relation to the other reviews presented in the Bulletins was the fact that the evaluations were written not only by experienced reviewers of the Office, but also by those aspiring to this role: *Piątka z ulicy Barskiej* was "used as test material for censor and reviewer candidates."[582]

Maybe this was the reason why out of eleven reviews prepared, as many as four gave an "explicitly negative"[583] assessments regarding the publication of the book; a book that had been successfully operating on the publishing market for several months. In 1952, the work received the Artistic State Award of the Third Degree, while a few months later – in April 1953 – it was recognized by the international film community thanks to Aleksander Ford's screen adaptation, which won a distinction at the Cannes Film Festival.[584] In addition, the film was evaluated in one of Bulletins the following year.[585]

The novel's recognition in Poland seemed to be well deserved, as the fate of the five friends, shown against the background of Warsaw ruined by the war, fully realized the postulates of socialist realism. From the material presented in the Bulletin, it seems that a few censors could be partly credited with that, as their comments "significantly influenced the final form of the book [...] and consequently contributed to the publication of a novel devoid of any major shortcomings."[586] We know that Koźniewski corrected the manuscript, but the Bulletin lacks information about what suggestions the author and the publishing house

---

[580] "Śladem naszych recenzji," *Biuletyn Informacyjno-Instrukcyjny* no. 1 (13), January 1953, pp. 45–50 (APG, WUKPPiW, file ref. no. 19). See also: K. Koźniewski, *Piątka z ulicy Barskiej*, Warszawa: PIW, 1952.

[581] "Śladem naszych recenzji," *Biuletyn Informacyjno-Instrukcyjny* no. 1 (13), January 1953, p. 45 (APG, 25WUKPPiW, file ref. no. 19).

[582] Ibidem.

[583] Ibidem, p. 46.

[584] The book was very successful, as evidenced by subsequent editions: Second Edition: Warszawa: PIW, 1952; Third Edition: ibidem 1953; Fourth Edition: ibidem 1954; Fifth Edition: ibidem 1954; Sixth Edition: ibidem 1955; Seventh Edition: ibidem 1962; Eighth Edition: ibidem 1964; Ninth Edition: ibidem 1964; Tenth Edition: Warszawa: "Czytelnik," 1968; Eleventh Edition: Warszawa: PIW, 1976. See also: *Five from Barska Street,* directed by A. Ford, script by A. Ford, K. Koźniewski, starring A. Śląska, T. Janczar, T. Łomnicki, Wytwórnia Filmów Fabularnych, Łódź 1953.

[585] "Znaczenie wtórnej kontroli filmów," *Biuletyn Informacyjno-Instrukcyjny* no. 6 (30), June 1954, pp. 21–23 (APG, WUKPPiW, file ref. no. 52).

[586] "Śladem naszych recenzji," *Biuletyn Informacyjno-Instrukcyjny* no. 1 (13), January 1953, p. 50 (APG, WUKPPiW, file ref. no. 19).

took into account, how many times the text was revised, and how far the version submitted to the Main Office differed from the one that appeared in print. This was certainly important data, but for the censor-readers of the Bulletin, it was equally important, if not more important, that their work could have a real impact on the final shape of the text. Such information must have mobilized them for further work and "lifted the spirits" of comrades who, as it has been illustrated, usually received negative feedback in the field of "censor criticism."

***

In February 1953, interferences and omissions in publications on Polish history were discussed.[587] Among the titles analyzed was the second edition of Stanisław Strumph-Wojtkiewicz's novel *Generał Komuny* [General of the Commune], which described the heroes of the January Uprising.[588] The author – for some, a great popularizer of history; for others, above all, a mythomaniac – operated quite freely with historical facts, interweaving them with unbridled literary fantasy. This loose approach to "historical truth" often made the writer the target of (justified) criticism.[589] On the other hand, this strategy brought him a group of loyal readers, making him one of the most widely read authors and popularizers of knowledge about Polish history in the PRL, especially during the interwar period and the Second World War (although *Generał Komuny*, which was subjected to reflection in the Bulletin, shows that the author also explored more distant times).

The book was first published in 1950; at the time, it passed inspection with minimal corrections, but this was considered an oversight by the censors. During the work on the reprint, a number of serious errors were noticed that had to be addressed. Generally speaking, the author was criticized for presenting certain aspects of the January Uprising falsely, that is, inconsistently with the prevailing interpretation. A comparison of both editions of the novel suggests that the censors' efforts were "fruitful," because the book was reprinted in an expanded version and with numerous changes in relation to the first edition.

***

---

[587] W.P., "Kilka uwag o niektórych ingerencjach i przeoczeniach w publikacjach z dziedziny historii Polski (artykuł dyskusyjny)," *Biuletyn Informacyjno-Instrukcyjny* no. 2 (14), February 1953, pp. 33–37 (APG, WUKPPiW, file ref. no. 18).

[588] S. Strumph-Wojtkiewicz, *Generał Komuny*, Warszawa: PIW, 1950; Second Expanded Edition: ibidem 1953.

[589] M. Wańkowicz, "Czaruś w grobowcu Szujskich. Polski Münchhausen," [in:] idem, *Przez cztery klimaty 1912–1972*, Second Edition, Warszawa: PIW, 1974, pp. 656–675.

The works of Stefan Żeromski were also discussed in 1953. A separate article devoted to the writer examined selected novels and short stories (e.g., *Doktor Piotr* [Doctor Piotr], *The Coming Spring, Syzyfowe prace* [Sisyphean works], *Walka z szatanem* [Fight with the devil], *Zapomnienie* Oblivion], *Zmierzch* [The dusk]), which the censors appreciated for their criticism of the capitalist system. The material quoted a number of excerpts from the diaries and works of the writer, who was showered with praise for the fact that "throughout his output, he has stood on the side of the worker exploited by the factory owner and the peasant oppressed by the worker."[590]

***

In 1954, several major articles on exercising control over books were published. One of them dealt with the extremely important problem of "cooperation of the National Department of Non-Periodical Publications with voivodeship offices,"[591] basically discussing only organizational issues (briefings, instructions, secondary inspection, etc.). The subsequent material, on the other hand, examined the collection of reportages *Ziemia i morze* [Land and sea] by the aforementioned Franciszek Gil.[592] Władysław Wierciak of the Kraków branch devoted an entire seven-page article to describing the difficult work on a footnote in the book about the "Brest protest."[593] The article did not go unnoticed, as the very next issue printed two letters from comrade-censors and presented the position of the Bulletin's editors on the problematic footnote; the first of them was accompanied by a quote from Charles Dickens' *The Pickwick Papers*, "This is a bit much."[594]

---

[590] Sowadski (Dept. Of Non-Periodical Publications GUKPPiW), "Stefan Żeromski," *Biuletyn Informacyjno-Instrukcyjny* no. 9 (21), September 1953, p. 529 (AAN, GUKPPiW, file ref. no. 22). See English edition: S. Żeromski, *The Coming Spring*, trans. B. Johnston, Budapest–New York: Central European University Press, 2007.

[591] "Wnioski z narady krajowej tyczące kontroli prewencyjnej książek," *Biuletyn Informacyjno-Instrukcyjny* no. 6 (30), June 1954, pp. 11–19 (APG, WUKPPiW, file ref. no. 52).

[592] W. Wierciak (WUKPPiw Kraków), "Na przykładzie jednego przypisu," *Biuletyn Informacyjno-Instrukcyjny* no. 7/8 (31/32), July/August 1954, pp. 37–43 (APG, WUK-PPiW, file ref. no. 65). See: F. Gil, *Ziemia i morze*, introduction by A. Polewka, Kraków: Wydawnictwo Literackie, 1954; I. Iwasiów, "Przesiedleni chłopi uruchamiają miasto," *Teksty Drugie* 2017, no. 5, pp. 181–192.

[593] The Brest Trial – a political trial of the leaders of the Centrolew (an alliance of centrist and left-wing parties, including the PPS and PSL, formed in 1929 to fight the Sanation system of government), held between October 1931 and January 1932 in Warsaw; almost all the defendants were sentenced to prison.

[594] K. Wachowiak, "Na przykładzie jednego przypisu"; J. Kupraszwili, "Odpowiedź na list Kolegi prasowca"; [Od Redakcji] (correspondence in "Dział Listów"), *Biuletyn*

Such focus on detail is rare in the Bulletins. Evidence of this can be found in another article from 1954, which discussed several novels, short stories and reportages that illustrated the "social, political and moral changes occurring in the countryside."[595] The material mentioned, for example, Witold Zalewski's "somewhat pioneering book"[596] *Traktory zdobędą wiosnę* [Tractors will win the spring], Jacek Bocheński's novellas from the collection *Zgodnie z prawem* [According to law], and Lesław Bartelski's novel *Ludzie zza rzeki* (after *Miejsce urodzenia*, this was the second book by this author discussed in the Bulletin).[597] The text raised problems typical of other reviews of that period; it once again emphasized the importance of a comprehensive assessment of works, and taking into account not only their ideological, but also artistic side. This time, the problem was approached in terms of form and content:

> The form is a concrete manifestation of the content. The form is not indifferent to the essence of the content; it is dependent on it. The form is not only dependent on the content, but also influences the very content.
> Content and form are one, with content always being the decisive element.[598]

In 1954, the censors' attention was also drawn to several short stories and novels, including *Opowiadania świętokrzyskie* [Short stories of Świętokrzyskie] by Kazimierz Dębnicki, published by "Czytelnik," and a book by Jan Dobraczyński, *Kościół w Chochołowie* [A church in Chochołów], published by "Pax" and reprinted within a year.[599]

Informacyjno-Instrukcyjny no. 9 (33), September 1954, pp. 38–40 (APG, WUKPPiW, file ref. no. 56).

[595] "Spółdzielczość produkcyjna w naszej literaturze," *Biuletyn Informacyjno-Instrukcyjny* no. 3 (27), March 1954, pp. 28–46 (APG, WUKPPiW, file ref. no. 45).

[596] Ibidem, p. 39.

[597] W. Zalewski, *Traktory zdobędą wiosnę*, Warszawa: "Czytelnik," 1950; Second Edition: ibidem 1951; Third Edition: ibidem 1953; J. Bocheński, *Zgodnie z prawem*, Warszawa: "Czytelnik," 1952; Second Edition: ibidem 1953; Third Edition: ibidem 1954; Fourth Edition: ibidem 1954.

[598] "Spółdzielczość produkcyjna w naszej literaturze," *Biuletyn Informacyjno-Instrukcyjny* no. 3 (27), March 1954, p. 45 (APG, WUKPPiW, file ref. no. 45).

[599] Both titles were discussed in the article "Przegląd ingerencji nr 3/54 Departamentu Publikacyj Nieperiodycznych GUKPPiW poświęcony omówieniu kilku różnorodnych zagadnień," *Biuletyn Informacyjno-Instrukcyjny* no. 4 (28), April 1954, pp. 34–35 (APG, WUKPPiW, file ref. no. 48). See also: K. Dębnicki, *Opowiadania Świętokrzyskie*, Warszawa: "Czytelnik," 1954; J. Dobraczyński, *Kościół w Chochołowie*, Warszawa: Instytut Wydawniczy "Pax," 1954.

5. DRAMATIC WORKS

It is time that this passive, consumerist attitude
towards the Bulletin was overcome and the field
became its host to a decidedly larger degree.[600]

Dramatic works published in book form were sometimes discussed in the Bulletins, but it was in the chapters devoted to the control of performances that the problem of the stage production of works was raised much more often (which will be discussed later). Nevertheless, the Bulletins provide some information about how the censor's work on dramatic texts proceeded.

In May 1949, the aforementioned plays *Ułan i Młynarka* by Robert Rydz and *Powrót* by Janina Matysiak were found to have been erroneously redacted. All religious phrases had been removed, which the superiors considered a harmful "zealotry."[601] In the March (May) Bulletin of the following year, two works, *Morgi* by Zofia Przęczek and *Przebudzenie* by Maria Witkowska,[602] were reviewed at length. The books were evaluated in the context of the ongoing debates about class struggle and the so-called rightist-nationalist deviation, which – as was illustrated by Stanisława Sowińska's *Lata Walki* – had a decisive influence on the accusations formulated against them.

The plays focused on rural problems during the implementation of the agricultural reform: *Morgi* described one day in the life of farmer Józef Walocha and his loved ones; *Przebudzenie* was about the family of another farmer, Antoni Gniewosz.

---

[600] WUKP Bydgoszcz, "Pięćdziesiąt numerów," *Biuletyn Informacyjno-Instrukcyjny* no. 2 (50), February 1956, p. 21 (APG, WUKPPiW, file ref. no. 6).

[601] "Stosunki między Kościołem a Państwem," *Biuletyn Informacyjno-Szkoleniowy* no. 4, May 1949, fol. 142r–142v (APP, WUKPPiW, file ref. no. 4). See also: R. Rydz, *Ułan i młynarka. Wodewil ludowy w trzech aktach*, Katowice: Wydawnictwo "Odrodzenie" (T. Nalepa i S-ka), 1947, series *Biblioteka Teatrów Amatorskich* no. 247; J. Matysiak, *Powrót. Obrazek sceniczny w 3 odsłonach dla świetlic*, Bydgoszcz: Pomorska Spółdzielnia Księgarska i Papiernicza "Nauka," 1947.

[602] Z. Przęczek, *Morgi…*; M. Witkowska, *Przebudzenie. Widowisko ludowe w trzech odsłonach*, Katowice: Wydawnictwo "Odrodzenie" (T. Nalepa i Ska), 1948, series *Teatr dla Wszystkich* no. 14 (in the description promoting the series, the title of the work is slightly changed: *Przebudzenie. Współczesna sztuka ludowa w 3 aktach* (ibidem, p. 3 of the cover).

The accusations against both titles focused on an allegedly false representation of rural problems at a time of change. According to the censors, the works failed to show the positive aspects of collectivization and instead, emphasized antagonisms within the peasantry, which could have had a demotivating effect on readers. The functionaries only gave their opinion on the ideological realization of the two texts; the issue of artistic value was completely ignored.

Both books reviewed did not stand out from other productions of this type, so it is difficult to say unequivocally why they were selected to be discussed in the magazine. Neither Zofia Przęczek – a writer representing peasant and folk art – nor Maria Witkowska seem to have been among the leading authors. The choice of *Przebudzenie* may have been determined by the fact that, firstly, the play was published by a private publishing house (during the period when the book market was being nationalized, publishing houses of this type were under the special "care" of the Office for the Control) and, secondly, it was published in the popular "Theatre for All" series.[603] Addressed to a wide, often uneducated audience, the series was intended to discuss contemporary issues in the most accessible way possible, providing theater companies with

> 1. a **repertoire** of old and contemporary stage literature, stage production, prose, poetry, and folk songs adapted to the needs and assumptions of the contemporary nonprofessional theater movement.
> 2. **assistance** in implementing the repertoire in the form of staging guidelines, blocking and illustrations[604] (original emphasis).

Thanks to such initiatives, "theatrical life continued in community theaters and centers adjacent to workplaces."[605] The evidence of this was supposed to be another play discussed in the Bulletin and published in this series, namely,

---

[603] See also other titles by Maria Witkowska published in this series: *Zbiór inscenizacji prozy, poezji i piosenek ludowych z ilustracją muzyczną i wzorem strojów ludowych wraz ze wstępem teoretycznym o pracy świetlicowej*, Katowice: Wydawnictwo "Odrodzenie" (T. Nalepa i Ska), 1948, series *Teatr dla Wszystkich* no. 2 and *Kłopoty sportowca, wesoła komedia współczesna w 3 aktach*, Katowice: Wydawnictwo "Odrodzenie" (T. Nalepa i Ska), 1948, series *Teatr dla Wszystkich* no. 9. See also the aforementioned short book by Robert Rydz, *Ułan i młynarka...*, published as part of the *Biblioteka Teatrów Amatorskich* series.

[604] M. Witkowska, *Przebudzenie...*, the reverse of the cover (n.p.).

[605] A. Wiśniewska-Grabarczyk, "Teatr i dramat okresu socrealizmu w świetle kryptotekstów (na materiale Ministerstwa Kultury i Sztuki oraz Wojewódzkiego Urzędu Kontroli Prasy, Publikacji i Widowisk w Poznaniu)," [in:] *Metateksty i parateksty teatru i dramatu. Od antyku do współczesności*, eds. J. Czerwińska, K. Chiżyńska, M. Budzowska, Łódź: Wydawnictwo UŁ, 2017, p. 101.

Szopka betleemska [Nativity scene of Bethlehem] by Jan Baranowicz.[606] Both titles included guidelines for staging the work, such as a musical setting based "on well-known folk melodies"[607] and a director's commentary by the author.[608] The plays published in series intended for various types of community theaters were revisited several more times. The importance of appropriately "adapting the work to the needs and possibilities of amateur groups, staging arrangements, etc." was emphasized.[609]

As noted earlier, in August 1952, the publication of a community center play *Głos Narodu*[610] was criticized. In that same year, the October issue broached the subject of the booklet *Obrazki i... obrazy, czyli pięć satyrycznych i łatwych do inscenizacji ataków na bramkę przeciwnika*[611] [Impressions and... insults, or five satirical and easily staged attacks on the opponent's goal]. This time the evaluators drew attention to a newspaper review of the work that made – what they considered – an unauthorized equation of U.S. imperialists with West German officials: according to the functionaries, it was wrong to treat all Germans as enemies.[612]

Several remarks on the control of dramatic creativity appeared in the report on the activity of the "Czytelnik" Publishing Cooperative. The evaluation of the achievements of Borejsza's publishing house in the field of contemporary Polish literature started with discussing theatrical plays. The report summarizes both the successes and failures of the initiative to publish works presented at the Festival of Contemporary Polish Plays. The festival was initiated in theaters across the country

---

[606] J. Baranowicz, *Szopka betleemska. Misterium ludowe w 3 obrazach*, with the director's commentary by the author and foreword, graphic design by S. Gawron, Katowice: Wyd. "Odrodzenie" (Nalepa i S-ka), 1947, series *Teatr dla Wszystkich* no. 8 (in the description promoting the series, the title of the work is expanded with the adjective "uwspółcześnione" (modernized): *Misterium ludowe uwspółcześnione w 3 obrazach*). See: *Biuletyn Informacyjno-Szkoleniowy* no. 1/3, January 1949, p. 41 (APG, WUKPPiW, file ref. no. 196).

[607] M. Witkowska, *Przebudzenie...*, the reverse of the cover (n.p.).

[608] J. Baranowicz, *Szopka Betleemska...*

[609] "Recenzja z pozycji literackiej, cz. I" (in the series *O wyższy poziom pracy nad książką*), *Biuletyn Informacyjno-Instrukcyjny* no. 8, August 1952, p. 22 (APG, WUKPPiW, file ref. no. 81).

[610] See the chapter "Books Discussed as Part of the Series *For a Higher Level of Work on the Book*: (Not Only) Nałkowska, Czeszko, Lācis, Meisner, and Jackiewicz."

[611] In the Bulletin – *Obrazy i obrazki* [Insults and impressions].

T. Chrzanowski, K. Rudzki, *Obrazki i... obrazy, czyli pięć satyrycznych i łatwych do inscenizacji ataków na bramkę przeciwnika*, Warszawa: Czytelnik, 1952, series *Biblioteka Świetlicowa 'Czytelnika.'*

[612] "Zabezpieczyć stałe i systematyczne szkolenie zespołów cenzorskich," *Biuletyn Informacyjno-Instrukcyjny* no. 10, October 1952, p. 4 (APG, WUKPPiW, file ref. no. 75).

on February 26, 1951, although "it was preceded by almost two years of preparation."[613] "Czytelnik" began publishing festival works as early as 1950 and continued throughout the following year, publishing "almost all the festival plays."[614] The theater review finished on July 18, 1951, and at the beginning of 1952, "Czytelnik" discontinued the project. Perhaps the reason for this was the fact that the festival received mostly negative reviews. This, however, was not mentioned in the report itself, which criticized only the selection of plays presented that Borejsza's publishing house may no longer have wanted to publish. In addition, only some of the negative opinions about the festival appeared in print at the time; others had to wait several decades to see the light of day, such as Leon Kruczkowski's editorial summation of the event, which was not published until 1974 in *Dialog*.[615]

This report also looks at the subject matter of the dramatic works published by Borejsza's publishing house. The most frequently discussed issue was "the breakthrough in the consciousness of an intellectual";[616] the following plays were to serve as examples: *Doktor Anna Leśna* [Doctor Anna Leśna] by Irena Krzywicka, *Pawilon pod sosnami* [Pavilion under the pine trees] by Michał Rusinek, *Próba sił* [A test of strength] by Jerzy Lutowski and *Śmierć Hamleta* [Hamlet's death] by Andrzej Wydrzyński – all of the aforementioned titles were published by "Czytelnik" in 1951, and stage productions took place at the festival between 1950 and 1951.

Other issues centered around several published dramatic works that were focused on matters related to production and the countryside. According to the censors, there were far too few plays devoted to these topics, and those that were published presented the subject in a highly incompetent manner, which was supposedly evidenced by such titles as: *Dobry człowiek* [A good man] by Krzysztof Gruszczyński, *Awans* [Promotion] by Wanda Żółkiewska, and *Zwycięstwo* [Victory] by Janusz Warmiński. The latter play, staged at the Teatr Nowy in Łódź, was judged quite differently by the festival jury, where it received the second prize (all of the aforementioned titles were published by "Czytelnik" in 1951).

Moreover, the report on "Czytelnik" examined the translation of dramatic works. Although the publishing house released "a number of contemporary Soviet plays,"[617] in the period under discussion, this was a drop in the ocean of needs, since

---

[613] M. Fik, *Kultura polska po Jałcie…*, p. 155.

[614] "Działalność wydawnictwa 'Czytelnik' w 1951 r.," *Biuletyn Informacyjno-Instrukcyjny* no. 5, May 1952, p. 20 (APG, WUKPPiW, file ref. no. 90).

[615] L. Kruczkowski, "Po Festiwalu Polskich Sztuk Współczesnych," *Dialog* 1974, issue 1, pp. 91–101.

[616] "Działalność wydawnictwa 'Czytelnik' w 1951 r." *Biuletyn Informacyjno-Instrukcyjny* no. 5, May 1952, p. 20 (APG, WUKPPiW, file ref. no. 90).

[617] Ibidem.

by drawing on the experience, especially of Soviet literature, as well as on the dramaturgical achievements of the fraternal countries of people's democracy, which are at a similar stage of development to ours, [translations] could be of great help to our dramaturgy arriving at a turning point.[618]

The authors of the report criticized the publishing house for excessive freedom and spontaneity in the selection of published works, at the expense of a lack of a stable, "defined conceptual line."[619] The authors were extremely critical of two of "Czytelnik's" publications: *Jacht Paradise* [Yacht Paradise] by the Lem-Hussarski tandem, and *Kąkol i pszenica* [The cockle and the wheat] by Tadeusz Łomnicki; both plays were published in 1951 and were accused of errors in their artistic and ideological realization.

As observed earlier, none of the analyzed Bulletins contained a separate article on the control of dramatic works. It would also be difficult to identify any longer statements on the subject beyond those discussed above. Some additional information is provided by brief remarks scattered here and there, such as one from May 1952, when, in a letter from the Wrocław branch, the censor mentioned two plays – Howard Fast's *Thirty Pieces of Silver* and Stefan Żeromski's *Grzech* [Sin].[620] However, the letter was primarily concerned with the organization of work in the Lower Silesian branch, so the functionary limited himself to listing the titles without discussing them.

Fast, who at that time was still a member of the Communist Party USA, was eagerly translated into Polish.[621] His *Thirty Pieces of Silver* was published in the series *Biblioteka Świetlicowa "Czytelnika"* in 1953, while from 1951, the play was successfully performed in several theaters in the country, including Teatr Dramatyczny in Wrocław, from which the correspondence in question was sent.[622] The play was also mentioned in a Bulletin from 1954, this time in the

---

[618] Ibidem.

[619] Ibidem, pp. 19–20.

[620] Z. Serafinowicz, "Jak odbywają się odprawy aparatu politycznego WUKP Wrocław," *Biuletyn Informacyjno-Instrukcyjny* no. 5, May 1952, p. 48 (APG, WUKP-PiW, file ref. no. 90). See: H. Fast, *Trzydzieści srebrników. Sztuka w trzech aktach*, trans. Z. Meissner, I. Babel, Warszawa: "Czytelnik," 1953, series *Biblioteka Świetlicowa "Czytelnika"*; see English edition: H. Fast, *Thirty Pieces of Silver*, New York: The Blue Heron Press, 1953; S. Żeromski, *Grzech. Dramat w 5 aktach*, Warszawa: "Czytelnik," 1950.

[621] H. Fast, *Amerykanin*, trans. J. Brodzki, Warszawa: "Wiedza," 1948; idem, *Dumni i wolni*, trans. M. Michałowska, Warszawa: "Czytelnik," 1952.

[622] See: the Polish Theater Encyclopedia, http://www.encyklopediateatru.pl/przedstawienie/17371/trzydziesci-srebrnikow and http://www.encyklopediateatru.pl/sztuki/wyszukaj?search=trzydzie%C5%9Bci+srebrnik%C3%B3w (accessed January 31, 2021).

context of staging by an amateur group of Związek Branżowych Spółdzielni Rzemieślniczych[623] [the Union of Craftsmen's Trade Cooperatives].

Żeromski was also among the authors published and staged at the time. Suffice to say that *Grzech* was successfully staged in more than a dozen theaters in Poland and abroad, including in Warsaw, Łódź, Wrocław (Teatr Dramatyczny), and London.[624] As indicated earlier, the writer was also the subject of one of the Bulletin articles.

---

[623] K. Zawistowska, "O współdziałaniu z ruchem amatorskim," *Biuletyn Informacyjno-Instrukcyjny* no. 9 (33), September 1954, pp. 18–19 (APG, WUKPPiW, file ref. no. 56).

[624] See the Polish Theater Encyclopedia, http://www.encyklopediateatru.pl/sztuki/2830/grzech and http://www.encyklopediateatru.pl/przedstawienie/32503/grzech (accessed January 31, 2021).

6. SATIRICAL WORKS

*It is important to remember that laughter is not an
end in itself, that it is a weapon.
And that is why you have to be constantly mindful
about how this weapon is used.*[625]

Material on satire appeared several times in the Bulletins. Four extensive articles
were published in October 1952, in the double issues from July and August, and
November and December 1954, plus in April 1955, which meant a departure "from
the rule of a strictly pragmatic approach to subject matter."[626] In the foreword to the
first text, the editors of the Bulletin justified the publication of such a long theoretical
elaboration with an exceptionally interesting framing of the problem. Perhaps the
decision was also influenced by the fact that the author was Jerzy Kleyny, who at
the time was not only a censor but also a satirist and regular contributor to *Szpilki*,
one of the key satirical magazines of the PRL.[627] This is how Jarosław Abramow-
-Newerly, co-founder of the legendary Students' Satirical Theatre (STS) established
in 1954, recalls his contacts with him: "My first censor from the STS, Jerzy Kleyny,
opened his eyes and became a satirist. After October, following in our footsteps, he

---

[625] J. Kleyny, "Uwagi na temat satyry," *Biuletyn Informacyjno-Instrukcyjny* no. 10, October 1952, p. 38 (APG, WUKPPiW, file ref. no. 75).

[626] Ibidem, p. 35. See also: J. Kleyny, "Z problemów satyry," *Biuletyn Informacyjno-Instrukcyjny* no. 7/8 (31/32), July/August 1954, pp. 21–36 (APG, WUKPPiW, file ref. no. 65); K. Bażańska, "Satyra w terenie. Uwagi o dyskusji nad tekstami Brzezińskiego," *Biuletyn Informacyjno-Instrukcyjny* no. 11/12 (35/36), November/December 1954, pp. 27–36 (APG, WUKPPiW, file ref. no. 59); J. Kleyny, "I jeszcze raz o satyrze," *Biuletyn Informacyjno-Instrukcyjny* no. 4 (40), April 1955, pp. 9–25 (APG, WUKPPiW, file ref. no. 65).

[627] See, e.g.: *"Biuletyn Informacyjno-Instrukcyjny." Wybór dokumentów z 1955 r...*, p. 125 et seq.; J.M. Bates, "Cenzura w epoce stalinowskiej," *Teksty Drugie* 2000, no. 1/2, p. 105; K. Budrowska, "Cenzura, tabu i wstyd. Cenzura obyczajowa PRL-u (1948–1958)," *Napis. Pismo poświęcone literaturze okolicznościowej i użytkowej* 2012, series 18, pp. 234–235. See also: R. Wolański, "Kleyny Jerzy," [in:] *Cyfrowa Biblioteka Polskiej Piosenki*, https://bibliotekapiosenki.pl/osoby/Kleyny_Jerzy (accessed January 31, 2021).
Szpilki (Pins) – a Polish satirical magazine established in 1936 by a group of leftist
literary people, including Zbigniew Mitzner (chief editor), Eryk Lipiński and Zenon Wasilewski; suspended during World War II, resumed in 1945, it was closed in 1990.

did a cabaret at the censorship's, which was the most splendid grotesque."[628] According to the Bulletins, Kleyny "did a cabaret at the censorship's" even earlier: his *Cicha woda brzegi rwie* [Still waters run deep] was staged on the "theater stage" of the Main Office on January 22, 1955, which will be discussed later in the book.

Kleyny spoke out about satire several times – probably also for personal, professional and literary reasons – because, as a censor and writer, he was perfectly aware that it was "a very strong and, at the same time, very attractive and broad means of educational and political influence, a means enjoying enormous popularity in the widest circles of society."[629] As a result, the questions he posed about the purpose, tasks, forms and state of Polish satire in the years 1952, 1954 and 1955 were justified, and they were intended to help set a direction in which the censorial evaluation of the genre should go. The articles he wrote are an interesting document of the era, in which the censor-satirist reviews his fellow writers and collaborators: Jerzy Jurandot, Janusz Minkiewicz and Józef Prutkowski. They were all regular contributors to *Szpilki* at the time.

In the first article, Kleyny presented the development and portrait of the genre, which was consistent with the theories of the time. He stressed the importance of realistic and progressive satire in the struggle of the revolutionary class against the backwardness and retrograde nature of a system based on exploitation and oppression, citing as examples the satire of Rabelais, Voltaire, Chekhov, Shchedrin, Gogol, and France. For Kleyny, the culmination of the genre's development was satire flowing from the spirit of Marxism-Leninism, constituting "a weapon of a new, consistently revolutionary class – the working class"[630] – as well as the most recent, post-war satire, which was born as a result of the creation of "a 200-million strong state of workers and peasants."[631]

The impetus for writing the second article was "the discussion of satire that began in the Soviet press after the 19th Congress of the Communist Party of the Soviet Union."[632] Kleyny referred to Malenkov's paper (which was also quoted in the material devoted to the competition on Wasilewska) and to the voices in the discussion published in the Soviet *Komunista*, also citing events that took place

---

[628] J. Abramow-Newerly, *Lwy STS-u…*, p. 404.

Polski październik 1956 (Październik '56, odwilż październikowa, odwilż gomułkowska; Polish October 1956, October '56, Polish Thaw, Gomułka's Thaw) – the culmination period of the Thaw, that is, the political, social and economic transformations related to the collapse of the communist dictatorship following the death of Joseph Stalin (1953).

[629] J. Kleyny, "Uwagi na temat satyry," *Biuletyn Informacyjno-Instrukcyjny* no. 10, October 1952, p. 35 (APG, WUKPPiW, file ref. no. 75).

[630] Ibidem, p. 36.

[631] Ibidem, p. 37.

[632] J. Kleyny, "Z problemów satyry," *Biuletyn Informacyjno-Instrukcyjny* no. 7/8 (31/32), July/August 1954, p. 21 (APG, WUKPPiW, file ref. no. 65).

in Poland, such as the All-Polish Satirists' Meeting in 1953 and the conventions of creative associations, such as the Writers' Congress and the Journalists' Congress.[633] In his last article, Kleyny reported on the "meteorological discussion" that was sweeping through the press at the time: "thaw, frost, a breath of fresh air,"[634] which is how the censor-satirist fit into the Bulletin debates over the "Thaw."

Kleyny's comments focused primarily on how to assess satirical works correctly. From the point of view of the censor's office, it was important to formulate the goals of the genre, which the authors could be held accountable for – and these goals differed depending on whether it was anti-imperialist satire (directed outward) or satire discussing Polish affairs (hence, directed inward). The task of the former was to fight against the imperialist external enemy, which should be presented in such a way as to arouse disgust and hatred in the audience. Works of this type were supposed to avoid irreverent "hilarity," which did not mean that the authors should lose humor completely and focus only on rendering the enemy as "disgusting":

> Take, for example, Soviet political caricature, where next to unquestionably serious whistle-blowing cartoons (e.g., the well-known drawing by Prorokov entitled "The Lynching United States") we can find, for example, political caricatures by the Kukryniksy that are meant to both whistle-blow and ridicule.[635]

Boris Ivanovich Prorokov, mentioned by Kleyny and awarded with the Stalin Prize, was the author of many graphics in the series *Oto Ameryka* [This is America], in which he presented the "real life" of Americans,[636] while the Kukryniksy were a group of three Soviet graphic artists and painters (the group was comprised of Mikhail Kupriyanov, Porfiri Krylov and Nikolai Sokolov), who before the war had contributed to the satirical *Krokodil*, among other journals, and specialized in creating (propaganda) posters, book illustrations and caricatures.[637]

---

[633] Ibidem.

[634] J. Kleyny, "I jeszcze raz o satyrze," *Biuletyn Informacyjno-Instrukcyjny* no. 4 (40), April 1955, p. 9 (APG, WUKPPiW, file ref. no. 65). On the censorship of satire during the "Thaw" period, see, e.g.: K. Smyczek, "Satyra w służbie 'odwilży.' O ingerencjach cenzury w felietonach 'Notatki naiwnego' Zygmunta Ościenia," [in:] *Życie społeczne, kultura i polityka w okresie PRL*, eds. P. Szymczyk, M. Maciąg, Lublin: Wydawnictwo Naukowe TYGIEL, 2018, pp. 20–29.

[635] J. Kleyny, "Uwagi na temat satyry," *Biuletyn Informacyjno-Instrukcyjny* no. 10, October 1952, p. 37 (APG, WUKPPiW, file ref. no. 75).

[636] See, e.g.: "Wystawa grafiki radzieckiej," *Katalog*, Warszawa: 1954, pp. 27–29, 36–37. Cf. Fig. 17. B.I. Prorokov, "'Pracownia' na bruku" (in the series *Oto Ameryka*), [in:] *Wystawa grafiki radzieckiej...*, Fig. 18.

[637] See: Fig. 18. The Kukryniksy, "Cziczikow: – Ja, mister Harriman...," [in:] *Wystawa grafiki radzieckiej...*, Fig. 9.

Fig. 17. B.I. Prorokov, "'Pracownia' na bruku" ["'Studio' on the streets"]
(in the series *Oto Ameryka*).

Fig. 18. The Kukryniksy, "Cziczikow: – Ja, mister Harriman…"

The aim of the second type of satire – that is, the one focused on Polish issues – should be to fight the baggage of the "bourgeois artistic workshop,"[638] namely, formalism. According to Kleyny, it was primarily on the "small stage" that the "traditions of bourgeois' cabaret 'tastes' and 'hilarity'"[639] lingered the most, namely, everything that Jan Szeląg[640] (quoted by Kleyny) called "muddling the water of old and putrid, musty wells."[641] Kleyny argued that every satire should skillfully juggle seriousness and humor. However, the words of the censor, who during the Stalinist period wrote about the laughter of "a free man building his happy tomorrow,"[642] sound bizarre and highly inappropriate. The passages in which laughter was not so strongly identified with freedom sound a little less disturbing:

> We must remember that in Poland there is still more than just the pure, healthy laughter of the creators and builders of socialism. We have the laughter interrupted by drunken hiccups, the cackle of someone listening to the silly *Voice of America* limericks, and the sneaky smile of spies and saboteurs.[643]

In all three articles, Kleyny discussed examples of tampering with satirical texts conducted by the Press and Radio Section and the Theater Department, among others. Most of the material dealt with internal satire, and one of the most common mistakes was the creation of texts without a precisely identified audience. An example of this kind of carelessness was found in the drawings "Ogonek i Boczek" [Queue and bacon] sent by *Szpilki*:

> the first cartoon shows a line in front of the CZPM[644] store, and the second one shows the interior of the store, where the shop assistant (who, by the way, looked like a typical butcher from a "private initiative") resells slices of bacon "under the counter" – almost right in front of the eyes of the citizens waiting to buy meat. In these drawings, the very manner of depiction, as well as the presentation of the CZPM as the seat of meat speculation, is inappropriate and definitely harmful, while the center of speculation is not the state or cooperative apparatus, but *kulak* elements and their urban counterparts. Nevertheless, the same topic presented in

---

[638] J. Kleyny, "Uwagi na temat satyry," *Biuletyn Informacyjno-Instrukcyjny* no. 10, October 1952, p. 39 (APG, WUKPPiW, file ref. no. 75).

[639] Ibidem.

[640] Jan Szeląg was the pseudonym of another satirist, journalist and writer Zbigniew Mitzner, the husband of Larysa Zajączkowska-Mitzner, who, in turn, was an author of detective stories popular in the PRL (also published under the pseudonym Barbara Gordon).

[641] J. Kleyny, "Uwagi na temat satyry," *Biuletyn Informacyjno-Instrukcyjny* no. 10, October 1952, p. 39 (APG, WUKPPiW, file ref. no. 75).

[642] Ibidem, p. 38.

[643] Ibidem.

[644] The CZPM stands for Centralny Urząd Przemysłu Mięsnego – the Central Office for the Meat Industry.

the form of a clearly addressed drawing pointing out a concrete fact of speculation would not have raised any objections; on the contrary, it would have helped with the daily struggle and mobilized for it.[645]

In addition to the lack of a target audience, another offense committed by satirists was "giving a platform to the enemy, quoting at length a hostile argument or rumor"[646] without any explanatory commentary. Kleyny cited two examples of this type of negligence that involved the "passport issue." In addition to the circus couplet, he quoted a poem by Jerzy Jurandot, the author of countless cabaret texts and song lyrics, an excellent poet and satirist who, along with his wife Stefania Grodzieńska, created the cultural image of post-war Poland.[647] For the analysis of the material in the Bulletin, it is also important that after the war, Jurandot – similarly to Minkiewicz and Kleyny – was a permanent contributor to *Szpilki*, from which comes the discussed redaction:

[Jerzy Jurandot's poem "Pułapka" [Trap], quoted in the Bulletin]

Ale zaraz pana trafię
po co aż trzy fotografie.
Jedna na dowodzie będzie
druga jest do akt w urzędzie,
Ale trzecia! W jakim celu!
Nie, nie, drogi przyjacielu!
Pan jak chce, to bardzo proszę,
Ale ja tam się nie zgłoszę.[648]

[Now this is just ridiculous
why as many as three pictures?
One will go on your ID card
The second's in your files secured,
but the third one! To what end?
It's not happening, my friend!
If you want, go ahead,
But I'm not going anywhere.]

---

645 J. Kleyny, "Uwagi na temat satyry," *Biuletyn Informacyjno-Instrukcyjny* no. 10, October 1952, pp. 41–42 (APG, WUKPPiW, file ref. no. 75).

646 Ibidem, p. 43.

647 Both Jurandot and Grodzieńska went through the hell of the Warsaw Ghetto, where their theatrical activity during that period was a form of escape, meager as it was. See, e.g.: J. Jurandot, *Miasto skazanych. Dwa lata w warszawskim getcie*, Warszawa: Muzeum Historii Żydów Polskich, 2014.

648 J. Kleyny, "Uwagi na temat satyry," *Biuletyn Informacyjno-Instrukcyjny* no. 10, October 1952, p. 43 (APG, WUKPPiW, file ref. no. 75).

[the circus couplet quoted in the Bulletin]

Ale szwagier mój o zgrozo
Zbladł i wpadł w histerię,
No i co, No i co, No i co.
Bo powiada, że wywiozą
Wszystkich na Syberię!
Nie rozumiem – Bo jesteś kiep
Mądrej głowie dość pałką w łeb.[649]

[My brother-in-law, horror of horrors
Turned pale and went hysterical,
Now what, now what, now what?
He says they're going to deport
Each and everyone to Siberia!
I don't understand – 'Cause you're stupid
The wise know when they're being booted.]

Among other redactions chosen by Kleyny, the one about coffee is noteworthy. The poem did not meet with the approval of the functionaries because it supposedly illustrated a complaint of "a typical bourgeois whose whole world is 'Bristol,' flat white and other accessories of kind."[650] The author of the poem was the aforementioned Janusz Minkiewicz, a satirist, writer, author of humorous sketches, political puppet shows, and works for children, and another contributor of *Szpilki* evaluated by Kleyny. The following poem was submitted to the Office:

[the poem by Janusz Minkiewicz "Więcej kawy" [More coffee]
quoted in the Bulletin]

Przychodzę do kawiarni,
by ranne zjeść śniadanko,
Zamawiam raz herbatę –
przynoszą… kawę z pianką.

Przychodzę do winiarni,
Bo chcę się napić winka,
zamawiam "Balatońskie" –
przynoszą mi… "murzynka".

---

[649] Ibidem.
[650] Ibidem, p. 45.
Bristol – a café opened in Warsaw in 1901, which still exists today; for a long time, it was one of the most popular and exclusive cafés in Poland.

Uciekam więc do klubu,
lecz tam niewielka zmiana:
zamawiam małe lody –
przynoszą mi… "szatana."

Przychodzę do "Bristolu"
Gdzie czeka na mnie Linke;
prosimy o dwa piwa –
przynoszą nam… "maszynkę."

Gdzie nie pójść, tam "okazja"
na człeka czyha wszędzie:
"Dostaliśmy dziś przydział…
Wieczorem już nie będzie…"

Nie wypić! to obraza…
Odmówić! Nie wypada…
Cóż robić! Trzeba żłopać
i truć się – trudna rada!

Wyjaśnić jakoś nijak
i jakoś się nie godzi,
że nienawidzę kawska,
że mi w dodatku szkodzi…

Więc pić truciznę muszę
przez całe dnie, niezmiennie
i trwam już od miesięcy,
w bezsennej mej gehennie…

Zaklinam: – O czynniki!
Zmiarkujcie się, pospieszcie
Niech będzie dużo kawy,
bym mógł jej nie pić wreszcie![651]

[I go to a bistro,
to have my morning breakfast,
I order tea –
they bring me… cappuccino.

---

[651] Ibidem, pp. 44–45. On Minkiewicz, see e.g.: *Sława i infamia. Z Bohdanem Korzeniewskim rozmawia Małgorzata Szejnert*, Kraków: Wydawnictwo Literackie, 1992, pp. 30 and 45; B. Urbankowski, *Czerwona msza, czyli uśmiech Stalina* vol. 2, Warszawa: Alfa, 1998, p. 315 and others.

I go to the wine bar,
For a glass of wine,
I order "Balatońskie" –
they bring me… a frappe.

So I run to the club,
but there's not much change:
I order some ice cream –
they bring me… a latte.

I make my way to "Bristol"
where Linke's waiting for me;
we ask for two beers –
they bring us… espressos.

Wherever you turn,
they say "You're in luck!
We just got a shipment.
It'll be gone by tonight…"

Don't drink it? It's an insult…
Refuse it! That's not right…
Then what? You guzzle it
– and suffer through this blight!

There's no way to explain,
it's somehow unbecoming
to admit I hate coffee,
and also it's bad for me...

So I must drink the poison
for days on end
and for months I have been
in this sleepless torment…

I beg you: O factors!
Show some mercy, hurry
Let coffee be abundant,
So I don't have to drink it!]

As noted earlier, there was far less interference in anti-imperialist satirical texts than in domestic satire discussing Polish affairs. However, Kleyny
offered several examples for this genre, too. Consider a work by another contributor to *Szpilki*, namely "Ballada pod psem" [The under-dog ballad] by
Józef Prutkowski. According to the evaluators, the poem presented "a false

picture of the balance of power in the international arena"[652] and lacked a whistle-blowing flair:

["Ballada pod psem" by Józef Prutkowski, quoted in the Bulletin]

Pokoju bardzo się boją,
Czekają więc w przedpokoju
I czują się marnie.

Służy psów wierny szereg:
Oto hitlerek-ratlerek
Pupilek psiarni.

John Buldog – wielki brytan
Warczy i pozwólcie, że spytam
Kiedy nam rzucą kości!

Ten brytan ma uwiąd starczy,
Lecz ciągle jeszcze warczy
I bardzo się złości.

Pies – policyjny szpic,
A właściwie szpicel, nic
nie szczekał i nie ujadał.

– Niech szczeka ta hołota
Jak zacznie się Moch-ra robota
Wtedy dopiero pogadam.

Wtem wszedł człowieczek mały,
Nazywał się Eisenhower
I wpadł od razu w gniew:

– Żółci, biali i czarni
– „Żółci, biali i czarni

Niech drżą na widok mej psiarni
Już dziś popłynie psia krew!

Za waszą śmierć ochotniczą…
(Nasi bankierzy obliczą)
Zapłacą nam bardzo drogo!

---

[652] J. Kleyny, "Uwagi na temat satyry," *Biuletyn Informacyjno-Instrukcyjny* no. 10, October 1952, p. 47 (APG, WUKPPiW, file ref. no. 75).

Naprzód dzielnie i walnie!”
Krzyknął. Lecz w poszczekalni
Już nie było nikogo.[653]

[They are terrified of peace,
So they wait in the hallway
And they feel unease.

A faithful line of dogs:
Here's a hitler-ratter
The pet of the doghouse.

John Bull – the great mastiff
He growls and demands to know
When they will throw the bones!

This mastiff is quite infirm
But he keeps on growling
And gets very angry.

One dog – a police Spitz,
Or rather, a spy,
he didn't bark or snarl.

– Let the rabble bark
When the wet work starts
Then I'll speak.

Then a little man came in,
His name was Eisenhower
And he got angry right away:

– Yellow, white and black
– "Yellow, white and black

Let them tremble at the sight of my pack
Today the canine blood will flow!

For your voluntary death…
(Our bankers will send a bill)
They will pay us dearly!

---

[653] Ibidem, pp. 46–47.

Forward bravely, attack!"
He shouted. But in the barking room
There was not a dog's soul.]

***

Apart from Kleyny's, a few more texts on the subject of satire censorship in the Bulletins can be found, although – apart from the aforementioned material devoted to Brzeziński's "Egzamin"[654] – none of them was as comprehensive as those written by the censor-satirist.

Some information is included in the material on Gałczyński and in the text on the activities of "Czytelnik" in 1951.[655] The former contained a reminder that the satirical literature of the author of *Zaczarowana dorożka* did not find the recognition of the critics immediately. In the article on "Czytelnik," the fact that Borejsza's publishing house took an interest in "this type of work, which is very rare in our publishing movement"[656] was appreciated and "due to its subject matter (exposing imperialism, fighting the internal enemy, etc.) and attractive form"[657] was "undoubtedly a very effective means of ideological influence."[658] As with many other genres, the censors were troubled by the small number of translations; a major oversight, of course, was the "omission of translations of contemporary Soviet literature";[659] of the translations, only *Niemiecka satyra antyfaszystowska* [The German anti-fascist satire] was listed.[660] The censors noted, however, the publication of Polish classics in the genre, such as Michał Bałucki's satires, but were especially pleased with the contemporary Polish works, such as *Bez pardonu* [No mercy] by Antoni Marianowicz or *Do żywego* [On the raw] by the above-quoted Prutkowski, even if many of these works could be accused of "lacking the necessary class focus,"[661] as was the case with

---

[654] K. Bażańska, "Satyra w terenie. Uwagi o dyskusji nad tekstami Brzezińskiego," *Biuletyn Informacyjno-Instrukcyjny* no. 11/12 (35/36), November/December 1954, pp. 27–36 (APG, WUKPPiW, file ref. no. 59).

[655] "Działalność wydawnictwa 'Czytelnik' w 1951 r.," *Biuletyn Informacyjno-Instrukcyjny* no. 5, May 1952, pp. 20–21 (APG, WUKPPiW, file ref. no. 90).

[656] Ibidem, p. 20.

[657] Ibidem.

[658] Ibidem.

[659] Ibidem, p. 21.

[660] See: *Niemiecka satyra antyfaszystowska*, compiled by A. Marianowicz, E. Osmańczyk, Warszawa: "Czytelnik," 1951.

[661] "Działalność wydawnictwa 'Czytelnik' w 1951 r.," *Biuletyn Informacyjno-Instrukcyjny* no. 5, May 1952, p. 21 (APG, WUKPPiW, file ref. no. 90).

Pigułki [Pills] by Janusz Minkiewicz and *Plagi i plażki* [Big and small plagues] by Stefania Grodeńska.[662]

In September and October 1952, a series of satirical programs entitled *Żądło mikrofonu* [The sting of the microphone], supposedly devoted to exposing profiteers and bureaucrats, was evaluated.[663] The "lively and appealing" formula of the program was appreciated, but it was noted that in several cases, the pursuit of attractiveness led "to a blunting of the political edge of these programs or to mere vulgarity."[664] The problem was found with an insufficiently strong rebuke of the speculative activities of shop assistants. It was not enough to offer an analysis of the language they used and formulate a caution: "Take this sincere advice, / Don't hide sausage under the counter, / Because it sets a bad example."[665]

There was one more interference which was decidedly "satirical." When reviewing daily press, an objection was made regarding a satirical editorial *Po prostu z nudów* [Simply out of boredom], which appeared to slander the anti-alcohol committee.[666] The censors found that it was groundless to suggest that all committee members were habitual drinkers and regulars at taverns.

---

[662] All the titles were published by "Czytelnik" in 1951.

[663] "Z terenowych prac ocenowych," *Biuletyn Informacyjno-Instrukcyjny* no. 9, September 1952, p. 45 (APG, WUKPPiW, file ref. no. 78); WUKP Bydgoszcz, "Radio Polskie – Bydgoszcz. Uwagi krytyczne za okres od 1–25.IX.52 r.," *Biuletyn Informacyjno-Instrukcyjny* no. 10, October 1952, pp. 19–20 (APG, WUKPPiW, file ref. no. 75; the issue also criticized the cheap political satire on Sanation deputies presented in the series *Z bliska i z daleka*, see p. 17).

[664] WUKP Bydgoszcz, "Radio Polskie – Bydgoszcz. Uwagi krytyczne za okres od 1–25.IX.52 r.," *Biuletyn Informacyjno-Instrukcyjny* no. 10, October 1952, p. 19 (APG, WUKPPiW, file ref. no. 75).

[665] Ibidem.

[666] "O sygnałach dziennych," *Biuletyn Informacyjno-Instrukcyjny* no. 10, October 1952, p. 33 (APG, WUKPPiW, file ref. no. 75; it was a signal from 1952's issue no. 225, sent by the WUKPPiW in Poznań).

7. CHILDREN'S AND YOUNG ADULT LITERATURE

The Poland you will have is the Poland
you will build.[667]
Bolesław Bierut

During the eleven years under review, children's and young adult literature appeared relatively rarely as the subject of more extensive Bulletin discussions. In fact, only one separate article was devoted to it (not counting the material on the magazine for young people *Dookoła świata*[668]); it appeared more commonly as a supplement to general discussions on art. While it is impossible to say for certain whether this was a sign of neglect to this type of writing, the editors of the Bulletin certainly did not treat it as a priority. It should be added that at this stage of research, questions about the status of children's literature at the Office for the Control also cannot be answered unequivocally.

Yet, from the very beginning of the communist regime, literature for the youngest readers, also called "fourth" and "separate" literature, remained under the scrutiny of the lawmakers of the new system.[669] On the indices of banned books, separate lists were created for titles representing this type of literature.[670] Furthermore,

---

[667] Statement by Bolesław Bierut quoted in *Błyskawica*, a newspaper of the Union of Polish Youth – an issue with this quotation was attached to the Bulletin from May 1952. ("Stajemy na apel [*Błyskawica*]," *Biuletyn Informacyjno-Instrukcyjny* no. 5, May 1952, pp. 52–53 (APG, WUKPPiW, file ref. no. 90)).

[668] L. Kimlowski, "Kilka uwag o tygodniku *Dookoła świata* (January–June 1954)," *Biuletyn Informacyjno-Instrukcyjny* no. 9 (33), September 1954, pp. 25–32 (APG, WUKPPiW, file ref. no. 56); M. M., "O lepszą metodę ocen" (correspondence in "Dział Listów"), *Biuletyn Informacyjno-Instrukcyjny* no. 10 (34), October 1954, pp. 44–45 and 48–49 (APG, WUKPPiW, file ref. no. 58; the article was mistakenly printed twice).

[669] On the "fourth," "separate" literature, see, e.g.: Z. Adamczykowa, "Literatura 'czwarta' – w kręgu zagadnień teoretycznych," [in:] *Literatura dla dzieci i młodzieży (po roku 1980)*, ed. K. Heska-Kwaśniewicz, Katowice: Wydawnictwo UŚ, 2008, pp. 13–43; S. Frycie, "Czy literatura dla dzieci i młodzieży jest literaturą 'osobną,'" *Guliwer* 1999, no. 6, pp. 73–75; J. Cieślikowski, *Literatura osobna*, selection by R. Waksmund, Warszawa: "Nasza Księgarnia," 1985.

[670] See "Wykaz nr 3 (książek dla dzieci)," [in:] *Cenzura PRL. Wykaz książek…*, pp. 58–76.

in trying to develop a new type of literature devoid of fantasy elements and kings and queens, which were incompatible with the socialist model of education, the press analyzed the tasks and goals of children's literature in great detail.[671] The complete elimination of these components, which were the backbone of the "fourth" literature, proved simply impossible, and attempts to "socialize" classic works for children, especially fairy tales, were reminiscent of the ancient paradox of the heap, from which we remove one grain after another until only one grain remains. Would the pile still remain a pile? If not, when did it stop being one?

Analogous doubts could be directed towards works mutilated by rationalizations, written or reworked according to the requirements of the new, socialist reality. A number of such productions were submitted to the censor's office, but they did not sufficiently saturate the market, so publishers also submitted many classic fairy tales. The result of such turmoil was devastating censorship reviews, accompanying the approval of publication.[672]

The section below will examine how issues of literature for the youngest readers were reported in the monthly.

***

Notes on children's books appeared in the June 1945 Bulletin. In the chapter, "The question of libraries," a CBKP functionary, comrade Grzeszczak, emphasized the preventive role that suitably selected literature could play: "The question of children's books is very important. A child must be protected from inappropriate influences."[673] This obvious statement of the censor was left without comment, but the topic resurfaced on the next page. This time, another employee

---

[671] See, among others, articles on literature for children and young adults (including materials on conferences devoted to works for young audiences) appearing in *Kuźnica* and *Odrodzenie* in the second half of the 1940s and the first half of the 1950s, e.g.: W. Grodzieńska, "Współczesna literatura dla dzieci," *Kuźnica* December 25, 1949, no. 51–52, p. 11; S. Wortman, "W obronie baśni ludowej," *Odrodzenie* October 17, 1948, no. 2, p. 7. I wrote about the censorship of children's and young adult literature in 1950 in my book *"Czytelnik" ocenzurowany. Literatura w kryptotekstach...* There I also provide a bibliography on this topic; see, e.g.: M. Nadolna-Tłuczykont, *Powrót książek "zakazanych" do współczesnych odbiorców (wybrane zagadnienia)*, Katowice: Wydawnictwo UŚ, 2013; M. Głowiński, "Stalin-czarodziej. (O baśni totalitarnej)," [in:] idem, *Dzień Ulissesa i inne szkice na tematy niemitologiczne*, Kraków: Wydawnictwo Literackie, 2000, pp. 98–110; M. Zawodniak, "Królewicz i murarz (socrealistyczne potyczki z fantazją)," *Teksty Drugie* 1994, no. 1, pp. 84–93.

[672] K. Budrowska, *Writers, Literature and Censorship...*, p. 237.

[673] "Kwestia bibliotek," *Biuletyn Instrukcyjny* no. 2, June 1945, p. 11 (APG, WUKP-PiW, file ref. no. 210).

of the Office, censor Papińska, was quoted, describing an inspection of Kielce libraries, during which "books for children and young adults emerged":[674]

> I believe that the issue of "what a child should read" is perhaps of greater importance than the same issue in relation to adults. A child is the future of the nation, a child is a developing person. Our society depends on how we raise our children. The period of occupation has also intruded on this sphere, poisoning our children with its venom. That is why I emphasize again: we must pay attention to the books that are intended for children. If you come across books in children's libraries that were published by Germans, you should absolutely inspect them. You will have no problem finding them. On the cover of the book or inside there is an inscription in German (edition, printing house). Recently, I came across a book with a beautiful and innocent title: *Świat baśni i czarów* [The world of fairy tales and spells] by Edmund Jezierski, published by Buchdrukerei "Pospieszna," Kraków. This book is a vivid picture of what was fed to young people so that they would grow up to be SS and Gestapo men…[675]

Papińska emphasized the important role that literature plays in the educational process and stressed the need to sort through children's literature, especially titles published by German publishing houses – the information that the book was published (or rather printed) by "Buchdruckerei 'Pospieszna'" was reason enough to withdraw it from libraries. If we add that Jezierski's work was published by the private publishing house Senzacja (more on that below) and bear in mind that work on the nationalization and monopolization of the book market had been going on since the end of World War II, Jezierski may be considered an example of the so-called censorship according to publishing house (publisher or printer).

The choice of Jezierski's fairy tales as a kind of anti-example was not accidental either: published by a private publishing house, the book's very title presented contents for which there was no place in the new literature for children. The decision was undoubtedly made easier by the author's background: Edmund Jezierski was the literary pseudonym of Edmund Krüger, a publicist, printer and writer, who died in 1935. He specialized in works for young readers, just like his daughter Maria (author of such novels as *Karolcia* and *Godzina pąsowej róży* [The hour of the crimson rose]).[676] He was one of the most popular authors of science fiction

---

[674] "Ze sprawozdań kierowników Wojewódzkich Biur," *Biuletyn Instrukcyjny* no. 2, June 1945, p. 12 (APG, WUKPPiW, file ref. no. 210).

[675] Ibidem.

[676] Jezierska was the maiden name of Krüger's mother; he also published under the pseudonym Janusz Kruk. See, e.g.: K. Kuliczkowska, "Krüger Edmund," [in:] *Polski Słownik Biograficzny*, ed. E. Rostworowski, in co-operation with W. Armon et al., vol. 15: *Kozłowska Zofia–Kubacki Stanisław*, Wrocław–Warszawa–Kraków: Ossolineum–PAN, 1970, pp. 449–450; "Krüger Edmund," [in:] *Słownik współczesnych pisarzy polskich* vol. 2, ed.

literature in the interwar period, which – considering the strategy of censorship according to when a work was created – may have been of great importance when evaluating his book. A significant part of his output consisted of books on historical and war themes – which were unacceptable in the new Poland because of their subject matter and interpretation of events – and novels in which he criticized the assumptions of the communist system. In this context, the negative assessment of the collection of tales seems understandable. Nevertheless, in the short fragment included in the 1945 Bulletin, the censor referred only to the writer's fairy tales and to the fact that the book was published by Germans. Perhaps the official decision to withdraw the book from libraries was influenced by the above-mentioned factors, that is, the book being associated with a private publisher, the author's views and attitude expressed in other publications, and the fact that the tales did not meet the ideological "standards" of writing for children (although the crusade against magic in literature for children was launched later).

The material preserved in the State Archive in Poznań shows that Jezierski's book, *Świat czarów*, was indeed included on *List 1 of Books and Brochures Subject to Immediate Removal*, created in 1945; the decision to withdraw this and other titles from public book collections was signed by Tadeusz Zabłudowski, director of the CBKP at the time.[677]

On the other hand, the fact that even in the 1950s, Jezierski could not count on the favor of the Office for the Control is evidenced by the aforementioned *List 1 of Books and Brochures Subject to Immediate Withdrawal*, prepared in 1951, which included a total of fifteen titles of his authorship: eight on *List 1* containing titles subject to immediate withdrawal, and seven on *List 2*, which narrowed the index to children's books; however, *Świat baśni i czarów* was not among them (perhaps because the work had already been withdrawn).[678] Instead, the list included Jezierski's fairy tales, science fiction, history and war books.

E. Korzeniewska, Warszawa: PWN, 1964, pp. 52–55; "Edmund Krüger," [in:] *Encyklopedia fantastyki*, http://encyklopediafantastyki.pl/index.php?title=Edward_Kr%C3%BCger (accessed January 31, 2021; in the title of the entry the incorrect name "Edward" was given).

[677] "Wykaz książek wycofanych z bibliotek 1945–1956" (APP, WUKPPiW, file ref. no. 13, pp. 1, 2). See: Fig. 19. Annex dated July 5, 1945 concerning list no.1 of books to be immediately withdrawn from public book collections; "Wykaz książek wycofanych z bibliotek 1945–1956" (APP, WUKPPiW, file ref. no. 13, p. 1); Fig. 20. A list of books and brochures subject to immediate removal; "Wykaz książek wycofanych z bibliotek 1945–1956" (APP, WUKPPiW, file ref. no. 13, p. 2).

[678] The following works of Jezierski were found on *List 3*: *Bajki polskie; Dla ciebie Polsko; Książę Józef Poniatowski; Legenda polska; Ludzie elektryczni; Ofiary. Opowiadania historyczne z r. 1846; Ojczyzna* (all editions); Jezierski's works put on *List 1*: *A gdy komunizm zapanuje; Bronisław Pieracki; Dla ciebie Polsko; Józef Piłsudski; Nieznani żołnierze; Palę Moskwę; Wyspa Lenina; Z życia obozowego skautów* (*Cenzura PRL. Wykaz książek…*, pp. 18, 65).

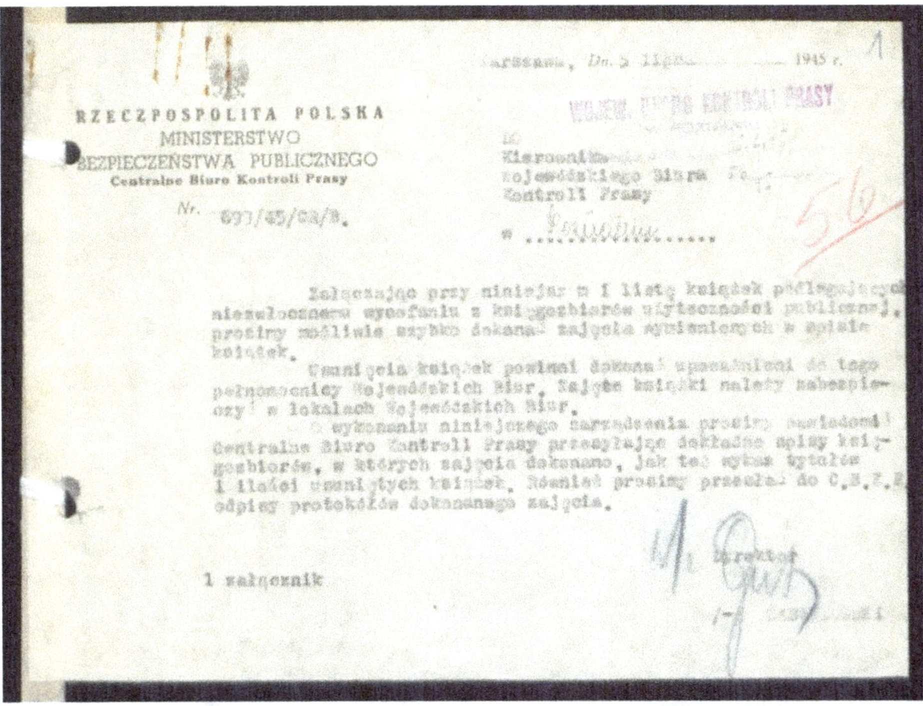

Fig. 19. Annex dated July 5, 1945 concerning list no.1 of books to be immediately withdrawn from public book collections (APP, WUKPPiW, file ref. no. 13, p. 1).

When Papińska noted *Świat baśni i czarów*, most likely she was referring to *Świat czarów. Zbiór baśni, podań i legend*. The book with this title was published in 1943, and the second edition came out the following year – both with the Senzacja publishing house in Kraków.[679] Thus, Papińska was most probably referring to one of these editions. Actually, the pre-war editions of the collection appeared under a slightly different title *Ze świata czarów. Zbiór baśni, podań i legend różnych narodów* [From the world of spells. A collection of tales, stories, and legends of various nations]. However, it seems that Papińska did not write about them, because, firstly, these were not editions from the time of the occupation, and secondly, none of them was printed by a "Buchdrukerei 'Pospieszna,'" but by the Polish publishing houses of Michał Arct and M. Ostaszewska.[680]

---

[679] *Świat czarów. Zbiór baśni, podań i legend*, compiled and arranged by E. Jezierski, il. A. Żmuda, Kraków: Wydawnictwo Senzacja, 1943; Second Edition: ibidem 1944.

[680] *Ze świata czarów. Zbiór baśni, podań i legend różnych narodów*, compiled and arranged by E. Jezierski, part 1, 2: Warszawa: M. Arct, 1911; Warszawa: Księgarnia M. Ostaszewskiej i S-ki, [1921].

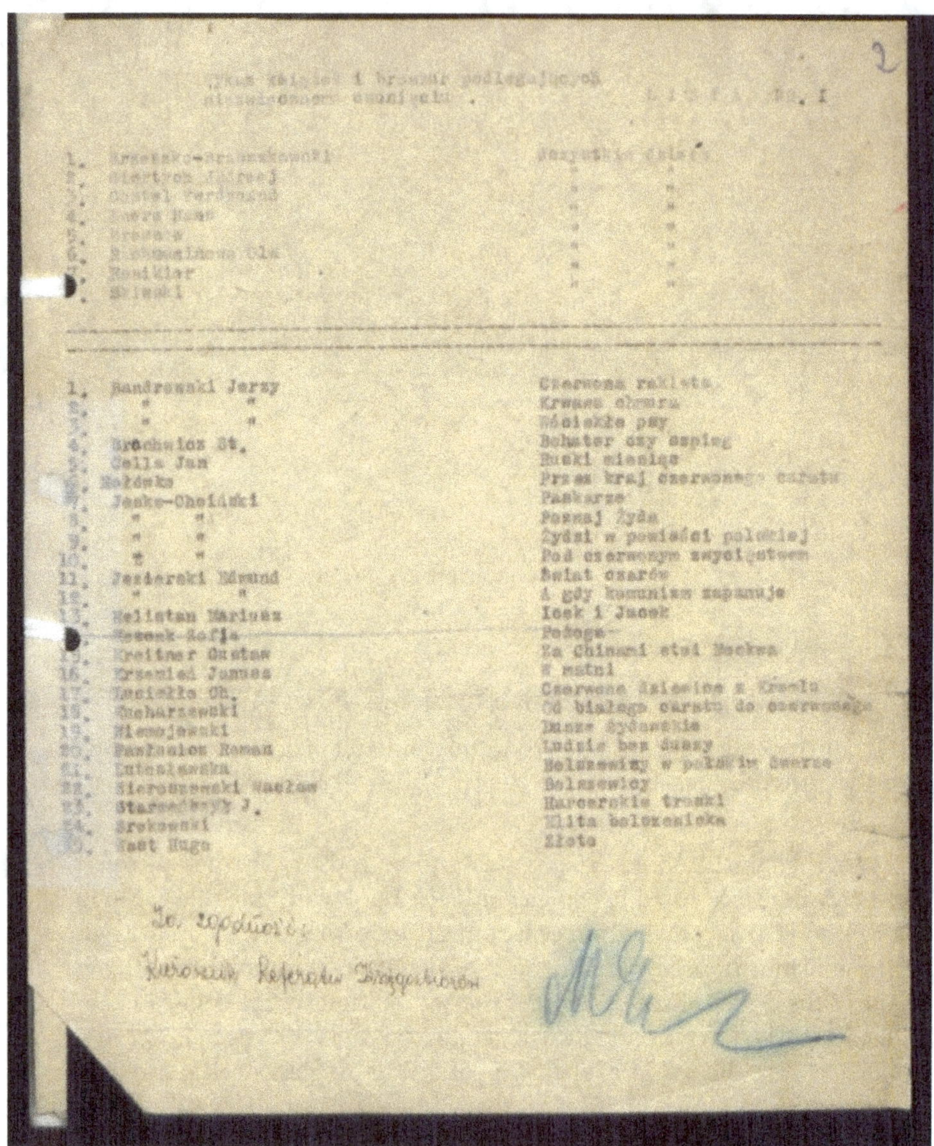

Fig. 20. A list of books and brochures subject to immediate removal, with E. Jezierski's *Świat czarów* under number 11 (APP, WUKPPiW, file ref. no. 13, p. 2).

Finally, Papińska's appeal to take the place of publication into account when assessing a book – in other words, censorship by publishing house (or publisher) – was a common strategy of the Office for the Control. The information about the place of publication was also important when drawing up the *List of Books and Brochures Subject to Immediate Removal*. Its section on children's literature reads:

When purging a book collection, close attention should be paid to the publishing address of the titles on the list (that is, the place, year, and publishing company), as in some cases, certain titles will be removed simply because of an incorrect edition.[681]

***

The recent "comic strips," with their extremely low artistic level, discredit both the magazine and the author of the texts.[682]

A laconic mention of Jezierski appeared in the June 1945 issue of the Bulletin, while another reference to his work for children was made in the January 1949 issue. This time the focus was on a comic book, or more precisely, on one of the episodes of the "cartoon film" *Psoty Kleksa* [Klek's gambols], printed in *Głos Wielkopolski*.

Artistic works as well as various kinds of drawings, graphics and tables were rarely published in the Bulletins, although there were a few cases where an illustration would perfectly complement the description or could even replace it.[683] Probably for technical reasons – even in the chapters devoted to the control of exhibitions, artworks or book and press illustrations – a description had to suffice. For instance, it would have been much more effective to include a photo of Bolesław Bierut greeting the crowd than provide a "dry" Bulletin description arguing that the photograph depicting this very moment should be removed because the president's hand was at a height resembling a Nazi salute.[684]

---

[681] *Cenzura PRL. Wykaz książek…*, p. 58.

[682] L. Kimlowski, "Kilka uwag o tygodniku *Dookoła świata* (January–June 1954)," *Biuletyn Informacyjno-Instrukcyjny* no. 9 (33), September 1954, p. 32 (APG, WUKPPiW, file ref. no. 56; evaluation of the comics presented in *Dookoła świata*).

[683] See, e.g.: "Na marginesie ogólnonarodowej dyskusji (materiał wysłany do WUKP dnia 6 II 52 r.)," *Biuletyn Informacyjno-Instrukcyjny* no. 2, February 1952, p. 26 (APG, WUKPPiW, file ref. no. 99). Cf. also reflections on Bolesław Zagała's book *Na przełaj przez świat*.

[684] "Kontrola ilustracyj," *Biuletyn Informacyjno-Szkoleniowy* no. 1/3, January 1949, p. 7 (APG, WUKPPiW, file ref. no. 196; the photograph was supposedly featured in the *Świat* magazine). See also: WUKP Szczecin, "Na odcinku propagandy poglądowej," *Biuletyn Informacyjno-Instrukcyjny* no. 10, October 1952, pp. 27–29 (APG, WUKPPiW, file ref. no. 75). Various illustration materials (graphics, posters, postcards, etc.) can be found in the issues: *Biuletyn Informacyjno-Szkoleniowy* no. 1/3, January 1949, p. 6

Furthermore, the February 1955 material on postcards sold at the "Dom Książki" would have been more interesting if illustrations had been included alongside the text.[685]

Unfortunately, the illustrative material was not included in the case of the above-mentioned series created by Adam Bilski and Zygmunt Jaski, entitled *Psoty Kleksa*. It was printed in *Głos Wielkopolski*, the press arm of the Ministry of Information and Propaganda. That is why the censors had to use the written word to recreate the story expressed in the picture. According to the Bulletin, the titular character Kleks

1. tied the lion's tail to a trellis and rejoiced as the lion roared desperately,
2. stuck a double-edged stake into the open mouth of a hippo,
3. painted a zebra black.[686]

This behavior did not gain recognition in the eyes of the superiors, who decided that "These 'gambols' can only arouse sadistic instincts in children. Therefore, this part of the 'cartoon film' qualified for confiscation."[687]

The series was published in 1948 from number 270 to 323.[688] I examined the issues from this period and found that all the infamous parts were printed in the magazine, thus, the example of Kleks could be treated as an oversight.[689] Note, however, that the way the remarks about Kleks were worded did not allow for a clear answer as to whether something "should have" been removed but was not, or whether something "ought to" be removed and it was. In the context of the training objectives, this ambiguity and the lack of illustrations were a bit of an "oversight," this time on the part of the Bulletin's editors. Below is one of the parts "salvaged" by the censor's inattention:

(APG, WUKPPiW, file ref. no. 196); *Biuletyn Informacyjno-Szkoleniowy* no. 4, May 1949, fol. 162r (APP, WUKPPiW, file ref. no. 4).

[685] S. Hardej (WUKPPiW Rzeszów), "Lekcja historii na pocztówkach (correspondence in "Dział Listów")," *Biuletyn Informacyjno-Instrukcyjny* no. 2 (38), February 1955, p. 46 (APG, WUKPPiW, file ref. no. 108).

[686] "Kontrola ilustracyj," *Biuletyn Informacyjno-Szkoleniowy* no. 1/3, January 1949, p. 8 (APG, WUKPPiW, file ref. no. 196).

[687] Ibidem.

[688] A. Rusek, *Od rozrywki do ideowego zaangażowania. Komiksowa rzeczywistość w Polsce w latach 1939–1955*, Warszawa: Biblioteka Narodowa, 2011, p. 237. On *Psoty Kleksa* see also: A. Rusek, *Leksykon polskich bohaterów i serii komiksowych*, Warszawa: Biblioteka Narodowa, 2007, p. 107.

[689] The episodes about a zebra, lion and hippopotamus appeared in the October 1948 issues no. 293 and 294, respectively (October 24, p. 6 and October 25, p. 6), 295 (October 26, 1948, p. 6), 296 and 297 (October 27, p. 6 and October 28, p. 4).

Fig. 21a. One of the strips of *Psoty Kleksa*, which was discussed in the Bulletin (*Głos Wielkopolski* October 27, 1948, no. 296, p. 6).

Fig. 21b. One of the strips of *Psoty Kleksa*, which was discussed in the Bulletin (*Głos Wielkopolski* October 28, 1948, no. 297, p. 4).

Finally, we should not forget the difficult fate of the comic book in the PRL. Already in the early post-war years, the communists began to combat this form of art, treating it as one of the "American contaminants in a healthy, socialist culture."[690] *Psoty Kleksa*, as a native work created before the censorship was tightened, was not subject to such harsh criticism as Western comics and the "American way of life" on the whole; as late as 1953, it was presented in the following way by the Polish Film Chronicle: "Literature – savagery, sadism, pornography. Seven deadly sins for one dollar. It is necessary to raise future gangsters from an early age – they will be needed in Korea, and they will be needed in Europe."[691]

---

[690] Fragment of a statement by Jacek Fedorowicz, satirist and cartoonist, recorded in the film *W ostatniej chwili – o komiksie w PRL-u*, directed by M. Szlachtycz, script by Sz. Holcman, M. Szlachtycz, produced by Telewizja Polska S.A., Freakshot, Szymon Holcman, Warszawa 2011, 1.10'.

[691] *Oto Ameryka*, Polska Kronika Filmowa, January 14, 1953, episode 3, http://www.repozytorium.fn.org.pl/?q=pl/node/7255 (accessed February 8, 2021).

That was the take of the reader who reported on the *Oto Ameryka* exhibition organized in Warsaw in 1953.

***

Also in subsequent material, this time devoted to a book for young adults entitled *Na przełaj przez świat* [Cross-country through the world], a reference was made to an image. Below is the "suggestive photograph"[692] of the British liner *Queen Elizabeth*, which was not included in the Bulletin.

In his book *Na przełaj przez świat*, published in 1948, Bolesław Zagała describes the achievements of technology that improved people's quality of life – the variety of examples can be seen in the titles of the chapters: "What would the world be like without iron and steel?"; "Lime, cement, ferroconcrete"; "Cork is not equal to cork"; "About a postage stamp"; "300 cans per minute"; "Clocks"; "How a gramophone record is made"; "About ships and shipyards," and others.

According to the censors, the book was an unsuccessful attempt to "objectively present the facts" because it actually served to "glorify the technical power of the Anglo-Saxons."[693] It is hard to agree with such a statement, because while in Zagała's view, we owe the progress of civilization largely to the countries of the West, the author repeatedly mentions the Polish contributions to the development of technology and science. The editors of the Bulletin omitted that fact and quoted only those passages that referred to American and English successes, including the one about the largest transatlantic liner of that time, the British *Queen Elizabeth*.

From literature about comic books (not only) of the Polish People's Republic, I found the following particularly useful: M. Krzanicki, *Komiks w PRL, PRL w komiksie*, Warszawa: Wydawnictwo IPN, 2011; M. Misiora, *Bibliografia komiksów wydanych w Polsce w latach 1905 (1859*)–1999. Albumy, magazyny komiksowe, fanziny i książki o komiksie*, Poznań: Fundacja Tranzyt / Centrala, 2010; W. Obremski, *Krótka historia sztuki komiksu w Polsce (1945–2003)*, Toruń: Wydawnictwo Adam Marszałek, 2005; K.T. Toeplitz, *Sztuka komiksu. Próba definicji nowego gatunku artystycznego*, Warszawa: "Czytelnik," 1985.

[692] "O tzw. 'obiektywizmie,'" *Biuletyn Informacyjno-Szkoleniowy* no. 4, May 1949, fol. 155v–156r (APP, WUKPPiW, file ref. no. 4). I write more on this subject in the article "Archiwalia 'pionierskiego' okresu powojennej cenzury. Literatura w poufnych biuletynach urzędu cenzury (1945–1951)," *Sztuka Edycji. Studia Tekstologiczne i Edytorskie* 2021, issue 2 (20), pp. 51–62.

[693] "O tzw. 'obiektywizmie,'" *Biuletyn Informacyjno-Szkoleniowy* no. 4, May 1949, fol. 155v ("*Biuletyny Instrukcyjno-Szkoleniowe 1945–1951*" (APP, WUKPPiW, file ref. no. 4)).

Fig. 22. "The largest ship in the world 'Queen Elizabeth' with a displacement of 85,000 tons." Photo of the British liner *Queen Elizabeth* published in the book by B. Zagała, *Na przełaj przez świat* (B. Zagała, *Na przełaj przez świat*, Warszawa: "Książka," 1948, n.p. (illustration placed between pages 80 and 81)).

***

For the next several months, artistic creations for children were either not featured at all on the pages of the discussed instructional manuals, or there were modest mentions of the subject.[694] A few comments were made in the April 1952 Bulletin; in this case, the material concerned radio programs aimed at young people, which also appeared in September of the same year and in the November/December 1954 double issue, which will be discussed later in the book.

The report on "Czytelnik" made no secret of the fact that in 1951, the offer addressed to young readers constituted only a fraction of the publishing house's activity. Most often, books for the youngest group of readers were published, and young adults' literature was treated with some distance. However, the functionaries were happy to see an increase in the number of domestic publications in comparison to 1950, especially those tackling current issues; as an example, they cited a collection of Lucyna Krzemieniecka's poetry entitled *Jaskółki* [Swallows][695] and Ewa Szelburg-Zarembina's *Wesoła praca* [Merry job].[696] However, the authors of the report were concerned about a decrease in the number of published translations; among those printed in 1951, the majority were "small Soviet titles,"[697] such as *Myszka Pik* [Little mouse Pik] and *W leśnych domkach* [Forest houses] by Vitaly Bianki, an author of books which were also popular in Poland.[698] Among the translations for young people, a novel entitled *Dzieci z Kobányi* [The children of Kobányi] by Kāto Acs was noted; it depicted "the life of Hungarian children at the crucial time when Hungary was being liberated by the Soviet Army."[699] Interestingly, in the case of Szelburg-Zarembina's and Bianki's titles, there is no mention that these were reprints.[700]

The authors of the report stressed that even though some books were not "free of many errors,"[701] as illustrated by Wanda Żółkiewska's *Droga przez ogień*

---

[694] "Uwagi na temat pracy wydawnictw w zakresie zagadnień społeczno-politycznych," *Biuletyn Informacyjno-Instrukcyjny* no. 1, January 1952, pp. 33–34 (APG, WUKPPiW, file ref. no. 100).

[695] In the Bulletin – *Jaskółka* – a swallow.

[696] L. Krzemieniecka, *Jaskółki*, Warszawa: "Czytelnik," 1951; E. Szelburg-Zarembina, *Wesoła praca*, Expanded Second Edition, Warszawa: "Czytelnik," 1951.

[697] "Działalność wydawnictwa 'Czytelnik' w 1951 r.," *Biuletyn Informacyjno-Instrukcyjny* no. 5, May 1952, p. 24 (APG, WUKPPiW, file ref. no. 90).

[698] W. Bianki, *Myszka Pik*, Second Edition, trans. H. Jarmolińska, Warszawa: "Czytelnik," 1951; W. Bianki, *W leśnych domkach*, Second Edition, trans. W. Grodzieńska, Warszawa: "Czytelnik," 1951.

[699] "Działalność wydawnictwa 'Czytelnik' w 1951 r.," *Biuletyn Informacyjno-Instrukcyjny* no. 5, May 1952, p. 24 (APG, WUKPPiW, file ref. no. 90). See: K. Acs, *Dzieci z Kobányi*, trans. C. Mondral, Warszawa: "Czytelnik," 1951.

[700] The first edition of *Wesoła praca* was published in 1947 ([s.l.] Drukarnia św. Wojciecha w Poznaniu), *Myszka Pik* and *W leśnych domkach* in 1949 by "Czytelnik."

[701] "Działalność wydawnictwa 'Czytelnik' w 1951 r.," *Biuletyn Informacyjno-Instrukcyjny* no. 5, May 1952, p. 24 (APG, WUKPPiW, file ref. no. 90).

[Path through fire] (reprinted numerous times), "the publishing house, which the previous year offered no Polish children's literature of greater educational value, has put this section of its publishing activity on the right path."[702]

***

Another, this time minor, mention of works for children appeared in the very next issue of the Bulletin, i.e., in June 1952. In the report on socio-political publications, a few sentences were devoted to articles on youth, noting – not without reproach – that in the entire reporting period, only one brochure closely related to the subject had been published: this was Mirosława Radłowska's *ŚFMD w walce o pokój i prawa młodzieży* [The World Federation of Democratic Youth's struggle for peace and youth rights] published by "Książka i Wiedza."[703] The World Federation of Democratic Youth, which sill exists today, was founded on November 10, 1945 in London as an organization for young people from all over the world. The year 1947 and the beginning of the Cold War put an end to the original plans, as most of the Western countries left its ranks and the Federation was completely dominated by communist youth groups and was henceforth perceived as pro-Soviet.[704]

In the years that followed, works for the youngest and teenage readers were sporadically broached. The next, extensive article on children's books was published in May 1955 by A. Purowska (analyzed below).

***

We say among ourselves that children's literature is not at
an adequate level in our country, that children's books are
boring, that they either teach nothing or provide an accessible
but schematic, slogan-based lecture on our reality.[705]

---

[702] Ibidem. See also: W. Żółkiewska, *Droga przez ogień*, Warszawa: "Czytelnik," 1951.

[703] "Publikacje społeczno-polityczne," *Biuletyn Informacyjno-Instrukcyjny* no. 6, June 1952, p. 35 (APG, WUKPPiW, file ref. no. 87). See: M. Radłowska, *ŚFMD w walce o pokój i prawa młodzieży*, Warszawa: "Książka i Wiedza," 1952.

[704] J. Kotek, "The Creation of the World Federation of Democratic Youth," [in:] idem, *Students and the Cold War*, trans. R. Blumenau, London: Palgrave Macmillan, 1996, pp. 62–85; „Światowa Federacja Młodzieży Demokratycznej," [in:] *Słownik organizacji młodzieżowych w Polsce 1918–1970*, ed. Z.J. Bolek, compiled by Cz. Kozłowski, Warszawa: Iskry, 1971, pp. 92–94.

[705] A. Purowska, "O pracy nad książką dziecięcą," *Biuletyn Informacyjno-Instrukcyjny* 1955, no. 5 (41), pp. 21–22 (APG, WUKPPiW, file ref. no. 131). "We say among ourselves" referred, of course, to the censor-employees of "Mysia Street and its environs."

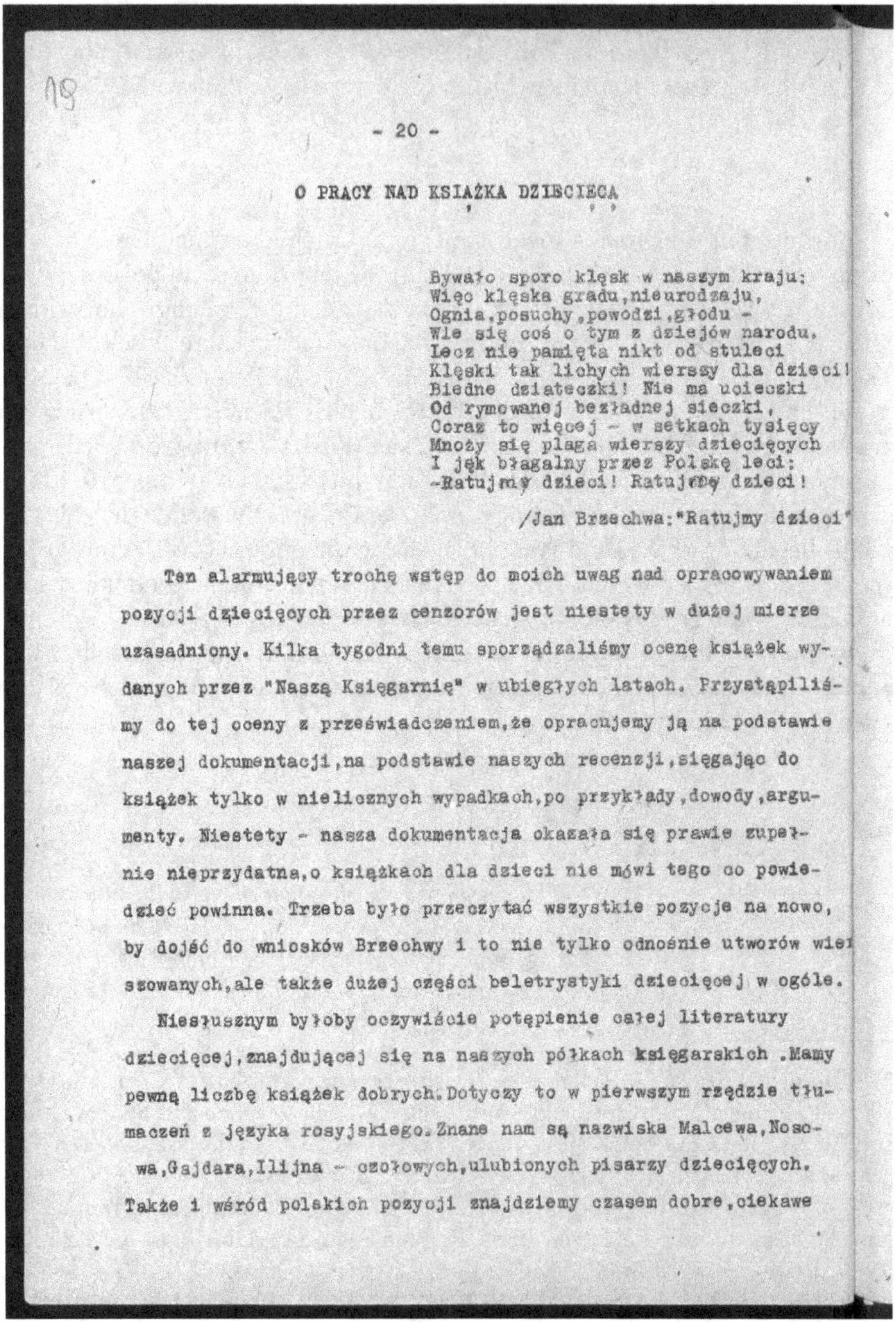

- 20 -

O PRACY NAD KSIĄŻKA DZIECIĘCA

> Bywało sporo klęsk w naszym kraju:
> Więc klęska gradu,nieurodzaju,
> Ognia,posuchy,powodzi,głodu -
> Wie się coś o tym z dziejów narodu.
> Lecz nie pamięta nikt od stuleci
> Klęski tak lichych wierszy dla dzieci!
> Biedne dziateczki! Nie ma ucieczki
> Od rymowanej bezładnej sieczki,
> Coraz to więcej - w setkach tysięcy
> Mnoży się plaga wierszy dziecięcych
> I jęk błagalny przez Polskę leci:
> -Ratujmy dzieci! Ratujmy dzieci!
>
> /Jan Brzechwa:"Ratujmy dzieci"

Ten alarmujący trochę wstęp do moich uwag nad opracowywaniem
pozycji dziecięcych przez cenzorów jest niestety w dużej mierze
uzasadniony. Kilka tygodni temu sporządzaliśmy ocenę książek wydanych przez "Naszą Księgarnię" w ubiegłych latach. Przystąpiliś-
my do tej oceny z przeświadczeniem,że opracujemy ją na podstawie
naszej dokumentacji,na podstawie naszych recenzji,sięgając do
książek tylko w nielicznych wypadkach,po przykłady,dowody,argu-
menty. Niestety - nasza dokumentacja okazała się prawie zupeł-
nie nieprzydatna,o książkach dla dzieci nie mówi tego co powiedzieć powinna. Trzeba było przeczytać wszystkie pozycje na nowo,
by dojść do wniosków Brzechwy i to nie tylko odnośnie utworów wier
szowanych,ale także dużej części beletrystyki dziecięcej w ogóle.

Niesłusznym byłoby oczywiście potępienie całej literatury
dziecięcej,znajdującej się na naszych półkach księgarskich .Mamy
pewną liczbę książek dobrych.Dotyczy to w pierwszym rzędzie tłu-
maczeń z języka rosyjskiego.Znane nam są nazwiska Malcewa,Noso-
wa,Gajdara,Ilijna - czołowych,ulubionych pisarzy dziecięcych.
Także i wśród polskich pozycji znajdziemy czasem dobre,ciekawe

Fig. 23a. The first page of the article by A. Purowska, "O pracy nad książką dziecięcą" (*Biuletyn Informacyjno-Instrukcyjny* no. 5 (41), May 1955, p. 19 (APG, WUKPPiW, file ref. no. 131)).

- 21 -

książki dla dzieci,np.utwory Brzechwy,niektóre bajki i opo-
wiastki Porazińskiej,"Ogniwo" Broniewskiej i kilka innych.Na
podstawie naszych recenzji nie można powiedzieć,czy lektura
dla dzieci jest dobra,czy zła,nie można powiedzieć nic. Nasza
ocena większości pozycji dziecięcych wygląda tak:

    "Zofia Sielecka - "Dwie minuty":

    To krótkie opowiadanie obrazujące niecierpliwe oczeki-
    wanie małej Ani na ojca,powracającego z wczasów.Utwór
    o ciekawej i wysokiej formie artystycznej uczy dzieci
    punktualności."

Oto cała recenzja. Co można powiedzieć na jej podstawie o książce Sieleckiej[2] Nie wiemy nawet dla jakiego wieku przeznaczone
zostało opowiadanie,czy forma odpowiada temu wiekowi,czy wytłu-
maczono w nim dlaczego trzeba się uczyć punktualności itd.Warto
chyba przytoczyć jeszcze kilka przykładów.

    "A.Szymankiewicz -"Chłopcy z cegielni":

    Bajka z życia dzieci chińskich w okresie władzy Kuomin-
    tangu i po wyzwoleniu.Posiada duże i głębokiej treści
    walory wychowawcze."

Chciałoby się tu zawołać: ładna bajka - życie dzieci w Kuomin-
tangowskich Chinach! I znowu pytanie - na czym polegają walory
wychowawcze tej"bajki",co rozumiemy pod stwierdzeniem głęboka
treść?O tym w recenzji nie ma ani słowa.Ani jednego zdania nie
poświęcono też w recenzji poziomowi książki,jej językowi i formie.

    A oto jeszcze "ciekawszy" wypadek. Dwie recenzje z pozycji
Borysa Żytkowa. Pierwsza,podpisana dnia 19.XI.52 r.brzmi:

    "Książeczka o słoniu stanowi kolejną pozycję cyklu"Od
    książeczki do biblioteczki". Zapoznaje ona dziecko z
    życiem chłopów hinduskich,z ich sposobem pracy za po-
    mocą słoni.W tok opowiadania autor umiejętnie wplótł
    fragment obrazujący stosunki anglo-hinduskie.Bez za-
    strzeżeń."

Fig. 23b. The second page of the article by A. Purowska, " O pracy nad książką dziecięcą" (*Biuletyn Informacyjno-Instrukcyjny* no. 5 (41), May 1955, p. 20 (APG, WUKPPiW, file ref. no. 131)).

Purowska's article "O pracy nad książką dziecięcą" [On the work on the children's book] was preceded by a quote from Jan Brzechwa's poem "Ratujmy dzieci" [We must save the children]:

> Bywało sporo klęsk w naszym kraju:
> Więc klęska gradu, nieurodzaju,
> Ognia, posuchy, powodzi, głodu –
> Wie się coś o tym z dziejów narodu.
> Lecz nie pamięta nikt od stuleci
> Klęski tak lichych wierszy dla dzieci!
> Biedne dziateczki! Nie ma ucieczki
> Od rymowanej bezładnej sieczki;
> Coraz to więcej – w setkach tysięcy
> Mnoży się plaga wierszy dziecięcych
> I jęk błagalny przez Polskę leci:
> – Ratujmy dzieci! Ratujmy dzieci![706]

> [This country has seen many a calamity:
> We have suffered hail, drought, and famine
> Crop failures, floods and fires –
> The history of our nation is familiar to me.
> But no one remembers throughout history
> The disaster of such miserable poems for children!
> Poor little children! There is no way to flee
> This rhyming chaotic debris;
> More and more – in hundreds of thousands
> The plague of children's poems is spreading
> And so everyone in Poland is pleading:
> – Save the children! Save the children!]

The author of the article admits that the choice of this quotation was not random. She was prompted to do so, first, by the evaluation she and her colleagues had made of the books published in the previous years by "Nasza Księgarnia," and second, by the state of the earlier censorship documentation, which was supposed to facilitate this task. Purowska and the rest of the censor collective hoped to base their evaluation at least in part on the findings of their predecessors. The use of censorship reviews for periodic, "retrospective" evaluations was a common and entirely understandable practice, especially in the context of the oft-repeated accusations of staff shortages and failure to keep up with evaluations. However, when the collective set to work, they were sorely disappointed:

---

[706] A. Purowska, "O pracy nad książką dziecięcą," *Biuletyn Informacyjno-Instrukcyjny* 1955, no. 5 (41), p. 19 (APG, WUKPPiW, file ref. no. 131). See also: Fig. 23a and J. Brzechwa, "Ratujmy dzieci," [in:] idem, *Wiersze wybrane*, Warszawa: PIW, 1955, pp. 215–216.

Unfortunately, our documentation turned out to be almost completely useless; it does not say what it should say about children's books. We had to re-read all the books in order to come to Brzechwa's conclusions – not only about verse, but also about a large part of children's fiction in general.[707]

So what were the conclusions of the committee's audit? Despite the above remarks, there were some positives. Above all, translations from Russian deserved praise. The quality of these translations was not the subject; what was important was that Soviet literature continued to supply the Polish children's book market. The importance of translations from people's democracies was mentioned repeatedly in the Bulletins. This time, attention was drawn to translations of the "leading, beloved children's authors,"[708] who were indeed popular at the time: Nosov, Gaydar, Ilyin,[709] and Maltsev.[710] Once again, the titles of specific books are not given. The list can be completed with the titles published in 1954 and in the preceding years, which may have been evaluated by the censor collective (incidentally, the titles cited by Purowska do not come exclusively from the catalog of "Nasza Księgarnia," even though this was the publisher under inspection). At that time, the works of the four above-mentioned authors were eagerly translated (and often reprinted), for instance: Elizar Maltsev's *Heart and Soul*; Nikolai Nosov's *Jolly Family*; Arkady Gaydar's *Timur and His Gang* and *Chuck and Geck*; and Mikhail Ilyin's *What Time Is It? The Story of Clocks*.[711] Of Polish authors, " works by Brzechwa, some fairy tales and stories by Porazińska, *Ogniwo* [The link] by Broniewska and some others"[712] were appreciated, but without specifying the details.

---

[707] A. Purowska, "O pracy nad książką dziecięcą," *Biuletyn Informacyjno-Instrukcyjny* 1955, no. 5 (41), p. 19 (APG, WUKPPiW, file ref. no. 131).

[708] Ibidem.

[709] In the Bulletin – Iliyn.

[710] See also K. Budrowska, *Writers, Literature and Censorship…*, p. 245.

[711] E. Maltsev, *Z całego serca*, trans. W. Dobaczewska, Warszawa: "Książa i Wiedza," 1951; see English edition: idem, *Heart and Soul*, Moscow: Foreign Languages Publishing House, 1953; N. Nosov, *Wesoła rodzinka*, trans. H. Rogalowa, Warszawa: "Nasza Księgarnia," 1952; see English edition: idem, *Jolly family*, Moscow: Foreign Languages Publishing House, 1930; A. Gaydar, *Timur i jego drużyna*, Second Edition, trans. A. Wat, Warszawa: "Nasza Księgarnia," 1952; see English edition: idem, *Timur and His Gang*, trans. Z. Voynov, New York: C. Scribner's Sons, 1943; idem, *Czuk i Hek i inne opowiadania*, Second Edition, Warszawa: "Nasza Księgarnia," 1952; idem, *Chuck and Geck*, Moscow: Foreign Languages Publishing House, 1953; M. Iljin, *Która godzina? Opowiadania o czasie*, trans. H. Jarmolińska, Warszawa: "Czytelnik," 1949; see English edition: idem, *What Time Is It? The Story of Clocks*, trans. B. Kincead, Philadelphia–London: J.B. Lippincott Co., 1932.

[712] A. Purowska, "O pracy nad książką dziecięcą," *Biuletyn Informacyjno-Instrukcyjny* 1955, no. 5 (41), p. 20 (APG, WUKPPiW, file ref. no. 131). See also: J. Broniewska, *Ogniwo*, Second Edition, Warszawa: "Nasza Księgarnia," 1952.

In fact, only the above-mentioned authors were worthy of praise. The rest of the article dealt not so much with the books themselves and the assessment of the publishing market as with the reviews created by fellow-censors. In the context of the smooth functioning of the Office on Mysia Street, this was a very important issue. As previously noted, the Bulletins repeatedly stressed staff shortages and the need to streamline work, so it was optimal to carry out periodic reviews on the basis of the previous documentation. However, as it turned out, this was not always possible because some of the censorship reviews were simply incomplete. There were complaints that most of the reviews lacked a conclusion and did not provide an answer to the question of whether a given"reading for children is good or bad,"[713] even though the decision (preceded by the reviewer's submission) was one of the most important elements of censorial evaluation.[714] The censorship review of Zofia Sielecka's book *Dwie minuty* [Two minutes] was cited as evidence of this malpractice: " This is a short story about little Ania impatiently waiting for her father to return from holiday. The work has an interesting and highly artistic form and teaches children punctuality."[715] The quoted evaluation lacked not only an unambiguous assessment, but also an indication of the age range of the children to whom the book was addressed, among other things.

Purowska noted that the censors' evaluations often failed to assess the work's aesthetic dimension: " In our reviews, we sometimes find a few words about the language of a children's book, but nothing about its graphic design, the cover, drawings or illustrations."[716] Indeed, the visual aspect could be much less important – meaning, ideologically dangerous – than the "word" (the storyline), but it was often forgotten that it could also convey a certain worldview, and for this reason alone, should be taken into account in any evaluation.

Jan Brzechwa (1898–1966) – a Polish poet of Jewish descent; author of many extremely popular works for children, and a translator of Russian literature.

Janina Porazińska (1882–1971) – a Polish prose writer and editor, author of many works for children, and a translator of Scandinavian literature.

Janina Broniewska (1904–1981) – a Polish writer, author of children's books; during the Stalinist period, one of the most important figures on the literary scene of the time – a promoter of socialist realism and an activist of the Union of Polish Writers.

[713] A. Purowska, "O pracy nad książką dziecięcą," *Biuletyn Informacyjno-Instrukcyjny* 1955, no. 5 (41), p. 20 (APG, WUKPPiW, file ref. no. 131).

[714] A. Wiśniewska-Grabarczyk, "Decyzja," [in:] eadem, *"Czytelnik" ocenzurowany. Literatura w kryptotekstach…*, pp. 147–149.

[715] A. Purowska, "O pracy nad książką dziecięcą," *Biuletyn Informacyjno-Instrukcyjny* 1955, no. 5 (41), p. 20 (APG, WUKPPiW, file ref. no. 131). See also: Z. Sielecka, *Dwie minuty*, Warszawa: "Nasza Księgarnia," 1951; Second Edition: ibidem 1952; Third Edition: ibidem 1954.

[716] A. Purowska, "O pracy nad książką dziecięcą," *Biuletyn Informacyjno-Instrukcyjny* 1955, no. 5 (41), p. 21 (APG, WUKPPiW, file ref. no. 131).

Another significant criticism of the inspected censorship reviews was their failure to assess the educational value of the works. This category was extremely important, especially when discussing literature for the youngest readers. A children's book, according to the Bulletin, was supposed to help parents, schools, and children's organizations form correct attitudes; it was meant to move, teach, and educate.[717] Purowska cited reviews that dismissed these issues with perfunctory remarks, as in the case of *Chłopcy z cegielni* [The boys from the brickyard] by Andrei Szmankiewicz:[718] "A story from the life of Chinese children during the period of Kuomintang rule and after liberation. It has great and profound educational value."[719]

The collective evaluating the works of their colleagues also drew attention to the disdainful attitude towards children's books, which manifested itself, among other things, in the duplication of reviews. Certainly, such a practice deserved to be condemned, but it should be emphasized that it also occurred when evaluating books for adult readers. Purowska's article obviously refers to an example from children's literature – it quotes the material from the Poznań branch where two identical reviews of Boris Żytkow's short book *O słoniu* [About an elephant] were written a year apart (the identical fragments are underscored):

A review from November 19, 1952, written by censor Wierzbiński

> A short book about an elephant is one of the titles in the series *Od książeczki do biblioteczki* [From a pop-up book to a library]. It familiarizes children with the life of Indian peasants and their way of working using elephants. In the course of the story, the author skillfully wove a fragment illustrating Anglo-Hindu relationships. No reservations.[720]

A review from November 28, 1953, written by censor Szulczewski

> The inspected title familiarizes children with the life of Indian peasants and their way of working using elephants. A fragment illustrating Anglo-Hindu relationships is skillfully woven in the story. Permission granted.[721]

---

[717] Ibidem.

[718] In the Bulletin – Szymankiewicz.

[719] A. Purowska, "O pracy nad książką dziecięcą," *Biuletyn Informacyjno-Instrukcyjny* 1955, no. 5 (41), p. 20 (APG, WUKPPiW, file ref. no. 131). See also: A. Szmankiewicz, *Chłopcy z cegielni*, Second Edition, trans. H. Broniatowska, Warszawa: "Nasza Księgarnia," 1952.

[720] A. Purowska, "O pracy nad książką dziecięcą," *Biuletyn Informacyjno-Instrukcyjny* 1955, no. 5 (41), p. 20 (APG, WUKPPiW, file ref. no. 131).

[721] Ibidem, p. 21. See also: B. Żytkow, *O słoniu*, trans. N. Gałczyńska, K.I. Gałczyński, Warszawa: "Nasza Księgarnia," 1950.

Finally, it is worth highlighting some general remarks and postulates formulated by Purowska. The censor emphasized the separateness of children's literature from literature for adult readers, and thus the need to develop separate tools for evaluating the former:

> In our several years of censorship practice, we have developed certain criteria, general as they are, for evaluating fiction. Of course, it is much more difficult to find them for children's literature. Children's literature has its own peculiarities – it requires a more careful, thorough, and – because of its role – stricter assessment than adult literature. But above all, it needs to be taken seriously, regardless of whether it is intended for a three-year-old or a twelve-year-old child, whether it is ten pages long or a hundred.[722]

This is why the censor postulated that "a briefing should be devoted to discussing reviews or remarks about a children's book, and if necessary, to discussing the whole book."[723] Unfortunately, the analyzed Bulletins were not invested in the realization of such postulates – none of the children's books was the subject of a separate presentation, for instance, in a series of nationwide debates on fiction. The conclusions drawn from the inspection suggested that such literature did not have full "citizenship rights" at the censor's office and that it was not taken seriously.[724] References were also made to literary criticism, which was believed to overlook the needs of the "juvenile reader."[725] While "Mysia Street and its environs" did not entirely ignore the "fourth" literature, this genre was certainly not prioritized in the Bulletins.

Throughout the article, Purowska was highly critical of the competence of her colleagues working with children's books and cited numerous examples. However, she ended her statement with a good, though not exemplary review – could she not find one? – of Anatoly Aleksin's *Dwa portrety* [Two portraits]:

> Aleksin's short story is about the misery of the people of India exploited by foreign and domestic capital. More specifically, the protagonist of the story is a member of the Communist Party of Indonesia, Mamurat, who teaches the little pariah Mochan to read and write and to love the leaders of the Revolution: Lenin and Stalin. The author leads us to believe that the former illiterate, humiliated pariah Mochan will become a conscious defender of the tormented and exploited proletariat of India. Aleksin's story is intended for children and young people. The language is colorful, vivid, figurative, with great ideological force.[726]

---

[722] A. Purowska, "O pracy nad książką dziecięcą," *Biuletyn Informacyjno-Instrukcyjny* 1955, no. 5 (41), p. 22 (APG, WUKPPiW, file ref. no. 131).

[723] Ibidem, p. 23.

[724] Ibidem, pp. 21–23.

[725] Ibidem, p. 22.

[726] Ibidem, p. 23. See also: A. Aleksin, *Dwa portrety*, trans. H. Broniatowska, Warszawa: "Nasza Księgarnia," 1953.

8. LITERATURE AND DISCUSSIONS OF THE "THAW"

Is this really the key to opening the rusty locks
of our censor mentality?[727]

The subject of the "Thaw" dominated the Bulletins in 1955. Remember that the Thaw was a period of changes lasting from 1953 (Stalin's death) to about 1957, aimed at liberalizing state policy (de-Stalinization, the release of political prisoners; in art, this meant a move away from socialist realism, among other things). A reversal to a harsher course already took place in late 1956 but despite a certain failure, the achievements of the Thaw cannot be overestimated, as the dark years of Stalinism in Poland were over. The first Thaw-related article was published in April, and in the following months, the topic was continued. The materials evaluated the phenomenon in various ways: from initial statements disregarding the "frost" (as it was put) to later, deeper and more serious reflections.[728]

The discussion of the "Thaw" continued in the following year. Apart from the previously signaled report on Flaszen, Andrzejewski and Rudnicki, three "serious" letters were published as a response to Kleyny's article "O sztuce dla dorosłych," and a less serious, humorous piece – a poem by one of the censors.[729] To clarify, the satire specialist from "Mysia Street" actually published two texts with the same title – in October and December 1955.[730] The second

---

[727] H. Landsberg, "Mój głos w dyskusji," *Biuletyn Informacyjno-Instrukcyjny* no. 1 (49), January 1956, p. 26 (APG, WUKPPiW, file ref. no. 4).

[728] Most of the material on the "Thaw" was reprinted in *"Biuletyn Informacyjno-Instrukcyjny." Wybór dokumentów z 1955 r...*, hence, here I focus on the previously unreviewed documents from 1956.

[729] H. Landsberg, "Mój głos w dyskusji," *Biuletyn Informacyjno-Instrukcyjny* no. 1 (49), January 1956, pp. 24–29 (APG, WUKPPiW, file ref. no. 4); L. Rutkowski (Dept. of Cultural Publications), A. Furmański (Dept. of Instruction and Supervision), "Dyskusji ciąg dalszy," *Biuletyn Informacyjno-Instrukcyjny* no. 1 (49), January 1956, pp. 30–39 (APG, WUKPPiW, file ref. no. 4); J. Ł., "O dorastaniu do sztuki (głos w dyskusji)"; W. J., "Towarzyszu Redaktorze," *Biuletyn Informacyjno-Instrukcyjny* no. 2 (50), February 1956, pp. 37–48 (APG, WUKPPiW, file ref. no. 6).

[730] J. Kleyny, "O sztuce dla dorosłych," *Biuletyn Informacyjno-Instrukcyjny* no. 10 (45), October 1955, pp. 10–22 (APG, WUKPPiW, file ref. no. 119); J. Kleyny, "O sztuce

was published as a "discussion paper," encouraging staff to send comments and reflections to "Mysia Street."

All three responses are evidence of the considerable chaos that prevailed during the Thaw in the censorship office and polemicized with Kleyny's diagnosis of the artistic achievements of the previous decade. The censor pointed out a few valuable phenomena (e.g., *Niemcy* – a previously mentioned book by Leon Kruczkowski and *Ostatni etap* – a film directed by Elżbieta Jakubowska), but the overall assessment was not very positive. The reason for this was believed to be the "ideological slumber" that everyone – the artists, the Party and the Main Office – succumbed to during those ten years. This resulted, according to Kleyny, in a number of either bad or terrible projects: from literary ones, such as *Nr 16 produkuje* [No. 16 produces] by Jan Wilczek; critical-literary ones, such as prescriptive reviews; and visual arts projects, such as Krajewski in painting (which is a reference to one of the practitioners and ideologues of socialist realist art, Juliusz Krajewski).[731]

Helena Landsberg, the aforementioned head of the Non-Periodicals, hence, a person holding a high position in the Office's structures, polemicized with Kleyny. While she could accept such an evaluation of art created in a time of errors and distortions, she could not remain indifferent to Kleyny's accusations against "Mysia Street." The censor pointed to the lack of a constructive dialogue between the rank-and-file employees and the management, who often did not listen to the arguments of the subordinates, passing their own, individual judgments on the evaluated texts. This is how Landsberg responded to her colleague's text, using the metaphor suggested by him:

> No flowers. Those that have grown hesitantly are too frail. Yes, it is a pity that we cannot decorate the shelves of our libraries with a larger bouquet of the 10th-anniversary masterpieces. Are the slumbering authors to blame? Probably not, or at least not exclusively.
> It was hard for the flowers of our Polish creativity to flourish; maybe it was the excess of "artificial fertilizers" and "entrenchment" in the form of ready-made, imposed patterns and misunderstood varnishes.
> Nevertheless, many a beautiful flower has blossomed in this way, and is still blossoming.
> [...]
> According to comrade Kleyny, everyone is asleep at the wheel: the authors, the party and us, the "censorial lot," and especially, the management of the office,

---

dla dorosłych (artykuł dyskusyjny)," *Biuletyn Informacyjno-Instrukcyjny* no. 12 (48), December 1955, pp. 4–18 (APG, WUKPPiW, file ref. no. 117).

[731] J. Kleyny, "O sztuce dla dorosłych (artykuł dyskusyjny)," *Biuletyn Informacyjno--Instrukcyjny* no. 12 (48), December 1955, p. 5 (APG, WUKPPiW, file ref. no. 117).

turning from the side of opportunism to the side of liberalism. And while there is a productive decompression in the creative world, the GUKP leadership continues to slumber.[732]

The accusation of a lack of understanding between the management and the rank-and-file employees appeared, for instance, in the assessment of Jerzy Lutowski's *Ostry dyżur* [Emergency Room] (praised by Kleyny). The "decision-makers" were bothered by such aspects as the anti-party nature of the work, while the "drones"[733] (as Kleyny called the rank-and-file functionaries) embraced the drama without waiting for their superiors to explain their position. Landsberg countered the attack by claiming that the play had been the subject of intense discussions not only in the Office, between the management and the censors, but also in the press. The functionary admitted that the decision to publish the piece was not easy, as it was ambiguous and, as she wrote, continued to evoke extreme emotions in her. What was so controversial about the play? *Ostry dyżur*, directed by Erwin Axer at the National Theatre in Warsaw in 1955, dealt with the issue of the rehabilitation of Polish underground soldiers, a topic that was absent in Stalinist Poland.[734] According to Kleyny, "fear of public speaking" prevented critics from evaluating the dilemma faced by the work's protagonist – a doctor and former Home Army soldier, who had to treat a communist dignitary. When the reviews finally appeared, they showed a range of extreme attitudes, from hedging through negative to… extremely creative – such as the one in *Dziś i Jutro*, where an attempt was made to prove by all means that the play was thoroughly Christian. In addition, Kleyny and the discussants referred (with extensive citations) to the play's press reviews written by Czanerle, Ludawska, Messer, Szczawiński and Szydłowski.[735] The censors accused the opponent of misunderstanding the

---

[732] H. Landsberg, "Mój głos w dyskusji," *Biuletyn Informacyjno-Instrukcyjny* no. 1 (49), January 1956, p. 24, 26 (APG, WUKPPiW, file ref. no. 4).

[733] J. Kleyny, "O sztuce dla dorosłych (artykuł dyskusyjny)," *Biuletyn Informacyjno-Instrukcyjny* no. 12 (48), December 1955, p. 12 (APG, WUKPPiW, file ref. no. 117).

[734] J. Lutowski, "Ostry dyżur," *Twórczość* 1955, no. 13, pp. 8–10 (excerpts from the play); idem, *Ostry dyżur. Sztuka w trzech aktach*, Warszawa: "Czytelnik," 1956; *Encyklopedia teatru polskiego*, https://encyklopediateatru.pl/kalendarium/1307/ostry-dyzur-jerzego-lutowskiego (accessed July 20, 2021).

[735] The reviews of the play *Ostry dyżur* mentioned by Kleyny and his discussants: M. Czanerle, "Ostry spór o *Ostry dyżur*," *Teatr* 1955, no. 22, pp. 18–19; R. Szydłowski, "Ostry dyżur," *Trybuna Ludu* October 15, 1955, no. 284, p. 4; J. Ludawska, "Ostry dyżur," *Nowa Kultura* October 23, 1955, no. 43, pp. 3, 6; J. Szczawiński, "Z perspektywy humanizmu," *Dziś i Jutro* November 6, 1955, no. 44, p. 8. See also: [Interview with Jerzy Lutowski conducted by L. Woy.], *Express Wieczorny* June 17, 1955, no. 143, p. 4 (the conversation mainly about *Ostry dyżur*).

analyzed materials and even of misrepresentations and inaccuracies elsewhere in his account. An example are the evaluations of the aforementioned important Thaw titles: "Trudny kunszt womitowania," "Wieczór z Henrykiem," "Deficyt" and "Poemat dla dorosłych," as well as the case of "Bardzo krótka historia" [A very short story] by Stanisław Zieliński (who a few years later took part in the famous smear campaign against Gombrowicz).[736] The story fit into the subject, present during the Thaw, of rehabilitating those who during the war, stood on the wrong side of the barricades, according to the authorities at the time.

Specific objections to Kleyny's text were accompanied by those of a general nature. The author of an article from February 1956, signed with the initials J. Ł., disagreed, for example, with the argument about the slumber, which according to him was "a product of the author's imagination or at least a lack of precision in its formulation."[737] It seems that both Landsberg and the other debaters wanted to show that at "Mysia Street," there were often difficult disputes and that the final decisions crystallized in lively and heated polemics between the rank-and-file employees and their superiors. Landsberg and her colleagues defended the Office, pointing to the many positive decisions taken (not only) during the Thaw.

As we can see, especially in 1956, the management of the Office "defended" its decisions, emphasizing that many of them were based on long, difficult and challenging debates. However, also in 1955, Kleyny's article was not left without an answer – the polemic was published in the same issue under a meaningful title "O zawodzie cenzora poważnie" [A serious take on the profession of a censor].[738] Signed M. M., essentially anonymous, the functionary made several counter-arguments in his dispute with Kleyny, but ultimately accepted his text as an expression of the author's positive attitude toward the censor's work and as evidence of a mental revival in the Office. M. M.'s statement is another interpretation of the events of the previous several months. From the Thaw discussions, it is not easy to draw unambiguous conclusions as to which of the texts published during this crucial period were considered an oversight in the Office, which only required corrections, and which were wrongly withheld. Complementing Kleyny's statement, one could say that fear paralyzed not only overt, but also "censorial" criticism. This is why there were so many different opinions about the above-mentioned texts in print, but also about those removed from print, which either never

---

[736] S. Zieliński, "Bardzo krótka historia," [in:] idem, *Kalejdoskop*, Warszawa: "Czytelnik", 1955, pp. 267–281. See also: J. Siedlecka, *Zlecenie na Gombrowicza*, [in:] eadem, *Biografie odtajnione. Z archiwów literackich bezpieki*, Poznań: Zysk i S-ka, 2015, pp. 112–130.

[737] J. Ł., "O dorastaniu do sztuki (głos w dyskusji)," *Biuletyn Informacyjno-Instrukcyjny* no. 2, February 1956, p. 33 (APG, WUKPPiW, file ref. no. 6).

[738] M. M., "O zawodzie cenzora poważnie," *Biuletyn Informacyjno-Instrukcyjny* no. 12 (48), December 1955, pp. 19–27 (APG, WUKPPiW, file ref. no. 117).

appeared, had to wait for a more opportune moment, or found their way to the list of titles banned after their initial publication. Examples included the removed article by Andrzejewski "O relatywizmie" [On relativism], and Leon Pasternak's poems "Moja rzecz" [My thing] and "Do działacza od kultury" [To the cultural activist]. According to Landsberg's testimony, "Moja rzecz" was not allowed to be published in *Nowa Kultura*, and the latter poem by the former Bereziak prisoner – in *Szpilki*.[739]

The discussions published in the Bulletins may be, on the one hand, a testimony to the confusion which reigned at "Mysia Street," and on the other, an attempt to present the Office's "final" position on issues which were ambiguous and triggered the most polemics. As early as October 1955, Kleyny warned that one should "always keep their ear to the ground" to prevent the publication of a statement which "in one way or another, reverted to an ill-conceived 'Thaw.'"[740] Clearly, the "Ministry of Truth" was still working on establishing the only correct narrative describing the unfolding changes.

---

[739] H. Landsberg, "Mój głos w dyskusji," *Biuletyn Informacyjno-Instrukcyjny* no. 1 (49), January 1956, pp. 26–27 (APG, WUKPPiW, file ref. no. 4).

[740] J. Kleyny, "O sztuce dla dorosłych," *Biuletyn Informacyjno-Instrukcyjny* no. 10 (45), October 1955, p. 11 (APG, WUKPPiW, file ref. no. 119).

9. CENSORSHIP ACCORDING TO PUBLISHER (NOT ONLY) "CZYTELNIK"

The changes taking place in the post-war publishing market ended with its almost complete nationalization around 1950. Most private and cooperative publishing houses shut down, not counting pseudo-cooperative shell presses and a few Church-run publishers, which functioned under strictly state-determined rules.[741] In the Bulletins issued up to 1951, we find little material describing the aforementioned changes (although the nationalization of printing houses and the press market was mentioned in briefings[742]). This absence is particularly surprising in the Bulletins from 1949 and 1950, because the nationalization of the printing industry reached its peak in 1949. Given the perhaps still incomplete database of the Bulletins from the early years of the Office, it must be assumed that these matters were discussed in the issues not yet found.

A few remarks about publishing houses were made in later issues. However, these subjects never became the primary focus, appearing rather as comments illustrating another, main topic. The longest statement concerning censorship according to publisher was announced in the July 1952 issue of the Bulletin. Nothing new was added beyond what had long been taught in training courses for Office employees, but in view of the recurring mistakes in this area, the inclusion of the following instruction was fully justified:

> We cannot approach every publisher equally. We have different requirements for a party publishing house such as "Książka i Wiedza" or a catalog of a mass party press, and different requirements for the "Czytelnik" publishing house, which to a large extent represents the Writers' Union and has to undertake a wider range of authors. A popular science publishing house such as "Wiedza Powszechna" may not publish positions that contain any ideological errors or represent the position of an unsettled, undecided author, because they are supposed to shape

---

[741] P. Nowak, "Wojewódzki Urząd Kontroli Prasy, Publikacji i Widowisk w okresie nacjonalizacji rynku książki…," pp. 170, 191; K. Budrowska, "Wewnętrzne pismo cenzury…," p. 100; M. Tobera, "Księgarstwo spółdzielcze i prywatne w okresie trójsektorowości polskiego rynku książki (1945–1950)," *Przegląd Biblioteczny* 2014, issue 3, pp. 329–364.

[742] See the "problematic" ["Materiały z odprawy"], fol. 33r (*"Biuletyny Instrukcyjno--Szkoleniowe 1945–1951"* (APP, WUKPPiW, file ref. no. 4)).

the worldview of the broad masses. Scientific associations may publish positions of a debatable nature, because the correct view of often wavering and hesitant scholars will crystallize more easily in a scientific discussion. Of course, these are errors within the bounds of tolerance, meaning, errors that are not the mouthpiece of a hostile worldview.[743]

To a large extent, the assessment criteria in the above passage overlap with those applied to the differences between the evaluation of fiction and other types of writing. Transferring these differences to the publishing world, publishers specializing in fiction and science essentially had more leeway than other publishers: the former because of the creative element that organizes literary expression; the latter because of limited distribution and thus a smaller audience.

General comments on the censorship of specific publishers were also accompanied by reports describing various segments of the publishing market. Most such summaries, however, discussed non-fiction works, explored later in this book. The evaluation of the activity of one of the key publishing houses in the discussed period is analyzed below.

***

The Activity of the "Czytelnik" Publishing House in 1951

In May 1952, an extensive, almost 10-page article was published under the title "The Activity of the 'Czytelnik' Publishing House in 1951."[744] The appearance of the material in the manual for censors is not surprising, as the publishing house, established in 1944 by Jerzy Borejsza, was one of the most important press businesses of the Polish People's Republic[745]; the publishing house was mentioned in

---

[743] "Uwagi ogólne o recenzji" (in the series *O wyższy poziom pracy nad książką*), *Biuletyn Informacyjno-Instrukcyjny* no. 7, July 1952, p. 27 (APG, WUKPPiW, file ref. no. 84).

[744] "Działalność wydawnictwa 'Czytelnik' w 1951 r.," *Biuletyn Informacyjno-Instrukcyjny* no. 5, May 1952, pp. 18–27 (APG, WUKPPiW, file ref. no. 90). See, e.g.: K. Budrowska, "Wewnętrzne pismo cenzury…," p. 100.

[745] In my book, "*Czytelnik" ocenzurowany. Literatura w kryptotekstach…*, I write about the censorship of "Czytelnik" in 1950. I also provide a bibliography on the subject of the publishing house there, see, e.g.: *Na rogu Stalina i Trzech Krzyży. Listy do Jerzego Borejszy 1944–1952*, selection, introduction, compilation and footnotes G.P. Bąbiak, Warszawa: "Czytelnik," 2014; B. Fijałkowska, *Borejsza i Różański. Przyczynek do dziejów stalinizmu w Polsce*, Olsztyn: Wydawnictwo Wyższej Szkoły Pedagogicznej w Olsztynie, 1995; *Literatura światowa w wydawnictwach "Czytelnika*," layout J. Jaworowski, Warszawa: "Czy-

numerous Bulletins,[746] and the majority of books evaluated by the functionaries or recommended for self-study came from the catalog of "Czytelnik."

Fragments of the report concerning contemporary drama, satire, poetry and children's literature were discussed in detail in earlier chapters. Moreover, in the opinion of the editors, the publishing house displayed

> a lively activity in such areas as poetry, the stage, and satire – all the while focusing mainly on contemporary publications dealing with issues that are close to our lives and development. Taking into account the errors and shortcomings indicated, one must conclude that the tendency of publishing policy in the field of the above-mentioned literary genres is generally correct.[747]

Bear this in mind as we look at how the other segments of the publishing house were evaluated.

***

The report devoted the most space to contemporary literature, which should not come as a surprise since, under the division of powers among state publishing houses, it was "Czytelnik" that was assigned this sector of the literary market.[748] This had an impact on the choice of topics in which the authors engaged: in their stories, the past often gave way to the present. The authors of the report paid attention to this fact, adding that the modest representation of titles dealing with historical issues was also a result of limiting the number of pre-1945 titles published by "Czytelnik."

Since classics were printed by other publishing houses, such as "Książka i Wiedza" and Państwowy Instytut Wydawniczy (PIW), the omission of this type of literature from the "Czytelnik's" publishing policy did not pose any significant threat to the book market, which the authors seemed to ignore. In fact, Borejsza's publishing house did not completely abandon this segment and published, as it was noted in the article, some Polish classics (mainly Żeromski and Kraszewski) and particular works of Russian literature rooted in tradition (Leskov, Gogol,

---

telnik," 1957; S. Siekierski, *Książka literacka. Potrzeby społeczne i ich realizacja w latach 1944–1986*, Warszawa: Wydawnictwo Naukowe PWN, 1992, pp. 146–150.

[746] See, e.g.: ["Materiały z odprawy"], fol. 35r (*"Biuletyny Instrukcyjno-Szkoleniowe 1945–1951"* (APP, WUKPPiW, file ref. no. 4)).

[747] "Działalność wydawnictwa 'Czytelnik' w 1951 r.," *Biuletyn Informacyjno-Instrukcyjny* no. 5, May 1952, pp. 21–22 (APG, WUKPPiW, file ref. no. 90).

[748] K. Budrowska, "Wewnętrzne pismo cenzury...," p. 100. See also: "Działalność wydawnictwa 'Czytelnik' w 1951 r.," *Biuletyn Informacyjno-Instrukcyjny* no. 5, May 1952, p. 18 (APG, WUKPPiW, file ref. no. 90).

Kuprin).[749] Once again, only surnames were listed, but in 1951 – the year discussed in the report – "Czytelnik" published such works as Stefan Żeromski's *Grzech, Wspomnienia* [Memories], and *Zamieć* [Blizzard]; Józef Ignacy Kraszewski's *Kawał literata* [A piece of a literati]; Nikolai Leskov's *Lefty. Being the Tale of Cross-Eyed Lefty from Tula and the Steel Flea, The Toupée Artist,* and *Selected Works;* and Nikolai Gogol and Alexander Kuprin's *Utwory wybrane* [Selected Works].[750] We cannot omit, of course, the publication of titles as part of the National Edition of Mickiewicz's Works (which is not mentioned in this report, but to which a few sentences were devoted in the January 1949 Bulletin).

Furthermore, the interwar reality – that is, the living conditions of the "working masses in capitalist Poland"[751] – could also be gleaned from the few reprints of books, such as Leon Kruczkowski's *Sidła* [Snares], published by "Czytelnik." Thanks to the recollections of Italian workers' activists, Giovani Germanetto (*Memoirs of a Barber*) and Mario Montagnana (*Wspomnienia robotnika turyńskiego* – Memoirs of a worker from Turin), who were mentioned in the Bulletin, the Polish reader had an opportunity to read about the Italian proletariat's struggle with fascism.[752] Furthermore, the second, expanded edition of the anthology *Dwa wieki poezji rosyjskiej* [Two centuries of Russian poetry], compiled by Mieczysław Jastrun and Seweryn Pollak, was particularly praised.[753] The collection, with an afterword by Leon Gomolicki, was first published in 1947, hence, in a very different political and cultural reality. The article omitted that the afterword was redacted from the new edition, noting only that the material was compiled "in such a way as to fully emphasize the realistic, progressive, and revolutionary elements in Russian poetry of the last two centuries."[754]

---

[749] "Działalność wydawnictwa 'Czytelnik' w 1951 r.," *Biuletyn Informacyjno-Instrukcyjny* no. 5, May 1952, p. 19 (APG, WUKPPiW, file ref. no. 90).

[750] N. Leskov, *Opowieść o tulskim mańkucie,* Warszawa: "Czytelnik," 1951. English version: N. Leskov, *Lefty. Being the Tale of Cross-Eyed Lefty from Tula and the Steel Flea,* trans. G. Hanna, Moscow: Progress Publishers, 1965; N. Leskov, *Balwierz-artysta,* Warszawa: "Czytelnik," 1951. English version: idem, *The Toupée Artist,* [in:] idem, *The Sentry and Other Stories,* trans. A.E. Chamot, London: The Bodley Lane, 1922.

[751] "Działalność wydawnictwa 'Czytelnik' w 1951 r.," *Biuletyn Informacyjno-Instrukcyjny* no. 5, May 1952, p. 22 (APG, WUKPPiW, file ref. no. 90).

[752] G. Germanetto, *Memoirs of a Barber,* trans. E. Stevens, London: Martin Lawrence, 1934.

[753] *Dwa wieki poezji rosyjskiej. Antologia,* Revised and Expanded Second Edition, arranged and compiled by M. Jastrun, S. Pollak, Warszawa: "Czytelnik," 1951.

[754] "Działalność wydawnictwa 'Czytelnik' w 1951 r.," *Biuletyn Informacyjno-Instrukcyjny* no. 5, May 1952, p. 19 (APG, WUKPPiW, file ref. no. 90). See also: *Dwa wieki poezji rosyjskiej. Antologia,* arranged and compiled by M. Jastrun, S. Pollak, afterword by L. Gomolicki, Warszawa: "Czytelnik," 1947; the excluded afterword was entitled *Etapy rozwojowe poezji rosyjskiej* (see: *Dwa wieki poezji rosyjskiej. Antologia…,* First Edition, pp. 443–471).

According to the authors of the report, this is exactly what was missing in the analogous publication on Polish classical poetry, that is, in the anthology *Wiersze, które lubimy,* compiled by Jan Kott and Adam Ważyk.[755] The Bulletin reads that "as a result of an improper selection of authors and works, the progressive, realistic trend in our poetry was not fully displayed."[756] The volume presents the works of several dozen poets, from Mikołaj Rej and Jan Kochanowski to a selection of works by Stanisław Wyspiański and Leopold Staff; it does not specify, however, which of them should not have been included in the discussed selection. Moreover, a review of the volume, which appeared in *Życie Literackie,* informs about the anthology's "extensive introduction justifying its arrangement and selection of poems, and characterizing the historical periods in which they were written."[757] As previously noted, authors and editors were often "asked" for such introductions – though not all of them were produced on "Mysia Street's" request.

On the other hand, there were no objections to "drawing on the classic literature of people's democracies."[758] The publication of *Selected Stories* by Ivan Vazov, one of the fathers of modern Bulgarian literature, and *Selections from the Poems of Alexander Petofi* was praised; the latter title was all the more valuable "because it reflected the traditions of the common revolutionary struggle of the Hungarian and Polish nations,"[759] which at least partly compensated for the lack of historical subject matter in the remaining titles (the profile of the Hungarian author was also presented in a book published the same year by "Czytelnik": *Wódz i poeta*[760] [A leader and poet]).

The report also commended the publication of *Nauka polskiego Oświecenia w walce o postęp* [The science of the Polish Enlightenment in the fight for progress] by Bogusław Leśnodorski and Kazimierz Opałek, as well as *The French Revolution 1787–1799* by Albert Soboul – books which, according to the authors of the

---

[755] *Wiersze, które lubimy. Antologia,* compiled by A. Ważyk, J. Kott, Warszawa: "Czytelnik," 1951.

[756] "Działalność wydawnictwa 'Czytelnik' w 1951 r.," *Biuletyn Informacyjno-Instrukcyjny* no. 5, May 1952, p. 19 (APG, WUKPPiW, file ref. no. 90).

[757] [Review: *Wiersze, które lubimy. Antologia,* compiled by A. Ważyk, J. Kott, Warszawa: "Czytelnik," 1951], *Życie Literackie* May 13, 1951, p. 11 (a review-note in the column "Literatura").

[758] "Działalność wydawnictwa 'Czytelnik' w 1951 r.," *Biuletyn Informacyjno-Instrukcyjny* no. 5, May 1952, p. 19 (APG, WUKPPiW, file ref. no. 90).

[759] Ibidem. See: S. Petőfi, *Wybór poezji,* compiled by J.W. Gomulicki, Warszawa: "Czytelnik," 1951; I. Wazow, *Wybór opowiadań,* trans. J. Anc, Warszawa: "Czytelnik", 1951.

[760] G. Illyés, *Wódz i poeta,* trans. J. Moszczeński, Warszawa: "Czytelnik," 1951.

Bulletin, were isolated but valuable attempts to popularize historical themes.[761] The few above-presented examples did not, however, significantly influence the evaluation of this segment of Borejsza's activity: "publications on historical issues appear only sporadically and infrequently. In 1951, 'Czytelnik' did not fulfill the task of making the progressive, revolutionary historical traditions – especially Polish – more accessible through either literary publications (both Polish and translated), scientific or popular science ones."[762]

***

The situation was quite different "as far as the publication of Polish contemporary literature is concerned,"[763] where probably the biggest quantitative increase in comparison to 1950 was observed. Already at the beginning of the article, this fact was appreciated by emphasizing the growing number of publications on domestic and current issues, in which Borejsza's empire was supposed to specialize. These tasks were accompanied by "the concern of the publishing house to use the widest possible range of forms to influence the masses of readers"[764] and introduce "literary genres that were previously underrepresented not only among 'Czytelnik's' publications, but also across the whole publishing establishment."[765] For this reason, the publisher's catalog was dominated by "attractive, popular forms, (most of all, diverse) kinds of literature that could easily reach the audience, such as prose, poetry, drama, satire, as well as a range of genres often bordering on fiction: reportage, memoir, etc."[766]

On the periphery of the main considerations, attention should be drawn to the above-proposed classification of literary kinds and genres. The traditional epic and lyric were replaced by prose and poetry, while a new literary kind – satire – emerged. In the context of deciding the fate of publishing specific titles, the terminological problems seem unimportant, although they could reveal the incompetence of the author of the article. Perhaps, in this case, the censor used the term "kind" not meaning "kind of literature" but simply a certain mode of expression. The fact that he treated satire as one of such forms rather than a lit-

---

[761] A. Soboul, *Rewolucja Francuska*, trans. P. Hertz, Warszawa: "Czytelnik," 1951; see English edition: A. Seboul, *The French Revolution 1787–1799*, trans. A. Forrest, C. Jones, New York: Vintage, 1975.

[762] "Działalność wydawnictwa 'Czytelnik' w 1951 r.," *Biuletyn Informacyjno-Instrukcyjny* no. 5, May 1952, p. 19 (APG, WUKPPiW, file ref. no. 90).

[763] Ibidem.

[764] Ibidem, p. 18.

[765] Ibidem, p. 19.

[766] Ibidem, p. 18; illegible fragment [AWG].

erary genre could be justified by the fact that after classicism, the term "lost its generic sense, encompassing works that represent a variety of lit[erary] kinds and genres."[767] However, further discussion of whether the censor was aware of these distinctions seems irrelevant.

The most space in the report in question was devoted to prose, which, "on account of its communicativeness and possibilities for wide distribution,"[768] was called a fundamental kind of literature. The report welcomed the publication of contemporary domestic prose, despite the still "relatively small number (3–4 per quarter)"[769] of titles published in this genre. Among "a whole range of new Polish novels published by 'Czytelnik'"[770] in 1951, the Bulletin listed Stanisław Wygodzki's *Opowiadanie buchaltera* [The tale of a bookkeeper], Joanna Żwirska's *Światło* [Light], Roman Hussarski's *Nowy mur* [A new wall] and Kuśmierek's volume *Uwaga! Człowiek*, the latter of which was well-known to the censors. None of the titles was discussed separately; rather, the focus was on formulating a general diagnosis of this part of the publishing catalog.

The authors of the report noted that "in comparison with the 'Czytelnik's' activity in previous years, there has been a clear breakthrough in the subject matter of novels, short stories, etc."[771] As a result, the titles started reflecting the effort "of the Polish working class and the Polish working masses to build the foundations of the socialist system."[772] In spite of some formal errors (a schematic presentation of characters and situations) or ideological shortcomings (insufficient emphasis or omission of some fundamental issues, such as the role of the Party or the ZMP[773]) signaled in the report, these publications were rated highly.

---

[767] *Słownik terminów literackich*, ed. J. Sławiński, Revised and Expanded Third Edition, Wrocław: Ossolineum, 1988, p. 457. Prose can be defined either as unbound speech (devoid of fixed rhythmic units in opposition to verse), or as common speech (with mainly cognitive-communicative functions, in contrast to poetic speech), or as "a body of narrative-fiction works (novels, novellas, stories, etc.) as distinct from lyric poetry and dramatic works" (ibidem, pp. 403–404), while poetry is defined either as the opposite of prose, that is, bound speech, works written in verse, or as a synonym for lyric; as a consequence, almost all drama (except for poetic drama) and almost all epic have become the domain of prose (ibidem, p. 371).

[768] "Działalność wydawnictwa 'Czytelnik' w 1951 r.," *Biuletyn Informacyjno-Instruk-cyjny* no. 5, May 1952, p. 18 (APG, WUKPPiW, file ref. no. 90).

[769] Ibidem.

[770] Ibidem.

[771] Ibidem.

[772] Ibidem.

[773] ZMP (Związek Młodzieży Polskiej) – the Union of Polish Youth, which existed from 1948 to 1957 and was modeled on the Soviet Komsomol, was one of many organizations of this type operating in People's Poland.

Contemporary Polish prose was dominated by current issues, but the authors of "Czytelnik" also reached back to the Nazi occupation, describing their own or their protagonists' wartime experiences. The authors of the report limited themselves to noting only two titles dealing with this subject matter: *Pokolenie* by Bohdan Czeszko and *Ostatnie ognie* [Last fires] by Stanisław Zieliński.

***

Translations from Eastern Bloc countries belonged to the standard repertoire of the publishing catalog at the time. Thus, it is not surprising that the report also devotes some attention to them. The authors of the article observed with regret that in 1951, "the publishing house did not develop a broader activity in the field of translations from Soviet literature."[774] However, despite this unsatisfactory situation, it was still possible to get acquainted with the works of the brotherly nation, thanks to reprints of twentieth-century novels, for example, Vera Panova's *Bright Shore,* Ivan Ryaboklyach's *Maksym z kołchozu "Zorza"* [Maxim from the kolkhoz "Aurora"], and Nikolai Virta's *Samotność* [Solitude].[775]

The report also notes the few new translations from Soviet literature appearing in the publisher's catalog. Among the titles published in Poland for the first time, the predominant themes were "related to the transformations taking place in the various Soviet republics, particularly in Asia,"[776] as exemplified by the novels of the Kyrgyzstani writer Tugelbay Sydykbekov entitled *Ludzie naszych dni* [People of our time] and the Kazakh writer Gabit Musrepov entitled *Żołnierz z Kazachstanu* [A soldier from Kazakhstan]. The everyday life and work of the "Soviet man"[777] was described by such authors as Alexander Voloshin in *Kuznetsk Land* and the Ukrainian poet and writer Jurij Yanovskij in his *Opowiadania kijowskie* [Kiev stories].[778]

---

[774] "Działalność wydawnictwa 'Czytelnik' w 1951 r.," *Biuletyn Informacyjno-Instrukcyjny* no. 5, May 1952, p. 23 (APG, WUKPPiW, file ref. no. 90).

[775] *Jasny brzeg* and *Maksym z kołchozu "Zorza"* were first published in Poland in 1950, while *Samotność* in 1949. All three titles were reprinted in 1951. See English edition: V. Panova, *Bright Shore,* trans. B. Isaacs.

[776] "Działalność wydawnictwa 'Czytelnik' w 1951 r.," *Biuletyn Informacyjno-Instrukcyjny* no. 5, May 1952, p. 23 (APG, WUKPPiW, file ref. no. 90).

[777] Ibidem.

[778] Cf. J. Janowski, *Opowiadania kijowskie,* trans. E. Kobylińska-Masiejewska, Warszawa: "Czytelnik," 1950; idem, *Nowe opowiadania kijowskie,* trans. J. Bielicki, K. Marska, Warszawa: "Czytelnik," 1951; for the record, *Opowiadania kijowskie* that was mentioned in the Bulletin was published in 1950, while *Nowe opowiadania kijowskie* was published in 1951, the year of the report.

While Soviet literature was translated relatively infrequently, the works of other people's democracies received more attention from publishers. Particularly noteworthy were the changes in the choice of subject matter: there was a departure from the so-called reckoning with the past, which was "limited exclusively to whistle-blowing criticism – often carried out from bourgeois positions,"[779] to "criticism from the perspective of the oppressed classes with appropriate emphasis on the struggle of the working class and its communist parties."[780] Three titles were cited as examples that fully realized this new perspective, two German and one Bulgarian, respectively: Anna Seghers' *Ocalenie* [Survival] and *List gończy* [Wanted], and Stoyan Daskalov's *Droga* [The road]. Unsuccessful attempts, according to the report's authors, included *Z notatnika lekarza wiejskiego* [From the notebook of a country doctor] by the Romanian writer George Ulieru and *Bunt w klasie* [Revolt in the class] by the Hungarian politician, soldier and writer Pál Ilku. Of the few books that dealt with current problems of the people's democracies, two Hungarian books were mentioned: *Nie ma dymu bez ognia* [There is no smoke without fire] by István Asztalos and *Fabryka budzi się* [The factory awakens] by Irén Egra, as well as *Ludzie spod złotego modrzewia* [People from under the golden larch] by Zhao Shula (who lost his mandate as a model Party writer during the Cultural Revolution in China and died under house arrest).[781]

According to the authors of the report, the situation of translations from the literature of capitalist countries was the worst. A rather severe quantitative decline from 1950 was observed. If titles from behind the Iron Curtain were selected, they were usually written by authors sympathetic to the communist movement who presented the situation of the working masses under capitalism in a negative light. American, French and Italian novels were mentioned as examples, namely: *With the Sun in Our Blood* by Myra Page, *Komuniści* [The communists] by Louis Aragon, and *W ręku wroga* [In the hand of the enemy] by Arturo Colombi. This excerpt, too, is limited to just listing the titles and a few sentences of summary.

***

---

[779] "Działalność wydawnictwa 'Czytelnik' w 1951 r.," *Biuletyn Informacyjno-Instrukcyjny* no. 5, May 1952, p. 23 (APG, WUKPPiW, file ref. no. 90).

[780] Ibidem.

[781] The Cultural Revolution initiated by Mao Zedong in 1966 destroyed the careers of many hitherto respected artists; some were put under house arrest, and thousands died in mass purges aimed at eliminating political opponents and introducing the new ideology, Maoism. See, e.g.: B.S. McDougall, K. Louise, *The Literature of China in the Twentieth Century*, New York: Colombia University Press, 1999.

The report on "Czytelnik's" activities also included a discussion of publications of a socio-political nature, which were published in the form of brochures, reports or more extensive journalistic works. While the former were easy to make and read, the latter were more time-consuming, and due to the specific nature of the material, they were more prone to mistakes. Such longer texts were criticized for not "keeping up with the development of events and the needs of the publishing movement"[782] and this was one of the basic objections formulated by the authors of the report against this type of publication.

Another complaint concerned the small number of titles showing the leading role of the USSR "in the peace camp"[783] – an accusation that requires no explanation. The poor range of titles reporting on the decolonization of Africa was also noted; indeed, the "scant coverage of the struggles of colonial and dependent peoples"[784] might have been surprising in the context of the enormous changes sweeping through Egypt, Tunisia, and Iran, among others. The Bulletin's editors, however, tried to use the subject as propaganda by occasionally publishing minor mentions of colonial countries and their predatory policies, also in *Biblioteczki Biuletynu*.[785]

The authors of the report confirmed that socio-political publications were dominated by topics in the fields of international politics (imperialism, the development of people's democratic countries) and domestic politics (the Six-Year Plan). To prove it, several examples were quoted, listing Polish and foreign (French, English) titles, e.g., *Obrazki węgierskie* [Hungarian pictures] by Ryszard Konarski, *ABC planu sześcioletniego* [The ABCs of the Six-Year Plan] by Janusz Litwin or *Imperializm nad przepaścią* [Imperialism over the precipice] by Henri Claude. One of the staunchest supporters of Stalin in the United Kingdom, Rajani Palme Dutt and his *India Today* and *Britain's Crisis of Empire*[786] were also mentioned. Incidentally, a printing error was found in the article. Or was it deliberate? Instead of *Britain's Crisis of Empire*, the Bulletin provided the title *Britain's Crisis of Imperialism*. In an era of struggle against the imperialism of Western countries, the proposed translation may not have been accidental, but essentially, both translations satisfied the senders of the message.

---

[782] "Działalność wydawnictwa 'Czytelnik' w 1951 r.," *Biuletyn Informacyjno-Instrukcyjny* no. 5, May 1952, p. 25 (APG, WUKPPiW, file ref. no. 90).

[783] Ibidem, p. 26.

[784] Ibidem.

[785] S. Siemiński (GUKPPiW), [the entire issue of the Supplement is devoted to the untitled article], *Biblioteczka Biuletynu Informacyjno-Instrukcyjnego GUKPPiW* no. 18, 1955 (APG, WUKPPiW, file ref. no. 215); "O tzw. 'obiektywizmie,'" *Biuletyn Informacyjno--Szkoleniowy* no. 4, May 1949, fol. 155r–155v (APP, WUKPPiW, file ref. no. 4).

[786] This title was published in 1950, not in 1951, which was the year of the report on "Czytelnik."

***

Concluding the report on the publishing house's activities, the authors of the Bulletin gave a telegraphic summary of popular science publications not covered earlier. On the one hand, they criticized publishing philosophical works without adequate commentary; on the other, they appreciated popular science publications in the field of film, medicine and astronomy, stressing that: "in general, all publications of this type fulfill their task of popularizing the latest research and scientific achievements and, as far as possible, link the issues raised with the practical needs dictated by the implementation of the Six-Year Plan."[787]

***

In general, the publishing activity of "Czytelnik" for 1951 was evaluated very well. The only failings were: not keeping up with current events (especially in socio-political works, which was the Achilles heel of many publications also in the following year), frequent randomness in the selection of presented titles (which suggested that the publishing concept had not been thought through entirely) and a small number of contemporary historical publications. As Kamila Budrowska aptly pointed out, the above-enumerated problems resulted from the restrictions imposed on the publishing house – and, more broadly, on literature – because at that time, the most strictly censored and redacted were contemporary topics (the introduction of a new political and social order), as well as Polish history (especially "Soviet" issues). However, the authors of the Bulletin did not seem to notice this contradiction.[788]

---

[787] "Działalność wydawnictwa 'Czytelnik' w 1951 r.," *Biuletyn Informacyjno-Instrukcyjny* no. 5, May 1952, p. 26 (APG, WUKPPiW, file ref. no. 90).
[788] K. Budrowska, "Wewnętrzne pismo cenzury...," p. 100.

10. LITERARY AND CULTURAL ISSUES IN THE PRESS

The censor who made the omission in Trybuna Ludu stated directly that while reading the article, he must have forgotten that he was a censor.[789]

In the analyzed cryptotexts, both non-periodical and serial publications were discussed. The most interest was taken in socio-political, religious (mainly Catholic) and specialized press, less frequently literary and cultural journals. Censors commented both on the widely available "mass ("Czytelnik"-related) press,"[790] but also the newsletters created by and for the employees of various plants and enterprises, for example, the *Echo Otmętu* newsletter, published by the Silesian Shoe Works in Otmęt.[791] Overall, more than 70 periodicals – mostly domestic, but also foreign – appeared in the Bulletins.[792]

---

[789] "Ulepszenie naszej pracy jest warunkiem sprostania naszym obecnym zadaniom," *Biuletyn Informacyjno-Instrukcyjny* no. 9, September 1952, p. 3 (APG, WUKPPiW, file ref. no. 78).

[790] "O wyższy poziom naszej pracy. O właściwe wykorzystywanie prasy periodycznej w naszej pracy codziennej," *Biuletyn Informacyjno-Instrukcyjny* no. 2, February 1952, p. 31 (APG, WUKPPiW, file ref. no. 99).

[791] "Kilka uwag o pracy WUKPPiW w okresie kampanii wyborczej," *Biuletyn Informacyjno-Instrukcyjny* no. 11, November 1952, p. 6 (APG, WUKPPiW, file ref. no. 72). See also, e.g.: *Biuletyn Głównego Urzędu Kontroli Prasy* no. 4 (APP WUKPPiW, file ref. no. 4, fol. 52r–53r); *Biuletyn Informacyjno-Instrukcyjny* no. 1 (25), January 1954, pp. 15–22 (APG, WUKPPiW, file ref. no. 39).

[792] Domestic: *Nowa Kultura, Twórczość, Życie Literackie, Odrodzenie, Zdroje, Szpilki, Przekrój, Dookoła świata, Przyjaciółka, Przegląd Skórzany, Przegląd Spawalnictwa, Przegląd Budowlany, Przegląd Mechaniczny, Przegląd Sportowy, Hutnik, Walczymy o stal, Technika Lotnicza, Życie Nauki, Rzemieślnik, Przyjaciel Rzemieślnika, Trybuna Ludu, Sztandar Ludu, Wola Ludu, Trybuna Robotnicza, Głos Robotniczy, Życie Robotnicze, Gazeta Robotnicza, Rzeczpospolita, Głos Narodu, Głos Pracy, Jedność Narodowa, Nowe Drogi, Chłopska Droga, Wieś, Rolnik Polski – Gromada, Nowy Rolnik, Ogólnopolski Tygodnik Gospodarczy, Zagadnienia Ekonomiki Rolnej, Leśnik, Zielony Sztandar, Notatnik Propagandysty, Prasa Polska, Słowo Polskie, Kurier Codzienny, Ilustrowany Kurier Polski, Express Wieczorny, Express Ilustrowany, Dziennik Polski, Dziennik Zachodni,*

The Bulletins repeatedly reminded the censors of the need to apply different assessment criteria, depending on which title was inspected. As early as 1945, it was instructed to respect the specific character of newspapers and to "approach the party, peasant and Church press with particular subtlety."[793] The accusations leveled at the various journals also differed; for example, when discussing articles from the specialized press, unjustified admiration for the state of Western industry and science, and underestimation of the achievements of the people's democracies were "stamped out." Many Bulletins presented evidence of such practices by quoting extensive excerpts from newspaper articles.

How was the issue of the literary and, more broadly, cultural press discussed at the censorship office? Usually individual articles were considered, but sometimes entire journals were evaluated, e.g., *Dookoła świata*[794] or cultural supplements to periodicals; in one of the materials, *Nowy Świat* and *Widnokręg*, that is, weekly supplements to, respectively, *Głos Wielkopolski* and *Gazeta Poznańska* were discussed.[795] There were also references to the emergence and closing of magazines, the relationship between various editors, and even editors and columnists, for instance, a handful of remarks about *Zdrój, Odrodzenie* and Jarosław Iwaszkiewicz and Wojciech Bąk as editors of *Życie Literackie*.[796] However, in most cases, the materials discussed a few selected interferences from various papers. For example, in April 1953, an extensive article was published that assessed texts from *Przegląd Kulturalny, Wieś* and *Nowa Kultura*.[797] It analyzed works on

---

Dziennik Łódzki, Dziennik Bałtycki, Życie Warszawy, Gazeta Krakowska, Gazeta Lubelska, Gazeta Tarnowska, Gazeta Pomorska, Kurier Szczeciński, Głos Szczeciński, Głos Koszaliński, Głos Wybrzeża, Głos Wielkopolski, Gazeta Poznańska, Gazeta Białostocka, Nowiny Rzeszowskie, Trybuna Opolska, Żołnierz Wolności, Żołnierz Polski, Żołnierz Ludu, Na straży wolności, Skrzydła Wolności, Naprzód, Za Polskę Ludową; foreign: *Krokodil, Izvestiya Sovetov Narodnykh Deputatov SSSR, Star, New York Herald Tribune*; and denominational ones, which are listed later.

[793] *Biuletyn Instrukcyjny* no. 2, June 1945, p. 3 (APG, WUKPPiW, file ref. no. 210); see also, e.g.: the "problematic" ["Materiały z odprawy"], *passim* ("*Biuletyny Instrukcyjno-Szkoleniowe 1945–1951*" (APP, WUKPPiW, file ref. no. 4)).

[794] L. Kimlowski, "Kilka uwag o tygodniku *Dookoła świata* (January–June 1954)," *Biuletyn Informacyjno-Instrukcyjny* no. 9 (33), September 1954, pp. 25–32 (APG, WUKPPiW, file ref. no. 56).

[795] Z. Beryt (WUKPPiW Poznań), "Uwagi o dodatkach kulturalnych poznańskiej prasy codziennej za I kwartał 1953 r.," *Biuletyn Informacyjno-Instrukcyjny* no. 4 (16), April 1953, pp. 43–49 (APG, WUKPPiW, file ref. no. 16).

[796] ["Materiały z odprawy"], fol. 25r–26r ("*Biuletyny Instrukcyjno-Szkoleniowe 1945–1951*" (APP, WUKPPiW, file ref. no. 4)).

[797] "Z doświadczeń prewencyjnej kontroli niektórych pism literackich," *Biuletyn Informacyjno-Instrukcyjny* no. 4 (16), April 1953, pp. 18–25 (APG, WUKPPiW, file ref. no. 16).

rural themes, as well as several reportages and short stories, including by Józef Kuśmierek, who had already been examined in the Bulletin.

In January 1954, the afore-cited weekly *Szpilki* appeared again in the censorship materials, this time in the surprising company of *Elektronowiec* – a newsletter of the Electron Lamp Manufacturing Plant. One error was pointed out in the evaluation of this newsletter, namely, the fact that it reprinted a satire from *Szpilki*.[798] Another interference related to the weekly included comments on an article in the series *7 Dni* by the previously mentioned Jan Szeląg. While the text did appear in *Szpilki* in January 1952, it was not in the first but in the sixteenth issue (as the Bulletin stated). Since it was written on the occasion of Bolesław Bierut's 60th birthday, the date of April 16, 1952, was given in parentheses.

A year later, hiding under the pseudonym "Jan Szeląg," Zbigniew Mitzner again became the editor-in-chief of the weekly, a post he held until 1955. After all, it was he, together with Eryk Lipiński and Andrzej Nowicki, who had founded the magazine in 1935. At that time, before the war, Szeląg had been subjected to a number of press lawsuits. For his views, he came close to sharing the fate of the aforementioned Leon Pasternak – but ultimately, he was not sent to Bereza Prison. One more detail, this time from the February 1955 Bulletin, is noteworthy. On January 22, 1955, Szeląg performed at the celebrations of the tenth anniversary of the GUKPPiW – the work prepared for the occasion can be read in the February issue of the monthly.[799] However, returning to 1952, it was not Szeląg himself, but a column written by him that found its way to "Mysia Street."

The way in which the interference in question is presented does not seem to be the most optimal, as only the first part of the text – before the redactions – is included; the censors had no opportunity to confront it with the edited version. The version submitted for evaluation to the Office for the Control is as follows:

> In our beautiful and great literature, there are no words to express our feelings today. No stanza from the past can help us say or write what we think, what we feel. [...]
> These were tragic times for those who did not use their love of the Fatherland as a cloak for personal and class egoism. [...]
> The memories of those who have fallen comprised the national history, the history of defeats, falls and failures. Today we speak of the one who has won, who

---

[798] "Próba oceny," *Biuletyn Informacyjno-Instrukcyjny* no. 1 (25), January 1954, p. 20 (APG, WUKPPiW, file ref. no. 39).

[799] Z. Mitzner (J. Szeląg), "Świtezianka" (material in "Dział Satyry"), *Biuletyn Informacyjno-Instrukcyjny* no. 2 (38), February 1955, pp. 51–53 (APG, WUKPPiW, file ref. no. 108).

triumphed by leading the working class and the nation. <u>Therefore, everything that was written about those people does not fit the present moment.</u> [...] Bolesław Bierut is the <u>happy</u> leader of the nation[800] (original emphasis).

The emphasis in the quotation was provided by the Office's functionaries; in censorship practice, it usually marked fragments that should be modified.[801] In this case, the underlined fragments had to be removed because, according to the evaluators, Szeląg used them to wrongly separate "the struggle of comrade Bierut and the revolutionary traditions of the Polish working class from the masses of progressive national traditions."[802] A comparison of the version submitted to the censorship office with the version of the article that appeared in *Szpilki* suggests that indeed, the underscored passages were removed, as a result of which "the happy leader of the nation" was stripped of the problematic modifier.

Another example of interference with press material concerning literature was a review of Fedor Panfierov's four-volume novel cycle *Bruski*, which was published in *Nowa Kultura* in 1952.[803] The Soviet writer, who supported the communist regime not only with his official works but also with frequent denunciations of his fellow writers,[804] had been translated into Polish even before the war. It was then that the translations of the first volumes of the novel, on which Panfierov worked for "over ten years (1926–1937)" were published.[805] The four volumes of the cycle referred to in the 1952 press review were published in 1950, thus, "*Bruski* waited long and patiently for critical attention."[806]

Once again, the presentation of the material left a lot to be desired; neither the author nor the title of that extensive review was given (it was easy to establish, however, that it was Waldemar Kiwilszo who penned "Nad epopeją socjalizmu").

---

[800] "O dobrych i złych przykładach pracy kontroli prewencyjnej w terenie," *Biuletyn Informacyjno-Instrukcyjny* no. 6, June 1952, p. 1 (APG, WUKPPiW, file ref. no. 87). Cf. J. Szeląg, "7 *dni* (19 kwietnia 1952 roku)", *Szpilki* April 20, 1952, no. 16, p. 2.

[801] In the Bulletins, we can find some underlining that is of a different nature. Authors use this kind of underlining to emphasize a passage that is important to their argument – in such cases, a footnote included the information "our emphasis"; "Szkolenie ideologiczne – podstawa naszej pracy," *Biuletyn Informacyjno-Instrukcyjny* no. 6, June 1952, pp. 24, 26 (APG, WUKPPiW, file ref. no. 87).

[802] "O dobrych i złych przykładach pracy kontroli prewencyjnej w terenie," *Biuletyn Informacyjno-Instrukcyjny* no. 6, June 1952, p. 1 (APG, WUKPPiW, file ref. no. 87).

[803] W. Kiwilszo, "Nad epopeją socjalizmu," *Nowa Kultura* March 23, 1952, no. 12, pp. 3–4, 11.

[804] J. Prokop, "Panfierow," *Arcana* 1996, no. 5, pp. 126–137.

[805] W. Kiwilszo, "Nad epopeją socjalizmu...," p. 3. See: F. Panfierow, *Bruski*, part 1, trans. K. Maliszewski, Warszawa: Wydawnictwo "Znicz," 1934; part 2: *Komuna nędzarzy*: ibidem 1935; vol. 1–4: trans. J. Brzęczkowski, Warszawa: "Książka i Wiedza," 1950.

[806] W. Kiwilszo, "Nad epopeją socjalizmu...," p. 3.

But given the training nature of the Bulletins, what is more important is the fact that only a fragment of the text before modifications was quoted, thus, the opportunity to compare it with the published version was not afforded. The comparison of the "problematic fragment" with the version that appeared in *Nowa Kultura* is below.

The version before the interference:

> Ale w życiu wsi wciąż jeszcze rolę pierwszorzędną grał drobny wytwórca, w którego osobistym, klasowym interesie leżało hamowanie postępu rewolucji, opór przed jej rozporządzeniami.[807]

> [But in village life, a primary role was still played by the small manufacturer, whose personal, class interest was to impede the progress of the revolution, to resist its decrees.]

The version after the interference:

> Ale w życiu wsi wciąż jeszcze rolę pierwszorzędną grał kułak, w którego osobistym, klasowym interesie leżała walka z postępem rewolucji, opór przed jej rozporządzeniami.[808]

> [But in village life, a primary role was still played by the kulak, whose personal, class interest was to fight the progress of the revolution, to resist its decrees.]

Although the superiors considered the interference of their colleagues to be correct, the latter "were unable to justify their position with appropriate arguments,"[809] which was obviously supposed to be the result of their inadequate ideological training. Therefore, the editors tried to provide a fairly comprehensive (though not easy) explanation of the error. By referring to, for instance, the history of the All-Union Communist Party (Bolsheviks) and the "triune formula" of Lenin (which divided the rural population into the poor, the middle-sized farmers and the kulaks),[810] they recapitulated that it was fundamentally wrong to "present the small manufacturer, that is, a working peasant, as an enemy of the revolution."[811]

---

[807] "Szkolenie ideologiczne – podstawa naszej pracy," *Biuletyn Informacyjno-Instrukcyjny* no. 6, June 1952, p. 25 (APG, WUKPPiW, file ref. no. 87).

[808] W. Kiwilszo, "Nad epopeją socjalizmu…," p. 3. In that same review, Kiwilszo also makes a reference to another novel discussed in the Bulletin: *Ludzie zza rzeki* by Lesław Bartelski (p. 3).

[809] "Szkolenie ideologiczne – podstawa naszej pracy," *Biuletyn Informacyjno-Instrukcyjny* no. 6, June 1952, p. 26 (APG, WUKPPiW, file ref. no. 87).

[810] Ibidem.

[811] Ibidem.

Fig. 24. A fragment of a review of Fedor Panfierov's novel *Bruski,* modified as a result of censorial interference (W. Kiwilszo, "Nad epopeją socjalizmu," *Nowa Kultura* 1952, no. 12, p. 3); I have marked the place that was interfered with in red; below is an article on the novel by another "Bulletin" writer, Vilis Lācis.

Another theme of the Bulletins was the fight against cosmopolitanism in literature and art, usually limited to general remarks of little value. One of the more lengthy statements on the subject appeared in August 1952, in material concerning technical-scientific periodicals. It featured a quote from Bolesław Bierut that was "succinct, but so fraught and profound,"[812] and as such, was provided with no commentary:

> In the field of culture, cosmopolitanism is expressed in the underestimation of national cultural achievements, in the renunciation of our own progressive traditions, in the reverence for declining capitalist culture and all of its degenerations, in an often undignified kneeling before American art, literature, and science, regardless of their essential values. In America, cosmopolitanism is super-nationalism; in Marshall countries, it takes the form of submissiveness and national treason. Here, the struggle against cosmopolitanism, national defeatism and national nihilism is combined with the struggle against nationalism and chauvinism, which until now have been the main form of anti-proletarian ideology.[813]

The final example of evaluating press material comes from November 1952. It was a summary of the discussion on the article entitled "Od Statutu Wiślickiego do Konstytucji Polskiej Rzeczpospolitej Ludowej," published in the supplement to *Dziennik Zachodni*.[814] The material reflected on an exhibition that was organized in the Bytom branch of the Silesian Library in Katowice on the occasion of Education, Book and Press Days. The exposition presented a review of Polish literature concerning political issues in Poland, starting with the Statute of Wiślica and ending with the Constitution of the Polish People's Republic *Anno Domini* 1952.

Since neither the "discussants nor the article's censor had seen the exhibition itself,"[815] the critical voices referred directly to the text (which, by the way, was attached to the Bulletin). One has to admit that this was quite a surprising practice. Moreover, it also astonished the censors, who signaled that "it is difficult to talk about the article if one is not familiar with the exhibition."[816] However, according

---

[812] "O niektórych przejawach kosmopolityzmu w czasopismach techniczno-naukowych," *Biuletyn Informacyjno-Instrukcyjny* no. 8, August 1952, p. 33 (APG, WUKPPiW, file ref. no. 81).

[813] Ibidem.

[814] "Podsumowanie dyskusji," *Biuletyn Informacyjno-Instrukcyjny* no. 11, November 1952, p. 24–36 (APG, WUKPPiW, file ref. no. 72). F. Szymiczek, "Od Statutu Wiślickiego do Konstytucji Polskiej Rzeczypospolitej Ludowej," *Dziennik Zachodni* May 11, 1952 (*Świat i Życie* supplement no. 19).

[815] "Podsumowanie dyskusji," *Biuletyn Informacyjno-Instrukcyjny* no. 11, November 1952, p. 24 (APG, WUKPPiW, file ref. no. 72).

[816] Ibidem.

to their superiors, "the evaluation, and therefore the critique of the exhibition as a whole and its shortcomings, should be the aim of the author of the article,"[817] which is why they considered similar suggestions groundless. Thus, only the press material was evaluated, which was basically criticized for its presentation of the history of the Polish nobility, which was inconsistent with the "historical truth." According to the functionaries, the inequality of the system, in which the oppression of the underprivileged, especially the peasantry, prevailed and successive statutes extended the rights and real power of the nobility, was not emphasized enough. The material discusses in detail many other allegations concerning Polish political history, pointing out both the omissions and incompetence of the censors, as well as praising interferences that were deemed "correct."

[817] Ibidem.

II. Non-fiction

1. SCIENTIFIC AND POPULAR SCIENCE PUBLICATIONS

> *How can you specialize when you read "Petroleum"*
> *for two hours, "Cement, Lime, and Gypsum"*
> *for another two, and, for example, Dembowski's*
> *Philosophical Views for the remainder?*[818]

The proper assessment of non-fiction, including scientific and popular science works, was discussed in the Bulletins several times. Although fiction was very often discussed during the work briefings, and belles-lettres dominated in the evaluations of the Non-Periodical Publications Department, the censors were cautioned against a dismissive attitude towards other types of writing:

> [...] it is wrong to underestimate the necessity of a good evaluation also in regards to non-fiction publications; an attitude which is not uncommon in our work. Many a censor who believes that a novel merits a good, thorough review, when preparing, let's say, a work on livestock management dismisses it with a general statement, such as: "The title indicative of the content. No objections." Such underestimation of the importance of non-fiction publications, which undeniably constitute the bulk of censored materials, is not only unjust but fundamentally harmful.[819]

In the case of certain scientific and popular science titles, a different critical apparatus was applied than when analyzing fiction; sometimes experts on the subject were called upon to assist in the evaluation of the text. However, for the most part, the assessment of fiction and science books followed a single pattern, which the "decision-makers" at the Office frequently bemoaned. Most often, the periodicals discussed titles in the fields of history and law. Social sciences were also represented by works on sociology and socio-economic geography. Apart

---

[818] K. Kudroń (WUKPPiW Kraków), "Czy specjalizacja to tylko podział na referaty" (in the series *Kierownicy referatów piszą…*), *Biuletyn Informacyjno-Instrukcyjny* no. 12 (48), December 1955, p. 53 (APG, WUKPPiW, file ref. no. 117).

[819] "Recenzja z pozycji literackiej, cz. I" (in the series *O wyższy poziom pracy nad książką*), *Biuletyn Informacyjno-Instrukcyjny* no. 8, August 1952, pp. 19–20 (APG, WUKPPiW, file ref. no. 81).

from history, publications in the humanities – texts on philosophy, culture and religion or, most interesting in the context of present deliberations, Polish and world literature – appeared relatively rarely. In addition, there were some book proposals from the engineering and technology sciences.

Here is a small selection of examples.[820]

1.1. Scientific and Popular Science Publications in the Humanities

1.1.1. Publications in the Field of Literature (and Culture)

Comrades, get yourselves spelling dictionaries;
they will come in handy.[821]

In the cryptotexts analyzed, issues of evaluating scholarly works on literature and, more broadly, culture were raised several times. Some of the titles served as clear exemplars of censorial carelessness. This was the case when a manuscript entitled *Odbudowa i rozwój życia kulturalnego w Polsce 1944–1948* [Reconstruction and development of cultural life in Poland 1944–1948] was submitted for evaluation. The editors of the Bulletin did not name its author, but it was not difficult to establish that the text had been edited and compiled by Zofia Jaremko-Żytyńska, and that the book had been published in 1948.[822] The periodical quoted excerpts from two reviews: the censor from Małopolska did not catch the work's errors and shortcomings, which his colleague from the capital's branch found. The main accusations were a lack of proper politicization of the content and careless editing, thus, the decision was inexorable: "to be rejected in its entirety."[823] However, after consultations with the publisher, that

---

[820] Below is a list of specific titles according to the current classification of fields and disciplines of science, but my classification proposal does not claim to be definitive. See "Rozporządzenie Ministra Nauki i Szkolnictwa Wyższego z dnia 20 września 2018 r. w sprawie dziedzin nauki i dyscyplin naukowych oraz dyscyplin artystycznych" (*Journal of Laws* 2018, item 1818, pp. 1–2, http://isap.sejm.gov.pl/isap.nsf/DocDetails. xsp?id=WDU20180001818 (accessed July 27, 2021)).

[821] "Na marginesie sprawozdań kwartalnych WUKPPiW," *Biuletyn Informacyjno-Instrukcyjny* no. 7/8 (31/32), July/August 1954, p. 11 (APG, WUKPPiW, file ref. no. 65).

[822] Z. Jaremko-Żytyńska, *Odbudowa i rozwój życia kulturalnego w Polsce 1944–1948,* Warszawa: Ministerstwo Kultury i Sztuki. Biuro Współpracy z Zagranicą, 1948.

[823] "Dwie recenzje," *Biuletyn Informacyjno-Szkoleniowy* no. 4, May 1949, fol. 157r (APP, WUKPPiW, file ref. no. 4).

is, the Ministry of Culture and Art, and probably indirectly with the author, the manuscript was corrected and published.

As previously mentioned, in November 1952, the editing of *Korespondencja Jana Śniadeckiego*[824] was criticized, whereas in the February 1953 Bulletin, an excerpt from a textbook on the history of Polish literature for the ninth grade was reviewed (the case was also revisited in March of that year).[825] However, the material did not deal with literary issues, but with the revolt of the masses in Mazovia, which took place in the 11th century under the leadership of Masław. The textbook lauded the merits of the prince, which was not met with the approval of the censors. The uprising – known in historiography as "Miecław's rebellion" – was interpreted in isolation from the figure of the leader, whose actions were assessed by the censors as decentralistic and separatist, aiming at tearing Mazovia away from the rest of the country.

In April 1954, Stanisław Kolbuszewski's work entitled *Autograf wiersza Słowackiego* Pośród niesnasków[826] [The autograph of Słowacki's poem *Pośród niesnasków*] received a small mention, while in June of that year, Jadwiga Kupraszwili, the head of the Non-Periodical Publications Division of the National Department, briefly presented several new publications. These included Ryszard Matuszewski's *Literatura międzywojenna* [Interwar literature], which was highly praised by the censor, and *Szkice o literaturze współczesnej* [Sketches on contemporary literature], edited by Matuszewski. The former title had already been regularly discussed at departmental briefings of the GUKPPiW, and Kupraszwili encouraged her colleagues from field branches (especially those from the Non-Periodicals) to read both.[827]

***

---

[824] See the chapter "Books Discussed as Part of the Series *For a Higher Level of Work on the Book*: (Not Only) Nałkowska, Czeszko, Lācis, Meisner, and Jackiewicz."

[825] Cf. W. P., "Kilka uwag o niektórych ingerencjach i przeoczeniach w publikacjach z dziedziny historii Polski (artykuł dyskusyjny)," *Biuletyn Informacyjno-Instrukcyjny* no. 2 (14), February 1953, pp. 35–36 (APG, WUKPPiW, file ref. no. 18); "Artykuł wstępny," *Biuletyn Informacyjno-Instrukcyjny* no. 3 (15), March 1953, p. 10 (APG, WUKPPiW, file ref. no. 17).

[826] "Przegląd ingerencji nr 3/54 Departamentu Publikacyj Nieperiodycznych GUKPPiW poświęcony omówieniu kilku różnorodnych zagadnień," *Biuletyn Informacyjno-Instrukcyjny* no. 4 (28), April 1954, pp. 35–36 (APG, WUKPPiW, file ref. no. 48).

[827] J. Kupraszwili (Naczelnik Wydziału Krajowego Departamentu Publikacji Nieperiodycznych), "Nowości wydawnicze," *Biuletyn Informacyjno-Instrukcyjny* no. 6 (30), June 1954, p. 42 (APG, WUKPPiW, file ref. no. 52). See: R. Matuszewski, *Literatura międzywojenna*, Warszawa: "Wiedza Powszechna", 1953; *Szkice o literaturze współczesnej. Praca zbiorowa*, ed. R. Matuszewski, Warszawa: "Czytelnik," 1954.

Publications in the Field of Philosophy

> *But under no circumstances can we put ourselves in the position of*
> *seeing the speck in the other's eye and not seeing the beam in our own.*
> *Once we remove the beam, the speck will be easier to remove.*[828]

Of the more substantial studies on philosophy, the one devoted to the medieval thinker, theologian and cardinal, Nicholas of Cusa, is noteworthy; beyond that, articles or even shorter texts on philosophical publications were scarce in the Bulletins.[829] A few remarks on this subject can be found in the material investigating the activities of the "Czytelnik" publishing house. The functionaries appreciated Howard Selsam's textbook *Co to jest filozofia* [What is philosophy?], with a foreword by Leszek Kołakowski; unfortunately, the title was only mentioned, and with a mistake, since the book was actually called *Problemy filozofii* [Problems of philosophy] (perhaps the censors were guided by the original title, *What is Philosophy? A Marxist Introduction*).[830]

Most titles on Marxist philosophy could not count on even such modest approval as Selsam's book. The main criticism often leveled against the translations was the lack of proper editing, which supposedly led to "a number of serious distortions,"[831] an example being *Marksizm współczesny i jego krytycy* [Modern Marxism and its critics] by the German philosopher Fred Oelssner. Once again, it turned out that the paratexts accompanying the main text played no small part in the assessment of the work.

***

Publications in the Field of History

> *Intensive studies are underway in Poland to refute the falsifications*
> *and simplifications of bourgeois historiosophy and to produce a new*
> *Marxist account of the history of our country.*[832]

---

[828] "O wyższy poziom pracy na odcinku widowisk," *Biuletyn Informacyjno-Instrukcyjny* no. 3 (15), March 1953, p. 38 (APG, WUKPPiW, file ref. no. 17).

[829] Wydział Instruktażu Departamentu Publikacji Nieperiodycznych, "Na temat pewnej recenzji," *Biuletyn Informacyjno-Instrukcyjny* no. 5 (41), May 1955, pp. 25–30 (APG, WUKPPiW, file ref. no. 131). See also: "Kilka uwag o pracy nad wstępem, przypisami i posłowiem," *Biuletyn Informacyjno-Instrukcyjny* no. 9 (21), September 1953, pp. 542–549 (AAN, GUKPPiW, file ref. no. 22).

[830] "Działalność wydawnictwa 'Czytelnik' w 1951 r.," *Biuletyn Informacyjno-Instrukcyjny* no. 5, May 1952, p. 26 (APG, WUKPPiW, file ref. no. 90).

[831] Ibidem.

[832] W. P., "Kilka uwag o niektórych ingerencjach i przeoczeniach w publikacjach z dziedziny historii Polski (artykuł dyskusyjny)," *Biuletyn Informacyjno-Instrukcyjny* no. 2 (14), February 1953, p. 33 (APG, WUKPPiW, file ref. no. 18). Cf. J. Wojdon, *Propaganda*

The Main Office played an invaluable role in shaping the only correct vision of history. The Bulletins published a great deal of material discussing the presentation of these topics in the press; far less space was devoted to the realization of the issues in textbooks and other non-serial publications, although a handful of examples can be given. The functionaries were interested in titles devoted to important events (often requiring a "new" interpretation adjusted to contemporary times) and problems from the history of the country (partitions, uprisings, the Borderlands, etc.),[833] the history of Silesia and other regions of Poland, as well as world history.[834] Due to the freshness of the war trauma, considerable space was devoted to publications on the subject of the Second World War.[835]

In February and March 1953, a chapter and a letter on interferences and omissions in publications on Polish history were published.[836] It examined the articles printed in *Wiedza i Życie* that discussed the beginnings of Polish statehood. A few words were also devoted to historical maps by Jan Natanson-Leski, a geographer and historian, and author of numerous school atlases and historical maps. According to the censors, the author represented revisionist tendencies, "classifying – contrary to historical truth – the lands in the vicinity of present-day Lviv as ethnically Polish territory."[837]

In the same Bulletin, the censors' attention was also drawn to an article by a renowned Church historian, Professor Tadeusz Silnicki, in which the author argued about the salutary influence of the baptism of Poland on the culture and progress

---

polityczna w podręcznikach dla szkół podstawowych Polski Ludowej (1944–1989), Toruń: Wydawnictwo Adama Marszałek, 2001.

[833] Of the numerous titles, see, e.g.: S. Kieniewicz, *Warszawa w powstaniu styczniowym*, Warszawa: "Wiedza Powszechna," 1954 (Bulletin no. 4 (28) from 1954, pp. 37–38).

[834] Of the numerous titles, see, e.g.: Z. Wróblewski, *Droga narodów radzieckich do komunizmu*, Warszawa: Iskry, 1954 (Bulletin no. 4 (28) from 1954, p. 33).

[835] Of the numerous titles, see, e.g.: T. Cyprian, J. Sawicki, *Walka z prasową propagandą wojenną*, Warszawa: Fundusz Wydawniczy Ligii do Walki z Rasizmem, 1949 and J. Sawicki, *"Ludobójstwo" – od pojęcia do konwencji 1933–1948*, Kraków: Księgarnia Wydawnicza L.J. Jaroszewski, 1949 (Bulletin no. 4 from 1949, fol. 154r–155v).

[836] W. P., "Kilka uwag o niektórych ingerencjach i przeoczeniach w publikacjach z dziedziny historii Polski (artykuł dyskusyjny)," *Biuletyn Informacyjno-Instrukcyjny* no. 2 (14), February 1953, pp. 33–37 (APG, WUKPPiW, file ref. no. 18); B. P. (Wrocław), "Szkolenie zawodowe rękojmią wyników pracy cenzorskiej (na marginesie uwag nad pracą w Dziale Publikacyj Nieperiodycznych)," *Biuletyn Informacyjno-Instrukcyjny* no. 3 (15), March 1953, pp. 65–68 (APG, WUKPPiW, file ref. no. 17).

[837] W. P., "Kilka uwag o niektórych ingerencjach i przeoczeniach w publikacjach z dziedziny historii Polski (artykuł dyskusyjny)," *Biuletyn Informacyjno-Instrukcyjny* no. 2 (14), February 1953, p. 35 (APG, WUKPPiW, file ref. no. 18). On the censorship of maps in the PRL, see, e.g.: B. Konopska, "Cenzura w kartografii okresu PRL na przykładzie map do użytku ogólnego," *Polski Przegląd Kartograficzny* 2007, vol. 39, no. 1, pp. 44–57.

of the country. Naturally, such an interpretation was out of the question.[838] Church history was also examined in other years, evoking, for example, *Mroki średniowiecza* [The darkness of the Middle Ages] by Józef Putek, published in 1935 and reprinted several times in People's Poland. His interpretation of the role of the Church in the state was obviously received more favorably than that of Silnicki.[839]

***

1.2. Scientific Publications in the Social Sciences

Titles representing the social sciences appeared in the Bulletins quite frequently, particularly when it came to issues of civil, criminal or canon law.[840] However, the Bulletins also contained materials on social and economic geography, an example of which was the book entitled *Norwegia, Szwecja, Finlandia i Dania* [Norway, Sweden, Finland and Denmark], reprimanded by the censors for excessive admiration of the Scandinavian lifestyle. The book's author was Maria Czekańska, an outstanding geographer and professor at Adam Mickiewicz University in Poznań, whose academic interests included not only Scandinavia, but also the Polish West Lands.[841]

***

1.3. Scientific and Popular Science Publications in Engineering and Technology

Every name of a Western scientist or a brand of Western machinery gives the censor anxiety.[842]

---

[838] W. P., "Kilka uwag o niektórych ingerencjach i przeoczeniach w publikacjach z dziedziny historii Polski (artykuł dyskusyjny)," *Biuletyn Informacyjno-Instrukcyjny* no. 2 (14), February 1953, p. 36 (APG, WUKPPiW, file ref. no. 18). T. Silnicki, "Millenium," *Życie i Myśl* 1952, no. 7/9, pp. 217–241.

[839] "Radio," *Biuletyn Informacyjno-Szkoleniowy* no. 2, November 30, 1948, fol. 91r (APP, WUKPPiW, file ref. no. 4). I write more on this subject in the article "Archiwalia 'pionierskiego' okresu powojennej cenzury…"

[840] Of the numerous titles, see, e.g.: J. Trzcieniecki, *Prawo pracy (według stanu prawnego z grudnia 1947 r.)*, Second Supplemented Edition, Warszawa: Ministerstwo Przemysłu i Handlu, 1948 (Bulletin no. 4 from 1949, fol. 154v).

[841] "O tzw. 'obiektywizmie,'" *Biuletyn Informacyjno-Szkoleniowy* no. 4, May 1949, fol. 156r–156v (APP, WUKPPiW, file ref. no. 4).

[842] "O wyższy poziom pracy nad książką (cd.)" (in the series *O wyższy poziom pracy nad książką*), *Biuletyn Informacyjno-Instrukcyjny* no. 11, November 1952, pp. 40–41 (APG, WUKPPiW, file ref. no. 72).

Scientific publications from engineering disciplines did not escape the attention of the censors and editors of the Bulletin. The censor's strategies used when evaluating these kind of texts, well known in the literature on the subject, were also present in the analyzed cryptotexts: the censors did not allow for excessive appreciation of Western achievements and made sure to present the state of science and industry in the countries of the people's democracy as favorably as possible. They were very careful about the works cited; it was acceptable to refer to Western scientists, but "our" scientists from the Eastern Bloc had to be given priority.[843] The matter of attributing inventions and discoveries was approached similarly. If there were any ambiguities, they had to be resolved in favor of socialist science. This was the case with the invention of Tesla/Marconi/Popov: in the literature of the Eastern Bloc, it was Popov who was the undisputed inventor of the radio.[844]

The Bulletins confirm the "validity" of the above-mentioned assessment strategies, since one of the most frequent accusations leveled against engineering and technology publications was fawning over the industry and scientific achievements of capitalist countries while underestimating native or Soviet solutions. These accusations appeared, among others, in relation to the review of Frank Twyman's textbook *Metal Spectroscopy*, which was published in *Hutnik* magazine in the segment *Wśród książek*.[845] The authors of the Bulletin considered the publication of this material an oversight because of the excessive admiration for the English textbook and the almost complete omission of Soviet instruments. Furthermore, the editors of the Bulletin drew attention to the fact that the aforementioned review was placed (perhaps not accidentally) next to another evaluation, this time of a Soviet book, which was written in a more restrained manner.

It is worth noting that the charge of excessive "admiration" for Twyman's textbook was probably unfounded. The review mentioned in the Bulletin is indeed positive, but the book was highly respected in the scientific community, and the first edition from 1941 became the primary textbook in the field. Moreover, this book was not the only work of the respected optician, who was both the author of scientific publications as well as designs for various optical instruments, such as the spectroscope.[846]

---

843 Ibidem, p. 41.

844 Ibidem.

845 "O niektórych przejawach kosmopolityzmu w czasopismach techniczno-naukowych," *Biuletyn Informacyjno-Instrukcyjny* no. 8, August 1952, pp. 36–37 (APG, WUKPPiW, file ref. no. 81); F. Twyman, *Metal Spectroscopy*, London: Charles Griffin & Company Limited, 1951; W. Klimecki "[Review: F. Twyman, *Metal Spectroscopy...*]" (in the series *Wśród Książek*), *Hutnik* 1952, no. 3, pp. 113–114. See also: "Z zagadnień tajemnicy państwowej," *Biuletyn Informacyjno-Instrukcyjny* no. 2 (14), February 1953, pp. 10–15 (APG, WUKPPiW, file ref. no. 18).

846 A.C. Menzies, *Frank Twyman 1876–1959*, "Royal Society Publishing," pp. 268–279, https://royalsocietypublishing.org/doi/pdf/10.1098/rsbm.1960.0020 (accessed March 27, 2021).

Bulletin materials confirm that when discussing issues on the borderline of science and technology, mistakes occurred quite often. Sometimes there was particular overzealousness on the part of publishers and censors; such was the case when the names of Volta, Galvani, and Hertz were deleted from a textbook on electromagnetics.[847] The superiors frequently rebuked this kind of censorial eagerness, since it made the Office, and sometimes the publisher, look ridiculous.

The next analyzed example is one of the more extensive Bulletin materials on science and engineering. In 1950, it discussed two censorship reviews of the last volume of *Urbanistyka* by the aforementioned renowned architect Tadeusz Tołwiński, who spoke with a great reserve about the post-war reconstruction plans of the Republic of Poland.[848] The fate of the professor's final work is quite dramatic. The volume in question was written during the occupation. Unfortunately, "this manuscript and the original illustrations were burned when Warsaw was being destroyed after the Warsaw Uprising."[849] From a conversation with Dr. Teresa Kotaszewicz, the author of the monograph on Tołwiński, I know that part of the manuscript was found in a dumpster and became – in a sense – the core around which the architect rebuilt his work.[850]

Regrettably, far from the socialist realist urban planning standards, the book was blocked by censorship for a dozen years. It was not published until 1963 as the third volume of *Urbanistyka* under the title *Zieleń w urbanistyce* [Greenery in urban planning]. The sentence quoted below comes from the preface to this edition; a preface that does not reveal the actual reasons why the publication was withheld: "The third volume of *Urbanistyka*, discussing the issues of greenery composition in urban planning, is being published more than twelve years after the death of the author, the honorary doctorate from the Warsaw University of Technology, Professor Tadeusz Tołwiński."[851]

---

[847] "O wyższy poziom pracy nad książką (cd.)" (in the series *O wyższy poziom pracy nad książką*), *Biuletyn Informacyjno-Instrukcyjny* no. 11, November 1952, p. 41 (APG, WUKPPiW, file ref. no. 72).

[848] "Walka klas," *Biuletyn Szkoleniowy* no. 1, March (May) 1950, pp. 41–46 (APG, WUKPPiW, file ref. no. 328).

[849] K. Wejchert, "Przedmowa," [in:] T. Tołwiński, *Urbanistyka* vol. 3: *Zieleń w urbanistyce*, Warszawa: PWN, 1963, p. 7.

[850] I would like to thank Dr. Teresa Kotaszewicz for the valuable information and goodwill shown to me during my work on this chapter. I conducted interviews with the author in September 2018.

[851] K. Wejchert, "Przedmowa…," p. 5.

2. PERIODIC REPORTS ON THE BOOK MARKET

We demand from the written word under inspection
accountability and communist integrity – purity
and flawlessness.[852]

As previously noted, the Bulletins presented a number of different types of reports on the publishing market. Most of them discussed non-fiction publications. This was the case in 1952, when the first issue presented a report on the activities of publishing houses from January 1 to October 31, 1951, while the June issue included a quarterly report for the period between January 1 and March 31, 1952, prepared by the Non-Periodical Publications Department of the GUKP in Warsaw.

The censors noticed that most of the socio-political publications were translations of Soviet titles, however, they formulated charges mainly against the original Polish publications, which – with few exceptions – were considered to have an exceptionally low standard and unattractive form.[853] This applied to "all publications, including the ones by "Książka i Wiedza," but especially the publications of the CRZZ [Central Trade Union Council – AWG], whose range of topics is poor and level is extremely low."[854]

According to both reports, the titles on international affairs were dominated by materials describing the achievements of the USSR, especially in industry and economy. However, in the June material, there were complaints about the insufficient number of titles analyzing the transformations that were taking place in the Soviet countryside. The authors of the compilation had expected (propagandistically tailored) texts about the disappearance of the urban-rural divide and the constant rise in living standards that resulted from Stalin's policy of systematic price reductions. The news about the increase in the number of publications describing the morality of Soviet people would have been welcome, as well.[855]

---

[852] J. Raczyński, J. Raczkowski (WUKPPiW Poznań), "W dyskusji nad uwagami krytycznymi tow. Bielińskiego," *Biuletyn Informacyjno-Instrukcyjny* no. 4 (16), April 1953, p. 55 (APG, WUKPPiW, file ref. no. 16).

[853] "Publikacje społeczno-polityczne," *Biuletyn Informacyjno-Instrukcyjny* no. 6, June 1952, p. 31 (APG, WUKPPiW, file ref. no. 87).

[854] Ibidem.

[855] Ibidem, p. 32.

High expectations were also placed on publications popularizing the achievements of people's democracies. There were complaints that only the People's Republic of China had been given attention, while in the first quarter of 1952, not even a brochure had been published on Bulgaria, Hungary, Romania or Czechoslovakia (despite the fact that a year earlier, in 1951, *Obrazki węgierskie* by Ryszard Konarski and *Rumunia na drodze do socjalizmu* [Romania on the path to socialism] by Vladimir Lesakov had been published). Although 1951 saw "a certain quantitative increase in publications on the GDR [East Germany – AWG],"[856] both then and in the following year, it was stressed that the number and range of topics of such publications was unsatisfactory, even alarming.[857] The lack of such publications was all the more surprising in view of the fact that "a whole series of meetings between Polish writers and publicists and democratic German activists took place, and that a considerable number of excursions to the GDR were organized."[858] The authors of the June report noted that the only book dealing with East Germany was *Z życia Niemieckiej Republiki Demokratycznej* (*Dlaczego za Odrą mamy przyjaciół*)[859] [From the life of the German Democratic Republic (Why we have friends beyond the Oder)]. Its author was Jacek Bocheński (later evaluated in the cryptotexts, as well): a writer and publicist who had been active in the opposition in the 1970s, as a consequence of which the Office for the Control had a "file on him."[860]

Problems concerning the Federal Republic of Germany appeared somewhat more frequently and were presented in accordance with the expectations of the authorities of the time, e.g., in the works of an outstanding expert on the subject, Marian Podkowiński. In the report covering the first quarter of 1952, two titles appeared – an original work entitled *Za amerykańskim kordonem* [Behind the American cordon] (published in 1952, but also mentioned in the report on the year 1951) and the translation *Niemcy zachodnie w służbie amerykańskich podżegaczy wojennych* [West Germany in the service of American warmongers].

---

[856] "Uwagi na temat pracy wydawnictw w zakresie zagadnień społeczno-politycznych," *Biuletyn Informacyjno-Instrukcyjny* no. 1, January 1952, p. 36 (APG, WUKPPiW, file ref. no. 100).

[857] Ibidem; "Publikacje społeczno-polityczne," *Biuletyn Informacyjno-Instrukcyjny* no. 6, June 1952, p. 32 (APG, WUKPPiW, file ref. no. 87).

[858] "Publikacje społeczno-polityczne," *Biuletyn Informacyjno-Instrukcyjny* no. 6, June 1952, p. 33 (APG, WUKPPiW, file ref. no. 87).

[859] In the Bulletin – *Z życia NRD*.

[860] T. Strzyżewski, *Wielka księga cenzury PRL w dokumentach…*, p. 95. Actually, Bocheński's book was published in 1951 and not, as the material suggested, in 1952. Moreover, another title cited later in the article was not published in 1952: M. Wasiljew, *Ameryka od strony schodów kuchennych*, Warszawa: "Książka i Wiedza," 1950; Second Supplemented Edition: ibidem, Warszawa, 1951.

In this case, it is also worth referring to the author's biography: this former soldier of the Home Army and Warsaw insurgent, a longtime journalist of *Trybuna Ludu*, author of several dozen books on history, was included by Tyrmand in the infamous group of "the manufacturers of lies"[861] and put on the "Kisiel list."[862]

The authors of the reports did not fail to mention the publications concerning the United States. The titles that allegedly exposed the face of American imperialism and the progressing fascistization of life in the USA were noteworthy.[863] Examples included translations of Soviet and English titles, such as Vladislav Minayev's *Amerykańskie Gestapo* [American Gestapo] and *Raj amerykański* [American paradise]: "an abridged edition of famous reportages about the United States, published in 1929 by one of the most famous journalists and reporters of the time,"[864] Egon Kisch. As we know, the works of "The Raging Reporter"[865] enjoyed a particular interest in Poland in the 1950s, not only because of the excellent technique and literary value of his reports. Kisch, a Czech-German Jew with leftist views, strongly criticized capitalism as well as the United States, while presenting a rather idealized picture of the Soviet Union. This set of views was perfectly suited to the propaganda of the PRL's regime.

The reports also referred to publications describing the liberation of dependent countries from the yoke of usurpers. There were still many specific examples to be explored, for instance, the case of Tunisia, Morocco, and Algiers, but in comparison with the report on "Czytelnik," the situation was much better. Among the titles worthy of recommendation, native works and translations were indicated, e.g: Henryk Kassyanowicz's *Egipt w walce z imperializmem* [Egypt in the struggle against imperialism], Lidia Watolina's *Współczesny Egipt* [Modern Egypt], Witold Lipski's *Wietnam i jego młodzież* [Vietnam and its youth], Vyacheslav Maslennikov's[866] *Pogłębienie kryzysu kolonialnego systemu imperializmu*[867] [Exacerbation of the crisis of the colonial system of imperialism], Krzysztof Wolicki's *Iran walczy*[868]

---

[861] L. Tyrmand, *Dziennik. 1954*, Warszawa: Wydawnictwo MG, 2015, pp. 128–129.

[862] S. Kisielewski, "Moje typy," *Tygodnik Powszechny* December 2, 1984, no. 49, p. 8. The material was published in place of Kisiel's weekly column entitled *Widziane inaczej*. The list included the names of those who with their attitude and activity clearly supported the actions of the communist regime.

[863] "Publikacje społeczno-polityczne," *Biuletyn Informacyjno-Instrukcyjny* no. 6, June 1952, p. 33 (APG, WUKPPiW, file ref. no. 87).

[864] [Review: E. Kisch, *Raj amerykański*, Warszawa: Wydawnictwo MON, 1952], *Nowe Książki* 1952, no. 5, pp. 271–272.

[865] In Europe, Kisch had a reputation of traveling to the far corners of the world and producing reports at a staggering rate.

[866] In the Bulletin – Meselnikow.

[867] The Bulletin provided an incomplete title – *Pogłębienie kryzysu kolonialnego*.

[868] The title was published not, as the material suggests, in 1952, but in 1951.

[Iran fights] and Vladimir Konstantinov's *Mapa Afryki opowiada*[869] [The map of Africa tells the story].

Overall, the publications on international issues were assessed quite well, although a number of problems were mentioned that still awaited proper elaboration. It was no different in the case of publications on domestic issues. Here, the emphasis was placed primarily on popularizing the Six-Year Plan and mobilizing "the masses to strive for the implementation of its third and decisive year."[870] This was to be achieved by increasing the number of publications, taking into account all the problems that had hitherto been overlooked and remedying numerous technical deficiencies. Among other things, several books on Poland's planned economy and pamphlets published by the CRZZ were subjected to succinct evaluation. However, because of their narrow and limited character, the latter did not represent any great mobilizing or propaganda value; they were used in work with middle and lower production assets, but could not "replace real, bellicose, mobilizing journalism."[871]

Another problem that appeared in publications on national issues was the then highly topical matter of the "struggle for peace," propagandistically played out by Poland and other communist countries. The notion was illustrated by titles in the field of political science, including a short collection by Jarosław Iwaszkiewicz entitled *Sprawa pokoju. Wiersze i przemówienia*[872] [The issue of peace. Poems and speeches]. Unfortunately, the work was only mentioned, which was the result of the writer's involvement in domestic politics and his engagement (to use the language of the propaganda) in the struggle to improve the international situation. Already in 1948, Iwaszkiewicz (along with Borejsza) participated in organizing the World Congress of Intellectuals in Defense of Peace in Wrocław, and two years later, he became a delegate to the Second World Congress of Peace Defenders, which this time took place in Warsaw.[873] Both events were intended to convince the public that only the countries of people's democracy cared about maintaining peace in the world, the greatest threat to which, of course, was supposedly the West. The events were organized with great panache: the first Congress was attended by some four hundred delegates from forty-six countries.

---

[869] The work from 1952 was a reprint of the work published in 1950.

[870] "Publikacje społeczno-polityczne," *Biuletyn Informacyjno-Instrukcyjny* no. 6, June 1952, p. 34 (APG, WUKPPiW, file ref. no. 87).

[871] Ibidem.

[872] J. Iwaszkiewicz, *Sprawa pokoju. Wiersze i przemówienia*, Warszawa: "Czytelnik," 1952.

[873] *Kongres Pokoju. Kongres Intelektualistów we Wrocławiu*, Polska Kronika Filmowa, episode 33, September 07, 1948, http://www.repozytorium.fn.org.pl/?q=pl/node/6435 (accessed March 8, 2021); The World Congress of Intellectuals in Defense of Peace took place between August 25 and 28, 1948; the Second World Congress of Peace Defenders between November 16 and 22, 1950.

The organizing committee included a number of eminent authors of literature and science, such as Maria Dąbrowska, Zofia Nałkowska, Tadeusz Kotarbiński and Kazimierz Ajdukiewicz; the congress was attended by Julian Tuwim, Antoni Słonimski, Kazimierz Nitsch, among others, as well as Pablo Picasso, Bertolt Brecht, Graham Greene and Martin Andersen Nexø.[874]

Summarizing publications on national themes, the authors of the reports noted that in this sector of publishing, the most work was needed on problems of the countryside, the Six-Year Plan, the issue of patriotism, and the "ideological and political education of youth."[875]

---

[874] Martin Andersen Nexø was a Danish author of the popular novel *Pelle the Conqueror*, reprinted many times in Poland. The novel was the subject of an article published in 1950 in the popular series *Dobra Książka. Informator dla Czytelników* [A good book: a reader's guide]; after the war, subsequent volumes of the novel were published; the award-winning film *Pelle the Conqueror*, directed by Bille August and starring Max von Sydow, was released in 1987.

See: *Martin Andersen Nexø i jego powieść "Pelle zwycięzca,"* Warszawa: "Czytelnik," 1950, series: *Dobra Książka. Informator dla Czytelników* no. 42.

[875] "Uwagi na temat pracy wydawnictw w zakresie zagadnień społeczno-politycznych," *Biuletyn Informacyjno-Instrukcyjny* no. 1, January 1952, p. 33 (APG, WUKP-PiW, file ref. no. 100); "Publikacje społeczno-polityczne," *Biuletyn Informacyjno-Instrukcyjny* no. 6, June 1952, p. 36 (APG, WUKPPiW, file ref. no. 87).

III. Other Topics Related to the Supervision of the Word

If Russian texts are rendered in translation as a potboiler libretto, a disservice is being done to Soviet songs, to the cause of popularizing them.[876]

Controlling the written word also involved monitoring translations, along with the area of proofreading, typesetting, and editing of texts. Furthermore, it presupposed the institutional base of control – the supervision of libraries and book collections, as well as cooperation with publishers, editors and control of printing houses. Scattered throughout the Bulletins, the handful of comments on the art of translation in the years 1945–1956 add very little to the previous exploration of the subject, as they replicate standard observations made in censorship reviews and other documents of the era.

Translations from the literature of friendly nations were the most frequently addressed issue. A report on "Czytelnik" argued that a pressing problem at the time, in 1951, was the "insufficient number of publications, especially from Soviet literature and the literature of the countries of people's democracy."[877] The problem of a lack of translations concerned almost all artistic fields: drama, satire, poetry, prose, and literature for children and young adults, but it seemed not to affect – or affect to a lesser extent – publications in the field of international politics, in which "particular emphasis was put on showing and exposing the policy of imperialism."[878] This observation is also corroborated by the material from January and June 1952, which highlighted that many translations of socio-political publications had appeared on the market.[879]

---

[876] "Kilka uwag o programach *Artosu*," *Biuletyn Informacyjno-Instrukcyjny* no. 1, January 1952, p. 45 (APG, WUKPPiW, file ref. no. 100).

[877] "Działalność wydawnictwa 'Czytelnik' w 1951 r.," *Biuletyn Informacyjno-Instrukcyjny* no. 5, May 1952, p. 20 (APG, WUKPPiW, file ref. no. 90). See also, e.g.: J. Królak, "Paratekst w służbie propagandy. Wprowadzenia w przekładach literatury pięknej na język polski i czeski w latach 50. XX wieku," *Przekłady Literatur Słowiańskich* vol. 8, part 1, pp. 159–177.

[878] "Działalność wydawnictwa 'Czytelnik' w 1951 r.," *Biuletyn Informacyjno-Instrukcyjny* no. 5, May 1952, p. 25 (APG, WUKPPiW, file ref. no. 90).

[879] "Uwagi na temat pracy wydawnictw w zakresie zagadnień społeczno-politycznych," *Biuletyn Informacyjno-Instrukcyjny* no. 1, January 1952, pp. 29–38 (APG, WUKPPiW, file ref. no. 100); "Publikacje społeczno-polityczne," *Biuletyn Informacyjno-Instrukcyjny* no. 6, June 1952, p. 31 (APG, WUKPPiW, file ref. no. 87).

In July 1952, it was argued that the editorial preparation of a given publication should play a major role in granting permission for the translation, since "a proper adjustment of the translation or its juxtaposition with the original can clear up a number of doubts"[880]; in this case, a reference was made to the specially understood creative inventiveness of the translator and the publisher. It should be noted that the Bulletins also assessed the actual artistic value of translations, but this was done rarely; suffice it to recall an extremely succinct opinion on the translation of the aforementioned novel *The Fisherman's Son* by Vilis Lācis': "translation is beyond reproach."[881]

One of the guidelines from 1952 seems quite bold in the context of the questionable competence of the censors, to say the least:

> As far as translation is concerned, the value of an excellent title is often diminished by an inept translation. It is the responsibility of the censor to show how the translation turned out, whether it does not distort the ideological sense, does not violate the structure, or does not warp the valid formulations of the original through an incompetent (sometimes literal) translation.[882]

Most likely, the non-polyglot censors who wanted to evaluate a translation were assisted by "external specialists" appointed by the Office, whose services were used, as I have noted, in the Non-Periodicals Department. However, such support was signaled extremely sparingly in the Bulletins.

***

The problem of errors in typesetting and proofreading appeared several times in the Bulletins.[883] Taking up this subject in an instructional magazine was highly

---

[880] "Uwagi ogólne o recenzji" (in the series *O wyższy poziom pracy nad książką*), *Biuletyn Informacyjno-Instrukcyjny* no. 7, July 1952, pp. 27–28 (APG, WUKPPiW, file ref. no. 84).

[881] "Recenzja z pozycji literackiej, cz. I" (in the series *O wyższy poziom pracy nad książką*), *Biuletyn Informacyjno-Instrukcyjny* no. 8, August 1952, p. 21 (APG, WUKPPiW, file ref. no. 81). Cf. also "Uwagi na temat pracy wydawnictw w zakresie zagadnień społeczno-politycznych"; "Kilka uwag o programach *Artosu*," *Biuletyn Informacyjno-Instrukcyjny* no. 1, January 1952, pp. 34, 45 (APG, WUKPPiW, file ref. no. 100); "Uwagi ogólne o recenzji" (in the series *O wyższy poziom pracy nad książką*), *Biuletyn Informacyjno-Instrukcyjny* no. 7, July 1952, p. 28 (APG, WUKPPiW, file ref. no. 84).

[882] "Uwagi ogólne o recenzji" (in the series *O wyższy poziom pracy nad książką*), *Biuletyn Informacyjno-Instrukcyjny* no. 7, July 1952, p. 28 (APG, WUKPPiW, file ref. no. 84).

[883] See, e.g.: "Błędy ortograficzne i stylistyczne"; "Układ graficzny," *Biuletyn Informacyjno-Szkoleniowy* no. 4, May 1949, fol. 160v (APP, WUKPPiW, file ref. no. 4); "O dobrych i złych przykładach pracy kontroli prewencyjnej w terenie. 4. Błędy korektorskie o charak-

justified, because –apart from the assessment of the ideological correctness of particular titles – the Office's functionaries' tasks also included textual control in terms of "diversionary" proofreading and typesetting mistakes, as well as control of graphic design (illustrations, drawings, tables, charts, etc.) and typesetting understood as a way presenting particular materials on a page (layout).

The importance of the problem is demonstrated by the articles published in the Bulletin devoted entirely to these issues. One example is an extensive text entitled "The Typesetter's Diversion as a Manifestation of Class Struggle,"[884] which linked the discussed errors to:

> some typesetters and proofreaders' improper attitude toward their professional duties; their sloppiness and lack of vigilance and understanding of the great responsibility for each printed word; their lack of sufficient supervision over the course of working with the word from the first to the last phase; and finally, the lack of work organization that would establish the full personal responsibility of each worker called upon to watch over the purity of each printed word and to protect themselves fully against errors.[885]

For what might seem like minor omissions, one could be held liable, which was reported elsewhere in the article:

> Although typesetting and proofreading errors may be of various kinds and gravity, regardless of the qualification of the act, the degree of "accidentality" or the "goodwill" of those responsible, they objectively constitute a diversion that plays into the hands of our class enemies. This diversion must be fought with full force. Of course, any fact of deliberate action in this direction is a crime prosecutable by the power and the rule of law.[886]

---

terze dywersyjnym," *Biuletyn Informacyjno-Instrukcyjny* no. 6, June 1952, pp. 12–13 (APG, WUKPPiW, file ref. no. 87); Rak (WUKP Poznań), "Brygada Młodzieżowa im. J. Bruna wita Zlot," *Biuletyn Informacyjno-Instrukcyjny* no. 7, July 1952, p. 3 (APG, WUKPPiW, file ref. no. 84); "O sygnałach dziennych," *Biuletyn Informacyjno-Instrukcyjny* no. 10, October 1952, p. 31 (APG, WUKPPiW, file ref. no. 75); J. Garlicki, "Kilka uwag na temat organizacji pracy w WUKPPiW" (correspondence in "Dział listów"), *Biuletyn Informacyjno-Instrukcyjny* no. 12, December 1952, p. 42 (APG, WUKPPiW, file ref. no. 70); "Z działu druków ulotnych," *Biuletyn Informacyjno-Instrukcyjny* no. 1 (13), January 1953, p. 52 (APG, WUKPPiW, file ref. no. 19); "Jakie ingerencje były konieczne w artykule pt. 'Czy socjalizm i komunizm to inne ustroje'" (*Kurier Szczeciński*, nr 297), *Biuletyn Informacyjno-Instrukcyjny* no. 2 (14), February 1953, p. 22 (APG, WUKPPiW, file ref. no. 18).

[884] "Dywersja zecerska jako przejaw walki klasowej," *Biuletyn Informacyjno-Instrukcyjny* no. 1, January 1952, pp. 39–40 (APG, WUKPPiW, file ref. no. 100).

[885] Ibidem, p. 39.

[886] Ibidem.

In the context of the instructional function of the Bulletins, examples illustrating the problem at hand and ways to prevent the above-mentioned mistakes would have been helpful. Unfortunately, the authors of this particular material opted not to give any examples, which made the article contribute little to the concrete censorship practice. The text was written in extremely general terms, and the problems of proofreading and typesetting errors played a servile role to the issue of class struggle.

However, the paucity of examples illustrating the "sloppiness" of proofreaders and typesetters was compensated for in other Bulletins. Many such interferences concerned the religious press, for example, discussions over "Psalm Wiary i Ufności" [Psalm of Faith and Confidence], interjected into an article by Father Jan Piwowarczyk, a founder of *Tygodnik Powszechny* and an author of antisemitic statements in the pre-war *Głos Narodu*.[887]

An increase in the number of intentional typesetting and proofreading distortions was observed "particularly often during periods of major political actions."[888] The problem of proofreading and typesetting errors, encrusted with concrete examples, appeared in the context of electoral slogans, agitational motives, etc.[889] From among a number of such examples, two can be highlighted. The first is the May Day slogan (submitted by *Głos Szczeciński*):

<u>Nie żyje</u> Wielka Partia Komunistów[890]

[Long <u>leave</u> the Great Party of Communists]

---

[887] See, e.g.: "Pierwsza wypowiedź o Kongresie Zjednoczeniowym," *Biuletyn Informacyjno-Szkoleniowy* no. 1/3, January 1949, pp. 27–29 (APG, WUKPPiW, file ref. no. 196); "Eliminowanie etyki z życia publicznego i prywatnego," *Biuletyn Informacyjno--Szkoleniowy* no. 4, May 1949, fol. 144r–144v (APP, WUKPPiW, file ref. no. 4). See also: J. Leociak, *Młyny Boże. Zapiski o Kościele i Zagładzie*, Wołowiec: Wydawnictwo Czarne, 2018, p. 63 et seq.

[888] "O dobrych i złych przykładach pracy kontroli prewencyjnej w terenie," *Biuletyn Informacyjno-Instrukcyjny* no. 6, June 1952, p. 12 (APG, WUKPPiW, file ref. no. 87). See also: "Rozumienie aktualnych zadań naszej propagandy warunkiem dobrej pracy cenzora," *Biuletyn Informacyjno-Instrukcyjny* no. 3, January 1952, pp. 7–13 (APG, WUKPPiW, file ref. no. 96); "Kilka uwag o pracy WUKPPiW w okresie kampanii wyborczej," *Biuletyn Informacyjno-Instrukcyjny* no. 11, November 1952, pp. 7–10 (APG, WUKPPiW, file ref. no. 72).

[889] "Na marginesie ogólnonarodowej dyskusji (materiał wysłany do WUKP dnia 6 II 52 r.)," *Biuletyn Informacyjno-Instrukcyjny* no. 2, February 1952, p. 27 (APG, WUKPPiW, file ref. no. 99).

[890] "O dobrych i złych przykładach pracy kontroli prewencyjnej w terenie," *Biuletyn Informacyjno-Instrukcyjny* no. 6, June 1952, p. 13 (APG, WUKPPiW, file ref. no. 87).

The second is an unfortunate layout of titles from the period of the Sejm election campaign in 1952 (submitted by *Kurier Szczeciński*):

Psy szczekają, karawana idzie dalej
W Polsce Ludowej wybory są prawdziwymi wyborami[891]

[The dogs are barking, the caravan keeps going
In People's Poland, elections are real.]

However, "typesetter diversion" was also attempted in quite different materials, e.g., on the industrial, communications, or food sectors. For instance, the censors felt that an issue of *Przemysł Spożywczy* [Food industry] displayed a biased selection and layout of articles; the text affirming this sector of the American economy was followed by material entitled "Przemysł spożywczy w ZSRR" [The food industry in the USSR] where "it was highlighted [in the beginning – AWG] that this article was delivered to the editors by the Soviet Information Bureau."[892] The Bulletin supported the thesis that it was not a simple oversight but a deliberate act on the part of the magazine considering that "the editors do not provide such 'explanations' before articles on other countries."[893]

***

During the period of People's Poland, several actions were taken to purge libraries of harmful and undesirable books, creating lists of banned authors and titles, as well as indices of topics and issues that required the special "care" of the censor. The question of the different provenance of book collections was also taken up in the Bulletin, although it was not one of the key matters.

The first materials on this subject were published in the June 1945 issue.[894] The emergence of the above-mentioned topic in this period was not accidental. Although the campaign to purge libraries and other book collections began in 1949, the first actions of this kind had already taken place in 1945; for instance, the book *Świat czarów* by the aforementioned Edmund Jezierski was on the list

---

[891] "Kilka uwag o pracy WUKPPiW w okresie kampanii wyborczej," *Biuletyn Informacyjno-Instrukcyjny* no. 11, November 1952, p. 7 (APG, WUKPPiW, file ref. no. 72).

[892] "Czasopisma techniczno-fachowe," *Biuletyn Informacyjno-Szkoleniowy* no. 1/3, January 1949, p. 33 (APG, WUKPPiW, file ref. no. 196).

[893] Ibidem.
See the previously mentioned – most likely deliberate – oversight in *Hutnik* magazine.

[894] "Kwestia bibliotek"; "Ze sprawozdań kierowników Wojewódzkich Biur (Biblioteki)," *Biuletyn Instrukcyjny* no. 2, June 1945, pp. 11–14 (APG, WUKPPiW, file ref. no. 210).

drawn up in 1945 of titles to be removed. In the June issue, information on the institutional base of the purges can be found: the authors of the Bulletin write about the action of purging libraries in Białystok and Kielce, the units created for this purpose, and describe subsequent stages of the process. The material also contains several proposals for the organization of book collections, such as the one about the creation of a "Library Department."[895] Some of the ideas never made it to the implementation stage, while others were put into practice, as evidenced, for example, by the decree on libraries and care of library collections, introduced a year later on April 17, 1946.[896]

The Bulletin's materials suggest that already at the initial stage of planning the supervision of libraries, there were efforts to introduce different types of control depending on the type of institution:

> libraries should be divided into two categories, namely:
> 1. Central and school libraries, which are not subject to our interference,
> 2. General and educational libraries, which must be controlled.[897]

This division coincides only partially with that adopted by the April decree, which distinguished between public institutions (school, scientific, and general), as well as community, private, and home ones.[898] It is possible that the school and general libraries distinguished by the censors were to perform similar, if not the

---

[895] "Kwestia bibliotek," *Biuletyn Instrukcyjny* no. 2, June 1945, p. 11 (APG, WUKP-PiW, file ref. no. 210).

[896] "Dekret z dnia 17 kwietnia 1946 r. o bibliotekach i opiece nad zbiorami biblio-tecznymi" (*Journal of Laws* 1946, no. 26, item 163, pp. 291–295, http://isap.sejm.gov.pl/isap.nsf/DocDetails.xsp?id=wdu19460260163 (accessed July 27, 2021)).
The bibliography of publications on the decree is extensive; the following texts are certainly worth mentioning: T. Zarzębski, "Geneza, życie i nauki Dekretu," *Przegląd Biblioteczny* 1986, no. 3/4, pp. 279–295; J. Puchalski, "Biblioteki w życiu naukowym PRL i poza krajem w latach 1939–1989," [in:] *Historia nauki polskiej 1944–1989* vol. 10: *Instytucje*, eds. L. Zasztowt, J. Schiller-Walicka, Warszawa: Oficyna Wydawnicza Aspra-JR, 2015, pp. 359–483.

[897] "Kwestia bibliotek," *Biuletyn Instrukcyjny* no. 2, June 1945, p. 11 (APG, WUKP-PiW, file ref. no. 210).

[898] "Dekret z dnia 17 kwietnia 1946 r. o bibliotekach i opiece nad zbiorami biblio-tecznymi, Dział I. Przepisy ogólne, art. 1, pkt. 3" (*Journal of Laws* 1946, no. 26, item 163, pp. 291–292, http://isap.sejm.gov.pl/isap.nsf/DocDetails.xsp?id=wdu19460260163 (accessed July 27, 2021)). It should be noted that "this decree does not apply to home libraries" (ibidem, p. 292) with some exceptions, namely: in exceptional cases, the Minister of Education, at the request of the State Library Board, could seize "private and home libraries and give them on deposit to school and scientific-research institutions" (ibidem), as long as the needs of education and science required it.

same, tasks as those delegated to the institutions, which were named identically in the decree of 1946. A greater interpretive difficulty is posed by the distinction between educational and central libraries, which were not mentioned in the decree, although even in these cases, it seems that the differences are merely in nomenclature.

Popular in the interwar period, educational libraries could have been the equivalent of community libraries, since both were run by various associations and social, cultural, educational, professional, youth, or religious organizations and institutions.[899] The choice of such a term would also have its historical justification – after all, these names functioned interchangeably in the interwar period. Moreover, the 1955 edition of *Podręczny słownik bibliotekarza* [The librarian's handbook] does not distinguish between educational and general libraries; along with the term "mass libraries," all three are used synonymously to describe a library accessible to all, promoting "the widest range of readership, social education, general and professional training, and cultural entertainment."[900]

What institutions could have been equivalent to the central libraries mentioned in the Bulletin? Establishing this is a difficult task, as it is an extremely general term – one definition states that a central library is "a library that compiles in a planned manner a possibly complete collection of writing in a specific branch of knowledge."[901] Piotr Lechowski, PhD, pointed out to me that a central library can also be treated as a particular type of scientific library, namely, a special (subject-related) library, which collects, elaborates and makes available literature from a given field of knowledge and science, which has been assigned specific (superior, coordinating) functions in the system of scientific information circulation. Perhaps the central libraries proposed in the Bulletin were scientific libraries, especially the largest and most significant ones, which were university libraries at that time. Certainly, in the work on the 1946 decree, there was no proposal to separate central libraries understood in this way as a component of the national library network; such a proposal, according to Dr. Lechowski

---

[899] I. Kaczmarek, "Biblioteki oświatowe i publiczne w Łodzi w dwudziestoleciu międzywojennym," *Acta Universitatis Lodziensis. Folia Librorum* 2013, no. 17, p. 76. See also: I. Kaczmarek, "Biblioteki szkolne w Łodzi w dwudziestoleciu międzywojennym. Przegląd działalności," *Acta Universitatis Lodziensis. Folia Librorum* 2015, no. 1, pp. 33–57; P. Lechowski, "Problemy i organizacja powszechnego bibliotekarstwa publicznego w Polsce w latach 1945–1951," *Roczniki Biblioteczne* 2011, no. 55, pp. 91–112.

[900] H. Więckowska, H. Pliszczyńska, *Podręczny słownik bibliotekarza*, Warszawa: PWN, 1955, p. 38. The same definition was offered in *Podręczny słownik bibliotekarza*, compiled by G. Czapnik and Z. Gruszka in cooperation with H. Tadeusiewicz, Warszawa: Wydawnictwo Stowarzyszenia Bibliotekarzy Polskich, 2011, p. 39.

[901] *Podręczny słownik bibliotekarza...*, p. 36, see also: H. Więckowska, H. Pliszczyńska, *Podręczny słownik bibliotekarza...*, p. 37.

appeared a few years later, in 1951, at the so-called Krynica Conference (the National Conference of Librarians in Krynica), which played an important role in the Sovietization of Polish librarianship. It passed a resolution on the necessity of creating a network of scientific libraries based on their specialization.[902]

Regardless of the terminological differences, the consequences of the proposed division are significant. Only certain book collections were going to be subject to the supervision of the censorship office, and one could say that these were libraries of a "mass" character[903] (in other words, libraries open to the public, universal, and today, also public). Each library, on the other hand, was to be subject to the control of the Book Evaluation Commission, the establishment of which was considered in the Bulletin: "A project has arisen for the Ministry of Education to establish the Book Evaluation Commission [which would assess] a book's suitability for use by libraries of various types."[904] The proposal formulated in the Bulletin in June 1945 was realized four years later; in 1949, the Ministry of Education established said Commission. The composition of this still informal body, active in 1945, was noted in the Bulletin independently by two censors, comrades Lewi and Papińska. The teams included representatives of the department of education, library, censorship office, Ministry of Information and Propaganda, Ministry of Culture and Arts, National Council and political parties.[905] The slight discrepancies in the composition listed by the censors may have stemmed from the imprecise message of one of them, but most likely, they prove that the final shape of these first commissions had not yet crystallized (hence, the different compositions in different field centers). Due to the particular post-war chaos of the period, the differences may have resulted simply from the lack of "competent" people – from the authorities' point of view – in a given area.

Thus, it can be said that the censorship office did not surrender control over book collections; in some cases, it was rather a matter of delegating at least part of the tasks to "special commissions"[906] and other institutions, but even so, the "mobilizing" presence of the functionaries of the prevention and repression apparatus was an integral part of the work. The first guidelines on the control of specific types of books were issued right after the war. In June 1945, libraries and

---

[902] Dr. Piotr Lechowski's response to my question about the interpretation of distinguishing central libraries, proposed in the Bulletin (e-mail correspondence, August 26–September 6, 2018).

[903] "Kwestia bibliotek," *Biuletyn Instrukcyjny* no. 2, June 1945, p. 11 (APG, WUKPPiW, file ref. no. 210).

[904] Ibidem.

[905] "Ze sprawozdań Kierowników Wojewódzkich Biur," *Biuletyn Instrukcyjny* no. 2, June 1945, pp. 12, 13 (APG, WUKPPiW, file ref. no. 210).

[906] Ibidem, p. 12.

bookstores were supposed to remove, first, "the books of an anti-democratic, anti-Soviet character, harmful books[907] that litter our reading rooms"[908]; second, the post-German collections and the Nazi books. In this case, an interesting distinction was made: the first collections could be "removed" while the Nazi books were to be "totally eliminated" (the difference between "removal" and "elimination" of books was not specified, though it seems that the effect of the latter procedure was meant as irreversible).[909]

The topic of book collections appeared in a few more Bulletins, but these were usually perfunctory remarks on the margins of other topics. This was the case, for example, in June 1952, when the GUKPPiW staff pledged to organize a book collection for one of the schools, all "to commemorate the anniversary of the July Manifesto and the Rally of Young Leaders – the Builders of People's Poland."[910] A remark on the subject of book collections also appeared in September of that year in the assessment of a radio program in Bydgoszcz, which discussed the need for better provisions of municipal libraries.[911]

Apart from these types of minor remarks, the Bulletins offer no major material describing the changes within the book collections. This may come as a surprise considering that during the period under study – between 1945 and 1956 – systemic and global measures were being taken toward these resources.[912] Work on the "appropriate" shape of the collections started already in 1945 and lasted for three consecutive years; however, "the purge of the book collections carried out in a way that was much more systematic, better organized and – unchangeably – confidential"[913] did not materialize until a few years later. Some

---

[907] The excerpt is unclear; new words were added above the deleted words; the first word is illegible, in the case of the second, it may be the word "harmful."

[908] "Kwestia bibliotek," *Biuletyn Instrukcyjny* no. 2, June 1945, p. 11 (APG, WUKPPiW, file ref. no. 210).

[909] Ibidem.

[910] "Wytyczne dla mobilizacji pracowników GUKP w Warszawie," *Biuletyn Informacyjno-Instrukcyjny* no. 6, June 1952, p. 44 (APG, WUKPPiW, file ref. no. 87).

[911] "Z terenowych prac ocenowych," *Biuletyn Informacyjno-Instrukcyjny* no. 9, September 1952, pp. 46–47 (APG, WUKPPiW, file ref. no. 78).

[912] See, e.g.: M. Korczyńska-Derkacz, "Książki szkodliwe politycznie, czyli akcja 'oczyszczania' księgozbiorów bibliotek szkolnych, pedagogicznych i publicznych w latach 1947–1956," [in:] *Niewygodne dla władzy...*, pp. 341–344; A. Obrębska, "Akcja usuwania książek z bibliotek województwa olsztyńskiego w 1949 r.," *Komunikaty Mazursko-Warmińskie* 2008, no. 2, pp. 145–153; A. Kempa, "Literatura źle obecna," *Poradnik Bibliotekarza* 1989, no. 5, pp. 28–29; P. Szulc, *Czy w Polsce palono książki?*, Dzieje.pl, July 28, 2017, https://dzieje.pl/artykuly-historyczne/czy-w-polsce-palono-ksiazki (accessed January 31, 2021).

[913] M. Korczyńska-Derkacz, "Książki szkodliwe politycznie...," pp. 340–341.

of the first decisions that had a significant impact on the shape of Polish book collections were made on March 2, 1949 during a library conference at the KC of the PZPR.[914] In June 1952, the library purge initiatives were extended to include private and parish bookshops.[915] The March Bulletin from that year merely mentions the subject;[916] the work, which lasted about four months, was not presented in detail. There was also no discussion on the selection carried out in the following year[917] nor the year after that, when the course of action changed, at least to some extent. In accordance with the Decree of December 20, 1954, titles that until recently had been the cornerstone of Polish libraries – constituting its most valuable component – became an unpleasant testimony to the dependence on the eastern neighbor and were being removed. Thanks to this Thaw-triggered selection, a number of Stalinist books disappeared from library shelves. The last library selection in the discussed period took place in 1956.[918]

Between 1945 and 1956, lists and indices of "inconvenient" authors and books appeared, not only as help to the censors. As Marcin Zaremba observes, between 1949 and 1957, at least three extensive lists of books intended for removal were drafted. Małgorzata Korczyńska-Derkacz complements them with a detailed list of minor indices.[919] The aforementioned, longest *List of Books Subject to Immediate Withdrawal* was drawn up on October 1, 1951. It included one thousand six hundred and eighty-two items, although there were many more specific titles, as sometimes a single number mandated that all works by a given author be removed; this was the fate of, for instance, the previously mentioned Marian Spychalski or Agatha Christie.[920]

It is difficult to say why the authors of the Bulletins were so selective and reported only certain changes and problems that affected Polish book collections.

---

[914] M. Zaremba, "Amputacja pamięci," *Polityka* November 23, 1996, p. 65, http://niniwa22.cba.pl/amputacja_pamieci.htm (accessed January 31, 2021); Zaremba writes about the session from February 2, 1949.

[915] Ibidem, p. 66.

[916] "Przez sprawniejszą organizację – do lepszej pracy" (in the series *O wyższy poziom naszej pracy*), *Biuletyn Informacyjno-Instrukcyjny* no. 3, March 1952, p. 23 (APG, WUKPPiW, file ref. no. 96).

[917] M. Korczyńska-Derkacz, "Książki szkodliwe politycznie…," pp. 348–352.

[918] Ibidem, p. 352.

[919] M. Zaremba, "Amputacja pamięci…," p. 65; M. Korczyńska-Derkacz, "Książki szkodliwe politycznie…," pp. 343, 345–353.

[920] See: *Cenzura PRL. Wykaz książek podlegających niezwłocznemu wycofaniu…*, pp. 8, 39. See also: E. Dąbrowicz, "Zdezaktualizowane: na marginesie *Wykazu książek podlegających niezwłocznemu wycofaniu 1 X 1951 r.*," *Acta Universitatis Lodziensis. Folia Litteraria Polonica* 2013, no. 19, pp. 43–57; M. Korczyńska-Derkacz, "Książki szkodliwe politycznie…," pp. 345–347.

The control of the written word is an extremely important segment of any total-itarian system and it seems that the reports of activities carried out in this field should be placed on the pages of periodicals intended for censors. It must be re-membered, however, that the confidential Bulletins of the Office for the Control were supposed to contain all the key problems faced by "Mysia Street's" func-tionaries. It can be said that the topic of "taking care" of book collections was, in a way, broached when identifying banned books and authors, drawing attention to matters and issues subject to special control, and specifying publishing houses for which there was no place on the nationalized book market. These were only some of the problems connected with the broadly understood topic of libraries and book collections.

***

The matters of work organization at "Mysia Street" and in the field branches – from personnel to financial problems – very often appeared in the Bulletins and were presented both by the authors of the journal and in the functionaries' letters published in the periodicals. In the context of reflections on literature, materials concerning cooperation with publishers and editors, as well as control and super-vision of printing houses are of particular interest. Several Bulletins mentioned what a model cooperation between the Office for the Control, editors and pub-lishing houses should look like.[921] The periodical tried to publish articles discuss-ing these matters, but it was not always possible to satisfy everyone's expectations:

> For example, Gdańsk believes that evaluations of the activities of publishers are useless to the WUKPPiW, as they have no contact with these publishers. Other Voivodeship Offices claim that, on the contrary, it gives them a comprehensive picture and ask for additional lists of noteworthy new publications, assessments of some of them, further bibliographic notes, etc.[922]

---

[921] See, e.g.: "Zadania biuletynu"; "Ocena pracy cenzury prewencyjnej. Uwagi ogól-ne," *Biuletyn Instrukcyjny* no. 1, May 1945, fol. 1r–1v (APP, WUKPPiW, file ref. no. 4); "Seminarium prasy. (Wyjątki z protokółu)"; "O stylu pracy w terenie"; "Przemówienie dyrektora ob. Zabłudowskiego," *Biuletyn Instrukcyjny* no. 2, June 1945, pp. 10, 18–19 (APG, WUKPPiW, file ref. no. 210); "O właściwe wykorzystywanie prasy periodycz-nej w naszej pracy codziennej" (in the series *O wyższy poziom naszej pracy*), *Biuletyn Informacyjno-Instrukcyjny* no. 2, February 1952, p. 34 (APG, WUKPPiW, file ref. no. 99); "Przez sprawniejszą organizację – do lepszej pracy" (in the series *O wyższy poziom naszej pracy*), *Biuletyn Informacyjno-Instrukcyjny* no. 3, March 1952, pp. 21–25 (APG, WUKP-PiW, file ref. no. 96).

[922] "Artykuł wstępny," *Biuletyn Informacyjno-Instrukcyjny* no. 1 (13), January 1953, p. 6 (APG, WUKPPiW, file ref. no. 19).

What proved helpful in researching the publishing market of the PRL and literary censorship is the material published in April 1952 and sent to the editors by two censors from Wrocław, Stanisław Art and Zofia Freidman. The employees of the Non-Periodical Publications Department of the Voivodeship Office in Wrocław suggested improvements in cooperation with publishers, pointing out the basic problems they faced on a daily basis:

> So far, the practice of our work has been characterized by haphazardness and passive waiting for a title to be submitted by a publisher. In many cases, when several publishers submitted a large number of titles in a short period of time, it resulted in bottlenecks and, inevitably, in more hasty control (e.g., at the end of the year, when a publisher working unsystematically, in spurts, tries to catch up). On the other hand, there have been periods of slack time, when the work of a censor of non-periodical publications was not used productively.
>
> In view of the above, it would be advisable for the WUKP to know the plans of field publishers and their schedules.
>
> This would make it possible to reach an agreement with the publishers on the distribution of work in a planned manner; it would increase the sense of responsibility on the part of both the publishing house and our office with regard to the timely processing of a given title, and it would possibly help determine who, in a specific case, is responsible for delaying the publishing process and disrupting the plans.[923]

"The initiative of the Wrocław team has been recognized by the management of the Non-Periodical Publications Department as legitimate and useful,"[924] as reported in the brief reply underneath the letter:

> The WUKP should request publication plans and schedules from field publishers. The WUKP should also send quarterly evaluations of these publications. The management of the Non-Periodical Publications Department requests other voivodeship offices to send projects that would streamline work, improve qualifications, etc.
>
> Non-Periodical Publications Department.[925]

It is worth stressing, however, that the conciliatory vision of cooperation with publishing houses, as presented in the letter, was only applicable at the stage of publishing plans; the publishing house did not decide what would eventually

---

[923] S. Art, Z. Freidman (Employees of the Non-Periodical Publications Department. WUKP Wrocław), "List do Redakcji," *Biuletyn Informacyjno-Instrukcyjny* no. 4, April 1952, p. 45 (APG, WUKPPiW, file ref. no. 93).

[924] Ibidem, p. 46.

[925] Ibidem.

be published. It was also unrealistic to assume that this solution would identify the culprit for the delays. Obstructions in the review process were often caused by the decisions of the Office for the Control or other institutions responsible for the control of the word, which often sought to delay the review process. In fact, the issue of timely processing of titles was raised several times in the Bulletins. Efforts were made to encourage the establishment of a precise reviewing schedule when "representatives of publishing houses or printing houses [delivered] titles for inspection."[926]

The Bulletins repeatedly reminded their readers that editors and publishers were obliged to introduce changes suggested by the Office in the assessed materials.[927] In doubtful cases, it was recommended to "intervene, make a phone call to editors, explain and persuade."[928] There were also materials that inquired about the point of "rampant censorship."[929] Such a question was posed in June 1945 by Tadeusz Zabłudowski, the director of what was then the Central Press Control Bureau. He warned his subordinates against encroaching on the competence of various editorial offices, the Department of Culture and the Arts, or the Office of Information and Propaganda. Most likely, rather than anything else, this was about establishing the prerogatives and scope of influence of individual institutions.

Continuous control of the entities involved in the publishing process was extremely important. It was no different in the case of printing companies, where, among other things, typesetter diversion – the censor's "torment" – occurred. To avoid this, it was suggested that, after appropriate training, censors should work as "printing house inspectors," so they could check, for example, the first issue of a newspaper coming off the press.[930] There were times when printing companies

---

[926] K. Dworecki, "O wyższy poziom organizacji pracy," *Biuletyn Informacyjno-Instrukcyjny* no. 1 (25), January 1954, p. 10 (APG, WUKPPiW, file ref. no. 39).

[927] See, e.g.: "Kilka uwag o pracy WUKPPiW w okresie kampanii wyborczej," *Biuletyn Informacyjno-Instrukcyjny* no. 11, November 1952, p. 9 (APG, WUKPPiW, file ref. no. 72); "Wzmóc ochronę tajemnicy wojskowej na wszystkich odcinkach naszej kontroli," *Biuletyn Informacyjno-Instrukcyjny* no. 1 (13), January 1953, p. 24 (APG, WUKPPiW, file ref. no. 19).

[928] "O niektórych przejawach kosmopolityzmu w czasopismach techniczno-naukowych," *Biuletyn Informacyjno-Instrukcyjny* no. 8, August 1952, p. 40 (APG, WUKPPiW, file ref. no. 81).

[929] "Przemówienie dyrektora ob. Zabłudowskiego," *Biuletyn Instrukcyjny* June 1945, p. 18 (APG, WUKPPiW, file ref. no. 210).

[930] "Kilka uwag o pracy WUKPPiW w okresie kampanii wyborczej," *Biuletyn Informacyjno-Instrukcyjny* no. 11, November 1952, p. 9 (APG, WUKPPiW, file ref. no. 72). On the control of printing houses, see also, e.g.: "Ze sprawozdań kierowników Wojewódzkich Biur," *Biuletyn Instrukcyjny* no. 2, June 1945, p. 12 (APG, WUKPPiW, file ref. no. 210); "Oszczędność – systemem w naszej pracy," *Biuletyn Informacyjno-Instrukcyjny*

removed "particular words or sentences thoughtlessly, sloppily and haphazardly"[931] – sometimes deliberately, other times as a result of simple carelessness of employees. More importantly, such a negligently laid out text made it immediately clear that "the text has been censored,"[932] which was obviously an unacceptable oversight. This is why there was such a strong emphasis on the need for good cooperation between field censorship offices and printing houses, and for the organization of training sessions during which the proper "removal of paragraphs, phrases or individual words" would be taught.[933]

For the publishing market and a literary creation, the changes concerning the functioning of "printing, stamping, and copying houses, as well as companies working with the photo-sensitive method"[934] were extremely important. The May 1952 Bulletin published a two-and-a-half-page article titled "Usprawnić i rozszerzyć kontrolę i inspekcję zakładów drukarskich"[935] [Improving and expanding the control and inspection of printing houses]. The material was published in connection with an amendment to the GUKPPiW Act. The changes introduced by the decree of April 22, 1952 concerned, among others, the inclusion of "announcements, notices, and posters" within the scope of controlled cultural texts. They also extended the powers of the GUKPPiW to include supervision over companies manufacturing stamps, publications and illustrations using a photo-sensitive method, and introduced control and registration of copying machines. A clause was also added, according to which anyone who evaded supervision or control "shall be punished with imprisonment of up to one year or a fine of up to 10,000 zloty, or both these penalties jointly."[936] The decree was mentioned in several other

---

no. 3, March 1952, p. 18 (APG, WUKPPiW, file ref. no. 96); "Po odprawie kierowników referatów widowisk i inspekcji WUKPPiW," *Biuletyn Informacyjno-Instrukcyjny* no. 1 (25), January 1954, pp. 33–34 (APG, WUKPPiW, file ref. no. 39); acting Head of Performance and Inspection Department of the WUKP Kraków Zofia Haraschin, "Nasz głos w dyskusji" (correspondence in "Dział Listów"), *Biuletyn Informacyjno-Instrukcyjny* no. 1 (25), January 1954, pp. 44–48 (APG, WUKPPiW, file ref. no. 39).

[931] "Wzmóc ochronę tajemnicy wojskowej na wszystkich odcinkach naszej kontroli," *Biuletyn Informacyjno-Instrukcyjny* no. 1 (13), January 1953, p. 24 (APG, WUKPPiW, file ref. no. 19).

[932] Ibidem.

[933] Ibidem.

[934] "Usprawnić i rozszerzyć kontrolę i inspekcję zakładów drukarskich," *Biuletyn Informacyjno-Instrukcyjny* no. 5, May 1952, p. 16 (APG, WUKPPiW, file ref. no. 90).

[935] Ibidem, pp. 15–17.

[936] "Dekret z dnia 22 kwietnia 1952 r. o częściowej zmianie dekretu z dnia 5 lipca 1946 r. o utworzeniu Głównego Urzędu Kontroli Prasy, Publikacyj i Widowisk" (*Journal of Laws* 1952, no. 19, item 114, p. 119). The decree came into force on April 26, 1952 and was repealed on July 1, 1984. The control of printing houses was also discussed

issues of the magazine, expressing the hope that the time when "the enemy roistered with impunity in the area of copying machines and stamps"[937] was irrevocably over, and that this would result in increased supervision of the hitherto neglected ephemera, such as posters, passes, personal files, official delegations, questionnaires, forms, certificates, etc."[938] It is worth mentioning that the authors indeed took advantage of "Mysia Street's" lack of supervision over printing houses. One of the ways of publishing a text blocked by the Office for the Control was turning it into a large stamp and making copies of it.[939]

in: "Z krajowej odprawy w GUKP," *Biuletyn Informacyjno-Instrukcyjny* no. 7, July 1952, pp. 15–20 (APG, WUKPPiW, file ref. no. 84).

[937] "Z krajowej odprawy w GUKP," *Biuletyn Informacyjno-Instrukcyjny* no. 7, July 1952, p. 16 (APG, WUKPPiW, file ref. no. 84).

[938] Ibidem, p. 17.

[939] Ibidem, p. 16.

PART THREE

"CAMERA CENSORICA."
WHAT ELSE WAS DISCUSSED
IN THE BULLETINS?

I. Other problems raised in the Bulletins

The censor did not notice the forest
among the trees.[1]

Over the course of the eleven years under review, the Bulletins dealt with a variety of topics: the literary issues discussed above were only one of them and not necessarily the most important. The journal was dominated by materials that were a response to changes occurring in the political, social, and economic reality of the time, as well as questions directly related to the organization of work in the Office for the Control. However, topics on culture – in the broadest sense of the term – appeared several more times in the Bulletins. The non-literary subjects featured in the confidential guides included discussions on the censorship of films, theatrical productions, radio broadcasts, and in one issue, the focus was on a board game.

***

Most of the information on film censorship appeared on the margins of other considerations. Only a few separate articles devoted to this matter were published.[2] The magazine discussed, above all, the achievements of Polish cinematography, although it also examined foreign films, including those presented at international film festivals; the monthly could not have overlooked the titles from the Soviet Union, but also mentioned productions from Czechoslovakia, the Netherlands, Italy and the United States.[3]

---

[1] [Materiały z odprawy], fol. 35r (*"Biuletyny Instrukcyjno-Szkoleniowe 1945–1951"* (APP, WUKPPiW, file ref. no. 4)); cf. the "horse blinkers" metaphor cited earlier. The phrase "camera censorica" comes from: "Camera censorica," *Biuletyn Informacyjno-Szkoleniowy* no. 1/3, January 1949, p. 43 (APG, WUKPPiW, file ref. no. 196).

[2] See, e.g.: "Kontrola wtórna filmów. Obowiązek zawodowy czy rozrywka?," *Biuletyn Informacyjno-Instrukcyjny* no. 9 (21), September 1953, pp. 550–556 (AAN, GUKPPiW, file ref. no. 22); "Znaczenie wtórnej kontroli filmów," *Biuletyn Informacyjno-Instrukcyjny* no. 6 (30), June 1954, pp. 20–25 (APG, WUKPPiW, file ref. no. 52). On the control of film, aside from the below-listed titles, see also M. Fik, "Film a cenzura. Z archiwum Głównego Urzędu Kontroli Prasy, Publikacji i Widowisk (6). Październik–grudzień 1968," *Kwartalnik Filmowy* 1995, no. 11, pp. 128–134.

[3] See, e.g.: "Recenzje"; "Prowokacje antyradzieckie"; "Camera censorica," *Biuletyn Informacyjno-Szkoleniowy* no. 1/3, January 1949, pp. 8–9, 14, 43–44 (APG, WUKPPiW,

The way the editors inspected the film industry was similar to the way the book market was presented: a discussion of current problems of the field was accompanied by a rather biased selection of training materials, which consisted of bad and terrible analyses and censorship opinions. Therefore, one had the impression that only a few employees passed the exam on writing literary and film reviews. According to their superiors, the majority of them penned erroneous reviews, as a result of which a work that was incorrect for various reasons could be sent for publication or distribution or, on the contrary, a work that was made "properly" could be stopped by the blithe decision of the censors. Obviously, all films were scrutinized according to the guidelines in force at the time, and the focus was mainly on the ideological realization, while the artistic dimension was treated as a secondary element (in exceptional cases, the proportions between the two components shifted).

Among the materials on the tenth muse, there was also room for accounts revealing the more technical behind-the-scenes work of controlling film. As it turned out, voivodeship offices were unable to keep up with the assessment of productions, of which there were simply too many, and the constant staff shortages exacerbated the situation. That is why changes were introduced to streamline film inspection and to help relieve the WUKPPiW of the burden of reviewing films subject to control.[4]

***

Aside from films, theatrical productions were also assessed. The evaluation of dramatic works, similarly to any other publications, was a two-stage process: they underwent primary and secondary inspection. The issue of evaluation was different "if a decision was made to stage a play: then the play was censored repeatedly at various steps of its preparation: before the production (as a script), during rehearsals and dress rehearsal, and at the premiere."[5]

---

file ref. no. 196); "Kontrola wtórna filmów. Obowiązek zawodowy czy rozrywka?," *Biuletyn Informacyjno-Instrukcyjny* no. 9 (21), September 1953, pp. 550–556 (AAN, GUKPPiW, file ref. no. 22).

[4] "Po odprawie kierowników referatów widowisk i inspekcji WUKPPiW," *Biuletyn Informacyjno-Instrukcyjny* no. 1 (25), January 1954, pp. 31–32 (APG, WUKPPiW, file ref. no. 39). See also: "Wypowiedzi w dyskusji. Grajewska (GUKPPiW, Wydz. Widowisk)," *Biuletyn Informacyjno-Instrukcyjny* no. 6/7 (18/19), June/July 1953, pp. 21–25 (APG, WUKPPiW, file ref. no. 14).

[5] A. Artysiewicz, "Cenzorska wizja dramatu i teatru na podstawie *Odpraw krajowych z lat 1945–1946*," [in:] *Dramat i teatr w dokumentach GUKPPiW*, eds. K. Budrowska, M. Budnik, K. Kościewicz, Białystok: Wydawnictwo Alter Studio, 2017, series *Cenzura w PRL. Archiwalia* vol. 2, p. 12.

Clearly, the evaluation of a show is only one component in a rather complicated process of censoring performances, which – according to the nomenclature adopted by the Main Office – included: texts of plays, scripts of performances and entertainment events, performances of professional theaters (permanent and touring) and amateur theaters, as well as various entertainment performances (musical, literary, and cabaret, etc.).[6] More than a dozen articles on the control of performances thus defined were published in the Bulletins, which mentioned fairly regularly the activities of the State Organization of Artistic Events "ARTOS," established at the time "to assemble and execute entertainment programs."[7]

However, a lot of space was also devoted to artistic activities that escaped the control of the censorship office, not being fully supervised by any of the existing institutions. A great challenge for the evaluators were the so-called rouge bands,[8] a perfect example of walking a tightrope on the edge of the law. Events organized by such groups usually "did not have an Artos license"[9] or "a program approved by the GUKP,"[10] therefore, problems arose at the moment of "catching the bands in the field."[11]

---

[6] K. Boroda, K. Kościewicz, "Cenzurowanie widowisk w 1949 r. w świetle statystyki Głównego Urzędu Kontroli Prasy, Publikacji i Widowisk," [in:] *Dramat i teatr w dokumentach GUKPPiW…*, p. 91.

[7] "Kilka uwag o programach 'Artosu,'" *Biuletyn Informacyjno-Instrukcyjny* no. 1, January 1952, p. 41 (APG, WUKPPiW, file ref. no. 100). See, e.g.: "Widowiska," *Biuletyn Informacyjno-Szkoleniowy* no. 4, May 1949, fol. 157v–158r (APP, WUKPPiW, file ref. no. 4); "Ze sprawozdań Kierowników Wojewódzkich Biur," *Biuletyn Instrukcyjny* June 1945, pp. 12–13 (APG, WUKPPiW, file ref. no. 210); "O wyższy poziom pracy na odcinku widowisk," *Biuletyn Informacyjno-Instrukcyjny* no. 3 (15), March 1953, pp. 36–46 (APG, WUKPPiW, file ref. no. 17); M. Grzybowska (WUKP Gdańsk), "Kilka uwag o próbach generalnych," *Biuletyn Informacyjno-Instrukcyjny* no. 3 (15), March 1953, pp. 60–64 (APG, WUKPPiW, file ref. no. 17); "Po odprawie kierowników referatów widowisk i inspekcji WUKPPiW," *Biuletyn Informacyjno-Instrukcyjny* no. 1 (25), January 1954, pp. 26–38 (APG, WUKPPiW, file ref. no. 39).

[8] "Widowiska" (in the series *Z naszych doświadczeń*), *Biuletyn Informacyjno-Instrukcyjny* no. 2, February 1952, p. 48 (APG, WUKPPiW, file ref. no. 99). See: B. Tyszkiewicz, "'Dzikie zespoły' i ocenzurowany cyrk. GUKPPiW wobec wybranych zjawisk kultury popularnej," [in:] *Kultura popularna w Polsce 1944–1989. Między projektem ideologicznym a kontestacją*, ed. K. Stańczak-Wiślicz, Warszawa: IBL PAN, 2015, pp. 11–41.

[9] "Z krajowej odprawy w GUKP," *Biuletyn Informacyjno-Instrukcyjny* no. 7, July 1952, p. 19 (APG, WUKPPiW, file ref. no. 84).

[10] Ibidem.

[11] "Widowiska" (in the series *Z naszych doświadczeń*), *Biuletyn Informacyjno-Instrukcyjny* no. 2, February 1952, p. 47 (APG, WUKPPiW, file ref. no. 99).

The Bulletins very often informed about problems with the control of various kinds of performances. The lists of withdrawn plays sent out by AGTIF (the Theatre and Film Agency) were supposed to help, but they did not solve the problem.[12] The briefings criticized the field officials for lacking "vigilance and political training,"[13] disregarding their duties and their "superficial treatment of the phenomena occurring specifically in professional theaters."[14] As a side note, the above-mentioned officials (social-administrative, social-political, and local) were so-called plenipotentiaries of the censorship office, appointed from among the employees of the presidiums of the national councils, whose tasks were to control these very local contents. "It should be noted that censorship was really only one of their duties and that is why the cooperation was not always satisfactory to the Office for the Control," observed Zbigniew Romek.[15] The Bulletins repeatedly complained about difficult contact with the officials, and their professional competence could be illustrated by the fact that in one of the articles, they were infamously called "nincompoops."[16] Finally, even circus programs merited attention in the Bulletin materials on censoring performances.[17]

***

On numerous occasions, the Bulletin looked into the censorship of radio broadcasts.[18] Materials about the radio were often published in the form of periodic reports sent to the editors from the "field." Some cultural events presented

---

[12] "Listy sztuk wycofanych," *Biuletyn Informacyjno-Instrukcyjny* no. 4, May 1949, fol. 158r (APP, WUKPPiW, file ref. no. 4).

[13] "Widowiska" (in the series *Z naszych doświadczeń*), *Biuletyn Informacyjno-Instrukcyjny* no. 2, February 1952, p. 47 (APG, WUKPPiW, file ref. no. 99).

[14] Ibidem, p. 46.

[15] E-mail correspondence between the author and Professor Zbigniew Romek, March 20–22, 2019.

[16] "Z krajowej odprawy w GUKP," *Biuletyn Informacyjno-Instrukcyjny* no. 7, July 1952, p. 18 (APG, WUKPPiW, file ref. no. 84). See also: "Stosunki między Kościołem a Państwem; Kontrola pracy referentów społeczno-politycznych," *Biuletyn Informacyjno-Szkoleniowy* no. 4, May 1949, fol. 142r–142v, 158v (APP, WUKPPiW, file ref. no. 4); S. Borowik (Gdańsk), "O pracy WUKP Gdańsk z referentami społeczno-administracyjnymi," *Biuletyn Informacyjno-Instrukcyjny* no. 4, April 1952, pp. 33–37 (APG, WUKPPiW, file ref. no. 93); "Z działu druków ulotnych," *Biuletyn Informacyjno-Instrukcyjny* no. 1 (13), January 1953, p. 56 (APG, WUKPPiW, file ref. no. 19).

[17] See, e.g.: "O pomocy zespołom amatorskim," *Biuletyn Informacyjno-Instrukcyjny* no. 4 (28), April 1954, p. 13 (APG, WUKPPiW, file ref. no. 48).

[18] See, e.g.: "Ocena pracy cenzury prewencyjnej. Podważenie jedności narodowej," *Biuletyn Instrukcyjny* no. 1, May 1945, fol. 2r (APP, WUKPPiW, file ref. no. 4); "Radio,"

in the radio broadcasts appeared in the reports not because of their artistic value. This was the case when a report from Katowice mentioned a radio program titled *Concert at the Central Miner's House*; it appreciated the organization of the event, which was combined "with the popularization of cyclicality and a multi-order (*wieloporządkowy*) [*sic*] system."[19] Thanks to consultation with Wacław Andrusikiewicz from the AGH University of Science and Technology in Kraków, it was possible to establish that what was meant was a multiface (*wieloprzodkowy*) system (not a *wieloporządkowy* system as it was spelled in the Bulletin); without going into details that are complicated for a literature specialist, it was a system which, as Andrusikiewicz explains, was aimed at

> increasing the concentration of coal extraction from a given area of the mine. Propaganda claimed that it was better than the systems used in the West or across the pond; except each deposit is different and requires an individual approach, but the activities to be performed (at least in the basic scope) are the same and repeatable. In so-called socialism, no one discovered America, it was more propaganda geared at demonstrating the superiority of the socialist labor system over the capitalist one. We must also remember that this was a post-war period, with a recovering economy. One of the keys to success was propaganda.[20]

This rather atypical example further emphasizes that manipulative and propagandistic imagery was applied to all topics covered in the Bulletins, from the creation of literature to the extraction of natural resources. However, returning to cultural broadcasts, most of the materials on radio programs that appeared in

---

Biuletyn Informacyjno-Szkoleniowy no. 2, 30 November 1948, fol. 89r–91r (APP, WUKP-PiW, file ref. no. 4); "O dobrych i złych przykładach pracy kontroli prewencyjnej w terenie," *Biuletyn Informacyjno-Instrukcyjny* no. 6, June 1952, pp. 6–7, 13 (APG, WUKPPiW, file ref. no. 87); "Lokalne audycje terenowych radiowęzłów," *Biuletyn Informacyjno-Instrukcyjny* no. 6, June 1952, pp. 28–30 (APG, WUKPPiW, file ref. no. 87); WUKP Bydgoszcz, "Radio Polskie – Bydgoszcz. Uwagi krytyczne za okres od 1–25.IX.52 r.," *Biuletyn Informacyjno-Instrukcyjny* no. 10, October 1952, pp. 16–21 (APG, WUKPPiW, file ref. no. 75); J. Garlicki, "Kilka uwag na temat organizacji pracy w WUKPPiW" (correspondence in "Dział listów"), *Biuletyn Informacyjno-Instrukcyjny* no. 12, December 1952, p. 42 (APG, WUKPPiW, file ref. no. 70); "Z zagadnień tajemnicy państwowej," *Biuletyn Informacyjno-Instrukcyjny* no. 2 (14), February 1953, pp. 10–11 (APG, WUKPPiW, file ref. no. 18); "O pracy radiowęzłów w woj. lubelskim," *Biuletyn Informacyjno-Instrukcyjny* no. 3 (27), March 1954, pp. 20–27 (APG, WUKPPiW, file ref. no. 45).

[19] "Ocena audycji radiowych rozgłośni Polskiego Radia w Katowicach za okres od 16.XII.51 r. do 15.II.52 r.," *Biuletyn Informacyjno-Instrukcyjny* no. 4, April 1952, p. 21 (APG, WUKPPiW, file ref. no. 93).

[20] Reply from Prof. Wacław Andrusikiewicz to my question on "cyclicality and multi-order/multiface systems" (e-mail correspondence, August 10–March 12, 2020).

the Bulletins, primarily raised issues of the accuracy of the formulated assessment and the problems of censoring the radio as a medium. The subject matter was dominated by contemporary socio-political problems; the topics of literature and broadly defined culture were found only in a few reports.

***

In March 1954, a board game called *Przygody w dżungli*[21] [Jungle adventures] was discussed, which, according to the evaluators, supposedly represented an idyllic version of the old imperialist world order.[22] The one-page material was accompanied by a photo of the game board, which shows a white man dressed in the traditional clothes of a colonizer.[23] He is looking at black inhabitants of a stereotypically depicted African village engage in a play, perhaps a ritual dance. This particular graphic element was controversial because, according to the Bulletin's editors, the concept of the drawing offered an idyllic version of the coexistence between the colonizers and the colonized, and idealized "white imperialist colonizers while showing the 'savagery' and 'inferiority' of dark-skinned people."[24]

The game *Przygody w dżungli* was therefore suspended, but not for long, as it already re-entered the market in 1956. It was not easy to find it, as unfortunately, other than the (imprecise) title, the Bulletin did not note the game's publisher or any other details. Moreover, in the case of PRL's board games, there are often problems with identifying the publisher, because, as board game enthusiast and expert Michał Stajszczak concludes:

> during the communist era, board games were produced by cooperatives of disabled workers and artisans' cooperatives. In the latter case, the game was produced by a particular artisan, who, however, could not sell it himself. Often the box provided no details outside the name and address of the cooperative.[25]

---

[21] In the Bulletin – *Przygoda w dżungli* – A jungle adventure.

[22] "O grze *Przygoda w dżungli*," *Biuletyn Informacyjno-Instrukcyjny* March 1954, no. 3 (27), p. 47 + n.p. game board (APG, WUKPPiW, file ref. no. 45). The following literature proved useful when working on this chapter: M. Wieczorek, "Kreatywność projektantów zabawek zatrudnionych w spółdzielniach pracy w okresie PRL a czynniki ją ograniczające," *Lubelski Rocznik Pedagogiczny* 2019, vol. 38, no. 1, pp. 97–112; E. Glonnegger, *Leksykon gier planszowych. Geneza, zasady i historia*, trans. J.A. Jerry, Warszawa: Świat Książki, 1997.

[23] See: Fig. 25a.

[24] "O grze *Przygoda w dżungli*," *Biuletyn Informacyjno-Instrukcyjny* March 1954, no. 3 (27), p. 47 (APG, WUKPPiW, file ref. no. 45).

[25] Excerpt from the author's correspondence with Michał Stajszczak about *Przygody w dżungli* (e-mail correspondence, January 25, 2020).

Courtesy of Marek Rutkowski, I was able to find the original game from 1956, which was published in Warsaw by the "Światowid" Artistic Industry Cooperative.[26]

Fig. 25a. A photograph of the game board of *Przygody w dżungli. Kombinacyjna gra dla młodzieży* [A combination game for the youth] in the March 1954 Bulletin ("O grze *Przygoda w dżungli*," *Biuletyn Informacyjno-Instrukcyjny* March 1954, no. 3 (27), p. 48 (APG, WUKPPiW, file ref. no. 45)).

The comparison of the boards illustrates a change introduced in the part of the drawing that shows the "white colonizer" surrounded by villagers. Evidently, one of the problems noticed by the censors in 1954 was removed, because instead of an adult man looking at the inhabitants with a clearly condescending face, a young girl who joined the play (ritual) was introduced. In the new version of the game board, the young girl is depicted with a characteristic red scarf tied around her neck – was the white colonizer replaced by a Soviet pioneer? Such an interpretation of the drawing seems highly probable and would justify allowing the game to be distributed.

---

[26] Locating the game published sixty-five years ago was not easy. I would like to thank users of the boardgamegeek.com and boardgamegeek.pl forums, as well as board game enthusiasts who helped me find the game: Marcin Leszczyński, Przemysław Gumułka, Wojciech Chuchla and the user nicked "hamanu." See, e.g.: *Przygody w dżungli (1956)*, Boardgamegeek.com, https://boardgamegeek.com/boardgame/38043/przygody-w-dzungli?fbclid=IwAR0C2ec2wKwIT_-vyF4Pg1Tg7Byx6yePFQAAhfQIe-Jek0s-6Y2asjo7UnJ4 (accessed January 31, 2021).

Fig. 25b. The game board of *Przygody w dżungli. Kombinacyjna gra dla młodzieży*, Warszawa: Spółdzielnia Przemysłu Artystycznego "Światowid," 1956. Material from the private collection of Marek Rutkowski.

***

It bears repeating that the above-discussed literary and cultural issues were only one of the topics dealt with by the functionaries of the "Mysia Street and it environs." The journal was dominated by materials that were a response to changes in the political, social, and economic reality of the time. Most of them focused on domestic issues, although the magazine also wrote about the situation of friendly countries: priority was given to news about the USSR, but there were also materials about the GDR, Bulgaria, Hungary, the People's Republic of China and Romania.[27]

In international politics, matters of defense against the "hostile imperialism" of the USA resurfaced,[28] as well as comparisons of living standards and conditions in America and the countries of people's democracy, obviously, in favor of the latter.[29] Several articles discussed the struggle against cosmopolitanism, as well as decolonization and the political-economic situation of post-colonial countries.[30]

Domestic topics included the problems of the Polish countryside. The Bulletins raised the subjects of class struggle, the struggle against the kulaks, and the ties between the countryside and the city. The successes of Polish agriculture were also highlighted; party organizations, production cooperatives and other forms of activity in the countryside were appreciated, such as "Samopomoc Chłopska" [Peasant Self-Help], country women's clubs, and State Agricultural Farms (PGR-y). The most attention was paid to censorial omissions and "harmful" interventions, but censors were also praised for their vigilance in evaluating materials devoted to agriculture and the living conditions in rural areas. Several materials also examined the cultural life of the Polish countryside and art that dealt with rural issues.[31]

---

[27] Among the numerous materials, see, e.g.: "Publikacje społeczno-polityczne," *Biuletyn Informacyjno-Instrukcyjny* no. 6, June 1952, pp. 31–36 (APG, WUKPPiW, file ref. no. 87). When presenting subsequent topics covered in the Bulletins, I include a reference to one sample of material addressing a given question (in exceptional cases, I provide more articles).

[28] Ibidem.

[29] Among the numerous materials, see, e.g.: "Czy Reformy Roosevelta były postępowe (z dyskusji nad artykułem w Dziale Prasy i Radia)," *Biuletyn Informacyjno-Instrukcyjny* no. 1 (13), January 1953, pp. 27–44 (APG, WUKPPiW, file ref. no. 19).

[30] Among the numerous materials, see, e.g.: "O niektórych przejawach kosmopolityzmu w czasopismach techniczno-naukowych," *Biuletyn Informacyjno-Instrukcyjny* no. 8, August 1952, pp. 30–41 (APG, WUKPPiW, file ref. no. 81); "Niektóre zagadnienia międzynarodowe w świetle naszych doświadczeń," *Biuletyn Informacyjno-Instrukcyjny* no. 11, November 1952, pp. 11–23 (APG, WUKPPiW, file ref. no. 72).

[31] See, e.g.: "Po odprawie kierowników referatów widowisk i inspekcji WUKPPiW," *Biuletyn Informacyjno-Instrukcyjny* no. 1 (25), January 1954, p. 27 (APG, WUKPPiW, file ref. no. 39); "Spółdzielczość produkcyjna w naszej literaturze," *Biuletyn Informacyjno-Instrukcyjny* no. 3 (27), March 1954, pp. 28–46 (APG, WUKPPiW, file ref. no. 45).

Considerable space was devoted to the most important events and phenomena from the point of view of the political interests of the authorities. One of them was, of course, the Constitution passed on July 22, 1952. The draft of the Basic Law and the Act itself were the subject of shorter and longer articles in the 1952 issues (more than half of the fifty-one-page February Bulletin was about the Constitution). Subsequent issues published materials about "the election campaign for the First Sejm of the Polish People's Republic."[32] In addition, the censors wishing to further educate themselves in the aforementioned topics were recommended to read the books of the "Ksiażka i Wiedza" publishing house in particular.[33]

Naturally, the Bulletins had to include materials on the Three-Year and Six-Year Plans: they not only reported on the implementation of tasks on construction sites scattered around Poland, but also on its execution in literature, assessing books and brochures published on this subject.[34] "Poland under construction" and current affairs, such as the protection of state secrets, were certainly the most important and appeared regularly in the periodical (an example of which is the "Military Instruction" discussed in detail in one of the Bulletins, that is, the GUK-PPiW's order from June 1948 on the protection of military secrets).[35] However, the crucial topics of the present day were also examined from a historical perspective, thanks to which the functionaries learned, for instance, about the history and present of the peasant and workers' movement as well as of the All-Union Communist Party.[36]

---

[32] See, e.g.: "Na marginesie ogólnonarodowej dyskusji konstytucyjnej" and "Na marginesie ogólnonarodowej dyskusji (materiał wysłany do WUKP dnia 6 II 52 r.)," *Biuletyn Informacyjno-Instrukcyjny* no. 2, February 1952, pp. 1–28 (APG, WUKPPiW, file ref. no. 99); "Ulepszenie naszej pracy jest warunkiem sprostania naszym obecnym zadaniom," *Biuletyn Informacyjno-Instrukcyjny* no. 9, September 1952, pp. 1–8 (APG, WUKPPiW, file ref. no. 78).

[33] "Na marginesie ogólnonarodowej dyskusji konstytucyjnej," *Biuletyn Informacyjno--Instrukcyjny* no. 2, February 1952, p. 21 (APG, WUKPPiW, file ref. no. 99).

[34] See, e.g.: *Biuletyn Głównego Urzędu Kontroli Prasy* no. 4, fol. 50r (APP WUKPPiW, file ref. no. 4); "Publikacje społeczno-polityczne," *Biuletyn Informacyjno-Instrukcyjny* no. 6, June 1952, p. 34 (APG, WUKPPiW, file ref. no. 87); "O pracy WUKP na odcinku ochrony tajemnicy gospodarczej," *Biuletyn Informacyjno-Instrukcyjny* no. 6, June 1952, pp. 18–20 (APG, WUKPPiW, file ref. no. 87).

[35] Among the numerous materials, see, e.g.: "Ochrona tajemnicy wojskowej," *Biuletyn Informacyjno-Szkoleniowy* no. 2, November 30, 1948, fol. 82r–88r (APP, WUKPPiW, file ref. no. 4).

[36] Among the numerous materials, see, e.g.: "Szkolenie ideologiczne – podstawa naszej pracy," *Biuletyn Informacyjno-Instrukcyjny* no. 6, June 1952, pp. 21–27 (APG, WUKPPiW, file ref. no. 87).

A different kind of history, describing the tragic experiences of the Polish nation during the Second World War, was also present in the magazine. All the relatively frequent materials, including those concerning Katyń and the Warsaw Uprising, were obviously constructed in accordance with the optics of the time, as evidenced by the following comment: "the cases of Katyń and the Warsaw Uprising are brilliantly exposed anti-Soviet intrigues."[37]

Matters related to faith were another frequent topic of the monthly. To a large extent, a more or less subtle fight was waged against the clergy and the Catholic Church, which in several places was explicitly described as the "enemy."[38] The presence of religious institutions in the public and media space as well as other matters concerning the relationship between the state and the Church were debated. Such materials invoked Article 71 of the Constitution, which provided citizens with the "freedom of speech, print, assembly and rallies, marches and demonstrations,"[39] and referred to the Agreement between the Government and the Episcopate.[40] Discussions on the evaluation of the religious press,[41] mainly Catholic, were interesting in the context of the "freedom of speech." On the one hand, the aggressive "corseting" of the titles was condemned; on the other, arguments were made about the diversionary activities of the Church.[42]

Since "the PRL loved to celebrate its anniversaries,"[43] the cryptotexts published numerous materials in connection with commemoration events or celebrations (usually state holidays). Over the course of the eleven-year period under

---

[37] "Trzy recenzje," *Biuletyn Informacyjno-Instrukcyjny* no. 11, November 1952, p. 63 (APG, WUKPPiW, file ref. no. 72). See also: "Na marginesie dyskusji nad *Pokoleniem* Czeszki," *Biuletyn Informacyjno-Instrukcyjny* no. 4, April 1952, p. 16 (APG, WUKPPiW, file ref. no. 93).

[38] *Biuletyn Informacyjno-Instrukcyjny* no. 5, May 1952, pp. 10, 12, 15 (APG, WUKP-PiW, file ref. no. 90).

[39] "Z doświadczeń naszej kontroli na odcinku niektórych pism katolickich," *Biuletyn Informacyjno-Instrukcyjny* no. 9, September 1952, p. 38 (APG, WUKPPiW, file ref. no. 78).

[40] See, e.g.: "Porozumienie między Rządem Polskiej Rzeczypospolitej Ludowej a Episkopatem podstawą słusznej linii kontroli pism i publikacji katolickich," *Biuletyn Informacyjno-Instrukcyjny* no. 12, December 1952, pp. 29–37 (APG, WUKPPiW, file ref. no. 70).

[41] References were made to the following periodicals: *Tygodnik Powszechny, Tygodnik Katolicki, Głos Katolicki, Słowo Powszechne, Niedziela, Dziś i Jutro, Ład Boży, Gość Niedzielny, Homo Dei, Wiadomości Diecezjalne Łódzkie, Kronika Diecezji Sandomierskiej, Ruch Biblijny i Liturgiczny,* and *Rycerz Niepokalanej.* See, e.g.: *Biuletyn Informacyjno-Instrukcyjny* no. 12, December 1952, p. 30 (APG, WUKPPiW, file ref. no. 70).

[42] See, e.g.: "Seminarium prasy (wyjątki z protokółu). Jedność narodowa"; "Ze sprawozdań kierowników Wojewódzkich Biur," *Biuletyn Instrukcyjny* no. 2, June 1945, pp. 3–4, 11 (APG, WUKPPiW, file ref. no. 210).

[43] W. Kot, *PRL – jak cudnie się żyło!,* Poznań: Wydawnictwo Publicat, 2010, p. 10.

review, there were multiple reminders of, for example, Bolesław Bierut's sixtieth birthday, the tenth anniversary of the founding of the Polish Workers' Party, the eighth anniversary of the founding of People's Poland, the eighth anniversary of the proclamation of the manifesto of the Polish Committee of National Liberation, and the seventh anniversary of the liberation of Katowice.[44] In addition, materials were published on the occasion of May First and the millennium of the Polish state.[45] Naturally, the Bulletin's "birthday" was celebrated with panache on its pages in 1956.[46]

There were also commemorations of events going beyond the local color, especially those which showed Poland as a member of the great socialist family of states. Thus, the anniversaries of Vladimir Lenin's birth and death were celebrated, as well as the founding of the People's Republic of China and the GDR, to name but a few.[47] Furthermore, the periodical commemorated, for example, the thirty-fifth anniversary of the October Revolution, but also the 19th Congress of the All-Union Communist Party, which lasted from October 5 to 14, 1952.[48] Perhaps the most significant symbolic proof of this community of nations was the portrait of the "Leader and Teacher, Great Stalin" and a condolence letter from the GUKPPiW to the USSR Embassy, which was posted in March 1953.[49]

Clearly, in spite of certain thematic shortcomings, the Bulletin proved to be a remarkably comprehensive magazine, with rich potential for further research.

---

[44] Among the numerous materials, see, e.g.: *Biuletyn Informacyjno-Instrukcyjny* no. 3, March 1952, p. 5 et seq. (APG, WUKPPiW, file ref. no. 96); *Biuletyn Informacyjno-Instrukcyjny* no. 4, April 1952, pp. 28–29 (APG, WUKPPiW, file ref. no. 93); *Biuletyn Informacyjno-Instrukcyjny* no. 5, May 1952, p. 50 (APG, WUKPPiW, file ref. no. 90); *Biuletyn Informacyjno-Instrukcyjny* no. 6, June 1952, p. 40 (APG, WUKPPiW, file ref. no. 87).

[45] See, e.g.: *Biuletyn Informacyjno-Instrukcyjny* no. 5, May 1952, pp. 10, 49–50 (APG, WUKPPiW, file ref. no. 90).

[46] S. Wilner, "I co dalej?… (refleksje redaktora *Biuletynu*)"; "Pięćdziesiąt numerów," *Biuletyn Informacyjno-Instrukcyjny* no. 2 (50), February 1956, pp. 2–21 (APG, WUKPPiW, file ref. no. 6).

[47] See, e.g.: "Ocena audycji radiowych rozgłośni Polskiego Radia w Katowicach za okres od 16.XII.51 r. do 15.II.52 r.," *Biuletyn Informacyjno-Instrukcyjny* no. 4, April 1952, pp. 25–26, 29 (APG, WUKPPiW, file ref. no. 93); B. Gutkowski, "O wyższy poziom pracy Urzędu," *Biuletyn Informacyjno-Instrukcyjny* no. 12, December 1952, pp. 4–5 (APG, WUKPPiW, file ref. no. 70).

[48] See, e.g.: "Z zobowiązań zespołu WUKPPiW Kraków," *Biuletyn Informacyjno-Instrukcyjny* no. 9, September 1952, p. 50, 52–56 (APG, WUKPPiW, file ref. no. 78).

[49] "Do Ambasady Związku Socjalistycznych Republik Radzieckich," *Biuletyn Informacyjno-Instrukcyjny* no. 3 (15), March 1953, pp. 1–2 (APG, WUKPPiW, file ref. no. 17). See also: Fig. 26 and Fig. 27.

Fig. 26. A portrait of Joseph Stalin featured in the March 1953 Bulletin
(APG, WUKPPiW, file ref. no. 17, p. 1).

Do

Ambasady   Związku   Socjalistycznych

Republik   Radzieckich

w Warszawie

Pracownicy Głównego Urzędu Kontroli Prasy, Publikacyj i Widowisk wraz z całym narodem polskim głęboko wstrząśnięci zgonem Największego Człowieka naszych czasów, Wodza i Nauczyciela całej ludzkości, Wielkiego Stalina, przesyłają na Wasze ręce narodom radzieckim wyrazy współczucia w tym wielkim nieszczęściu. W tej ciężkiej chwili łączymy się z Wami w bólu i żałobie .

Pomni historycznych zasług Wielkiego Stalina, który był naszemu narodowi szczególnie bliski i drogi jako ten, który na różnych etapach walki polskiej klasy robotniczej wskazywał jej właściwą drogę, jako ten, dzięki któremu naród polski dwukrotnie odzyskał niepodległość i dzięki któremu suwerenność naszego narodu jest zabezpieczona, ślubujemy - jak uczy nas Towarzysz Bierut - dochować wierności jego naukom i codzienną twórczą i ofiarną pracą przyczynić się do zwycięstwa wielkich idei Lenina—Stalina.

Rozwijając pracę polityczną wśród naszego zespołu, wzmagając czujność rewolucyjną całego naszego aparatu w walce o wyższy poziom naszej pracy, przyczynimy się do jeszcze silniejszego scementowania naszych szeregów wokół bastionu pokoju, przewodniej siły ludzkości Związku Radzieckiego i Jego Wielkiej okrytej chwałą Partii Lenina—Stalina.

Imię WIELKIEGO STALINA było jest i będzie natchnieniem dla naszej walki i pracy.

W imieniu załogi:

NACZELNY DYREKTOR
[M. MIKOŁAJCZYK]

SEKRETARZ P. O. P.   PRZEWODNICZĄCY
P. Z. P. R   RADY MIEJSCOWEJ
[J. Tajer]   [M. Michlewicz]

6 marca 1953 r.

Fig. 27. The condolence letter from the GUKPPiW to the USSR Embassy in Warsaw, published in the March 1953 Bulletin on the death of Joseph Stalin (APG, WUKPPiW, file ref. no. 17, p. 2).

To the Embassy of the Union of Soviet Socialist Republics in Warsaw

Deeply shocked by the death of the Greatest Man of our time, the Leader and Teacher of all mankind, the Great Stalin, we – the staff of the Main Office for the Control of the Press, Publications and Public Performances, along with the entire Polish nation – are expressing our sympathy to the Soviet people in this sheer misfortune. At this grave moment, we join you in pain and mourning. Mindful of the historical merits of the Great Stalin – a man particularly close and dear to our people as the one who showed the right path to the Polish working class at various stages of its struggle; as the one thanks to whom the Polish nation regained its independence twice, and thanks to whom the sovereignty of our nation has been secured – we vow, as Comrade Bierut guides us, to remain faithful to Stalin's teachings and to contribute with our daily creative and devoted work to the victory of the great ideas of Lenin-Stalin.

By developing political work among our team, by increasing the revolutionary vigilance of our entire apparatus in the struggle for a higher level of our work, we contribute to cementing our ranks even more firmly around the bastion of peace, the guiding force of humanity of the Soviet Union and Its Great glorified Party Lenin-Stalin.

The name of the GREAT STALIN has been and will continue to be an inspiration for our struggle and work.

On behalf of the crew:

CHIEF EXECUTIVE
[M. MIKOŁAJCZYK]

SECRETARY P.O.P.　　　　　　　　　　CHAIRMAN OF THE
P.Z.P.R　　　　　　　　　　　　　　　　LOCAL COUNCIL
[J. Tajer].　　　　　　　　　　　　　　[M. Michlewicz]

March 6, 1953

II. Before the Proper Summary, or...
the Censor as an Artist:
The Literary Work of the Functionaries
of "Mysia Street and Its Environs"

Censorship is necessary.
Censorship is an art.
A good censor should be an artist.[50]

Before a proper summary of the considerations about the Bulletins, those censors who aspired to be artists merit attention. It is no secret that some censors combined their work at the Office with literary and artistic pursuits outside it; Jerzy Kleyny, for example, published his texts both in the Bulletins and in *Szpilki*. Admittedly, there is not much information about this aspect of the censors' literary activity, this peculiar "local folklore,"[51] which was directly connected with their work at the Main Office and constituted an "artistic" testimony to their professional experience. Nonetheless, the functionaries had a creative side: over the course of eleven years, several such artistic proposals appeared in the Bulletins.[52]

For instance, '"Wnikliwe' spojrzenie" [An "insightful" look] was a story about one "of the more prominent censors."[53] In January 1955, two satirical pieces written by functionaries to commemorate the tenth anniversary of the existence of the censorship office were published: the first one, "Nasz Bilans" [Our balance], was submitted by the WUKPPiW in Łódź;[54] the second, "Cicha woda brzegi

---

[50] A line opening the film *Ucieczka z kina wolność* delivered by a censor (played by Janusz Gajos): *Ucieczka z kina "Wolność,"* directed by W. Marczewski, script by W. Marczewski, starring J. Gajos, P. Fronczewski, T. Marczewska, Z. Zamachowski, M. Bajon, Warszawa: Studio Filmowe "Tor," 1990.

[51] This term was suggested to me by an anonymous reviewer of the Preludium grant.

[52] I discuss these materials in a forthcoming book *Cenzor jako artysta. Twórczość literacka funkcjonariuszy "Mysiej i okolic" ogłoszona w Biuletynach urzędu cenzury z lat 1945–1956.*

[53] J. Garlicki (Łódź), '"Wnikliwe' spojrzenie" (material in "Dział Satyry"), *Biuletyn Informacyjno-Instrukcyjny* no. 6 (30), June 1954, p. 35 (APG, WUKPPiW, file ref. no. 52).

[54] "Nasz Bilans," *Biuletyn Informacyjno-Instrukcyjny* no. 1 (37), January 1955, pp. 66–81 (APG, WUKPPiW, file ref. no. 110).

rwie," was prepared by the Satirical Committee at the GUKPPiW.[55] Both texts were prepared for the stage, as evidenced by the blocking and the musical setting (the first production was supposed to be accompanied by recorded music). The Satirical Committee's work premiered at the GUKPPiW on January 22, 1955, as stated in the annotation. Did Jan Szeląg – who took an active part in the "Mysia Street's" jubilee – along with invited "friends" of the Office watch the show?

In the following months, further "artistic"[56] materials were published, and in September 1955, several literary texts from a newspaper published by the WUKP in Łódź were presented.[57] In addition to short, humorous pieces, a song and a dramatic work were published. Perhaps a fitting conclusion to the discussion of the Bulletins is this "farewell poem" from the Łódź branch, written for a colleague who was leaving his job:

> *Pieśń pobożna* [A pious song]
>
> Żył sobie jeden święty w Urzędzie
> Co chadzał bez aureoli.
> Ach jego pamięć zawsze żyć będzie
> Pośród cenzorskich pokoleń.
>
> Bowiem w swym życiu, w tym WoUKaPe
> Grzechów on nie miał nijakich.
> I zawsze słuszne wygłaszał sądy
> W mnogich dyskusjach wszelakich.
>
> Lecz i świętemu Urząd się znudził,
> Więc rzecz gruntowne przemyślał.
> Po cóż mam kreślić, gdy inni piszą?
> Chcę pisać, niech inni kreślą!
>
> I tak nam odszedł bez aureoli
> Ten socjalistyczny święty,
> I pozostawił nam łzy niedoli
> I serca bólem przejęte.

---

[55] "Cicha woda brzegi rwie," *Biuletyn Informacyjno-Instrukcyjny* no. 1 (37), January 1955, pp. 82–106 (APG, WUKPPiW, file ref. no. 110).

[56] See, e.g.: J. Kleyny, "Tego jeszcze nie było"; "Tylko dla kobiet," *Biuletyn Informacyjno-Instrukcyjny* no. 3 (39), March 1955, pp. 41–46 (APG, WUKPPiW, file ref. no. 107).

[57] S. Horowska [the surname is illegible – AWG] (WUKP Łódź), "Nasze ingerencje świadczą o nas," *Biuletyn Informacyjno-Instrukcyjny* no. 9 (45), September 1955, pp. 49–56 (APG, WUKPPiW, file ref. no. 120).

Od tego czasu w Urzędzie naszym
Coś się po nocach panoszy
To ex-cenzora pamięć tu straszy
I spokój Urzędu płoszy.[58]

[There lived a saint in the Office
Who walked without a halo.
And his memory will live on
Among the generations of censors.

For in his life, at this WUKP
He had no sins of any kind.
And his judgements were always right
In many discussions of all types.

But even the holy get bored with the Office,
So he thought things over.
Why should I delete, when others write?
I want to write, let others redact!

And so he quit without a halo
This socialist saint,
And left us with tears of misery
And our hearts filled with pain.

Ever since then, something
Has been prowling the Office at night
It's the ex-censor's memory that haunts here
Disturbing those who stayed behind.]

---

[58] Ibidem, p. 50.

SUMMARY

The Bulletin has been embraced – not without difficulty – and has undoubtedly contributed to the expansion of censorship issues, to the exchange of experiences, to a deeper look at the shortcomings and deficiencies in our work.[1]

The Bulletins for censors are an extremely interesting document of an epoch – an epoch in which the Main Office for the Control of the Press, Publications and Public Performances supervised creativity of all kinds. The materials presented on the pages of these confidential periodicals reveal the behind-the-scenes functioning of institutionalized censorship, often supplementing our knowledge of how "Mysia Street and its environs" operated.

I have analyzed the Bulletins created over a period of eleven years, between 1945 and 1956. I was primarily interested in matters related to literary life, and it is them that formed the core of the book. I have devoted each chapter to a separate topic, but I have always discussed the material in the context of the political and cultural situation in which it was created. The inclusion of both systems – problem-based and chronological – proved to be an optimal choice for at least several reasons.

Firstly, out of several thousand pages of Bulletins, it allowed me to extract a corpus of texts discussing the literary and cultural life of the country. This was a labor-intensive task and one which required a close reading, since many of the comments concerning creativity were made on the margins of the "more important" – that is, strictly political – topics which dominated the materials covered by the magazine. However, several matters related to the literary and cultural postwar period were discussed in more detail, and some of them were afforded separate articles.

Applying the problem-based and chronological orders made it possible for me to discuss the recurring topics from a diachronic perspective, which highlighted the changes in the evaluation and interpretation of selected topics. One example is the question of the criteria that should guide censors when assessing

---

[1] Redakcja, "50 numerów *Biuletynu,*" *Biuletyn Informacyjno-Instrukcyjny* no. 12 (48), December 1955, p. 2 (APG, WUKPPiW, file ref. no. 117).

a work. Essentially, throughout the entire period of institutional censorship, the ideological realization was unquestionably the most important measure of a work's evaluation; however, from time to time, there were reminders that it could not be the only one. This peculiar "struggle for the quality of literature" became the subject of several articles from the first half of 1952 and recurred with varying intensity in subsequent years.

Ultimately, the overlapping of the two perspectives, problem-based and chronological, helped me establish that the materials presented in the Bulletins were very often a response to the changes taking place in the country and in the world. The hypothesis of a strong dependence of the Bulletins on the (cultural) policy of the state is confirmed by a number of articles that raise matters relevant to a given period, e.g., the question of right-wing-nationalist deviation steered the assessment of literary and film works in the Bulletin from March 1950; the draft Constitution, the electoral campaign and the already passed Basic Law were discussed in the Bulletins from 1952 and 1953; in subsequent issues, a great deal was written about the situation of the country after the victory of the National Front. The Bulletins also referred to the changes that were unfolding in the economy and in the broadly defined everyday life of the citizens, for example, information about the resolution regulating prices and abolishing food stamps.[2] Furthermore, the magazine's editors reacted to institutional and legal changes within the Office for the Control itself. This was the case when, less than a month after the Act on the GUKPPiW was amended, the May 1952 issue published the content of the relevant decree.[3]

The Bulletins discussed, reviewed or simply quoted as examples several dozen cultural works. Prose enjoyed particular interest; there was a focus on contemporary novels, short stories and reportage, but there were also materials evaluating poetry collections and dramatic works. Non-fiction was also inspected, with particular attention paid to works on history and law, but also to those that "explained" the contemporary world. Polish literature constituted the largest percentage of reviewed titles, although translated works, especially from the countries of the Eastern Bloc, were also analyzed.

It should be stressed, however, that it is not always possible to determine what had a greater influence on the selection of the presented examples: was it

---

[2] "O realizację wyników odprawy grudniowej GUKPPiW," *Biuletyn Informacyjno-Instrukcyjny* no. 1 (13), January 1953, p. 13 (APG, WUKPPiW, file ref. no. 19; this was the Resolution of the Council of Ministers of January 3, 1953 on the abolition of food stamps, price regulation, general wage increases and the abolition of restrictions on trade in surplus agricultural products).

[3] "Pełny tekst Dekretu o utworzeniu GUKPPiW z dnia 5 lipca 1946 r. Rozporządzenie Prezesa Rady Ministrów z dnia 22 kwietnia 1952 r. Zarządzenie Nr 1/52 Naczelnego Dyrektora GUKPPiW z dnia 5 maja 1952 r.," *Biuletyn Informacyjno-Instrukcyjny* no. 5, May 1952, pp. 1–4 (APG, WUKPPiW, file ref. no. 90).

a decision dictated more by political or cultural factors? Perhaps there is no need to make such subtle distinctions; it is difficult to do so, considering that literary production was nationalized and creativity was made dependent on the whims of the state authorities. It is true that certain topics appeared periodically, while others were addressed only once, but an attempt was usually made to present material that corresponded to the literary and cultural reality of the country; suffice it to mention the turn of 1956, when literary topics were dominated by reflections on the course and consequences of the "Thaw."

Over the course of eleven years, guidelines meant to improve censorship practice were regularly formulated. The materials addressed the specificity of working with literary texts, providing examples of works published usually only several months earlier, or those that had not passed the censor's sieve. This practice was, of course, deeply justified; the idea was to arm the censors with tools suitable for assessing what the current publishing market offered and to sensitize them to topics that should be absent from it.

Similar goals were pursued when discussing the work of debutants and established authors, those writing along party lines and those who still needed some "training." Literary obedience was demanded from all of them, and not always enforced in the same way because external circumstances, such as the biography and attitude of the author, had an impact on the assessment of a work.

The periodical reviewed works published by newly established publishing houses and, until the book market was nationalized, also by private ones. Against this background, "Czytelnik," mentioned numerous times in the Bulletins, came to the fore; an extensive article was devoted to it, summing up its activity in 1951. In several places, there were also brief remarks on the profile of other publishing houses, e.g., Wiedza Powszechna or "Książka i Wiedza"; Wydawnictwo Literackie, established in 1953, also did not escape the censors' attention.

Press inspection was most often discussed on the basis of socio-political titles, both nationwide, e.g., *Trybuna Ludu* and local ones. Cultural periodicals were examined much less frequently; the articles that got reviewed came from *Szpilki, Nowa Kultura, Życie Literackie*, but also, for example, from *Teatr*.

Considerable space was devoted to cooperation with the "field." There were keen reactions to problems with controlling non-stationary theaters and so-called "rogue bands," as well as reports on the deficiencies in the work of inspectors of local content, printing companies and publishing houses. Censorial attention was attuned to the matters of controlling film and radio, and even board games.

The magazine published editorials and articles submitted by functionaries or entire censorship teams. The layout of the periodical usually remained unchanged. A certain deviation from this was the inclusion of additional materials, complementing the topics presented in the issue, such as peer-reviewed articles, postcards, or game boards.

Considering that the magazine was published once a month, the selection of material had to be quite scrupulous as a result of which not all current cultural and literary events were covered. Still, it may come as some surprise that not much space was devoted to works for children, which at the time were an important component of a young reader's education program. What is less surprising, however, is that literary tradition was also scarcely presented: the Bulletins clearly show that adapting the cultural past to the requirements of the present turned out to be less important than the education of censors skilled in the art of evaluating literature and contemporary art.

In analyzing the Bulletins, I focused primarily on capturing, understanding, and describing the censorship strategies used by the employees of the "Ministry of Truth." The (literary) text was undoubtedly the starting point of my considerations, but it was not possible, nor was it my intention, to study it in isolation from its author. The Bulletins are yet another testimony to the difficult choices artists had to make and the tough consequences they had to face.

ACKNOWLEDGEMENTS

The book would not have been written without the support of Prof. Marzena Woźniak-Łabieniec, whom I would like to thank sincerely for her help and for joining me in my explorations of the Bulletin's corridors.

I would also like to express my gratitude to the first reviewers of the book, Prof. Kamila Budrowska, Prof. Sławomir Buryła, Dr. John M. Bates, Prof. Kamila Kamińska-Chełminiak, Prof. Mariusz Zawodniak.

My thanks also go to the translator, Katarzyna Szuster-Tardi, who translated the text with great care. While working on the book, I could always count on her kindness and attentive translations of linguistic intricacies.

At the subsequent stages of writing, I received great support from many people: selfless help in scholarly issues from Prof. Wacław Andrusikiewicz, Dr. Teresa Kotaszewicz, Dr. Piotr Lechowski, Dr. Tomasz Majda, Prof. Iwona Loewe, Prof. Zbigniew Romek, Prof. Grzegorz Strauchold; help in reaching the library and archival resources that became unavailable due to the pandemic from Ewelina Chmielewska, Arkadiusz Morawiec, Natalia Popłonikowska, Katarzyna Smyczek, Marcin Bogusławski, Tadeusz Ciecierski Ewa Ciszewska and the staff of the Library of the University of Łódź, Anna Zatora, Aleksandra Chruściel, Kamila Jędrychowska and Tomasz Czajka; I would also like to thank Marek Rutkowski, Michał Stajszczak, Marcin Leszczyński, Przemysław Gumułka, Wojciech Chuchla and a user named hamanu for their valuable tips about communist-era board games.

I extend my thanks to Prof. Joanna Wojdon, Iwona Krasowska, Agnieszka Przybyszewska, Bożena Tuchołka, Magdalena Michałowska, Elwira Kaczyńska, Krzysztof Tomasz Witczak, Małgorzata Kąkiel, Patrycja Zborowska and Maria Garda.

A thank you to my grandparents, Danuta and Bolesław Budyń and to my parents, Ewa and Marek Wiśniewscy.

Antoś, Paweł, Amiga… without you there would be nothing.

INDEX OF FIGURES AND TABLES

LIST OF ABBREVIATIONS

AAN – Archiwum Akt Nowych (Central Archives of Modern Records)
AL – Armia Ludowa (People's Army)
APG – Archiwum Państwowe Gdańsk (State Archives in Gdańsk)
APP – Archiwum Państwowe w Poznaniu (State Archives in Poznań)
CBKP – Centralne Biuro Kontroli Prasy (Central Press Control Bureau)
GL – Gwardia Ludowa (People's Guard)
Glavlit – Central Board for Literature and Press Affairs
GUKPiW – Główny Urząd Kontroli Publikacji i Widowisk (The Main Office for the Control of Publications and Public Performances)
GUKPPiW – Główny Urząd Kontroli Prasy, Publikacji i Widowisk (The Main Office for the Control of the Press, Publications and Public Performances)
KPP – Komunistyczna Partia Polski (the Communist Party of Poland)
PPR – Polska Partia Robotnicza (the Polish Workers' Party)
PPS – Polska Partia Socjalistyczna (the Polish Socialist Party)
PRL – Polska Rzeczpospolita Ludowa (the Polish People's Republic)
PZPR – Polska Zjednoczona Partia Robotnicza (the Polish United Workers' Party)
RP – Rzeczpospolita Polska (the Republic of Poland)
UPA – Ukraińcza Powstańcza Armia (The Ukrainian Insurgent Army)
WUKPPiW – Wojewódzki Urząd Kontroli Prasy, Publikacji i Widowisk (The Voivodeship Office for the Control of the Press, Publications and Public Performances)
ZWM – Związek Walki Młodych (Union of Youth Struggle)

BIBLIOGRAPHY[1]

> In conclusion, I find the "Bulletin" very useful
> for the daily work of censors.[2]

The compilation of a *Bibliography* in the case of a journal such as the Bulletin for censors is not easy. That is why I would like to, perhaps rather surprisingly at this point, offer a brief introduction to this last part of the book.

I treat the following *Bibliography* and its accompanying indexes as another chapter of the book, the purpose of which is not only to record the literature used in the book – its primary goal is to show the enormity of the damage that the PRL's censorship did to Polish culture. That is why I decided to present the bibliography in a manner slightly different from the customary approach, but one that seemed to me the most beneficial to the subject at hand.

Subject literature

The subject literature is comprised of two parts: List of Authors and Works Documented in the Bulletins for Censors from 1945–1956 (Selection) and List of the Bulletins for Censors and *Biblioteczki Biuletynu Informacyjno-Instrukcyjnego GUKPPiW*.

The purpose of the subject literature thus compiled is to identify authors and works whose existence in the "censorial circuit" is attested to by the resources of the Bulletins and about which I have written in this book. A list of all the authors and works appearing in the Bulletins will be included in the aforementioned *Appendix*.

The discussion so far has shown that the editors of the Bulletin were far from being reliable in quoting the titles of the works in question – these were often omitted or the versions given were wrong (sometimes the titles may not have been determined yet). As a result, we rarely see accurately cited titles of works in

---

[1] I would like to thank Prof. Mariusz Zawodniak for his valuable guidance in compiling the bibliography and indexes.

[2] K. Rosadziński (WUKPPiW w Gdańsku), "O naszym *Biuletynie* (kilka uwag marginesowych)" (correspondence in "Dział Listów"), *Biuletyn Informacyjno-Instrukcyjny* no. 6 (30), June 1954, p. 29 (APG, WUKPPiW, file ref. no. 52).

the Bulletins, and so I reconstruct most of them on the basis of an analysis of the Bulletin material. Titles whose reconstruction needs to be confirmed are marked with an asterisk (*).

List of Authors and Works Documented in the Bulletins for Censors from 1945–1956 (Selection)

[*Ale szwagier mój o zgrozo*]
Bąk brzmi… w trzcinie
Głos Narodu
Lotny finisz
Acs Kāto, *Dzieci z Kobányi*
Aleksin Anatolij, *Dwa portrety*
Andrzejewski Jerzy, *O relatywizmie*
Andrzejewski Jerzy, *Wieczór z Henrykiem*
Andrzejewski Jerzy, *Wielki lament papierowej głowy*
Aragon Louis, *Komuniści*
Asztalos Istvan, *Nie ma dymu bez ognia*
Baranowicz Jan, *Szopka betleemska. Misterium ludowe w 3 obrazach*
Bartelski Lesław, *Ludzie zza rzeki*
Bartelski Lesław, *Miejsce urodzenia. Opowiadania*
Bednorz Zbyszko, *Decyzja, czyli rzecz o człowieku odzyskanym*
Bianki Vitalij, *Myszka Pik*
Bianki Vitalij, *W leśnych domkach*
Bocheński Jacek, *Z życia Niemieckiej Republiki Demokratycznej (Dlaczego za Odrą mamy przyjaciół)*
Bocheński Jacek, *Zgodnie z prawem*
*Borowski Tadeusz, *Utwory zebrane*
Broniewska Janina, *Ogniwo*
Brzechwa Jan, *Ratujmy dzieci*
Brzeziński Bogdan, *Egzamin*
Carnegie Dale, *Jak uszczęśliwiać innych i samemu być szczęśliwym?*
Chrzanowski Tadeusz, Rudzki Kazimierz, *Obrazki i… obrazy, czyli pięć satyrycznych i łatwych do inscenizacji ataków na bramkę przeciwnika*
Claude Henri, *Imperializm nad przepaścią*
Colombi Arturo, *W ręku wroga*
Cyprian Tadeusz, Sawicki Jerzy, *Walka z prasową propagandą wojenną*
Czanerle Maria, *Ostry spór o* Ostry dyżur
Czekańska Maria, *Norwegia, Szwecja, Finlandia i Dania*
Czeszko Bohdan, *Pokolenie*
Daskałow Stojan, *Droga*
Dębnicki Kazimierz, *Opowiadania świętokrzyskie*
Dickens Charles, *Klub Pickwicka*
Dobraczyński Jan, *Kościół w Chochołowie*

Dom na pustkowiu, directed by Jan Rybkowski
Droga narodów radzieckich do komunizmu
Dróżdż-Satanowska Zofia, *Pod wiatr*
Dutt Rajani Palme, *Indie dzisiejsze*
Dutt Rajani Palme, *Kryzys Imperium Brytyjskiego*
Dwa wieki poezji rosyjskiej. Antologia, arranged and compiled by Mieczysław Jastrun, Seweryn Pollak
Egry Irén, *Fabryka budzi się*
Fast Howard, *Trzydzieści srebrników. Sztuka w 3 aktach*
*Fenikowski Franciszek, *Lewy brzeg*
Flaszen Ludwik, *O trudnym kunszcie womitowania*
*Gaworski Henryk, *Przed nami życie*
Germanetto Giovani, *Pamiętnik fryzjera*
Gil Franciszek, *Ziemia i morze*
*Ginczanka Zuzanna, *Wiersze wybrane*
*Gisges Jan Maria, *Pierwsza miłość*
Goethe Johann Wolfgang, *Egmont*
Grodzieńska Stefania, *Plagi i plażki*
Gruszczyński Krzysztof, *Dobry człowiek*
*Hollender Tadeusz, *Wiersze. Satyry. Fraszki*
Hussarski Roman, *Nowy mur*
Hussarski Roman, Lem Stanisław, *Jacht „Paradise"*
Igiszew Władimir, *Gwiazda nad kopalnią*
Ilku Pál, *Bunt w klasie*
Illyés Gyula, *Wódz i poeta*
Iłłakowiczówna Kazimiera, *Ballady bohaterskie*
Iłłakowiczówna Kazimiera, *Opowieść o moskiewskim męczeństwie. Złoty wianek*
Iłłakowiczówna Kazimiera, *Poezje. 1940–1954*
Iłłakowiczówna Kazimiera, *Słowik litewski*
Iłłakowiczówna Kazimiera, *Ścieżka obok drogi*
Iłłakowiczówna Kazimiera, *Trzy struny*
Iłłakowiczówna Kazimiera, *Wiersze o Marszałku Piłsudskim. 1912–1935*
Iłłakowiczówna Kazimiera, *Wiersze religijne. 1912–1954*
Iłłakowiczówna Kazimiera, *Z głębi serca*
Iłłakowiczówna Kazimiera, *Z wycieczki jesiennej*
Iwaszkiewicz Jarosław, *Sprawa pokoju. Wiersze i przemówienia*
Jackiewicz Aleksander, *Wiedeńska wiosna*
Janowski Jurij, *Opowiadania kijowskie*
Jaremko-Żytyńska Zofia, *Odbudowa i rozwój życia kulturalnego w Polsce 1944–1948*
*Jastrun Mieczysław, *Wiersze dawne i nowe*
Jurandot Jerzy, *Pułapka*
Kariera, directed by Karel Steklý
Kassyanowicza Henryk, *Egipt w walce z imperializmem*
Kieniewicz Stefan, *Warszawa w powstaniu styczniowym*
Kieroński Marek, *Nos czy tabakiera*

Kish Egon, *Raj amerykański*
Kiwilszo Waldemar, *Nad epopeją socjalizmu*
Klimecki Wojciech, [Rec. F. Twyman, *Metal Spectroscopy*]
Kolbuszewski Stanisław, *Autograf wiersza Słowackiego „Pośród niesnasków"*
Konarski Ryszard, *Obrazki węgierskie*
*Konopnicka Maria, *Stefek Burczymucha*
Konstantinow Władimir, *Mapa Afryki odpowiada*
Korespondencja Jana Śniadeckiego, t. 2: Listy z Krakowa 1787–1807
Korzeniowski Józef, *Karpaccy górale*, stage version: sports club „Stella" in Żabikowo
*Kowalewski Stanisław, *Dwa pokoje*
Koźniewski Kazimierz, *Piątka z ulicy Barskiej*
Kruczkowski Leon, *Niemcy*
Kruczkowski Leon, *Sidła*
Krzemieniecka Lucyna, *Jaskółki*
Krzywicka Irena, *Doktor Anna Leśna*
Kubalski Zdzisław, *Wyrok*
Kuśmierek Józef, *Uwaga! Człowiek*
Kuśmierek Józef, *Uwaga, wielkie niebezpieczeństwo*
Lācis Vilis, *Syn rybaka. Powieść z życia łotewskiego*
Leśnodorski Bogusław, Opałek Kazimierz, *Nauka polskiego Oświecenia w walce o postęp*
Lipski Witold, *Wietnam i jego młodzież*
Litwin Janusz, *ABC planu sześcioletniego*
Ludawska Janina, *Ostry dyżur*
Lutowski Jerzy, *Ostry dyżur*, stage version: Państwowy Teatr Narodowy in Kraków
Lutowski Jerzy, *Próba sił*
Łomnicki Tadeusz, *Kąkol i pszenica*
Majakowski Władimir, *Nie wierzymy*, translated by Bruno Jasieński
Majakowski Władimir, *Posiedzeniarze*
*Malenkow Gieorgij Maksimilianowicz, *Referat sprawozdawczy na XIX Zjeździe Partii o działalności KC WKP(b)*
*Mandalian Andrzej, *Dzisiaj*
*Mandalian Andrzej, *Słowa na co dzień*
Marianowicz Antoni, *Bez pardonu*
Maslennikow Wiaczesław, *Pogłębienie kryzysu kolonialnego systemu imperializmu*
Matuszewski Ryszard, *Literatura międzywojenna*
Matuszewski Ryszard, *Szkice o literaturze współczesnej. Praca zbiorowa*
Matysiak Janina, *Powrót. Obrazek sceniczny w 3 odsłonach dla świetlic*
Meisner Zofia, *Wrak 103*
Miasto nieujarzmione (Robinson warszawski), directed by Jerzy Zarzycki
Miller Arthur, *Synowie*, stage version: „Placówka" Theatre in Warszawa
Miller Arthur, *Synowie*, stage version: Vakhtangov Theatre in Moscow
*Miller Jerzy, *Słowa na pozycji*
Minajew Władysław, *Amerykańskie gestapo*
Minkiewicz Janusz, *Pigułki*
Minkiewicz Janusz, *Więcej kawy*

Montagnany Mario, *Wspomnienia robotnika turyńskiego*
Morcinek Gustaw, *Zabłąkane ptaki*
Musrepow Gabit, *Żołnierz z Kazachstanu*
Na dziesięciolecie ZWM
Nałkowska Zofia, *Medaliony*
Niemiecka satyra antyfaszystowska, oprac. Antoni Marianowicz, Edmund Osmańczyk
Norwid Cyprian, *Do lilii polnej* (*Do Najświętszej Panny Maryi Litania*)
O W.I. Leninie. Zbiór recytacji i pieśni w 30-tą rocznicę śmierci W.I. Lenina, translated by Adam Ważyk et al.
Oelssner Fred, *Marksizm współczesny i jego krytycy*
Ostatni etap, directed by Wanda Jakubowska
Page Myra, *Słońce nad kopalnią*
Pan Nowak, directed by Bořivoj Zeman
Panfierow Fiedor, *Bruski*
Panowa Wiera, *Jasny brzeg*
Pasternak Leon, *Do działacza od kultury*
Pasternak Leon, *Moja rzecz*
Pasternak Leon, *Warszawskoje szosse*
Petőfi Sándor, *Wybór poezji*
Piątka z ulicy Barskiej, directed by Aleksander Ford
Podkowiński Marian, *Niemcy zachodnie w służbie amerykańskich podżegaczy wojennych*
Podkowiński Marian, *Za amerykańskim kordonem*
Promiński Marian, *Toreador i mściciel*
Prorokow Boris Iwanowicz, *Linczujące Stany Zjednoczone*
Prutkowski Józef, *Ballada pod psem*
Prutkowski Józef, *Do żywego*
Przęczek Zofia, *Morgi. Współczesna sztuka obyczajowa w 3 aktach*
Przygody w dżungli. Kombinacyjna gra dla młodzieży
Przyjdą nowi bojownicy, directed by Jiří Weiss
Psoty Kleksa, illustrated by Adam Bilski, text by Zygmunt Jaski
Putek Józef, *Mroki średniowiecza*
Riaboklacz Iwan, *Maksym z kołchozu „Zorza"*
Rostworowski Mikołaj, *Oskarżam*
*Różewicz Tadeusz, *Czas, który idzie*
*Różewicz Tadeusz, *Pięć poematów*
Rudnicki Adolf, *Deficyt (1)*
Rudnicki Adolf, *Kartki z dziennika*
Rusinek Michał, *Pawilon pod sosnami*
*Rydz Robert, *Ułan i młynarka. Wodewil ludowy w trzech aktach*
Sawicki Jerzy, *„Ludobójstwo" – od pojęcia do konwencji 1933–1948*
Seghers Anna, *List gończy*
Seghers Anna, *Ocalenie*
*Selsam Howard, *Co to jest filozofia* (*Problemy filozofii*)
Shuli Zhao, *Ludzie spod złotego modrzewia*
Sielecka Zofia, *Dwie minuty*

Sinclair Upton Beall, *Król węgiel. Powieść osnuta na tle wydarzeń w zagłębiu węglowym w Colorado*

Skarb, directed by Leonard Buczkowski

Słonimski Antoni, *Poezje*

Soboul Albert, *Rewolucja francuska*

Sowińska Stanisława, *Lata walki*

Srebrne kolczyki, directed by Alex Benno

Stadnicki Jerzy, *Badania dodatkowe*

Stadnicki Jerzy, *Prawo do skargi*

Stone Irving, *Pasja życia. Powieść na tle życia van Gogha*

Strumph-Wojtkiewicz Stanisław, *Generał Komuny*

Sydybekow Tugelbaj, *Ludzie naszych dni*

Syrena, directed by Karel Steklý

Szczawiński Józef, *Z perspektywy humanizmu*

Szeląg Jan [Zbigniew Mitzner], *7 dni (18 kwietnia 1952 r.)*

Szelburg-Zarembina Ewa, *Wesoła praca*

Szmankiewicz Andriej, *Chłopcy z cegielni*

Szydłowski Roman, *Ostry dyżur*

Szymiczek Franciszek, *Od Statutu Wiślickiego do Konstytucji Polskiej Rzeczypospolitej Ludowej*

Ścibor-Rylski Aleksander, *Węgiel*

Świat czarów. Zbiór baśni, podań i legend, compilation and layout Edmund Jezierski

Tamási Áron, *Abel w puszczy*

Tołstoj Lew, *Anna Karenina*

*Tołwiński Tadeusz, *Urbanistyka* (*Urbanistyka, t. 3: Zieleń w urbanistyce*)

Trzcieniecki Janusz, *Prawo pracy*

Ulieru George, *Z notatnika lekarza wiejskiego*

Warmiński Janusz, *Zwycięstwo*

Wasilewska Wanda, *Rzeki płoną*

Wasiljew Nikołaj, *Ameryka od strony schodów kuchennych*

Watolina Lidia, *Współczesny Egipt*

Wazow Iwan, *Wybór opowiadań*

Ważyk Adam, *Nowy wybór wierszy*

Ważyk Adam, *Oczy i usta*

Ważyk Adam, *Poemat dla dorosłych*

Wiersze, które lubimy. Antologia, compiled by Adam Ważyk, Jan Kott

Wilczek Jan, *Nr 16 produkuje*

Wirta Mikołaj, *Samotność*

Witkowska Maria, *Przebudzenie. Widowisko ludowe w trzech odsłonach*

Wolicki Krzysztof, *Iran walczy*

Wołoszyn Aleksander, *Ziemia kuźniecka*

Wydrzyński Andrzej, *Śmierć Hamleta*

Wygodzki Stanisław, *Opowiadanie buchaltera*

Zagała Bolesław, *Na przełaj przez świat*

*Zagórski Jerzy, *Wiersze wybrane*

Zakazane piosenki, directed by Leonard Buczkowski

Zalewski Witold, *Traktory zdobędą wiosnę*

Zieliński Stanisław, *Bardzo krótka historia*

Zieliński Stanisław, *Ostatnie ognie*

**Zrodził nas czyn. Zbiór wierszy i pieśni na dziesięciolecie ZWM*, compiled by Tadeusz Drewnowski, introduction Bohdan Czeszko

„Żądło mikrofonu" (series of radio broadcasts)

Żelazny dziadek, directed by Vaclav Kubásek

Żeromski Stefan, *Doktor Piotr*

Żeromski Stefan, *Grzech. Dramat w 5 aktach*

Żeromski Stefan, *Przedwiośnie*

Żeromski Stefan, *Syzyfowe prace*

Żeromski Stefan, *Walka z szatanem*

Żeromski Stefan, *Zapomnienie*

Żeromski Stefan, *Zmierzch*

Żółkiewska Wanda, *Awans*

Żółkiewska Wanda, *Droga przez ogień. Powieść dla młodzieży*

Żwirska Joanna, *Światło*

Żytkow Boris, *O słoniu*

List of the Bulletins for Censors and *Biblioteczki Biuletynu Informacyjno-Instrukcyjnego GUKPPiW*

Biuletyn Instrukcyjny no. 1, May 1945 (APP, WUKPPiW, file ref. no. 4, fol. 1r–3r).

Biuletyn Instrukcyjny no. 2, June 1945 (APG, WUKPPiW, file ref. no. 210).

Biuletyn Głównego Urzędu Kontroli Prasy no. 4 (APP WUKPPiW, file ref. no. 4, fol. 49r–56r i 57r–64r.).

Biuletyn Informacyjno-Szkoleniowy no. 1, October 30, 1948 (APP, WUKPPiW, file ref. no. 4, fol. 65r–80r).

Biuletyn Informacyjno-Szkoleniowy no. 2, November 30, 1948 (APP, WUKPPiW, file ref. no. 4, fol. 81r–91r).

Biuletyn Informacyjno-Szkoleniowy no. 1/3, January 1949 (APG, WUKPPiW, file ref. no. 196).

Biuletyn Informacyjno-Szkoleniowy no. 4, May 1949 (APP, WUKPPiW, file ref. no. 4, fol. 139r–163v).

Biuletyn Szkoleniowy no. 1, March (May) 1950 (APG, WUKPPiW, file ref. no. 328).

Biuletyn Informacyjno-Szkoleniowy no. 1, 1951 (APP, WUKPPiW, file ref. no. 4, fol. 254r–291r).

Biuletyn Informacyjno-Instrukcyjny no. 1, January 1952 (APG, WUKPPiW, file ref. no. 100).

Biuletyn Informacyjno-Instrukcyjny no. 2, February 1952 (APG, WUKPPiW, file ref. no. 99).

Biuletyn Informacyjno-Instrukcyjny no. 3, March 1952 (APG, WUKPPiW, file ref. no. 96).

Biuletyn Informacyjno-Instrukcyjny no. 4, April 1952 (APG, WUKPPiW, file ref. no. 93).

Biuletyn Informacyjno-Instrukcyjny no. 5, May 1952 (APG, WUKPPiW, file ref. no. 90).

Biuletyn Informacyjno-Instrukcyjny no. 6, June 1952 (APG, WUKPPiW, file ref. no. 87).

Biuletyn Informacyjno-Instrukcyjny no. 7, July 1952 (APG, WUKPPiW, file ref. no. 84).

Biuletyn Informacyjno-Instrukcyjny no. 8, August 1952 (APG, WUKPPiW, file ref. no. 81).

Biuletyn Informacyjno-Instrukcyjny no. 9, September 1952 (APG, WUKPPiW, file ref. no. 78).

Biuletyn Informacyjno-Instrukcyjny no. 10, October 1952 (APG, WUKPPiW, file ref. no. 75).

Biuletyn Informacyjno-Instrukcyjny no. 11, November 1952 (APG, WUKPPiW, file ref. no. 72).

Biuletyn Informacyjno-Instrukcyjny no. 12, December 1952 (APG, WUKPPiW, file ref. no. 70).

Biuletyn Informacyjno-Instrukcyjny no. 1 (13), January 1953 (APG, WUKPPiW, file ref. no. 19).

Biuletyn Informacyjno-Instrukcyjny no. 2 (14), February 1953 (APG, WUKPPiW, file ref. no. 18).

Biuletyn Informacyjno-Instrukcyjny no. 3 (15), March 1953 (APG, WUKPPiW, file ref. no. 17).

Biuletyn Informacyjno-Instrukcyjny no. 4 (16), April 1953 (APG, WUKPPiW, file ref. no. 16).

Biuletyn Informacyjno-Instrukcyjny no. 5 (17), May 1953 (APG, WUKPPiW, file ref. no. 15).

Biuletyn Informacyjno-Instrukcyjny no. 6/7 (18/19), June/July 1953 (APG, WUKPPiW, file ref. no. 14).

Biuletyn Informacyjno-Instrukcyjny no. 8 (20), August 1953 (APG, WUKPPiW, file ref. no. 13).

Biuletyn Informacyjno-Instrukcyjny no. 9 (21), September 1953 (AAN, GUKPPiW, file ref. no. 22).

Biuletyn Informacyjno-Instrukcyjny no. 10 (22), October 1953 (APG, WUKPPiW, file ref. no. 11).

Biuletyn Informacyjno-Instrukcyjny no. 11/12 (23/24), November/December 1953 (APG, WUKPPiW, file ref. no. 9).

Biuletyn Informacyjno-Instrukcyjny no. 1 (25), January 1954 (APG, WUKPPiW, file ref. no. 39).

Biuletyn Informacyjno-Instrukcyjny no. 2 (26), February 1954 (APG, WUKPPiW, file ref. no. 42).

Biuletyn Informacyjno-Instrukcyjny no. 3 (27), March 1954 (APG, WUKPPiW, file ref. no. 45).

Biuletyn Informacyjno-Instrukcyjny no. 4 (28), April 1954 (APG, WUKPPiW, file ref. no. 48).

Biuletyn Informacyjno-Instrukcyjny no. 5 (29), May 1954 (APG, WUKPPiW, file ref. no. 49).

Biuletyn Informacyjno-Instrukcyjny no. 6 (30), June 1954 (APG, WUKPPiW, file ref. no. 52).

Biuletyn Informacyjno-Instrukcyjny no. 7/8 (31/32), July/August 1954 (APG, WUKPPiW, file ref. no. 65).

Biuletyn Informacyjno-Instrukcyjny no. 9 (33), September 1954 (APG, WUKPPiW, file ref. no. 56).

Biuletyn Informacyjno-Instrukcyjny no. 10 (34), October 1954 (APG, WUKPPiW, file ref. no. 58).

Biuletyn Informacyjno-Instrukcyjny no. 11/12 (35/36), November/December 1954 (APG, WUKPPiW, file ref. no. 59).

Biuletyn Informacyjno-Instrukcyjny no. 1 (37), January 1955 (APG, WUKPPiW, file ref. no. 110).

Biuletyn Informacyjno-Instrukcyjny no. 2 (38), February 1955 (APG, WUKPPiW, file ref. no. 108).

Biuletyn Informacyjno-Instrukcyjny no. 3 (39), March 1955 (APG, WUKPPiW, file ref. no. 107).

Biuletyn Informacyjno-Instrukcyjny no. 4 (40), April 1955 (APG, WUKPPiW, file ref. no. 106).

Biuletyn Informacyjno-Instrukcyjny no. 5 (41), May 1955 (APG, WUKPPiW, file ref. no. 131).

Biuletyn Informacyjno-Instrukcyjny no. 6 (42), June 1955 (APG, WUKPPiW, file ref. no. 126).

Biuletyn Informacyjno-Instrukcyjny no. 7 (43), July 1955 (APG, WUKPPiW, file ref. no. 103).

Biuletyn Informacyjno-Instrukcyjny no. 8 (44), August 1955 (APG, WUKPPiW, file ref. no. 124).

Biuletyn Informacyjno-Instrukcyjny no. 9 (45), September 1955 (APG, WUKPPiW, file ref. no. 120).

Biuletyn Informacyjno-Instrukcyjny no. 10 (46), October 1955 (APG, WUKPPiW, file ref. no. 119).

Biuletyn Informacyjno-Instrukcyjny no. 11 (47), November 1955 (APG, WUKPPiW, file ref. no. 118).

Biuletyn Informacyjno-Instrukcyjny no. 12 (48), December 1955 (APG, WUKPPiW, file ref. no. 117).

Biuletyn Informacyjno-Instrukcyjny no. 1 (49), January 1956 (APG, WUKPPiW, file ref. no. 4).

Biuletyn Informacyjno-Instrukcyjny no. 2 (50), February 1956 (APG, WUKPPiW, file ref. no. 6).

Biblioteczka Biuletynu Informacyjno-Instrukcyjnego GUKPPiW no. 18, 1955 (APG, WUKPPiW, file ref. no. 215).

Biblioteczka Biuletynu Informacyjno-Instrukcyjnego GUKPPiW no. 19, 1955 (APG, WUKPPiW, file ref. no. 213).

Biblioteczka Biuletynu Informacyjno-Instrukcyjnego GUKPPiW no. 20, 1955 (APG, WUKPPiW, file ref. no. 214).

Biblioteczka Biuletynu Informacyjno-Instrukcyjnego GUKPPiW no. 21, 1955 (APG, WUKPPiW, file ref. no. 212).

Biblioteczka Biuletynu Informacyjno-Instrukcyjnego GUKPPiW no. 22, 1955 (APG, WUKPPiW, file ref. no. 195).

Biblioteczka Biuletynu Informacyjno-Instrukcyjnego GUKPPiW no. 23, 1955 (APG, WUKPPiW, file ref. no. 194).

Biblioteczka Biuletynu Informacyjno-Instrukcyjnego GUKPPiW no. 24, 1955 (APG, WUKPPiW, file ref. no. 193).

Literary Texts, Journalism (Literary and Film Criticism Interviews, etc.) Made Before 1945

Fiedler A., *Dywizjon 303*, London: M.I. Kolin, 1942.

Gaydar A., *Timur and His Gang*, trans. Z. Voynov, New York: C. Scribner's Sons, 1943.

Ginczanka Z., *O centaurach*, Warszawa: Wydawnictwo J. Przeworskiego, 1936.

Iljin M., *What Time Is It? The Story of Clocks*, trans. B. Kincead, Philadelphia–London: J.B. Lippincott Co., 1932.

Kłos J., "Grymas szatana," *Wiadomości dla Duchowieństwa* 1923, no. 4, pp. 60–63.

Korespondencja Jana Śniadeckiego vol. 1: *Listy z Krakowa 1780–1787*, compiled by L. Kamykowski, Kraków: PAU, 1932.

Leskov N., *The Sentry and Other Stories*, trans. A.E. Chamot, New York: Alfred A. Knopf, 1923.

Nosov N., *Jolly family*, Moscow: Foreign Languages Publishing House, 1930.

Pasternak L., *Słowa z daleka*, Moscow: Związek Patriotów Polskich w ZSRR, 1944.

Pruszyński K., *Droga wiodła przez Narvik*, London: M.I. Kolin, 1941.

Twain M., *Following the Equator. A Journey Around the world*, Hartford–New York: The American Publishing Co., Doubleday&McClure Co., 1897.

Ważyk A., *Serce granatu*, Moscow: Związek Patriotów Polskich w ZSRR, 1943; Second Edition expanded with poems written in 1944: Lublin: Związek Zawodowy Literatów Polskich, 1944.

Wielopolska M.J., *Pliszka w jaskini lwa. Rozważania nad książką panny Iłłakowiczówny Ścieżka obok drogi*, Warszawa: Drukarnia J. Zielony, 1939.

"Zamordowanie księdza prałata Budkiewicza," *Kurier Warszawski* April 4, 1923, no. 92, p. 1.

Ze świata czarów. Zbiór baśni, podań i legend różnych narodów compiled and arranged by E. Jezierski, part 1, 2: Warszawa: M. Arct, 1911; Warszawa: Księgarnia M. Ostaszewskiej i S-ki, [1921].

"Zmiana Rządu. Gen. dr. Sławoj-Składkowski premjerem i ministrem spraw wewn.," *Gazeta Lwowska* May 17, 1936, no. 113, p. 1.

Literary Texts, Journalism (Literary and Film Criticism Interviews, etc.), Radio Programs and Films Made Between 1945–1956

6643 Nel Siedlecki J., 75817 Olszewski K., 119198 Borowski T., *Byliśmy w Oświęcimiu*, Munich: Oficyna Warszawska na Obczyźnie, 1946.

"XIX Zjazd KPZR. O sprawach kultury i sztuki," *Życie Literackie* October 26, 1952, no. 22, pp. 2, 15.

Andrzejewski J., "O *Niebieskich kartkach* Adolfa Rudnickiego" (in the series *Kartki z dziennika lektury*), *Nowa Kultura* April 24, 1955, no. 17, p. 2.

Andrzejewski J., *Złoty Lis*, Expanded Second Edition, Warszawa: PIW, 1956.

Banderczak Z., "Przeciw nocy," *Tygodnik Powszechny* February 7, 1954, no. 6, pp. 5–6.

Bąk W., "Kazimiera Iłłakowiczwna," *Świat* October 24, 1948, no. 43, p. 2.

Berman J., "Pokażcie wielkość naszych czasów," *Materiały do Studiów i Dyskusji z Zakresu Teorii i Historii Sztuki, Krytyki Artystycznej oraz Badań nad Sztuką* 1952, no. 1, pp. 33–37.

Bieńkowski Z., "Po plenum krytyki," *Twórczość* 1952, no. 3, pp. 141–143.

Błaut S., "Poezja Jerzego Zagórskiego," *Tygodnik Powszechny* February 10, 1952, no. 6, pp. 4–5.

Błoński J., "Pogłosy i zapowiedzi, " *Wieś* 1950, no. 25, p. 5.

Błoński J., "U poetów (I)," *Życie Literackie* September 16, 1951, no. 17, pp. 4, 11.

Błoński J., "U poetów (III)," *Życie Literackie* December 9, 1951, no. 23, p. 10.

Borowski T., "Małe i wielkie legendy," *Odrodzenie* February 29, 1948, no. 9, pp. 1, 3.

Borowski T., *Pewien żołnierz. Opowieści szkolne*, Warszawa: Spółdzielnia Wydawnicza "Płomienie," 1947.

Borowski T., *Pożegnanie z Marią. Opowiadania*, Warszawa: "Wiedza," 1948.

Borowski T., "Rozmowy. Dla towarzyszy: Jerzego Andrzejewskiego i Wiktora Woroszylskiego," *Odrodzenie* 1950, no. 8, pp. 5–6.

Brandys K., "Nim będzie zapomniany," *Nowa Kultura* September 18, 1955, no. 38, pp. 1, 4–5, 7.

Brzechwa J., *Wiersze wybrane*, Warszawa: PIW, 1955.

Brzeziński B., *Satyryk w terenie*, Warszawa: Wydawnictwo Literackie, 1954.

Drawicz A., "Jeszcze o *Pokoleniu*," *Wieś* May 11, 1952, no. 19, p. 6.

Drewnowski T., "Uwaga! Nowy człowiek," *Nowa Kultura* October 14, 1951, no. 41, p. 5.

Dwa wieki poezji rosyjskiej. Antologia, arranged and compiled by M. Jastrun, S. Pollak, afterword by L. Gomolicki, Warszawa: "Czytelnik," 1947.

"Dyskusja o poezji Różewicza," *Życie Literackie* August 8, 1954, no. 31, p. 10.

Fast H., *Amerykanin*, trans. J. Brodzki, Warszawa: "Wiedza," 1948.

Fast H., *Dumni i wolni*, trans. M. Michałowska, Warszawa: "Czytelnik," 1952.

Fiedler A., *Rio de Oro. Na ścieżkach Indian brazylijskich*, Warszawa: "Nasza Księgarnia," 1950.

Flaszen L., "Nowy Zoil, czyli o schematyzmie," *Życie Literackie* January 6, 1952, no. 1, pp. 3–4.

Flaszen L., "Odpowiedź Zoila, czyli o akcentach," *Życie Literackie* June 8, 1952, no. 12, pp. 7, 13.

Flaszen L., "Rozmowa o *Pokoleniu*," *Życie Literackie* February 17, 1952, no. 4, p. 5.

Gaydar A., *Chuck and Geck*, Moscow: Foreign Languages Publishing House, 1953.

Gaydar A., *Czuk i Hek i inne opowiadania*, Second Edition, Warszawa: "Nasza Księgarnia," 1952.

Gaydar A., *Timur i jego drużyna*, Second Edition, trans. A. Wat, Warszawa: "Nasza Księgarnia," 1952.

Głowiński M., "O sztuce miniatury" (in the series *Wśród Książek*), *Twórczość* 1955, no. 7, pp. 162–165.

Głowiński M., "Od katastrofizmu do poezji politycznej" (in the series *Wśród książek*), *Twórczość* 1956, no. 1, pp. 140–144.

Gogol M., *Utwory wybrane*, Warszawa: "Czytelnik", 1951.

Goliński L., Fenikowski F., *Odra szumi po polsku*, Poznań: Wydawnictwo Zachodnie, 1946.

Górski J., "Moje trzy grosze," *Dziś i Jutro* April 11, 1954, no. 15, p. 4.

Grochowiak S., "Opowiadania okrutne," *Wrocławski Tygodnik Katolicki* June 19, 1955, no. 25, p. 11.

Grodzieńska W., "Współczesna literatura dla dzieci," *Kuźnica* December 25, 1949, no. 51–52, p. 11.

Grzeniewski L., "Nowelistyka Promińskiego," *Życie Literackie* December 16, 1956, no. 51, p. 4.

Herdegen L., "Dwa tomiki poezji" (in the series *Świat Książek*), *Świat. Tygodnik Ilustrowany* 1953, no. 27, p. 14.

Herdegen L., "'Pierścienie strof' Jerzego Zagórskiego," *Życie Literackie* September 30, 1951, no. 18, p. 12.

Herdegen L., "Poemat Andrzeja Mandaliana," *Życie Literackie* June 22, 1952, no. 13, p. 6.

Hoffman P., "O niektórych problemach realizmu socjalistycznego," *Nowa Kultura* November 18, 1951, no. 46, pp. 1–2.

Iljin M., *Która godzina? Opowiadania o czasie*, trans. H. Jarmolińska, Warszawa: "Czytelnik," 1949.

Iłłakowiczówna K., *Lekkomyślne serce*, Warszawa: "Czytelnik," 1959.

Iłłakowiczówna K., *Wiersze wybrane. 1912–1947*, Łódź–Poznań: Wydawnictwo W. Bąka, 1949.

[Interview with Jerzy Lutowski conducted by L. Woy.], *Express Wieczorny* June 17, 1955, no. 143, p. 4.

[Interview with Tadeusz Borowski after the publication of *Opowiadania z książek i gazet*], Polskie Radio 1951, https://www.polskieradio.pl/39/156/Artykul/1469874,Tadeusz-Borowski-zdac-relacje-w-obronie-umarlych (accessed January 31, 2021).

Janion M., "'Dopływy' krytyki literackiej," *Wieś* January 10, 1952, no. 6, p. 4.

Jarochowska M., *Niebieskie okulary. Reportaże z huty Częstochowa*, Warszawa: "Czytelnik," 1952.

Jarochowska M., "Pierwsze kombajny" (in the series *Wycieczka Chłopów do ZSRR*), *Przekrój* July 22, 1950, no. 276, p. 4.

Jastrzębski Z., "Sprawy trudne i bliskie," *Tygodnik Powszechny* February 7, 1954, no. 6, p. 5.

Kamieńska A., [Review: J.M. Gisges, *Pierwsza miłość*, Warszawa: "Czytelnik," 1951] (in the series *Wśród Książek*), *Twórczość* 1951, no. 2, pp. 144–147.

Kierczyńska M., "O schematyzmie," *Nowa Kultura* January 20, 1952, no. 3, p. 2.

Kijowski A., "Opowiadania niecierpliwe," *Życie Literackie* February 17, 1952, no. 4, p. 6.

Kongres Pokoju. Kongres Intelektualistów we Wrocławiu, Polska Kronika Filmowa, episode 33, September 07, 1948, http://www.repozytorium.fn.org.pl/?q=pl/node/6435 (accessed March 8, 2021).

Konwicki T., "Z zapisków schematysty," *Nowa Kultura* November 23, 1952, no. 47, p. 6.

Kott J., "Świadomość i pasja (O *Pokoleniu* Bohdana Czeszki)," *Nowa Kultura* January 27, 1952, no. 4, p. 6.

Kowalewski S., *Kiedy mija noc. Opowiadania*, Warszawa: "Czytelnik," 1955.

Kraszewski J.I., *Kawał literata*, Warszawa: "Czytelnik", 1951.

Kubalski Z., "O głośnym wydarzeniu w cichej wsi Skorupki," *Zielony Sztandar* December 27, 1953, no. 52, p. 16 (part one); January 1–3, 1954, no. 1, p. 11 (part two).

Kubalski Z., *W Redłowie i gdzie indziej. Opowiadania*, Warszawa: Ludowa Spółdzielnia Wydawnicza, 1954.

Kuczawa J., "Bumerang stalinowskiej laureatki," *Orzeł Biały* [London] 1952, no. 31/32, pp. 6–7; no. 34, pp. 4–5.

Kuprin A., *Utwory wybrane*, Warszawa: "Czytelnik", 1951.

Kuśmierek J., *Opowiadania reportera*, Warszawa: "Czytelnik," 1954.

Kuśmierek J., *Uwaga! Człowiek i inne opowiadania*, Warszawa: "Książka i Wiedza," 1955.

Lācis V., *The Fisherman's Son*, trans. I. and T. Litvinov, Moscow: Foreign Languages Publishing House, 1954.

Lasota G., "Patos walki," *Nowa Kultura* May 11, 1952, no. 19, pp. 9–10.

Lichniak Z., "Z dziejów zwycięskiej generacji," *Dziś i Jutro* March 9, 1952, no. 10, pp. 5–6.

Lipski J.J., "O czytankach," *Nowa Kultura* July 11, 1954, no. 28, p. 7.

Lipski J.J., [Review: F. Fenikowski, Warszawa: *Lewy brzeg*, "Czytelnik," 1951] (in the series *Wśród Książek*), *Twórczość* 1952, no. 6, pp. 166–168.

Maciąg W., [Review: T. Różewicz, *Pięć poematów*, Warszawa: "Czytelnik," 1950], *Życie Literackie* April 1, 1951, no. 5, p. 3.

Macużanka Z., "Powieść o bohaterskiej młodzieży," *Polonistyka* 1952, no. 5, pp. 55–57.

Maltsev E., *Heart and Soul*, Moscow: Foreign Languages Publishing House, 1953.

Maltsev E., *Z całego serca*, trans. W. Dobaczewska, Warszawa: "Książka i Wiedza," 1951.

Mamoń B., "O wierszach Kazimiery Iłłakowiczówny," *Tygodnik Powszechny* Easter 1955, no. 15, p. 12.

Markiewicz H., "Krytyka literacka w latach 1945–1951. Referat wygłoszony na plenum ZLP poświęconym zagadnieniom krytyki literackiej," *Twórczość* 1952, no. 3, pp. 117–140.

Martin Andersen Nexø i jego powieść "Pelle zwycięzca," Warszawa: "Czytelnik," 1950.

Materiały do Studiów i Dyskusji z Zakresu Teorii i Historii Sztuki, Krytyki Artystycznej oraz Badań nad Sztuką 1952, no. 1.

Matuszewski R., "Trylogia Wasilewskiej," *Nowa Kultura* May 18, 1952, no. 20, pp. 2, 11.

Mauersberger A., [Review: J. Kuśmierek, *Uwaga! Człowiek*, Warszawa: "Czytelnik," 1951], *Twórczość* 1952, no. 2, pp. 150–153.

Meissner J., *Wraki*, Warszawa: Iskry, 1953.

Miłosz Cz., *Światło dzienne*, Paris: Instytut Literacki, 1953.

Miłosz Cz., *Zniewolony umysł*, Paris: Instytut Literacki, 1953.

Mrożek S., "Młode Miasto," *Przekrój* July 22, 1950, no. 276, pp. 8–9.

Nosov N., *Wesoła rodzinka*, trans. H. Rogalowa, Warszawa: "Nasza Księgarnia," 1952.

Orwell G., *1984*, London: Secker & Warburg, 1949.

Orwell G., *1984*, trans. J. Mieroszewski, Paris: Instytut Literacki, 1953.

Ostromęcki B., "Niepokój," *Nowiny Literackie* October 5, 1947, no. 29, p. 6.

Oto Ameryka, Polska Kronika Filmowa, January 14, 1953, episode 3, http://www.repozytorium.fn.org.pl/?q=pl/node/7255 (accessed March 8, 2021).

Pędziński Z., "Piórkiem Promińskiego," *Nowe Sygnały* November 25, 1956, no. 8, p. 5.

Płoszewski L., "O Wydaniu Narodowym *Dzieł* Mickiewicza," *Pamiętnik Literacki* 1956, issue 2, pp. 317–340.

Pokolenie (A Generation), directed by A. Wajda, script by B. Czeszko, starring T. Łomnicki, U. Modrzyńska, Z. Cybulski, R. Polański, prod. Wytwórnia Filmów Fabularnych, 1954.

Polska poezja Maryjna, anthology laid out by T. Jodełka, preface by J. Zawieyski, cover and vignettes by T. Gronowski, Niepokalanów: Centrala "Milicji Niepokalanej," 1949.

Preger J., [Review: J. Zagórski, *Wiersze wybrane*, Warszawa: "Czytelnik," 1951] (in the series *Wśród Książek*), *Twórczość* 1951, no. 11, pp. 165–167.

Promiński M., *Salamandra*, Kraków: Wydawnictwo Literackie, 1956.

Putrament J., "Idea staje się życiem," *Nowa Kultura* October 5, 1952, no. 40, pp. 1–2.

[Review: E. Kisch, *Raj amerykański*, Warszawa: Wydawnictwo MON, 1952], *Nowe Książki* 1952, no. 5, pp. 271–272.

[Review: *Wiersze, które lubimy. Antologia*, compiled by A. Ważyk, J. Kott, Warszawa: "Czytelnik," 1951], *Życie Literackie* May 13, 1951, p. 11.

Rostworowski M., *Przeciw nocy*, Warszawa: Instytut Wydawniczy "Pax," 1953.

Różewicz T., *Kartki z Węgier*, Warszawa: "Czytelnik," 1953.

Rudnicki A., *Niebieskie kartki. Ślepe lustro tych lat*, Kraków: Wydawnictwo Literackie, 1956.

Rudnicki A., *Szekspir*, Warszawa: "Książka," 1948.

Sandauer A., "O typowości i schematyzmie," *Nowa Kultura* May 18, 1952, no. 20, pp. 5–6.

Sokorski W., "Wnioski z narady," *Nowa Kultura* November 18, 1951, no. 46, pp. 3–4.

Stadnicki J., *Kurz na miłości. Opowiadania*, preface S. Lichański, Warszawa: Instytut Wydawniczy "Pax," 1955.

Swiatlo J., *Behind the Scene of the Party and Bezpieka: Josef Swiatlo Reveals the Secrets of the Regime and Security Apparatus*, New York: Free Europe Committee, 1955.

Szczepański J.J., *Polska jesień*, Kraków: Wydawnictwo Literackie, 1955.

Ścibor-Rylski A., *Górnicze gołębie pokoju. O Wiktorze Markiefce*, Warszawa: "Książka i Wiedza," 1950.

Ścibor-Rylski A., "W poszukiwaniu epickiego klucza," *Nowa Kultura* October 30, 1955, no. 44, p. 3.

Śpiewak J., [Review: A. Mandalian, *Dzisiaj*, Warszawa: "Czytelnik," 1951] (in the series *Wśród Książek*), *Twórczość* 1952, no. 3, pp. 150–152.

Śpiewak J., [Review: H. Gaworski, *Przed nami życie*, Warszawa: "Czytelnik," 1951] (in the series *Wśród Książek*), *Twórczość* 1952, no. 5, pp. 207–211.

Wańkowicz M., *Ziele na kraterze*, New York: Roy, 1951.

Wasilewska W., *Wieczór literacki*, compiled by A. Naborowska, Warszawa: "Czytelnik," 1954.

Wasilewski A., "O kilku problemach typowości," *Nowa Kultura* August 23, 1953, no. 34, pp. 1–2.

Wieczny płomień. Wybór wierszy poetów radzieckich i polskich o Feliksie Dzierżyńskim, compiled by W. Woroszylski, Warszawa: PIW, 1951.

Wiersze i Pieśni Pierwszej Armii Polskiej w ZSRR, Łódź: Wydawnictwo Oddziału Propagandy Głównego Zarządu Polityczno-Wychowawczego Wojska Polskiego, 1945.

Wiersze i pieśni poświęcone pracownikom bezpieczeństwa, Warszawa 1954.

Witkowska M., *Kłopoty sportowca, wesoła komedia współczesna w 3 aktach*, Katowice: Wydawnictwo "Odrodzenie" (T. Nalepa i Ska), 1948, series *Teatr dla Wszystkich* no. 9.

Witkowska M., *Zbiór inscenizacji prozy, poezji i piosenek ludowych z ilustracją muzyczną i wzorem strojów ludowych wraz ze wstępem teoretycznym o pracy świetlicowej*, Katowice: Wydawnictwo "Odrodzenie" (T. Nalepa i Ska), 1948, series *Teatr dla Wszystkich* no. 2.

Wortman S., "W obronie baśni ludowej," *Odrodzenie* October 17, 1948, no. 2, p. 7.

Zawieyski J., "Poezja niepokoju," *Odrodzenie* October 19, 1947, no. 42, p. 5.

Zaworska H., "Wokół 'schematyzmu,'" *Wieś* January 13, 1952, no. 2, p. 4.

Zaworska-Trznadlowa H., "O powojennej twórczości Adolfa Rudnickiego," *Pamiętnik Literacki* 1953, issue 3–4, pp. 151–189.

"Zmarła Zofia Meisner," *Głos Wybrzeża* October 8–9, 1955, no. 240, p. 2.

"Zofia Meisner-Denis nie żyje," *Dziennik Bałtycki* October 9–10, 1955, no. 241, p. 4.

Żeromski S., *Zamieć*, Warszawa: "Czytelnik", 1951.

Żółkiewski S., "Pamiętnik 'Barbary' Sowińskiej," *Kuźnica* June 6, 1948, no. 23, p. 10.

Żukrowski W., "Walczące pokolenie," *Nowa Kultura* January 27, 1952, no. 4, p. 7.

"Życie przeciwko schematowi. List do redakcji dziennika *Prawda* w sprawie krytyki powieści W. Łacisa," *Nowa Kultura* March 23, 1952, no. 12, p. 3.

Literary Texts, Journalism (Literary and Film Criticism Interviews, etc.), Radio Programs and Films Made Between 1957–1990

Barańczak S., *Książki najgorsze i parę innych ekscesów krytycznoliterackich*, Second Revised Edition, Poznań: Wydawnictwo a5, 1990.

Bednorz Z., *Na zapiecku trzy okna*, Warszawa: Instytut Wydawniczy "Pax", 1978.

Błoński J., "Piekła Borowskiego," *Teksty* 1972, no. 6, pp. 156–161.

Błoński J., "Krakowska szkoła krytyki," the interview with Jan Błoński conducted by Maciej Szybist, *Gazeta Krakowska* January 1, 1981, no. 11, pp. 3, 5.

Borowski T., *Opowiadania wybrane*, selection and layout by T. Drewnowski, Warszawa: PIW, 1971.

Borowski T., *Poezje*, selection and preface by T. Drewnowski, Warszawa: PIW, 1972.

Borowski T., *Wspomnienia, wiersze, opowiadania*, afterword, selection and illustrations by T. Drewnowski, footnotes W. Jesionowska, Warszawa: PIW, 1974.

Gaworski H., *Jelenie jedzą klejnoty*, Warszawa: Iskry, 1978.

Giedroyc J., Stempowski J., *Listy 1946–1969. Część 1*, selection, introduction, and footnotes by A.S. Kowalczyk, Warszawa: "Czytelnik," 1998.

Kisielewski S., "Moje typy," *Tygodnik Powszechny* December 2, 1984, no. 49, p. 8.

Kisielewski S., "Przeciw cenzurze – legalnie (garść wspomnień)," *Zapis* 1977, no. 4, pp. 58–68.

Kruczkowski L., "Po Festiwalu Polskich Sztuk Współczesnych," *Dialog* 1974, issue 1, pp. 91–101.

Kuśmierek J., *Obecny (reportaże 1945–1990)*, London: Wydawnictwo Aneks, 1991.

Leskov N., *Lefty. Being the Tale of Cross-Eyed Lefty from Tula and the Steel Flea*, trans. G. Hanna, Moscow: Progress Publishers, 1965.

"List 34" – *reakcja zachodnich mediów na list wystosowany do premiera Cyrankiewicza*, RWE 1964, https://www.polskieradio.pl/39/156/Artykul/565503,Trzydziestu-czterech-w-obronie-kultury-polskiej (accessed January 31, 2021).

Markiewicz H., "O typowości w literaturze. Z historii problemu," *Pamiętnik Literacki* 1957, issue 1, pp. 46–82.

Meisner Z., *Obrońcy Westerplatte*, Warszawa: Wydawnictwo MON, 1957.

Orwell G., *Rok 1984*, trans. T. Mirkowicz, Warszawa: PIW, 1988.

Petőfi S., *Poezje*, Warszawa: PIW, 1971.

"Protest pisarzy przeciw antypolskiej kampanii. Polityka kulturalna jest wspólną sprawą inteligencji twórczej i kierownictwa politycznego," *Dziennik Polski* May 12, 1964, no. 111, p. 2.

Przymanowski J., *Ze 101 frontowych nocy*, Warszawa: "Książka i Wiedza," 1961.

Putrament J., "Pół wieku," vol. 4: *Literaci*, Warszawa: "Czytelnik," 1970.

Sandauer A., *Bez taryfy ulgowej*, Warszawa: "Czytelnik," 1959.

Słonimski A., *Poezje wybrane*, Warszawa: Ludowa Spółdzielnia Wydawnicza, 1972.

Słonimski A., *Poezje zebrane*, Warszawa: PIW, 1964.

Szkic do portretu Tadeusza Hollendra, Polskie Radio August 19, 1978, https://www.polskieradio.pl/39/156/Artykul/1452163,Tadeusz-Hollender-satyra-w-czasach-Apokalipsy (accessed January 31, 2021).

Śpiewak J., *Przyjaźnie i animozje*, Warszawa: PIW, 1965.

Światło J., *Za kulisami bezpieki i partii. Józef Światło ujawnia tajniki partii, reżymu i aparatu bezpieczeństwa*, Warszawa: Niezależna Oficyna Wydawnicza NOWA, 1981.

Tadeusz Hollender – poeta rozstrzelany, compiled by T. Żółciński, Polskie Radio May 30, 1973, https://www.polskieradio.pl/39/156/Artykul/1452163,Tadeusz-Hollender-satyra-w-czasach-Apokalipsy (accessed January 31, 2021).

[Tadeusz Drewnowski reminisces about Tadeusz Borowski], Polskie Radio October 16, 1973, https://www.polskieradio.pl/39/156/Artykul/1469874,Tadeusz-Borowski-zdac-relacje-w-obronie-umarlych (accessed January 31, 2021).

Ucieczka z kina "Wolność," directed by W. Marczewski, script by W. Marczewski, starring J. Gajos, P. Fronczewski, T. Marczewska, Z. Zamachowski, M. Bajon, Studio Filmowe "Tor," Warszawa 1990.

Wańkowicz W., *Przez cztery klimaty 1912–1972*, Second Edition, Warszawa: PIW, 1974.

Wraki, directed by E. Petelska, Cz. Petelski, script by E. Petelska, Cz. Petelski, J. Meissner, dialogues J. Meissner, B. Czeszko, starring Z. Józefowicz, Z. Cybulski, U. Modrzyńska, produced by Wytwórnia Filmów Fabularnych w Łodzi, Polska 1957.

Wybór poezji o żołnierzach PSZ na Zachodzie, związanych z żołnierzami Polski Podziemnej i Powstania Warszawskiego wspólną ideą wywalczenia Polski wolnej i niepodległej (in the series *Dodatek Literacki* no. 774), compiled by E. Romiszewski, Polskie Radio May 10, 1975, https://www.polskieradio.pl/13/3707/Audio/291108,Dodatek-literacki-nr-774 (accessed January 31, 2021).

Literary Texts, Journalism (Literary and Film Criticism Interviews, etc.), Radio Programs and Films Made After 1990

Abramow-Newerly J., *Lwy STS-u*, Warszawa: Wydawnictwo Rosner&Wspólnicy, 2005.

Bohdan Czeszko (in the series *Literackie Portrety*), prepared by W. Holewiński, guests: A. Robiński, J. Termer, Polskie Radio program 2 June 14, 2018, https://polskieradio24.pl/8/3869/Artykul/2149212,Literackie-portrety-Bohdan-Czeszko (accessed January 31, 2021).

Borowski T., *Pisma w czterech tomach* vol. 1: *Poezja*, compiled by T. Drewnowski, J. Szczęsna, Kraków: Wydawnictwo Literackie, 2003; vol. 2: *Proza (1)*, compiled by S. Buryła, ibidem 2004; vol. 3: *Proza (2)*, compiled by S. Buryła, ibidem 2004; vol. 4: *Krytyka*, compiled by T. Drewnowski, ibidem 2005.

Borowski T., *Rozmowa z przyjacielem. Wiersze*, submitted for print and prefaced by T. Drewnowski, Wrocław: Wydawnictwo Dolnośląskie, 1999.

Boruszkowski P., Eisler J., *Towarzysz Wiesław* (in the series *Cafe Historia*), interview conducted by A. Górniakowska, ed. U. Dubowska, prod. APTiF for TVP Historia, TVP SA 2014, https://vod.tvp.pl/video/cafe-historia,towarzysz-wieslaw,17022431 (accessed January 10, 2021).

Buryła S., [Review: J. Wróbel, *Miara cierpienia. O pisarstwie Adolfa Rudnickiego*, Kraków: Universitas, 2004], *Pamiętnik Literacki* 2006, issue 2, pp. 233–238.

Buryła S., "Artyści i ich opiekunowie," *Znak* 2009, no. 7/8, pp. 138–143.

Carnegie D., *Jak zjednywać przyjaciół i osiągnąć sukces w życiu*, edition revised, amended, trans. into Polish and summarized by K. Iłłakowiczówna, Warszawa: Oficyna Literatów "Rój," 1991.

Dąbrowska M., *Dzienniki powojenne* vol. 1: *1945–1949*; vol. 2: *1950–1954*, selection, introduction and footnotes by T. Drewnowski, Warszawa: "Czytelnik," 1996.

Ginczanka Z., *Udźwignąć własne szczęście. Poezje*, introduction and compilation by I. Kiec, Poznań: "Brama" – Książnica Włóczęgów i Uczonych, 1991.

Grochowska M., "Uwaga! Kuśmierek. Opowieść o szlachetnym warchole," *Gazeta Wyborcza* March 31–April 1, 2012, no. 77, pp. 34–37.

"Iłła" – opowieść o Kazimierze Iłłakowiczównie [Joanna Kuciel-Frydryszak interviewed by Agata Szwedowicz (PAP)], Dzieje.pl, October 7, 2017, https://dzieje.pl/ksiazki/illa-opowiesc-o-kazimierze-illakowiczownie (accessed January 22, 2021).

Jaworska M., "Prababka polskiej rewolucji kobiecej – Maria Jehanne Wielopolska," *Akant* 2007, no. 12, pp. 22–23.

Jurandot J., *Miasto skazanych. Dwa lata w warszawskim getcie*, Warszawa: Muzeum Historii Żydów Polskich, 2014.

Kaliski B., "Jedynie donos jest ciekawy?," *Nowe Książki* 2009, no. 4, pp. 49–50.

Kotarba R., "Śmierć poetki. Historia okupacyjna," *Ale Historia. Tygodnik Historyczny* December 14, 2015, no. 50, pp. 12–13.

List 34 (in the series *Dźwiękowy Przewodnik Po Historii Najnowszej – Polska*), compiled by K. Kobylecka, Polskie Radio February 4, 1997, https://www.polskieradio.pl/39/156/Artykul/565503,Trzydziestu-czterech-w-obronie-kultury-polskiej (accessed January 31, 2021).

Mrozik A., "Czy komunistka może być ofiarą?," *Bez dogmatu* 2017, no. 112, pp. 29–31.

Poręba S., "Zofia Meisner – między szkołą i literaturą," *Nowości. Gazeta Pomorza i Kujaw* July 9, 1997, no. 158, p. 9.

Prokop J., "Panfierow," *Arcana* 1996, no. 5, pp. 126–137.

Przeperski M., "Suwerenność komunistki," *Nowe Książki* 2017, no. 9, pp. 28–29.

Ratajczak J., "*Wspomnienia* Barbary Czerwijowskiej," *W Drodze* 1991, no. 2, pp. 60–64.

"Sam na sam z Polską Ludową," interview with an anonymous censor conducted by Joanna Pruszyńska," *Rzeczpospolita* April 15–16, 2000, no. 90, pp. D4–D5.

Sandauer A., *Byłem...*, Warszawa: PIW, 1991.

Sowińska S., *Gorzkie lata. Z wyżyn władzy do stalinowskiego więzienia*, edited and compiled by Ł. Bertram, Warszawa: Wydawnictwo Ośrodek Karta, 2017.

Szczęsna J., *Tadeusz Borowski – poeta*, Poznań: Poznańskie Studia Polonistyczne, 2000.

Towarzysz Wiesław, script and direction by P. Boruszkowski, produced by Telewizja Polska, 2013, https://www.cda.pl/video/1306845d5 (accessed March 31, 2021).

Tunak M., *1953–1955 – trudne lata dla środowiska Pax*, Historia.org.pl, February 26, 2018, https://historia.org.pl/2018/02/26/1953-1956-trudne-lata-dla-srodowiska-pax/ (accessed January 31, 2021).

Tyrmand L., *Dziennik. 1954*, Warszawa: Wydawnictwo MG, 2015.

Zaremba M., "Amputacja pamięci," *Polityka* November 23, 1996, pp. 64–68, http://niniwa22.cba.pl/amputacja_pamieci.htm (accessed January 31, 2021).

Żaryn J., *Endecja – cenne dziedzictwo* (in the series *Spory historyków*) Biuletyn IPN "Pamięć.pl" 2012, no. 9, pp. 30–34, http://www.polska1918-89.pl/pdf/endecja---cenne-dziedzictwo,2095.pdf (accessed January 31, 2021).

Scholarly and Popular Science Texts

Adamczykowa Z., "Literatura 'czwarta' – w kręgu zagadnień teoretycznych," [in:] *Literatura dla dzieci i młodzieży (po roku 1980)*, ed. K. Heska-Kwaśniewicz, Katowice: Wydawnictwo UŚ, 2008, pp. 13–43.

Ajdukiewicz K., "W sprawie artykułu prof. A. Schaffa o moich poglądach filozoficznych," *Myśl Filozoficzna* 1953, no. 2, pp. 292–334.

Araszkiewicz A., *Wypowiadam wam moje życie. Melancholia Zuzanny Ginczanki*, Warszawa: Fundacja Ośka, 2001.

Artysiewicz A., "Cenzorska wizja dramatu i teatru na podstawie *Odpraw krajowych* z lat 1945–1946," [in:] *Dramat i teatr w dokumentach GUKPPiW*, eds. K. Budrowska, M. Budnik, K. Kościewicz, Białystok: Wydawnictwo Alter Studio, 2017, series *Cenzura w PRL. Archiwalia* vol. 2, pp. 9–20.

Bartelski L., *Genealogia ocalonych. Szkice o latach 1939–1944*, Warszawa: Wydawnictwo Literackie, 1963.

Bartelski L., *Termopile literackie. Polska 1939–1945*, Warszawa: Instytut Wydawniczy "Pax," 2002.

Bartelski L., *W kręgu bliskich. Szkice do portretów*, Kraków: Wydawnictwo Literackie, 1967.

Bates J.M., "Cenzura w epoce stalinowskiej," *Teksty Drugie* 2000, no. 1/2, pp. 95–120.

Bates J.M., "Cenzura wobec problemu niemieckiego w literaturze polskiej (1948–1955)," [in:] *Presja i ekspresja. Zjazd szczeciński i socrealizm*, eds. D. Dąbrowska, P. Michałowski, Szczecin: Wydawnictwo Naukowe US, 2002, pp. 79–92.

Bereś S., *Gajcy. W pierścieniu śmierci*, Wołowiec: Wydawnictwo Czarne, 2016.

Bikont A., Szczęsna J., *Lawina i kamienie. Pisarze wobec komunizmu*, Warszawa: Prószyński i S-ka, 2006.

"Biuletyn Informacyjno-Instrukcyjny." Wybór dokumentów z 1955 r., eds. K. Budrowska, M. Budnik, W. Gardocki, Białystok: Wydawnictwo Alter Studio, 2018, series *Cenzura w PRL. Archiwalia* vol. 3.

Boroda K., Kościewicz K., "Cenzurowanie widowisk w 1949 r. w świetle statystyki Głównego Urzędu Kontroli Prasy, Publikacji i Widowisk," [in:] *Dramat i teatr w dokumentach GUKPPiW*, eds. K. Budrowska, M. Budnik, K. Kościewicz, Białystok: Wydawnictwo Alter Studio, 2017, series *Cenzura w PRL. Archiwalia* vol. 2, pp. 91–107.

Budnik M., *"Książka Nowego Czytelnika." Literatura dla byłych analfabetów przeszkolonych w Polsce w latach 1948–1951*, Białystok: Wydawnictwo UwB, 2014.

Budnik M., "Przedwojenna pisarka w realiach wczesnego PRL-u. Przypadek Zofii Meisner," [in:] *Kariera pisarza w PRL-u*, eds. M. Budnik, K. Budrowska, E. Dąbrowicz, K. Kościewicz, Warszawa: IBL PAN, 2014, series *Badania Filologiczne nad Cenzurą PRL* vol. 4, pp. 212–231.

Budrowska K., "Cenzura, tabu i wstyd. Cenzura obyczajowa PRL-u (1948–1958)," *Napis. Pismo poświęcone literaturze okolicznościowej i użytkowej* 2012, series 18, pp. 234–235.

Budrowska K., "Cenzurowanie tematyki pogranicza w Polsce Ludowej w latach 1945–1956. Przegląd problematyki badań," *Studia Wschodniosłowiańskie* 2015, vol. 15, pp. 533–542.

Budrowska K., "O twórczości Kazimiery Iłłakowiczówny. Materiał archiwalny z zespołu Głównego Urzędu Kontroli Prasy, Publikacji i Widowisk z połowy 1955 r.," *Napis. Pismo poświęcone literaturze okolicznościowej i użytkowej* 2017, series 23, pp. 364–386.

Budrowska K., "Od orderu do 'zapisu.' Jak GUKPPiW oceniał pisarzy w latach 1952–1955?," [in:] *Kariera pisarza w PRL-u*, eds. M. Budnik, K. Budrowska, E. Dąbrowicz, K. Kościewicz, Warszawa: IBL PAN, 2014, series *Badania Filologiczne nad Cenzurą PRL* vol. 4, pp. 78–95.

Budrowska K., *Studia i szkice o cenzurze w Polsce Ludowej w latach 40. i 50. XX wieku*, Białystok: Wydawnictwo Alter Studio, 2014.

Budrowska K., "Tajne pismo cenzury. *Biuletyn Informacyjno-Instrukcyjny* w latach 1952–1955," [in:] *Komunikowanie się Polaków w latach 1944–1989*, eds. K. Stępnik, M. Rajewski, Lublin: Wydawnictwo UMCS, 2011, pp. 51–61.

Budrowska K., *Writers, Literature and Censorship in Poland. 1948–1956*, Berlin: Peter Lang, 2020.

Budrowska K., *Zatrzymane przez cenzurę. Inedita z połowy wieku XX*, Warszawa: IBL PAN, 2013, series *Badania Filologiczne nad Cenzurą PRL* vol. 2.

Budzyńska C., "Hoffman Paweł Maksymilian," [in:] *Słownik biograficzny działaczy polskiego ruchu robotniczego*, ed. F. Tych, vol. 2: *E–J*, Warszawa: "Książka i Wiedza," 1987, pp. 635–636.

Burkot S., *Literatura polska 1939–2009*, Third Revised Edition, Warszawa: PWN, 2014.

Buryła S., *Prawda mitu i literatury. O pisarstwie Tadeusza Borowskiego i Leopolda Buczkowskiego*, Kraków: Universitas, 2003.

Cenzura PRL. Wykaz książek podlegających niezwłocznemu wycofaniu 1 X 1951 r., afterword by Z. Żmigrodzki, Wrocław: Wydawnictwo "Nortom," 2002.

Chojnowski Z., *Postacie kobiecości. O poezji Kazimiery Iłłakowiczówny*, Kraków–Bielsko-Biała: Instytut Literacki–Wydawnictwo Naukowe UKSW, 2019.

Chwastyk-Kowalczyk J., "Tadeusz Hollender – enfant terrible de Léopo," *Respectus Philologicus* 2007, no. 12, pp. 64–76.

Cieśla A.B., *Mania – cenzorka z Ryk,* http://www.ryki-dawniej.com/yewish-ryki/ zide-z-ryk-ve-svete/mania---cenzorka-z-ryk?tmpl=%2Fsystem%2Fapp%2Ftemplates%2Fprint%2F&showPrintDialog=1 (accessed March 31, 2021).

Cieślikowski J., *Literatura osobna,* selection by R. Waksmund, Warszawa: "Nasza Księgarnia," 1985.

Czachowska J. [J. Cz.], "Hollender Tadeusz," [in:] *Współcześni polscy pisarze i badacze literatury. Słownik biobibliograficzny* vol. 3: *G–J,* eds. J. Czachowska, A. Szałagan, Warszawa: WSiP, 1994, pp. 264–265.

Czachowska J. [J. Cz.], "Kowalewski Janusz," [in:] *Współcześni polscy pisarze i badacze literatury. Słownik biobibliograficzny* vol. 4: *K,* eds. J. Czachowska, A. Szałagan, Warszawa: WSiP, 1994, pp. 317–318.

Czarniawski M., *Sławoj Składkowski w legendzie,* Białystok: Wydawca Marek Czarniawski, 2007.

Czuchnowski W., *Blizna. Proces kurii krakowskiej 1953,* Kraków: Społeczny Instytut Wydawniczy "Znak," 2003.

Dakowicz P., "Walka ideologiczna z Norwidem i o Norwida (1944–1948)," *Pamiętnik Literacki* 2009, issue 2, pp. 5–30.

Dąbrowicz E., "Zdezaktualizowane: na marginesie *Wykazu książek podlegających niezwłocznemu wycofaniu 1 X 1951 r.*," *Acta Universitatis Lodziensis. Folia Litteraria Polonica* 2013, no. 19, pp. 43–57.

Dorosz B. [B. D.], "Kuśmierek Józef," [in:] *Współcześni polscy pisarze i badacze literatury. Słownik biobibliograficzny* vol. 4: *K,* eds. J. Czachowska, A. Szałagan, Warszawa: WSiP, 1994, pp. 498–501.

Drewnowski T., *Próba scalenia. Obiegi-Wzorce-Style,* Warszawa: PWN, 1997.

Drewnowski T., *Ucieczka z kamiennego świata (o Tadeuszu Borowskim),* Warszawa: PIW, 1961.

Drewnowski T., *Walka o oddech. O pisarstwie Tadeusza Różewicza,* Warszawa: Wydawnictwa Artystyczne i Filmowe, 1990.

Dygul J., "Parateksty polskich przekładów z literatury włoskiej w czasach stalinowskich," *Italica Wratislaviensia* 2010, no. 1, pp. 80–92.

Dziki S. [SD], "Biuletyn," [in:] *Słownik terminologii medialnej,* ed. W. Pisarek, Kraków: Universitas, 2006, p. 18.

Dziki S. [S. Dz.], Michalski B. [B. M.], "Biuletyn," [in:] *Encyklopedia wiedzy o prasie,* ed. J. Maślanka, Wrocław: Ossolineum, 1976, pp. 33–34.

"Edmund Krüger," [in:] *Encyklopedia fantastyki,* http://encyklopediafantastyki.pl/index.php?title=Edward_Kr%C3%BCger (accessed January 31, 2021).

Eisler J., *List 34,* Warszawa: PWN, 1993.

Encyklopedia wiedzy o książce, eds. A. Birkenmajer, B. Kocowski, J. Trzynadlowski, Wrocław: Ossolineum, 1971.

Faryna-Paszkiewicz H., *Polemira. Niesłusznie zapomniana,* Warszawa: Wydawnictwo Nisza i Narodowe Centrum Kultury, 2016.

Fijałkowska B., *Borejsza i Różański. Przyczynek do dziejów stalinizmu w Polsce,* Olsztyn: Wydawnictwo Wyższej Szkoły Pedagogicznej w Olsztynie, 1995.

Fik M., "Film a cenzura. Z archiwum Głównego Urzędu Kontroli Prasy, Publikacji i Widowisk (6). Październik–grudzień 1968," *Kwartalnik Filmowy* 1995, no. 11, pp. 128–134.

Fik M., *Kultura polska po Jałcie. Kronika lat 1944–1981*, London: Polonia Book Fund, 1989.

Flisikowska A., *Gdańsk literacki: od kontrolowanego do wolnego słowa (1945–2005)*, Gdańsk: Wydawnictwo "Mestwin" i Wojewódzka i Miejska Biblioteka Publiczna im. Josepha Conrada-Korzeniowskiego w Gdańsku, 2011.

Friszke A., *Grzechy endecji* (in the series *Spory historyków*), Biuletyn IPN "Pamięć.pl" 2012, no. 9, pp. 25–29, http://www.polska1918-89.pl/pdf/grzechy-endecji,2094.pdf (accessed January 31, 2021).

Frycie S., "Czy literatura dla dzieci i młodzieży jest literaturą 'osobną,'" *Guliwer* 1999, no. 6, pp. 73–75.

Gall A., "Kresy w polskiej literaturze," [in:] *Interakcje. Leksykon komunikowania polsko-niemieckiego*, http://www.polska-niemcy-interakcje.pl/articles/show/3 (accessed January 31, 2021).

Gardocki W., *Cenzura wobec literatury polskiej w latach osiemdziesiątych XX w.*, Warszawa: IBL PAN, 2019, series *Badania Filologiczne nad Cenzurą PRL* vol. 8.

Gdańsk w literaturze. Bibliografia od roku 997 do dzisiaj vol. 5: *1945–1979*, ed. L. Rybicki, Gdańsk: Wydawnictwo słowo/obraz terytoria, 2007.

Genette G., "Palimpsesty. Literatura drugiego stopnia," trans. A. Milecki, [in:] *Współczesna teoria badań literackich za granicą. Antologia* vol. 4, part 2: *Literatura jako produkcja i ideologia. Poststrukturalizm. Badanie intertekstualne. Problemy syntezy historycznoliterackiej*, compiled by H. Markiewicz, Kraków: Wydawnictwo Literackie, 1992, pp. 319–321.

Genette G., *Palimpsesty. Literatura drugiego stopnia*, trans. T. Stróżyński, A. Milecki, Gdańsk: Wydawnictwo słowo/obraz terytoria, 2014.

Gieba K., "Próba epopei. O narracjach założycielskich tzw. Ziem Odzyskanych," *Teksty Drugie* 2015, no. 5, pp. 321–335.

Ginczanka. Na stulecie poetki, eds. K. Kuczyńska-Kochany, K. Szymańska, Kraków: Wydawnictwo Pasaże, 2018.

Glonnegger E., *Leksykon gier planszowych. Geneza, zasady i historia*, trans. J.A. Jerry, Warszawa: Świat Książki, 1997.

Głębicka E. [E. G.], "Gisges Jan Maria," [in:] *Współcześni polscy pisarze i badacze literatury. Słownik biobibliograficzny* vol. 5: *L–M*, eds. J. Czachowska, A. Szałagan, Warszawa: WSiP, 1997, pp. 50–52.

Głębicka E. [E. G.], "Kowalewski Stanisław," [in:] *Współcześni polscy pisarze i badacze literatury. Słownik biobibliograficzny* vol. 4: *K*, eds. J. Czachowska, A. Szałagan, Warszawa: WSiP, 1994, pp. 319–322.

Głowiński M., *Dzień Ulissesa i inne szkice na tematy niemitologiczne*, Kraków: Wydawnictwo Literackie, 2000.

Głowiński M., *Rytuał i demagogia. Trzynaście szkiców o sztuce zdegradowanej*, Warszawa: Wydawnictwo "Open," 1992.

Główny Urząd Kontroli Prasy 1945–1949, compiled by D. Nałęcz, Warszawa: ISP PAN, 1994, series *Dokumenty do Dziejów PRL* issue 6.

Gogol B., *"Fabryka fałszywych tekstów." Z działalności Wojewódzkiego Urzędu Kontroli Prasy, Publikacji i Widowisk w Gdańsku w latach 1945–1958*, Warszawa: Wydawnictwo Neriton, 2012.

Grabarczyk P., *Directival Theory of Meaning. From Syntax and Pragmatics to Narrow Linguistic Content*, Cham: Springer, 2019.

Hadaczek B., *Kresy w literaturze polskiej XX wieku. Szkice*, Szczecin: Wydawnictwo Ottonianum, 1993.

Hemar M., *Moja przekora. Satyry polityczne z lat 1943–1971*, selected and compiled by A.K. Kunert, Kraków: Wydawnictwo Literackie, 2001.

Hobot J., *Gra z cenzurą w poezji Nowej Fali (1968–1976)*, Kraków: Wydawnictwo Literackie, 2000.

Hollender T., *Wiersze. Satyry. Fraszki*, selection and introduction by A. Maliszewski, recollections about the author by J. Zagórski, critical supplement by J.W. Gomulicki, Warszawa: "Książka i Wiedza," 1949.

Inglot M., *Polska kultura literacka Lwowa lat 1939–1941*, Wrocław: Towarzystwo Przyjaciół Polonistyki Wrocławskiej, 1995.

Iwasiów I., "Przesiedleni chłopi uruchamiają miasto," *Teksty Drugie* 2017, no. 5, pp. 181–192.

Jagiełło J., *O polską drogę do socjalizmu. Dyskusje w PPR i PPS w latach 1944–1948*, Second Edition, Warszawa–Kraków: PWN, 1983.

Janowski W., "Główny Urząd Kontroli Prasy, Publikacji i Widowisk w latach 1945–1947. Problemy wewnątrzorganizacyjne," [in:] *Literatura w granicach prawa (XIX–XX w.)*, eds. K. Budrowska, E. Dąbrowicz, M. Lul, Warszawa: IBL PAN, 2013, series *Badania Filologiczne nad Cenzurą PRL* vol. 3, pp. 152–156.

Jarosz D., "Zapisy cenzury z lat 1948–1955," *Regiony* 1996, no. 3, pp. 2–37.

Kaczmarek I., "Biblioteki oświatowe i publiczne w Łodzi w dwudziestoleciu międzywojennym," *Acta Universitatis Lodziensis. Folia Librorum* 2013, no. 17, pp. 75–95.

Kaczmarek I., "Biblioteki szkolne w Łodzi w dwudziestoleciu międzywojennym. Przegląd działalności," *Acta Universitatis Lodziensis. Folia Librorum* 2015, no. 1, pp. 33–57.

Kajtoch W. [W. K.], "Drugi obieg," [in:] *Encyklopedia książki* vol. 1: *Eseje. A–J*, eds. A. Żbikowska-Migoń, M. Skalska-Zlat, Wrocław: Wydawnictwo UWr, 2017, pp. 539–540.

Kamińska-Chełminiak K., *Cenzura w Polsce 1944–1960. Organizacja. Kadry. Metody pracy*, Warszawa: Wydział Dziennikarstwa, Informacji i Bibliologii UW i Oficyna Wydawnicza ASPRA-JR, 2019.

Kąkolewski K., "Reportaż," [in:] *Słownik literatury polskiej XX wieku*, eds. A. Brodzka, M. Puchalska, M. Semczuk, A. Sobolewska, E. Szary-Matywiecka, Wrocław: Ossolineum, 1995, pp. 930–935.

Kempa A., "Literatura źle obecna," *Poradnik Bibliotekarza* 1989, no. 5, pp. 28–29.

Kiec I., *Ginczanka. Życie i twórczość*, Poznań: Wydawnictwo Obserwator, 1991.

Kienzler I., *Kobiety w życiu Marszałka Piłsudskiego*, Warszawa: Bellona, 2014.

Kienzler I., *Prowokatorka. Fascynujące życie Marii Dąbrowskiej*, Warszawa: Bellona, 2017.

Kloc A., *Cenzura wobec tematu II wojny światowej i podziemia powojennego w literaturze polskiej 1956–1958*, Warszawa: Wydawnictwo IPN, 2018.

Kłak T., *Spojrzenia. Szkice o poezji Tadeusza Różewicza*, Katowice: Wydawnictwo Biblioteka Śląska, 1999.

Kochanowska E., *Odeszli w cień*, Gdańsk: Wydawnictwo Morskie, 1981.

Kolbuszewski J., *Kresy*, Wrocław: Wydawnictwo Dolnośląskie, 2006.

Kołakowski P., Krzak A., *Sprawa majora Jerzego Sosnowskiego w świetle dokumentów analitycznych Oddziału II SGWP i zeznań Franza Heinricha Pfeifera*, Warszawa: Wydawnictwo Demart, 2015.

Kołodziejczyk A., "Bolesław Piasecki i jego idea," [in:] *Komu służył PAX. Materiały z sympozjum "Od Pax-u do Civitas Christiana" zorganizowanego przez Katolickie Stowarzyszenie Civitas Christiana, 30–31 stycznia 2008 roku*, ed. S. Bober, Warszawa: Instytut Wydawniczy "Pax," 2008, pp. 27–50.

Kondek S.A., *Papierowa rewolucja. Oficjalny obieg książek w Polsce w latach 1948–1955*, Warszawa: Biblioteka Narodowa, 1999.

Kondek S.A., *Władza i wydawcy. Polityczne uwarunkowania produkcji książek w Polsce w latach 1944–1949*, Warszawa: Biblioteka Narodowa, 1993.

Konopska B., "Cenzura w kartografii okresu PRL na przykładzie map do użytku ogólnego," *Polski Przegląd Kartograficzny* 2007, vol. 39, no. 1, pp. 44–57.

Korczyńska-Derkacz M., "Książki szkodliwe politycznie, czyli akcja 'oczyszczania' księgozbiorów bibliotek szkolnych, pedagogicznych i publicznych w latach 1947–1956," [in:] *Niewygodne dla władzy. Ograniczanie wolności słowa na ziemiach polskich w XIX i XX wieku. Zbiór studiów*, eds. D. Degen, J. Gzella, Toruń 2010, pp. 335–356.

Korzeniowski M., Latawiec K., Gabryś-Sławińska M., Tarasiuk D., *Leksykon uchodźstwa polskiego w Rosji w latach I wojny światowej*, Lublin: Wydawnictwo UMCS, 2018.

Kotek J., *Students and the Cold War*, trans. R. Blumenau, London: Palgrave Macmillan, 1996.

Kozłowski W., "Jaroszewicz Zofia," [in:] *Słownik biograficzny działaczy polskiego ruchu robotniczego*, ed. F. Tych, vol. 2: *E–J*, Warszawa: "Książka i Wiedza," 1987, p. 661.

Kozłowski W., *Pola zakwitną makami*, Warszawa: Wydawnictwo Harcerskie "Horyzonty," 1970; Second Edition: Warszawa: Młodzieżowa Agencja Wydawnicza, 1978; Third Edition: ibidem 1983.

Kresy – pojęcie i rzeczywistość. Zbiór studiów, ed. K. Handke, Warszawa: Slawistyczny Ośrodek Wydawniczy, 1997.

"Kronika życia literackiego w PRL. 1951," compiled by M. Wosiek, [in:] *Kronika życia literackiego Polski Ludowej 1944–1969. Materiały*, collaborative work edited by E. Korzeniewska (until 1963) and J. Stradecki (1964–1969), written between 1963–1970.

"Kronika życia literackiego w PRL. 1952," compiled by H. Filipkowska, [in:] *Kronika życia literackiego Polski Ludowej 1944–1969. Materiały*, collaborative work edited by E. Korzeniewska (until 1963) and J. Stradecki (1964–1969), written between 1963–1970.

Królak J., "Paratekst w służbie propagandy. Wprowadzenia w przekładach literatury pięknej na język polski i czeski w latach 50. XX wieku," *Przekłady Literatur Słowiańskich* vol. 8, part 1, pp. 159–177.

"Krüger Edmund," [in:] *Słownik współczesnych pisarzy polskich* vol. 2, ed. E. Korzeniewska, Warszawa: PWN, 1964, pp. 52–55.

Krzanicki M., *Komiks w PRL, PRL w komiksie*, Warszawa: Wydawnictwo IPN, 2011.

Kto był kim w Drugiej Rzeczypospolitej, ed. J.M. Majchrowski in cooperation with G. Mazur and K. Stepan, Warszawa: "BGW" 1994.

Kuciel-Frydryszak J., "Antoni Słonimski i *List 34*," Biuletyn IPN "Pamięć.pl," 2012, no. 1, pp. 38–41.

Kuciel-Frydryszak J., *Iłła. Opowieść o Kazimierze Iłłakowiczównie*, Warszawa: Marginesy, 2017.

Kuciel-Frydryszak J., *Słonimski. Heretyk na ambonie*, Warszawa: W.A.B., 2012.

Kuliczkowska K., "Krüger Edmund," [in:] *Polski Słownik Biograficzny*, ed. E. Rostworowski, in co-operation with W. Armon et al., vol. 15: *Kozłowska Zofia–Kubacki Stanisław*, Wrocław–Warszawa–Kraków: Ossolineum–PAN, 1970, pp. 449–450.

Kulińska L., Ostrowski M., Sierchuła R., *Narodowcy. Myśl polityczna i społeczna Obozu Narodowego w Polsce w latach 1944–47*, Warszawa: PWN, 2001.

Kumaniecka J., *Saga rodu Słonimskich*, Warszawa: Iskry, 2003.

"Lancetem, a nie maczugą". Cenzura wobec literatury i jej twórców w latach 1945–1965, eds. K. Budrowska, M. Woźniak-Łabieniec, Warszawa: IBL PAN, 2012, series *Badania Filologiczne nad Cenzurą PRL* vol. 1.

Landau Z., "Sławoj Felicjan Składkowski," [in:] *Polski Słownik Biograficzny*, ed. H. Markiewicz, co-operation with M. Adrianek et al., vol. 38: *Skarbek Aleksander–Słomka Jan*, Warszawa–Kraków: PAN, 1997–1998, pp. 193–197.

Lechowski P., "Problemy i organizacja powszechnego bibliotekarstwa publicznego w Polsce w latach 1945–1951," *Roczniki Biblioteczne* 2011, no. 55, pp. 92–112.

Leociak J., *Młyny Boże. Zapiski o Kościele i Zagładzie*, Wołowiec: Wydawnictwo Czarne, 2018.

Leśniakowska M., *Architektura w Warszawie*, Third Revised Edition, Warszawa: Arkada. Pracownia Historii Sztuki, 2005.

Lisiecka A., *Pokolenie "pryszczatych,"* Warszawa: PIW, 1964.

Literatura światowa w wydawnictwach *"Czytelnika,"* layout by J. Jaworowski, Warszawa: "Czytelnik," 1957.

Loewe I., *Gatunki paratekstowe w komunikacji medialnej*, Kraków: Wydawnictwo UŚ, 2007.

Looby R., *Censorship, Translation and English Language Fiction in People's Poland*, Leiden (Netherlands)–Boston (Massachusetts): Brill Rodopi, 2015.

Łobodowski J., *Pamięci Sulamity*, Toronto: Polski Fundusz Wydawniczy w Kanadzie, 1987.

Makowiecki A.Z., *"Odrodzenie" (1944–1950)*, [in:] *Słownik literatury polskiej XX wieku*, eds. A. Brodzka, M. Puchalska, M. Semczuk, A. Sobolewska, E. Szary-Matywiecka, Wrocław: Ossolineum, 1995, pp. 754–756.

Malenkow G.M., *Referat sprawozdawczy na XIX Zjeździe Partii o działalności KC WKP(b)*, Warszawa: "Książka i Wiedza," 1952.

Marzec L., *Maria-Jehanne Wielopolska, Wielkopolski Słownik Pisarek*, https://pisarki.fandom.com/wiki/Maria-Jehanne_Wielopolska (accessed January 31, 2021).

Matuszewski R., *Literatura na przełomie*, Warszawa: "Czytelnik," 1951.

Mazur E., "'Składam słowa/dźwigam swój czas.' Kilka uwag do dyskursu o ocaleniu w poezji Tadeusza Różewicza (na lekcjach języka polskiego w szkołach ponadgimnazjalnych)," *Zeszyty Naukowe Uniwersytetu Rzeszowskiego* 2014, issue 86, pp. 35–46.

McCullagh F., *Prześladowanie chrześcijaństwa przez bolszewizm rosyjski*, trans. K. Iłłakowiczówna, Kraków: Wydawnictwo Księży Jezuitów, 1924.

McCullagh F., *The Bolshevik Persecution of Christianity*, London 1924.

Menzies A.C., *Frank Twyman 1876–1959*, "Royal Society Publishing," pp. 268–279, https://royalsocietypublishing.org/doi/pdf/10.1098/rsbm.1960.0020 (accessed March 27, 2021).

Mielczarek T., "Pisarze w PRL: 'pieszczochy władzy' czy ofiary systemu," [in:] *Niewygodne dla władzy. Ograniczanie wolności słowa na ziemiach polskich w XIX i XX wieku*, eds. D. Degen, J. Gzella, Toruń: Wydawnictwo Naukowe UMK, 2010, pp. 213–231.

Mikołajewski J., *Cień w cień. Za cieniem Zuzanny Ginczanki*, Warszawa: Wydawnictwo Dowody na Istnienie, 2019.

Misiora M., *Bibliografia komiksów wydanych w Polsce w latach 1905 (1859*)–1999. Albumy, magazyny komiksowe, fanziny i książki o komiksie*, Poznań: Fundacja Tranzyt / Centrala, 2010.

Mojsak K., *Wczesna twórczość Stanisława Mrożka w dokumentach cenzury*, [in:] idem, *Cenzura wobec prozy nowoczesnej. 1956–1965*, IBL PAN, Warszawa 2016, series: *Badania Filologiczne nad Cenzurą PRL* vol. 7, pp. 123–154.

Molisak A., "Adolfa Rudnickiego odmiany żydowskości," [in:] *Pisarze polsko-żydowscy. Przybliżenia*, eds. M. Dąbrowski, A. Molisak, Warszawa: Dom Wydawniczy Elipsa, 2006, pp. 67–79.

Morawiec A., "Brr, Bereza. Polish Literature towards the Confinement Centre in Bereza Kartuska. 1934–1939," *Acta Universitatis Lodziensis. Folia Litteraria Polonica* 2019, no. 4, pp. 231–271.

Możejko E., *Realizm socjalistyczny. Teoria. Rozwój. Upadek*, Kraków: Universitas, 2001.

Na rogu Stalina i Trzech Krzyży. Listy do Jerzego Borejszy 1944–1952, selection, introduction, compilation and footnotes by G.P. Bąbiak, Warszawa: "Czytelnik," 2014.

Nadolna-Tłuczykont M., *Powrót książek "zakazanych" do współczesnych odbiorców (wybrane zagadnienia)*, Katowice: Wydawnictwo UŚ, 2013.

Nasalska A., "Reportaż," [in:] *Słownik realizmu socjalistycznego*, eds. Z. Łapiński, W. Tomasik, Kraków: Universitas, 2004, pp. 286–292.

Nasiłowska A., "Problemowo czy chronologicznie? Kilka argumentów," *Zeszyty Szkolne. Edukacja humanistyczna* 2007, no. 2, pp. 46–49.

Nowak P., *Cenzura wobec rynku książki. Wojewódzki Urząd Kontroli Prasy, Publikacji i Widowisk w Poznaniu w latach 1946–1955*, Poznań: Wydawnictwo Naukowe UAM, 2012.

Nowak P., "Skuteczna czy nieskuteczna. Socjalistyczna cenzura w czasach terroru stalinowskiego. Studium przypadku poznańskiego wydawnictwa Albertinum," *Toruńskie Studia Bibliologiczne* 2013, no. 2, pp. 31–47.

Nowak P., "Wojewódzki Urząd Kontroli Prasy, Publikacji i Widowisk w okresie nacjonalizacji rynku książki w Poznaniu (1946–1955)," *Biblioteka* 2011, no. 15, pp. 163–193.

Obremski W., *Krótka historia sztuki komiksu w Polsce (1945–2003)*, Toruń: Wydawnictwo Adam Marszałek, 2005.

Obrębska A., "Akcja usuwania książek z bibliotek województwa olsztyńskiego w 1949 r.," *Komunikaty Mazursko-Warmińskie* 2008, no. 2, pp. 145–153.

Owczarek B., "Realizm socjalistyczny," [in:] *Słownik literatury polskiej XX wieku*, eds. A. Brodzka, M. Puchalska, M. Semczuk, A. Sobolewska, E. Szary-Matywiecka, Wrocław: Ossolineum, 1995, pp. 922–925.

Paczkowski A., "Cenzura 1946–1949. Statystyka działalności," *Zeszyty Historyczne* 1996, issue 116, pp. 22–57.

Pawlicki A., *Kompletna szarość. Cenzura w latach 1965–1972. Instytucja i ludzie*, Warszawa: Wydawnictwo Trio, 2001.

Pietrych P., "*Niepokój* – niemal zapomniany tom poetycki Tadeusza Różewicza z 1947 roku," *Pamiętnik Literacki* 2017, issue 2, pp. 143–166.

Pietrych P., "Tadeusz Różewicz pisze wiersze w roku 1946, czyli poeta modernistyczny wobec wojny," *Poznańskie Studia Polonistyczne. Seria Literacka* 2014, no. 24, pp. 256–267.

Pietrzak M., "Socrealistyczna krytyka literacka w ujęciu diachronicznym," *Acta Universitatis Lodziensis. Folia Litteraria Polonica* 2008, no. 10, pp. 237–251.

Podręczny słownik bibliotekarza, compiled by G. Czapnik, Z. Gruszka in cooperation with H. Tadeusiewicz, Warszawa: Wydawnictwo Stowarzyszenia Bibliotekarzy Polskich, 2011.

Pogranicza, Kresy, Wschód a idee Europy, series 2: *Wiktor Choriew in memoriam*, concept and introduction by J. Ławski, scholarly edition A. Janicka, G. Kowalski, Ł. Zabielski, Białystok: Książnica Podlaska im. Łukasza Górnickiego, 2013.

Poppa A., "Siostra znanej siostry czy poetka nieusłyszana? Twórczość Barbary Czerwijowskiej," [in:] *Twórczość niepozorna. Szkice o literaturze*, eds. J. Grądziel-Wójcik, A. Kwiatkowska, L. Marzec, Kraków: Wydawnictwo Pasaże, 2015, pp. 52–62.

Presja i ekspresja. Zjazd szczeciński i socrealizm, eds. D. Dąbrowska, P. Michałowski, Szczecin: Wydawnictwo Naukowe US, 2002, pp. 79–92.

Prokop-Janiec E., "Żyd – Polak – artysta. O budowaniu tożsamości po Zagładzie," *Teksty Drugie* 2001, no. 1, pp. 120–134.

Przetakiewicz Z., *Od ONR-u do Pax-u*, Warszawa: Wydawnictwo Prasy Lokalnej, 2010.

Puchalski J., "Biblioteki w życiu naukowym PRL i poza krajem w latach 1939–1989," [in:] *Historia nauki polskiej 1944–1989* vol. 10: *Instytucje*, eds. L. Zasztowt, J. Schiller-Walicka, Warszawa: Oficyna Wydawnicza Aspra-JR, 2015, pp. 359–483.

Radłowska M., *ŚFMD w walce o pokój i prawa młodzieży*, Warszawa: "Książka i Wiedza," 1952.

Redlich S., *Na rozdrożu. Żydzi w powojennej Łodzi 1945–1950*, Łódź: Wydawnictwo IPN, 2012.

Romanowski A., "'My, Pierwsza Brygada': powstanie pieśni – przemiany – recepcja społeczna," *Pamiętnik Literacki* 1988, issue 2, pp. 267–296.

Romek Z., *Cenzura a nauka historyczna w Polsce 1944–1970*, Warszawa: Wydawnictwo Neriton, 2010.

Rosiek S., "Mówienie a milczenie. O biografii duchowej krytyka literackiego w Polsce," [in:] S. Chwin, S. Rosiek, *Bez autorytetu*, Gdańsk: Wydawnictwo Gdańskie, 1981, pp. 70–82.

Rusek A., *Leksykon polskich bohaterów i serii komiksowych*, Warszawa: Biblioteka Narodowa, 2007.

Rusek A., *Od rozrywki do ideowego zaangażowania. Komiksowa rzeczywistość w Polsce w latach 1939–1955*, Warszawa: Biblioteka Narodowa, 2011.

Rutkowska J., Zdziarska R., Szwankowska H., *Warszawa. Przewodnik*, Warszawa: Wydawnictwo Sport i Turystyka, 1966.

Rygielska M., "O 'tekście kultury,'" *Zeszyty Etnologii Wrocławskiej* 2015, no. 1, pp. 27–43.

Shore M., *Kawior i popiół. Życie i śmierć pokolenia oczarowanych i rozczarowanych marksizmem*, trans. M. Szuster, Warszawa: Świat Książki, 2008.

Shore M., *The Taste of Ashes: The Afterlife of Totalitarianism in Eastern Europe*, London: Windmill Books, 2014.

Siedlecka J. *Biografie odtajnione. Z archiwów literackich bezpieki*, Poznań: Zysk i S-ka, 2015.

Siedlecka J., *Kryptonim "Liryka." Bezpieka wobec literatów*, Warszawa: Prószyński Media, 2009.

Siekierski S., *Książka literacka. Potrzeby społeczne i ich realizacja w latach 1944–1986*, Warszawa: Wydawnictwo Naukowe PWN, 1992.

Sioma M., "Obcy wśród swoich: losy gen. dyw. Sławoja Felicjana Składkowskiego w latach 1939–1941," *Annales Universitatis Mariae Curie-Skłodowska* 2005, vol. 60, pp. 193–207.

Składkowski F.S., *Strzępy meldunków*, Warszawa: Instytut Badania Najnowszej Historii Polski, 1936.

Skrendo A., *Poezja modernizmu. Interpretacje*, Kraków: Universitas, 2005.

Sława i infamia. Z Bohdanem Korzeniewskim rozmawia Małgorzata Szejnert, Kraków: Wydawnictwo Literackie, 1992.

Słownik organizacji młodzieżowych w Polsce 1918–1970, ed. Z.J. Bolek, compiled by Cz. Kozłowski, Warszawa: Iskry, 1971.

Słownik pojęć i tekstów kultury. Terytoria słowa, Third Revised Edition, ed. E. Szczęsna, WSiP, Warszawa [2004].

Słownik terminologii medialnej, ed. W. Pisarek, Kraków: Universitas, 2006.

Słownik terminów literackich, ed J. Sławiński, Revised and Expanded Third Edition, Wrocław: Ossolineum, 1988.

Smulski J., "Odwilżowe w formie, stalinowskie w treści (o opowiadaniu Kazimierza Brandysa 'Nim będzie zapomniany')," *Acta Universitatis Nicolai Copernici. Nauki Humanistyczno-Społeczne. Filologia Polska* 1996, no. 47, pp. 47–60.

Smulski J., *Pękanie lodów. (Krótkie formy narracyjne w literaturze polskiej 1954–1955)*, Toruń: Wydawnictwo UMK, 1995.

Smyczek K., "Satyra w służbie 'odwilży.' O ingerencjach cenzury w felietonach 'Notatki naiwnego' Zygmunta Ościenia," [in:] *Życie społeczne, kultura i polityka w okresie PRL*, eds. P. Szymczyk, M. Maciąg, Lublin: Wydawnictwo Naukowe TYGIEL, 2018, pp. 20–29.

Strauchold G., "Ludność rodzima pod 'opieką' cenzury (1945–1948). Przyczynek do polityki informacyjnej lat 40," *Wrocławskie Studia z Historii Najnowszej* 2001, vol. 8, pp. 277–286.

Strzyżewski T., *Czarna Księga Cenzury PRL* vol. 1: London: Wydawnictwo Aneks, 1977, vol. 2: ibidem 1978.

Strzyżewski T., *Czarna Księga Cenzury PRL*, Warszawa: Niezależna Oficyna Wydawnicza "Nowa," 1981.

Strzyżewski T., *The Black Book of Polish Censorship*, trans. and ed. by J. Leftwich Curry, New York: Vintage Books, 1984.

Strzyżewski T., *Wielka Księga Cenzury PRL w dokumentach*, Warszawa: Wydawnictwo Prohibita, 2015.

Swat T., *Niewinnie straceni w Warszawie 1944–1956*, Warszawa: Fundacja Ochrony Zabytków, 1994.

Szałagan A. [A. Sz.], "Bartelski Lesław Marian," [in:] *Współcześni polscy pisarze i badacze literatury. Słownik biobibliograficzny* vol. 1: *A–B*, eds. J. Czachowska, A. Szałagan, Warszawa: WSiP, 1994, pp. 108–112.

Szałagan A. [A. Sz.], "Fenikowski Franciszek," [in:] *Współcześni polscy pisarze i badacze literatury. Słownik biobibliograficzny* vol. 2: *C–F*, eds. J. Czachowska, A. Szałagan, Warszawa: WSiP, 1994, pp. 285–288.

Szulc P., *Czy w Polsce palono książki?*, Dzieje.pl, July 28, 2017, https://dzieje.pl/artykuly-historyczne/czy-w-polsce-palono-ksiazki (accessed January 31, 2021).

Szumna M., "Uczeń Kazimierza Wyki," *Nowa Dekada Krakowska* 2018, no. 1, pp. 16–26.

Szwagrzyk K., *Zbrodnie w majestacie prawa 1944–1955*, Warszawa: Wydawnictwo ABC Future, 2000.

Szydłowska J., *Narracje pojałtańskiego Okcydentu. Literatura polska wobec pogranicza na przykładzie Warmii i Mazur (1945–1989)*, Olsztyn: Wydawnictwo UWM, 2013.

Ściepuro A., "Wobec stalinizmu. Wiersze Tadeusza Różewicza z lat 1949–1956," *Pamiętnik Literacki* 1997, issue 2, pp. 33–49.

Terech Z., "Zofia Dróżdż-Satanowska," [in:] *Pisarze regionu świętokrzyskiego*, series 1, vol. 3, ed. J. Pacławski, Kielce: Kieleckie Towarzystwo Naukowe i Wyższa Szkoła Pedagogiczna im. J. Kochanowskiego w Kielcach, 1990, pp. 32–47.

Tobera M., "Księgarstwo spółdzielcze i prywatne w okresie trójsektorowości polskiego rynku książki (1945–1950)," *Przegląd Biblioteczny* 2014, issue 3, pp. 329–364.

Toeplitz K.T., *Sztuka komiksu. Próba definicji nowego gatunku artystycznego*, Warszawa: "Czytelnik," 1985.

Tołwiński T., *Urbanistyka* vol. 3: *Zieleń w urbanistyce*, Warszawa: PWN, 1963.

Tomasik W., *Słowo o socrealizmie. Szkice*, Bydgoszcz: Wydawnictwo Wyższej Szkoły Pedagogicznej w Bydgoszczy, 1993.

Trembicka K., "Dwie wizje komunistycznej Polski czy spór o sposób sprawowania władzy? Refleksje o myśli politycznej Władysława Gomułki i Bolesława Bieruta," *Annales Universitatis Paedagogicae Cracoviensis. Studia Politologica* 2013, no. 9, pp. 32–45.

Twyman F., *Metal Spectroscopy*, London: Charles Griffin & Company Limited, 1951.

Tyszkiewicz B. [B. T.], "Ginczanka Zuzanna," [in:] *Współcześni polscy pisarze i badacze literatury. Słownik biobibliograficzny* vol. 3: *G–J*, eds. J. Czachowska, A. Szałagan, Warszawa: WSiP, 1994, pp. 46–47.

Tyszkiewicz B., "'Dzikie zespoły' i ocenzurowany cyrk. GUKPPiW wobec wybranych zjawisk kultury popularnej," [in:] *Kultura popularna w Polsce 1944–1989. Między projektem ideologicznym a kontestacją*, ed. K. Stańczak-Wiślicz, Warszawa: IBL PAN, 2015, pp. 11–41.

Tyszkiewicz B., "'Pod prąd.' Jerzy Zawieyski wobec zmian w polityce kulturalnej państwa w latach 1945–1955," [in:] *"Lancetem, a nie maczugą". Cenzura wobec literatury i jej twórców w latach 1945–1965*, eds. K. Budrowska, M. Woźniak-Łabieniec, Warszawa: IBL PAN, 2012, series *Badania Filologiczne nad Cenzurą PRL* vol. 1, pp. 11–41.

Tyszkiewicz B., "Sztuka czytania między wierszami. Z problematyki cenzorskich instruktaży drugiej połowy lat 70.," [in:] *"Sztuka czytania między wierszami." Cenzura w komunikacji literackiej w Polsce w latach 1965–1989*, eds. K. Budrowska, M. Kotowska-Kachel, Warszawa: IBL PAN, 2016, series *Badania Filologiczne nad Cenzurą PRL* vol. 6, pp. 127–158.

W ostatniej chwili – o komiksie w PRL-u, directed by M. Szlachtycz, script by Sz. Holcman, M. Szlachtycz, produced by Telewizja Polska S.A., Freakshot, Szymon Holcman, Warszawa 2011.

Wakar M., "Mit Ziem Odzyskanych – geneza i tropy w literaturze," [in:] *"Ziemie Odzyskane." W poszukiwaniu nowych narracji*, eds. E. Kledzik, M. Michalski, M. Praczyk, Poznań: Instytut Historii UAM, 2018, pp. 127–143.

Wal A., *Twórczość w cieniu menory. O prozie Adolfa Rudnickiego*, Rzeszów: Wydawnictwo URz, 2001.

Ważyk A., *W stronę humanizmu*, Warszawa: "Książka," 1949.

Wieczorek M., "Kreatywność projektantów zabawek zatrudnionych w spółdzielniach pracy w okresie PRL a czynniki ją ograniczające," *Lubelski Rocznik Pedagogiczny* 2019, vol. 38, no. 1, pp. 97–112.

Więckowska H., Pliszczyńska H., *Podręczny słownik bibliotekarza*, Warszawa: PWN, 1955.

Wincławski W., "*Studia Socjologiczne* – okoliczności powstania i status czasopisma w socjologii polskiej," *Studia Socjologiczne* 2011, no. 1, pp. 11–38.

Wiśniewska-Grabarczyk A., "Archiwalia 'pionierskiego' okresu powojennej cenzury. Literatura w poufnych biuletynach urzędu cenzury (1945–1951)," *Sztuka Edycji. Studia Tekstologiczne i Edytorskie* 2021, issue 2 (20), pp. 51–62.

Wiśniewska-Grabarczyk A., "Bulletins of the Polish censorship office from 1945 to 1956. A reconnaissance study," *Acta Universitatis Lodziensis. Folia Litteraria Polonica* 2019, no. 4, pp. 311–331.

Wiśniewska-Grabarczyk A., "'Cenzura jest jak stara kochanka…,' czyli o czym pisano w poufnych poradnikach dla cenzorów," *Informator Polski* 2020, no. 3–4, pp. 13–16, https://www.federacja-polonia.dk/pliki/pdf/IP-110.pdf (accessed January 21, 2021).

Wiśniewska-Grabarczyk A., "*Czytelnik" ocenzurowany. Literatura w kryptotekstach – recenzjach cenzorskich okresu stalinizmu (na materiale GUKPPiW z 1950 roku)*, Warszawa: Wydawnictwo IPN, 2018.

Wiśniewska-Grabarczyk A., "Konkurs na recenzję cenzorską powieści Wandy Wasilewskiej pt. *Rzeki płoną*. Materiał archiwalny z poufnego biuletynu dla cenzorów z roku 1952," *Bibliotekarz Podlaski* 2020, issue 1, pp. 215–233, https://bibliotekarzpodlaski.pl/index.php/bp/article/view/427/489 (accessed January 21, 2021).

Wiśniewska-Grabarczyk A., "'O wyższy poziom pracy nad książką' – biuletyny urzędu cenzury z lat 1945–1956 w perspektywie literaturoznawczej. Rekonesans," [in:] *Cenzura w PRL. Analiza zjawiska*, eds. Z. Romek, K. Kamińska-Chełminiak, Warszawa: Oficyna Wydawnicza ASPRA-JR, 2017, pp. 61–74.

Wiśniewska-Grabarczyk A., "Recenzja cenzorska Polski Ludowej," *Zagadnienia Rodzajów Literackich* 2016, vol. 59, no. 1 (117), pp. 97–103.

Wiśniewska-Grabarczyk A., "Teatr i dramat okresu socrealizmu w świetle kryptotekstów (na materiale Ministerstwa Kultury i Sztuki oraz Wojewódzkiego Urzędu Kontroli Prasy, Publikacji i Widowisk w Poznaniu)," [in:] *Metateksty i parateksty teatru i dramatu. Od antyku do współczesności*, eds. J. Czerwińska, K. Chiżyńska, M. Budzowska, Łódź: Wydawnictwo UŁ, 2017, pp. 61–74.

Wiśniewska-Grabarczyk A., "The censorship review in the Polish People's Republic as cryptotext," *The Polish Review* 2019, vol. 64, no. 1, pp. 31–49.

Wojdon J., *Propaganda polityczna w podręcznikach dla szkół podstawowych Polski Ludowej (1944–1989)*, Toruń: Wydawnictwo Adama Marszałek, 2001.

Wojtak M., *Analiza gatunków prasowych*, Lublin: Wydawnictwo UMCS, 2010.

Wolański R., "Kleyny Jerzy," [in:] *Cyfrowa Biblioteka Polskiej Piosenki*, https://bibliotekapiosenki.pl/osoby/Kleyny_Jerzy (accessed January 31, 2021).

Woźniak-Łabieniec M., "Cenzura w okresie odwilży jako temat tabu," *Acta Universitatis Lodziensis. Folia Litteraria Polonica* 2013, no. 1, pp. 89–97.

Woźniak-Łabieniec M., *Obecny nieobecny. Krajowa recepcja Czesława Miłosza w krytyce literackiej lat pięćdziesiątych w świetle dokumentów cenzury*, Łódź: Wydawnictwo UŁ, 2012.

Wróbel J., *Miara cierpienia. O pisarstwie Adolfa Rudnickiego*, Kraków: Universitas, 2004.

Wróbel Ł., "Korespondencja Jana Śniadeckiego jako źródło w edukacji historycznej," *Wiadomości Historyczne. Czasopismo dla nauczycieli* 2013, no. 3, pp. 17–21.

Zaleski M., *Przygoda drugiej awangardy*, Second Revised and Supplemented Edition, Wrocław: Ossolineum, 2000.

Zarzębski T., "Geneza, życie i nauki Dekretu," *Przegląd Biblioteczny* 1986, no. 3/4, pp. 279–295.

Zawadzka J. [J. Z.], "Kowalewski Mirosław," [in:] *Współcześni polscy pisarze i badacze literatury. Słownik biobibliograficzny* vol. 4: *K*, eds. J. Czachowska, A. Szałagan, Warszawa: WSiP, 1994, pp. 318–319.

Zawadzka J. [J. Z.], "Matuszewski Ryszard," [in:] *Współcześni polscy pisarze i badacze literatury. Słownik biobibliograficzny* vol. 5: *L–M*, eds. J. Czachowska, A. Szałagan, WSiP, Warszawa 1997, pp. 327–331.

Zawadzka J. [J. Z.], "Miller Jerzy," [in:] *Współcześni polscy pisarze i badacze literatury. Słownik biobibliograficzny* vol. 5: *L–M*, eds. J. Czachowska, A. Szałagan, WSiP, Warszawa 1997, pp. 396–398.

Zawodniak M., "Klasycy literatury i klasycy marksizmu. Dwa w jednym," [in:] *Komunistyczni bohaterowie* vol. 1: *Tradycja, kult, rytuał*, eds. M. Bogusławska, Z. Grębecka, E. Wróblewska-Trochimiuk, Warszawa–Kraków: Wydział Polonistyki UW and Wydawnictwo Libron, 2011, series *Wschód–Zachód–Konfrontacje*, pp. 13–20.

Zawodniak M., "Królewicz i murarz (socrealistyczne potyczki z fantazją)," *Teksty Drugie* 1994, no. 1, pp. 84–93.

Zawodniak M., "Zaraz po wojnie, a nawet przed… O przygotowaniach do socrealizmu," *Teksty Drugie* 2000, no. 1–2, pp. 141–151.

Zrodził nas czyn. Szlakiem bojowym ZWM, compiled by A. Drożdżyński, Warszawa: Wydawnictwo RSW "Prasa," 1953.

Zrodził nas czyn. W 30-lecie powstania Związku Walki Młodych, Warszawa: Wydawca Miesięcznik "Kultura i Ty," 1973.

Zrodził nas czyn. W XX rocznicę powstania Związku Walki Młodych i ZMP "Grunwald," Warszawa: Związek Młodzieży Socjalistycznej, 1963.

Żółkiewski S., *Teksty kultury. Studia*, Warszawa: PWN, 1988.

Żurek S.J., "Koncepcja podstawy programowej z języka polskiego," [in:] *Podstawa programowa z komentarzami* vol. 2: *Język polski w szkole podstawowej, gimnazjum i liceum*, Warszawa: Ministerstwo Edukacji Narodowej, 2009, pp. 55–59.

Other Archival Sources

"*Biuletyn Informacyjno-Instrukcyjny* no. 1 (I 1953)–nr 11/12 (XI–XII 1953)" (AAN, GUKPPiW, file ref. no. 22).

"*Biuletyn Informacyjno-Instrukcyjny* no. 1 (I 1955)–nr 11/12 (XI–XII 1955)" (AAN, GUKPPiW, file ref. no. 24).

"*Biuletyny Instrukcyjno-Szkoleniowe* 1945–1951" (APP, WUKPPiW, file ref. no. 4).

"Ingerencje cenzorskie GUKPPiW, WUKPPiW w Bydgoszczy, Gdańsku, Katowicach, Krakowie, Łodzi w okresie VI 1950–XI 1950, IV 1951–XII 1951 w publikacjach nieperiodycznych Spółdzielni Wydawniczej 'Czytelnik.' Recenzje prewencyjne i wtórne" (AAN, GUKPPiW, file ref. no. 2854).

"Ingerencje cenzorskie GUKPPiW, WUKPPiW w Bydgoszczy, Krakowie, Wrocławiu w okresie VII 1951, I 1952–II 1953 w publikacjach nieperiodycznych. Recenzje prewencyjne i wtórne" (AAN, GUKPPiW, file ref. no. 2919).

"Materiały dyskusyjno-szkoleniowe 1954–1955" (APP, WUKPPiW, file ref. no. 18).

"Narady i odprawy naczelników WUKP i kierowników referatów widowisk w dniach: 7–9 II 1949, 26–28 VI 1949, 5 VIII 1949, 11 XII 1949. Protokoły, stenogramy" (AAN, GUKPPiW, file ref. no. 4).

"Recenzje książkowe 1949" (APP, WUKPPiW, file ref. no. 234).

"Wykaz książek wycofanych z bibliotek 1945–1956" (APP, WUKPPiW, file ref. no. 13).

Electronic Sources

Przygody w dżungli (1956), Boardgamegeek.com, https://boardgamegeek.com/boardgame/38043/przygody-w-dzungli?fbclid=IwAR0C2ec2wKwIT_-vyF4Pg1Tg-7Byx6yePFQAAhfQIeJek0s-6Y2asjo7UnJ4 (accessed January 31, 2021).

Legal Acts

"Dekret z dnia 17 kwietnia 1946 r. o bibliotekach i opiece nad zbiorami bibliotecznymi" (Dz.U. 1946, nr 26, poz. 163, s. 291–295) [Decree of April 17, 1946 on libraries and care of library collections (*Journal of Laws* 1946, no. 26, item 163, pp. 291–295)].

"Dekret z dnia 5 lipca 1946 r. o utworzeniu Głównego Urzędu Kontroli Prasy, Publikacji i Widowisk" (Dz.U. 1946, nr 34, poz. 210, s. 379) ["Decree of July 5, 1946 on the establishment of the Main Office for the Control of the Press, Publications and Public Performances" (*Journal of Laws* 1946, no. 34, item 210, p. 379)].

"Konstytucja Polskiej Rzeczypospolitej Ludowej uchwalona przez Sejm Ustawodawczy w dniu 22 lipca 1952 r.," http://libr.sejm.gov.pl/tek01/txt/kpol/e1952a.html (accessed September 1, 2021) ["Constitution of the Polish People's Republic, July 22, 1952"].

"Obwieszczenie Marszałka Sejmu Rzeczypospolitej Polskiej z dnia 14 września 2018 r. w sprawie ogłoszenia jednolitego tekstu ustawy – Prawo prasowe" (Dz.U. 2018, poz. 1914, s. 1–17) ["Notice of the Speaker of the Sejm of the Republic of Poland of September 14, 2018 on the announcement of the uniform text of the act – The Press Law Act" (*Journal of Laws* 2018, item 1914, pp. 1–17)].

"Rozporządzenie Ministra Nauki i Szkolnictwa Wyższego z dnia 20 września 2018 r. w sprawie dziedzin nauki i dyscyplin naukowych oraz dyscyplin artystycznych" (Dz.U. 2018, poz. 1818, s. 1–2) ["Regulation of the Minister of Science and Higher Education of September 20, 2018 on the fields of science and scientific disciplines and artistic disciplines" (*Journal of Laws* 2018, item 1818, pp. 1–2)].

"Ustawa z dnia 11 kwietnia 1990 r. o uchyleniu ustawy o kontroli publikacji i widowisk, zniesieniu organów tej kontroli oraz o zmianie ustawy – Prawo prasowe" (Dz.U. 1990, nr 27, poz. 173, s. 378–389) [The act of April 11, 1990 on the repeal of the act on the control of publications and performances, on the abolition of the bodies of this control, and on the amendment of the act – Press Law (*Journal of Laws* 1990, no. 27, item 173, pp. 378–389)].

"Ustawa z dnia 17 marca 1921 r. – Konstytucja Rzeczypospolitej Polskiej," http://libr.sejm.gov.pl/tek01/txt/kpol/e1921.html (accessed September 1, 2021) ["Constitution of the Republic of Poland, March 17, 1921"].

Author's E-Mail Correspondence

The author's e-mail correspondence with Prof. Iwona Loewe on the censorship review as a paratextual genre (April 10, 2018).

The author's e-mail correspondence with Dr. Piotr Lechowski on library control (August 26–September 6, 2018).

The author's e-mail correspondence and phone conversations with Dr. Teresa Kotaszewicz on Tadeusz Tolwiński's *Urbanistyka* (September 2018).

The author's e-mail correspondence with Prof. Zbigniew Romek on field officials (local content supervisors) in national councils (March 20–22, 2019).

The author's e-mail correspondence with Michał Stajszczak regarding *Przygody w dżungli. Kombinacyjna gra dla młodzieży* (January 24–February 14, 2020).

The author's e-mail correspondence with Prof. Wacław Andrusikiewicz on "cyclicality and multi-seam systems" (March 10–12, 2020).

The author's e-mail correspondence with Prof. Gregory Strauchold on the literature of the Recovered Territories (March 20–29, 2020).

The author's e-mail correspondence with Dr. Tomasz Majda on the GUKPPiW's building at 5 Mysia Street (August 19–22, 2021).

REVIEWERS
John Bates, Sławomir Buryła, Kamila Kamińska-Chełminiak

ENGLISH TRANSLATION
Katarzyna Szuster-Tardi

INITIATING EDITOR
Urszula Dzieciątkowska

TECHNICAL EDITOR
Wojciech Grzegorczyk

TYPESETTING
Munda – Maciej Torz

COVER DESIGN
Polkadot Studio Graficzne
Aleksandra Woźniak, Hanna Niemierowicz

The book was written as part of a grant project entitled *Powojenna literatura polska w świetle kryptotekstów (na podstawie biuletynów Głównego Urzędu Kontroli Prasy, Publikacji i Widowisk z lat 1945–1956)* [Post-war Polish literature in the light of cryptotexts (on the basis of bulletins of the Main Office of Control of Press, Publications and Shows 1945–1956)] funded by the National Science Center (Preludium 12, UMO-2016/23/N/HS2/01798 period of implementation 2017–2021, project leader – Anna Wiśniewska-Grabarczyk)

Publisher's sheets 20.7; printing sheets 23.375